Paramahansa Yogananda
(January 5, 1893–March 7, 1952)
A Premavatar, "Incarnation of Love" (see page 290 n.)

Autobiography of a Yogi

by
Paramahansa Yogananda

With a Preface by
W. Y. Evans-Wentz, M.A., D.Litt., D.Sc.

---

*"Except ye see signs and wonders,
ye will not believe."*—John 4:48

Self-Realization Fellowship
FOUNDED 1920
Paramahansa Yogananda

Autobiography of a Yogi has been published in English, Bengali, Gujarati, Hindi, Kannada, Malayalam, Marathi, Oriya, Tamil, Telugu, Urdu, Japanese, Arabic, Greek, Icelandic, Danish, Dutch, Finnish, French, German, Italian, Nepali, Polish, Portuguese, Spanish, and Swedish.

An audiobook edition is available in English (read by Sir Ben Kingsley).

 Authorized by the International Publications Council of Self-Realization Fellowship

Library of Congress Catalog Card Number: 80-52927
ISBN-13: 978-0-87612-082-8 (hardcover)
ISBN-10: 0-87612-082-6 (hardcover)
ISBN-13: 978-0-87612-083-5 (quality paperback)
ISBN-10: 0-87612-083-4 (quality paperback)
Printed in the United States of America
1050-J772

THE SPIRITUAL LEGACY OF
PARAMAHANSA YOGANANDA

His Complete Writings, Lectures, and Informal Talks

Paramahansa Yogananda founded Self-Realization Fellowship in 1920 to disseminate his teachings worldwide and to preserve their purity and integrity for generations to come. A prolific writer and lecturer from his earliest years in America, he created a renowned and voluminous body of works on the yoga science of meditation, the art of balanced living, and the underlying unity of all great religions. Today this unique and far-reaching spiritual legacy lives on, inspiring millions of truth-seekers all over the world.

In accord with the express wishes of the great master, Self-Realization Fellowship has continued the ongoing task of publishing and keeping permanently in print *The Complete Works of Paramahansa Yogananda*. These include not only the final editions of all the books he published during his lifetime, but also many new titles—works that had remained unpublished at the time of his passing in 1952, or which had been serialized over the years in incomplete form in Self-Realization Fellowship's magazine, as well as hundreds of profoundly inspiring lectures and informal talks recorded but not printed before his passing.

Paramahansa Yogananda personally chose and trained those close disciples who head the Self-Realization Fellowship Publications Council, and gave them specific guidelines for the preparation and publishing of his teachings. The members of the SRF Publications Council (monks and nuns who have taken lifelong vows of renunciation and selfless service) honor these guidelines as a sacred trust, in order that the universal message of this beloved world teacher will live on in its original power and authenticity.

The Self-Realization Fellowship emblem (shown above) was designated by Paramahansa Yogananda to identify the nonprofit society he founded as the authorized source of his teachings. The SRF name and emblem appear on all Self-Realization Fellowship publications and recordings, assuring the reader that a work originates with the organization founded by Paramahansa Yogananda and conveys his teachings as he himself intended they be given.

—*Self-Realization Fellowship*

Dedicated to the Memory of

LUTHER BURBANK

"An American Saint"

AUTHOR'S ACKNOWLEDGMENTS

I am deeply indebted to Miss L. V. Pratt [Tara Mata] for her long editorial labors over the manuscript of this book. My thanks are due also to Mr. C. Richard Wright for permission to use extracts from his Indian travel diary. To Dr. W. Y. Evans-Wentz I am grateful not only for his Preface, but also for suggestions and encouragement.

PARAMAHANSA YOGANANDA

October 28, 1945

CONTENTS

List of Illustrations ix

Preface, by W. Y. Evans-Wentz xiii

Introduction xv

Chapter

1. My Parents and Early Life 3
2. My Mother's Death and the Mystic Amulet 13
3. The Saint With Two Bodies 19
4. My Interrupted Flight Toward the Himalayas 25
5. A "Perfume Saint" Displays His Wonders 37
6. The Tiger Swami 45
7. The Levitating Saint 53
8. India's Great Scientist, J. C. Bose 58
9. The Blissful Devotee and His Cosmic Romance
   (Master Mahasaya) 66
10. I Meet My Master, Sri Yukteswar 73
11. Two Penniless Boys in Brindaban 83
12. Years in My Master's Hermitage 91
13. The Sleepless Saint 118
14. An Experience in Cosmic Consciousness 125
15. The Cauliflower Robbery 132
16. Outwitting the Stars 142
17. Sasi and the Three Sapphires 152
18. A Mohammedan Wonder-Worker 158
19. My Master, in Calcutta, Appears in Serampore 163
20. We Do Not Visit Kashmir 167
21. We Visit Kashmir 172
22. The Heart of a Stone Image 181
23. I Receive My University Degree 187
24. I Become a Monk of the Swami Order 194
25. Brother Ananta and Sister Nalini 202

26. The Science of *Kriya Yoga* 207

27. Founding a Yoga School in Ranchi 216

28. Kashi, Reborn and Discovered 224

29. Rabindranath Tagore and I Compare Schools 229

30. The Law of Miracles 233

31. An Interview With the Sacred Mother
(Kashi Moni Lahiri) 244

32. Rama Is Raised From the Dead 253

33. Babaji, Yogi-Christ of Modern India 261

34. Materializing a Palace in the Himalayas 269

35. The Christlike Life of Lahiri Mahasaya 281

36. Babaji's Interest in the West 292

37. I Go to America 301

38. Luther Burbank—A Saint Amid the Roses 308

39. Therese Neumann, the Catholic Stigmatist 313

40. I Return to India 321

41. An Idyl in South India 328

42. Last Days With My Guru 340

43. The Resurrection of Sri Yukteswar 352

44. With Mahatma Gandhi at Wardha 369

45. The Bengali "Joy-Permeated Mother"
(Ananda Moyi Ma) 385

46. The Woman Yogi Who Never Eats 390

47. I Return to the West 400

48. At Encinitas in California 404

49. The Years 1940–1951 408

Paramahansa Yogananda: A Yogi in Life and Death 422

Commemorative stamp issued by Government of India
in honor of Paramahansa Yogananda 423

The Line of Self-Realization Fellowship Gurus 431

Aims and Ideals of Self-Realization Fellowship 432

Index 433

ILLUSTRATIONS

Facing page

The author *(frontispiece)*

Sri Yogananda's mother, Gurru (Gyana Prabha) Ghosh 8
Sri Yogananda's father, Bhagabati Charan Ghosh 8
Yoganandaji at age of six 9
Jitendra Mazumdar, companion in Brindaban 9
Sri Yogananda's sisters: Uma, Roma, and Nalini 9
Nagendra Nath Bhaduri, "the levitating saint" 16
Swami Kebalananda, Yogananda's Sanskrit tutor 16
Swami Pranabananda, the Banaras "saint with two bodies" 17
Master Mahasaya (Mahendra Nath Gupta) 17
Lord Krishna, India's greatest prophet 48
Yoganandaji at age of sixteen 48
Sri Yogananda's family home, Calcutta 49
Ananta, Yoganandaji's elder brother 49
Ram Gopal Muzumdar, the "sleepless saint" 49
Sri Yukteswar, guru of Yogananda 80
Sri Yukteswar Meditation Temple, Serampore 81
Sri Yogananda, 1915 81
Sri Yukteswar in lotus posture 112
Sri Yukteswar's seaside ashram, Puri, Orissa 112
Yoganandaji and his cousin, Prabhas Chandra Ghosh 113
Sri Yukteswar and Sri Yogananda, Calcutta, 1935 144
Sri Yukteswar Memorial Temple in Puri 145
Krishnananda with tame lioness at *Kumbha Mela* 145
Group on dining balcony of Serampore ashram, 1935 145
International Headquarters, Self-Realization Fellowship/
    Yogoda Satsanga Society of India 176
Sri Rajarsi Janakananda, past president (1952–55), Self-
    Realization Fellowship/Yogoda Satsanga Society of India 177
Sri Daya Mata, president, Self-Realization Fellowship/
    Yogoda Satsanga Society of India 177
Sri Jagadguru Shankaracharya at SRF/YSS headquarters, 1958 208

A Westerner in *samadhi* — Sri Rajarsi Janakananda
    (Mr. J. J. Lynn) 209
Shankari Mai Jiew, disciple of Trailanga Swami 240
Panchanon Bhattacharya, disciple of Lahiri Mahasaya 240
Kashi, student at Ranchi school 240
Yogoda Math, Dakshineswar, India 241
Rabindranath Tagore 241
Jagadis Chandra Bose, great Indian scientist 241
Mahavatar Babaji, guru of Lahiri Mahasaya 272
Lahiri Mahasaya 273
Cave occasionally occupied by Mahavatar Babaji 273
Lahiri Mahasaya, guru of Sri Yukteswar 304
Sri Yogananda's passport photo, 1920 305
Center Photo Section .... *following text page* 336
    Delegates, Congress of Religions,
        Boston, 1920 .... *photo page*   1
    Easter sunrise service, SRF/YSS International
        Headquarters, 1925   1
    Yoganandaji at Lake Xochimilco, Mexico, 1929   2
    Emilio Portes Gil, president of Mexico,
        with Sri Yogananda   2
    Yoga class in Denver   3
    Sri Yogananda at George Washington's crypt, 1927   4
    Sri Yogananda at the White House   4
    Luther Burbank and Yoganandaji, Santa Rosa, 1924   5
    Sri Yogananda en route to Alaska, summer of 1924   5
    A class of yoga students, Los Angeles   6
    Sri Yukteswar and Yoganandaji
        in religious procession, 1935   7
    Group in courtyard of Serampore ashram, 1935   8
    Mahatma Gandhi and Sri Yogananda,
        Wardha ashram, 1935   9
    The Lord as Shiva, "King of Yogis" 10
    The Divine Mother 10
    Sri Yogananda at Damodar, India, 1935 11

Yogoda Branch Math and Ashram, Ranchi.............................. 11
Sri Yogananda at School for Aborigine Girls, 1936 12
Yogoda Satsanga school for boys, Ranchi 12
Yogoda Satsanga schools in Ranchi... 13
Ananda Moyi Ma, "Joy-Permeated Mother,"
    and Paramahansa Yogananda 14
Swami Dayananda and Sri Yogananda.................................... 15
Ramana Maharshi and Yoganandaji.. 15
Sri Yogananda and companions on Yamuna River
    at Mathura, 1935 16
Sri Yogananda and C. Richard Wright, his secretary,
    with Swami Keshabananda, Brindaban, 1936................... 16
Yoga class in Calcutta, 1935 17
Sri Yogananda at the Taj Mahal, Agra, 1936 18
Giri Bala, non-eating saint of Bengal..................................... 19
Therese Neumann, C. R. Wright, and Yoganandaji............... 19
Sri Yogananda, Encinitas, California, 1950 20

Paramahansa Yogananda and Sri Rajarsi
Janakananda, 1933..................................... *following text page* 368
Paramahansa Yogananda and Sri Daya Mata, 1939..................... 368
Sri Daya Mata in divine communion 368
Hon. Goodwin J. Knight, Lt. Governor of California,
    with Yoganandaji at India Center opening, 1951.................... 368
Self-Realization Fellowship Temple, Hollywood, California 368
Sri Yogananda on grounds of SRF Encinitas
    Hermitage, 1940... 368
Ambassador of India, Mr. B. R. Sen,
    at SRF International Headquarters..................................... 368
Paramahansa Yogananda at dedication of
    SRF Lake Shrine, 1950.. 400
Self-Realization Fellowship Lake Shrine and
    Gandhi World Peace Memorial.. 401
Sri Yogananda, one hour before his *mahasamadhi*,
    March 7, 1952... 416
Self-Realization Fellowship Hermitage, Encinitas, California..... 417

PREFACE

By W. Y. Evans-Wentz, M.A., D.Litt., D.Sc.
Jesus College, Oxford
Author and translator of many classic works on yoga and the
wisdom traditions of the East, including *Tibetan Yoga and
Secret Doctrines, Tibet's Great Yogi Milarepa,*
and *The Tibetan Book of the Dead.*

The value of Yogananda's *Autobiography* is greatly enhanced
by the fact that it is one of the few books in English about the wise
men of India which have been written, not by a journalist or for-
eigner, but by one of their own race and training—in short, a book
about yogis *by* a yogi. As an eyewitness recountal of the extraordinary lives and powers of modern Hindu saints, the book has importance both timely and timeless. To its illustrious author, whom
I have had the pleasure of knowing in both India and America, may
every reader render due appreciation and gratitude. His unusual life
document is certainly one of the most revealing of the depths of the
Hindu mind and heart, and of the spiritual wealth of India, ever to
be published in the West.

It has been my privilege to meet one of the sages whose life
history is herein narrated—Sri Yukteswar Giri. A likeness of the
venerable saint appeared as part of the frontispiece of my *Tibetan
Yoga and Secret Doctrines.** It was at Puri, in Orissa, on the Bay of
Bengal, that I encountered Sri Yukteswar. He was then the head of a
quiet *ashrama* near the seashore there, and was chiefly occupied in
the spiritual training of a group of youthful disciples. He expressed
keen interest in the welfare of the people of the United States and
of all the Americas, and of England, too, and questioned me concerning the distant activities, particularly those in California, of his
chief disciple, Paramahansa Yogananda, whom he dearly loved, and
whom he had sent, in 1920, as his emissary to the West.

Sri Yukteswar was of gentle mien and voice, of pleasing pres-

* Oxford University Press, 1958.

ence, and worthy of the veneration that his followers spontaneously accorded to him. Every person who knew him, whether of his own community or not, held him in the highest esteem. I vividly recall his tall, straight, ascetic figure, robed in the saffron-colored garb of one who has renounced worldly quests, as he stood at the entrance of the hermitage to give me welcome. His hair was long and somewhat curly, and his face bearded. His body was muscularly firm, but slender and well-formed, and his step energetic. He had chosen as his place of earthly abode the holy city of Puri, whither multitudes of pious Hindus, representative of every province of India, come daily on pilgrimage to the famed Temple of Jagannath, "Lord of the World." It was at Puri that Sri Yukteswar closed his mortal eyes, in 1936, to the scenes of this transitory state of being and passed on, knowing that his incarnation had been carried to a triumphant completion.

I am glad, indeed, to be able to record this testimony to the high character and holiness of Sri Yukteswar. Content to remain afar from the multitude, he gave himself unreservedly and in tranquillity to that ideal life which Paramahansa Yogananda, his disciple, has now described for the ages.

INTRODUCTION

*"The experience of meeting Paramahansa Yogananda is
etched in my memory as one of the unforgettable events of
my life....As I looked into his face, my eyes were almost dazzled by a radiance—a light of spirituality that literally shone
from him. His infinite gentleness, his gracious kindliness,
enveloped me like warm sunshine....I could see that his
understanding and insight extended to the most mundane
of problems, even though he was a man of Spirit. In him I
found a true ambassador of India, carrying and spreading the
essence of India's ancient wisdom to the world."*

—Dr. Binay R. Sen, former Ambassador
of India to the United States

To those who were personally acquainted with Paramahansa
Yogananda, his own life and being were convincing testimony to
the power and authenticity of the ancient wisdom he presented to
the world. Countless readers of his autobiography have attested to
the presence in its pages of that same light of spiritual authority
that radiated from his person. Hailed as a masterpiece when it first
appeared in print more than sixty years ago, the book sets forth not
only the story of a life of unmistakable greatness but a fascinating
introduction to the spiritual thought of the East—especially its
unique science of direct personal communion with God—opening
up to the Western public a realm of knowledge hitherto accessible
only to a few.

Today *Autobiography of a Yogi* is recognized around the world
as a classic of spiritual literature. In this introduction, we would
like to share some of the book's extraordinary history.

❖ ❖ ❖

The writing of the work had been prophesied long ago. One of
the seminal figures in the renaissance of yoga in modern times, the
revered nineteenth-century master Lahiri Mahasaya, had foretold:
"About fifty years after my passing, an account of my life will be
written because of a deep interest in yoga that will arise in the

West. The message of yoga will encircle the globe. It will aid in establishing the brotherhood of man: a unity based on humanity's direct perception of the One Father."

Many years later, Lahiri Mahasaya's exalted disciple Swami Sri Yukteswar related this prophecy to Sri Yogananda. "You must do your part in spreading that message," he declared, "and in writing that sacred life."

It was in 1945, exactly fifty years after Lahiri Mahasaya's passing, that Paramahansa Yogananda completed his *Autobiography of a Yogi*, which amply fulfilled both of his guru's injunctions: providing the first detailed presentation in English of Lahiri Mahasaya's remarkable life, and introducing to a world audience India's age-old science of the soul.

❖ ❖ ❖

The creation of *Autobiography of a Yogi* was a project that Paramahansa Yogananda worked on over a period of many years. Sri Daya Mata, one of his earliest and closest disciples,* recalls:

"When I came to Mount Washington in 1931, Paramahansaji had already begun to work on the *Autobiography*. Once when I was in his study attending to some secretarial duties, I was privileged to see one of the first chapters he wrote—it was on 'The Tiger Swami.' He asked me to save it, and explained that it would be going into a book he was writing. Most of the book was composed later, between 1937 and 1945."

From June 1935 through October 1936, Sri Yogananda had made a return trip to India (via Europe and Palestine) for a last visit with his guru, Swami Sri Yukteswar. While there, he had compiled much factual data for the *Autobiography*, as well as stories about some of the saints and sages whom he had known and whose lives he was to describe so memorably in the book. "I had never forgotten Sri Yukteswar's request that I write the life of Lahiri Mahasaya," he later wrote. "During my stay in India I was taking every opportunity to contact direct disciples and relatives of the Yogavatar. Recording their conversations in voluminous notes, I verified facts and dates, and collected photographs, old letters, and documents."

Upon his return to the United States at the end of 1936, he began to spend much of his time at the hermitage that had been

---

* Sri Daya Mata joined the monastic community Paramahansa Yogananda had established atop Mount Washington, overlooking the city of Los Angeles, in 1931. She has served as president of Self-Realization Fellowship since 1955.

built for him in his absence, in Encinitas on the southern California coast. It proved to be an ideal place to concentrate on completing the book he had begun years before.

"Still vivid in my memory are the days spent in that peaceful seaside hermitage," recounts Sri Daya Mata. "He had so many other responsibilities and commitments that he was not able to work on the *Autobiography* every day; but in general he devoted the evenings to it, and whatever free time he could spare. Beginning around 1939 or '40, he was able to concentrate full time on the book. And full time it was—from early morning until early morning! A small group of us disciples—Tara Mata; my sister, Ananda Mata; Sraddha Mata; and myself—were present to assist him. After each part was typed, he would give it to Tara Mata, who served as his editor.

"What treasured memories! As he wrote he relived inwardly the sacred experiences he was recording. His divine intent was to share the joy and revelations encountered in the company of saints and great masters and in one's own personal realization of the Divine. Often he would pause for a time, his gaze uplifted and his body motionless, rapt in the *samadhi* state of deep communion with God. The whole room would be filled with a tremendously powerful aura of divine love. For us disciples, merely to be present at such times was to be lifted into a higher state of consciousness.

"Finally, in 1945, came the jubilant day of the book's completion. Paramahansaji wrote the last words, 'Lord, Thou hast given this monk a large family'; then laid down his pen and joyously exclaimed:

"'All done; it is finished. This book will change the lives of millions. It will be my messenger when I am gone.'"

❖ ❖ ❖

It then became Tara Mata's responsibility to find a publisher. Paramahansa Yogananda had met Tara Mata while conducting a series of lectures and classes in San Francisco in 1924. Possessed of rare spiritual insight, she became one of the small circle of his most advanced disciples. He held her editorial abilities in highest esteem, and used to say that she had one of the most brilliant minds of anyone he had ever met. He appreciated her vast knowledge and understanding of India's scriptural wisdom, and remarked on one occasion: "Excepting my great guru, Sri Yukteswarji, there is no one with whom I have more enjoyed talking of Indian philosophy."

Tara Mata took the manuscript to New York City. But finding a publisher was not an easy task. As can often be observed, the true stature of a great work may not at first be recognized by those of a more conventional cast of mind. Despite the newly born atomic age having enlarged the collective consciousness of humanity with a growing understanding of the subtle unity of matter, energy, and thought, the publishers of the day were hardly ready for such chapters as "Materializing a Palace in the Himalayas" and "The Saint With Two Bodies"!

For a year, Tara Mata lived in a sparsely furnished, unheated cold-water flat while making the rounds of publishing houses. At last she was able to send a cable with news of success. The Philosophical Library, a respected New York publisher, had accepted the *Autobiography* for publication. "What [she] has done for this book I cannot begin to describe...," Sri Yogananda said. "But for her, the book would never have gone through."

Shortly before Christmas 1946, the long-awaited books reached Mount Washington.

❖ ❖ ❖

The book was greeted by readers and by the world press with an outpouring of appreciative praise. "There has been nothing before, written in English or in any other language, like this presentation of Yoga," wrote Columbia University Press in its *Review of Religions*. *The New York Times* proclaimed it "a rare account." *Newsweek* reported, "Yogananda's book is rather an autobiography of the soul than of the body....It is a fascinating and clearly annotated study of a religious way of life, ingenuously described in the lush style of the Orient."

Following are excerpts from some of the other reviews that appeared:

> *San Francisco Chronicle:* "In a very readable style...Yogananda presents a convincing case for yoga, and those who 'came to scoff' may remain 'to pray.'"

> *United Press:* "Yogananda expounds the so-called esoteric doctrines of the East with the utmost frankness and good humor. His book is rewarding for its account of a life filled with spiritual adventure."

> *The Times of India:* "The autobiography of this sage makes captivating reading."

> *Saturday Review:* "...cannot but impress and interest the Western reader."

> *Grandy's Syndicated Book Reviews:* "Engrossing, inspiring; a 'literarity'!"

West Coast Review of Books: "Whatever your own religious beliefs, you'll find *Autobiography of a Yogi* a joyous affirmation of the power of the human soul."

News-Sentinel, Fort Wayne, Indiana: "Sheer revelation.... intensely human account....should help the human race to understand itself better....autobiography at its best....breathtaking.... told with delightful wit and compelling sincerity....as fascinating as any novel."

Sheffield Telegraph, England: "...a monumental work."

With the translation of the book into other languages, many more reviews began appearing in newspapers and periodicals around the world.

Il Tempo del Lunedì, Rome: "Pages that will enthrall the reader, because they appeal to the aspiration and longing that slumber in the heart of every man."

China Weekly Review, Shanghai: "The contents of this book are unusual...particularly to the contemporary Christian whose comfortable habit is to relegate miracles to past centuries....The philosophical passages are extremely interesting. Yogananda is on a spiritual plane above religious differences....The book is well worth reading."

Haagsche Post, Holland: "...fragments of a wisdom so deep that one feels spellbound, permanently moved."

Welt und Wort, German literary monthly: "Extremely impressive....The singular value of *Autobiography of a Yogi* is that here, for the first time, a yogi breaks his silence and tells of his spiritual experiences. Heretofore, such an account would have been viewed with skepticism. But today the world situation is such that one is forced to acknowledge the value of such a book. ...The whole aim of the author is not to present Indian Yoga in opposition to the Christian teaching, but as allied with it—as companions traveling toward the same great goal."

Eleftheria, Greece: "It is a book by which a reader...will see his horizon of thoughts enlarged to the infinite, and will realize that his heart is capable of beating for all human beings, irrespective of color and race. It is a book that can be called inspired."

Neue Telta Zeitung, Austria: "One of the deepest and most important messages of this century."

La Paz, Bolivia: "The reader of our present times will seldom find such a beautiful, deep, and truthful book as *Autobiography of a Yogi*....Full of knowledge and rich in personal experiences.... One of the most dazzling chapters of the book is one that deals with the mysteries of life beyond physical death."

Schleswig-Holsteinische Tagespost, Germany: "These pages reveal, with incomparable strength and clarity, a fascinating life, a personality of such unheard-of greatness that from beginning to end the reader is left breathless....We must credit this important biography with the power to bring about a spiritual revolution."

A second edition was quickly prepared, and in 1951 a third. In addition to revising and updating portions of the text, and deleting some passages describing organizational activities and plans that were no longer current, Paramahansa Yogananda added a final chapter—one of the longest in the book—covering the years 1940–1951. In a footnote to the new chapter, he wrote, "Much new material in Chapter 49 has been added to the third edition of this book (1951). In response to requests made by a number of readers of the first two editions, I have answered, in this chapter, various questions about India, yoga, and Vedic philosophy." *

* Additional revisions made by Paramahansa Yogananda were included in the seventh edition (1956), as described in a Publisher's Note to this edition:

"This 1956 American edition contains revisions made by Paramahansa Yogananda in 1949 for the London, England, edition; and additional revisions made by the author in 1951. In a 'Note to the London Edition,' dated October 25, 1949, Paramahansa Yogananda wrote: 'The arrangement for a London edition of this book has given me an opportunity to revise, and slightly to enlarge, the text. Besides new material in the last chapter, I have added a number of footnotes in which I have answered questions sent me by readers of the American edition.'

"Later revisions, made by the author in 1951, were intended to appear in the fourth (1952) American edition. At that time the rights in *Autobiography of a Yogi* were vested in a New York publishing house. In 1946 in New York each page of the book had been made into an electrotype plate. Consequently, to add even a comma requires that the metal plate of an entire page be cut apart and resoldered with a new line containing the desired comma. Because of the expense involved in resoldering many plates, the New York publisher did not include in the fourth edition the author's 1951 revisions.

"In late 1953 Self-Realization Fellowship (SRF) bought from the New York publisher all rights in *Autobiography of a Yogi*. SRF reprinted the book in 1954 and 1955 (fifth and sixth editions); but during those two years other duties prevented the SRF editorial department from undertaking the formidable task of incorporating the author's revisions on the electrotype plates. The work, however, has been accomplished in time for the seventh edition."

After 1956, some further editorial revisions were made, in accordance with guidance Tara Mata had received from Paramahansa Yogananda before his passing.

Early editions of *Autobiography of a Yogi* gave the author's title as "Paramhansa," reflecting the common Bengali practice of omitting silent or near-silent *a*'s in spelling. To ensure that the sacred significance of this Veda-based title would be conveyed, in later editions the standard Sanskrit transliteration has been used: "Paramahansa," from *parama*, "highest or supreme" and *hansa*, "swan"—signifying one who has attained highest realization of his true divine Self, and of the unity of that Self with Spirit.

❖ ❖ ❖

"I have been intensely moved," Sri Yogananda wrote in an Author's Note to the 1951 edition, "to receive letters from thousands of readers. Their comments, and the fact that the book has been translated into many languages, encourages me to believe that the West has found in these pages an affirmative answer to the question: 'Has the ancient science of yoga any worthwhile place in the life of the modern man?'"

With the passing years "thousands of readers" became millions, and the enduring and universal appeal of *Autobiography of a Yogi* has become increasingly apparent. Sixty years after the book was first published, it is still appearing on metaphysical and inspirational best-seller lists. A rare phenomenon! Available in many translations, it is now being used in colleges and universities all over the world in courses ranging from Eastern philosophy and religion to English literature, psychology, sociology, anthropology, history, and even business management. As predicted more than a century ago by Lahiri Mahasaya, the message of yoga and its ancient tradition of meditation has indeed encircled the globe.

"Perhaps best known for his *Autobiography of a Yogi*, which has inspired countless millions around the world," writes the metaphysical journal *New Frontier* (October 1986), "Paramahansa Yogananda, like Gandhi, brought spirituality into the mainstream of society. It is reasonable to say that Yogananda did more to put the word 'yoga' into our vocabulary than any other person."

The respected scholar Dr. David Frawley, Director of the American Institute of Vedic Studies, writing in the bimonthly journal *Yoga International* (October/November 1996), states, "Yogananda can be said to be the father of yoga in the West—not the mere physical yoga that has become popular, but the spiritual yoga, the science of Self-realization that is the real meaning of yoga."

Professor Ashutosh Das, Ph.D., D.Litt., of Calcutta University, declares, "*Autobiography of a Yogi* is regarded as an Upanishad of the new age....It has satisfied the spiritual thirst of truth-seekers throughout the world. We in India have watched with wonder and fascination the phenomenal spread of the popularity of this book about India's saints and philosophy. We have felt great satisfaction and pride that the immortal nectar of India's *Sanatana Dharma*, the eternal laws of truth, has been stored in the golden chalice of *Autobiography of a Yogi*."

Even in the former Soviet Union, the book apparently made a

deep impression on the relative few who had access to it under the communist regime. Justice V. R. Krishna Iyer, former judge of India's Supreme Court, tells of visiting a town near St. Petersburg (then Leningrad) and asking a group of professors there "whether they had thought about what happens when man dies....One of the professors quietly went inside and came out with a book—*Autobiography of a Yogi*. I was surprised. In a country ruled by the materialistic philosophy of Marx and Lenin, here is an official of a government institute showing me Paramahansa Yogananda's book! 'Please realize that the spirit of India is not alien to us,' he said. 'We accept the authenticity of everything recorded in this book.'"

"Among the thousands of books that are published each year," concluded an article in *India Journal* (April 21, 1995), "there are those that entertain, those that instruct, those that edify. A reader can consider himself fortunate if he finds one that does all three. *Autobiography of a Yogi* is rarer still—it is a book that opens windows of the mind and spirit."

In recent years, the book has been hailed by booksellers, reviewers, and readers alike as one of the most influential spiritual books of modern times. In a 1999 HarperCollins panel of authors and scholars, *Autobiography of a Yogi* was selected as one of the "100 Best Spiritual Books of the Century," and in his *50 Spiritual Classics* which was released in 2005, Tom Butler-Bowden wrote that the book was "justifiably celebrated as one of the most entertaining and enlightening spiritual books ever written."

❖ ❖ ❖

In the book's final chapter, Paramahansa Yogananda writes of the profound assurance which has been affirmed by saints and sages of all the world's religions down through the ages:

> *"God is Love; His plan for creation can be rooted only in love. Does not that simple thought, rather than erudite reasonings, offer solace to the human heart? Every saint who has penetrated to the core of Reality has testified that a divine universal plan exists and that it is beautiful and full of joy."*

As *Autobiography of a Yogi* continues in its second half-century, it is our hope that all readers of this inspiring work—those who are encountering it for the first time as well as those for whom it has become a long-cherished companion on life's path—will find their own souls opening to a deeper faith in the transcendent truth that lies at the heart of life's seeming mysteries.

SELF-REALIZATION FELLOWSHIP

Los Angeles, California
July 2007

THE ETERNAL LAW OF RIGHTEOUSNESS

The flag of a newly independent India (1947) has bands of deep saffron, white, and dark green. The navy blue *Dharma Chakra* ("Wheel of the Law") is a reproduction of the design appearing on the Sarnath Stone Pillar erected in the third century B.C. by Emperor Asoka.

The wheel was chosen as a symbol of the eternal law of righteousness; and, incidentally, as an honor to the memory of the world's most illustrious monarch. "His reign of forty years is without a parallel in history," writes the English historian, H. G. Rawlinson. "He has been compared at various times to Marcus Aurelius, St. Paul, and Constantine....250 years before Christ, Asoka had the courage to express his horror and remorse at the results of a successful campaign, and deliberately to renounce war as a means of policy."

Asoka's inherited dominions included India, Nepal, Afghanistan, and Baluchistan. The first internationalist, he sent religious and cultural missions, with many gifts and blessings, to Burma, Ceylon, Egypt, Syria, and Macedonia.

"Asoka, the third king of the Maurya line, was one...of the great philosopher-kings of history," the scholar P. Masson-Oursel observed. "No one has combined energy and benevolence, justice and charity, as he did. He was the living embodiment of his own time, and he comes before us as quite a modern figure. In the course of a long reign he achieved what seems to us to be a mere aspiration of the visionary: enjoying the greatest possible material power, he organized peace. Far beyond his own vast dominions he realized what has been the dream of some religions—universal order, an order embracing mankind."

"*Dharma* (cosmic law) aims at the happiness of all creatures." In his rock edicts and stone pillars, surviving to this day, Asoka lovingly advises the subjects of his far-flung empire that happiness is rooted in morality and godliness.

Modern India, aspiring to renew the eminence and prosperity that for millenniums enveloped the land, pays homage in her new flag to the memory of Asoka, sovereign "dear to the gods."

India

Khyber Pass
Peshawar· Taxila
KASHMIR
·SRINAGAR
·Rawalpindi

PUNJAB
Lahore·
·Amritsar
·SIMLA
TIBET

BALUCHISTAN
Moradabad·
·Dehra Dun
·Hardwar
·Naini Tal
Ranikhet
NEPAL
⛰ Mt. Everest

RAJPUTANA
Mohenjodaro
DELHI·
UNITED PROVINCES
Muttra·
·Bareilly
·Brindaban
·AGRA
·Gorakhpur
Patna
·DARJEELING
Cooch Behar·

·KARACHI
·Chitor
CENTRAL INDIA
Allahabad·
BANARAS
Purulia·
BENGAL
·Biur
·Ghurni
·Serampore

Ujjain
Ranchi·
Dakshineswar·
CALCUTTA
BIHAR
AND
ORISSA

·Baroda
CENTRAL PROVINCES
Wardha

Nasik·
BOMBAY
·Ajanta
·Ellora

BOMBAY
·Poona
HYDERABAD
Puri

·HYDERABAD
MADRAS PRESIDENCY
Bay of Bengal

MYSORE
Bangalore·
·Mysore
MADRAS
Conjeeveram·

Arabian Sea
·Tanjore

Madura·
Rameswaram·
CEYLON

Colombo·

N

*(Prior to 1947. Sections in the northwest now compose Pakistan;
in the northeast, Bangladesh.)*

AUTOBIOGRAPHY OF A YOGI

CHAPTER 1

My Parents and Early Life

The characteristic features of Indian culture have long been a search for ultimate verities and the concomitant disciple-guru* relationship.

My own path led to a Christlike sage; his beautiful life was chiseled for the ages. He was one of the great masters who are India's truest wealth. Emerging in every generation, they have bulwarked their land against the fate of ancient Egypt and Babylonia.

I find my earliest memories covering the anachronistic features of a previous incarnation. Clear recollections came to me of a distant life in which I had been a yogi† amid the Himalayan snows. These glimpses of the past, by some dimensionless link, also afforded me a glimpse of the future.

I still remember the helpless humiliations of infancy. I was resentfully conscious of being unable to walk and to express myself freely. Prayerful surges arose within me as I realized my bodily impotence. My strong emotional life was mentally expressed in words of many languages. Amid the inward confusion of tongues, I gradually became accustomed to hearing the Bengali syllables of my people. The beguiling scope of an infant's mind! adultly considered to be limited to toys and toes.

Psychological ferment and my unresponsive body brought me to many obstinate crying spells. I recall the general family bewilderment at my distress. Happier memories, too, crowd in on me: my mother's caresses, and my first attempts at lisping phrase and toddling step. These early triumphs, usually forgotten quickly, are yet a natural basis of self-confidence.

My far-reaching memories are not unique. Many yogis are known to have retained their self-consciousness without interruption by the dramatic transition to and from "life" and "death." If

---

* Spiritual teacher. The *Guru Gita* (verse 17) aptly describes the guru as "dispeller of darkness" (from *gu*, "darkness," and *ru*, "that which dispels").

† Practitioner of yoga, "union," ancient science of meditation on God. (See chapter 26: "The Science of Kriya Yoga.")

3

man be solely a body, its loss indeed ends his identity. But if prophets down the millenniums spake with truth, man is essentially a soul, incorporeal and omnipresent.

Although odd, clear memories of infancy are not extremely rare. During travels in numerous lands, I have heard very early recollections from the lips of veracious men and women.

I was born on January 5, 1893, in Gorakhpur in northeastern India near the Himalaya Mountains. There my first eight years were passed. We were eight children: four boys and four girls. I, Mukunda Lal Ghosh,* was the second son and the fourth child.

Father and Mother were Bengalis, of the *Kshatriya* caste.† Both were blessed with saintly nature. Their mutual love, tranquil and dignified, never expressed itself frivolously. A perfect parental harmony was the calm center for the revolving tumult of eight young lives.

Father, Bhagabati Charan Ghosh, was kind, grave, at times stern. Loving him dearly, we children yet observed a certain reverential distance. An outstanding mathematician and logician, he was guided principally by his intellect. But Mother was a queen of hearts, and taught us only through love. After her death, Father displayed more of his inner tenderness. I noticed then that his gaze often seemed to be metamorphosed into my mother's gaze.

In Mother's presence we children made an early bittersweet acquaintance with the scriptures. Mother would resourcefully summon from the *Mahabharata* and the *Ramayana*‡ suitable tales to meet the exigencies of discipline; on these occasions chastisement and instruction went hand in hand.

As a gesture of respect for Father, in the afternoons Mother would dress us children carefully to welcome him home from the office. He held a position, similar to that of a vice-president, in one of India's large companies: Bengal-Nagpur Railway. His work involved traveling; our family lived in several cities during my childhood.

Mother held an open hand toward the needy. Father was also kindly disposed, but his respect for law and order extended to the budget. One fortnight Mother spent, in feeding the poor, more than Father's monthly income.

"All I ask, please," Father said, "is that you keep your charities

---

* My name was changed to Yogananda in 1915 when I entered the ancient monastic Swami Order. In 1935 my guru bestowed on me the further religious title of *Paramahansa* (see pp. 195 and 341).

† The second caste, originally that of rulers and warriors.

‡ These ancient epics are a hoard of India's history, mythology, and philosophy.

within a reasonable limit." Even a gentle rebuke from her husband was grievous to Mother. Not hinting to the children at any disagreement, she ordered a hackney carriage.

"Good-bye, I am going away to my mother's home." Ancient ultimatum!

We broke into astounded lamentations. Our maternal uncle arrived opportunely; he whispered to Father some sage counsel, garnered no doubt from the ages. After Father had made a few conciliatory remarks, Mother happily dismissed the cab. Thus ended the only trouble I ever noticed between my parents. But I recall a charactcristic discussion.

"Please give me ten rupees for a hapless woman who has just arrived at the house." Mother's smile had its own persuasion.

"Why ten rupees? One is enough." Father added a justification: "When my father and grandparents died suddenly, I had my first experience of poverty. My only breakfast, before walking miles to my school, was a small banana. Later, at the university, I was in such need that I applied to a wealthy judge for aid of one rupee per month. He declined, remarking that even a rupee is important."

"How bitterly you recall the denial of that rupee!" Mother's heart had an instant logic. "Do you want this woman also to remember painfully your refusal of ten rupees, which she needs urgently?"

"You win!" With the immemorial gesture of vanquished husbands, he opened his wallet. "Here is a ten-rupee note. Give it to her with my goodwill."

Father tended first to say "No" to any new proposal. His attitude toward the stranger who so readily had won Mother's sympathy was an example of his customary caution. An aversion to instant acceptance is really only honoring the principle of "due reflection." I always found Father reasonable and evenly balanced in his judgments. If I could bolster up my numerous requests with one or two good arguments, he would invariably put within my reach the coveted goal—whether a vacation trip or a new motorcycle.

Father was a strict disciplinarian to his children in their early years, but his attitude toward himself was truly Spartan. He never visited the theater, for instance, but sought his recreation in various spiritual practices and in reading the Bhagavad Gita.* Shunning all

---

* This noble Sanskrit poem, which forms part of the *Mahabharata* epic, is the Hindu Bible. Mahatma Gandhi wrote: "Those who will meditate on the Gita will derive fresh joy and new meanings from it every day. There is not a single spiritual tangle which the Gita cannot unravel."

luxuries, he would cling to one old pair of shoes until they were useless. His sons bought automobiles after they came into popular use, but Father was content with the trolley car for his daily ride to the office.

Father was not interested in the accumulation of money for the sake of power. On one occasion, after he had organized the Calcutta Urban Bank, he refused to benefit himself by holding any of its shares. He had simply wished to perform a civic duty in his spare time.

Several years after Father had retired on a pension, an accountant from England came to India to examine the books of Bengal-Nagpur Railway. The amazed investigator discovered that Father had never applied for overdue bonuses.

"He did the work of three men!" the accountant told the company. "He has rupees 125,000 ($41,250) owing to him as back compensation." The treasurer sent Father a check for that amount. My parent thought so little about the matter that he forgot to mention it to the family. Much later he was questioned by my youngest brother Bishnu, who had noticed the large deposit on a bank statement.

"Why be elated by material profit?" Father replied. "The one who pursues a goal of evenmindedness is neither jubilant with gain nor depressed by loss. He knows that man arrives penniless in this world, and departs without a single rupee."

Early in their married life, my parents became disciples of a great master, Lahiri Mahasaya of Banaras. This association strengthened Father's naturally ascetical temperament. Mother once made a remarkable admission to my eldest sister Roma: "Your father and I sleep together as man and wife only once a year, for the purpose of having children."

Father met Lahiri Mahasaya through Abinash Babu,* an employee of a branch line of Bengal-Nagpur Railway. In Gorakhpur, Abinash Babu instructed my young ears with engrossing tales of many Indian saints. He invariably concluded with a tribute to the superior glories of his own guru.

"Did you ever hear of the extraordinary circumstances under which your father became a disciple of Lahiri Mahasaya?" It was on a lazy summer afternoon, as Abinash and I sat together in the compound of my home, that he put this intriguing question. I shook my head with a smile of anticipation.

---

* *Babu* (Mister) is placed in Bengali names at the end.

"Years ago, before you were born, I asked my superior officer—
your father—to give me a week's leave from my office duties in
order to visit my guru in Banaras. Your father ridiculed my plan.

"'Are you going to become a religious fanatic?' he inquired.
'Concentrate on your office work if you want to forge ahead.'

"Sadly walking home along a woodland path that day, I met
your father in a palanquin. He dismissed his servants and con-
veyance, and fell into step beside me. Seeking to console me, he
pointed out the advantages of striving for worldly success. But I
heard him listlessly. My heart was repeating: 'Lahiri Mahasaya! I
cannot live without seeing you!'

"Our path took us to the edge of a tranquil field, where the rays
of the late afternoon sun were crowning the tall ripple of the wild
grass. We paused in admiration. There in the field, only a few yards
from us, the form of my great guru suddenly appeared!*

"'Bhagabati, you are too hard on your employee!' His voice
was resonant in our astounded ears. He vanished as mysteriously
as he had come. On my knees I was exclaiming, 'Lahiri Mahasaya!
Lahiri Mahasaya!' For a few moments your father was motionless
with stupefaction.

"'Abinash, not only do I give *you* leave, but I give *myself* leave
to start for Banaras tomorrow. I must know this great Lahiri Mahasaya, who is able to materialize himself at will in order to intercede
for you! I will take my wife and ask this master to initiate us in his
spiritual path. Will you guide us to him?'

"'Of course.' Joy filled me at the miraculous answer to my
prayer, and the quick, favorable turn of events.

"The next evening your parents and I entrained for Banaras.
Reaching there on the following day, we took a horse cart for some
distance, then had to walk through narrow lanes to my guru's secluded home. Entering his little parlor, we bowed before the master,
enlocked in his habitual lotus posture. He blinked his piercing eyes
and leveled them on your father. 'Bhagabati, you are too hard on
your employee!' His words were the same as those he had used two
days before in the grassy field. He added, 'I am glad that you have
permitted Abinash to visit me, and that you and your wife have
accompanied him.'

"To their joy, he initiated your parents in the spiritual practice

* The phenomenal powers possessed by great masters are explained in chapter 30,
"The Law of Miracles."

of *Kriya Yoga*.* Your father and I, as brother disciples, have been close friends since the memorable day of the vision. Lahiri Mahasaya took a definite interest in your own birth. Your life shall surely be linked with his own; the master's blessing never fails."

Lahiri Mahasaya left this world shortly after I had entered it. His picture, in an ornate frame, always graced our family altar in the various cities to which Father was transferred by his office. Many a morning and evening found Mother and me meditating before an improvised shrine, offering flowers dipped in fragrant sandalwood paste. With frankincense and myrrh as well as our united devotions, we honored the divinity that had found full expression in Lahiri Mahasaya.

His picture had a surpassing influence over my life. As I grew, the thought of the master grew with me. In meditation I would often see his photographic image emerge from its small frame and, taking a living form, sit before me. When I attempted to touch the feet of his luminous body, it would change and again become the picture. As childhood slipped into boyhood, I found Lahiri Mahasaya transformed in my mind from a little image, cribbed in a frame, to a living, enlightening presence. I frequently prayed to him in moments of trial or confusion, finding within me his solacing direction.

At first I grieved because he was no longer physically living. As I began to discover his secret omnipresence, I lamented no more. He had often written to those of his disciples who were over-anxious to see him: "Why come to view my flesh and bones, when I am ever within range of your *kutastha* (spiritual sight)?"

At about the age of eight I was blessed with a wonderful healing through the photograph of Lahiri Mahasaya. This experience gave intensification to my love. While at our family estate in Ichapur, Bengal, I was stricken with Asiatic cholera. My life was despaired of; the doctors could do nothing. At my bedside, Mother frantically motioned me to look at Lahiri Mahasaya's picture on the wall above my head.

"Bow to him mentally!" She knew I was too feeble even to lift my hands in salutation. "If you really show your devotion and inwardly kneel before him, your life will be spared!"

---

* A yogic technique, taught by Lahiri Mahasaya, whereby the sensory tumult is stilled, permitting man to achieve an ever-increasing identity with cosmic consciousness. (See chapter 26.)

BHAGABATI CHARAN GHOSH (1853–1942)
Father of Yoganandaji; disciple of Lahiri Mahasaya

GURRU (Gyana Prabha) GHOSH (1868–1904)
Mother of Yoganandaji; disciple of Lahiri Mahasaya

(*Left*) Sri Yogananda at age six. (*Right*) Jitendra Mazumdar, Yoganandaji's companion in the "penniless test" in Brindaban (ch. 11).

(*Left*) Yoganandaji's elder sister Uma as a young girl, Gorakhpur. (*Right*) Eldest sister Roma (*left*) and younger sister Nalini, with Paramahansa Yogananda at his boyhood home, Calcutta, 1935.

I gazed at his photograph and saw there a blinding light, enveloping my body and the entire room. My nausea and other uncontrollable symptoms disappeared; I was well. At once I felt strong enough to bend over and touch Mother's feet in appreciation of her immeasurable faith in her guru. Mother pressed her head repeatedly against the little picture.

"O Omnipresent Master, I thank thee that thy light hath healed my son!"

I realized that she too had witnessed the luminous blaze through which I had instantly recovered from a usually fatal disease.

One of my most precious possessions is that same photograph. Given to Father by Lahiri Mahasaya himself, it carries a holy vibration. The picture had a miraculous origin. I heard the story from Father's brother disciple, Kali Kumar Roy.

It appears that the master had an aversion to being photographed. Over his protest, a picture was once taken of him and a group of devotees, including Kali Kumar Roy. It was an amazed photographer who discovered that the plate, which had clear images of all the disciples, revealed nothing more than a blank space in the center where he had reasonably expected to find the outlines of Lahiri Mahasaya. The phenomenon was widely discussed.

A student who was an expert photographer, Ganga Dhar Babu, boasted that the fugitive figure would not escape him. The next morning, as the guru sat in lotus posture on a wooden bench with a screen behind him, Ganga Dhar Babu arrived with his equipment. Taking every precaution for success, he greedily exposed twelve plates. On each one he soon found the imprint of the wooden bench and screen, but once again the master's form was missing.

With tears and shattered pride, Ganga Dhar Babu sought out his guru. It was many hours before Lahiri Mahasaya broke his silence with a pregnant comment:

"I am Spirit. Can your camera reflect the omnipresent Invisible?"

"I see it cannot! But, Holy Sir, I lovingly desire a picture of your bodily temple. My vision has been narrow; until today I did not realize that in you the Spirit fully dwells."

"Come, then, tomorrow morning. I will pose for you."

Again the photographer focused his camera. This time the sacred figure, not cloaked with mysterious imperceptibility, was sharp on the plate. The master never posed for another picture; at least, I have seen none.

The photograph is reproduced in this book.* Lahiri Mahasaya's fair features, of a universal cast, hardly suggest to what race he belonged. The joy of God-communion is slightly revealed in his enigmatic smile. His eyes, half open to denote a nominal interest in the outer world, are also half closed, indicating his absorption in inner bliss. Oblivious of the poor lures of the earth, he was fully awake at all times to the spiritual problems of seekers who approached for his bounty.

Shortly after my healing through the potency of the guru's picture, I had an influential spiritual vision. Sitting on my bed one morning, I fell into a deep reverie.

"What is behind the darkness of closed eyes?" This probing thought came powerfully into my mind. An immense flash of light at once manifested to my inner gaze. Divine shapes of saints, sitting in meditation posture in mountain caves, formed like miniature cinema pictures on the large screen of radiance within my forehead.

"Who are you?" I spoke aloud.

"We are the Himalayan yogis." The celestial response is difficult to describe; my heart was thrilled.

"Ah, I long to go to the Himalayas and become like you!" The vision vanished, but the silvery beams expanded in ever-widening circles to infinity.

"What is this wondrous glow?"

"I am Ishwara.† I am Light." The Voice was as murmuring clouds.

"I want to be one with Thee!"

Out of the slow dwindling of my divine ecstasy, I salvaged a permanent legacy of inspiration to seek God. "He is eternal, ever-new Joy!" This memory persisted long after the day of rapture.

Another early recollection is outstanding; and literally so, for I bear the scar to this day. My elder sister Uma and I were seated in the

---

* Opposite page 273. Copies of the photograph are available from Self-Realization Fellowship. See also painting of Lahiri Mahasaya opposite page 304. While in India in 1935–36, Sri Paramahansa Yogananda instructed a Bengali artist to paint this rendering of the original photograph, and later designated it as the formal portrait of Lahiri Mahasaya for use in SRF publications. (This painting hangs in Paramahansa Yogananda's sitting room at Mt. Washington.) *(Publisher's Note)*

† A Sanskrit name for the Lord in His aspect of Cosmic Ruler; from the root *is*, to rule. The Hindu scriptures contain a thousand names for God, each one carrying a different shade of philosophical meaning. The Lord as Ishwara is He by whose will all universes, in orderly cycles, are created and dissolved.

early morning under a *neem* tree in our Gorakhpur compound. She was helping me in my study of a Bengali primer, what time I could spare my gaze from the nearby parrots eating ripe margosa fruit.

Uma complained of a boil on her leg, and fetched a jar of ointment. I smeared a bit of the salve on my forearm.

"Why do you use medicine on a healthy arm?"

"Well, Sis, I feel I am going to have a boil tomorrow. I am testing your ointment on the spot where the boil will appear."

"You little liar!"

"Sis, don't call me a liar until you see what happens in the morning." Indignation filled me.

Uma, unimpressed, thrice repeated her taunt. An adamant resolution sounded in my voice as I made slow reply.

"By the power of will in me, I say that tomorrow I shall have a fairly large boil in this exact place on my arm; and *your* boil shall swell to twice its present size!"

Morning found me with a stalwart boil on the indicated spot; the dimensions of Uma's boil had doubled. With a shriek, my sister rushed to Mother. "Mukunda has become a necromancer!" Gravely, Mother instructed me never to use the power of words for doing harm. I have always remembered her counsel, and followed it.

My boil was surgically treated. A noticeable scar, left by the doctor's incision, is present today. On my right forearm is a constant reminder of the power in man's sheer word.

Those simple and apparently harmless phrases to Uma, spoken with deep concentration, had possessed sufficient hidden force to explode like bombs and to produce definite, though injurious, effects. I understood later that the explosive vibratory power in speech could be wisely directed to free one's life from difficulties and thus operate without scar or rebuke.*

Our family moved to Lahore in the Punjab. There I acquired a picture of the Divine Mother in the form of the Goddess Kali.† It sanctified a small informal shrine on the balcony of our home. An unequivocal conviction came over me that fulfillment would crown any of my prayers uttered in that sacred spot. Standing there with Uma one day, I watched two boys flying kites over the roofs of

---

* The infinite potencies of sound derive from the Creative Word, *Aum*, the cosmic vibratory power behind all atomic energies. Any word spoken with clear realization and deep concentration has a materializing value. Loud or silent repetition of inspiring words has been found effective in Couéism and similar systems of psychotherapy; the secret lies in the stepping-up of the mind's vibratory rate.

† Kali is a symbol of God in the aspect of eternal Mother Nature.

two buildings that were separated from our house by an extremely narrow lane.

"Why are you so quiet?" Uma pushed me playfully.

"I am just thinking how wonderful it is that Divine Mother gives me whatever I ask."

"I suppose She would give you those two kites!" My sister laughed derisively.

"Why not?" I began silent prayers for their possession.

Matches are played in India with kites whose strings are covered with glue and ground glass. Each player attempts to sever the string held by his opponent. A freed kite sails over the roofs; there is great fun in catching it. As Uma and I were on a roofed, recessed balcony, it seemed impossible that a loosed kite could come into our hands; its string would naturally dangle over the roof.

The players across the lane began their match. One string was cut; immediately the kite floated in my direction. Owing to a sudden abatement of the breeze the kite remained stationary for a moment, during which its string became firmly entangled with a cactus plant on top of the opposite house. A long, perfect loop was formed for my seizure. I handed the prize to Uma.

"It was just an extraordinary accident, and not an answer to your prayer. If the other kite comes to you, then I shall believe." Sister's dark eyes conveyed more amazement than her words. I continued my prayers with intensity. A forcible tug by the other player resulted in the abrupt loss of his kite. It headed toward me, dancing in the wind. My helpful assistant, the cactus plant, again secured the kite string in the necessary loop by which I could grasp it. I presented my second trophy to Uma.

"Indeed, Divine Mother listens to you! This is all too uncanny for me!" Sister bolted away like a frightened fawn.

CHAPTER 2

My Mother's Death
and the Mystic Amulet

My mother's greatest desire was the marriage of my elder brother. "Ah, when I behold the face of Ananta's wife, I shall find heaven on this earth!" I frequently heard Mother express in these words her strong Indian sentiment for family continuity.

I was about eleven years old at the time of Ananta's betrothal. Mother was in Calcutta, joyously supervising the wedding preparations. Father and I alone remained at our home in Bareilly in northern India, whence Father had been transferred after two years at Lahore.

I had previously witnessed the splendor of nuptial rites for my two elder sisters, Roma and Uma; but for Ananta, as the eldest son, plans were truly elaborate. Mother was welcoming numerous relatives, daily arriving in Calcutta from distant homes. She lodged them comfortably in a large, newly acquired house at 50 Amherst Street. Everything was in readiness—the banquet delicacies, the gay throne on which Brother was to be carried to the home of the bride-to-be, the rows of colorful lights, the mammoth cardboard elephants and camels, the English, Scottish, and Indian orchestras, the professional entertainers, the priests for the ancient rituals.

Father and I, in gala spirits, were planning to join the family in time for the ceremony. Shortly before the great day, however, I had an ominous vision.

It was in Bareilly on a midnight. As I slept beside Father on the piazza of our bungalow, I was awakened by a peculiar flutter of the mosquito netting over the bed. The flimsy curtains parted and I saw the beloved form of my mother.

"Awaken your father!" Her voice was only a whisper. "Take the first available train, at four o'clock this morning. Rush to Calcutta if you would see me!" The wraithlike figure vanished.

"Father, Father! Mother is dying!" The terror in my tone aroused him instantly. I sobbed out the fatal tidings.

"Never mind that hallucination of yours." Father gave his char-

13

acteristic negation to a new situation. "Your mother is in excellent health. If we get any bad news, we shall leave tomorrow."

"You shall never forgive yourself for not starting now!" Anguish caused me to add bitterly, "Nor shall I ever forgive you!"

The melancholy morning came with explicit words: "Mother dangerously ill; marriage postponed; come at once."

Father and I left distractedly. One of my uncles met us en route at a transfer point. A train thundered toward us, looming with telescopic increase. From my inner tumult, an abrupt determination arose to hurl myself on the railway tracks. Already bereft, I felt, of my mother, I could not endure a world suddenly bare to the bone. I loved Mother as my dearest friend on earth. Her solacing black eyes had been my refuge in the trifling tragedies of childhood.

"Does she yet live?" I stopped for one last question to my uncle.

He was not slow to interpret the desperation in my face. "Of course she is alive!" But I scarcely believed him.

When we reached our Calcutta home, it was only to confront the stunning mystery of death. I collapsed into an almost lifeless state. Years passed before any reconciliation entered my heart. Storming the very gates of heaven, my cries at last summoned the Divine Mother. Her words brought final healing to my suppurating wounds:

"It is I who have watched over thee, life after life, in the tenderness of many mothers. See in My gaze the two black eyes, the lost beautiful eyes, thou seekest!"

Father and I returned to Bareilly soon after the crematory rites for the well-beloved. Early every morning I made a pathetic memorial-pilgrimage to a large *sheoli* tree which shaded the smooth, green-gold lawn before our bungalow. In poetical moments, I thought that the white *sheoli* flowers were strewing themselves with a willing devotion over the grassy altar. Mingling tears with the dew, I often observed a strange other-worldly light emerging from the dawn. Intense pangs of longing for God assailed me. I felt powerfully drawn to the Himalayas.

One of my cousins, fresh from a period of travel in the holy hills, visited us in Bareilly. I listened eagerly to his tales about the high mountain abode of yogis and swamis.*

"Let us run away to the Himalayas." My suggestion one day to Dwarka Prasad, the young son of our landlord in Bareilly, fell on

---

* Sanskrit root meaning of *swami* is "he who is one with his Self (*Swa*)." (See chapter 24.)

unsympathetic ears. He revealed my plan to my elder brother, who had just arrived to see Father. Instead of laughing lightly over this impractical scheme of a small boy, Ananta made it a definite point to ridicule me.

"Where is your orange robe? You can't be a swami without that!"

But I was inexplicably thrilled by his words. They brought me a clear picture: that of myself as a monk, roaming about India. Perhaps they awakened memories of a past life; in any case, I realized with what natural ease I would wear the garb of the anciently founded monastic order.

Chatting one morning with Dwarka, I felt a love for God descending with avalanchelike force. My companion was only partly attentive to the ensuing eloquence, but I was wholeheartedly listening to myself.

I fled that afternoon toward Naini Tal in the Himalayan foothills. Ananta gave determined chase; I was forced to return sadly to Bareilly. The only pilgrimage permitted me was the customary one at dawn to the *sheoli* tree. My heart wept for my two lost mothers: one human, one Divine.

The rent left in the family fabric by Mother's death was irreparable. Father never remarried during his nearly forty remaining years. Assuming the difficult role of father-mother to his little flock, he grew noticeably more tender, more approachable. With calmness and insight, he solved the various family problems. After office hours he retired like a hermit to the cell of his room, practicing *Kriya Yoga* in a sweet serenity. Long after Mother's death, I attempted to engage an English nurse to attend to details that would make my parent's life more comfortable. But Father shook his head.

"Service to me ended with your mother." His eyes were remote with a lifelong devotion. "I will not accept ministrations from any other woman."

Fourteen months after Mother's passing, I learned that she had left me a momentous message. Ananta had been present at her deathbed and had recorded her words. Though she had asked that the disclosure be made to me in one year, my brother had delayed. He was soon to leave Bareilly for Calcutta, to marry the girl that Mother had chosen for him.* Once evening he summoned me to his side.

---

* The Indian custom, whereby parents choose the life partner for their child, has resisted the blunt assaults of time. The percentage is high of happy Indian marriages.

"Mukunda, I have been reluctant to give you strange tidings." Ananta's tone held a note of resignation. "My fear was to inflame your desire to leave home. But in any case you are bristling with divine ardor. When I captured you recently on your way to the Himalayas, I came to a definite resolve. I must not further postpone the fulfillment of my solemn promise." My brother handed me a small box, and delivered Mother's message.

"Let these words be my final blessing, my beloved son Mukunda!" Mother had said. "The hour is here when I must relate a number of phenomenal events following your birth. I first knew your destined path when you were but a babe in my arms. I carried you then to the home of my guru in Banaras. Almost hidden behind a throng of disciples, I could barely see Lahiri Mahasaya as he sat in deep meditation.

"While I patted you, I was praying that the great guru take notice and bestow a blessing. As my silent devotional demand grew in intensity, he opened his eyes and beckoned me to approach. The others made a way for me; I bowed at the sacred feet. Lahiri Mahasaya seated you on his lap, placing his hand on your forehead by way of spiritually baptizing you.

"'Little mother, thy son will be a yogi. As a spiritual engine, he will carry many souls to God's kingdom.'

"My heart leaped with joy to find my secret prayer granted by the omniscient guru. Shortly before your birth, he had told me you would follow his path.

"Later, my son, your vision of the Great Light was known to me and your sister Roma, as from the next room we observed you motionless on the bed. Your little face was illuminated; your voice rang with iron resolve as you spoke of going to the Himalayas in quest of the Divine.

"In these ways, dear son, I came to know that your road lies far from worldly ambitions. The most singular event in my life brought further confirmation—an event which now impels my deathbed message.

"It was an interview with a sage in the Punjab. While our family was living in Lahore, one morning the servant came into my room. 'Mistress, a strange sadhu* is here. He insists that he "see the mother of Mukunda."'

"These simple words struck a profound chord within me; I went at once to greet the visitor. Bowing at his feet, I sensed that

---

* An anchorite; one devoted to asceticism and spiritual discipline.

SWAMI KEBALANANDA
Yoganandaji's beloved Sanskrit tutor

NAGENDRA NATH BHADURI
"The Levitating Saint"

MASTER MAHASAYA
"The Blissful Devotee"

SWAMI PRANABANANDA
The Banaras "Saint With Two Bodies"

before me was a true man of God.

"'Mother,' he said, 'the great masters wish you to know that your stay on earth shall not be long. Your next illness shall prove to be your last.'* There was a silence, during which I felt no alarm but only a vibration of great peace. Finally he addressed me again:

"'You are to be the custodian of a certain silver amulet. I will not give it to you today; to demonstrate the truth in my words, the talisman shall materialize in your hands tomorrow as you meditate. On your deathbed, you must instruct your eldest son Ananta to keep the amulet for one year and then to hand it over to your second son. Mukunda will understand the meaning of the talisman from the great ones. He should receive it about the time he is ready to renounce all worldly hopes and to start his vital search for God. When he has retained the amulet for some years, and when it has served its purpose, it shall vanish. Even if kept in the most secret spot, it shall return whence it came.'

"I proffered alms† to the saint, and bowed before him in great reverence. Not taking the offering, he departed with a blessing. The next evening, as I sat with folded hands in meditation, a silver amulet materialized between my palms, even as the sadhu had promised. It made itself known by a cold, smooth touch. I have jealously guarded it for more than two years, and now leave it in Ananta's keeping. Do not grieve for me, as I shall have been ushered by my great guru into the arms of the Infinite. Farewell, my child; the Cosmic Mother will protect you."

A blaze of illumination came over me with possession of the amulet; many dormant memories awakened. The talisman, round and anciently quaint, was covered with Sanskrit characters. I understood that it came from teachers of past lives, who were invisibly guiding my steps. A further significance there was, indeed; but one may not fully unveil the heart of an amulet.‡

---

* When I discovered by these words that Mother had possessed secret knowledge of a short life, I understood for the first time why she had been insistent on hastening the plans for Ananta's marriage. Though she died before the wedding, her natural maternal wish had been to witness the rites.

† A customary gesture of respect to sadhus.

‡ The amulet was an astrally produced object. Structurally evanescent, such objects must finally disappear from our earth. (See chapter 43.)

A *mantra* or sacred chant words were inscribed on the talisman. The potencies of sound and of *vach*, the human voice, have nowhere else been so profoundly investigated as in India. The *Aum* vibration that reverberates throughout the universe (the "Word" or "voice of many waters" of the Bible) has three manifestations or *gunas*, those of creation, preservation, and destruction (*Taittiriya Upanishad* I:8).

How the talisman finally vanished amidst deeply unhappy circumstances of my life, and how its loss was a herald of my gain of a guru, may not be told in this chapter.

But the small boy, thwarted in his attempts to reach the Himalayas, daily traveled far on the wings of his amulet.

Each time a man utters a word he puts into operation one of the three qualities of *Aum.* This is the lawful reason behind the injunction of all scriptures that man should speak the truth.

The Sanskrit *mantra* on the amulet possessed, when correctly pronounced, a spiritually beneficial vibratory potency. The Sanskrit alphabet, ideally constructed, consists of fifty letters, each one carrying a fixed invariable pronunciation. George Bernard Shaw wrote a wise, and of course witty, essay on the phonetic inadequacy of the Latin-based English alphabet, in which twenty-six letters struggle unsuccessfully to bear the burden of sound. With his customary ruthlessness ("If the introduction of an English alphabet for the English language costs a civil war...I shall not grudge it"), Mr. Shaw urges the adoption of a new alphabet with forty-two characters (see his preface to Wilson's *The Miraculous Birth of Language,* Philosophical Library, N.Y.). Such an alphabet would approximate the phonetic perfection of the Sanskrit, whose use of fifty letters prevents mispronunciations.

The discovery of seals in the Indus Valley is leading a number of scholars to abandon the current theory that India "borrowed" her Sanskrit alphabet from Semitic sources. A few great Hindu cities have been recently unearthed at Mohenjo-Daro and Harappa, affording proof of an eminent culture that "must have had a long antecedent history on the soil of India, taking us back to an age that can only be dimly surmised" (Sir John Marshall, *Mohenjo-Daro and the Indus Civilization,* 1931).

If the Hindu theory of the extremely great antiquity of civilized man on this planet be correct, it becomes possible to explain why the world's most *ancient* tongue, Sanskrit, is also the most *perfect.* (See p. 74 n.) "The Sanskrit language," said Sir William Jones, founder of the Asiatic Society, "whatever be its antiquity, is of a wonderful structure; more perfect than the Greek, more copious than the Latin, and more exquisitely refined than either."

"Since the revival of classical learning," the *Encyclopedia Americana* states, "there has been no other event in the history of culture as important as the discovery of Sanskrit [by Western scholars] in the latter part of the 18th century. Linguistic science, comparative grammar, comparative mythology, the science of religion... either owe their very existence to the discovery of Sanskrit or were profoundly influenced by its study."

CHAPTER 3

The Saint With Two Bodies

"Father, if I promise to return home without coercion, may I take a sight-seeing trip to Banaras?"

My keen love of travel was seldom hindered by Father. He permitted me, even as a mere boy, to visit many cities and pilgrimage spots. Usually one or more of my friends accompanied me; we would travel comfortably on first-class passes provided by Father. His position as a railroad official was fully satisfactory to the nomads in the family.

Father promised to give my request due consideration. The next day he summoned me and held out a round-trip pass from Bareilly to Banaras, a number of rupee notes, and two letters.

"I have a business matter to propose to a Banaras friend, Kedar Nath Babu. Unfortunately I have lost his address. But I believe you will be able to get this letter to him through our common friend, Swami Pranabananda. The swami, my brother disciple, has attained an exalted spiritual stature. You will benefit by his company; this second note will serve as your introduction."

Father's eyes twinkled as he added, "Mind, no more flights from home!"

I set forth with the zest of my twelve years (though time has never dimmed my delight in new scenes and strange faces). Reaching Banaras, I proceeded immediately to the swami's residence. The front door was open; I made my way to a long, hall-like room on the second floor. A rather stout man, wearing only a loincloth, was seated in lotus posture on a slightly raised platform. His head and unwrinkled face were clean-shaven; a beatific smile played about his lips. To dispel my thought that I had intruded, he greeted me as an old friend.

"*Baba anand* (bliss to my dear one)." His welcome was given heartily in a childlike voice. I knelt and touched his feet.

"Are you Swami Pranabananda?"

He nodded. "Are you Bhagabati's son?" His words were out before I had had time to get Father's letter from my pocket. In astonishment, I handed him the note of introduction, which now seemed superfluous.

"Of course I will locate Kedar Nath Babu for you." The saint again surprised me by his clairvoyance. He glanced at the letter, and made a few affectionate references to my parent.

"You know, I am enjoying two pensions. One is by the recommendation of your father, for whom I once worked in the railway office. The other is by the recommendation of my Heavenly Father, for whom I have conscientiously finished my earthly duties in life."

I found this remark very obscure. "What kind of pension, sir, do you receive from the Heavenly Father? Does He drop money in your lap?"

He laughed. "I mean a pension of fathomless peace—a reward for many years of deep meditation. I never crave money now. My few material needs are amply provided for. Later you will understand the significance of a second pension."

Abruptly terminating our conversation, the saint became gravely motionless. A sphinxlike air enveloped him. At first his eyes sparkled, as if observing something of interest, then grew dull. I felt abashed at his pauciloquy; he had not yet told me how I might meet Father's friend. A trifle restlessly, I looked about me in the bare room, empty except for us two. My idle gaze took in his wooden sandals, lying under the platform seat.

"Little sir,* don't get worried. The man you wish to see will be with you in half an hour." The yogi was reading my mind—a feat not too difficult at the moment!

Again he fell into inscrutable silence. When my watch informed me that thirty minutes had elapsed, the swami aroused himself.

"I think Kedar Nath Babu is nearing the door," he said.

I heard somebody coming up the stairs. An amazed incomprehension arose suddenly; my thoughts raced in confusion: "How is it possible that Father's friend has been summoned to this place without the help of a messenger? The swami has spoken to no one but me since my arrival!"

I unceremoniously quitted the room and descended the steps. Halfway down I met a thin, fair-skinned man of medium height. He appeared to be in a hurry.

"Are you Kedar Nath Babu?" Excitement colored my voice.

---

* *Choto Mahasaya* is the term by which a number of Indian saints addressed me. It means "little sir."

"Yes. Are you not Bhagabati's son who has been waiting here to meet me?" He smiled in friendly fashion.

"Sir, how do you happen to come here?" I felt baffled resentment over his inexplicable presence.

"Everything is mysterious today! Less than an hour ago I had just finished my bath in the Ganges when Swami Pranabananda approached me. I have no idea how he knew I was there at that time.

"'Bhagabati's son is waiting for you in my apartment,' he said. 'Will you come with me?' I gladly agreed. As we proceeded hand in hand, the swami in his wooden sandals was strangely able to outpace me, though I wore these stout walking shoes.

"'How long will it take you to reach my place?' Pranabanandaji suddenly halted to ask me this question.

"'About half an hour.'

"'I have something else to do at present.' He gave me an enigmatical glance. 'I must leave you behind. You can join me in my house, where Bhagabati's son and I will be awaiting you.'

"Before I could remonstrate, he dashed swiftly past me and disappeared in the crowd. I walked here as fast as possible."

This explanation only increased my bewilderment. I inquired how long he had known the swami.

"We met a few times last year, but not recently. I was very glad to see him again today at the bathing *ghat*."

"I cannot believe my ears! Am I losing my mind? Did you meet him in a vision, or did you actually see him, touch his hand, and hear the sound of his feet?"

"I don't know what you're driving at!" He flushed angrily. "I am not lying to you. Can't you understand that only through the swami could I have known you were waiting at this place for me?"

"Why, that man, Swami Pranabananda, has not left my sight a moment since I first came about an hour ago." I blurted out the whole story, and repeated the conversations the swami and I had had.

His eyes opened wide. "Are we living in this material age, or are we dreaming? I never expected to witness such a miracle in my life! I thought this swami was just an ordinary man, and now I find he can materialize an extra body and work through it!" Together we entered the saint's room. Kedar Nath Babu pointed to the shoes under the platform seat.

"Look, those are the very sandals he was wearing at the *ghat*," he whispered. "He was clad only in a loincloth, just as I see him now."

As the visitor bowed before him, the saint turned to me with a quizzical smile.

"Why are you stupefied at all this? The subtle unity of the phenomenal world is not hidden from true yogis. I instantly see and converse with my disciples in distant Calcutta. They can similarly transcend at will every obstacle of gross matter."

It was probably in an effort to stir spiritual ardor in my young breast that the swami had condescended to tell me of his powers of astral radio and television.* But instead of enthusiasm, I experienced only an awestricken fear. Inasmuch as I was destined to undertake my divine search through one particular guru—Sri Yukteswar, whom I had not yet met—I felt no inclination to accept Pranabananda as my teacher. I glanced at him doubtfully, wondering if it were he or his counterpart before me.

The master sought to banish my disquietude by bestowing a soul-awakening gaze, and by some inspiring words about his guru.

"Lahiri Mahasaya was the greatest yogi I ever knew. He was Divinity Itself in the form of flesh."

If a disciple, I reflected, could materialize an extra fleshly form at will, what miracles indeed could be barred to his master?

"I will tell you how priceless is a guru's help. I used to meditate with another disciple for eight hours every night. We had to work at the railway office during the day. Finding difficulty in carrying on my clerical duties, I desired to devote my whole time to God. For eight years I persevered, meditating half the night. I had wonderful results; tremendous spiritual perceptions illumined my mind. But a little veil always remained between me and the Infinite. Even with superhuman earnestness, I found the final irrevocable union to be denied me. One evening I paid a visit to Lahiri Mahasaya and pleaded for his divine intercession. My importunities continued during the entire night.

---

* In its own way, physical science is affirming the validity of laws discovered by yogis through mental science. For example, a demonstration that man has televisional powers was given on Nov. 26, 1934, at the Royal University of Rome. "Dr. Giuseppe Calligaris, professor of neuro-psychology, pressed certain parts of a subject's body and the subject responded with minute descriptions of persons and objects on the opposite side of a wall. Dr. Calligaris told the professors that if certain areas on the skin are agitated, the subject is given super-sensorial impressions enabling him to see objects that he could not otherwise perceive. To enable his subject to discern things on the other side of a wall, Professor Calligaris pressed a spot to the right of the thorax for fifteen minutes. Dr. Calligaris said that when certain spots of the body are agitated, the subjects can see objects at any distance, regardless of whether they have ever before seen those objects."

"'Angelic Guru, my spiritual anguish is such that I can no longer bear my life without meeting the Great Beloved face to face!'

"'What can I do? You must meditate more profoundly.'

"'I am appealing to Thee, O God my Master! I see Thee materialized before me in a physical body; bless me that I may perceive Thee in Thine infinite form!'

"Lahiri Mahasaya extended his hand in a benign gesture. 'You may go now and meditate. I have interceded for you with Brahma.'*

"Immeasurably uplifted, I returned to my home. In meditation that night, the burning Goal of my life was achieved. Now I ceaselessly enjoy the spiritual pension. Never from that day has the Blissful Creator remained hidden from my eyes behind any screen of delusion."

Pranabananda's face was suffused with divine light. The peace of another world entered my heart; all fear had fled. The saint made a further confidence.

"Some months later I returned to Lahiri Mahasaya and tried to thank him for his bestowal of the infinite gift. Then I mentioned another matter.

"'Divine Guru, I can no longer work in the office. Please release me. Brahma keeps me continuously intoxicated.'

"'Apply for a pension from your company.'

"'What reason shall I give, so early in my service?'

"'Say what you feel.'

"The next day I made my application. The doctor inquired the grounds for my premature request.

"'At work, I find an overpowering sensation rising in my spine. It permeates my whole body, unfitting me for the performance of my duties.'†

---

* God in His aspect of Creator; from Sanskrit root *brih*, to expand. When Emerson's poem "Brahma" appeared in the *Atlantic Monthly* in 1857, most of the readers were bewildered. Emerson chuckled. "Tell them," he said, "to say 'Jehovah' instead of 'Brahma' and they will not feel any perplexity."

† In deep meditation, the first experience of Spirit is on the altar of the spine, and then in the brain. The torrential bliss is overwhelming, but the yogi learns to control its outward manifestations.

At the time of our meeting, Pranabananda was, indeed, a fully illumined master. But the closing days in his business life had occurred many years earlier; he had not then become irrevocably established in *nirbikalpa samadhi* (see pp. 210, 353 n.). In that perfect and unshakable state of consciousness, a yogi finds no difficulty in performing any of his worldly duties.

After his retirement, Pranabananda wrote *Pranab Gita*, a profound commentary

"Without further questioning the physician recommended me highly for a pension, which I soon received. I know the divine will of Lahiri Mahasaya worked through the doctor and the railroad officials, including your father. Automatically they obeyed the great guru's spiritual direction, and freed me for a life of unbroken communion with the Beloved."

After this extraordinary revelation, Swami Pranabananda retired into one of his long silences. As I was taking leave, touching his feet reverently, he gave me his blessing:

"Your life belongs to the path of renunciation and yoga. I shall see you again, with your father, later on." The years brought fulfillment to both these predictions.*

Kedar Nath Babu walked by my side in the gathering darkness. I delivered Father's letter, which my companion read under a street lamp.

"Your father suggests that I take a position in the Calcutta office of his railway company. How pleasant to look forward to one, at least, of the pensions that Swami Pranabananda enjoys! But it is impossible; I cannot leave Banaras. Alas, two bodies are not yet for me!"

---

on the Bhagavad Gita, available in Hindi and Bengali.

The power of appearing in more than one body is a *siddhi* (yogic power) mentioned in Patanjali's *Yoga Sutras* (see p. 201 n.). The phenomenon of bilocation has been exhibited in the lives of many saints down the ages. In *The Story of Therese Neumann* (Bruce Pub. Co.), A. P. Schimberg describes several occasions on which this Christian saint has appeared before, and conversed with, distant persons needing her help.

* See chapter 27.

CHAPTER 4

My Interrupted Flight Toward the Himalayas

"Leave your classroom on some trifling pretext, and engage a hackney carriage. Stop in the lane where no one in my house can see you."

These were my final instructions to Amar Mitter, a high school friend who planned to accompany me to the Himalayas. We had chosen the following day for our flight. Precautions were necessary, as my brother Ananta exercised a vigilant eye. He was determined to foil the plans of escape that he suspected were uppermost in my mind. The amulet, like a spiritual yeast, was silently at work within me. I hoped to find, amid the Himalayan snows, the master whose face often appeared to me in visions.

The family was living now in Calcutta, where Father had been permanently transferred. Following the patriarchal Indian custom, Ananta had brought his bride to live in our home. There in a small attic room I engaged in daily meditations and prepared my mind for the divine search.

The memorable morning arrived with inauspicious rain. Hearing the wheels of Amar's carriage in the road, I hastily tied together a blanket, a pair of sandals, two loincloths, a string of prayer beads, Lahiri Mahasaya's picture, and a copy of the Bhagavad Gita. This bundle I threw from my third-story window. I ran down the steps and passed my uncle, buying fish at the door.

"What is the excitement?" His gaze roved suspiciously over my person.

I gave him a noncommittal smile and walked to the lane. Retrieving my bundle, I joined Amar with conspiratorial caution. We drove to Chandni Chauk, a merchandise center. For months we had been saving our tiffin money to buy English clothes. Knowing that my clever brother could easily play the part of a detective, we thought to outwit him by wearing European garb.

On the way to the station, we stopped for my cousin, Jotin Ghosh, whom I called Jatinda. He was a new convert, longing for a guru in the Himalayas. He donned the new suit we had in readiness. Well camouflaged, we hoped! A deep elation possessed our hearts.

"All we need now are canvas shoes." I led my companions to a shop displaying rubber-soled footwear. "Articles of leather, got only through the slaughter of animals, should be absent on this holy trip." I halted on the street to remove the leather cover from my Bhagavad Gita, and the leather straps from my English-made *sola topee* (helmet).

At the station we bought tickets to Burdwan, where we planned to transfer for Hardwar in the Himalayan foothills. As soon as the train, like ourselves, was in flight, I gave utterance to a few of my glorious anticipations.

"Just imagine!" I ejaculated. "We shall be initiated by the masters and experience the trance of cosmic consciousness. Our flesh will be charged with such magnetism that wild animals of the Himalayas will come tamely near us. Tigers will be no more than meek house cats awaiting our caresses!"

This remark—picturing a prospect I considered entrancing, both metaphorically and literally—brought an enthusiastic smile from Amar. But Jatinda averted his gaze, directing it through the window at the scampering landscape.

"Let the money be divided in three portions." Jatinda broke a long silence with this suggestion. "Each of us should buy his own ticket at Burdwan. Thus no one at the station will surmise that we are running away together."

I unsuspectingly agreed. At dusk our train stopped at Burdwan. Jatinda entered the ticket office; Amar and I sat on the platform. We waited fifteen minutes, then made unavailing inquiries. Searching in all directions, we shouted Jatinda's name with the urgency of fright. But he had faded into the dark unknown surrounding the little station.

I was completely unnerved, shocked to a peculiar numbness. That God would countenance this depressing episode! The romantic occasion of my first carefully planned flight after Him was cruelly marred.

"Amar, we must return home." I was weeping like a child. "Jatinda's callous departure is an ill omen. This trip is doomed to failure."

"Is this your love for the Lord? Can't you stand the little test of a treacherous companion?"

Through Amar's suggestion of a divine test, my heart steadied itself. We refreshed ourselves with famous Burdwan sweetmeats, *sitabhog* (food for the goddess) and *motichur* (nuggets of sweet pearl). In a few hours we entrained for Hardwar, via Bareilly. Changing trains the following day at Moghul Serai, we discussed a vital matter as we waited on the platform.

"Amar, we may soon be closely questioned by railroad officials. I am not underrating my brother's ingenuity! No matter what the outcome, I will not speak untruth."

"All I ask of you, Mukunda, is to keep still. Don't laugh or grin while I am talking."

At this moment a European station-agent accosted me. He waved a telegram whose import I immediately grasped.

"Are you running away from home in anger?"

"No!" I was glad his choice of words permitted me to make emphatic reply. Not anger but "divinest melancholy" was responsible, I knew, for my unconventional behavior.

The official then turned to Amar. The duel of wits that followed hardly permitted me to maintain the counseled stoic gravity.

"Where is the third boy?" The man injected a full ring of authority into his voice. "Come now—speak the truth!"

"Sir, I notice you are wearing eyeglasses. Can't you see that we are only two?" Amar smiled impudently. "I am not a magician; I can't conjure up a third boy."

The official, noticeably disconcerted by this impertinence, sought a new field of attack. "What is your name?"

"I am called Thomas. I am the son of an English mother and a converted Christian Indian father."

"What is your friend's name?"

"I call him Thompson."

By this time my inward mirth had reached a zenith; I unceremoniously made for the train, which was providentially whistling for departure. Amar followed with the official, who was credulous and obliging enough to put us into a European compartment. It evidently pained him to think of two half-English boys traveling in the section allotted to natives. After his polite exit, I lay back on the seat and laughed uproariously. Amar wore an expression of blithe satisfaction at having outwitted a veteran European official.

On the platform I had contrived to read the telegram. From my brother Ananta, it went thus: "Three Bengali boys in English clothes running away from home toward Hardwar via Moghul Serai. Please detain them until my arrival. Ample reward for your services."

"Amar, I told you not to leave marked timetables in your home."
My glance was reproachful. "Brother must have found one there."

My friend sheepishly acknowledged the thrust. We halted
briefly in Bareilly, where Dwarka Prasad* awaited us with a telegram from Ananta. Dwarka tried valiantly to detain us; I convinced
him that our flight had not been undertaken lightly. As on a previous occasion, Dwarka refused my invitation to set out for the
Himalayas.

While our train stood in a station that night, and I was half
asleep, Amar was awakened by another questioning official. He, too,
fell a victim to the hybrid charms of "Thomas" and "Thompson."
The train bore us triumphantly into a dawn arrival at Hardwar. The
majestic mountains loomed invitingly in the distance. We dashed
through the station and entered the freedom of city crowds. Our
first act was to change into native costume, as Ananta had somehow
penetrated our European disguise. A premonition of capture weighed
on my mind.

Deeming it advisable to leave Hardwar at once, we bought tickets to proceed north to Rishikesh, a soil long hallowed by the feet of
many masters. I had already boarded the train, while Amar lagged
on the platform. He was brought to an abrupt halt by a shout from
a policeman. An unwelcome guardian, the officer escorted Amar
and me to a police-station bungalow and took charge of our money.
He explained courteously that it was his duty to hold us until my
elder brother arrived.

Learning that the truants' destination had been the Himalayas,
the officer related a strange story.

"I see you are crazy about saints! You will never meet a greater
man of God than the one I saw only yesterday. My brother officer
and I first encountered him five days ago. We were patrolling by the
Ganges, on a sharp lookout for a certain murderer. Our instructions
were to capture him, alive or dead. He was known to be masquerading as a sadhu in order to rob pilgrims. A short way before us, we
spied a figure which resembled the description of the criminal. He
ignored our command to stop; we ran to overpower him. Approaching his back, I wielded my ax with tremendous force; the man's
right arm was severed almost completely from his body.

"Without outcry or any glance at the ghastly wound, the
stranger astonishingly continued his swift pace. As we jumped in
front of him, he spoke quietly.

* Mentioned on page 14.

"'I am not the murderer you are seeking.'

"I was deeply mortified to see I had injured the person of a divine-looking sage. Prostrating myself at his feet, I implored his pardon, and offered my turban cloth to staunch the heavy spurts of blood.

"'Son, that was just an understandable mistake on your part.' The saint regarded me kindly. 'Run along, and don't reproach yourself. The Beloved Mother is taking care of me.' He pushed his dangling arm into its stump and lo! it adhered; the blood inexplicably ceased to flow.

"'Come to me under yonder tree in three days and you will find me fully healed. Thus you will feel no remorse.'

"Yesterday my brother officer and I went eagerly to the designated spot. The sadhu was there and allowed us to examine his arm. It bore no scar nor trace of hurt!

"'I am going via Rishikesh to the Himalayan solitudes.' The sadhu blessed us as he departed quickly. I feel that my life has been uplifted through his sanctity."

The officer concluded with a pious ejaculation; his experience had obviously moved him beyond his usual depths. With an impressive gesture, he handed me a printed clipping about the miracle. In the usual garbled manner of the sensational type of newspaper (not missing, alas! even in India), the reporter's version was slightly exaggerated: it indicated that the sadhu had been almost decapitated!

Amar and I lamented that we had missed the great yogi who could forgive his persecutor in such a Christlike way. India, materially poor for the last two centuries, yet has an inexhaustible fund of divine wealth; spiritual "skyscrapers" may occasionally be encountered by the wayside, even by worldly men like this policeman.

We thanked the officer for relieving our tedium with his marvelous story. He was probably intimating that he was more fortunate than we: he had met an illumined saint without effort; our earnest search had ended, not at the feet of a master, but in a coarse police station!

So near the Himalayas and yet, in our captivity, so far, I told Amar I felt doubly impelled to seek freedom.

"Let us slip away when opportunity offers. We can go on foot to holy Rishikesh." I smiled encouragingly.

But my companion had turned pessimist as soon as the stalwart prop of our money had been taken from us.

"If we started a trek over such dangerous jungle land, we should finish, not in the city of saints, but in the stomachs of tigers!"

Ananta and Amar's brother arrived after three days. Amar greeted his relative with affectionate relief. I was unreconciled; Ananta got no more from me than a severe upbraiding.

"I understand how you feel." My brother spoke soothingly. "All I ask of you is to accompany me to Banaras to meet a certain sage, and go on to Calcutta to visit our grieving father for a few days. Then you may resume your search here for a master."

Amar entered the conversation at this point to disclaim any intention of returning to Hardwar with me. He was enjoying the familial warmth. But I knew I would never abandon the quest for my guru.

Our party entrained for Banaras. There I had a singular and instant response to a prayer.

A clever scheme had been prearranged by Ananta. Before seeing me in Hardwar he had stopped in Banaras to ask a scriptural authority to interview me later. The pundit, and his son also, had promised Ananta that they would attempt to dissuade me from becoming a *sannyasi.**

Ananta took me to their home. The son, a young man of ebullient manner, greeted me in the courtyard. He engaged me in a lengthy philosophic discourse. Professing to have a clairvoyant knowledge of my future, he discountenanced my idea of being a monk.

"You will meet continual misfortune, and be unable to find God, if you insist on deserting your ordinary responsibilities! You cannot work out your past karma† without worldly experiences."

Immortal words from the Bhagavad Gita‡ rose to my lips in reply: "'Even he with the worst of karma who ceaselessly meditates on Me quickly loses the effects of his past bad actions. Becoming a high-souled being, he soon attains perennial peace. Know this for certain: the devotee who puts his trust in Me never perishes!'"

But the forceful prognostications of the young man had slightly shaken my confidence. With all the fervor of my heart I prayed silently to God:

"Please solve my bewilderment and answer me, right here and now, if Thou dost desire me to lead the life of a renunciant or a worldly man!"

I noticed a sadhu of noble countenance standing just outside

---

* Literally, "renunciant"; from Sanskrit verb roots, "to cast aside."
† Effects of past actions, in this or a former life; from the Sanskrit verb *kri*, "to do."
‡ Chapter IX, verses 30–31.

the compound of the pundit's house. Evidently he had overheard the spirited conversation between the self-styled clairvoyant and me, for the stranger called me to his side. I felt a tremendous power flowing from his calm eyes.

"Son, don't listen to that ignoramus. In response to your prayer, the Lord tells me to assure you that your sole path in this life is that of the renunciant."

With astonishment as well as gratitude, I smiled happily at this decisive message.

"Come away from that man!" The "ignoramus" was calling me from the courtyard. My saintly guide raised his hand in blessing and slowly departed.

"That sadhu is just as crazy as you are." It was the hoary-headed pundit who made this charming observation. He and his son were gazing at me lugubriously. "I have heard that he, too, has left his home in a vague search for God."

I turned away. To Ananta I remarked that I would not engage in further discussion with our hosts. My discouraged brother agreed to an immediate departure; we soon entrained for Calcutta.

"Mr. Detective, how did you discover I had fled with two companions?" I vented my lively curiosity to Ananta during our homeward journey. He smiled mischievously.

"At your school, I found that Amar had left his classroom and had not returned. I went to his home the next morning and unearthed a marked timetable. Amar's father was just leaving by carriage and was talking to the coachman.

"'My son will not ride with me to his school this morning. He has disappeared!' the father moaned.

"'I heard from a brother coachman that your son and two others, dressed in European suits, boarded the train at Howrah Station,' the man stated. 'They made a present of their leather shoes to the cab driver.'

"Thus I had three clues—the timetable, the trio of boys, and the English clothing."

I was listening to Ananta's disclosures with mingled mirth and vexation. Our generosity to the coachman had been slightly misplaced!

"Of course I rushed to send telegrams to station officials in all the cities that Amar had underlined in the timetable. He had checked Bareilly, so I wired your friend Dwarka there. After inquiries in our Calcutta neighborhood, I learned that cousin Jatinda had

been absent one night but had arrived home the following morning in European garb. I sought him out and invited him to dinner.
He accepted, quite disarmed by my friendly manner. On the way I
led him unsuspectingly to a police station. He was surrounded by
several officers whom I had previously selected for their ferocious
appearance. Under their formidable gaze, Jatinda agreed to account
for his mysterious conduct.

"'I started for the Himalayas in a buoyant spiritual mood,'
he explained. 'Inspiration filled me at the prospect of meeting the
masters. But as soon as Mukunda said, "During our ecstasies in
the Himalayan caves, tigers will be spellbound and sit around us
like tame pussies," my spirits froze; beads of perspiration formed
on my brow. "What then?" I thought. "If the vicious nature of the
tigers be not changed through the power of our spiritual trance,
shall they treat us with the kindness of house cats?" In my mind's
eye, I already saw myself the compulsory inmate of some tiger's
stomach—entering there not at once with the whole body, but by
installments of its several parts!'"

My anger at Jatinda's vanishment evaporated in laughter. The
hilarious explanation on the train was worth all the anguish he had
caused me. I must confess to a slight feeling of satisfaction: Jatinda,
too, had not escaped an encounter with the police!

"Ananta,* you are a born sleuthhound!" My glance of amusement was not without some exasperation. "And I shall tell Jatinda
I am glad he was prompted by no mood of treachery, as it appeared,
but only by the prudent instinct of self-preservation!"

At home in Calcutta, Father touchingly requested me to curb
my roving feet until, at least, the completion of my high school
studies. In my absence, he had lovingly hatched a plot by arranging
for a saintly pundit, Swami Kebalananda, to come regularly to the
house.

"The sage will be your Sanskrit tutor," my parent announced
confidently.

Father hoped to satisfy my religious yearnings by instruction
from a learned philosopher. But the tables were subtly turned: my
new teacher, far from offering intellectual aridities, fanned the
embers of my God-aspiration. Unknown to Father, Swami Kebalananda was an exalted disciple of Lahiri Mahasaya. The peerless
guru had possessed thousands of disciples, silently drawn to him

---

* I always addressed him as Ananta-da. *Da* is a respectful suffix that brothers and
sisters add to the name of their eldest brother.

by the irresistibility of his divine magnetism. I learned later that Lahiri Mahasaya had often characterized Kebalananda as rishi or illumined sage.*

Luxuriant curls framed my tutor's handsome face. His dark eyes were guileless, with the transparency of a child's. All the movements of his slight body were marked by a restful deliberation. Ever gentle and loving, he was firmly established in the infinite consciousness. Many of our happy hours together were spent in deep *Kriya* meditation.

Kebalananda was a noted authority on the ancient *shastras* or sacred books; his erudition had earned him the title of "Shastri Mahasaya," by which he was usually addressed. But my progress in Sanskrit scholarship was unnoteworthy. I sought every opportunity to forsake prosaic grammar and to talk of yoga and Lahiri Mahasaya. My tutor obliged me one day by telling me something of his own life with the master.

"Rarely fortunate, I was able to remain near Lahiri Mahasaya for ten years. His Banaras home was my nightly goal of pilgrimage. The guru was always present in a small front parlor on the first floor. As he sat in lotus posture on a backless wooden seat, his disciples garlanded him in a semicircle. His eyes sparkled and danced with the joy of the Divine. They were ever half closed, peering through the inner telescopic orb into a sphere of eternal bliss. He seldom spoke at length. Occasionally his gaze would focus on a student in need of help; healing words poured then like an avalanche of light.

"An indescribable peace blossomed within me at the master's glance. I was permeated with his fragrance, as though from a lotus of infinity. To be with him, even without exchanging a word for days, was experience which changed my entire being. If any invisible barrier rose in the path of my concentration, I would meditate at the guru's feet. There the most tenuous states came easily within my grasp. Such perceptions eluded me in the presence of lesser teachers. The master was a living temple of God, whose secret doors were open to all disciples through devotion.

* At the time of our meeting, Kebalananda had not yet joined the Swami Order and was generally called "Shastri Mahasaya." To avoid confusion with the name of Lahiri Mahasaya and of Master Mahasaya (chapter 9), I am referring to my Sanskrit tutor only by his later monastic name of Swami Kebalananda. His biography has been recently published in Bengali. Born in the Khulna district of Bengal in 1863, Kebalananda gave up his body in Banaras at the age of sixty-eight. His family name was Ashutosh Chatterji.

"Lahiri Mahasaya was no bookish interpreter of the scriptures. Effortlessly he dipped into the 'divine library.' Foam of words and spray of thoughts gushed from the fountain of his omniscience. He had the wondrous clavis that unlocked the profound philosophical science hidden ages ago in the Vedas.* If asked to explain the different planes of consciousness mentioned in the ancient texts, he would smilingly assent.

"'I will undergo those states, and presently tell you what I perceive.' He was thus diametrically unlike the teachers who commit scripture to memory and then give forth unrealized abstractions.

"'Please expound the holy stanzas as the meaning occurs to you.' The taciturn guru often gave this instruction to a nearby disciple. 'I will guide your thoughts, that the right interpretation be uttered.' In this way many of Lahiri Mahasaya's perceptions came to be recorded, with voluminous commentaries by various students.

"The master never counseled slavish belief. 'Words are only shells,' he said. 'Win conviction of God's presence through your own joyous contact in meditation.'

"No matter what the disciple's problem, the guru advised *Kriya Yoga* for its solution.

"'The yogic key will not lose its efficiency when I am no longer present in the body to guide you. This technique cannot be bound, filed, and forgotten, in the manner of theoretical inspirations. Continue ceaselessly on your path to liberation through *Kriya*, whose power lies in practice.'

"I myself consider *Kriya* the most effective device of salvation through self-effort ever to be evolved in man's search for the Infinite." Kebalananda concluded with this earnest testimony. "Through its use, the omnipotent God, hidden in all men, became visibly incarnated in the flesh of Lahiri Mahasaya and of a number of his disciples."

A Christlike miracle by Lahiri Mahasaya took place in Kebalananda's presence. My saintly tutor recounted the story one day, his eyes remote from the Sanskrit texts on the table before us.

---

* Over 100 canonical books of the ancient four Vedas are extant. In his *Journal* Emerson paid this tribute to Vedic thought: "It is sublime as heat and night and a breathless ocean. It contains every religious sentiment, all the grand ethics which visit in turn each noble poetic mind.... It is of no use to put away the book; if I trust myself in the woods or in a boat upon the pond, Nature makes a *Brahmin* of me presently: eternal necessity, eternal compensation, unfathomable power, unbroken silence.... This is her creed. Peace, she saith to me, and purity and absolute abandonment— these panaceas expiate all sin and bring you to the beatitude of the Eight Gods."

"A blind disciple, Ramu, aroused my active pity. Should he have no light in his eyes, when he faithfully served our master, in whom the Divine was fully blazing? One morning I sought to speak to Ramu, but he sat for patient hours fanning the guru with a handmade palm-leaf *punkha.* When the devotee finally left the room, I followed him.

"'Ramu, how long have you been blind?'

"'From my birth, sir! Never have my eyes been blessed with a glimpse of the sun.'

"'Our omnipotent guru can help you. Please make a supplication.'

"The following day Ramu diffidently approached Lahiri Mahasaya. The disciple felt almost ashamed to ask that physical wealth be added to his spiritual superabundance.

"'Master, the Illuminator of the cosmos is in you. I pray you to bring His light into my eyes, that I perceive the sun's lesser glow.'

"'Ramu, someone has connived to put me in a difficult position. I have no healing power.'

"'Sir, the Infinite One within you can certainly heal.'

"'That is indeed different, Ramu. God's limit is nowhere! He who ignites the stars and the cells of flesh with mysterious life-effulgence can surely bring the luster of vision into your eyes.' The master touched Ramu's forehead at the point between the eyebrows.*

"'Keep your mind concentrated there, and frequently chant the name of the prophet Rama† for seven days. The splendor of the sun shall have a special dawn for you.'

"Lo! in one week it was so. For the first time, Ramu beheld the fair face of nature. The Omniscient One had unerringly directed his disciple to repeat the name of Rama, adored by him above all other saints. Ramu's faith was the devotionally ploughed soil in which the guru's powerful seed of permanent healing sprouted." Kebalananda was silent for a moment, then paid a further tribute to his guru.

"It was evident in all miracles performed by Lahiri Mahasaya that he never allowed the ego-principle‡ to consider itself a causative

---

* The seat of the "single" or spiritual eye. At death the consciousness of man is usually drawn to this holy spot, accounting for the upraised eyes found in the dead.

† The central sacred figure of the Sanskrit epic, *Ramayana.*

‡ The ego-principle, *ahamkara* (lit., "I do") is the root cause of dualism or the seeming separation between man and his Creator. *Ahamkara* brings human beings under the sway of *maya* (cosmic delusion), by which the subject (ego) falsely appears as object; the creatures imagine themselves to be creators. (See pp. 38 n., 234–35, 242 n.)

force. By the perfection of his surrender to the Prime Healing Power, the master enabled It to flow freely through him.

"The numerous bodies that were spectacularly healed through Lahiri Mahasaya eventually had to feed the flames of cremation. But the silent spiritual awakenings he effected, the Christlike disciples he fashioned, are his imperishable miracles."

I never became a Sanskrit scholar; Kebalananda taught me a diviner syntax.

"Naught of myself I do!"
Thus will he think, who holds the truth of truths....
Always assured: "This is the sense-world plays
With senses." (V:8–9)
Seeing, he sees, indeed, who sees that works
Are Nature's wont, for Soul to practice by;
Acting, yet not the agent. (XIII:29)

Albeit I be
Unborn, undying, indestructible,
The Lord of all things living; not the less—
By Maya, by My magic which I stamp
On floating Nature-forms, the primal vast—
I come, and go, and come. (IV:6)

Hard it is
To pierce that veil divine of various shows
Which hideth Me; yet they who worship Me
Pierce it and pass beyond. (VII:14)

—Bhagavad Gita *(Arnold's translation)*

CHAPTER 5

A "Perfume Saint"
Displays His Wonders

"To every thing there is a season, and a time to every purpose under the heaven."*

I did not have this wisdom of Solomon to comfort me; I gazed searchingly about me, on any excursion from home, for the face of my destined guru. But my path did not cross his until after the completion of my high school studies.

Two years elapsed between my flight with Amar toward the Himalayas, and the great day of Sri Yukteswar's arrival into my life. During that interim I met a number of sages — the "Perfume Saint," the "Tiger Swami," Nagendra Nath Bhaduri, Master Mahasaya, and the famous Bengali scientist Jagadis Chandra Bose.

My encounter with the "Perfume Saint" had two preambles, one harmonious and the other humorous.

"God is simple. Everything else is complex. Do not seek absolute values in the relative world of nature."

These philosophical finalities gently entered my ear as I stood silently before a temple image of Kali.† Turning, I confronted a tall man whose garb, or lack of it, revealed him a wandering sadhu.

"You have indeed penetrated the bewilderment of my thoughts!" I smiled gratefully. "The confusion of benign and terrible aspects in nature, as symbolized by Kali, has puzzled wiser heads than mine!"

"Few there be who solve her mystery! Good and evil is the challenging riddle which life places sphinxlike before every intelligence. Attempting no solution, most men pay forfeit with their lives, penalty now even as in the days of Thebes. Here and there, a

---

* Ecclesiastes 3:1.

† Kali represents the Eternal Principle in nature. She is traditionally pictured as a four-armed woman, standing on the recumbent form of the God Shiva or the Infinite; because the activities of nature or the phenomenal world spring from the latent Spirit. The four arms symbolize cardinal attributes: two beneficent, two destructive; the essential duality of matter or creation.

towering lonely figure never cries defeat. From the *maya** of duality he plucks the cleaveless truth of unity."

"You speak with conviction, sir."

"I have long exercised an honest introspection, the exquisitely painful approach to wisdom. Self-scrutiny, relentless observance of one's thoughts, is a stark and shattering experience. It pulverizes the stoutest ego. But true self-analysis mathematically operates to produce seers. The way of 'self-expression,' individual acknowledgments, results in egotists, sure of the right to their private interpretations of God and the universe."

"Truth humbly retires, no doubt, before such arrogant originality." I was enjoying the discussion.

"Man can understand no eternal verity until he has freed himself from pretensions. The human mind, bared to a centuried slime, is teeming with the repulsive life of countless world-delusions. Struggles of the battlefield pale into insignificance here, when man first contends with inner enemies! No mortal foes these, to be overcome by a harrowing array of might! Omnipresent, unresting, pursuing man even in sleep, subtly equipped with miasmic weapons, these soldiers of ignorant lusts seek to slay us all. Thoughtless is the man who buries his ideals, surrendering to the common fate. May he seem other than impotent, wooden, ignominious?"

"Respected sir, have you no sympathy for the bewildered masses?"

The sage was silent for a moment, then answered obliquely.

"To love both the invisible God, Repository of All Virtues, and visible man, apparently possessed of none, is often baffling! But ingenuity is equal to the maze. Inner research soon exposes a unity of all human minds—the stalwart kinship of selfish motive. In one sense at least, the brotherhood of man stands revealed. An aghast humility follows this leveling discovery. It ripens into compassion for one's fellows, blind to the healing potencies of the soul awaiting exploration."

* Cosmic illusion; literally, "the measurer." *Maya* is the magical power in creation by which limitations and divisions are apparently present in the Immeasurable and Inseparable.

Emerson wrote the following poem about *Maya* (which he spelled *Maia*):

> Illusion works impenetrable,
> Weaving webs innumerable;
> Her gay pictures never fail,
> Crowd each other, veil on veil;
> Charmer who will be believed
> By man who thirsts to be deceived.

"The saints of every age, sir, have felt like yourself for the sorrows of the world."

"Only the shallow man loses responsiveness to the woes of others' lives, as he sinks into narrow suffering of his own." The sadhu's austere face was noticeably softened. "The one who practices a scalpel self-dissection will know an expansion of universal pity. Release is given him from the deafening demands of his ego. The love of God flowers on such soil. The creature finally turns to his Creator, if for no other reason than to ask in anguish: 'Why, Lord, why?' By ignoble whips of pain, man is driven at last into the Infinite Presence, whose beauty alone should lure him."

The sage and I were present in the Calcutta Kalighat Temple, whither I had gone to view its famed magnificence. With a sweeping gesture, my chance companion dismissed the ornate dignity.

"Bricks and mortar sing us no audible tune; the heart opens only to the human chant of being."

We strolled to the inviting sunshine at the entrance, where throngs of devotees were passing to and fro.

"You are young." The sage surveyed me thoughtfully. "India too is young. The ancient rishis* laid down ineradicable patterns of spiritual living. Their hoary dictums suffice for this day and land. Not outmoded, not unsophisticated against the guiles of materialism, the disciplinary precepts mold India still. By millenniums—more than embarrassed scholars care to compute!—the skeptic Time has validated Vedic worth. Take it for your heritage."

As I was reverently bidding farewell to the eloquent sadhu, he revealed a clairvoyant perception:

"After you leave here today, an unusual experience will come your way."

I quitted the temple precincts and wandered along aimlessly. Turning a corner, I ran into an old acquaintance—one of those fellows whose conversational powers ignore time and embrace eternity.

"I shall let you go in a very short while," he promised, "if you will tell me all that has happened during the years of our separation."

"What a paradox! I must leave you now."

But he held me by the hand, forcing out tidbits of information. He was like a ravenous wolf, I thought in amusement; the longer I spoke, the more hungrily he sniffed for news. Inwardly I petitioned the Goddess Kali to devise a graceful means of escape.

---

* The rishis, literally "seers," were the authors of the Vedas in an indeterminable antiquity.

My companion left me abruptly. I sighed with relief and doubled my pace, dreading any relapse into the garrulous fever. Hearing rapid footsteps behind me, I quickened my speed. I dared not look back. But with a bound, the youth rejoined me, jovially clasping my shoulder.

"I forgot to tell you of Gandha Baba ('Perfume Saint'), who is gracing yonder house." He pointed to a dwelling a few yards distant. "Do meet him; he is interesting. You may have an unusual experience. Good-bye," and he actually left me.

The similarly worded prediction of the sadhu at Kalighat Temple flashed to my mind. Intrigued, I entered the house and was ushered into a commodious parlor. A crowd of people were sitting, Orientwise, here and there on a thick orange-colored carpet. An awed whisper reached my ear:

"Behold Gandha Baba on the leopard skin. He can give the natural perfume of any flower to a scentless one, or revive a wilted blossom, or make a person's skin exude delightful fragrance."

I looked directly at the saint; his quick gaze rested on mine. He was plump and bearded, with dark skin and large, gleaming eyes.

"Son, I am glad to see you. Say what you want. Would you like some perfume?"

"What for?" I thought his remark rather childish.

"To experience the miraculous way of enjoying perfumes."

"Harnessing God to make odors?"

"What of it? God makes perfume anyway."

"Yes, but He fashions frail bottles of petals for fresh use and discard. Can you materialize flowers?"

"Yes. But usually I produce perfumes, little friend."

"Then scent factories will go out of business."

"I will permit them to keep their trade! My own purpose is to demonstrate the power of God."

"Sir, is it necessary to prove God? Isn't He performing miracles in everything, everywhere?"

"Yes, but we too should manifest some of His infinite creative variety."

"How long did it take to master your art?"

"Twelve years."

"For manufacturing scents by astral means! It seems, my honored saint, you have been wasting a dozen years for fragrances which you can obtain with a few rupees from a florist's shop."

"Perfumes fade with flowers."

"Perfumes fade with death. Why should I desire that which pleases the body only?"

"Mr. Philosopher, you please my mind. Now, stretch forth your right hand." He made a gesture of blessing.

I was a few feet away from Gandha Baba; no one else was near enough to contact my body. I extended my hand, which the yogi did not touch.

"What perfume do you want?"

"Rose."

"Be it so."

To my great surprise, the charming fragrance of rose was wafted strongly from the center of my palm. I smilingly took a large white scentless flower from a nearby vase.

"Can this odorless blossom be permeated with jasmine?"

"Be it so."

A jasmine fragrance instantly shot from the petals. I thanked the wonder-worker and seated myself by one of his students. He informed me that Gandha Baba, whose proper name was Vishuddhananda, had learned many astonishing yoga secrets from a master in Tibet. The Tibetan yogi, I was assured, had attained the age of over a thousand years.

"His disciple Gandha Baba does not always perform his perfume feats in the simple verbal manner you have just witnessed." The student spoke with obvious pride in his master. "His procedure differs widely, to accord with diversity in temperaments. He is marvelous! Many members of the Calcutta intelligentsia are among his followers."

I inwardly resolved not to add myself to their number. A guru too literally "marvelous" was not to my liking. With polite thanks to Gandha Baba, I departed. Sauntering home, I reflected on the three varied encounters the day had brought forth.

My sister Uma met me as I entered the door.

"You are getting quite stylish, using perfumes!"

Without a word, I motioned her to smell my hand.

"What an attractive rose fragrance! It is unusually strong!"

Thinking it was "strongly unusual," I silently placed the astrally scented blossom under her nostrils.

"Oh, I love jasmine!" She seized the flower. A ludicrous bafflement passed over her face as she repeatedly sniffed the odor of jasmine from a type of flower she well knew to be scentless. Her reactions disarmed my suspicion that Gandha Baba might have induced in me an autosuggestive state whereby I alone could detect the fragrances.

Later I heard from a friend, Alakananda, that the "Perfume Saint" had a power which I wish were possessed by the starving millions of the world.

"I was present with a hundred other guests at Gandha Baba's home in Burdwan," Alakananda told me. "It was a gala occasion. Because the yogi was reputed to have the power of extracting objects out of thin air, I laughingly requested him to materialize some out-of-season tangerines. Immediately the *luchis** that had been served on all the banana-leaf plates became puffed up. Each of the bread-envelopes proved to contain a peeled tangerine. I bit into my own with some trepidation, but found it delicious."

Years later I understood by inner realization how Gandha Baba accomplished his materializations. The method, alas, is beyond the reach of the world's hungry hordes.

The different sensory stimuli to which man reacts—tactual, visual, gustatory, auditory, and olfactory—are produced by vibratory variations in electrons and protons. The vibrations in turn are regulated by *prana*, "lifetrons," subtle life forces or finer-than-atomic energies intelligently charged with the five distinctive sensory idea-substances.

Gandha Baba, attuning himself with the pranic force by certain yoga practices, was able to guide the lifetrons to rearrange their vibratory structure and to objectify the desired result. His perfume, fruit, and other miracles were actual materializations of mundane vibrations, and were not inner sensations hypnotically produced.

Hypnotism has been used by physicians in minor operations as a sort of psychical chloroform for persons who might be endangered by an anesthetic. But a hypnotic state is harmful to those often subjected to it; a negative psychological effect ensues that in time deranges the brain cells. Hypnotism is trespass into the territory of another's consciousness.† Its temporary phenomena have nothing

* Flat, round Indian bread.

† Studies in consciousness by Western psychologists are largely confined to investigations of the subconscious mind and of mental diseases that are treated through psychiatry and psychoanalysis. There is little research into the origin and fundamental formation of normal mental states and their emotional and volitional expressions—a truly basic subject not neglected in Indian philosophy. Precise classifications are made, in the *Sankhya* and *Yoga* systems, of the various links in normal mental modifications and of the characteristic functions of *buddhi* (discriminative intellect), *ahamkara* (egoistic principle), and *manas* (mind or sense-consciousness).

in common with the miracles performed by men of divine realization. Awake in God, true saints effect changes in this dream-world
by means of a will harmoniously attuned to the Creative Cosmic
Dreamer.*

Wonder-workings such as those shown by the "Perfume Saint"
are spectacular but spiritually useless. Having little purpose beyond
entertainment, they are digressions from a serious search for God.

Ostentatious display of unusual powers is decried by masters. The Persian mystic, Abu Said, once laughed at certain *fakirs*
(Moslem ascetics) who were proud of their miraculous powers over
water, air, and space.

"A frog is also at home in the water!" Abu Said pointed out
in gentle scorn. "The crow and the vulture easily fly in the air;
the Devil is simultaneously present in the East and in the West! A
true man is he who dwells in righteousness among his fellowmen,
who may buy and sell, yet is never for a single instant forgetful
of God!"† On another occasion the great Persian teacher gave his

---

* "The universe is represented in every one of its particles. Everything is made
of one hidden stuff. The world globes itself in a drop of dew....The true doctrine
of omnipresence is that God appears with all His parts in every moss and
cobweb."—*Emerson, in "Compensation."*

† "To buy and sell, yet never to forget God!" The ideal is that hand and heart work
harmoniously together. Certain Western writers claim that the Hindu goal is one of
timid "escape," of inactivity and antisocial withdrawal. The fourfold Vedic plan for
man's life, however, is a well-balanced one for the masses, allotting half the span to
study and householder duties; the second half to contemplation and meditational
practices. (See p. 217 n.)

Solitude is necessary to become established in the Self, but masters then return
to the world to serve it. Even saints who engage in no outward work bestow, through
their thoughts and holy vibrations, more precious benefits on the world than can
be given by the most strenuous humanitarian activities of unenlightened men. The
great ones, each in his own way and often against bitter opposition, strive selflessly to
inspire and uplift their fellows. No Hindu religious or social ideal is merely negative.
Ahimsa, "noninjury," called "virtue entire" (*sakalo dharma*) in the *Mahabharata*, is
a positive injunction by reason of its conception that one who is not helping others
in some way is injuring them.

The Bhagavad Gita (III:4–8) points out that activity is inherent in man's very
nature. Sloth is simply "wrong activity."

> "No man shall 'scape from act
> By shunning action; nay, and none shall come
> By mere renouncements unto perfectness.
> Nay, and no jot of time, at any time,
> Rests any actionless; his nature's law
> Compels him, even unwilling, into act.
> (For thought is act in fancy).
> ...He who, with strong body serving mind,

views on the religious life thus: "To lay aside what you have in your head (selfish desires and ambitions); to bestow freely what you have in your hand; and never to flinch from the blows of adversity!"

Neither the impartial sage at Kalighat Temple nor the Tibetan-trained yogi had satisfied my yearning for a guru. My heart needed no tutor for its recognitions, and cried a spontaneous "Bravo!" the more resoundingly because it was unoften summoned from silence. When I finally met my master, by sublimity of example alone he taught me the measure of a true man.

Gives up his mortal powers to worthy work,
Not seeking gain, Arjuna! such a one
Is honorable. Do thine allotted task!"

(Arnold's translation)

CHAPTER 6

The Tiger Swami

"I have discovered the Tiger Swami's address. Let us visit him tomorrow."

This welcome suggestion came from Chandi, one of my high school friends. I was eager to meet the saint who, in his premonastic life, had caught and fought tigers with his naked hands. A boyish enthusiasm over such remarkable feats was strong within me.

The next day dawned wintry cold, but Chandi and I sallied forth gaily. After much vain hunting in Bhowanipur, outside Calcutta, we arrived at the right house. The door held two iron rings, which I sounded piercingly. Notwithstanding the clamor, a servant approached with leisurely gait. His ironical smile implied that noisy visitors were powerless to disturb the calmness of a saint's home.

Feeling the silent rebuke, my companion and I were thankful to be invited into the parlor. Our long wait there beset us with misgivings. India's unwritten law for the truth seeker is patience; a master may purposely make a test of one's eagerness to meet him. This psychological ruse is freely employed in the West by doctors and dentists!

Finally summoned by the servant, Chandi and I entered a sleeping apartment. The famous Sohong* Swami was seated on his bed. The sight of his tremendous body affected us strangely. With bulging eyes, we stood speechless. We had never before seen such a chest or such football-like biceps. On an immense neck, the swami's fierce yet calm face was adorned with flowing locks, beard, and moustache. A hint of dovelike and tigerlike qualities shone in his dark eyes. He was unclothed, save for a tiger skin about his muscular waist.

Finding our voices, my friend and I greeted the monk, expressing our admiration for his prowess in the extraordinary feline arena.

"Will you not tell us, please, how it is possible to subdue with bare fists the most ferocious of jungle beasts, the royal Bengals?"

* *Sohong* was his monastic name. He was popularly known as the "Tiger Swami."

"My sons, it is nothing to me to fight tigers. I could do it today if necessary." He gave a childlike laugh. "You look upon tigers as tigers; I know them as pussycats."

"Swamiji, I think I could impress my subconsciousness with the thought that tigers are pussycats, but could I make tigers believe it?"

"Of course strength also is necessary! One may not expect victory from a baby who imagines a tiger to be a house cat! Powerful hands are my sufficient weapon."

He asked us to follow him to the patio, where he struck the edge of a wall. A brick crashed to the floor; the sky peered boldly through the gape, the lost-tooth space in the wall. I staggered in astonishment; he who can remove a mortared brick from a solid wall with one blow, I thought, must surely be able to displace the teeth of tigers!

"A number of men have physical power such as mine, but still lack in cool confidence. Those who are bodily but not mentally stalwart may find themselves fainting at the mere sight of a wild beast bounding freely in the jungle. The tiger in its natural ferocity and habitat is vastly different from the opium-fed circus animal!

"Many a man with herculean strength has nonetheless been terrorized into abject helplessness before the onslaught of a royal Bengal. Thus the tiger has converted the man, in his own mind, to a state as fearful as the pussycat's. It is possible for a man, owning a fairly strong body and an immensely strong determination, to turn the tables on the tiger, and force it to a conviction of pussycat defenselessness. How often I have done just that!"

I was quite willing to believe that the titan before me was able to perform the tiger-pussycat metamorphosis. He seemed to be in a didactic mood; Chandi and I listened respectfully.

"Mind is the wielder of muscles. The force of a hammer blow depends on the energy applied; the power expressed by a man's bodily instrument depends on his aggressive will and courage. The body is literally manufactured and sustained by mind. Through pressure of instincts from past lives, strengths or weaknesses percolate gradually into human consciousness. They express as habits, which in turn manifest as a desirable or an undesirable body. Outward frailty has a mental origin; in a vicious circle, the habit-bound body thwarts the mind. If the master allows himself to be commanded by a servant, the latter becomes autocratic; the mind is similarly enslaved by submitting to bodily dictation."

At our entreaty, the impressive swami consented to tell us something of his own life.

"My earliest ambition was to fight tigers. My will was mighty, but my body was feeble."

An ejaculation of surprise broke from me. It appeared incredible that this man, now "with Atlantean shoulders, fit to bear," could ever have known weakness.

"It was by indomitable persistency in thoughts of health and strength that I overcame my handicap. I have every reason to extol the compelling mental vigor which I found to be the real subduer of royal Bengals."

"Do you think, revered Swami, that I could ever fight tigers?" This was the first time, and the last, that the bizarre ambition ever visited my mind!

"Yes." He was smiling. "But there are many kinds of tigers; some roam in jungles of human desires. No spiritual benefit accrues by knocking beasts unconscious. Rather be victor over the inner prowlers."

"May we hear, sir, how you changed from a tamer of wild tigers to a tamer of wild passions?"

The Tiger Swami fell into silence. Remoteness came into his gaze, summoning visions of bygone years. I discerned his slight mental struggle to decide whether to grant my request. Finally he smiled in acquiescence.

"When my fame reached a zenith, it brought the intoxication of pride. I decided not only to fight tigers but to display them in various tricks. My ambition was to force savage beasts to behave like domesticated ones. I began to perform my feats publicly, with gratifying success.

"One evening my father entered my room in pensive mood.

"'Son, I have words of warning. I would save you from coming ills, produced by the grinding wheels of cause and effect.'

"'Are you a fatalist, Father? Should superstition be allowed to discolor the powerful waters of my activities?'

"'I am no fatalist, son. But I believe in the just law of retribution, as taught in the holy scriptures. There is resentment against you in the jungle family; sometime it may act to your cost.'

"'Father, you astonish me! You well know what tigers are—beautiful but merciless! Who knows? my blows may inject some slight sanity of consideration into their thick heads. I am headmaster in a forest finishing school to teach them gentle manners!

"'Please, Father, think of me as tiger tamer and never as tiger killer. How could my good actions bring ill upon me? I beg you not to impose any command that I change my way of life.'"

Chandi and I were all attention, understanding the past dilemma. In India a child does not lightly disobey his parents' wishes. The Tiger Swami went on:

"In stoic silence Father listened to my explanation. He followed it with a disclosure which he uttered gravely.

"'Son, you compel me to relate an ominous prediction from the lips of a saint. He approached me yesterday as I sat on the veranda in my daily meditation.

"'"Dear friend, I come with a message for your belligerent son. Let him cease his savage activities. Otherwise, his next tiger-encounter shall result in his severe wounds, followed by six months of deathly sickness. He shall then forsake his former ways and become a monk."'

"This tale did not impress me. I considered that Father had been the credulous victim of a deluded fanatic."

The Tiger Swami made this confession with an impatient gesture, as though at some stupidity. Grimly silent for a long time, he seemed oblivious of our presence. When he took up the dangling thread of his narrative, it was suddenly, with subdued voice.

"Not long after Father's warning, I visited the capital city of Cooch Behar. The picturesque territory was new to me, and I expected a restful change. As usual everywhere, a curious crowd followed me on the streets. I would catch bits of whispered comment:

"'This is the man who fights wild tigers.'

"'Has he legs, or tree-trunks?'

"'Look at his face! He must be an incarnation of the king of tigers himself!'

"You know how village urchins function like final editions of a newspaper! With what speed do the even later speech-bulletins of the women circulate from house to house! Within a few hours, the whole city was in a state of excitement over my presence.

"I was relaxing quietly in the evening, when I heard the hoof-beats of galloping horses. They stopped in front of my dwelling place. In came a number of tall, turbaned policemen.

"I was taken aback. 'All things are possible unto these creatures of human law,' I thought. 'I wonder if they are going to take me to task about matters utterly unknown to me.' But the officers bowed with unwonted courtesy.

Sri Yogananda at the age of sixteen

BHAGAVAN (LORD) KRISHNA
India's beloved avatar

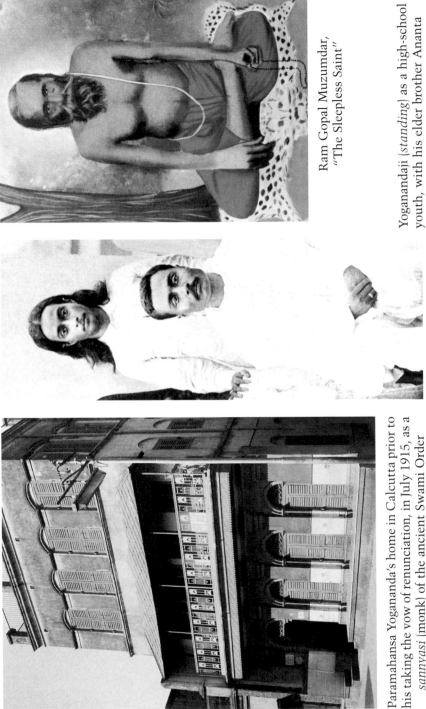

Ram Gopal Muzumdar,
"The Sleepless Saint"

Yoganandaji (*standing*) as a high-school
youth, with his elder brother Ananta

Paramahansa Yogananda's home in Calcutta prior to
his taking the vow of renunciation, in July 1915, as a
sannyasi (monk) of the ancient Swami Order

"'Honored Sir, we are sent to welcome you on behalf of the Prince of Cooch Behar. He is pleased to invite you to his palace tomorrow morning.'

"I speculated awhile on the prospect. For some obscure reason I felt sharp regret at this interruption in my quiet trip. But the suppliant manner of the policemen moved me; I agreed to go.

"I was bewildered the next day to be obsequiously escorted from my door into a magnificent coach drawn by four horses. A servant held an ornate umbrella to protect me from the scorching sunlight. I enjoyed the pleasant ride through the city and its woodland outskirts. The royal scion himself was at the palace door to welcome me. He proffered his own gold-brocaded seat, smilingly placing himself in a chair of simpler design.

"'All this politeness is certainly going to cost me something!' I thought in mounting astonishment. The prince's motive emerged after a few casual remarks.

"'My city is filled with the rumor that you can fight wild tigers with nothing more than your naked hands. Is it a fact?'

"'It is quite true.'

"'I can scarcely believe it! You are a Calcutta Bengali, nurtured on the white rice of cityfolk. Be frank, please; have you not been fighting only spineless, opium-fed animals?' His voice was loud and sarcastic, his speech tinged with provincial accent.

"I vouchsafed no reply to his insulting question.

"'I challenge you to fight my newly caught tiger, Raja Begum.* If you can successfully resist him, bind him with a chain, and depart his cage in a conscious state, you shall have this royal Bengal! Several thousand rupees and many other gifts shall also be bestowed. If you refuse to meet him in combat, I shall blazon your name throughout the state as an impostor!'

"His insolent words struck me like a volley of bullets. I shot an angry acceptance. Half risen from the chair in his excitement, the prince sank back with a sadistic smile. I was reminded of the Roman emperors who delighted in setting Christians in bestial arenas. He said:

"'The match will be set for a week hence. I regret that I cannot give you permission to view the tiger in advance.'

"Whether the prince feared I might seek to hypnotize the beast, or secretly feed him opium, I know not.

---

* "Prince Princess"—so named to indicate that this beast possessed the combined ferocity of tiger and tigress.

"I left the palace, noting with amusement that the royal umbrella and panoplied coach were now missing.

"The following week I methodically prepared my mind and body for the coming ordeal. Through my servant I learned of fantastic tales. The saint's direful prediction to my father had somehow got abroad, enlarging as it ran. Many simple villagers believed that an evil spirit, cursed by the gods, had reincarnated as a tiger which took various demoniac forms at night, but remained a striped animal during the day. This demon-tiger was supposed to be the one sent to humble me.

"Another imaginative version was that animal prayers to Tiger Heaven had achieved a response in the shape of Raja Begum. He was to be the instrument to punish me—the audacious biped, so insulting to the entire tiger species! A furless, fangless man daring to challenge a claw-armed, sturdy-limbed tiger! The force of concentrated venom of all humiliated tigers—the villagers declared—had gathered momentum sufficient to operate hidden laws and bring about the fall of the proud tiger tamer.

"My servant further apprised me that the prince was in his element as manager of the bout between man and beast. He had supervised the erection of a storm-proof pavilion, designed to accommodate thousands. Its center held Raja Begum in an enormous iron cage, surrounded by an outer safety room. The captive emitted a ceaseless series of blood-curdling roars. He was fed sparingly, to kindle a wrathful appetite. Perhaps the prince expected me to be the meal of reward!

"Crowds from the city and suburbs bought tickets eagerly in response to the beat of drums announcing the unique contest. The day of battle saw hundreds turned away for lack of seats. Many men broke through the tent openings, or crowded any space below the galleries."

As the Tiger Swami's story approached a climax, my excitement mounted with it; Chandi also was raptly mute.

"Amidst piercing sound-explosions from Raja Begum, and the hubbub of the terrified crowd, I quietly made my appearance. Scantily clad around the waist, I was otherwise unprotected by clothing. I opened the bolt on the door of the safety room and calmly locked it behind me. The tiger sensed blood. Leaping with a thunderous crash on the bars, he sent forth a ferocious welcome. The audience was hushed with pitiful fear; I seemed a meek lamb before the raging beast.

"In a trice I was within the cage; but as I slammed the door, Raja Begum was headlong upon me. My right hand was desperately torn. Human blood, the greatest treat a tiger can know, fell in appalling streams. The prophecy of the saint seemed about to be fulfilled.

"I rallied instantly from the shock of the first serious injury I had ever received. Banishing the sight of my gory fingers by thrusting them beneath my waist cloth, I swung my left arm in a bone-cracking blow. The beast reeled back, swirled around the rear of the cage, and sprang forward convulsively. My famous fistic punishment rained on his head.

"But Raja Begum's taste of blood had acted like the maddening first sip of wine to a dipsomaniac long-deprived. Punctuated by deafening roars, the brute's assaults grew in fury. My inadequate defense of only one hand left me vulnerable before claws and fangs. But I dealt out dazing retribution. Mutually ensanguined, we struggled as to the death. The cage was pandemonium, as blood splashed in all directions, and blasts of pain and lethal lust came from the bestial throat.

"'Shoot him!' 'Kill the tiger!' Shrieks arose from the audience. So fast did man and beast move, that a guard's bullet went amiss. I mustered all my will force, bellowed fiercely, and landed a final concussive blow. The tiger collapsed and lay quietly."

"Like a pussycat!" I interjected.

The swami laughed in hearty appreciation, then continued the engrossing tale.

"Raja Begum was vanquished at last. His royal pride was further humbled: with my lacerated hands, I audaciously forced open his jaws. For a dramatic moment, I held my head within the yawning deathtrap. I looked around for a chain. Pulling one from a pile on the floor, I bound the tiger by his neck to the cage bars. In triumph I moved toward the door.

"But that fiend incarnate, Raja Begum, had stamina worthy of his supposed demoniac origin. With an incredible lunge, he snapped the chain and leaped on my back. My shoulder fast in his jaws, I fell violently. But in a trice I had him pinned beneath me. Under merciless blows, the treacherous animal sank into semiconsciousness. This time I secured him more carefully. Slowly I left the cage.

"I found myself in a new uproar, this time one of delight. The crowd's cheer broke as though from a single gigantic throat. Disastrously mauled, I had yet fulfilled the three conditions of the fight—stunning the tiger, binding him with a chain, and leaving him without requiring assistance for myself. In addition, I had so drastically injured and frightened the aggressive beast that he had been content to overlook the opportune prize of my head in his mouth!

"After my wounds had been treated, I was honored and garlanded; many gold pieces were showered at my feet. The whole city entered a holiday period. Endless discussions were heard on all sides about my victory over one of the largest and most savage tigers ever seen. Raja Begum was presented to me, as promised, but I felt no elation. A spiritual change had entered my heart. It seemed that with my final exit from the cage I had also closed the door on my worldly ambitions.

"A woeful period followed. For six months I lay near death from blood poisoning. As soon as I was well enough to leave Cooch Behar, I returned to my native town.

"'I know now that my teacher is the holy man who gave the wise warning.' I humbly made this confession to my father. 'Oh, if I could only find him!' My longing was sincere, for one day the saint arrived unheralded.

"'Enough of tiger taming.' He spoke with calm assurance. 'Come with me; I will teach you to subdue the beasts of ignorance roaming in jungles of the human mind. You are used to an audience: let it be a galaxy of angels, entertained by your thrilling mastery of yoga!'

"I was initiated into the spiritual path by my saintly guru. He opened my soul doors, rusty and resistant with long disuse. Hand in hand, we soon set out for my training in the Himalayas."

Chandi and I bowed at the swami's feet, grateful for his outline of a cyclonic life. My friend and I felt amply repaid for the long probationary wait in the cold parlor!

CHAPTER 7

The Levitating Saint

"I saw a yogi remain in the air, several feet above the ground, last night at a group meeting." My friend, Upendra Mohun Chowdhury, spoke impressively.

I gave him an enthusiastic smile. "Perhaps I can guess his name. Was it Bhaduri Mahasaya, of Upper Circular Road?"

Upendra nodded, a little crestfallen not to be a news-bearer. My inquisitiveness about saints was well known to my friends; they delighted in setting me on a fresh track.

"The yogi lives so close to my home that I often visit him." My words brought keen interest to Upendra's face, and I made a further confidence.

"I have seen him in remarkable feats. He has expertly mastered the various *pranayamas** mentioned in the ancient eightfold yoga outlined by Patanjali.† Once Bhaduri Mahasaya performed the *Bhastrika Pranayama* before me with such amazing force that it seemed an actual storm had arisen in the room! Then he extinguished the thundering breath and remained motionless in a high state of superconsciousness.‡ The aura of peace after the storm was vivid beyond forgetting."

* Methods of controlling life force (*prana*) through regulation of breath. The *Bhastrika* ("Bellows") *Pranayama* makes the mind steady.

† The foremost ancient exponent of yoga.

‡ Professor Jules-Bois of the Sorbonne said in 1928 that French psychologists have investigated and accorded recognition to the superconsciousness, which, in its grandeur, "is the exact opposite of the subconscious mind as conceived of by Freud; and which comprises the faculties that make man really man and not just a super-animal." The French savant explained that the awakening of the higher consciousness is "not to be confused with Couéism or hypnotism. The existence of a superconscious mind has long been recognized philosophically, being in reality the Over-Soul spoken of by Emerson; but only recently has it been recognized scientifically." (See page 108 n.)

In "The Over-Soul," Emerson wrote: "A man is the facade of a temple wherein all wisdom and all good abide. What we commonly call man, the eating, drinking, planting, counting man, does not, as we know him, represent himself, but misrepresents himself. Him we do not respect; but the soul, whose organ he is, would he let it appear through his actions, would make our knees bend....We lie open on one side to the deeps of spiritual nature, to all the attributes of God."

"I have heard that the saint never leaves his home." Upendra's tone was a trifle incredulous.

"Indeed it is true! He has lived indoors for the past twenty years. He slightly relaxes his self-imposed rule at the times of our holy festivals, when he goes as far as his front sidewalk! The beggars gather there, because Saint Bhaduri is known for his tender heart."

"How does he remain in the air, defying the law of gravitation?"

"A yogi's body loses its grossness after use of certain *pranayamas.* Then it will levitate or hop about like a leaping frog. Even saints who do not practice a formal yoga have been known to levitate during a state of intense devotion to God."

"I would like to know more of this sage. Do you attend his evening meetings?" Upendra's eyes were sparkling with curiosity.

"Yes, I go often. I am vastly entertained by the wit in his wisdom. Occasionally my prolonged laughter mars the solemnity of his gatherings. The saint is not displeased, but his disciples look daggers!"

On my way home from school that afternoon, I passed Bhaduri Mahasaya's cloister and decided on a visit. The yogi was inaccessible to the general public. A lone disciple, occupying the ground floor, guarded his master's privacy. The student was something of a martinet; he now inquired formally if I had an "engagement." His guru put in an appearance just in time to save me from summary ejection.

"Let Mukunda come when he will." The sage's eyes twinkled. "My rule of seclusion is not for my own comfort, but for that of others. Worldly people do not like the candor that shatters their delusions. Saints are not only rare but disconcerting. Even in scripture, they are often found embarrassing!"

I followed Bhaduri Mahasaya to his austere quarters on the top floor, from which he seldom stirred. Masters often ignore the panorama of the world's ado, out of focus till centered in the ages. The contemporaries of a sage are not only those of the narrow present.

"Maharishi,* you are the first yogi I have known who always stays indoors."

"God plants His saints sometimes in unexpected soil, lest we think we may reduce Him to a rule!"

The sage locked his vibrant body in the lotus posture. In his seventies, he displayed no unpleasing signs of age or sedentary life.

---

* "Great sage."

Stalwart and straight, he was ideal in every respect. His face was that of a rishi, as described in the ancient texts. Noble-headed, abundantly bearded, he always sat firmly upright, his quiet eyes fixed on Omnipresence.

The saint and I entered the meditative state. After an hour his gentle voice roused me.

"You go often into the silence, but have you developed *anubhava*?"* He was reminding me to love God more than meditation. "Do not mistake the technique for the Goal."

He offered me some mangoes. With the good-humored wit that I found so delightful in his grave nature, he remarked, "People in general are more fond of *Jala Yoga* (union with food) than of *Dhyana Yoga* (union with God)."

His yogic pun affected me uproariously.

"What a laugh you have!" An affectionate gleam came into his gaze. His own face was always serious, yet subtly touched with an ecstatic smile. His large, lotus eyes held a hidden divine laughter.

"Those letters come from far-off America." The sage indicated several thick envelopes on a table. "I correspond with a few societies there whose members are interested in yoga. They are discovering India anew, with a better sense of direction than Columbus! I am glad to help them. A knowledge of yoga, like the daylight, is free to all who will receive it.

"What rishis perceived as essential for human salvation need not be diluted for the West. Alike in soul though diverse in outer experience, neither West nor East will flourish if some form of disciplinary yoga be not practiced."

The saint held me with his tranquil eyes. I did not realize that his speech was a veiled prophetic guidance. It is only now, as I write these words, that I understand the full meaning in the casual intimations he often gave me that someday I would carry India's teachings to America.

"Maharishi, I wish you would write a book on yoga for the benefit of the world."

"I am training disciples. They and their line of students will serve as living volumes, proof against the natural disintegrations of time and the unnatural interpretations of the critics."

I remained alone with the yogi until his disciples arrived in the evening. Bhaduri Mahasaya began one of his inimitable discourses. Like a peaceful flood he swept away the mental debris of his listeners,

---

* Actual perception of God.

floating them Godward. His striking parables were expressed in a flawless Bengali.

This evening Bhaduri expounded various philosophical points connected with the life of Mirabai, a medieval Rajputani princess who had abandoned her court life to seek the company of saints. One great *sannyasi*, Sanatana Goswami, refused to receive her because she was a woman; her reply brought him humbly to her feet.

"Tell the master," she had said, "that I did not know there was any Male in the universe save God; are we all not females before Him?" (A scriptural conception of the Lord as the only Positive Creative Principle, His creation being naught but a passive *maya*.)

Mirabai composed many ecstatic songs, which are still treasured in India. I translate one of them here:

> If by bathing daily God could be realized
> Sooner would I be a whale in the deep;
> If by eating roots and fruits He could be known
> Gladly would I choose the form of a goat;
> If the counting of rosaries uncovered Him
> I would say my prayers on mammoth beads;
> If bowing before stone images unveiled Him
> A flinty mountain I would humbly worship;
> If by drinking milk the Lord could be imbibed
> Many calves and children would know Him;
> If abandoning one's wife could summon God
> Would not thousands be eunuchs?
> Mirabai knows that to find the Divine One
> The only indispensable is Love.

Several students put rupees in Bhaduri's slippers, which lay by his side as he sat in yoga posture. This respectful offering, customary in India, indicates that the disciple places his material goods at the guru's feet. Grateful friends are only the Lord in disguise, looking after His own.

"Master, you are wonderful!" A student, taking his leave, gazed ardently at the patriarchal sage. "You have renounced riches and comforts to seek God and teach us wisdom!" It was well known that Bhaduri Mahasaya had forsaken great family wealth in his early childhood, when single-mindedly he had entered the yogic path.

"You are reversing the case!" The saint's face held a mild rebuke. "I have left a few paltry rupees, a few petty pleasures, for a cosmic empire of endless bliss. How then have I denied myself anything? I know the joy of sharing the treasure. Is that a sacrifice? The shortsighted worldly folk are verily the real renunciants! They relinquish an unparalleled divine possession for a poor handful of earthly toys!"

I chuckled over this paradoxical view of renunciation—one that puts the cap of Croesus on any saintly beggar, whilst transforming all proud millionaires into unconscious martyrs.

"The divine order arranges our future more wisely than any insurance company." The master's concluding words were the realized creed of his faith. "The world is full of uneasy believers in an outward security. Their bitter thoughts are like scars on their foreheads. The One who gave us air and milk from our first breath knows how to provide day by day for His devotees."

I continued my after-school pilgrimages to the saint's door. With silent zeal he aided me to attain *anubhava*. One day he moved to Ram Mohan Roy Road, away from the neighborhood of my home. His loving disciples had built him a new hermitage, known as Nagendra Math.*

Although it throws me ahead of my story by a number of years, I will recount here the last words given to me by Bhaduri Mahasaya. Shortly before I embarked for the West, I sought him out and humbly knelt for his farewell blessing:

"Son, go to America. Take the dignity of hoary India for your shield. Victory is written on your brow; the noble distant people will well receive you."

---

* His full name was Nagendra Nath Bhaduri. A *math* is, strictly speaking, a monastery, but the term is often applied to an *ashram* or hermitage.

Among "levitating saints" of the Christian world was the 17th-century St. Joseph of Cupertino. His feats received ample attestation from eyewitnesses. St. Joseph exhibited a worldly absentmindedness that was really a divine recollectedness. His monastery brothers could not permit him to serve at the common table, lest he ascend to the ceiling with the crockery. The saint, indeed, was uniquely disqualified for earthly duties by his inability to remain, for any long period, on the earth! Often the sight of a holy statue was enough to exalt St. Joseph in vertical flight; the two saints, one of stone and the other of flesh, would be seen circling together in the upper air.

St. Teresa of Avila, she of the great elevation of soul, found physical elevation very disconcerting. Charged with heavy organizational duties, she vainly tried to prevent her "uplifting" experiences. "But little precautions are unavailing," she wrote, "when the Lord will have it otherwise." The body of St. Teresa, which lies in a church at Alba in Spain, has for four centuries manifested incorruptibility, accompanied by a perfume of flowers. The site has witnessed innumerable miracles.

CHAPTER 8

India's Great Scientist,
J. C. Bose

"Jagadis Chandra Bose's wireless inventions antedated those of Marconi."

Overhearing this provocative remark, I walked closer to a sidewalk group of professors engaged in scientific discussion. If my motive in joining them was racial pride, I regret it. I cannot deny my keen interest in evidence that India can play a leading part in physics, and not metaphysics alone.

"What do you mean, sir?"

The professor obligingly explained. "Bose was the first one to invent a wireless coherer and an instrument for indicating the refraction of electric waves. But the Indian scientist did not exploit his inventions commercially. He soon turned his attention from the inorganic to the organic world. His revolutionary discoveries as a plant physiologist are outpacing even his radical achievements as a physicist."

I politely thanked my mentor. He added, "The great scientist is one of my brother professors at Presidency College."

I paid a visit the next day to the sage at his home, which was close to mine. I had long admired him from a respectful distance. The grave and retiring botanist greeted me graciously. He was a handsome, robust man in his fifties, with thick hair, broad forehead, and the abstracted eyes of a dreamer. The precision in his tones revealed the lifelong scientific habit.

"I have recently returned from an expedition to scientific societies of the West. Their members exhibited intense interest in delicate instruments of my invention which demonstrate the indivisible unity of all life.* The Bose crescograph has the enormousness of ten million magnifications. The microscope enlarges only a few thousand times, yet it brought vital impetus to biological science. The crescograph opens incalculable vistas."

* "All science is transcendental or else passes away. Botany is now acquiring the right theory—the avatars of Brahma will presently be the textbooks of natural history."—*Emerson.*

"You have done much, sir, to hasten the embrace of East and West with the impersonal arms of science."

"I was educated at Cambridge. How admirable is the Western method of submitting all theory to scrupulous experimental verification! That empirical procedure has gone hand in hand with the gift for introspection that is my Eastern heritage. Together they have enabled me to sunder the silences of natural realms long uncommunicative. The telltale charts of my crescograph* are evidence for the most skeptical that plants have a sensitive nervous system and a varied emotional life. Love, hate, joy, fear, pleasure, pain, excitability, stupor, and countless other appropriate responses to stimuli are as universal in plants as in animals."

"The unique throb of life in all creation could seem only poetic imagery before your advent, Professor! A saint I once knew would never pluck flowers. 'Shall I rob the rosebush of its pride in beauty? Shall I affront its dignity by my rude divestment?' His sympathetic words are verified literally through your discoveries."

"The poet is intimate with truth, while the scientist approaches awkwardly. Come someday to my laboratory and see the unequivocal testimony of the crescograph."

Gratefully I accepted the invitation, and took my departure. I heard later that the botanist had left Presidency College, and was planning a research center in Calcutta.

When the Bose Institute was opened, I attended the dedicatory services. Enthusiastic hundreds strolled over the premises. I was charmed with the artistry and spiritual symbolism of the new home of science. Its front gate is a centuried relic from a distant shrine. Behind a lotus† pool, a sculptured female figure with a torch conveys the Indian respect for woman as the immortal light-bearer. A small temple in a garden is consecrated to the Noumenon beyond phenomena. Thought of the Divine Incorporeity is suggested by the absence of any altar-image.

Bose's speech on this great occasion might have issued from the lips of one of the inspired ancient rishis.

"I dedicate today this Institute as not merely a laboratory but a temple." His reverent solemnity stole like an unseen cloak over the crowded auditorium. "In the pursuit of my investigations I was unconsciously led into the border region of physics and physiology.

---

* From the Latin root *crescere*, to increase. For his crescograph and other inventions, Bose was knighted in 1917.

† The lotus flower is an ancient divine symbol in India; its unfolding petals suggest the expansion of the soul; the growth of its pure beauty from the mud of its origin holds a benign spiritual promise.

To my amazement, I found boundary lines vanishing, and points of contact emerging, between the realms of the living and the non-living. Inorganic matter was perceived as anything but inert; it was athrill under the action of multitudinous forces.

"A universal reaction seemed to bring metal, plant, and animal under a common law. They all exhibited essentially the same phenomena of fatigue and depression, with possibilities of recovery and of exaltation, as well as the permanent unresponsiveness associated with death. Filled with awe at this stupendous generalization, it was with great hope that I announced my results before the Royal Society—results demonstrated by experiments. But the physiologists present advised me to confine myself to investigations in physics, in which my success had been assured, rather than to encroach on their preserves. I had unwittingly strayed into the domain of an unfamiliar caste system and had offended its etiquette.

"An unconscious theological bias was also present, which confounds ignorance with faith. It is often forgotten that He who has surrounded us with this ever-evolving mystery of creation has also implanted in us the desire to question and understand. Through many years of miscomprehension from others, I came to know that the life of a devotee of science is inevitably filled with unending struggle. It is for him to cast his life as an ardent offering—regarding gain and loss, success and failure, as one.

"In time the leading scientific societies of the world accepted my theories and results, and recognized the importance of the Indian contribution to science.* Can anything small or circumscribed ever satisfy the mind of India? By a continuous living tradition and a vital power of rejuvenescence, this land has readjusted itself through unnumbered transformations. Indians have always arisen who, discarding the immediate and absorbing prize of the hour, have sought for the realization of the highest ideals in life—not through passive renunciation but through active struggle. The weakling who has refused the conflict, acquiring nothing, has had nothing to renounce. He alone who has striven and won can enrich the world by bestowing the fruits of his victorious experience.

"The work already carried out in the Bose laboratory on the re-

* "We believe...that no department of study, particularly in the humanities, in any major university can be fully equipped without a properly trained specialist in the Indic phases of its discipline. We believe, too, that every college which aims to prepare its graduates for intelligent work in the world which is to be theirs to live in, must have on its staff a scholar competent in the civilization of India."—Extracts from an article by Professor W. Norman Brown of the University of Pennsylvania which appeared in the May 1939 issue of the *Bulletin* of the American Council of Learned Societies, Washington, D.C.

sponse of matter, and the unexpected revelations in plant life, have opened out very extended regions of inquiry in physics, in physiology, in medicine, in agriculture, and even in psychology. Problems hitherto regarded as insoluble have now been brought within the sphere of experimental investigation.

"But high success is not to be obtained without rigid exactitude. Hence the long battery of supersensitive instruments and apparatus of my design, which stand before you today in their cases in the entrance hall. They tell you of the protracted efforts to get behind the deceptive seeming into the reality that remains unseen, of the continuous toil and persistence and resourcefulness called forth to overcome human limitations. All creative scientists know that the true laboratory is the mind, where behind illusions they uncover the laws of truth.

"The lectures given here will not be mere repetitions of secondhand knowledge. They will announce new discoveries, demonstrated for the first time in these halls. Through regular publication of the work of the Institute, these Indian contributions will reach the whole world. They will become public property. No patents will ever be taken. The spirit of our national culture demands that we should forever be free from the desecration of utilizing knowledge only for personal gain.

"It is my further wish that the facilities of this Institute be available, so far as possible, to workers from all countries. In this I am attempting to carry on the traditions of my country. As far back as twenty-five centuries, India welcomed to its ancient universities, at Nalanda and Taxila, scholars from all parts of the world.

"Although science is neither of the East nor of the West but rather international in its universality, yet India is specially fitted to make great contributions.* The burning Indian imagination,

* The atomic structure of matter was well known to the ancient Hindus. One of the six systems of Indian philosophy is *Vaisesika*, from the Sanskrit root *visesas*, "atomic individuality." One of the foremost *Vaisesika* expounders was Aulukya, also called Kanada, "the atom-eater," born about 2800 years ago.

In an article by Tara Mata in *East-West*, April 1934, a summary of *Vaisesika* scientific knowledge was given as follows: "Though the modern 'atomic theory' is generally considered a new advance of science, it was brilliantly expounded long ago by Kanada, 'the atom-eater.' The Sanskrit *anus* can be properly translated as 'atom' in the latter's literal Greek sense of 'uncut' or indivisible. Other scientific expositions of *Vaisesika* treatises of the B.C. era include (1) the movement of needles toward magnets, (2) the circulation of water in plants, (3) *akash* or ether, inert and structureless, as a basis for transmitting subtle forces, (4) the solar fire as the cause of all other forms of heat, (5) heat as the cause of molecular change, (6) the law of gravitation as caused by the quality that inheres in earth-atoms to give them their attractive power or downward pull, (7) the kinetic nature of all energy; causation as which can extort new order out of a mass of apparently contradictory facts, is held in check by the habit of concentration. This restraint confers the power to hold the mind to the pursuit of truth with an infinite patience."

Tears stood in my eyes at the scientist's concluding words. Is "patience" not indeed a synonym of India, confounding Time and the historians alike?

I visited the research center again, soon after the day of opening. The great botanist, mindful of his promise, took me to his quiet laboratory.

"I will attach the crescograph to this fern; the magnification is tremendous. If a snail's crawl were enlarged in the same proportion, the creature would appear to be traveling like an express train!"

My gaze was fixed eagerly on the screen which reflected the magnified fern-shadow. Minute life-movements were now clearly perceptible; the plant was growing very slowly before my fascinated eyes. The scientist touched the tip of the fern with a small metal bar. The developing pantomime came to an abrupt halt, resuming its eloquent rhythms as soon as the rod was withdrawn.

"You saw how any slight outside interference is detrimental to the sensitive tissues," Bose remarked. "Watch; I will now administer chloroform, and then give an antidote."

The effect of the chloroform discontinued all growth; the antidote was revivifying. The evolutionary gestures on the screen held me more raptly than a "movie" plot. My companion (here in the role of villain) thrust a sharp instrument through a part of the fern; pain was indicated by spasmodic flutters. When he passed a razor partially through the stem, the shadow was violently agitated, then stilled itself with the final punctuation of death.

"By first chloroforming a huge tree, I achieved a successful transplantation. Usually, such monarchs of the forest die very quickly after being moved." Jagadis smiled happily as he recounted the life-saving maneuver. "Graphs of my delicate apparatus have proved that trees possess a circulatory system; their sap movements

always rooted in an expenditure of energy or a redistribution of motion, (8) universal dissolution through the disintegration of atoms, (9) the radiation of heat and light rays, infinitely small particles, darting forth in all directions with inconceivable speed (the modern 'cosmic rays' theory), (10) the relativity of time and space.

"*Vaisesika* assigned the origin of the world to atoms, eternal in their nature, i.e., their ultimate peculiarities. These atoms were regarded as possessing an incessant vibratory motion....The recent discovery that an atom is a miniature solar system would be no news to the old *Vaisesika* philosophers, who also reduced time to its furthest mathematical concept by describing the smallest unit of time (*kala*) as the period taken by an atom to traverse its own unit of space."

correspond to the blood pressure of animal bodies. The ascent of sap is not explicable on the mechanical grounds ordinarily advanced, such as capillary attraction. The phenomenon has been revealed through the crescograph as the activity of living cells. Peristaltic waves issue from a cylindrical tube which extends down a tree and serves as an actual heart! The more deeply we perceive, the more striking becomes the evidence that a uniform plan links every form in manifold nature."

The great scientist pointed to another Bose instrument.

"I will show you experiments on a piece of tin. The life force in metals responds adversely or beneficially to stimuli. Ink markings will register the various reactions."

Deeply engrossed, I watched the graph which recorded the characteristic waves of atomic structure. When the professor applied chloroform to the tin, the vibratory writings stopped. They recommenced as the metal slowly regained its normal state. My companion dispensed a poisonous chemical. Simultaneously with the quivering end of the tin, the needle dramatically wrote on the chart a death notice. The scientist said:

"Bose instruments have demonstrated that metals, such as the steel used in scissors and machinery, are subject to fatigue, and regain efficiency by periodic rest. The life pulse in metals is seriously harmed or even extinguished through the application of electric currents or heavy pressure."

I looked around the room at the numerous inventions, eloquent testimony of a tireless ingenuity.

"Sir, it is lamentable that mass agricultural development is not speeded by fuller use of your marvelous mechanisms. Would it not be easily possible to employ some of them in quick laboratory experiments to indicate the influence of various types of fertilizers on plant growth?"

"You are right. Countless uses of Bose instruments will be made by future generations. The scientist seldom knows contemporaneous reward; it is enough to possess the joy of creative service."

With expressions of unreserved gratitude to the indefatigable sage, I took my leave. "Can the astonishing fertility of his genius ever be exhausted?" I thought.

No diminution came with the years. Inventing an intricate instrument, the "Resonant Cardiograph," Bose then pursued extensive researches on innumerable Indian plants. An enormous unsuspected pharmacopoeia of useful drugs was revealed. The cardiograph is constructed with an unerring accuracy by which a one-hundredth part of a second is indicated on a graph. Resonant records measure infinitesimal pulsations in plant, animal, and human structure. The great botanist predicted that use of his cardiograph will lead to vivisection on plants instead of animals.

"Side by side recordings of the effects of a medicine given simultaneously to a plant and an animal have shown astounding unanimity in result," he pointed out. "Everything in man has been foreshadowed in the plant. Experimentation on vegetation will contribute to the lessening of animal and human suffering."

Years later Bose's pioneer plant findings were substantiated by other scientists. Work done in 1938 at Columbia University was reported by *The New York Times* as follows:

> It has been determined within the past few years that when the nerves transmit messages between the brain and other parts of the body, tiny electrical impulses are being generated. These impulses have been measured by delicate galvanometers and magnified millions of times by modern amplifying apparatus. Until now no satisfactory method had been found to study the passage of the impulses along the nerve fibers in living animals or man because of the great speed with which these impulses travel.
>
> Drs. K. S. Cole and H. J. Curtis reported having discovered that the long single cells of the fresh-water plant nitella, used frequently in goldfish bowls, are virtually identical with those of single nerve fibers. Furthermore, they found that nitella fibers, on being excited, propagate electrical waves that are similar in every way, except velocity, to those of the nerve fibers in animals and man. The electrical nerve impulses in the plant were found to be much slower than those in animals. This discovery was therefore seized upon by the Columbia workers as a means for taking slow-motion pictures of the passage of the electrical impulses in nerves.
>
> The nitella plant thus may become a sort of Rosetta stone for deciphering the closely guarded secrets close to the very borderland of mind and matter.

The poet Rabindranath Tagore was a stalwart friend of India's idealistic scientist. To him, the sweet Bengali singer addressed the following lines:

> O Hermit, call thou in the authentic words
> Of that old hymn called *Sama:* "Rise! Awake!"
> Call to the man who boasts his Shastric lore;
> From vain pedantic wranglings profitless,
> Call to that foolish braggart to come forth
> Out on the face of nature, this broad earth;
> Send forth this call unto thy scholar band.

Together round thy sacrifice of fire
Let them all gather. So may our India,
Our ancient land unto herself return
O once again return to steadfast work,
To duty and devotion, to her trance
Of earnest meditation; let her sit
Once more unruffled, greedless, strifeless, pure,
O once again upon her lofty seat
And platform, teacher of all lands.*

---

* Translated by Manmohan Ghosh from the Bengali of Rabindranath Tagore, in *The Visvabharati Quarterly,* Santiniketan, India.

The "hymn called *Sama*" mentioned in Tagore's poem is one of the four Vedas. The other three are the Rig, Yajur, and Atharva. The sacred texts expound the nature of Brahma, God the Creator, whose expression in the individual man is termed *atma,* soul. The verb root of Brahma is *brih,* "to expand," conveying the Vedic concept of the divine power of spontaneous growth, of bursting forth into creative activity. The cosmos, like a spider's web, is said to evolve (*vikurute*) out of His being. The conscious fusion of *atma* with Brahma, soul with Spirit, may be said to be the whole import of the Vedas.

The *Vedanta,* summaries in the Vedas, have inspired many great Western thinkers. The French historian, Victor Cousin, said: "When we read with attention the philosophical monuments of the Orient—above all, those of India—we discover there many a truth so profound...that we are constrained to bend the knee before the philosophy of the East, and to see in this cradle of the human race the native land of the highest philosophy." Schlegel observed: "Even the loftiest philosophy of the Europeans, the idealism of reason as set forth by the Greek philosophers, appears—in comparison with the abundant life and vigor of Oriental idealism—like a feeble Promethean spark against a full flood of sunlight."

In the immense literature of India, the Vedas (root *vid,* to know) are the only texts to which no author is ascribed. The Rig Veda (X:90,9) assigns a divine origin to the hymns and tells us (III:39,2) they have come down from "ancient times," reclothed in new language. Divinely revealed from age to age to the rishis, "seers," the Vedas are said to possess *nityatva,* "timeless finality."

The Vedas were a revelation by sound, "directly heard" (*shruti*) by the rishis. It is essentially a literature of chant and recitation. For millenniums, therefore, the 100,000 couplets of the Vedas were not written down, but were orally transmitted by *Brahmin* priests. Paper and stone alike are subject to the obliterating effects of time. The Vedas have persisted down the ages because the rishis understood the superiority of mind over matter as the proper means of transmittal. What can excel the "tablets of the heart"?

By observing the particular order (*anupurvi*) in which the Vedic words occur, and with the aid of phonological rules for combinations of sounds (*sandhi*) and for the relation of letters (*sanatana*), and by proving in certain mathematical ways the accuracy of the memorized texts, the *Brahmins* have uniquely preserved, from a dim antiquity, the original purity of the Vedas. Each syllable (*akshara*) of a Vedic word is endowed with significance and efficacy. (See pp. 288–9.)

CHAPTER 9

The Blissful Devotee
and His Cosmic Romance

"Little sir, please be seated. I am talking to my Divine Mother."

Silently I had entered the room in great awe. The angelic appearance of Master Mahasaya fairly dazzled me. With silky white beard and large lustrous eyes, he seemed an incarnation of purity. His upraised chin and folded hands apprised me that my first visit had disturbed him in the midst of his devotions.

His simple words of greeting produced the most violent effect my nature had so far experienced. The bitterness of separation at my mother's death I had thought the measure of all anguish. Now a consciousness of separation from my Divine Mother was an indescribable torture of the spirit. I fell moaning to the floor.

"Little sir, quiet yourself!" The saint was sympathetically distressed.

Abandoned in some oceanic desolation, I clutched his feet as the sole raft of my rescue.

"Holy sir, thine intercession! Ask Divine Mother if I find any favor in Her sight!"

The sacred promise of intercession is one not easily bestowed; the master was constrained to silence.

Beyond reach of doubt, I was convinced that Master Mahasaya was in intimate converse with the Universal Mother. It was deep humiliation to realize that my eyes were blind to Her who even at this moment was perceptible to the faultless gaze of the saint. Shamelessly gripping his feet, deaf to his gentle remonstrances, I besought him again and again for his intervening grace.

"I will make your plea to the Beloved." The master's capitulation came with a slow, compassionate smile.

What power in those few words, that my being should know release from its stormy exile!

"Sir, remember your pledge! I shall return soon for Her message." Joyful anticipation rang in my voice, which only a moment ago had been sobbingly choked with sorrow.

Descending the long stairway, I was overwhelmed by memories. This house in Calcutta at 50 Amherst Street, now the residence of Master Mahasaya, had once been my family home, the scene of my mother's death. Here my human heart had broken for the vanished mother; and here today my spirit had been as though crucified by the absence of the Divine Mother. Hallowed walls! silent witness of my grievous hurts and final healing.

My steps were eager as I returned to my home. Seeking the seclusion of my small attic, I remained in meditation until ten o'clock. The darkness of the warm Indian night was suddenly lit with a wondrous vision.

Haloed in splendor, the Divine Mother stood before me. Her face, tenderly smiling, was beauty itself.

"Always have I loved thee! Ever shall I love thee!"

The celestial tones still ringing in the air, She disappeared.

The sun on the following morning had hardly risen to an angle of decorum when I paid my second visit to Master Mahasaya. Climbing the staircase in the house of poignant memories, I reached his fourth-floor room. The knob of the closed door was wrapped around with a cloth; a hint, I felt, that the saint desired privacy. As I stood irresolutely on the landing, the door was opened by the master's welcoming hand. I knelt at his holy feet. In a playful mood, I wore a solemn mask over my face, hiding the divine elation.

"Sir, I have come—very early, I confess!—for your message. Did the Beloved Mother say anything about me?"

"Mischievous little sir!"

Not another remark would he make. Apparently my assumed gravity was unimpressive.

"Why so mysterious, so evasive? Do saints never speak plainly?" Perhaps I was a little provoked.

"Must you test me?" His calm eyes were full of understanding. "Might I add a single word this morning to the assurance you received last night at ten o'clock from the Beautiful Mother Herself?"

Master Mahasaya possessed control over the floodgates of my soul: again I plunged prostrate at his feet. But this time my tears welled from a bliss, and not a pain, past bearing.

"Think you that your devotion did not touch the Infinite Mercy? The Motherhood of God, which you have worshiped in forms both human and divine, could never fail to answer your forsaken cry."

Who was this simple saint, whose least request to the Universal Spirit met with sweet acquiescence? His role in the world was humble, as befitted the greatest man of humility I ever knew. In this Amherst Street house, Master Mahasaya* conducted a small high school for boys. No words of chastisement passed his lips; no rule and ferule maintained his discipline. Higher mathematics indeed was taught in these modest classrooms, and a chemistry of love absent from the textbooks.

He spread his wisdom by spiritual contagion rather than by impermeable precept. Consumed by an unsophisticated passion for the Divine Mother, the saint no more demanded the outward forms of respect than a child.

"I am not your guru; he shall come a little later," he told me. "Through his guidance, your experiences of the Divine in terms of love and devotion will be translated into his terms of fathomless wisdom."

Every late afternoon, I betook myself to Amherst Street. I sought Master Mahasaya's divine cup, so full that its drops daily overflowed on my being. Never before had I bowed in utter reverence; now I felt it an immeasurable privilege even to tread the same ground that Master Mahasaya's footsteps sanctified.

"Sir, please wear this champak garland I have fashioned especially for you." I arrived one evening, holding my chain of flowers. But shyly he drew away, repeatedly refusing the honor. Perceiving my hurt, he finally smiled consent.

"Since we are both devotees of the Mother, you may put the garland on this bodily temple, as offering to Her who dwells within." His vast nature lacked space in which any egotistical consideration could gain foothold.

"Let us go tomorrow to Dakshineswar to the Temple of Kali, forever hallowed by my guru." The saint was a disciple of a Christlike master, Sri Ramakrishna Paramahansa.

The four-mile journey on the following morning was taken by boat on the Ganges. We entered the nine-domed Temple of Kali, where the figures of the Divine Mother and Shiva rest on a burnished silver lotus, its thousand petals meticulously chiseled. Master Mahasaya beamed in enchantment. He was engaged in his inexhaustible romance with the Beloved. As he chanted Her name, my enraptured heart seemed shattered, like the lotus, into a thousand pieces.

We strolled later through the sacred precincts, halting in a tamarisk grove. The manna characteristically exuded by this tree

---

* These are respectful titles by which he was customarily addressed. His name was Mahendra Nath Gupta; he signed his literary works simply "M."

was symbolic of the heavenly food Master Mahasaya was bestowing. His divine invocations continued. I sat rigidly motionless on the grass amid the pink feathery tamarisk flowers. Temporarily absent from the body, I soared in a supernal visit.

This was the first of many pilgrimages to Dakshineswar with the holy teacher. From him I learned the sweetness of God in the aspect of Mother, or Divine Mercy. The childlike saint found little appeal in the Father aspect, or Divine Justice. Stern, exacting, mathematical judgment was alien to his gentle nature.

"He can serve as an earthly prototype for the very angels of heaven!" I thought fondly, watching him one day at his prayers. Without a breath of censure or criticism, he surveyed the world with eyes long familiar with the Primal Purity. His body, mind, speech, and actions were effortlessly harmonized with his soul's simplicity.

"My Master told me so." Shrinking from personal assertion, the saint usually ended his sage counsel with this tribute. So deep was his sense of identity with Sri Ramakrishna that Master Mahasaya no longer considered his thoughts to be his own.

Hand in hand, the saint and I walked one evening on the block of his school. My joy was dimmed by the arrival of a conceited acquaintance. He burdened us with a lengthy discourse.

"I see this man doesn't please you." The saint's whisper to me was unheard by the egotist, spellbound by his own monologue. "I have spoken to Divine Mother about it; She realizes our sad predicament. As soon as we get to yonder red house, She has promised to remind him of more urgent business."

My eyes were glued to the site of salvation. Reaching its red gate, the man unaccountably turned and departed, neither finishing his sentence nor saying good-bye. Peace descended on the assaulted air.

Another day found me walking alone near the Howrah railway station. I stood for a moment by a temple, silently criticizing a small group of men with drum and cymbals who were violently reciting a chant.

"How undevotionally they use the Lord's divine name in mechanical repetition," I reflected. Suddenly I was astonished to see Master Mahasaya rapidly approaching me.

"Sir, how come you here?"

The saint, ignoring my question, answered my thought. "Isn't it true, little sir, that the Beloved's name sounds sweet from all lips, ignorant or wise?" He passed his arm around me affectionately; I found myself carried on his magic carpet to the Merciful Presence.

"Would you like to see some bioscopes?" This question one afternoon from the reclusive Master Mahasaya was mystifying to me; the term was then used in India to signify motion pictures. I agreed, glad to be in his company in any circumstances. A brisk walk brought us to the garden fronting Calcutta University. My companion indicated a bench near the *goldighi* or pond.

"Let us sit here for a few minutes. My Master asked me to meditate whenever I saw an expanse of water. Here its placidity reminds us of the vast calmness of God. As all things can be reflected in water, so the whole universe is mirrored in the lake of the Cosmic Mind. So my gurudeva* often said."

Soon we entered a university hall where a lecture was in progress. It proved abysmally dull, though varied occasionally by lantern slide illustrations, equally uninteresting.

"So this is the kind of bioscope the master wanted me to see!" My thought was impatient, yet I would not hurt the saint by revealing boredom in my face. But he leaned toward me confidentially.

"I see, little sir, that you don't like this bioscope. I have mentioned it to Divine Mother; She is in full sympathy with us both. She tells me that the electric lights will now go out and won't be relit until we have a chance to leave the room."

As his whisper ended, the hall was plunged into darkness. The professor, whose strident voice had been stilled for a moment in astonishment, said, "The electrical system of this hall appears to be defective." By this time Master Mahasaya and I were already across the threshold. Glancing back from the corridor, I saw that the hall was again illuminated.

"Little sir, you were disappointed in that bioscope, but I think you will like a different one." The saint and I were standing on the sidewalk in front of the university building. He gently slapped my chest over the heart.

A transforming silence ensued. Just as the modern "talkies" become inaudible motion pictures when the sound apparatus goes out of order, so the Divine Hand, by some strange miracle, stifled the earthly bustle. Pedestrians as well as the passing trolley cars, automobiles, bullock carts, and iron-wheeled hackney carriages were all in noiseless transit. As though possessing an omnipresent eye, I beheld the scenes that were behind me, and to each side,

---

* "Divine teacher," the customary Sanskrit term for one's spiritual preceptor. *Deva* ("god") combined with *guru* ("illumined teacher") indicates profound reverence and respect. I have rendered it in English as simply "Master."

as easily as those in front. The whole spectacle of activity in that small section of Calcutta passed before me without a sound. Like a glow of fire dimly seen beneath a thin coat of ashes, a mellow luminescence permeated the panoramic view.

My own body seemed nothing more than one of the many shadows; though it was motionless, while the others flitted mutely to and fro. Several boys, friends of mine, approached and passed on; though they had looked directly at me, it was without recognition.

The unique pantomime brought me an inexpressible ecstasy. I drank deep from some blissful fount. Suddenly my chest received another soft blow from Master Mahasaya. The pandemonium of the world burst upon my unwilling ears. I staggered, as though harshly awakened from a gossamer dream. The transcendental wine was removed beyond my reach.

"Little sir, I see you found the second bioscope* to your liking." The saint was smiling. I started to kneel in gratitude on the ground before him. "You can't do that to me now," he said. "You know God is in your temple also! I won't let Divine Mother touch my feet through your hands!"

If anyone observed the unpretentious master and me as we slowly walked away from the crowded pavement, the onlooker surely suspected us of intoxication. I felt that the falling shades of evening were sympathetically drunk with God.

Trying with poor words to do justice to his benignity, I wonder if Master Mahasaya, and others among the saints whose paths crossed mine, knew that years later, in a Western land, I would be writing about their lives as divine devotees. Their foreknowledge would not surprise me, nor, I hope, my readers, who have come thus far with me.

Saints of all religions have attained God-realization through the simple concept of the Cosmic Beloved. Because the Absolute is *nirguna*, "without qualities," and *acintya*, "inconceivable," human thought and yearning have ever personalized It as the Universal Mother. A combination of personal theism and the philosophy of the Absolute is an ancient achievement of Hindu thought, expounded in the Vedas and the Bhagavad Gita. This "reconciliation of opposites" satisfies heart and head; *bhakti* (devotion) and *jnana* (wisdom) are essentially one. *Prapatti*, "taking refuge" in God, and *sharanagati*,

---

* Webster's New International Dictionary (1934) gives, as rare, this definition: "A view of life; that which gives such a view." Master Mahasaya's choice of a word was, then, peculiarly justified.

"flinging oneself on the Divine Compassion," are really paths of the highest knowledge.

The humility of Master Mahasaya and of all other saints springs from a recognition of their total dependence (*seshatva*) on the Lord as the sole Life and Judge. Because the very nature of God is Bliss, the man in attunement with Him experiences a native boundless joy. "The first of the passions of the soul and the will is joy."*

Devotees of all the ages, approaching the Mother in a childlike spirit, testify that they find Her ever at play with them. In Master Mahasaya's life the manifestations of divine play occurred on occasions important and unimportant. In God's eyes nothing is large or small. Were it not for His perfect nicety in constructing the tiny atom, could the skies wear the proud structures of Vega, Arcturus? Distinctions of "important" and "unimportant" are surely unknown to the Lord, lest, for want of a pin, the cosmos collapse!

---

* St. John of the Cross. The body of this lovable Christian saint, who died in 1591, was exhumed in 1859 and found to be in a state of incorruptibility.

Sir Francis Younghusband (*Atlantic Monthly*, Dec. 1936) told of his own experience of cosmic joy: "There came upon me what was far more than elation or exhilaration; I was beside myself with an intensity of joy, and with this indescribable and almost unbearable joy came a revelation of the essential goodness of the world. I was convinced past all refutation that men at heart were good, that the evil in them was the superficial."

CHAPTER 10

I Meet My Master, Sri Yukteswar

"Faith in God can produce any miracle except one—passing an examination without study." Distastefully I closed the "inspirational" book I had picked up in an idle moment.

"The writer's exception shows his complete lack of faith," I thought. "Poor chap, he has great respect for the midnight oil!"

My promise to Father had been that I would complete my high school studies. I cannot pretend to diligence. The passing months found me less frequently in the classroom than in secluded spots along the Calcutta bathing *ghats*. The adjoining crematory grounds, especially gruesome at night, are considered highly attractive by the yogi. He who would find the Deathless Essence must not be dismayed by a few unadorned skulls. Human inadequacy becomes clear in the gloomy abode of miscellaneous bones. My midnight vigils were thus of a different nature from the scholar's.

The week of final examinations at the Hindu High School was fast approaching. This interrogatory period, like the sepulchral haunts, inspires a well-known terror. My mind was nevertheless at peace. Braving the ghouls, I was exhuming a knowledge not found in lecture halls. But I lacked the art of Swami Pranabananda, who easily appeared in two places at one time. My reasoning (though to many, alas, it seems illogic) was that the Lord would notice my dilemma and would extricate me from it. The devotee's irrationality springs from a thousand inexplicable demonstrations of God's instancy in trouble.

"Hello, Mukunda! I catch hardly a glimpse of you these days!" A classmate accosted me one afternoon on Garpar Road.

"Hello, Nantu! My invisibility at school seems to have placed me there in a decidedly awkward position." I unburdened myself under his friendly gaze.

Nantu, who was a brilliant student, laughed heartily; my predicament was not without a comic aspect.

"You are utterly unprepared for the finals!" he said. "I suppose it is up to me to help you!"

73

The simple words conveyed divine promise to my ears; with alacrity I visited my friend's home. He kindly outlined the solutions to various problems he considered likely to be set by the instructors.

"These questions are the bait that will catch many trusting boys in the examination trap. Remember my answers and you will escape without injury."

The night was far gone when I departed. Bursting with unseasoned erudition, I devoutly prayed it would remain for the next few critical days. Nantu had coached me in my various subjects, but, under press of time, had forgotten my course in Sanskrit. Fervently I reminded God of the oversight.

I set out on a walk the next morning, assimilating my new knowledge to the rhythm of swinging footsteps. As I took a shortcut through the weeds of a corner lot, my eye fell on a few loose printed sheets. A triumphant pounce; in my hand were Sanskrit verses! I sought out a pundit for aid in my stumbling interpretation. His rich voice filled the air with the edgeless, honeyed beauty of the ancient tongue.*

"These exceptional stanzas cannot possibly be of aid in your Sanskrit test." The scholar dismissed them skeptically.

But familiarity with that particular poem enabled me on the following day to pass the Sanskrit examination. Through the discerning help Nantu had given, I also attained the minimum grade for success in all my other subjects.

Father was pleased that I had kept my word and concluded my secondary school course. My gratitude sped to the Lord, whose sole guidance I perceived in my visit to Nantu's home and in my walk by the unhabitual route of the debris-filled lot. Playfully He had given a dual expression to His timely design for my rescue.

I came across the discarded book whose author had denied God precedence in the examination halls. I could not restrain a chuckle at my own silent comment:

"It would only add to this fellow's confusion if I were to tell him that divine meditation among the cadavers is a shortcut to a high school diploma!"

In my new dignity, I was now openly planning to leave home.

---

* *Sanskrita*, "polished, complete." Sanskrit is the elder sister of all Indo-European tongues. Its alphabetical script is called *Devanagari*; literally, "divine abode." "Who knows my grammar knows God!" Panini, great philologist of ancient India, paid that tribute to the mathematical and psychological perfection of Sanskrit. He who would track language to its lair must indeed end as omniscient.

Together with a young friend, Jitendra Mazumdar,* I decided to join a Banaras† hermitage, Sri Bharat Dharma Mahamandal, and receive its spiritual discipline.

A desolation fell over me one day at the thought of separation from my family. Since Mother's death, my affection had grown especially tender for my two younger brothers, Sananda and Bishnu, and for Thamu, my youngest sister. I rushed to my retreat, the little attic that had witnessed so many scenes in my turbulent *sadhana.*‡ After a two-hour flood of tears I felt singularly transformed, as by some alchemical cleanser. All attachment§ disappeared; my resolution to seek God as the Friend of friends became adamantine.

"I make one last plea." Father was distressed as I stood before him for his blessing. "Do not forsake me and your grieving brothers and sisters."

"Revered Father, how can I tell my love for you? But even greater is my love for the Heavenly Father, who has given me the gift of a perfect father on earth. Let me go, that I someday return with a more divine understanding."

With reluctant parental consent, I set out to join Jitendra, already in Banaras at the hermitage. On my arrival the young head swami, Dayananda, greeted me cordially. Tall and thin, of thoughtful mien, he impressed me favorably. His fair face had a Buddhalike composure.

I was pleased that my new home possessed an attic, where I managed to spend the dawn and morning hours. The ashram members, knowing little of meditation practices, thought I should employ my whole time in organizational duties. They gave me praise for my afternoon work in their office.

"Don't try to catch God so soon!" This ridicule from a fellow resident accompanied one of my early departures toward the attic. I went to Dayananda, busy in his small sanctum overlooking the Ganges.

* He was not Jatinda (Jotin Ghosh), who will be remembered for his timely aversion to tigers.

† Since India gained her independence, the original Indian spellings have been restored to many words that had become anglicized during British rule. Thus Banaras is now more commonly spelled Varanasi, or is referred to by its more ancient name, Kashi.

‡ Path or preliminary road to God.

§ Hindu scriptures teach that family attachment is delusive if it prevents the devotee from seeking the Giver of all boons, including the one of loving relatives, not to mention life itself. Jesus similarly taught: "He that loveth father or mother more than me is not worthy of me."—Matthew 10:37.

"Swamiji,* I don't understand what is required of me here. I am seeking direct perception of God. Without Him, I cannot be satisfied with affiliation or creed or performance of good works."

The orange-robed ecclesiastic gave me an affectionate pat. Staging a mock rebuke, he admonished a few nearby disciples. "Don't bother Mukunda. He will learn our ways."

I politely concealed my doubt. The students left the room, not noticeably bent with their chastisement. Dayananda had further words for me.

"Mukunda, I see your father is regularly sending you money. Please return it to him; you require none here. A second injunction for your discipline concerns food. Even when you feel hunger, do not mention it."

Whether famishment gleamed in my eye, I knew not. That I was hungry, I knew only too well. The invariable hour for the first hermitage meal was twelve noon. I had been accustomed in my own home to a large breakfast at nine o'clock.

The three-hour gap became daily more interminable. Gone were the Calcutta years when I could rebuke the cook for a ten-minute delay. Now I tried to control my appetite; I completed a twenty-four-hour fast. With doubled zest I awaited the following midday.

"Dayanandaji's train is late; we are not going to eat until he arrives." Jitendra brought me this devastating news. As a gesture of welcome to the swami, who had been absent for two weeks, many delicacies were in readiness. An appetizing aroma filled the air. Nothing else offering, what could be swallowed except my pride in yesterday's fast?

"Lord, hasten the train!" The Heavenly Provider, I thought, could hardly have been included in the interdiction with which Dayananda had silenced me. Divine Attention was elsewhere, however; the plodding clock covered the hours. Darkness was descending as our leader entered the door. My greeting was one of sheer joy.

"Dayanandaji will bathe and meditate before we can serve food." Jitendra approached me again as a bird of ill omen.

I was in near collapse. My young stomach, new to deprivation, protested with gnawing vigor. Pictures I had seen of famine victims passed wraithlike before me.

"The next Banaras death from starvation is due at once in this

---

* *Ji* is a customary respectful suffix, particularly used in direct address; thus, "swamiji," "guruji," "Sri Yukteswarji."

hermitage," I thought. Impending doom was averted at nine o'clock. Ambrosial summons! In memory that evening meal is vivid as one of life's perfect hours.

Intense absorption had not prevented me from observing that Dayananda ate absentmindedly. He was apparently above my gross pleasures.

"Swamiji, weren't you hungry?" Happily surfeited, I was alone with the leader in his study.

"Oh, yes!" he said. "I spent the last four days without food or drink. I never eat on trains, filled with the heterogeneous vibrations of worldly people. Strictly I observe the shastric* rules for monks of my particular order.

"Certain problems of our organizational work lie on my mind. Tonight at home I neglected my dinner. What's the hurry? Tomorrow I'll make it a point to have a proper meal." He laughed merrily.

Shame spread within me like a suffocation. But the past day of my torture was not easily forgotten; I ventured a further remark.

"Swamiji, I am puzzled about following your instruction. Suppose I never ask for food, and nobody gives me any. I should starve to death."

"Die, then!" This alarming counsel split the air. "Die if you must, Mukunda! Never believe that you live by the power of food and not by the power of God! He who has created every form of nourishment, He who has bestowed appetite, will inevitably see that His devotee is maintained. Do not imagine that rice sustains you nor that money or men support you. Could they aid if the Lord withdraws your life breath? They are His instruments merely. Is it by any skill of yours that food digests in your stomach? Use the sword of your discrimination, Mukunda! Cut through the chains of agency and perceive the Single Cause!"

I found his incisive words entering some deep marrow. Gone was an age-old delusion by which bodily imperatives outwit the soul. Then and there I tasted the Spirit's all-sufficiency. In how many

---

* Pertaining to the *shastras*, literally, "sacred books," comprising four classes of scripture: the *shruti*, *smriti*, *purana*, and *tantra*. These comprehensive treatises cover every aspect of religious and social life, and the fields of law, medicine, architecture, art, etc. The *shrutis* are the "directly heard" or "revealed" scriptures, the Vedas. The *smritis* or "remembered" lore were finally written down in a remote past as the world's longest epic poems, the *Mahabharata* and the *Ramayana*. *Puranas*, eighteen in number, are literally "ancient" allegories; *tantras* literally means "rites" or "rituals": these treatises convey profound truths under a veil of detailed symbolism.

strange cities, in my later life of ceaseless travel, did occasion arise to prove the serviceability of this lesson in a Banaras hermitage!

The sole treasure which had accompanied me from Calcutta was the sadhu's silver amulet bequeathed to me by Mother. Guarding it for years, I now had it carefully hidden in my ashram room. To renew my joy in the talismanic testimony, one morning I opened the locked box. The sealed covering untouched, lo! the amulet was gone. Mournfully I tore open the envelope and made unmistakably sure. It had vanished, in accordance with the sadhu's prediction, into the ether whence he had summoned it.

My relationship with Dayananda's followers grew steadily worse. The household was alienated, hurt by my determined aloofness. My strict adherence to meditation on the very Ideal for which I had left home and all worldly ambitions called forth shallow criticism from all sides.

Torn by spiritual anguish, I entered the attic one dawn, resolved to pray until an answer was vouchsafed.

"Merciful Mother of the Universe, teach me Thyself through visions, or through a guru sent by Thee!"

The passing hours found my sobbing pleas without response. Suddenly I felt lifted as though bodily to a sphere uncircumscribed.

"Thy Master cometh today!" A divine womanly voice came from everywhere and nowhere.

The supernal experience was shattered by a shout from a definite locale. A young priest nicknamed Habu was calling me from the downstairs kitchen.

"Mukunda, enough of meditation! You are needed for an errand."

Another day I might have replied impatiently; now I wiped my tear-swollen face and meekly obeyed the summons. Together Habu and I set out for a distant marketplace in the Bengali section of Banaras. The ungentle Indian sun was not yet at zenith as we made our purchases in the bazaars. We pushed our way through the colorful medley of housewives, guides, priests, simply clad widows, dignified *Brahmins*, and ubiquitous holy bulls. As Habu and I moved on, I turned my head to survey a narrow, inconspicuous lane.

A Christlike man in the ocher robes of a swami stood motionless at the end of the lane. Instantly and anciently familiar he seemed; for a trice my gaze fed hungrily. Then doubt assailed me.

"You are confusing this wandering monk with someone known to you," I thought. "Dreamer, walk on."

After ten minutes, I felt heavy numbness in my feet. As though turned to stone, they were unable to carry me farther. Laboriously I turned around; my feet regained normality. I faced the opposite direction; again the curious weight oppressed me.

"The saint is magnetically drawing me to him!" With this thought, I heaped my parcels into the arms of Habu. He had been observing my erratic footwork with amazement, and now burst into laughter.

"What ails you? Are you crazy?"

My tumultuous emotion prevented any retort; I sped silently away.

Retracing my steps as though wing-shod, I reached the narrow lane. My quick glance revealed the quiet figure, steadily gazing in my direction. A few eager steps and I was at his feet.

"Gurudeva!" The divine face was the one I had seen in a thousand visions. These halcyon eyes, in a leonine head with pointed beard and flowing locks, had oft peered through the gloom of my nocturnal reveries, holding a promise I had not fully understood.

"O my own, you have come to me!" My guru uttered the words again and again in Bengali, his voice tremulous with joy. "How many years I have waited for you!"

We entered a oneness of silence; words seemed the rankest superfluities. Eloquence flowed in soundless chant from the heart of master to disciple. With an antenna of irrefragable insight I sensed that my guru knew God and would lead me to Him. The obscuration of this life disappeared in a fragile dawn of prenatal memories. Dramatic time! Past, present, and future are its cycling scenes. This was not the first sun to find me at these holy feet!

My hand in his, my guru led me to his temporary residence in the Rana Mahal section of the city. His athletic figure moved with firm tread. Tall, erect, about fifty-five at this time, he was active and vigorous as a young man. His dark eyes were large, beautiful with plumbless wisdom. Slightly curly hair softened a face of striking power. Strength mingled subtly with gentleness.

As we made our way to the stone balcony of a house overlooking the Ganges, he said affectionately:

"I shall give you my hermitages and all I possess."

"Sir, I come for wisdom and God-realization. Those are your treasure troves I am after!"

The swift Indian twilight had dropped its half-curtain before my master spoke again. His eyes held unfathomable tenderness.

"I give you my unconditional love."

Precious words! A quarter-century elapsed before I had another auricular proof of his love. His lips were strange to ardor; silence suited his oceanic heart.

"Will you give me the same unconditional love?" He gazed at me with childlike trust.

"I will love you eternally, Gurudeva!"

"Ordinary love is selfish, darkly rooted in desires and satisfactions. Divine love is without condition, without boundary, without change. The flux of the human heart is gone forever at the transfixing touch of pure love." He added humbly, "If ever you find me falling from a state of God-realization, please promise to put my head on your lap and help to bring me back to the Cosmic Beloved we both worship."

He rose then in the gathering darkness and guided me to an inner room. As we ate mangoes and almond sweetmeats, he unobtrusively wove into his conversation an intimate knowledge of my nature. I was awestruck at the grandeur of his wisdom, exquisitely blended with an innate humility.

"Do not grieve for your amulet. It has served its purpose." Like a divine mirror, my guru apparently had caught a reflection of my whole life.

"The living reality of your presence, Master, is joy beyond any symbol."

"It is time for a change, inasmuch as you are unhappily situated in the hermitage."

I had made no references to my life; they now seemed superfluous! By his natural, unemphatic manner, I understood that he wished no astonished ejaculations at his clairvoyance.

"You should go back to Calcutta. Why exclude relatives from your love of humanity?"

His suggestion dismayed me. My family was predicting my return, though I had been unresponsive to many pleas by letter. "Let the young bird fly in the metaphysical skies," Ananta had remarked. "His wings will tire in the heavy atmosphere. We shall yet see him swoop toward home, fold his pinions, and humbly rest in our family nest." This discouraging simile fresh in my mind, I was determined to do no "swooping" in the direction of Calcutta.

"Sir, I am not returning home. But I will follow you anywhere. Please give me your address, and your name."

"Swami Sri Yukteswar Giri. My chief hermitage is in Serampore, on Rai Ghat Lane. I am visiting my mother here for only a few days."

SRI YUKTESWAR (1855–1936)
A Jnanavatar, "Incarnation of Wisdom"
Disciple of Lahiri Mahasaya; Guru of Sri Yogananda
Paramguru of all SRF-YSS *Kriya Yogis*

Swami Sri Yukteswar Meditation Temple, dedicated in 1977, on site of his ashram in Serampore. Several bricks from the original ashram were used in its construction. The temple architecture is patterned after a design by Paramahansa Yogananda.

Yoganandaji in 1915, on back seat of motorcycle given by his father. "I rode everywhere on it," he said, "especially to visit my master, Sri Yukteswarji, in his Serampore hermitage."

I wondered at God's intricate play with His devotees. Serampore is but twelve miles from Calcutta, yet in those regions I had never caught a glimpse of my guru. We had had to travel for our meeting to the ancient city of Kashi (Banaras), hallowed by memories of Lahiri Mahasaya. Here too the feet of Buddha, Shankaracharya,* and many other Yogi-Christs had blessed the soil.

"You will come to me in four weeks." For the first time, Sri Yukteswar's voice was stern. "Now that I have told you of my eternal affection and have shown my happiness at finding you, you feel free to disregard my request. The next time we meet, you shall have to reawaken my interest. I won't easily accept you as a disciple: there must be complete surrender by obedience to my strict training."

* Shankaracharya (Shankara), India's greatest philosopher, was a disciple of Govinda Jati and of the latter's guru Gaudapada. Shankara wrote a famous commentary on a treatise, *Mandukya Karika*, by Gaudapada. With unanswerable logic, and in a style of charm and grace, Shankara interpreted *Vedanta* philosophy in a strictly *advaita* (non-dual, monistic) spirit. The great monist also composed poems of devotional love. His *Prayer to the Divine Mother for Forgiveness of Sins* bears the refrain: "Though bad sons are many, never has there been a bad mother."

Sanandana, a disciple of Shankara's, wrote a commentary on the *Brahma Sutras* (*Vedanta* philosophy). The manuscript was lost by fire, but Shankara (who had once glanced through it) repeated it word for word to his disciple. The text, known as *Panchapadika*, is studied by scholars to this day.

The *chela* Sanandana received a new name after a beautiful incident. Seated one day on a riverbank, he heard Shankara calling him from the opposite shore. Sanandana entered the water forthwith. His faith and his feet were simultaneously supported when Shankara materialized, in the swirling river, a series of lotus flowers. The disciple was thereafter known as Padmapada, "lotus-foot."

In the *Panchapadika* Padmapada offers many loving tributes to his guru. Shankara himself wrote the following beautiful lines: "No known comparison exists in the three worlds for a true guru. If the philosophers' stone be assumed as truly such, it can only turn iron into gold, not into another philosophers' stone. The venerated teacher, on the other hand, creates equality with himself in the disciple who takes refuge at his feet. The guru is therefore peerless, nay, transcendental" (*Century of Verses*, 1).

Lord Shankara was a rare combination of saint, scholar, and man of action. Though he lived only thirty-two years, many of them were spent in arduous travel to every part of India, spreading his *advaita* doctrine. Millions gathered eagerly to hear the solacing flow of wisdom from the lips of the barefooted young monk.

Shankara's reforming zeal included the reorganization of the ancient monastic Swami Order (see pp. 196 n., 197). He also founded *maths* (monastic educational centers) in four localities—Sringeri in the south, Puri in the east, Dwarka in the west, and Badrinath in the Himalayan north.

The four *maths* of the great monist, liberally endowed by princes and the common people, gave free instruction in Sanskrit grammar, logic, and *Vedanta* philosophy. Shankara's object in locating his *maths* in the four corners of India was the promotion of religious and national unity throughout the vast land. Now as in the past, the pious Hindu finds free room and board at *choultries* and *sattrams* (resting places along the pilgrimage roads), maintained by public benefactors.

I remained obstinately silent. My guru quickly penetrated my difficulty.

"Do you think your relatives will laugh at you?"

"I will not return."

"You will return in thirty days."

"Never."

The controversial tension unrelieved, I bowed reverently at his feet and departed. Walking in the midnight darkness toward the hermitage, I wondered why the miraculous meeting had ended on an inharmonious note. The dual scales of *maya*, that balance every joy with a grief! My young heart was not yet malleable to the transforming fingers of my guru.

The next morning I noticed increased hostility in the attitude of the hermitage members. They spiked my days with invariable rudeness. Three weeks passed; Dayananda then left the ashram to attend a conference in Bombay. Pandemonium broke over my hapless head.

"Mukunda is a parasite, accepting hermitage hospitality without making proper return." Overhearing this remark, I regretted for the first time that I had obeyed the request to send back my money to Father. With heavy heart, I sought out my sole friend, Jitendra.

"I am leaving. Please convey my respectful regrets to Dayanandaji when he returns."

"I will leave also! My attempts to meditate here meet with no more favor than your own." Jitendra spoke with determination.

"I have met a Christlike saint. Let us visit him in Serampore."

And so the "bird" prepared to "swoop" perilously close to Calcutta!

CHAPTER 11

Two Penniless Boys in Brindaban

"It would serve you right if Father disinherited you, Mukunda! How foolishly you are throwing away your life!" An elder-brother sermon was assaulting my ears.

Jitendra and I, fresh from the train (a figure of speech merely; we were covered with dust), had just arrived at the home of Ananta, recently transferred from Calcutta to the ancient city of Agra. Brother was a supervising accountant for the Public Works Department of the Government.

"You well know, Ananta, I seek my inheritance from the Heavenly Father."

"Money first; God can come later! Who knows? Life may be too long."

"God first; money is His slave! Who can tell? Life may be too short."

My retort was summoned by the exigencies of the moment and held no presentiment. (Alas, Ananta's life did come to an early close.)*

"Wisdom from the hermitage, I suppose! But I see you have left Banaras." Ananta's eyes gleamed with satisfaction; he was yet hoping to secure my pinions in the family nest.

"My sojourn in Banaras was not in vain! I found there everything my heart had been longing for. You may be sure it was not your pundit or his son!"

Ananta joined me in reminiscent laughter; he had had to admit that the Banaras "clairvoyant" he selected had proved a shortsighted one.

"What are your plans, my wandering brother?"

"Jitendra persuaded me to Agra. We shall view the beauties of the Taj Mahal† here," I explained. "Then we are going to my newly found guru, who has a hermitage in Serampore."

Ananta hospitably arranged for our comfort. Several times dur-

* See chapter 25.

† The world-famous mausoleum.

83

ing the evening I noticed his eyes fixed on me reflectively.

"I know that look," I thought. "A plot is brewing!"

The denouement took place during our early breakfast.

"So you feel quite independent of Father's wealth." Ananta's gaze was innocent as he resumed the barbs of yesterday's conversation.

"I am conscious of my dependence on God."

"Words are cheap! Life has shielded you thus far. What a plight if you were forced to look to the Invisible Hand for your food and shelter! You would soon be begging on the streets."

"Never! I would not put faith in passers-by rather than in God! He can devise for His devotee a thousand resources besides the begging bowl."

"More rhetoric! Suppose I suggest that your vaunted philosophy be put to a test in this tangible world?"

"I would agree! Do you confine God to a speculative world?"

"We shall see; today you shall have opportunity either to enlarge or to confirm my own views." Ananta paused for a dramatic moment, then spoke slowly and seriously.

"I propose that I send you and your fellow disciple Jitendra this morning to the nearby city of Brindaban. You must not take a single rupee; you must not beg, either for food or money; you must not reveal your predicament to anyone; you must not go without your meals; and you must not be stranded in Brindaban. If you return to my bungalow here before twelve o'clock tonight, without having broken any rule of the test, I shall be the most astonished man in Agra!"

"I accept the challenge." No hesitation was in my words or in my heart. Grateful memories flashed of the Instant Beneficence: my healing of deadly cholera through an appeal to Lahiri Mahasaya's picture; the playful gift of the two kites on the Lahore roof; the opportune amulet amidst my discouragement in Bareilly; the decisive message through the sadhu outside the courtyard of the pundit's house in Banaras; the vision of Divine Mother and Her majestic words of love; Her swift heed through Master Mahasaya to my trifling embarrassments; the last-minute guidance that had materialized my high school diploma; and the ultimate boon, my living Master from the mist of my lifelong dreams. Never would I admit my "philosophy" unequal to any tussle on the world's harsh proving-grounds!

"Your willingness does you credit. I'll escort you to the train at once," Ananta said.

He turned to the openmouthed Jitendra. "You must go along—as a witness and, very likely, a fellow victim!"

A half hour later Jitendra and I were in possession of one-way tickets for the trip. We submitted, in a secluded corner of the station, to a search of our persons. Ananta was quickly satisfied that we were carrying no hidden hoard; our simple *dhotis** concealed nothing more than was necessary.

As faith invaded the serious realms of finance, my friend spoke protestingly. "Ananta, give me one or two rupees as a safeguard. Then I can telegraph you in case of misfortune."

"Jitendra!" My ejaculation was sharply reproachful. "I will not proceed with the test if you take any money as final security."

"There is something reassuring about the clink of coins." Jitendra said no more as I regarded him sternly.

"Mukunda, I am not heartless." A hint of humility had crept into Ananta's voice. It may be that his conscience was smiting him: perhaps for sending two penniless boys to a strange city; perhaps for his own religious skepticism. "If by any chance or grace you pass successfully through the Brindaban ordeal, I shall ask you to initiate me as your disciple."

This promise had a certain irregularity, in keeping with the unconventional occasion. The eldest brother in an Indian family seldom bows before his juniors; he receives respect and obedience second only to a father. But no time remained for my comment; our train was at point of departure.

Jitendra maintained a lugubrious silence as the train covered the miles. Finally he bestirred himself; leaning over, he pinched me painfully on a tender spot.

"I see no sign that God is going to supply our next meal!"

"Be quiet, doubting Thomas; the Lord is working with us."

"Can you also arrange that He hurry? Already I am famished merely at the prospect before us. I left Banaras to view the Taj mausoleum, not to enter my own!"

"Cheer up, Jitendra! Are we not to have our first glimpse of the sacred wonders of Brindaban?† I am in deep joy at the thought of treading the ground hallowed by the feet of Lord Krishna."

The door of our compartment opened; two men seated themselves. The next train stop would be the last.

* A *dhoti*-cloth is knotted around the waist and covers the legs.

† Brindaban, by the Yamuna River, is the Hindu Jerusalem. Here the avatar Lord Krishna displayed his glories for the benefit of mankind.

"Young lads, do you have friends in Brindaban?" The stranger opposite me was taking a surprising interest.

"None of your business!" Rudely I averted my gaze.

"You are probably flying away from your families under the enchantment of the Stealer of Hearts.* I am of devotional temperament myself. I will make it my positive duty to see that you receive food, and shelter from this overpowering heat."

"No, sir, let us alone. You are very kind; but you are mistaken in judging us to be truants from home."

No further conversation ensued; the train came to a halt. As Jitendra and I descended to the platform, our chance companions linked arms with us and summoned a horse cab.

We alit before a stately hermitage, set amidst the evergreen trees of well-kept grounds. Our benefactors were evidently known here; a smiling lad led us without comment to a parlor. We were soon joined by an elderly woman of dignified bearing.

"Gauri Ma, the princes could not come." One of the men addressed the ashram hostess. "At the last moment their plans went awry; they send deep regrets. But we have brought two other guests. As soon as we met on the train, I felt drawn to them as devotees of Lord Krishna."

"Good-bye, young friends." Our two acquaintances walked to the door. "We shall meet again, if God be willing."

"You are welcome here." Gauri Ma smiled in motherly fashion. "You could not have come on a better day. I was expecting two royal patrons of this hermitage. What a shame if my cooking had found none to appreciate it!"

The pleasant words had a surprising effect on Jitendra: he burst into tears. The "prospect" he had feared in Brindaban was turning out as royal entertainment; his sudden mental adjustment proved too much for him. Our hostess looked at him with curiosity, but without remark; perhaps she was familiar with adolescent quirks.

Lunch was announced; Gauri Ma led the way to a dining patio, spicy with savory odors. She vanished into an adjoining kitchen.

I had been premeditating this moment. Selecting the appropriate spot on Jitendra's body, I gave him a pinch as painful as the one he had given me on the train.

"Doubting Thomas, the Lord works—in a hurry, too!"

The hostess reentered with a *punkha*. She steadily fanned us in the Oriental fashion as we squatted on ornate blanket seats.

* Hari; an endearing name by which Sri Krishna is known to his devotees.

Ashram disciples passed to and fro with some thirty courses. Rather than "meal," the description may be only "sumptuous repast." Since arriving on this planet, Jitendra and I had never before tasted such delicacies.

"Dishes fit for princes indeed, Honored Mother! What your royal patrons could have found more urgent than attending this banquet, I cannot imagine. You have given us a memory for a lifetime!"

Silenced as we were by Ananta's requirement, we could not explain to the gracious lady that our thanks held a double significance. Our sincerity at least was patent. We departed with her blessing and an attractive invitation to revisit the hermitage.

The heat outdoors was merciless. My friend and I made for the shelter of a lordly cadamba tree at the ashram gate. Sharp words followed; once again Jitendra was beset with misgivings.

"A fine mess you have got me into! Our luncheon was only accidental good fortune! How can we see the sights of this city, without a single *pice* between us? And how on earth are you going to take me back to Ananta's place?"

"You forget God quickly, now that your stomach is filled." My words, not bitter, were accusatory. How short is human memory for divine favors! No man lives who has not seen some of his prayers granted.

"I am not likely to forget my folly in venturing out with a madcap like you!"

"Be quiet, Jitendra! The same Lord who fed us will show us Brindaban, and return us to Agra."

A slight young man of pleasing countenance approached at rapid pace. Halting under our tree, he bowed before me.

"Dear friend, you and your companion must be strangers here. Permit me to be your host and guide."

It is scarcely possible for an Indian to pale, but Jitendra's face was suddenly sickly. I politely declined the offer.

"You are surely not banishing me?" The stranger's alarm would have been comic in any other circumstances.

"Why not?"

"You are my guru." His eyes sought mine trustfully. "During my midday devotions, the blessed Lord Krishna appeared in a vision. He showed me two forsaken figures under this very tree. One face was yours, my master! Often have I seen it in meditation. What joy if you accept my humble services!"

"I too am glad you have found me. Neither God nor man has

forsaken us!" Though I was motionless, smiling at the eager face before me, an inward obeisance cast me at the Divine Feet.

"Dear friends, will you not honor my home with a visit?"

"You are kind; but the plan is unfeasible. Already we are guests of my brother in Agra."

"At least give me memories of touring Brindaban with you."

I gladly consented. The young man, who said his name was Pratap Chatterji, hailed a horse carriage. We visited Madanamohana Temple and other Krishna shrines. Night descended before we had finished our temple devotions.

"Excuse me while I get *sandesh.*"* Pratap entered a shop near the railway station. Jitendra and I sauntered along the wide street, crowded now in the comparative coolness. Our friend was absent for some time, but finally returned with gifts of many sweetmeats.

"Please allow me to gain this religious merit." Pratap smiled pleadingly as he held out a bundle of rupee notes and two tickets, just purchased, to Agra.

The reverence of my acceptance was for the Invisible Hand. Scoffed at by Ananta, had Its bounty not far exceeded necessity?

We sought out a secluded spot near the station.

"Pratap, I will instruct you in the *Kriya* of Lahiri Mahasaya, the greatest yogi of modern times. His technique will be your guru."

The initiation was concluded in half an hour. "*Kriya* is your *chintamani*,"† I told the new student. "The technique, which as you see is simple, embodies the art of quickening man's spiritual evolution. Hindu scriptures teach that the incarnating ego requires a million years to obtain liberation from *maya*. This natural period is greatly shortened through *Kriya Yoga*. Just as plant growth can be accelerated far beyond its normal rate, as Jagadis Chandra Bose has demonstrated, so man's psychological development also can be speeded by scientific means. Be faithful in your practice; you will approach the Guru of all gurus."

"I am transported to find this yogic key, long sought!" Pratap spoke thoughtfully. "Its unshackling effect on my sensory bonds will free me for higher spheres. The vision today of Lord Krishna could only mean my highest good."

We sat awhile in silent understanding, then walked slowly to the station. Joy was within me as I boarded the train, but this was Jitendra's day for tears. My affectionate farewell to Pratap had been

---

* An Indian sweetmeat.

† A mythological gem with power to grant desires; also, a name of God.

punctuated by stifled sobs from both my companions. The journey once more found Jitendra in a welter of grief. Not for himself this time, but against himself.

"How shallow my trust; my heart has been stone! Never in future shall I doubt God's protection."

Midnight was approaching. The two "Cinderellas," sent forth penniless, entered Ananta's bedroom. Just as he had lightly predicted, his face was a study in astonishment. Silently I showered a table with rupee notes.

"Jitendra, the truth!" Ananta's tone was jocular. "Has not this youngster been staging a holdup?"

But as the tale was unfolded, my brother turned sober, then solemn.

"The law of demand and supply reaches into subtler realms than I had supposed." Ananta spoke with a spiritual enthusiasm never before noticeable. "I understand for the first time your indifference to the vaults and vulgar accumulations of the world."

Late as it was, my brother insisted that he receive *diksha** into *Kriya Yoga*. The "guru" Mukunda had to shoulder, in one night, the responsibility of two unsought "disciples."

Breakfast on the following day was eaten in a harmony that had been absent on the preceding morning.

I smiled at Jitendra. "You shall not be cheated of the Taj. Let us view it before starting for Serampore."

Bidding farewell to Ananta, my friend and I were soon before the glory of Agra, the Taj Mahal. White marble dazzling in the sun, it stands a vision of pure symmetry. The perfect setting is dark cypress, glossy lawn, and tranquil lagoon. The interior is exquisite with lacelike carvings inlaid with semiprecious stones. Delicate wreaths and scrolls emerge intricately from marbles, brown and violet. Illumination from the dome falls on the cenotaphs of emperor Shah Jehan and Mumtaz-i-Mahal, queen of his realm and his heart.

Enough of sight-seeing! I was longing for my guru. Jitendra and I were shortly traveling south by train toward Bengal.

"Mukunda, I have not seen my family for months. I have changed my mind; perhaps later I shall visit your master in Serampore."

My friend, who may mildly be described as vacillating in temperament, left me in Calcutta. By local train I soon reached Serampore, twelve miles to the north.

---

* Spiritual initiation; from the Sanskrit verb-root *diksh*, "to dedicate oneself."

A throb of wonderment stole over me as I realized that twenty-eight days had elapsed since the Banaras meeting with my guru. "You will come to me in four weeks!" Here I was, heart pounding, standing within his courtyard on quiet Rai Ghat Lane. I entered for the first time the hermitage where I was to spend the best part of the next ten years with India's *Jnanavatar*, "incarnation of wisdom."

CHAPTER 12

Years in My Master's Hermitage

"You have come." Sri Yukteswar greeted me from a tiger skin on the floor of a balconied sitting room. His voice was cold, his manner unemotional.

"Yes, dear Master, I am here to follow you." Kneeling, I touched his feet.

"How can that be? You ignore my wishes."

"No longer, Guruji! Your wish shall be my law."

"That is better! Now I can assume responsibility for your life."

"I willingly transfer the burden, Master."

"My first request, then, is that you return home to your family. I want you to enter college in Calcutta. Your education should be continued."

"Very well, sir." I hid my consternation. Would importunate books pursue me down the years? First Father, now Sri Yukteswar!

"Someday you will go to the West. Its people will be more receptive to India's ancient wisdom if the strange Hindu teacher has a university degree."

"You know best, Guruji." My gloom departed. The reference to the West I found puzzling, remote; but my opportunity to please Master by obedience was vitally immediate.

"You will be near in Calcutta; come here whenever you find time."

"Every day if possible, Master! Gratefully I accept your authority in every detail of my life—on one condition."

"Yes?"

"That you promise to reveal God to me!"

An hour-long verbal tussle ensued. A master's word cannot be falsified; it is not lightly given. The implications in the pledge open out vast metaphysical vistas. A guru must be on intimate terms indeed with the Creator before he can obligate Him to appear! I sensed Sri Yukteswar's divine unity, and was determined, as his disciple, to press my advantage.

"You are of exacting disposition." Then Master's consent rang out with compassionate finality:

"Let your wish be my wish."

A lifelong shadow lifted from my heart; the vague search, hither and yon, was over. I had found eternal shelter in a true guru.

"Come, I will show you the hermitage." Master rose from his tiger mat. In glancing about I noticed, on a wall, a picture that was garlanded with a spray of jasmine.

"Lahiri Mahasaya!" I said in astonishment.

"Yes, my divine guru." Sri Yukteswar's tone was reverently vibrant. "Greater he was, as man and yogi, than any other teacher whose life came within the range of my investigations."

Silently I bowed before the familiar picture. Soul homage sped to the peerless master who, blessing my infancy, had guided my steps to this hour.

Led by my guru, I strolled about the house and its grounds. Large, ancient, and well built, the massive-pillared hermitage surrounded a courtyard. Outer walls were moss-covered; pigeons fluttered over the flat gray roof, unceremoniously sharing the ashram quarters. A rear garden was pleasant with jackfruit, mango, and plantain trees. Balustraded balconies of upper rooms in the two-storied building faced the courtyard from three sides. A spacious ground-floor hall, with high ceiling supported by colonnades, was used, Master said, chiefly during the annual festivities of *Durgapuja.** A narrow stairway led to Sri Yukteswar's sitting room, whose small balcony overlooked the street. The ashram was plainly furnished; everything was simple, clean, and utilitarian. Several Western-style chairs, benches, and tables were in evidence.

Master invited me to stay overnight. A supper of vegetable curry was served by two young disciples who were receiving hermitage training.

"Guruji, please tell me something of your life." I was squatting on a straw mat near his tiger skin. The friendly stars were very close, it seemed, beyond the balcony.

"My family name was Priya Nath Karar. I was born† here in Serampore, where Father was a wealthy businessman. He left me this ancestral mansion, now my hermitage. My formal schooling was little; I found it slow and shallow. In early manhood, I under-

---

* "Worship of Durga." This is the chief festival of the Bengali almanac, and at most places lasts for nine days in the month of Asvina (September–October). Durga, literally, "the Inaccessible," is an aspect of the Divine Mother, Shakti, the female creative force personified. She is traditionally the destroyer of all evils.

† Sri Yukteswar was born on May 10, 1855.

took the responsibilities of a householder, and have one daughter, now married. My middle life was blessed with the guidance of Lahiri Mahasaya. After my wife died, I joined the Swami Order and received the new name of Sri Yukteswar Giri.* Such are my simple annals."

Master smiled at my eager face. Like all biographical sketches, his words had given the outward facts without revealing the inner man.

"Guruji, I would like to hear some stories of your childhood."

"I will tell you a few—each one with a moral!" Sri Yukteswar's eyes twinkled with his warning. "My mother once tried to frighten me with an appalling story of a ghost in a dark chamber. I went there immediately, and expressed my disappointment at having missed the ghost. Mother never told me another horror tale. Moral: Look fear in the face and it will cease to trouble you.

"Another early memory is my wish for an ugly dog belonging to a neighbor. I kept my household in turmoil for weeks to get that dog. My ears were deaf to offers of pets with more prepossessing appearance. Moral: Attachment is blinding; it lends an imaginary halo of attractiveness to the object of desire.

"A third story concerns the plasticity of the youthful mind. I heard my mother remark occasionally: 'A man who accepts a job under anyone is a slave.' That impression became so indelibly fixed that even after my marriage I refused all positions. I met expenses by investing my family endowment in land. Moral: Good and positive suggestions should instruct the sensitive ears of children. Their early ideas long remain sharply etched."

Master fell into tranquil silence. Around midnight he led me to a narrow cot. Sleep was sound and sweet the first night under my guru's roof.

Sri Yukteswar chose the following morning to grant me his *Kriya Yoga* initiation. The technique I had already received from two disciples of Lahiri Mahasaya—Father and my tutor, Swami Kebalananda. But Master possessed a transforming power; at his touch a great light broke upon my being, like the glory of countless suns blazing together. A flood of ineffable bliss overwhelmed my heart to an innermost core.

It was late in the afternoon of the following day before I could bring myself to leave the hermitage.

---

* *Yukteswar* means "united to Ishwara" (a name of God). *Giri* is the classificatory distinction of one of the ten ancient Swami branches. *Sri* means "holy"; it is not a name but a respectful title.

"You will return in thirty days." As I entered the door of my Calcutta home, the fulfillment of Master's prediction entered with me. None of my relatives made the pointed remarks I had feared about the reappearance of the "soaring bird."

I climbed to my little attic and bestowed affectionate glances, as though on a living presence. "You have witnessed my meditations, and the tears and storms of my *sadhana.* Now I have reached the harbor of my divine teacher."

"Son, I am happy for us both." Father and I sat together in the evening calm. "You have found your guru, as in miraculous fashion I once found my own. The holy hand of Lahiri Mahasaya is guarding our lives. Your master has proved to be no inaccessible Himalayan saint, but one nearby. My prayers have been answered: in your search for God you have not been permanently removed from my sight."

Father was also pleased that my formal studies would be resumed; he made suitable arrangements. I was enrolled the following day at nearby Scottish Church College in Calcutta.

Happy months sped by. My readers have doubtless made the perspicacious surmise that I was little seen in the college classrooms. The Serampore hermitage held a lure too irresistible. Master accepted my constant presence without comment. To my relief, he seldom referred to the halls of learning. Though it was plain to all that I was never cut out for a scholar, I managed to attain minimum passing grades from time to time.

Daily life at the ashram flowed smoothly, infrequently varied. My guru awoke before dawn. Lying down, or sometimes sitting on the bed, he entered a state of *samadhi.* * It was simplicity itself to discover when Master had awakened: abrupt halt of stupendous snores.† A sigh or two; perhaps a bodily movement. Then a soundless state of breathlessness: he was in deep yogic joy.

Breakfast did not follow; first came a long walk by the Ganges. Those morning strolls with my guru—how real and vivid still! In the easy resurrection of memory, I often find myself by his side. The early sun is warming the river; his voice rings out, rich with the authenticity of wisdom.

A bath, then the midday meal. Its preparation, according to Master's daily directions, had been the careful task of young disciples. My

---

* Lit., "to direct together." *Samadhi* is a blissful superconscious state in which a yogi perceives the identity of the individualized soul and Cosmic Spirit.

† Snoring, according to physiologists, is an indication of perfect relaxation.

guru was a vegetarian. Before embracing monkhood, however, he had eaten eggs and fish. His advice to students was to follow any simple diet which proved suited to one's constitution.

Master ate little; often rice, colored with turmeric or juice of beets or spinach and lightly sprinkled with buffalo *ghee* or melted butter. Another day he might have lentil-*dal* or *channa** curry with vegetables. For dessert, mangoes or oranges with rice pudding, or jackfruit juice.

Visitors appeared in the afternoons. A steady stream poured from the world into the tranquil hermitage. My guru treated all guests with courtesy and kindness. A master—one who has realized himself as the omnipresent soul, not the body or the ego—perceives in all men a striking similarity.

The impartiality of saints is rooted in wisdom. They are no longer influenced by the alternating faces of *maya*, no longer subject to the likes and dislikes that confuse the judgment of unenlightened men. Sri Yukteswar showed no special consideration to those who were powerful, rich, or accomplished; neither did he slight others for their poverty or illiteracy. He would listen respectfully to words of truth from a child; and, on occasion, would openly ignore a conceited pundit.

Eight o'clock was the supper hour, and sometimes found lingering guests. My guru would not excuse himself to eat alone; none left his ashram hungry or dissatisfied. Sri Yukteswar was never at a loss, never dismayed by unexpected visitors; under his resourceful directions to the disciples, scanty food would emerge a banquet. Yet he was economical; his modest funds went far. "Be comfortable within your purse," he often said. "Extravagance will bring you discomfort." Whether in the details of hermitage entertainment or of building and repair work or of other practical concerns, Master manifested the originality of a creative spirit.

Quiet evening hours often brought one of my guru's discourses: treasures against time. His every utterance was chiseled by wisdom. A sublime self-assurance marked his mode of expression: it was unique. He spoke as none other in my experience ever spoke. His thoughts were weighed in a delicate balance of discrimination before he permitted them the outward garb of speech. The essence of truth, all-pervasive with even a physiological aspect, came from him like a fragrant exudation of the soul. I was conscious always

---

* *Dal* is a thick soup made from split peas or other pulses. *Channa* is a cheese of fresh milk, curdled; often cubed and curried with potatoes.

that I was in the presence of a living manifestation of God. The weight of his divinity automatically bowed my head before him.

If guests detected that Sri Yukteswar was becoming engrossed with the Infinite, he quickly engaged them in conversation. He was incapable of striking a pose or of flaunting his inner withdrawal. Always one with the Lord, he needed no separate time for communion. A Self-realized master has already left behind the steppingstone of meditation. "The flower falls when the fruit appears." But saints often cling to spiritual forms in order to set an example for disciples.

As midnight approached, my guru might fall into a doze with the naturalness of a child. There was no fuss about bedding. He often lay down, without even a pillow, on a narrow davenport which was the background for his customary tiger-skin seat.

A night-long philosophical discussion was not rare; any disciple could summon it by intensity of interest. I felt no tiredness then, no desire for sleep; Master's living words were sufficient. "Oh, it is dawn! Let us walk by the Ganges." So ended many of my periods of nocturnal edification.

My early months with Sri Yukteswar culminated in a useful lesson: "How to Outwit a Mosquito." At home my family always used protective curtains at night. I was dismayed to discover that in the Serampore hermitage this prudent custom was honored in the breach. Yet the insects were in full residence; I was bitten from head to foot. My guru took pity on me.

"Buy yourself a curtain, and also one for me." He laughed and added, "If you buy only one, for yourself, all mosquitoes will concentrate on me!"

I was more than thankful to comply. On every night that I spent in Serampore, my guru would ask me to arrange the bedtime curtains.

One night, when a cloud of mosquitoes surrounded us, Master failed to issue his usual instructions. I listened nervously to the anticipatory hum of the insects. Getting into bed, I threw a propitiatory prayer in their general direction. A half hour later, I coughed pretentiously to attract my guru's attention. I thought I would go mad with the bites and especially the singing drone as the mosquitoes celebrated bloodthirsty rites.

No responsive stir from Master; I approached him cautiously. He was not breathing. This was my first close observation of him in the yogic trance; it filled me with fright.

"His heart must have failed!" I placed a mirror under his nose; no breath vapor appeared. To make doubly certain, for minutes I closed his mouth and nostrils with my fingers. His body was cold and motionless. In a daze, I turned toward the door to summon help.

"So! A budding experimentalist! My poor nose!" Master's voice was shaky with laughter. "Why don't you go to bed? Is the whole world going to change for you? Change yourself: be rid of the mosquito consciousness."

Meekly I returned to my bed. Not one insect ventured near. I realized that my guru had previously agreed to the curtains only to please me; he had had no fear of mosquitoes. By yogic power he could prevent them from biting him; or, if he chose, he could escape to an inner invulnerability.

"He was giving me a demonstration," I thought. "That is the yogic state I must strive to attain." A true yogi is able to pass into and maintain the superconscious state, regardless of multitudinous distractions never absent from this earth—the buzz of insects! the pervasive glare of daylight! In the first state of *samadhi* (*sabikalpa*), the devotee shuts off all sensory testimony of the outer world. He is rewarded then by sounds and scenes of inner realms fairer than the pristine Eden.*

The instructive mosquitoes served for another early lesson at the ashram. It was the gentle hour of dusk. My guru was matchlessly interpreting the ancient texts. At his feet, I was in perfect peace. A rude mosquito entered the idyl and competed for my attention. As it dug a poisonous "hypodermic needle" into my thigh, I automatically raised an avenging hand. Reprieve from impending execution! An opportune memory had come to me of Patanjali's aphorism on *ahimsa* (harmlessness).†

"Why didn't you finish the job?"

"Master! Do you advocate taking life?"

"No, but in your mind you had already struck the deathblow."

"I don't understand."

"By *ahimsa* Patanjali meant removal of the *desire* to kill." Sri Yukteswar had found my mental processes an open book. "This world is inconveniently arranged for a literal practice of *ahimsa*. Man may be compelled to exterminate harmful creatures. He is not

---

* The omnipresent powers of a yogi, whereby he sees, tastes, smells, touches, and hears without the use of outward sensory organs, have been described as follows in *Taittiriya Aranyaka:* "The blind man pierced the pearl; the fingerless put a thread through it; the neckless wore it; and the tongueless praised it."

† "In the presence of a man perfected in *ahimsa* (nonviolence), enmity [in any creature] does not arise."—*Yoga Sutras* II:35.

under a similar compulsion to feel anger or animosity. All forms of life have an equal right to the air of *maya*. The saint who uncovers the secret of creation will be in harmony with Nature's countless bewildering expressions. All men may understand this truth by overcoming the passion for destruction."

"Guruji, should one offer himself a sacrifice rather than kill a wild beast?"

"No, man's body is precious. It has the highest evolutionary value because of unique brain and spinal centers. These enable the advanced devotee fully to grasp and express the loftiest aspects of divinity. No lower form is so equipped. It is true that a man incurs the debt of a minor sin if he is forced to kill an animal or any other living thing. But the holy *shastras* teach that wanton loss of a human body is a serious transgression against the karmic law."

I sighed in relief; scriptural reinforcement of one's natural instincts is not always forthcoming.

Master, so far as I know, was never at close quarters with a leopard or a tiger. But a deadly cobra once confronted him, only to be conquered by his love. The encounter took place in Puri, where my guru had a seaside hermitage. Prafulla, a young disciple of Sri Yukteswar's later years, was with Master on this occasion.

"We were seated outdoors near the ashram," Prafulla told me. "A cobra appeared nearby, a four-foot length of sheer terror. Its hood was angrily expanded as it raced toward us. Master gave a welcoming chuckle, as though to a child. I was filled with consternation to see Sri Yukteswarji engage in a rhythmical clapping of hands.* He was entertaining the dread visitor! I remained completely quiet, inwardly ejaculating fervent prayers. The serpent, very close to Master, was now motionless, seemingly magnetized by his caressing attitude. The frightful hood gradually contracted; the snake slithered between Sri Yukteswarji's feet and disappeared into the bushes.

"Why Master would move his hands and why the cobra would not strike them were inexplicable to me then," Prafulla concluded. "I have since come to realize that our divine guru is beyond fear of hurt from any creature."

One afternoon during my early months at the ashram, I found Sri Yukteswar's eyes fixed on me piercingly.

---

* The cobra swiftly strikes at any moving object within its range. In most cases, complete immobility is one's sole hope of safety.

  The cobra is much feared in India, where it causes annually about five thousand deaths.

"You are too thin, Mukunda."

His remark struck a sensitive point; my sunken eyes and emaciated appearance were not to my liking. Chronic dyspepsia had afflicted me since childhood. Many bottles of tonics stood on a shelf in my room at home; none had helped me. Occasionally I would sadly ask myself if life were worthwhile with a body so unsound.

"Medicines have limitations; the divine creative life force has none. Believe that: you shall be well and strong."

Master's words instantly convinced me that I could successfully apply their truth in my own life. No other healer (and I had tried many) had been able to arouse in me such profound faith.

Day by day I waxed in health and strength. Through Sri Yukteswar's hidden blessing, in two weeks I gained the weight that I had vainly sought in the past. My stomach ailments vanished permanently.

On later occasions I was privileged to witness my guru's divine healings of persons suffering from diabetes, epilepsy, tuberculosis, or paralysis.

"Years ago, I, too, was anxious to put on weight," Master told me shortly after he had healed me. "During convalescence after a severe illness, I visited Lahiri Mahasaya in Banaras.

"'Sir,' I said, 'I have been very sick and have lost many pounds.'

"'I see, Yukteswar,* you made yourself unwell, and now you think you are thin.'

"This reply was far from the one I had expected; my guru, however, added encouragingly:

"'Let me see; I am sure you ought to feel better tomorrow.'

"My receptive mind accepted his words as a hint that he was secretly healing me. The next morning I sought him out and exclaimed exultingly, 'Sir, I feel much better today.'

"'Indeed! Today you invigorate yourself.'

"'No, Master!' I protested. 'It is you who have helped me; this is the first time in weeks that I have had any energy.'

"'Oh, yes! Your malady has been quite serious. Your body is frail yet; who can say how it will be tomorrow?'

"The thought of a possible return of my weakness brought me a shudder of cold fear. The following morning I could hardly drag myself to Lahiri Mahasaya's home.

---

* Lahiri Mahasaya actually said "Priya" (Master's first name), not "Yukteswar" (monastic name, not taken by my guru during Lahiri Mahasaya's lifetime). (See p. 92.) "Yukteswar" is substituted here and in a few other places in this book in order to avoid the confusion of two names.

"'Sir, I am ailing again.'

"My guru's glance was quizzical. 'So! Once more you indispose yourself.'

"My patience was exhausted. 'Gurudeva,' I said, 'I realize now that day by day you have been ridiculing me. I don't understand why you disbelieve my truthful reports.'

"'Really, it has been your thoughts that have made you feel alternately weak and strong.' My guru looked at me affectionately. 'You have seen how your health has exactly followed your subconscious expectations. Thought is a force, even as electricity or gravitation. The human mind is a spark of the almighty consciousness of God. I could show you that whatever your powerful mind believes very intensely would instantly come to pass.'

"Knowing that Lahiri Mahasaya never spoke idly, I addressed him with great awe and gratitude: 'Master, if I think that I am well and that I have regained my former weight, shall those things come to pass?'

"'It is so, even at this moment.' My guru spoke gravely, his gaze concentrated on my eyes.

"I instantly felt an increase not only of strength but of weight. Lahiri Mahasaya retreated into silence. After a few hours at his feet, I returned to my mother's house, where I stayed during my visits to Banaras.

"'My son! What is the matter? Are you swelling with dropsy?' Mother could hardly believe her eyes. My body was now as full and robust as it had been before my illness.

"I weighed myself and found that in one day I had gained fifty pounds; they have remained permanently. Friends and acquaintances who had seen my thin figure were overcome with amazement. A number of them changed their mode of life and became disciples of Lahiri Mahasaya as a result of this miracle.

"My guru, awake in God, knew this world to be nothing but an objectivized dream of the Creator. Because he was completely aware of his unity with the Divine Dreamer, Lahiri Mahasaya could materialize or dematerialize or make any other change he wished in the dream atoms of the phenomenal world.*

"All creation is governed by law," Sri Yukteswar concluded.

* "What things soever ye desire, when ye pray, believe that ye receive them, and ye shall have them."—Mark 11:24. God-united masters are fully able to transfer their divine realizations to advanced disciples, as Lahiri Mahasaya did for Sri Yukteswar on this occasion.

"The principles that operate in the outer universe, discoverable by scientists, are called natural laws. But there are subtler laws that rule the hidden spiritual planes and the inner realm of consciousness; these principles are knowable through the science of yoga. It is not the physicist but the Self-realized master who comprehends the true nature of matter. By such knowledge Christ was able to restore the servant's ear after it had been severed by one of the disciples."*

My guru was a peerless interpreter of the scriptures. Many of my happiest memories are centered in his discourses. But his jeweled thoughts were not cast into the ashes of heedlessness or stupidity. One restless movement of my body, or my slight lapse into absentmindedness, would suffice to put an abrupt period to Master's exposition.

"You are not here." Sri Yukteswar interrupted himself one afternoon with this observation. As usual, he was keeping relentless track of my attention.

"Guruji!" My tone was a protest. "I have not stirred; my eyelids have not moved; I can repeat each word you have uttered!"

"Nevertheless you were not fully with me. Your objection forces me to remark that in your mental background you were creating three institutions. One was a sylvan retreat on a plain, another on a hilltop, still another by the ocean."

Those vaguely formulated thoughts had indeed been present almost subconsciously. I glanced at him apologetically.

"What can I do with such a master—one who penetrates my random musings?"

"You have given me that right. The subtle truths I am expounding cannot be grasped without your complete concentration. Unless necessary I do not invade the seclusion of others' minds. Man has the natural privilege of roaming secretly among his thoughts. The unbidden Lord does not enter there; neither do I venture intrusion."

"You are ever welcome, Master!"

"Your architectural dreams will materialize later. Now is the time for study!"

Thus incidentally, in his simple way, my guru revealed his knowledge of the coming of three important events in my life. Since early youth I had had enigmatic glimpses of three buildings,

---

* "And one of them smote the servant of the high priest, and cut off his right ear. And Jesus answered and said, Suffer ye thus far. And he touched his ear and healed him."—Luke 22:50–51.

each in a different setting. In the exact sequence Sri Yukteswar had indicated, these visions took ultimate form. First came my founding of a boys' yoga school on a plain in Ranchi, then an American headquarters on a Los Angeles hilltop, and then a hermitage in Encinitas, California, overlooking the vast Pacific.

Master never arrogantly said: "I prophesy that such and such an event shall occur!" He would rather hint: "Don't you think it may happen?" But his simple speech hid vatic power. There was no recanting; never did his slightly veiled predictions prove false.

Sri Yukteswar was reserved and matter-of-fact in demeanor. There was naught of the vague or daft visionary about him. His feet were firm on the earth, his head in the haven of heaven. Practical people aroused his admiration. "Saintliness is not dumbness! Divine perceptions are not incapacitating!" he would say. "The active expression of virtue gives rise to the keenest intelligence."

My guru was reluctant to discuss the superphysical realms. His only "marvelous" aura was that of perfect simplicity. In conversation he avoided startling references; in action he was freely expressive. Many teachers talked of miracles but could manifest nothing; Sri Yukteswar seldom mentioned the subtle laws but secretly operated them at will.

"A man of realization does not perform any miracle until he receives an inward sanction," Master explained. "God does not wish the secrets of His creation revealed promiscuously.* Also, every individual in the world has an inalienable right to his free will. A saint will not encroach on that independence."

The silence habitual to Sri Yukteswar was caused by his deep perceptions of the Infinite. No time remained for the interminable "revelations" that occupy the days of teachers without Self-realization. A saying from the Hindu scriptures is: "In shallow men the fish of little thoughts cause much commotion. In oceanic minds the whales of inspiration make hardly a ruffle."

Because of my guru's unspectacular guise, only a few of his contemporaries recognized him as a superman. The adage: "He is a fool that cannot conceal his wisdom," could never be applied to my profound and quiet master.

Though born a mortal like all others, Sri Yukteswar achieved identity with the Ruler of time and space. Master found no insuperable obstacle to the mergence of human and Divine. No such barrier exists,

---

* "Give not that which is holy unto the dogs, neither cast ye your pearls before swine, lest they trample them under their feet, and turn again and rend you."—Matthew 7:6.

I came to understand, save in man's spiritual unadventurousness.

I always thrilled at the touch of Sri Yukteswar's holy feet. A disciple is spiritually magnetized by reverent contact with a master; a subtle current is generated. The devotee's undesirable habit-mechanisms in the brain are often as if cauterized; the grooves of his worldly tendencies are beneficially disturbed. Momentarily at least he may find the secret veils of *maya* lifting, and glimpse the reality of bliss. My whole body responded with a liberating glow whenever I knelt in the Indian fashion before my guru.

"Even when Lahiri Mahasaya was silent," Master told me, "or when he conversed on other than strictly religious topics, I discovered that nonetheless he had transmitted to me ineffable knowledge."

Sri Yukteswar affected me similarly. If I entered the hermitage in a worried or indifferent frame of mind, my attitude imperceptibly changed. A healing calm descended at the mere sight of my guru. Each day with him was a new experience in joy, peace, and wisdom. Never did I find him deluded or emotionally intoxicated with greed, anger, or human attachment.

"The darkness of *maya* is silently approaching. Let us hie homeward within." With these cautionary words Master constantly reminded his disciples of their need for *Kriya Yoga*. A new student occasionally expressed doubts regarding his own worthiness to engage in yoga practice.

"Forget the past," Sri Yukteswar would console him. "The vanished lives of all men are dark with many shames. Human conduct is ever unreliable until man is anchored in the Divine. Everything in future will improve if you are making a spiritual effort now."

Master always had young *chelas* (disciples) in his ashram. Their intellectual and spiritual education was his lifelong interest. Even shortly before he passed on, he accepted, as hermitage residents, two six-year-old boys and a youth of sixteen. All those in his charge were carefully trained; "disciple" and "discipline" are etymologically and practically related.

The ashram residents loved and revered their guru; a slight clap of his hands sufficed to bring them eagerly to his side. When his mood was silent and withdrawn, no one ventured to speak; when his laugh rang jovially, children looked upon him as their own.

Sri Yukteswar seldom asked others to render him a personal service, nor would he accept a *chela's* help unless it was offered cheerfully. Master himself would wash his clothes if the disciples forgot the privileged task.

His usual garment was the traditional ocher-colored swami robe. For indoor use he wore laceless shoes that had been made, in accordance with yogi-custom, of tiger or deer skin.

Sri Yukteswar spoke fluent English, French, Bengali, and Hindi; his Sanskrit was fair. He patiently instructed his young disciples by certain shortcuts that he had ingeniously devised for the study of English and Sanskrit.

Master was not solicitously attached to his body, but he was cautious of it. The Divine, he pointed out, is properly manifested through physical and mental soundness. He discountenanced all extremes. To a disciple who wanted to fast for a long period, my guru said laughingly, "Why not throw the dog a bone?"*

Sri Yukteswar's health was excellent; I never saw him unwell.† To show respect for a worldly custom he permitted his students, if they wished, to consult doctors. "Physicians," he said, "should carry on their work of healing through God's laws as applied to matter." But he extolled the superiority of mental therapy, and often repeated: "Wisdom is the greatest cleanser." He told his *chelas:*

"The body is a treacherous friend. Give it its due; no more. Pain and pleasure are transitory; endure all dualities with calmness, trying at the same time to remove yourself beyond their power. Imagination is the door through which disease as well as healing enters. Disbelieve in the reality of sickness even when you are ill; an unrecognized visitor will flee!"

Master numbered many doctors among his disciples. "Those who have studied physiology should go further and investigate the science of the soul," he told them. "A subtle spiritual structure is hidden just behind the bodily mechanism."‡

---

* My guru approved of fasting as the ideal natural cleansing method; but that particular disciple was overly preoccupied with his body.

† He was once ill in Kashmir, when I was absent from him (see p. 177).

‡ A courageous medical man, Charles Robert Richet, awarded the Nobel Prize in physiology, wrote as follows: "Metaphysics is not yet officially a science, recognized as such. But it is going to be....At Edinburgh, I was able to affirm before 100 physiologists that our five senses are not our only means of knowledge and that a fragment of reality sometimes reaches the intelligence in other ways....Because a fact is rare is no reason that it does not exist. Because a study is difficult, is that a reason for not understanding it? ...Those who have railed at metaphysics as an occult science will be as ashamed of themselves as those who railed at chemistry on the ground that pursuit of the philosophers' stone was illusory....In the matter of principles there are only those of Lavoisier, Claude Bernard, and Pasteur—the *experimental* everywhere and always. Greetings, then, to the new science which is going to change the orientation of human thought."

Sri Yukteswar counseled his students to be living liaisons of Western and Eastern virtues. Himself an executive Occidental in outer habits, inwardly he was the spiritual Oriental. He praised the progressive, resourceful, and hygienic ways of the West, and the religious ideals that give a centuried halo to the East.

Discipline had not been unknown to me; at home Father was strict, Ananta often severe. But Sri Yukteswar's training may not be described as other than drastic. A perfectionist, my guru was hypercritical of his disciples, whether in matters of moment or in the subtle nuances of ordinary behavior.

"Good manners without sincerity are like a beautiful dead lady," he remarked on suitable occasion. "Straightforwardness without civility is like a surgeon's knife, effective but unpleasant. Candor with courtesy is helpful and admirable."

Master was apparently satisfied with my spiritual progress, for he seldom referred to it; in other matters my ears were no strangers to reproof. My chief offenses were absentmindedness, intermittent indulgence in sad moods, nonobservance of certain rules of etiquette, and occasional unmethodical ways.

"Observe how the activities of your father Bhagabati are well organized and well balanced," my guru pointed out. The two disciples of Lahiri Mahasaya had met, soon after my first visit to the Serampore hermitage. Father and Master deeply admired each other. Both had built a beautiful inner life on foundations of spiritual granite, insoluble against the ages.

From a transient teacher of my earlier life I had imbibed a few erroneous lessons. A *chela*, I had been told, need not concern himself strenuously with worldly duties; when I had neglected or carelessly performed my tasks, I had not been chastised. Human nature finds such instruction very easy of assimilation. Under Master's unsparing rod, however, I soon recovered from the agreeable delusions of irresponsibility.

"Those who are too good for this world are adorning some other," Sri Yukteswar remarked one day. "So long as you breathe the free air of earth, you are under obligation to render grateful service. Only he who has fully mastered the breathless state* is freed from cosmic imperatives." He added dryly, "I shall not fail to let you know when you have attained the final perfection."

My guru could not be bribed, even by love. He showed no leniency to anyone who, like myself, had willingly offered to become

* *Samadhi:* superconsciousness.

a disciple. Whether Master and I were surrounded by his students or by strangers, or were alone together, he always spoke plainly and upbraided sharply. No trifling lapse into shallowness or inconsistency escaped his rebuke. This flattening-to-the-ego treatment was hard to endure, but my unchangeable resolve was to allow Sri Yukteswar to iron out all of my psychological kinks. As he labored at this titanic transformation, I shook many times under the weight of his disciplinary hammer.

"If you don't like my words, you are at liberty to leave at any time," Master assured me. "I want nothing from you but your own improvement. Stay only if you feel benefited."

I am immeasurably grateful for the humbling blows he dealt my vanity. I sometimes felt that, metaphorically, he was discovering and uprooting every diseased tooth in my jaw. The hard core of egotism is difficult to dislodge except rudely. With its departure, the Divine finds at last an unobstructed channel. In vain It seeks to percolate through flinty hearts of selfishness.

Sri Yukteswar's intuition was penetrating; heedless of remarks, he often replied to one's unexpressed thoughts. The words a person uses, and the actual thoughts behind them, may be poles apart. "By calmness," my guru said, "try to feel the thoughts behind the confusion of men's verbiage."

The disclosures of divine insight are often painful to worldly ears; Master was not popular with superficial students. The wise, always few in number, deeply revered him.

I daresay Sri Yukteswar would have been the most sought-after guru in India had his speech not been so candid and so censorious.

"I am hard on those who come for my training," he admitted to me. "That is my way. Take it or leave it; I never compromise. But you will be much kinder to your disciples; that is your way. I try to purify only in fires of severity; these are searing beyond the average toleration. The gentle approach of love is also transfiguring. The inflexible and the yielding methods are equally effective if applied with wisdom." He added, "You will go to foreign lands, where blunt assaults on the ego are not appreciated. A teacher could not spread India's message in the West without an ample fund of accommodative patience and forbearance." (I refuse to say how often, in America, I have remembered Master's words!)

Though my guru's undissembling speech prevented a large following during his years on earth, nevertheless, through an ever-growing number of sincere students of his teachings, his spirit lives on in the world today. Warriors like Alexander the Great seek sovereignty over the soil; masters like Sri Yukteswar win a farther dominion—in men's souls.

It was Master's practice to point out the simple, negligible shortcomings of his disciples with an air of portentous gravity. One day my father visited Serampore to pay his respects to Sri Yukteswar. My parent expected, very likely, to hear some words in my praise. He was shocked to be given a long account of my imperfections. He rushed to see me.

"From your guru's remarks I thought to find you a complete wreck!" My parent was between tears and laughter.

The only cause of Sri Yukteswar's displeasure at the time was that I had been trying, against his gentle hint, to convert a certain man to the spiritual path.

With indignant speed I sought out my guru. He received me with downcast eyes, as though conscious of guilt. It was the only time I ever saw the divine lion meek before me. The unique moment was savored to the full.

"Sir, why did you judge me so mercilessly before my astounded father? Was that just?"

"I will not do it again." Sri Yukteswar's tone was apologetic.

Instantly I was disarmed. How readily had the great man admitted a fault! Though he never again upset Father's peace of mind, Master relentlessly continued to dissect me whenever and wherever he chose.

New disciples often joined Sri Yukteswar in exhaustive criticism of others. Wise like the guru! Models of flawless discrimination! But he who takes the offensive should not be defenseless. The carping students themselves fled precipitantly as soon as Master publicly unloosed in their direction a few shafts from his analytical quiver.

"Tender inner weaknesses, revolting at mild touches of censure, are like diseased parts of the body, recoiling before even delicate handling." This was Sri Yukteswar's amused comment on the flighty ones.

Many disciples have a preconceived image of a guru, by which they judge his words and actions. Such persons often complained that they did not understand Sri Yukteswar.

"Neither do you understand God!" I retorted on one occasion. "If a saint were clear to you, you would be one!" Among the trillion mysteries, breathing every second the inexplicable air, may one venture to ask that the fathomless nature of a master be instantly grasped?

Students came, and generally went. Those who craved an easy path—that of instant sympathy and comforting recognitions of one's merits—did not find it at the hermitage. Master offered his disciples shelter and shepherding for the aeons, but many students miserly demanded ego-balm as well. They departed; preferring, before any humility, life's countless humiliations. Sri Yukteswar's blazing rays, the open penetrating sunshine of his wisdom, were too powerful for their spiritual sickness. They sought out some lesser teacher, who, shading them with flattery, permitted the fitful sleep of ignorance.

During my early months with Master I experienced a sensitive fear of his reprimands. I soon saw that his verbal vivisections were performed only on persons who, like myself, had asked him to discipline them. If any writhing student made a protest, Sri Yukteswar, unoffended, would fall into silence. His words were never wrathful, but impersonal with wisdom.

Master's rebukes were not aimed at casual visitors; he seldom remarked on their defects, even if conspicuous. But toward students who sought his counsel, Sri Yukteswar felt a serious responsibility. Brave indeed is the guru who undertakes to transform the crude ore of ego-permeated humanity! A saint's courage is rooted in his compassion for *maya*-bewildered men, the stumbling eyeless of the world.

After I had abandoned underlying resentment, I found a marked decrease in my chastisement. In a very subtle way, Master melted into comparative clemency. In time I demolished every wall of rationalization and subconscious* reservation behind which the human personality generally shields itself. The reward was an effortless harmony with my guru. I discovered him then to be trusting, considerate, and silently loving. Undemonstrative, however, he bestowed no word of affection.

My own temperament is principally devotional. It was disconcerting at first to find that my guru, saturated with *jnana* but seemingly dry of *bhakti*,† expressed himself chiefly in terms of cold spiritual mathematics. But, as I attuned myself to his nature, I discovered no diminution but rather an increase in my devotional

---

* "Our conscious and subconscious being is crowned by a superconsciousness," Rabbi Israel H. Levinthal pointed out in a lecture in New York. "Many years ago the English psychologist, F. W. H. Myers, suggested that 'hidden in the deep of our being is a rubbish heap as well as a treasure house.' In contrast to the psychology that centers all its researches on the subconscious in man's nature, the new psychology of the superconscious focuses its attention upon the treasure house—the region that alone can explain the great, unselfish, heroic deeds of men."

† *Jnana*, wisdom; and *bhakti*, devotion: two of the main paths to God.

approach to God. A Self-realized master is fully able to guide his various disciples along the natural lines of their essential bias.

My relationship with Sri Yukteswar was somewhat inarticulate, yet possessed a hidden eloquence. Often I found his silent signature on my thoughts, rendering speech inutile. Quietly sitting beside him, I would feel his bounty pouring peacefully over my being.

Master's impartial justice was notably demonstrated during the summer vacation of my first college year. I had been looking forward to uninterrupted months in Serampore with my guru.

"You may be in charge of the hermitage." Sri Yukteswar was pleased over my enthusiastic arrival. "Your duties will be the reception of guests, and supervision of the work of the other disciples."

Kumar, a young villager from east Bengal, was accepted a fortnight later for ashram training. Remarkably intelligent, he quickly won Master's affection. For some unfathomable reason, Sri Yukteswar adopted an uncritical attitude toward the new resident.

"Mukunda, let Kumar assume your duties. Employ your own time in sweeping and cooking." Master issued these instructions after the new boy had been with us for a month.

Exalted to leadership, Kumar exercised a petty household tyranny. In silent mutiny, the other disciples continued to seek me out for daily counsel. This situation continued for three weeks; then I overheard a conversation between Kumar and Master.

"Mukunda is impossible!" the boy said. "You made me supervisor, yet the others go to him and obey him."

"That's why I assigned him to the kitchen and you to the parlor—so you might come to realize that a worthy leader has the desire to serve, not to dominate." Sri Yukteswar's withering tones were new to Kumar. "You wanted Mukunda's position, but could not maintain it by merit. Return now to your earlier work as cook's assistant."

After this humbling incident, Master resumed toward Kumar a former attitude of unwonted indulgence. Who may solve the mystery of attraction? In Kumar our guru discovered a charming fount—one, however, that did not spurt for the fellow disciples. Though the new boy was obviously Sri Yukteswar's favorite, I felt no dismay. Personal idiosyncrasies, possessed even by masters, lend a rich complexity to the pattern of life. My nature is seldom commandeered by a detail; I was seeking from Sri Yukteswar a higher benefit than outward praise.

Kumar spoke venomously to me one day without reason; I was deeply hurt.

"Your head is swelling to the bursting point!" I added a warning whose truth I felt intuitively: "Unless you mend your ways, someday you will be asked to leave this ashram."

Laughing sarcastically, Kumar repeated my remark to our guru, who had just entered the room. Fully expecting to be scolded, I retired meekly to a corner.

"Maybe Mukunda is right." Master's reply to the boy came with unusual coldness.

A year later, Kumar set out for a visit to his childhood home. He ignored the quiet disapproval of Sri Yukteswar, who never authoritatively controlled his disciples' movements. On the boy's return to Serampore in a few months, a change was unpleasantly apparent. Gone was the stately Kumar with serenely glowing face. Only an undistinguished peasant stood before us, one who had lately acquired a number of evil habits.

Master summoned me and brokenheartedly discussed the fact that the boy was now unsuited to the monastic hermitage life.

"Mukunda, I will leave it to you to instruct Kumar to leave the ashram tomorrow; I can't do it!" Tears stood in Sri Yukteswar's eyes, but he controlled himself quickly. "The boy would never have fallen to these depths had he listened to me and not gone away to mix with undesirable companions. He has rejected my protection; the callous world must be his guru still."

Kumar's departure brought me no elation; sadly I wondered how one with the power to win a master's love could readily respond to worldly allures. Enjoyments of wine and sex are rooted in the natural man; to appreciate them one requires no delicacy of perception. Sense wiles are comparable to the evergreen oleander, fragrant with its rosy-colored flowers: every part of the plant is poisonous.* The land of healing lies within, radiant with the happiness that is blindly sought in a thousand outer directions.

"Keen intelligence is two-edged," Master once remarked in reference to Kumar's brilliant mind. "It may be used constructively or destructively, like a knife, either to cut the boil of ignorance, or to decapitate oneself. Intelligence is rightly guided only after the mind has acknowledged the inescapability of spiritual law."

My guru mixed freely with men and women disciples, treat-

* "Man in his waking state puts forth innumerable efforts for experiencing sensual pleasures; when the entire group of sensory organs is fatigued, he forgets even the pleasure on hand and goes to sleep in order to enjoy rest in the soul, his own nature," Shankara, the great Vedantist, has written. "Ultrasensual bliss is thus extremely easy of attainment and is far superior to sense delights, which always end in disgust."

ing all as his children. Perceiving their soul equality, he made no distinction and showed no partiality.

"In sleep, you do not know whether you are a man or a woman," he said. "Just as a man, impersonating a woman, does not become one, so the soul, impersonating both man and woman, remains changeless. The soul is the immutable, unqualified image of God."

Sri Yukteswar never avoided or blamed women as the cause of "man's downfall." He pointed out that women, too, have to face temptation from the opposite sex. I once asked Master why a great ancient saint had called women "the door to hell."

"A girl must have proved very troublesome to his peace of mind in his early life," my guru answered caustically. "Otherwise he would have denounced, not woman, but some imperfection in his own self-control."

If a visitor dared to relate a suggestive story in the hermitage, Master would maintain an unresponsive silence. "Do not allow yourself to be thrashed by the provoking whip of a beautiful face," he told the disciples. "How can sense slaves enjoy the world? Its subtle flavors escape them while they grovel in primal mud. All nice discriminations are lost to the man of elemental lusts."

Students seeking to escape from the *maya*-induced sex delusion received from Sri Yukteswar patient and understanding counsel.

"Just as hunger, not greed, has a legitimate purpose, so the sexual instinct has been implanted by Nature solely for the propagation of the species, not for the kindling of insatiable longings," he said. "Destroy wrong desires now; otherwise they will remain with you after the astral body has been separated from its physical casing. Even when the flesh is weak, the mind should be constantly resistant. If temptation assails you with cruel force, overcome it by impersonal analysis and indomitable will. Every natural passion can be mastered.

"Conserve your powers. Be like the capacious ocean, absorbing quietly all the tributary rivers of the senses. Daily renewed sense yearnings sap your inner peace; they are like openings in a reservoir that permit vital waters to be wasted in the desert soil of materialism. The forceful, activating impulse of wrong desire is the greatest enemy to the happiness of man. Roam in the world as a lion of self-control; don't let the frogs of sense weakness kick you around!"

A true devotee is finally freed from all instinctive compulsions. He transforms his need for human affection into aspiration for God alone—a love solitary because omnipresent.

Sri Yukteswar's mother lived in the Rana Mahal district of Banaras where I had first visited my guru. Gracious and kindly, she was yet a woman of very decided opinions. I stood on her balcony one day and watched mother and son talking together. In his quiet, sensible way, Master was trying to convince her about something. He was apparently unsuccessful, for she shook her head with great vigor.

"Nay, nay, my son, go away now! Your wise words are not for me! I am not your disciple!"

Sri Yukteswar backed away without further argument, like a scolded child. I was touched at his great respect for his mother even in her unreasonable moods. She saw him only as her little boy, not as a sage. There was a charm about the trifling incident; it supplied a sidelight on my guru's unusual nature, inwardly humble and outwardly unbendable.

The monastic regulations do not permit a swami to retain connection with worldly ties after their formal severance. He may not perform the ceremonial family rites that are obligatory on the householder. Yet Shankara, reorganizer of the ancient Swami Order, disregarded the injunctions. After the death of his beloved mother, he cremated her body with heavenly fire that he caused to spurt from his upraised hand.

Sri Yukteswar also ignored the restrictions — in a fashion less spectacular. When his mother passed on, he arranged for crematory services by the holy Ganges in Banaras and fed many *Brahmins*, in conformance with householder customs.

The shastric prohibitions were intended to help swamis to overcome narrow identifications. Shankara and Sri Yukteswar had wholly merged their being in the Impersonal Spirit; they needed no rescue by rule. Sometimes, too, a master purposely ignores a canon in order to uphold its principle as superior to and independent of form. Thus Jesus plucked ears of corn on the day of rest. To the inevitable critics he said: "The sabbath was made for man, and not man for the sabbath." *

With the exception of the scriptures, Sri Yukteswar read little. Yet he was invariably acquainted with the latest scientific discoveries and other advancements of knowledge.† A brilliant conversationalist, he enjoyed an exchange of views on countless topics

---

* Mark 2:27.

† When he so desired, Master could instantly attune himself to the mind of any man (a yogic power mentioned in Patanjali's *Yoga Sutras* III:19). His powers as a human radio, and the nature of thoughts, are explained on p. 134.

Sri Yukteswar's seaside ashram in Puri, Orissa, near the Bay of Bengal. (See also photo opposite p. 109.)

Swami Sri Yukteswar in lotus posture

Prabhas Chandra Ghosh and Paramahansa Yogananda, Calcutta, December 1919. Sri Ghosh, a cousin and lifelong friend and disciple of Sri Yogananda's, was vice-president of Yogoda Satsanga Society of India for nearly forty years, until his passing in 1975.

with his guests. My guru's ready wit and rollicking laugh enlivened every discussion. Often grave, Master was never gloomy. "To seek the Lord, men need not 'disfigure their faces,'" he would say, quoting from the Bible.* "Remember that finding God will mean the funeral of all sorrows."

Among the philosophers, professors, lawyers, and scientists who came to the hermitage, a number arrived for their first visit with the thought of meeting an orthodox religionist. Occasionally a supercilious smile or a glance of amused tolerance would betray that the newcomers expected nothing more than a few pious platitudes. After talking with Sri Yukteswar and discovering that he possessed precise insight into their specialized fields of knowledge, the visitors would depart reluctantly.

My guru ordinarily was gentle and affable to guests; his welcome was given with charming cordiality. Yet inveterate egotists sometimes suffered an invigorating shock. They confronted in Master either a frigid indifference or a formidable opposition: ice or iron!

A noted chemist once crossed swords with Sri Yukteswar. The visitor would not admit the existence of God, inasmuch as science has devised no means of detecting Him.

"So you have inexplicably failed to isolate the Supreme Power in your test tubes!" Master's gaze was stern. "I recommend a new experiment: examine your thoughts unremittingly for twenty-four hours. Then wonder no longer at God's absence."

A celebrated scholar received a similar jolt. It came during his first visit to the ashram. The rafters resounded as the guest recited passages from the *Mahabharata, Upanishads,*† and *bhasyas* (commentaries) of Shankara.

"I am waiting to hear you." Sri Yukteswar's tone was inquiring, as though silence had reigned. The pundit was puzzled.

"Quotations there have been, in superabundance." Master's words convulsed me with mirth, as I squatted in my corner at a respectful distance from the visitor. "But what original commentary can you supply, from the uniqueness of your particular life? What holy text have you absorbed and made your own? In what ways have

---

* Matthew 6:16.

† The *Upanishads* or *Vedanta* (lit., "end of the Vedas"), which occur in certain parts of the four Vedas, are essential summaries that form the doctrinal basis of the Hindu religion. Schopenhauer praised their "deep, original, and sublime thoughts," and said: "Access to the Vedas [through Western translations of the *Upanishads*] is, in my eyes, the greatest privilege this century may claim over all previous centuries."

these timeless truths renovated your nature? Are you content to be a hollow victrola, mechanically repeating the words of other men?"

"I give up!" The scholar's chagrin was comical. "I have no inner realization."

For the first time, perhaps, he understood that discerning placement of a comma does not atone for a spiritual coma.

"These bloodless pedants smell unduly of the lamp," my guru remarked after the departure of the chastened one. "They consider philosophy to be a gentle intellectual setting-up exercise. Their elevated thoughts are carefully unrelated either to the crudity of outward action or to any scourging inner discipline!"

Master stressed on other occasions the futility of mere book learning.

"Do not confuse understanding with a larger vocabulary," he remarked. "Sacred writings are beneficial in stimulating desire for inward realization, if one stanza at a time is slowly assimilated. Otherwise, continual intellectual study may result in vanity, false satisfaction, and undigested knowledge."

Sri Yukteswar related one of his own experiences in scriptural edification. The scene was a forest hermitage in eastern Bengal, where he observed the procedure of a renowned teacher, Dabru Ballav. His method, at once simple and difficult, was common in ancient India.

Dabru Ballav had gathered his disciples around him in the sylvan solitudes. The holy Bhagavad Gita was open before them. Steadfastly they looked at one passage for half an hour, then closed their eyes. Another half hour slipped away. The master gave a brief comment. Motionless, they meditated again for an hour. Finally the guru spoke.

"Do you now understand the stanza?"

"Yes, sir." One in the group ventured this assertion.

"No, not fully. Seek the spiritual vitality that has given these words the power to rejuvenate India century after century." Another hour passed in silence. The master dismissed the students, and turned to Sri Yukteswar.

"Do you know the Bhagavad Gita?"

"No, sir, not really; though my eyes and mind have run through its pages many times."

"Hundreds have replied to me differently!" The great sage smiled at Master in blessing. "If one busies himself with an outer display of scriptural wealth, what time is left for silent inward diving after the priceless pearls?"

Sri Yukteswar directed the study of his own disciples by the same intensive method of one-pointedness. "Wisdom is not assimilated with the eyes, but with the atoms," he said. "When your conviction of a truth is not merely in your brain but in your being, you may diffidently vouch for its meaning." He discouraged any tendency a student might have to consider book knowledge a necessary step to spiritual realization.

"The rishis wrote in one sentence profundities that commentating scholars busy themselves over for generations," he said. "Endless literary controversy is for sluggard minds. What more quickly liberating thought than 'God is'—nay, 'God'?"

But man does not easily return to simplicity. It is seldom "God" for an intellectualist, but rather learned pomposities. His ego is pleased, that he can grasp such erudition.

Men who were pridefully conscious of their wealth or worldly position were likely, in Master's presence, to add humility to their other possessions. On one occasion a local magistrate requested an interview at the seaside hermitage in Puri. The man, who was reputed to be ruthless, had it well within his power to dispossess us of the ashram. I mentioned this fact to my guru. But he seated himself with an uncompromising air, and did not rise to greet the visitor.

Slightly nervous, I squatted near the door. Sri Yukteswar failed to ask me to fetch a chair for the magistrate, who had to be content with a wooden box. There was no fulfillment of the man's obvious expectation that his importance would be ceremoniously acknowledged.

A metaphysical discussion ensued. The guest blundered through misinterpretations of the scriptures. As his accuracy sank, his ire rose.

"Do you know that I stood first in the M.A. examination?" Reason had forsaken him, but he could still shout.

"Mr. Magistrate, you forget that this is not your courtroom," Master replied evenly. "From your childish remarks one would surmise that your college career had been unremarkable. A university degree, in any case, is not related to Vedic realization. Saints are not produced in batches every semester like accountants."

After a stunned silence, the visitor laughed heartily.

"This is my first encounter with a heavenly magistrate," he said. Later he made a formal request, couched in the legal terms that were evidently part and parcel of his being, to be accepted as a "probationary" disciple.

On several occasions Sri Yukteswar, like Lahiri Mahasaya, discouraged "unripe" students who wished to join the Swami Order.

"To wear the ocher robe when one lacks God-realization is misleading to society," the two masters said. "Forget the outward symbols of renunciation, which may injure you by inducing a false pride. Nothing matters except your steady, daily spiritual advancement; for that, use *Kriya Yoga.*"

In measuring the worth of a man, a saint employs an invariable criterion, one far different from the shifting yardsticks of the world. Humanity—so variegated in its own eyes!—is seen by a master to be divided into only two classes: ignorant men who are not seeking God, and wise men who are.

My guru personally attended to the details connected with the management of his property. Unscrupulous persons on various occasions attempted to secure possession of Master's ancestral land. With determination and even by instigating lawsuits, Sri Yukteswar outwitted every opponent. He underwent these painful experiences from a desire never to be a begging guru, or a burden on his disciples.

His financial independence was one reason why my alarmingly outspoken master was innocent of the cunnings of diplomacy. Unlike teachers who have to flatter their supporters, my guru was impervious to the influences, open or subtle, of others' wealth. Never did I hear him ask or even hint for money for any purpose. His hermitage training was given free to all disciples.

A court deputy arrived one day at the Serampore ashram to serve a legal summons. A disciple named Kanai and I ushered the man into Master's presence.

The officer's attitude toward Sri Yukteswar was offensive. "It will do you good to leave the shadows of your hermitage and breathe the honest air of a courtroom," he said contemptuously.

I could not contain myself. "Another word of your insolence and you will be on the floor!" I advanced threateningly.

Kanai, also, was shouting at the deputy. "You wretch! Dare you bring your blasphemies into this sacred ashram?"

But Master stood protectingly in front of his abuser. "Don't get excited over nothing. This man is only doing his rightful duty."

The officer, dazed at his varying reception, respectfully offered a word of apology and sped away.

Amazing it was to find that a master with such a fiery will could be so calm within. He fitted the Vedic definition of a man of God: "Softer than the flower, where kindness is concerned; stronger than the thunder, where principles are at stake."

There are always those in this world who, in Browning's words, "endure no light, being themselves obscure." Occasionally an outsider, fevered over some imaginary grievance, would berate Sri Yukteswar. My imperturbable guru would listen politely, analyzing himself to see if any shred of truth lay within the denunciation. These scenes would bring to my mind one of Master's inimitable observations: "Some people try to be tall by cutting off the heads of others!"

The unfailing composure of a saint is impressive beyond any sermon. "He that is slow to anger is better than the mighty; and he that ruleth his spirit than he that taketh a city."*

I often reflected that my majestic master could easily have been an emperor or world-shaking warrior had his mind been centered on fame or worldly achievement. He had chosen instead to storm those inner citadels of wrath and egotism whose fall is the height of a man.

---

* Proverbs 16:32.

CHAPTER 13

The Sleepless Saint

"Please permit me to go to the Himalayas. I hope in unbroken solitude to achieve continuous divine communion."

I actually once addressed these ungrateful words to my master. Seized by one of the unpredictable delusions that occasionally assail the devotee, I felt a growing impatience with hermitage duties and college studies. A feebly extenuating circumstance is that my proposal was made when I had known Sri Yukteswar for only six months. Not yet had I fully surveyed his towering stature.

"Many hillmen live in the Himalayas, yet possess no God-perception." My guru's answer came slowly and simply. "Wisdom is better sought from a man of realization than from an inert mountain."

Ignoring Master's plain hint that he, and not a hill, was my teacher, I repeated my plea. Sri Yukteswar vouchsafed no reply. I took his silence for consent — a precarious but convenient interpretation.

In my Calcutta home that evening, I busied myself with travel preparations. Tying a few articles inside a blanket, I remembered a similar bundle, surreptitiously dropped from my attic window a few years earlier. I wondered if this were to be another ill-starred flight toward the Himalayas. The first time my spiritual elation had been high; tonight my conscience smote me at the thought of leaving my guru.

The following morning I sought out Behari Pundit, my Sanskrit professor at Scottish Church College.

"Sir, you have told me of your friendship with a great disciple of Lahiri Mahasaya. Please give me his address."

"You mean Ram Gopal Muzumdar. I call him the 'sleepless saint.' He is always awake in an ecstatic consciousness. His home is in Ranbajpur, near Tarakeswar."

I thanked the pundit and entrained immediately for Tarakeswar. I hoped to silence my misgivings by getting permission from the "sleepless saint" to engage myself in lonely meditation in the Himalayas. Behari Pundit had told me that Ram Gopal had received illumination after many years of *Kriya Yoga* practice in isolated caves in Bengal.

In Tarakeswar I made my way to a famous shrine. Hindus regard it with veneration, such as Catholics feel for the Lourdes sanctuary in France. Innumerable healing miracles have occurred in Tarakeswar, including one for a member of my family.

"I sat in the temple there for a week," my eldest aunt once told me. "Observing a complete fast, I prayed for the recovery of your Uncle Sarada from a chronic malady. On the seventh day I found an herb materialized in my hand! I made a brew from the leaves and gave it to your uncle. His disease vanished at once and has never reappeared."

I entered the sacred Tarakeswar shrine; the altar contains nothing but a round stone. Its circumference, beginningless and endless, makes it aptly significant of the Infinite. In India cosmic abstractions are understood even by the unlettered peasant; in fact, Westerners have sometimes accused him of living on abstractions!

My own mood at the moment was so austere that I felt disinclined to bow before the stone symbol. God should be sought, I reflected, only within the soul.

I left the temple without genuflection and walked briskly toward the outlying village of Ranbajpur. I was not sure of the way. My appeal to a passer-by for information caused him to sink into long cogitation.

"When you come to a crossroad, turn right and keep going," he finally pronounced oracularly.

Obeying the directions, I wended my way alongside the banks of a canal. Darkness fell; the outskirts of the jungle village were alive with winking fireflies and the howls of nearby jackals. The moonlight was too faint to be helpful; I stumbled on for two hours.

Welcome clang of a cowbell! My repeated shouts eventually brought a peasant to my side.

"I am looking for Ram Gopal Babu."

"No such person lives in our village." The man's tone was surly. "You are probably a lying detective."

Hoping to allay suspicion in his politically troubled mind, I touchingly explained my predicament. He took me to his home and offered a hospitable welcome.

"Ranbajpur is far from here," he remarked. "At the crossroad, you should have turned left, not right."

My earlier informant, I thought sadly, was a definite menace to travelers. After a relishable meal of coarse rice, lentil-*dal*, and curry of potatoes with raw bananas, I retired to a small hut adjoining the courtyard. In the distance, villagers were singing to the loud accompaniment of *mridangas** and cymbals. Sleep was inconsiderable that night; I prayed deeply to be directed to the secluded yogi, Ram Gopal.

As the first streaks of dawn penetrated the fissures of my hut, I set out for Ranbajpur. Crossing rough paddy fields, I trudged over sickled stumps of the prickly plant and around mounds of dried clay. An occasionally met peasant would inform me, invariably, that my destination was "only a *krosha*" (two miles). In six hours the sun traveled victoriously from horizon to meridian, but I began to feel that I would ever be distant from Ranbajpur by one *krosha*.

At midafternoon my world was still an endless paddy field. Heat pouring from the inescapable sky was bringing me to near-collapse. I saw a man approaching me at a leisurely pace. I hardly dared utter my usual question, lest it summon the monotonous: "Just a *krosha*."

The stranger halted beside me. Short and slight, he was physically unimpressive save for an extraordinary pair of piercing dark eyes.

"I was planning to leave Ranbajpur, but your purpose was good, so I awaited you." He shook his finger in my astounded face. "Aren't you clever to think that, unannounced, you could pounce on me? That professor Behari had no right to give you my address."

Considering that introduction of myself would be mere verbosity in the presence of this master, I stood speechless, somewhat hurt at my reception. His next remark was abruptly put.

"Tell me, where do you think God is?"

"Why, He is within me and everywhere." I doubtless looked as bewildered as I felt.

"All-pervading, eh?" The saint chuckled. "Then why, young sir, did you fail to bow before the Infinite in the stone symbol at the Tarakeswar temple yesterday?† Your pride caused you the punishment of being misdirected by the passer-by who was not bothered by fine distinctions between left and right. Today, too, you have had a fairly uncomfortable time of it!"

---

* Hand-played drums, commonly used to accompany devotional chanting (*kirtan*) during religious ceremonies and processions.

† "A man who bows down to nothing can never bear the burden of himself."— Dostoyevsky, *The Possessed.*

I agreed wholeheartedly, wonder-struck that an omnipresent eye hid within the unremarkable body before me. Healing strength emanated from the yogi; I was instantly refreshed in the scorching field.

"The devotee inclines to think his path to God is the only way," he said. "Yoga, through which divinity is found within, is doubtless the highest road, as Lahiri Mahasaya has told us. But, discovering the Lord within, we soon perceive Him without. Holy shrines in Tarakeswar and elsewhere are rightly venerated as nuclear centers of spiritual power."

The saint's censorious attitude vanished; his eyes became compassionately soft. He patted my shoulder.

"Young yogi, I see you are running away from your master. He has everything you need; you should return to him." He added, "Mountains cannot be your guru"—the same thought that Sri Yukteswar had expressed two days earlier.

"Masters are under no cosmic compulsion to live on mountains only." My companion glanced at me quizzically. "The Himalayas in India and Tibet have no monopoly on saints. What one does not trouble to find within will not be discovered by transporting the body hither and yon. As soon as the devotee is *willing* to go even to the ends of the earth for spiritual enlightenment, his guru appears nearby."

I silently agreed, recalling my prayer in the Banaras hermitage, followed by the meeting with Sri Yukteswar in a crowded lane.

"Are you able to have a little room where you can close the door and be alone?"

"Yes." I reflected that this saint descended from the general to the particular with disconcerting speed.

"That is your cave." The yogi bestowed on me a gaze of illumination which I have never forgotten. "That is your sacred mountain. That is where you will find the kingdom of God."

His simple words instantaneously banished my lifelong obsession for the Himalayas. In a burning paddy field I awoke from the dream of mountains and eternal snows.

"Young sir, your divine thirst is laudable. I feel great love for you." Ram Gopal took my hand and led me to a quaint hamlet within a jungle clearing. The adobe houses were covered with coconut leaves and rustically adorned over their entrances with fresh tropical flowers.

The saint seated me on the umbrageous bamboo platform of his small cottage. After he had given me sweetened lime juice and a piece of rock candy, we entered his patio and assumed the lotus posture. Four hours of meditation passed. I opened my eyes and saw that the moonlit figure of the yogi was still motionless. As I was sternly reminding my stomach that man does not live by bread alone, Ram Gopal rose from his seat.

"I see you are famished," he said. "Food will be ready soon."

He kindled a fire under a clay oven on the patio. In a short time we were eating rice and *dal,* served on large banana-tree leaves. My host had courteously refused my aid in all cooking chores. "The guest is God," a Hindu proverb, has commanded devout observance in India since time immemorial. In my later world travels, I was charmed to see that a similar respect for visitors is manifested in the rural sections of many countries. The city dweller finds the keen edge of hospitality blunted by a superabundance of strange faces.

The marts of men seemed almost unimaginably remote as I squatted by the yogi in the isolation of the tiny jungle village. The cottage room was mysteriously lit with a mellow glow. Ram Gopal arranged some torn blankets on the floor for my bed, and seated himself on a straw mat. Overwhelmed by his spiritual magnetism, I ventured a request.

"Sir, why don't you grant me a *samadhi*?"

"Dear one, I would be glad to convey the divine contact, but it is not my place to do so." The saint looked at me with half closed eyes. "Your master will bestow that experience on you shortly. Your body is not tuned just yet. As a small lamp-bulb would be shattered by excessive electrical voltage, so your nerves are unready for the cosmic current. If I gave you the infinite ecstasy right now, you would burn as though every cell were on fire.

"You are asking illumination from me," the yogi continued musingly, "while I am wondering—inconsiderable as I am, and with the little meditation I have done—if I have succeeded in pleasing God, and what worth I may find in His eyes at the final reckoning."

"Sir, have you not been singleheartedly seeking God for a long time?"

"I have not done much. Behari must have told you something of my life. For twenty years I occupied a secret grotto, meditating eighteen hours a day. Then I moved to a more inaccessible cave and stayed there for twenty-five years, remaining in yoga union for twenty hours daily. I did not need sleep, for I was ever with God. My body was more rested by the complete calmness of superconsciousness than it could have been by the imperfect peace of the ordinary subconscious state.

"The muscles relax during sleep; but the heart, lungs, and circulatory system are constantly at work; they get no rest. In superconsciousness, all internal organs remain in a state of suspended animation, electrified by the cosmic energy. By such means I have found it unnecessary to sleep for years." He added, "The time will come when you, too, will dispense with sleep."

"My goodness, you have meditated for so long and yet are unsure of the Lord's favor!" I remarked with astonishment. "Then what about us poor mortals?"

"Well, don't you see, my dear boy, that God is Eternity Itself? To assume that one may fully know Him by forty-five years of meditation is rather a preposterous expectation. Babaji assures us, however, that even a little meditation saves us from the dire fear of death and of after-death states. Do not fix your spiritual ideal on small mountains, but hitch it to the star of unqualified divine attainment. If you work hard, you will get there."

Enthralled by the prospect, I asked him for further enlightening words. He related a wondrous story of his first meeting with Lahiri Mahasaya's guru, Babaji.* Around midnight Ram Gopal fell into silence, and I lay down on my blankets. Closing my eyes, I saw flashes of lightning; the vast space within me was a chamber of molten light. I opened my eyes and observed the same dazzling radiance. The room became a part of the infinite vault that I was beholding with interior vision.

The yogi said, "Why don't you go to sleep?"

"Sir, how can I sleep when lightning is blazing around me, whether my eyes are shut or open?"

"You are blessed to be having this experience. The spiritual radiations are not easily seen." The saint added a few words of affection.

At dawn Ram Gopal gave me rock candies and said I must depart. I felt such reluctance to bid him farewell that tears coursed down my cheeks.

"I will not let you go empty-handed." The yogi spoke tenderly. "I will do something for you."

He smiled and looked at me steadfastly. I became immobile, as though rooted to the ground; vibrations of peace that emanated from the saint flooded my being. I was instantaneously healed of a pain in my back that had been troubling me intermittently for years.

* See pages 265–68.

Renewed, bathed in a sea of luminous joy, I wept no more. After touching Ram Gopal's feet, I entered the jungle. I made my way through its tropical tangle and over many paddy fields until I reached Tarakeswar.

There I made a second pilgrimage to the famous shrine, and prostrated myself fully before the altar. The round stone enlarged before my inner vision until it became the cosmical spheres: ring within ring, zone after zone, all dowered with divinity.

I entrained happily an hour later for Calcutta. My travels ended, not in the lofty mountains, but in the Himalayan presence of my master.

CHAPTER 14

An Experience in Cosmic Consciousness

"I am here, Guruji." My shamefacedness spoke more eloquently for me.

"Let us go to the kitchen and find something to eat." Sri Yukteswar's manner was as casual as though hours and not days had separated us.

"Master, I must have disappointed you by my abrupt departure from my duties here; I thought you might be angry with me."

"No, of course not! Wrath springs only from thwarted desires. I do not expect anything from others, so their actions cannot be in opposition to wishes of mine. I would not use you for my own ends; I am happy only in your own true happiness."

"Sir, one hears of divine love in a vague way, but today I am indeed having a concrete example of it from your angelic self! In the world, even a father does not easily forgive his son if he leaves his parent's business without warning. But you show not the slightest vexation, though you must have been put to great inconvenience by the many unfinished tasks I left behind."

We looked into each other's eyes, where tears were shining. A blissful wave engulfed me; I was conscious that the Lord, in the form of my guru, was expanding the limited ardors of my heart to vast reaches of cosmic love.

A few mornings later I made my way to Master's empty sitting room. I planned to meditate, but my laudable purpose was unshared by disobedient thoughts. They scattered like birds before the hunter.

"Mukunda!" Sri Yukteswar's voice sounded from a distant balcony.

I felt as rebellious as my thoughts. "Master always urges me to meditate," I muttered to myself. "He should not disturb me when he knows why I came to his room."

He summoned me again; I remained obstinately silent. The third time his tone held rebuke.

"Sir, I am meditating," I shouted protestingly.

"I know how you are meditating," my guru called out, "with your mind distributed like leaves in a storm! Come here to me."

Thwarted and exposed, I made my way sadly to his side.

"Poor boy, mountains cannot give you what you want." Master spoke caressingly, comfortingly. His calm gaze was unfathomable. "Your heart's desire shall be fulfilled."

Sri Yukteswar seldom indulged in riddles; I was bewildered. He struck gently on my chest above the heart.

My body became immovably rooted; breath was drawn out of my lungs as if by some huge magnet. Soul and mind instantly lost their physical bondage and streamed out like a fluid piercing light from my every pore. The flesh was as though dead; yet in my intense awareness I knew that never before had I been fully alive. My sense of identity was no longer narrowly confined to a body but embraced the circumambient atoms. People on distant streets seemed to be moving gently over my own remote periphery. The roots of plants and trees appeared through a dim transparency of the soil; I discerned the inward flow of their sap.

The whole vicinity lay bare before me. My ordinary frontal vision was now changed to a vast spherical sight, simultaneously all-perceptive. Through the back of my head I saw men strolling far down Rai Ghat Lane, and noticed also a white cow that was leisurely approaching. When she reached the open ashram gate, I observed her as though with my two physical eyes. After she had passed behind the brick wall of the courtyard, I saw her clearly still.

All objects within my panoramic gaze trembled and vibrated like quick motion pictures. My body, Master's, the pillared courtyard, the furniture and floor, the trees and sunshine, occasionally became violently agitated, until all melted into a luminescent sea; even as sugar crystals, thrown into a glass of water, dissolve after being shaken. The unifying light alternated with materializations of form, the metamorphoses revealing the law of cause and effect in creation.

An oceanic joy broke upon calm endless shores of my soul. The Spirit of God, I realized, is exhaustless Bliss; His body is countless tissues of light. A swelling glory within me began to envelop towns, continents, the earth, solar and stellar systems, tenuous nebulae, and floating universes. The entire cosmos, gently luminous, like a city seen afar at night, glimmered within the infinitude of my being. The dazzling light beyond the sharply etched global outlines faded slightly at the farthest edges; there I saw a mellow radiance, ever undiminished. It was indescribably subtle; the planetary pictures were formed of a grosser light.*

The divine dispersion of rays poured from an Eternal Source, blazing into galaxies, transfigured with ineffable auras. Again and again I saw the creative beams condense into constellations, then resolve into sheets of transparent flame. By rhythmic reversion, sextillion worlds passed into diaphanous luster, then fire became firmament.

I cognized the center of the empyrean as a point of intuitive perception in my heart. Irradiating splendor issued from my nucleus to every part of the universal structure. Blissful *amrita,* nectar of immortality, pulsated through me with a quicksilverlike fluidity. The creative voice of God I heard resounding as *Aum,*† the vibration of the Cosmic Motor.

Suddenly the breath returned to my lungs. With a disappointment almost unbearable, I realized that my infinite immensity was lost. Once more I was limited to the humiliating cage of a body, not easily accommodative to the Spirit. Like a prodigal child, I had run away from my macrocosmic home and had imprisoned myself in a narrow microcosm.

My guru was standing motionless before me; I started to prostrate myself at his holy feet in gratitude for his having bestowed on me the experience in cosmic consciousness that I had long passionately sought. He held me upright and said quietly:

"You must not get overdrunk with ecstasy. Much work yet remains for you in the world. Come, let us sweep the balcony floor; then we shall walk by the Ganges."

I fetched a broom; Master, I knew, was teaching me the secret of balanced living. The soul must stretch over the cosmogonic abysses, while the body performs its daily duties.

When Sri Yukteswar and I set out later for a stroll, I was still entranced in unspeakable rapture. I saw our bodies as two astral pictures, moving over a road by the river whose essence was sheer light.

"It is the Spirit of God that actively sustains every form and force in the universe; yet He is transcendental and aloof in the bliss-

---

* Light as the essence of creation is explained in chapter 30.

† "In the beginning was the Word, and the Word was with God, and the Word was God." — John 1:1.

ful uncreated void beyond the worlds of vibratory phenomena,"* Master explained. "Those who attain Self-realization on earth live a similar twofold existence. Conscientiously performing their work in the world, they are yet immersed in an inward beatitude.

"The Lord has created all men from the illimitable joy of His being. Though they are painfully cramped by the body, God nevertheless expects that men made in His image shall ultimately rise above all sense identifications and reunite with Him."

The cosmic vision left many permanent lessons. By daily stilling my thoughts, I could win release from the delusive conviction that my body was a mass of flesh and bones, traversing the hard soil of matter. The breath and the restless mind, I saw, are like storms that lash the ocean of light into waves of material forms—earth, sky, human beings, animals, birds, trees. No perception of the Infinite as One Light can be had except by calming those storms.

As often as I quieted the two natural tumults, I beheld the multitudinous waves of creation melt into one lucent sea; even as the waves of the ocean, when a tempest subsides, serenely dissolve into unity.

A master bestows the divine experience of cosmic consciousness when his disciple, by meditation, has strengthened his mind to a degree where the vast vistas would not overwhelm him. Mere intellectual willingness or open-mindedness is not enough. Only adequate enlargement of consciousness by yoga practice and devotional *bhakti* can prepare one to absorb the liberating shock of omnipresence.

---

* "For the Father judgeth no man, but hath committed all judgment unto the Son."—John 5:22. "No man hath seen God at any time; the only begotten Son, which is in the bosom of the Father, he hath declared him."—John 1:18. "God...created all things by Jesus Christ."—Ephesians 3:9. "He that believeth on me, the works that I do shall he do also; and greater works than these shall he do; because I go unto my Father."—John 14:12. "The Comforter, which is the Holy Ghost, whom the Father will send in my name, he shall teach you all things, and bring all things to your remembrance, whatsoever I have said to you."—John 14:26.

These Biblical words refer to the threefold nature of God as Father, Son, Holy Ghost (*Sat, Tat, Aum* in the Hindu scriptures). God the Father is the Absolute, Unmanifested, existing *beyond* vibratory creation. God the Son is the Christ Consciousness (Brahma or *Kutastha Chaitanya*) existing *within* vibratory creation; this Christ Consciousness is the "only begotten" or sole reflection of the Uncreated Infinite. The outward manifestation of the omnipresent Christ Consciousness, its "witness" (Revelation 3:14), is *Aum*, the Word or Holy Ghost: invisible divine power, the only doer, the sole causative and activating force that upholds all creation through vibration. *Aum* the blissful Comforter is heard in meditation and reveals to the devotee the ultimate Truth, bringing "all things to...remembrance."

The divine experience comes with a natural inevitability to the sincere devotee. His intense craving begins to pull at God with an irresistible force. The Lord as the Cosmic Vision is drawn by that magnetic ardor into the seeker's range of consciousness.

I wrote, in my later years, the following poem, "Samadhi," endeavoring to convey a glimpse of its glory:

Vanished the veils of light and shade,
Lifted every vapor of sorrow,
Sailed away all dawns of fleeting joy,
Gone the dim sensory mirage.
Love, hate, health, disease, life, death:
Perished these false shadows on the screen of duality.
The storm of *maya* stilled
By magic wand of intuition deep.
Present, past, future, no more for me,
But ever-present, all-flowing I, I, everywhere.
Planets, stars, stardust, earth,
Volcanic bursts of doomsday cataclysms,
Creation's molding furnace,
Glaciers of silent X-rays, burning electron floods,
Thoughts of all men, past, present, to come,
Every blade of grass, myself, mankind,
Each particle of universal dust,
Anger, greed, good, bad, salvation, lust,
I swallowed, transmuted all
Into a vast ocean of blood of my own one Being.
Smoldering joy, oft-puffed by meditation
Blinding my tearful eyes,
Burst into immortal flames of bliss,
Consumed my tears, my frame, my all.
Thou art I, I am Thou,
Knowing, Knower, Known, as One!
Tranquilled, unbroken thrill, eternally living, ever-new peace.
Enjoyable beyond imagination of expectancy, *samadhi* bliss!
Not an unconscious state
Or mental chloroform without willful return,
Samadhi but extends my conscious realm
Beyond limits of the mortal frame
To farthest boundary of eternity
Where I, the Cosmic Sea,
Watch the little ego floating in Me.
Mobile murmurs of atoms are heard,
The dark earth, mountains, vales, lo! molten liquid!
Flowing seas change into vapors of nebulae!

Aum blows upon vapors, opening wondrously their veils,
Oceans stand revealed, shining electrons,
Till, at the last sound of the cosmic drum,*
Vanish the grosser lights into eternal rays
Of all-pervading bliss.
From joy I came, for joy I live, in sacred joy I melt.
Ocean of mind, I drink all creation's waves.
Four veils of solid, liquid, vapor, light,
Lift aright.
I, in everything, enter the Great Myself.
Gone forever: fitful, flickering shadows of mortal memory;
Spotless is my mental sky —below, ahead, and high above;
Eternity and I, one united ray.
A tiny bubble of laughter, I
Am become the Sea of Mirth Itself.

Sri Yukteswar taught me how to summon the blessed experience at will, and also how to transmit it to others† when their intuitive channels are developed.

For months, after the first time, I entered the state of ecstatic union, comprehending daily why the *Upanishads* say that God is *rasa,* "the most relishable." One morning, however, I took a problem to Master.

"I want to know, sir—when shall I find God?"

"You have found Him."

"Oh, no, sir, I don't think so!"

My guru was smiling. "I am sure you aren't expecting a venerable Personage, adorning a throne in some antiseptic corner of the cosmos! I see, however, that you are imagining that possession of miraculous powers is proof that one has found God. No. One might gain the power to control the whole universe—yet find the Lord elusive still. Spiritual advancement is not to be measured by one's displays of outward powers, but solely by the depth of his bliss in meditation.

"*Ever-new Joy is God.* He is inexhaustible; as you continue your meditations during the years, He will beguile you with an infinite ingenuity. Devotees like yourself who have found the way to God never dream of exchanging Him for any other happiness; He is seductive beyond thought of competition.

---

* *Aum,* the creative vibration that externalizes all creation.
† I have transmitted the Cosmic Vision to a number of *Kriya Yogis* in East and West. One of them, Mr. James J. Lynn, is shown in *samadhi* in the picture opposite page 209.

"How quickly we weary of earthly pleasures! Desire for material things is endless; man is never satisfied completely, and pursues one goal after another. The 'something else' he seeks is the Lord, who alone can grant lasting joy.

"Outward longings drive us from the Eden within; they offer false pleasures that only impersonate soul happiness. The lost paradise is quickly regained through divine meditation. As God is unanticipatory Ever-Newness, we never tire of Him. Can we be surfeited with bliss, delightfully varied throughout eternity?"

"I understand now, sir, why saints call the Lord unfathomable. Even everlasting life could not suffice to appraise Him."

"That is true; but He is also near and dear. After the mind has been cleared by *Kriya Yoga* of sensory obstacles, meditation furnishes a twofold proof of God. Ever-new joy is evidence of His existence, convincing to our very atoms. Also, in meditation one finds His instant guidance, His adequate response to every difficulty."

"I see, Guruji; you have solved my problem." I smiled gratefully. "I do realize now that I have found God, for whenever the joy of meditation has returned subconsciously during my active hours, I have been subtly directed to adopt the right course in everything, even in minor details."

"Human life is beset with sorrow until we know how to tune in with the Divine Will, whose 'right course' is often baffling to the egoistic intelligence," Master said.

"God alone gives unerring counsel; who but He bears the burden of the cosmos?"

CHAPTER 15

The Cauliflower Robbery

"Master, a gift for you! These six huge cauliflowers were planted with my hands; I have watched over their growth with the tender care of a mother nursing her child." I presented the basket of vegetables with a ceremonial flourish.

"Thank you!" Sri Yukteswar's smile was warm with appreciation. "Please keep them in your room; I shall need them tomorrow for a special dinner."

I had just arrived in Puri* to spend my college summer vacation with my guru at his seaside hermitage. Built by Master and his disciples, the cheerful little two-storied retreat fronts on the Bay of Bengal.

I awoke early the following morning, refreshed by the salty sea breezes and the quiet charm of the ashram. My guru's melodious voice was calling; I took a look at my cherished cauliflowers and stowed them neatly under my bed.

"Come, let us go to the beach." Master led the way; several young disciples and I followed in a scattered group. Our guru surveyed us in mild criticism.

"When our Western brothers walk, they usually take pride in unison. Now, please march in two rows; keep rhythmic step with one another." Sri Yukteswar watched as we obeyed; he began to sing: "Boys go to and fro, in a pretty little row." I could not but admire the ease with which Master was able to match the brisk pace of his young students.

"Halt!" My guru's eyes sought mine. "Did you remember to lock the back door of the hermitage?"

"I think so, sir."

Sri Yukteswar was silent for a few minutes, a half suppressed smile on his lips. "No, you forgot," he said finally. "Divine contemplation must not be made an excuse for material carelessness. You

* Puri, about 310 miles south of Calcutta, is a famous pilgrimage city for devotees of Krishna; his worship is celebrated there with two immense annual festivals, *Snanayatra* and *Rathayatra*.

have neglected your duty in safeguarding the ashram; you must be punished."

I thought he was obscurely joking when he added: "Your six cauliflowers will soon be only five."

We turned around at Master's orders and marched back until we were close to the hermitage.

"Rest awhile. Mukunda, look across the compound on our left; observe the road beyond. A certain man will arrive there presently; he will be the means of your chastisement."

I concealed my vexation at these incomprehensible remarks. A peasant soon appeared on the road; he was dancing grotesquely and flinging his arms about with meaningless gestures. Almost paralyzed with curiosity, I glued my eyes on the hilarious spectacle. As the man reached a point in the road where he would vanish from our view, Sri Yukteswar said, "Now, he will return."

The peasant at once changed his direction and made for the rear of the ashram. Crossing a sandy tract, he entered the building by the back door. I had left it unlocked, even as my guru had said. The man emerged shortly, holding one of my prized cauliflowers. He now strode along respectably, invested with the dignity of possession.

The unfolding farce, in which my role appeared to be that of bewildered victim, was not so disconcerting that I failed in indignant pursuit of the thief. I was halfway to the road when Master called me back. He was shaking from head to foot with laughter.

"That poor crazy man has been longing for a cauliflower," he explained between outbursts of mirth. "I thought it would be a good idea if he got one of yours, so ill-guarded!"

I dashed to my room, where I found that the thief, evidently one with a vegetable fixation, had left untouched my gold rings, watch, and money, all lying openly on the blanket. He had crawled instead under the bed, where the basket of cauliflowers, completely hidden from casual sight, had yielded the object of his singlehearted desire.

I asked Sri Yukteswar that evening to explain the incident (which had, I thought, a few baffling features).

My guru shook his head slowly. "You will understand it someday. Science will soon discover a number of these hidden laws."

When the wonders of radio burst some years later on an astounded world, I remembered Master's prediction. Age-old concepts of time and space were annihilated; no person's home so narrow that London or Calcutta could not enter! The dullest intelligence enlarged before indisputable proof of one aspect of man's omnipresence.

The "plot" of the cauliflower comedy may be best understood by a radio analogy.* My guru was a perfect human radio. Thoughts are no more than very subtle vibrations moving in the ether. Just as a correctly tuned radio picks up a desired musical number out of thousands of other programs from every direction, so Sri Yukteswar had been sensitively receptive to a certain pertinent thought (that of the half-witted man who was hankering for a cauliflower), out of the countless thoughts of broadcasting human minds in the world. During the walk toward the beach, no sooner had Master become aware of the peasant's simple yearning than he was willing to gratify it. Sri Yukteswar's divine eye had discovered the man, dancing down the road, before he had become visible to the disciples. My forgetfulness about locking the ashram door had given Master a convenient excuse to deprive me of one of my valued vegetables.

After thus functioning as a receiving instrument, Sri Yukteswar then operated, through his powerful will, as a broadcaster or sending instrument.† In that role he had successfully directed the peasant to reverse his steps and go to a certain room for a single cauliflower.

Intuition is soul guidance, appearing naturally in man during those instants when his mind is calm. Nearly everyone has had the experience of an inexplicably correct "hunch" or has transferred his thoughts accurately to another person.

The human mind, freed from the disturbances or "static" of restlessness, is empowered to perform all the functions of compli-

* A radio microscope devised in 1939 revealed a new world of hitherto unknown rays. "Man himself as well as all kinds of supposedly inert matter constantly emits the rays that this instrument 'sees,' " reported the *Associated Press.* "Those who believe in telepathy, second sight, and clairvoyance, have in this announcement the first scientific proof of the existence of invisible rays that really travel from one person to another. The radio device actually is a radio-frequency spectroscope. It does the same thing for cool, non-glowing matter that the spectroscope does when it discloses the kinds of atoms that make the stars....The existence of such rays coming from man and all living things has been suspected by scientists for many years. Today is the first experimental proof of their existence. The discovery shows that every atom and every molecule in nature is a continuous radio-broadcasting station....Thus even after death the substance that was a man continues to send out its delicate rays. The wavelengths of these rays range from shorter than anything now used in broadcasting to the longest kind of radio waves. The jumble of these waves is almost inconceivable. There are millions of them. A single very large molecule may give off 1,000,000 different wavelengths at the same time. The longer wavelengths of this sort travel with the ease and speed of radio-waves....There is one amazing difference between the new radio-rays and familiar rays like light. This is the prolonged time, amounting to thousands of years, that these radio waves will keep on emitting from undisturbed matter."

† See footnote on page 226.

cated radio mechanisms—sending as well as receiving thoughts and tuning out undesirable ones. As the power of a radio-broadcasting station is regulated by the amount of electrical current it can utilize, so the effectiveness of a human radio depends on the degree of will power possessed by each person.

All thoughts vibrate eternally in the cosmos. By deep concentration a master is able to detect the thoughts of any man, living or dead. Thoughts are universally and not individually rooted; a truth cannot be created, but only perceived. Any erroneous thought of man is a result of an imperfection, large or small, in his discernment. The goal of yoga science is to calm the mind, that without distortion it may hear the infallible counsel of the Inner Voice.

Radio and television have brought the instantaneous sound and sight of remote persons to the firesides of millions: the first faint scientific intimations that man is an all-pervading spirit. Though the ego in most barbaric ways conspires to enslave him, man is not a body confined to a point in space but is essentially the omnipresent soul.

"Very strange, very wonderful, seemingly very improbable phenomena may yet appear which, when once established, will not astonish us more than we are now astonished at all that science has taught us during the last century," Charles Robert Richet,* Nobel laureate in physiology, has declared. "It is assumed that the phenomena which we now accept without surprise, do not excite our astonishment because they are understood. But this is not the case. If they do not surprise us, it is not because they are understood, it is because they are familiar; for if that which is not understood ought to surprise us, we should be surprised at everything—the fall of a stone thrown into the air, the acorn which becomes an oak, mercury which expands when it is heated, iron attracted by a magnet.

"The science of today is a light matter.... Those amazing truths that our descendants will discover are even now all around us, staring us in the eyes, so to speak; and yet we do not see them. But it is not enough to say that we do not see them; we do not wish to see them—for as soon as an unexpected and unfamiliar fact appears, we try to fit it into the framework of the commonplaces of accepted knowledge, and are indignant that anyone should dare to experiment further."

A humorous occurrence took place a few days after I had been so implausibly robbed of a cauliflower. A certain kerosene lamp

---

* Author of *Our Sixth Sense* (London: Rider & Co.).

could not be found. Having so lately witnessed my guru's omniscient insight, I thought he would demonstrate that it was child's play to find the lamp.

Master perceived my expectation. With exaggerated gravity he questioned all ashram residents. A young disciple confessed that he had used the lamp to go to the well in the back yard.

Sri Yukteswar gave the solemn counsel: "Seek the lamp near the well."

I rushed there; no lamp! Crestfallen, I returned to my guru. He was now laughing heartily, without compunction for my disillusionment.

"Too bad I couldn't direct you to the vanished lamp; I am not a fortune-teller!" With twinkling eyes, he added, "I am not even a satisfactory Sherlock Holmes!"

I realized that Master would never display his powers when challenged, or for a triviality.

Delightful weeks sped by. Sri Yukteswar was planning a religious procession. He asked me to lead the disciples across the town and beach of Puri. The festive day (the summer solstice) dawned in intense heat.

"Guruji, how can I take the barefooted students over the fiery sands?" I asked despairingly.

"I will tell you a secret," Master said. "The Lord shall send an umbrella of clouds; you all shall walk in comfort."

I happily organized the procession; our group started from the ashram with a Satsanga* banner. Designed by Sri Yukteswar, it bore the symbol of the single eye,† the telescopic gaze of intuition.

No sooner had we left the hermitage than the sky became filled with clouds as though by magic. To the accompaniment of astonished ejaculations from all observers, a light shower fell, cooling the city streets and the scorching seashore.

The soothing drops descended during the two hours of the parade. The exact instant at which our group returned to the ashram, the clouds and rain disappeared.

"You see how God feels for us," Master replied after I had

---

* *Sat* is literally "being," hence "essence, truth, reality"; *sanga* is "association." Sri Yukteswar called his hermitage organization *Satsanga*, "fellowship with truth."

† "If therefore thine eye be single, thy whole body shall be full of light."—Matthew 6:22. During deep meditation, the single or spiritual eye becomes visible within the central part of the forehead. This omniscient eye is variously referred to in scriptures as the third eye, star of the East, inner eye, dove descending from heaven, eye of Shiva, eye of intuition, and so on.

expressed my gratitude. "The Lord responds to all and works for all. Just as He sent rain at my plea, so He fulfills any sincere desire of the devotee. Seldom do men realize how often God heeds their prayers. He is not partial to a few, but listens to everyone who approaches Him trustfully. His children should ever have implicit faith in the loving-kindness of their Omnipresent Father."*

Sri Yukteswar sponsored four yearly festivals, at the equinoxes and solstices, when his students gathered from far and near. The winter solstice celebration was held in Serampore; the first one I attended left me with a permanent blessing.

The festivities started in the morning with a barefoot procession along the streets. The voices of a hundred students rang out with sweet religious songs; a few musicians played the flute and *khol kartal* (drums and cymbals). Enthusiastic townspeople strewed the path with flowers, glad to be summoned from prosaic tasks by our resounding praise of the Lord's blessed name. The long tour ended in the courtyard of the hermitage. There we encircled our guru, while students on upper balconies showered us with marigold blossoms.

Many guests went upstairs to receive a pudding of *channa* and oranges. I made my way to a group of brother disciples who were serving today as cooks. Food for such large gatherings had to be cooked outdoors in huge cauldrons. The improvised wood-burning brick stoves were smoky and tear-provoking, but we laughed merrily at our work. Religious festivals in India are never considered troublesome; each devotee gladly does his part, supplying money, or rice and vegetables, or his personal services.

Master was soon in our midst, supervising the details of the feast. Busy every moment, he kept pace with the most energetic young student.

A *sankirtan* (group chanting), accompanied by the harmonium and hand-beaten Indian drums, was in progress on the second floor. Sri Yukteswar listened appreciatively; his musical sense was acutely perfect.

"They are off key!" Master left the cooks and joined the musicians. The melody was heard again, this time correctly rendered.

The Sama Veda contains the world's earliest writings on musical science. In India, music, painting, and the drama are considered divine arts. Brahma, Vishnu, and Shiva, the Eternal Trinity, were the first musicians. Shiva in His aspect of Nataraja, the Cosmic

---

* "He that planted the ear, shall he not hear? he that formed the eye, shall he not see?... he that teacheth man knowledge, shall not he know?"—Psalms 94:9–10.

Dancer, is scripturally represented as having worked out the infinite modes of rhythm in the processes of universal creation, preservation, and destruction, while Brahma and Vishnu accentuated the time beat: Brahma clanging the cymbals and Vishnu sounding the *mridanga* or holy drum.

Saraswati, goddess of wisdom, is symbolized as performing on the *vina*, mother of all stringed instruments. Krishna, an incarnation of Vishnu, is shown in Hindu art with a flute; on it he plays the enrapturing song that recalls to their true home the human souls wandering in *maya*-delusion.

The foundation stones of Hindu music are *ragas* or fixed melodic scales. The six basic *ragas* branch out into 126 derivative *raginis* (wives) and *putras* (sons). Each *raga* has a minimum of five notes: a leading note (*vadi* or king), a secondary note (*samavadi* or prime minister), helping notes (*anuvadi*, attendants), and a dissonant note (*vivadi*, the enemy).

Each of the six basic *ragas* has a natural correspondence with a certain hour of the day, season of the year, and a presiding deity who bestows a particular potency. Thus, (1) the *Hindole Raga* is heard only at dawn in the spring, to evoke the mood of universal love; (2) *Deepaka Raga* is played during the evening in summer, to arouse compassion; (3) *Megha Raga* is a melody for midday in the rainy season, to summon courage; (4) *Bhairava Raga* is played in the mornings of August, September, October, to achieve tranquility; (5) *Sri Raga* is reserved for autumn twilights, to attain pure love; (6) *Malkounsa Raga* is heard at midnights in winter, for valor.

The ancient rishis discovered these laws of sound alliance between nature and man. Because nature is an objectification of *Aum*, the Primal Sound or Vibratory Word, man can obtain control over all natural manifestations through the use of certain *mantras* or chants.* Historical documents tell of the remarkable powers possessed by Miyan Tan Sen, sixteenth-century court musician for Akbar the Great. Commanded by the Emperor to sing a night

---

* Folklore of all peoples contains references to incantations with power over Nature. The American Indians developed effective sound rituals for rain and wind. Tan Sen, the great Hindu musician, was able to quench fire by the power of his song.

Charles Kellogg, the California naturalist, gave a demonstration of the effect of tonal vibration on fire in 1926 before a group of New York firemen. "Passing a bow, like an enlarged violin bow, swiftly across an aluminum tuning fork, he produced a screech like intense radio static. Instantly the yellow gas flame, two feet high, leaping inside a hollow glass tube, subsided to a height of six inches and became a sputtering blue flare. Another attempt with the bow, and another screech of vibration, extinguished it."

raga while the sun was overhead, Tan Sen intoned a *mantra* that instantly caused the whole palace precincts to become enveloped in darkness.

Indian music divides the octave into twenty-two *srutis* or demi-semitones. These microtonal intervals permit fine shades of musical expression unattainable by the Western chromatic scale of twelve semitones. Each of the seven basic notes of the octave is associated in Hindu mythology with a color, and the natural cry of a bird or beast—*Do* with green, and the peacock; *Re* with red, and the sky-lark; *Mi* with gold, and the goat; *Fa* with yellowish white, and the heron; *Sol* with black, and the nightingale; *La* with yellow, and the horse; *Si* with a combination of all colors, and the elephant.

Indian music outlines seventy-two *thatas* or scales. A musician has creative scope for endless improvisation around the fixed traditional melody or *raga*; he concentrates on the sentiment or definitive mood of the structural theme and embroiders it to the limits of his own originality. The Hindu musician does not read set notes; at each playing he clothes anew the bare skeleton of the *raga*, often confining himself to a single melodic sequence, stressing by repetition all its subtle microtonal and rhythmic variations.

Bach, among Western composers, understood the charm and power of repetitious sound slightly differentiated in a hundred complex ways.

Sanskrit literature describes 120 *talas* or time measures. The traditional founder of Hindu music, Bharata, is said to have isolated thirty-two kinds of *tala* in the song of a lark. The origin of *tala* or rhythm is rooted in human movements—the double time of walking, and the triple time of respiration in sleep, when inhalation is twice the length of exhalation.

India has long recognized the human voice as the most perfect instrument of sound. Hindu music therefore largely confines itself to the voice range of three octaves. For the same reason, melody (relation of successive notes) is stressed, rather than harmony (relation of simultaneous notes).

Hindu music is a subjective, spiritual, and individualistic art, aiming not at symphonic brilliance but at personal harmony with the Over-Soul. All the celebrated songs of India have been composed by devotees of the Divine. The Sanskrit word for "musician" is *bhagavathar*, "he who sings the praises of God."

The *sankirtans* or musical gatherings are an effective form of yoga or spiritual discipline, necessitating intense concentration, absorption in the seed thought and sound. Because man himself is an expression of the Creative Word, sound exercises on him a potent and immediate effect. Great religious music of East and West bestows joy on man because it causes a temporary vibratory awakening of one of his occult spinal centers.* In those blissful moments a dim memory comes to him of his divine origin.

The *sankirtan* issuing from Sri Yukteswar's second-story sitting room on the day of the festival was inspiring to the cooks amid the steaming pots. My brother disciples and I joyously sang the refrains, beating time with our hands.

By sunset we had served our hundreds of visitors with *khichuri* (rice and lentils), vegetable curry, and rice pudding. We laid cotton blankets over the courtyard; soon the assemblage was squatting under the starry vault, quietly attentive to the wisdom pouring from Sri Yukteswar's lips. His public speeches emphasized the value of *Kriya Yoga*, and a life of self-respect, calmness, determination, simple diet, and regular exercise.

A group of very young disciples then chanted a few sacred hymns; the meeting concluded with fervent *sankirtan*. From ten o'clock until midnight, ashram residents washed pots and pans and cleared the courtyard. My guru called me to his side.

"I am pleased over your cheerful labors today and during the past week of preparations. I want you with me; you may sleep in my bed tonight."

This was a privilege I had never thought would fall to my lot.

---

* Awakening of the occult cerebrospinal centers (*chakras*, astral lotuses) is the sacred goal of the yogi. Western exegetes have not understood that the New Testament chapter of Revelation contains the symbolic exposition of a yogic science, taught to John and other close disciples by Lord Jesus. John mentions (Rev. 1:20) the "mystery of the seven stars" and the "seven churches"; these symbols refer to the seven lotuses of light, described in yoga treatises as the seven "trap doors" in the cerebrospinal axis. Through these divinely planned "exits," the yogi, by scientific meditation, escapes from the bodily prison and resumes his true identity as Spirit. (See chapter 26.)

The seventh center, the "thousand-petaled lotus" in the brain, is the throne of the Infinite Consciousness. In the state of divine illumination the yogi is said to perceive Brahma or God the Creator as Padmaja, "the One born of the lotus."

The "lotus posture" is so called because in that traditional pose the yogi views the varicolored lotuses (*padmas*) of the cerebrospinal centers. Each lotus possesses a characteristic number of petals or rays composed of *prana* (life force). The *padmas* are also known as *chakras* or wheels.

The lotus posture (*padmasana*) holds the spine upright and locks the body securely against the danger of falling, backward or forward, during the trance state (*sabikalpa samadhi*); it is therefore the yogi's favorite meditation posture. However, *padmasana* may present some difficulties for the beginner, and should not be attempted without the guidance of a *Hatha Yoga* expert.

We sat a while in a state of intense divine tranquility. About ten minutes after we had lain down to sleep, Master rose and began to dress.

"What is the matter, sir?" The joy of sleeping beside my guru was suddenly tinged with unreality.

"I think that a few students who missed their proper train connections will be here soon. Let us have some food ready."

"Guruji, no one would come at one o'clock in the morning!"

"Stay in bed; you have been working very hard. But I am going to cook."

At Sri Yukteswar's resolute tone, I jumped up and followed him to the small daily used kitchen adjacent to the second-floor inner balcony. Rice and *dal* were soon boiling.

My guru smiled affectionately. "Tonight you have conquered fatigue and fear of hard work; you shall never be bothered by them in the future."

As he uttered these words of lifelong blessing, footsteps sounded in the courtyard. I ran downstairs and admitted a group of students.

"Dear brother," one man said, "how reluctant we are to disturb Master at this hour! We made a mistake about train schedules, but felt we could not return home without a glimpse of our guru."

"He has been expecting you and is even now preparing your food."

Sri Yukteswar's welcoming voice rang out; I led the astonished visitors to the kitchen. Master turned to me with twinkling eyes.

"Now that you have finished comparing notes, no doubt you are satisfied that our guests really did miss their train!"

I followed him to his bedroom a half hour later, anticipating happily the honor of sleeping beside a godlike guru.

CHAPTER 16

Outwitting the Stars

"Mukunda, why don't you get an astrological armlet?"

"Should I, Master? I don't believe in astrology."

"It is not a question of *belief*; the scientific attitude one should take on any subject is whether it is *true*. The law of gravitation worked as efficiently before Newton as after him. The cosmos would be fairly chaotic if its laws could not operate without the sanction of human belief.

"Charlatans have brought the ancient stellar science to its present disrepute. Astrology is too vast, both mathematically* and philosophically, to be rightly grasped except by men of profound understanding. If ignoramuses misread the heavens, and see there a scrawl instead of a script, that is to be expected in this imperfect world. One should not dismiss the wisdom with the 'wise.'

"All parts of creation are linked together and interchange their influences. The balanced rhythm of the universe is rooted in reciprocity," my guru continued. "Man, in his human aspect, has

---

* From astronomical references in ancient Hindu literature, scholars have been able to ascertain the dates of the authors. The scientific knowledge of the rishis was very great; in the *Kaushitaki Brahmana* we find precise astronomical passages indicating that in 3100 B.C. the Hindus were far advanced in astronomy, which had a practical value in determining the auspicious times for astrological ceremonies. An article by Tara Mata in *East-West*, February 1934, says of the *Jyotish* or body of Vedic astronomical expositions: "It contains the scientific lore that kept India at the forefront of all ancient nations and made her the mecca of seekers after knowledge. *Brahmagupta*, one of the *Jyotish* works, is an astronomical treatise dealing with such matters as the heliocentric motion of the planetary bodies in our solar system, the obliquity of the ecliptic, the earth's spherical form, the reflected light of the moon, the earth's daily axial revolution, the presence of fixed stars in the Milky Way, the law of gravitation, and other scientific facts that did not dawn in the Western world until the time of Copernicus and Newton."

The so-called "Arabic numerals," invaluable in the development of Western mathematics, came to Europe in the ninth century, via the Arabs, from India, where that system of notation had been anciently formulated. Further light on India's vast scientific heritage will be found in Sir P. C. Roy's *History of Hindu Chemistry*, in B. N. Seal's *Positive Sciences of the Ancient Hindus*, in B. K. Sarkar's *Hindu Achievements in Exact Science* and his *The Positive Background of Hindu Sociology*, and in U. C. Dutt's *Materia Medica of the Hindus*.

to combat two sets of forces—first, the tumults within his being, caused by the admixture of earth, water, fire, air, and ethereal elements; second, the outer disintegrating powers of nature. So long as man struggles with his mortality, he is affected by the myriad mutations of heaven and earth.

"Astrology is the study of man's response to planetary stimuli. The stars have no conscious benevolence or animosity; they merely send forth positive and negative radiations. Of themselves, these do not help or harm humanity, but offer a lawful channel for the outward operation of cause-effect equilibriums that each man has set into motion in the past.

"A child is born on that day and at that hour when the celestial rays are in mathematical harmony with his individual karma. His horoscope is a challenging portrait, revealing his unalterable past and its probable future results. But the natal chart can be rightly interpreted only by men of intuitive wisdom: these are few.

"The message boldly blazoned across the heavens at the moment of birth is not meant to emphasize fate—the result of past good and evil—but to arouse man's will to escape from his universal thralldom. What he has done, he can undo. None other than himself was the instigator of the causes of whatever effects are now prevalent in his life. He can overcome any limitation, because he created it by his own actions in the first place, and because he possesses spiritual resources that are not subject to planetary pressure.

"Superstitious awe of astrology makes one an automaton, slavishly dependent on mechanical guidance. The wise man defeats his planets—which is to say, his past—by transferring his allegiance from the creation to the Creator. The more he realizes his unity with Spirit, the less he can be dominated by matter. The soul is ever free; it is deathless because birthless. It cannot be regimented by stars.

"Man *is* a soul, and *has* a body. When he properly places his sense of identity, he leaves behind all compulsive patterns. So long as he remains confused in his ordinary state of spiritual amnesia, he will know the subtle fetters of environmental law.

"God is Harmony; the devotee who attunes himself will never perform any action amiss. His activities will be correctly and naturally timed to accord with astrological law. After deep prayer and meditation he is in touch with his divine consciousness; there is no greater power than that inward protection."

"Then, dear Master, why do you want me to wear an astrological bangle?" I ventured this question after a long silence; I had tried to assimilate Sri Yukteswar's noble exposition, which contained thoughts very new to me.

"It is only when a traveler has reached his goal that he is justified in discarding his maps. During the journey, he takes advantage of any convenient shortcut. The ancient rishis discovered many ways to curtail the period of man's exile in delusion. There are certain mechanical features in the law of karma that can be skillfully adjusted by the fingers of wisdom.

"All human ills arise from some transgression of universal law. The scriptures point out that man must satisfy the laws of nature, while not discrediting the divine omnipotence. He should say: 'Lord, I trust in Thee, and know Thou canst help me, but I too will do my best to undo any wrong I have done.' By a number of means—by prayer, by will power, by yoga meditation, by consultation with saints, by use of astrological bangles—the adverse effects of past wrongs can be minimized or nullified.

"Just as a house may be fitted with a copper rod to absorb the shock of lightning, so the bodily temple can be protected in certain ways.

"Electrical and magnetic radiations are ceaselessly circulating in the universe; they affect man's body for good and ill. Ages ago our rishis pondered the problem of combating the adverse effects of subtle cosmic influences. The sages discovered that pure metals emit an astral light which is powerfully counteractive to negative pulls of the planets. Certain plant combinations were also found to be helpful. Most effective of all are faultless jewels of not less than two carats.

"The practical preventive uses of astrology have seldom been seriously studied outside of India. One little-known fact is that the proper jewels, metals, and plant preparations are valueless unless the required weight is secured and unless the remedial agent is worn next to the skin."

"Sir, of course I shall take your advice and get a bangle. I am intrigued at the thought of outwitting a planet!"

"For general purposes I counsel the use of an armlet made of gold, silver, and copper. But for a specific purpose I want you to get one of silver and lead." Sri Yukteswar added careful directions.

"Guruji, what 'specific purpose' do you mean?"

"The stars are about to take an 'unfriendly' interest in you, Mukunda. Fear not; you shall be protected. In about a month your liver will cause you much trouble. The illness is scheduled to last for six months, but your use of an astrological armlet will shorten the period to twenty-four days."

SRI YUKTESWAR AND YOGANANDAJI, CALCUTTA, 1935

"Because of my guru's unspectacular guise, only a few of his contemporaries recognized him as a superman," Sri Yogananda said. "Though born a mortal like all others, Sri Yukteswar achieved identity with the Ruler of time and space. Master found no insuperable obstacle to the mergence of human and Divine. No such barrier exists, I came to understand, save in man's spiritual unadventurousness."

SRI YUKTESWAR MEMORIAL TEMPLE
In garden of his Puri ashram (see page 350)

(*Left*) Swami Krishnananda, at the 1936 *Kumbha Mela* in Allahabad, with his tame vegetarian lioness that utters *Aum* in a deep, attractive growl (see page 344).
(*Right*) Second-floor dining balcony of Sri Yukteswar's hermitage at Serampore, 1935. Sri Yogananda (*center*) is seated near his guru (*standing, right*).

I sought out a jeweler the next day, and was soon wearing the bangle. My health was excellent; Master's prediction slipped from my mind. He left Serampore to visit Banaras. Thirty days after our conversation, I felt a sudden pain in the region of my liver. The following weeks were a nightmare of excruciating pain. Reluctant to disturb my guru, I thought I would bravely endure my trial alone.

But twenty-three days of torture weakened my resolution; I entrained for Banaras. There Sri Yukteswar greeted me with unusual warmth, but gave me no opportunity to tell him my woes in private. Many devotees visited Master that day, just for a *darshan.**
Ill and neglected, I sat in a corner. It was not until after the evening meal that all guests had departed. My guru summoned me to the octagonal balcony of the house.

"You must have come about your liver disorder." Sri Yukteswar's gaze was averted; he walked to and fro, occasionally intercepting the moonlight. "Let me see, you have been ailing for twenty-four days, haven't you?"

"Yes, sir."

"Please do the stomach exercise I taught you."

"If you knew the extent of my suffering, Master, you would not ask me to exercise." Nevertheless I made a feeble attempt to obey him.

"You say you have pain; I say you have none. How can such contradictions exist?" My guru looked at me inquiringly.

I was dazed and then overcome with joyful relief. No longer could I feel the continuous torment that had kept me nearly sleepless for weeks; at Sri Yukteswar's words the agony vanished as though it had never been.

I started to kneel at his feet in gratitude, but he quickly prevented me.

"Don't be childish. Get up and enjoy the beauty of the moon over the Ganges." But Master's eyes were twinkling happily as I stood in silence beside him. I understood by his attitude that he wanted me to feel that not he, but God, had been the Healer.

I wear even now the heavy silver and lead bangle, a memento of that day—long past, ever cherished—when I found anew that I was living with a personage indeed superhuman. On later occasions, when I brought my friends to Sri Yukteswar for healing, he invariably recommended jewels or the bangle,† extolling their use as an act of astrological wisdom.

* The blessing that flows from the mere sight of a saint.
† See page 206 n.

I had been prejudiced against astrology from my childhood, partly because I observed that many people are sequaciously attached to it, and partly because of a prediction made by our family astrologer: "You will marry three times, being twice a widower." I brooded over the matter, feeling like a goat awaiting sacrifice before the temple of triple matrimony.

"You may as well be resigned to your fate," my brother Ananta had remarked. "Your written horoscope has correctly stated that you would fly from home toward the Himalayas during your early years, but would be forcibly returned. The forecast of your marriages is also bound to be true."

A clear intuition came to me one night that the prophecy was wholly false. I set fire to the horoscope scroll, placing the ashes in a paper bag on which I wrote: "Seeds of past karma cannot germinate if they are roasted in the fires of divine wisdom." I put the bag in a conspicuous spot; Ananta immediately read my defiant comment.

"You cannot destroy truth as easily as you have burnt this paper scroll." My brother laughed scornfully.

It is a fact that on three occasions before I reached manhood, my family tried to arrange my betrothal. Each time I refused to fall in with the plans,* knowing that my love for God was more overwhelming than any astrological persuasion from the past.

"The deeper the Self-realization of a man, the more he influences the whole universe by his subtle spiritual vibrations, and the less he himself is affected by the phenomenal flux." These words of Master's often returned inspiringly to my mind.

Occasionally I told astrologers to select my worst periods, according to planetary indications, and I would still accomplish whatever task I set myself. It is true that my success at such times has been preceded by extraordinary difficulties. But my conviction has always been justified: faith in divine protection, and right use of man's God-given will, are forces more formidable than are influences flowing from the heavens.

The starry inscription at one's birth, I came to understand, is not that man is a puppet of his past. Its message is rather a prod to pride; the very heavens seek to arouse man's determination to be free from every limitation. God created each man as a soul, dowered with

---

* One of the girls whom my family selected as a possible bride for me afterward married my cousin, Prabhas Chandra Ghosh. (See photo opposite page 113.) [Sri Ghosh was vice-president of Yogoda Satsanga Society of India (see pages 325–27) from 1936 until his death in 1975.]

individuality, hence essential to the universal structure, whether in the temporary role of pillar or parasite. His freedom is final and immediate, if he so wills; it depends not on outer but inner victories.

Sri Yukteswar discovered the mathematical application of a 24,000-year equinoctial cycle to our present age.* The cycle is divided into an Ascending Arc and a Descending Arc, each of 12,000 years. Within each Arc fall four *Yugas* or Ages, called *Kali, Dwapara, Treta,* and *Satya,* corresponding to the Greek ideas of Iron, Bronze, Silver, and Golden Ages.

My guru determined by various calculations that the last *Kali Yuga* or Iron Age, of the Ascending Arc, started about A.D. 500. The Iron Age, 1200 years in duration, is a span of materialism; it ended about A.D. 1700. That year ushered in *Dwapara Yuga,* a 2400-year period of electrical and atomic-energy developments: the age of telegraphy, radio, airplanes, and other space-annihilators.

The 3600-year period of *Treta Yuga* will start in A.D. 4100; the age will be marked by common knowledge of telepathic communications and other time-annihilators. During the 4800 years of *Satya Yuga,* final age in an Ascending Arc, the intelligence of man will be highly developed; he will work in harmony with the divine plan.

A Descending Arc of 12,000 years, starting with a Descending Golden Age of 4800 years, then begins for the world (in A.D. 12,500); man gradually sinks into ignorance. These cycles are the eternal rounds of *maya,* the contrasts and relativities of the phenomenal universe.† Men, one by one, escape from creation's prison of duality as they awaken to consciousness of their inseverable divine unity with the Creator.

---

* These cycles are expounded in the first part of Sri Yukteswar's book, *The Holy Science* (published by Self-Realization Fellowship).

† The Hindu scriptures place the present world-age as occurring within the *Kali Yuga* of a much longer universal cycle than the simple 24,000-year equinoctial cycle with which Sri Yukteswar was concerned. The universal cycle of the scriptures is 4,300,560,000 years in extent, and measures out a Day of Creation. This vast figure is based on the relationship between the length of the solar year and a multiple of pi (3.1416, the ratio of the circumference to the diameter of a circle).

The life span for a whole universe, according to the ancient seers, is 314,-159,000,000,000 solar years, or "One Age of Brahma."

The Hindu scriptures declare that an earth such as ours is dissolved for one of two reasons: the inhabitants as a whole become either completely good or completely evil. The world mind thus generates a power that releases the captive atoms held together as an earth.

Dire pronouncements are occasionally published regarding an imminent "end of the world." Planetary cycles, however, proceed according to an orderly divine plan. No earthly dissolution is in sight; many ascending and descending equinoctial cycles are yet in store for our planet in its present form.

Master enlarged my understanding not only of astrology but of the world's scriptures. Placing the holy texts on the spotless table of his mind, he was able to dissect them with the scalpel of intuitive reasoning, and to separate errors and interpolations of scholars from the truths as originally expressed by the prophets.

"Fix one's vision on the end of the nose." This inaccurate interpretation of a Bhagavad Gita stanza,* widely accepted by Eastern pundits and Western translators, used to arouse Master's droll criticism.

"The path of a yogi is singular enough as it is," he remarked. "Why counsel him that he must also make himself cross-eyed? The true meaning of *nasikagram* is 'origin of the nose,' not 'end of the nose.' The nose originates at the point between the eyebrows, the seat of spiritual vision."†

One *Sankhya‡* aphorism reads: *Ishwar asiddhe*§ ("A Lord of Creation cannot be deduced" or "God is not proved"). Chiefly on the basis of this sentence, most scholars call the whole philosophy atheistical.

"The verse is not atheistical," Sri Yukteswar explained. "It merely signifies that to the unenlightened man, dependent on his senses for all final judgments, proof of God must remain unknown and therefore nonexistent. True *Sankhya* followers, with unshakable insight born of meditation, understand that the Lord is both existent and knowable."

Master expounded the Christian Bible with a beautiful clarity. It was from my Hindu guru, unknown to the roll call of Christian membership, that I learned to perceive the deathless essence of the Bible, and to understand the truth in Christ's assertion—surely the most thrillingly intransigent ever uttered: "Heaven and earth shall pass away, but my words shall not pass away."¶

The great masters of India mold their lives by the same godly ideals that animated Jesus; these men are his proclaimed kin: "Whosoever shall do the will of my Father which is in heaven, the

---

* Chapter VI:13.

† "The light of the body is the eye: therefore when thine eye is single, thy whole body also is full of light; but when thine eye is evil, thy body also is full of darkness. Take heed therefore that the light which is in thee be not darkness."—Luke 11:34–35.

‡ One of the six systems of Hindu philosophy. *Sankhya* teaches final emancipation through knowledge of twenty-five principles, starting with *prakriti* or nature and ending with *purusha* or soul.

§ *Sankhya Aphorisms*, 1:92.

¶ Matthew 24:35.

same is my brother, and sister, and mother."* "If ye continue in my word," Christ pointed out, "then are ye my disciples indeed; and ye shall know the truth, and the truth shall make you free."† Freemen all, lords of themselves, the Yogi-Christs of India are part of the immortal fraternity: those that attain a liberating knowledge of the One Father.

"The Adam and Eve story is incomprehensible to me!" I observed with considerable heat one day in my early struggles with the allegory. "Why did God punish not only the guilty pair, but also the innocent unborn generations?"

Master was amused, more by my vehemence than by my ignorance. "Genesis is deeply symbolic, and cannot be grasped by a literal interpretation," he explained. "Its 'tree of life' is the human body. The spinal cord is like an upturned tree, with man's hair as its roots, and afferent and efferent nerves as branches. The tree of the nervous system bears many enjoyable fruits, or sensations of sight, sound, smell, taste, and touch. In these, man may rightfully indulge; but he was forbidden the experience of sex, the 'apple' at the center of the body ('in the midst of the garden').‡

"The 'serpent' represents the coiled-up spinal energy that stimulates the sex nerves. 'Adam' is reason, and 'Eve' is feeling. When the emotion or Eve-consciousness in any human being is overpowered by the sex impulse, his reason or Adam also succumbs.§

"God created the human species by materializing the bodies of man and woman through the force of His will; He endowed the new species with the power to create children in a similar 'immaculate' or divine manner.¶ Because His manifestation in the individualized soul had hitherto been limited to animals, instinct-bound and lacking the potentialities of full reason, God made the first human bodies, symbolically called Adam and Eve. To these, for advantageous

---

* Matthew 12:50.

† John 8:31–32. St. John testified: "But as many as received him, to them gave he power to become the sons of God, even to them that believe on his name (even to them that are established in the omnipresent Christ Consciousness)."—John 1:12.

‡ "We may eat of the fruit of the trees of the garden: but of the fruit of the tree which is in the midst of the garden, God hath said, Ye shall not eat of it, neither shall ye touch it, lest ye die."—Genesis 3:2–3.

§ "The woman whom thou gavest to be with me, she gave me of the tree, and I did eat. The woman said, The serpent beguiled me, and I did eat."—Gen. 3:12–13.

¶ "So God created man in his own image, in the image of God created he him; male and female created he them. And God blessed them, and God said unto them, Be fruitful and multiply, and replenish the earth, and subdue it."—Gen. 1:27–28.

upward evolution, He transferred the souls or divine essence of two animals.* In Adam or man, reason predominated; in Eve or woman, feeling was ascendant. Thus was expressed the duality or polarity that underlies the phenomenal worlds. Reason and feeling remain in a heaven of cooperative joy so long as the human mind is not tricked by the serpentine energy of animal propensities.

"The human body was therefore not solely a result of evolution from beasts, but was produced through an act of special creation by God. The animal forms were too crude to express full divinity; man was uniquely given the potentially omniscient 'thousand-petaled lotus' in the brain, as well as acutely awakened occult centers in the spine.

"God, or the Divine Consciousness present within the first created pair, counseled them to enjoy all human sensibilities, with one exception: sex sensations.† These were banned, lest humanity enmesh itself in the inferior animal method of propagation. The warning not to revive subconsciously present bestial memories was unheeded. Resuming the way of brute procreation, Adam and Eve fell from the state of heavenly joy natural to the original perfect man. When 'they knew that they were naked,' their consciousness of immortality was lost, even as God had warned them; they had placed themselves under the physical law by which bodily birth must be followed by bodily death.

"The knowledge of 'good and evil,' promised Eve by the 'serpent,' refers to the dualistic and oppositional experiences that mortals under *maya* must undergo. Falling into delusion through misuse of his feeling and reason, or Eve- and Adam-consciousness, man relinquishes his right to enter the heavenly garden of divine self-sufficiency.‡ The personal responsibility of every human being is to restore his 'parents' or dual nature to a unified harmony or Eden."

As Sri Yukteswar ended his discourse, I glanced with new respect at the pages of Genesis.

* "And the Lord God formed man of the dust of the ground, and breathed into his nostrils the breath of life; and man became a living soul."—Gen. 2:7.

† "Now the serpent (sex force) was more subtil than any beast of the field" (any other sense of the body).—Gen. 3:1.

‡ "And the Lord God planted a garden eastward in Eden; and there he put the man whom he had formed."—Gen. 2:8. "Therefore the Lord God sent him forth from the garden of Eden, to till the ground from whence he was taken."—Gen. 3:23. The divine man first made by God had his consciousness centered in the omnipotent single eye in the forehead (eastward). The all-creative powers of his will, focused at that spot, were lost to man when he began to "till the ground" of his physical nature.

"Dear Master," I said, "for the first time I feel a proper-filial obligation toward Adam and Eve!"*

---

* The "Adam and Eve" story of the Hindus is recounted in the hoary *purana, Srimad Bhagavata.* The first man and woman (beings in physical form) are called Swayambhuva Manu ("man born of the Creator") and his wife Shatarupa ("having a hundred images or forms"). Their five children intermarried with *Prajapatis* (perfect beings who could assume corporeal form); from these first divine families was born the human race.

Never in East or West have I heard anyone else expound the Christian scriptures with so deep a spiritual insight as Sri Yukteswar's. "Theologians have misinterpreted Christ's words," Master said, "in such passages as 'I am the way, the truth, and the life: no man cometh unto the Father, but by me' (John 14:6). Jesus meant, never that he was the sole Son of God, but that no man can attain the unqualified Absolute, the transcendent Father *beyond* creation, until he has first manifested the 'Son' or activating Christ Consciousness *within* creation. Jesus, who had achieved entire oneness with that Christ Consciousness, identified himself with it inasmuch as his own ego had long since been dissolved." (See page 128 n.)

When Paul wrote: "God...created all things by Jesus Christ" (Ephesians 3:9), and when Jesus said: "Before Abraham was, I am" (John 8:58), the sheer essence of the words is impersonality.

A form of spiritual cowardice leads many worldly people to believe comfortably that only one man was the Son of God. "Christ was uniquely created," they reason, "so how can I, a mere mortal, emulate Him?" But all men have been divinely created, and must someday obey Christ's command: "Be ye therefore perfect, even as your Father which is in heaven is perfect" (Matt. 5:48). "Behold, what manner of love the Father hath bestowed upon us, that we should be called the sons of God" (I John 3:1).

Understanding of the law of karma and of its corollary, reincarnation (see pp. 227 n., 281–82, and chapter 43), is displayed in numerous Biblical passages; e.g., "Whoso sheddeth man's blood, by man shall his blood be shed" (Gen. 9:6). If every murderer must himself be killed "by man," the reactive process obviously requires, in many cases, more than one lifetime. The contemporary police are just not quick enough!

The early Christian church accepted the doctrine of reincarnation, which was expounded by the Gnostics and by numerous church fathers, including Clement of Alexandria, the celebrated Origen (both 3rd century), and St. Jerome (5th century). The doctrine was first declared a heresy in A.D. 553 by the Second Council of Constantinople. At that time many Christians thought the doctrine of reincarnation afforded man too ample a stage of time and space to encourage him to strive for immediate salvation. But truths suppressed lead disconcertingly to a host of errors. The millions have not utilized their "one lifetime" to seek God, but to enjoy this world—so uniquely won, and so shortly to be forever lost! The truth is that man reincarnates on earth until he has consciously regained his status as a son of God.

CHAPTER 17

Sasi and the Three Sapphires

"Because you and my son think so highly of Swami Sri Yukteswar, I will take a look at him." The tone of voice used by Dr. Narayan Chunder Roy implied that he was humoring the whim of half-wits. I concealed my indignation, in the best tradition of the proselyter.

My companion, a veterinary surgeon, was a confirmed agnostic. His young son Santosh had implored me to take an interest in his father. So far, my invaluable aid had been a bit on the invisible side.

Dr. Roy accompanied me the following day to the Serampore hermitage. After Master had granted him a brief interview, marked for the most part by stoic silence on both sides, the visitor brusquely departed.

"Why bring a dead man to the ashram?" Sri Yukteswar looked at me inquiringly as soon as the door had closed on the Calcutta skeptic.

"Sir! The doctor is very much alive!"

"But in a short time he will be dead."

I was shocked. "Sir, this will be a terrible blow to his son. Santosh yet hopes for time to change his father's materialistic views. I beseech you, Master, to help the man."

"Very well—for your sake." My guru's face was impassive. "The proud horse doctor is far gone in diabetes, although he does not know it. In fifteen days he will take to his bed. The physicians will give him up for lost; his natural time to leave this earth is six weeks from today. Owing to your intercession, however, on that date he will recover. But there is one condition: you must get him to wear an astrological bangle. He will doubtless object as violently as one of his horses before an operation." Master chuckled.

After a silence, during which I wondered how Santosh and I might best employ the arts of cajolery on the doctor, Sri Yukteswar made further disclosures.

"As soon as the man gets well, advise him not to eat meat. He will not heed this counsel, however; and in six months, just as he is feeling at his best, he will drop dead." My guru added, "The six-month extension of life is granted him only because of your plea."

The following day I suggested to Santosh that he order an armlet at the jeweler's. It was ready in a week, but Dr. Roy refused to put it on.

"I am in the best of health. You will never impress me with these astrological superstitions." The doctor glanced at me belligerently.

I recalled with amusement that Master had justifiably compared the man to a balky horse. Another seven days passed; the doctor, suddenly ill, meekly consented to wear the bangle. Two weeks later the physician in attendance told me that his patient's case was hopeless. He supplied harrowing details of the ravages inflicted by diabetes.

I shook my head. "My guru has said that, after a sickness lasting one month, Dr. Roy will be well."

The physician stared at me incredulously. But he sought me out a fortnight later, with an apologetic air.

"Dr. Roy has made a complete recovery!" he exclaimed. "It is the most amazing case in my experience. Never before have I seen a dying man show such an inexplicable comeback. Your guru must indeed be a healing prophet!"

After one interview with Dr. Roy, during which I repeated Sri Yukteswar's advice about a meatless diet, I did not see the man again for six months. He stopped for a chat one evening as I sat on the piazza of my family home.

"Tell your teacher that by eating meat frequently, I have wholly regained my strength. His unscientific ideas on diet have not influenced me." It was true that Dr. Roy looked a picture of health.

But the next day Santosh came running to me from his home on the next block. "This morning Father dropped dead!"

This case was one of my strangest experiences with Master. He healed the rebellious veterinary surgeon in spite of his disbelief, and extended the man's natural term on earth by six months, just because of my earnest supplication. Sri Yukteswar was boundless in his kindness when responding to an urgent prayer of a devotee.

It was my proudest privilege to bring college friends to meet my guru. Many of them would lay aside—at least in the ashram!—their fashionable academic cloak of religious skepticism.

One of my friends, Sasi, spent a number of happy weekends in Serampore. Master became immensely fond of the boy, and lamented that his private life was wild and disorderly.

"Sasi, unless you reform, one year hence you will be dangerously ill." Sri Yukteswar gazed at my friend with affectionate exasperation.

"Mukunda is the witness; don't say later that I didn't warn you."

Sasi laughed. "Master, I will leave it to you to interest a sweet charity of cosmos in my own sad case! My spirit is willing but my will is weak. You are my only savior on earth; I believe in nothing else."

"At least you should wear a two-carat blue sapphire. It will help you."

"I can't afford one. Anyhow, dear Guruji, if trouble comes, I fully believe you will protect me."

"In a year you will bring three sapphires," Sri Yukteswar replied. "They will be of no use then."

Variations on this conversation took place regularly. "I can't reform!" Sasi would say in comical despair. "And my trust in you, Master, is more precious to me than any stone!"

A year passed. One day I was visiting my guru at the Calcutta home of his disciple, Naren Babu. About ten o'clock in the morning, as Sri Yukteswar and I were sitting in the second-floor parlor, I heard the front door open. Master straightened stiffly.

"It is that Sasi," he remarked gravely. "The year is now up; both his lungs are gone. He has ignored my counsel; tell him I don't want to see him."

Half stunned by Sri Yukteswar's sternness, I raced down the stairway. Sasi was ascending.

"O Mukunda! I do hope Master is here; I had a hunch he might be."

"Yes, but he doesn't wish to be disturbed."

Sasi burst into tears and brushed past me. He threw himself at Sri Yukteswar's feet, placing there three beautiful sapphires.

"Omniscient Guru, the doctors say I have pulmonary tuberculosis. They give me only three months to live! I humbly implore your aid; I know you can heal me!"

"Isn't it a bit late now to be worrying over your life? Depart with your jewels; their time of usefulness is past." Master then sat sphinxlike in an unrelenting silence, punctuated by the boy's sobs for mercy.

An intuitive conviction came to me that Sri Yukteswar was merely testing the depth of Sasi's faith in the divine healing power. I was not surprised a tense hour later when Master turned a sympathetic gaze on my prostrate friend.

"Get up, Sasi; what a commotion you make in another person's house! Return the sapphires to the jeweler's; they are an unnecessary expense now. But get an astrological bangle and wear it. Fear not; in a few weeks you shall be well."

Sasi's smile illumined his tear-marred face like sudden sun over a sodden landscape. "Beloved Guru, shall I take the medicines prescribed by the doctors?"

"Just as you wish — drink them or discard them; it does not matter. It is as impossible for you to die of tuberculosis as it would be for the sun and moon to interchange their positions." Sri Yukteswar added abruptly, "Go now, before I change my mind!"

With an agitated bow, my friend hastily departed. I visited him several times during the next few weeks, and was aghast to find his condition increasingly worse.

"Sasi cannot last through the night." These words from his physician, and the spectacle of my friend, now reduced almost to a skeleton, sent me posthaste to Serampore. My guru listened coldly to my tearful report.

"Why do you come here to bother me? You have already heard me assure Sasi of his recovery."

I bowed before him in great awe, and retreated to the door. Sri Yukteswar said no parting word, but sank into silence, his unwinking eyes half open, their vision fled to another world.

I returned at once to Sasi's home in Calcutta. With astonishment I found my friend sitting up, drinking milk.

"O Mukunda! What a miracle! Four hours ago I felt Master's presence in the room; my terrible symptoms immediately disappeared. I feel that through his grace I am entirely well."

In a few weeks Sasi was stouter and in better health than ever before.* But his reaction to his healing was tinged with ingratitude: he seldom visited Sri Yukteswar again! My friend told me one day that he so deeply regretted his previous mode of life that he was ashamed to face Master.

I could only conclude that Sasi's illness had had the contrasting effect of stiffening his will and impairing his manners.

The first two years of my course at Scottish Church College were drawing to a close. My classroom attendance had been very spasmodic; what little studying I did was only to keep peace with my family. My two private tutors came regularly to my house; I was regularly absent: I discern at least this one regularity in my scholastic career!

In India two successful years of college bring an Intermediate Arts diploma; the student may then look forward to another two years and his A.B. degree.

---

* In 1936 I heard from a friend that Sasi was still in excellent health.

The Intermediate Arts final examinations loomed ominously ahead. I fled to Puri, where my guru was spending a few weeks. Vaguely hoping that he would say I need not appear at the finals, I told him of my unpreparedness.

Sri Yukteswar smiled consolingly. "You have wholeheartedly pursued your spiritual duties, and could not help neglecting your college work. Apply yourself diligently to your books for the next week; you shall get through your ordeal without failure."

I returned to Calcutta, firmly suppressing the reasonable doubts that occasionally assailed me. Surveying the mountain of books on my table, I felt like a traveler lost in a wilderness.

A long period of meditation brought me a labor-saving inspiration. Opening each book at random, I studied only those pages that lay thus exposed. After I had pursued this course during eighteen hours a day for one week, I considered myself an expert on the art of cramming.

The following days in the examination halls were a justification of my seemingly haphazard procedure. I passed all the tests, though by a hairbreadth. The congratulations of my friends and family were ludicrously mixed with ejaculations betraying their astonishment.

On his return from Puri, Sri Yukteswar gave me a pleasant surprise.

"Your Calcutta studies are now over," he said. "I shall see that you pursue your last two years of university work right here in Serampore."

I was puzzled. "Sir, there is no Bachelor of Arts course in this town." Serampore College, the sole institution of higher learning, offered only a two-year course in Intermediate Arts.

Master smiled mischievously. "I am too old to go about collecting donations to establish an A.B. college for you. I guess I shall have to arrange the matter through someone else."

Two months later Professor Howells, president of Serampore College, publicly announced that he had succeeded in raising sufficient funds to offer a four-year course. Serampore College became an affiliated branch of Calcutta University. I was one of the first students to enroll in Serampore as an A.B. candidate.

"Guruji, how kind you are to me! I have been longing to leave Calcutta and be near you every day in Serampore. Professor Howells does not dream how much he owes to your silent help!"

Sri Yukteswar gazed at me with mock severity. "Now you won't have to spend so many hours on trains; what a lot of free time for your studies! Perhaps you will become less of a last-minute crammer and more of a scholar."

But somehow his tone lacked conviction.*

---

* Sri Yukteswar, like many another sage, grieved at the materialistic trend of modern education. Few schools expound the spiritual laws for happiness or teach that wisdom consists in guiding one's life in the "fear of God," that is, in awe of one's Maker.

Young people, who today hear in high schools and colleges that man is merely a "higher animal," often become atheists. They do not attempt any soul exploration or consider themselves, in their essential nature, to be "images of God." Emerson observed: "That only which we have within, can we see without. If we meet no gods, it is because we harbor none." He who imagines his animal nature to be his only reality is cut off from divine aspirations.

An educational system that does not present Spirit as the central Fact of man's existence is offering *avidya*, false knowledge. "Thou sayest, I am rich, and increased with goods, and have need of nothing; and knowest not that thou art wretched, and miserable, and poor, and blind, and naked" (Revelation 3:17).

The education of youth in ancient India was ideal. At the age of nine, the pupil was received "as a son" in a *gurukula* (guru's family home as a seat of learning). "The modern boy spends [annually] an eighth of his time at school; the Indian spent his whole time there," Professor S. V. Venkateswara writes in *Indian Culture Through the Ages* (Vol. I; Longmans, Green & Co.). "There was a healthy feeling of solidarity and responsibility, and ample opportunity for the exercise of self-reliance and individuality. There was a high standard of culture, self-imposed discipline, and stern regard for duty, selfless action, and sacrifice, combined with self-respect and reverence for others; a high standard of academic dignity, and a sense of...the nobility and the great purpose of human life."

CHAPTER 18

A Mohammedan Wonder-Worker

"Years ago, right in this very room you now occupy, a Mohammedan wonder-worker performed four miracles before me!"

Sri Yukteswar made this statement during his first visit to my new quarters. Immediately after entering Serampore College, I had taken a room in a nearby boardinghouse, called Panthi.* It was an old-fashioned brick mansion, fronting the Ganges.

"Master, what a coincidence! Are these newly decorated walls really ancient with memories?" I looked around my simply furnished room with awakened interest.

"It is a long story." My guru smiled reminiscently. "The name of the *fakir*† was Afzal Khan. He had acquired his extraordinary powers through a chance encounter with a Hindu yogi.

"'Son, I am thirsty; fetch me some water.' A dust-covered *sannyasi* made this request of Afzal one day during his early boyhood in a small village of eastern Bengal.

"'Master, I am a Mohammedan. How could you, a Hindu, accept a drink from my hands?'

"'Your truthfulness pleases me, my child. I do not observe the ostracizing rules of ungodly sectarianism. Go, bring me water quickly.'

"Afzal's reverent obedience was rewarded by a loving glance from the yogi.

"'You possess good karma from former lives,' he observed solemnly. 'I am going to teach you a certain yoga method that will give you command over one of the invisible realms. The great powers that will be yours should be exercised for worthy ends; never employ them selfishly! I perceive, alas! that you have brought over from the past some seeds of destructive tendencies. Do not allow them to sprout by watering them with fresh evil actions. The complexity of your previous karma is such that you must use

---

* Residence for students; from *pantha*, wanderer, seeker of knowledge.

† A Moslem yogi; from the Arabic *faqir*, poor; originally applied to dervishes under a vow of poverty.

this life to reconcile your yogic accomplishments with the highest humanitarian goals.'

"After instructing the amazed boy in a complicated technique, the master vanished.

"Afzal faithfully followed his yoga exercise for twenty years. His miraculous feats began to attract widespread attention. It seems that he was always accompanied by a disembodied spirit whom he called 'Hazrat.' This invisible entity was able to fulfill the *fakir's* slightest wish.

"Ignoring his master's warning, Afzal began to misuse his powers. Whatever object he took up and then replaced would soon disappear without a trace. This disconcerting eventuality usually made the Mohammedan an objectionable guest!

"He visited large jewelry stores in Calcutta from time to time, representing himself as a possible purchaser. Any jewel he handled would vanish shortly after he had left the shop.

"Afzal was often surrounded by several hundred students, attracted by the hope of learning his secrets. The *fakir* occasionally invited them to travel with him. At the railway station he would manage to touch a roll of tickets. These he would push toward the clerk, remarking: 'I have changed my mind, and won't buy them now.' But when he boarded the train with his retinue, Afzal would be in possession of the required tickets. [*]

"These exploits created an indignant uproar; Bengali jewelers and ticket-sellers were succumbing to nervous breakdowns! The police who sought to arrest Afzal found themselves helpless; the *fakir* could remove incriminating evidence merely by saying: 'Hazrat, take this away.'"

Sri Yukteswar rose from his seat and walked to the balcony of my room, which overlooked the Ganges. I followed him, eager to hear more of the baffling Mohammedan Raffles.

"This Panthi house formerly belonged to a friend of mine. He became acquainted with Afzal and asked him here. My friend also invited about twenty neighbors, including myself. I was only a youth then, and felt a lively curiosity about the notorious *fakir*." Master laughed. "I took the precaution of not wearing anything valuable! Afzal looked me over inquisitively, then remarked:

"'You have powerful hands. Go downstairs to the garden; get a smooth stone and write your name on it with chalk; then throw

---

[*] My father later told me that his company, the Bengal-Nagpur Railway, had been one of the firms victimized by Afzal Khan.

the stone as far as possible into the Ganges.'

"I obeyed. As soon as the stone had vanished under distant waves, the Mohammedan addressed me again:

"'Fill a pot with Ganges water near the front of this house.'

"After I had returned with a vessel of water, the *fakir* cried, 'Hazrat, put the stone in the pot!'

"The stone appeared at once. I removed it from the vessel and found my signature as legible as when I had written it.

"Babu,* one of my friends in the room, was wearing a heavy antique gold watch and chain. The *fakir* examined them with ominous admiration. Soon they were missing!

"'Afzal, please return my prized heirloom!' Babu was nearly in tears.

"The Mohammedan was stoically silent for a while, then said, 'You have five hundred rupees in an iron safe. Bring them to me, and I will tell you where to locate your timepiece.'

"The distraught Babu left immediately for his home. He came back shortly and handed Afzal the required sum.

"'Go to the little bridge near your house,' the *fakir* instructed Babu. 'Call on Hazrat to give you the watch and chain.'

"Babu rushed away. On his return, he was wearing a smile of relief and no jewelry whatever.

"'When I commanded Hazrat as directed,' he announced, 'my watch came tumbling down the air into my right hand! You may be sure I locked the heirloom in my safe before rejoining the group here!'

"Babu's friends, witnesses of the comicotragedy of the ransom for a watch, were staring with resentment at Afzal. He now spoke placatingly.

"'Please name any drink you want; Hazrat will produce it.'

"A number asked for milk, others for fruit juices. I was not too much shocked when the unnerved Babu requested whisky! The Mohammedan gave an order; the obliging Hazrat sent sealed containers sailing down and thudding to the floor. Each man found his desired beverage.

"The promise of the fourth spectacular feat of the day was doubtless gratifying to our host: Afzal offered to supply an instantaneous lunch!

"'Let us order the most expensive dishes,' Babu suggested

---

* I do not recall the name of Sri Yukteswar's friend, and must refer to him simply as "Babu" (Mister).

gloomily. 'I want an elaborate meal for my five hundred rupees. Everything should be served on gold plates!'

"As soon as each man had expressed his preferences, the *fakir* addressed himself to the inexhaustible Hazrat. A great rattle ensued; gold platters filled with intricately prepared curries, hot *luchis,* and many out-of-season fruits landed from nowhere at our feet. All the food was delicious. After feasting for an hour, we started to leave the room. A tremendous noise, as though dishes were being piled up, caused us to turn around. Lo! there was no sign of the glittering plates or the remnants of the meal."

"Guruji," I interrupted, "if Afzal could easily secure such things as gold dishes, why did he covet the property of others?"

"The *fakir* was not highly developed spiritually," Sri Yukteswar explained. "His mastery of a certain yoga technique gave him access to an astral plane where any desire is immediately materialized. Through the agency of an astral being, Hazrat, the Mohammedan could summon the atoms of any object from etheric energy by an act of powerful will. But such astrally produced objects are structurally evanescent; they cannot be long retained.* Afzal still yearned for worldly wealth, which, though more hardly earned, has a more dependable durability."

I laughed. "It, too, sometimes vanishes unaccountably!"

"Afzal was not a man of God-realization," Master went on. "Miracles of a permanent and beneficial nature are performed by true saints because they have attuned themselves to the omnipotent Creator. Afzal was merely an ordinary man with an extraordinary power of penetrating a subtle realm not usually entered by mortals until death."

"I understand now, Guruji. The afterworld appears to have some charming features."

Master agreed. "I never saw Afzal after that day, but a few years later Babu came to my home to show me a newspaper account of the Mohammedan's public confession. From it I learned the facts I have just told you about Afzal's early initiation from a Hindu guru."

The gist of the latter part of the published document, as recalled by Sri Yukteswar, was as follows: "I, Afzal Khan, am writing these words as an act of penance and as a warning to those who seek the possession of miraculous powers. For years I have been misusing the wondrous abilities imparted to me through the grace

* Just as my silver amulet, an astrally produced object, finally vanished from this earth. (The astral world is described in chapter 43.)

of God and my master. I became drunk with egotism, feeling that I was beyond the ordinary laws of morality. My day of reckoning finally arrived.

"Recently I met an old man on a road outside Calcutta. He limped along painfully, carrying a shining object that looked like gold. I addressed him with greed in my heart.

"'I am Afzal Khan, the great *fakir*. What have you there?'

"'This ball of gold is my sole material wealth; it can be of no interest to a *fakir*. I implore you, sir, to heal my limp.'

"I touched the ball and walked away without reply. The old man hobbled after me. He soon raised an outcry: 'My gold is gone!'

"As I paid no attention, he suddenly spoke in a stentorian voice that issued oddly from his frail body:

"'Do you not recognize me?'

"I stood speechless, aghast at the belated discovery that this unimpressive old cripple was none other than the great saint who, long, long ago, had initiated me into yoga. He straightened himself; his body instantly became strong and youthful.

"'So!' My guru's glance was fiery. 'I see with my own eyes that you use your powers, not to help suffering humanity; but to prey on it like a common thief! I withdraw your occult gifts; Hazrat is now freed from you. No longer shall you be a terror in Bengal!'

"I called on Hazrat in anguished tones; for the first time, he did not appear to my inner sight. But a dark veil suddenly lifted; I saw clearly the blasphemy of my life.

"'My guru, I thank you for coming to banish my long delusion.' I was sobbing at his feet. 'I promise to forsake my worldly ambitions. I will retire to the mountains for lonely meditation on God, hoping to atone for my evil past.'

"My master regarded me with silent compassion. 'I feel your sincerity,' he said finally. 'Because of your earlier years of strict obedience, and because of your present repentance, I will grant you one boon. Your other powers are now gone, but whenever food and clothing are needed, you may still call successfully on Hazrat to supply them. Devote yourself wholeheartedly to divine understanding in the mountain solitudes.'

"My guru then vanished; I was left to my tears and reflections. Farewell, world! I go to seek the forgiveness of the Cosmic Beloved."

CHAPTER 19

My Master, in Calcutta, Appears in Serampore

"I am often beset by atheistic doubts. Yet a torturing surmise sometimes haunts me: may not untapped soul possibilities exist? Is man not missing his real destiny if he fails to explore them?"

These remarks of Dijen Babu, my roommate at the Panthi boardinghouse, were called forth by my invitation that he meet my guru.

"Sri Yukteswarji will initiate you into *Kriya Yoga*," I replied. "It calms the dualistic turmoil by a divine inner certainty."

That evening Dijen accompanied me to the hermitage. In Master's presence my friend received such spiritual peace that he was soon a constant visitor.

The trivial preoccupations of daily life do not satisfy our deepest needs; for wisdom, too, man has native hunger. By Sri Yukteswar's words Dijen was inspired to try to discover within him a realer self than the shallow ego of a transient incarnation.

As Dijen and I were both pursuing the A.B. course at Serampore College, we got into the habit of walking together to the ashram as soon as classes were over. We would often see Sri Yukteswar standing on his second-floor balcony, welcoming our approach with a smile.

One afternoon Kanai, a young hermitage resident, met Dijen and me at the door with disappointing news.

"Master is not here; he was summoned to Calcutta by an urgent note."

The following day I received a postcard from my guru. "I shall leave Calcutta Wednesday morning," he had written. "You and Dijen meet the nine a.m. train at Serampore station."

About eight-thirty on Wednesday morning, a telepathic message from Sri Yukteswar flashed insistently to my mind: "I am delayed; don't meet the nine o'clock train."

I conveyed the latest instructions to Dijen, who was already dressed for departure.

"You and your intuition!" My friend's voice was edged in scorn. "I prefer to trust Master's written word."

I shrugged my shoulders and seated myself with quiet finality. Muttering angrily, Dijen made for the door and closed it noisily behind him.

As the room was rather dark, I moved nearer to a window overlooking the street. The scant sunlight suddenly increased to an intense brilliancy in which the iron-barred window completely vanished. Against this dazzling background appeared the clearly materialized figure of Sri Yukteswar!

Bewildered to the point of shock, I rose from my chair and knelt before him. With my customary gesture of respectful greeting at my guru's feet, I touched his shoes. These were a pair familiar to me, of orange-dyed canvas, soled with rope. His ocher swami cloth brushed against me; I distinctly felt not only the texture of his robe, but also the gritty surface of the shoes, and the pressure of his toes within them. Too much astounded to utter a word, I stood up and gazed at him questioningly.

"I was pleased that you got my telepathic message." Master's voice was calm, entirely normal. "I have now finished my business in Calcutta, and shall arrive in Serampore by the ten o'clock train."

As I still stared mutely, Sri Yukteswar went on, "This is not an apparition, but my flesh and blood form. I have been divinely commanded to give you this experience, rarely known on earth. Meet me at the station; you and Dijen will see me coming toward you, dressed as I am now. I shall be preceded by a fellow passenger—a little boy carrying a silver jug."

My guru placed both hands on my head, with a murmured blessing. As he concluded with the words, *"Tabe asi,"*[*] I heard a peculiar rumbling sound.[†] His body began to melt gradually within the piercing light. First his feet and legs vanished, then his torso and head, like a scroll being rolled up. To the very last, I could feel his fingers resting lightly on my hair. The effulgence faded; nothing remained before me but the barred window and a pale stream of sunlight.

* The Bengali "Good-bye"; literally, it is a hopeful paradox: "Then I come."
† The characteristic sound of dematerialization of bodily atoms.

I remained in a half-stupor, questioning whether I had not been the victim of a hallucination. A crestfallen Dijen soon entered the room.

"Master was not on the nine o'clock train or even the nine-thirty." My friend made his announcement with a slightly apologetic air.

"Come, I know he will arrive at ten o'clock." I took Dijen's hand and rushed him forcibly along with me, heedless of his protests. In about ten minutes we entered the station, where the train was already puffing to a halt.

"The whole train is filled with the light of Master's aura! He is there!" I exclaimed joyfully.

"You dream so?" Dijen laughed mockingly.

"Let us wait here." I told my friend details of the way in which our guru would approach us. As I finished my description, Sri Yukteswar came into view, wearing the same clothes I had seen a short time earlier. He walked slowly in the wake of a small lad bearing a silver jug.

For a moment a wave of cold fear passed through me, at the incredible strangeness of my experience. I felt the materialistic twentieth-century world slipping from me; was I back in the ancient days when Jesus appeared before Peter on the sea?

As Sri Yukteswar, a modern Yogi-Christ, neared the place where Dijen and I were standing speechless, Master smiled at my friend and remarked:

"I sent you a message too, but you were unable to grasp it."

Dijen was silent, but glared at me suspiciously. After we had escorted our guru to his hermitage, my friend and I proceeded toward Serampore College. Dijen halted in the street, indignation streaming from his every pore.

"So! Master sent me a message! Yet you concealed it! I demand an explanation!"

"Can I help it if your mental mirror oscillates with such restlessness that you cannot register our guru's instructions?" I retorted.

The anger vanished from Dijen's face. "I see what you mean," he said ruefully. "But please explain how you could know about the child with the jug."

By the time I had finished the story of Master's phenomenal appearance at the boardinghouse that morning, my friend and I had reached Serampore College.

"The account I have just heard of our guru's powers," Dijen said, "makes me feel that any university in the world is only a kindergarten."*

* "Such things have been revealed to me that now all I have written appears in my eyes as of no greater value than straw."

So spoke St. Thomas Aquinas, the "Prince of Scholastics," in answer to his secretary's anxious urgings that *Summa Theologiae* be completed. One day in 1273, during Mass in a Naples church, St. Thomas experienced a profound mystical insight. The glory of divine knowledge so overwhelmed him that henceforth he took no interest in intellectuality.

Cf. Socrates' words (in Plato's *Phaedrus*): "As for me, all I know is that I know nothing."

CHAPTER 20

We Do Not Visit Kashmir

"Father, I want to invite Master and four friends to accompany me to the Himalayan foothills during my summer vacation. May I have six railway passes to Kashmir and enough money to cover our travel expenses?"

As I had expected, Father laughed heartily. "This is the third time you have given me the same cock-and-bull story. Didn't you make a similar request last summer, and the year before that? At the last moment, Sri Yukteswarji refuses to go."

"It is true, Father; I don't know why my guru will not give me his definite word about Kashmir.* But if I tell him that I have already secured the passes from you, somehow I think that this time he will consent to make the journey."

Father was unconvinced at the moment, but the following day, after some good-humored gibes, he handed me six passes and a roll of ten-rupee bills.

"I hardly think your theoretical trip needs such practical props," he remarked, "but here they are."

That afternoon I exhibited my booty to Sri Yukteswar. Though he smiled at my enthusiasm, his words were noncommittal: "I would like to go; we shall see." He made no comment when I asked his little hermitage disciple, Kanai, to accompany us. I also invited three other friends—Rajendra Nath Mitra, Jotin Auddy, and one other boy. Our date of departure was set for the following Monday.

On Saturday and Sunday I stayed in Calcutta, where marriage rites for a cousin were being celebrated at my family home. I arrived in Serampore with my luggage early Monday morning. Rajendra met me at the hermitage door.

"Master is out, walking. He has refused to go."

I was equally grieved and obdurate. "I will not give Father a

* Although Master failed to make any explanation, his reluctance to visit Kashmir during those two summers may have been a foreknowledge that the time was not ripe for his illness there (see pp. 176 ff.).

third chance to ridicule my chimerical plans for Kashmir. The rest of us should go."

Rajendra agreed; I left the ashram to find a servant. Kanai, I knew, would not take the trip without Master, and someone was needed to look after the luggage. I bethought myself of Behari, previously a servant in my family home, who was now employed by a Serampore schoolmaster. As I walked along briskly, I met my guru in front of the Christian church near Serampore Courthouse.

"Where are you going?" Sri Yukteswar's face was unsmiling. "Sir, I hear that you and Kanai will not take the trip we have been planning. I am seeking Behari. You will recall that last year he was so desirous of seeing Kashmir that he even offered to serve without pay."

"I remember. Nevertheless, I don't think Behari will be willing to go."

I was exasperated. "He is just eagerly waiting for this opportunity!"

My guru silently resumed his walk; I soon reached the schoolmaster's house. Behari, in the courtyard, greeted me with a friendly warmth that abruptly vanished as soon as I mentioned Kashmir. With a murmured word of apology, the servant left me and entered his employer's house. I waited half an hour, nervously assuring myself that Behari's delay was being caused by preparations for his trip. Finally I knocked at the front door.

"Behari left by the back stairs about thirty minutes ago," a man informed me. A slight smile hovered about his lips.

I departed sadly, wondering whether my invitation had been too coercive or whether Master's unseen influence were at work. Passing the Christian church, again I saw my guru walking slowly toward me. Without waiting to hear my report, he exclaimed:

"So Behari would not go! Now, what are your plans?"

I felt like a recalcitrant child who is determined to defy his masterful father. "Sir, I am going to ask my uncle to lend me his servant, Lal Dhari."

"See your uncle if you want to," Sri Yukteswar replied with a chuckle. "But I hardly think you will enjoy the visit."

Apprehensive but rebellious, I left my guru and entered Serampore Courthouse. My paternal uncle, Sarada Ghosh, a government attorney, welcomed me affectionately.

"I am leaving today with some friends for Kashmir," I told him. "For years I have been looking forward to this Himalayan trip."

"I am happy for you, Mukunda. Is there anything I can do to

make your journey more comfortable?"

These kind words gave me a lift of encouragement. "Dear Uncle," I said, "could you possibly spare me your servant, Lal Dhari?"

My simple request had the effect of an earthquake. Uncle jumped so violently that his chair overturned, the papers on the desk flew in every direction, and his pipe, a long, coconut-stemmed hubble-bubble, fell to the floor with a great clatter.

"You selfish young man," he shouted, quivering with wrath, "what a preposterous idea! Who will look after me, if you take my servant on one of your pleasure jaunts?"

I concealed my surprise, reflecting that my amiable uncle's sudden change of front was only one more enigma in a day fully devoted to incomprehensibility. My retreat from the courthouse office was more alacritous than dignified.

I returned to the hermitage, where my friends were expectantly gathered. A conviction was growing in me that some sufficient, if exceedingly recondite, motive was behind Master's attitude. Remorse seized me for having tried to thwart my guru's will.

"Mukunda, wouldn't you like to stay a while longer with me?" Sri Yukteswar inquired. "Rajendra and the others may go ahead now, and wait for you in Calcutta. There will be plenty of time to catch the last evening train leaving Calcutta for Kashmir."

"Sir, I don't care to go without you," I said mournfully.

My friends paid not the slightest attention to my remark. They summoned a hackney carriage and departed with all the luggage. Kanai and I sat quietly at our guru's feet. After a half hour of silence, Master rose and walked toward the second-floor dining balcony.

"Kanai, please serve Mukunda's food. His train leaves soon."

Getting up from my blanket seat, I staggered suddenly with nausea and a ghastly churning sensation in my stomach. The stabbing pain was so intense that I felt I had been abruptly hurled into some violent hell. Groping blindly toward my guru, I collapsed before him, exhibiting all symptoms of the dread Asiatic cholera. Sri Yukteswar and Kanai carried me to the sitting room.

I cried in agony: "Master, I surrender my life to you"; for I believed it was indeed fast ebbing from the shores of my body.

Sri Yukteswar put my head on his lap, stroking my forehead with angelic tenderness.

"You see now what would have happened if you were at the station with your friends," he said. "I had to look after you in this

strange way, because you chose to doubt my judgment about taking
the trip at this particular time."

I understood at last. As great masters seldom see fit to display
their powers openly, a casual observer of the day's events would
have considered them quite natural. My guru's intervention had
been too subtle to be detected. He had inconspicuously worked
his will through Behari and my uncle and Rajendra and the others.
Probably everyone but me had thought the situations logical and
normal.

As Sri Yukteswar never failed to observe his social obligations, he instructed Kanai to summon a physician and to notify
my uncle.

"Master," I protested, "only you can heal me. I am too far gone
for any doctor."

"Child, you are protected by the Divine Mercy. Don't worry
about the doctor; he will not find you in this state. You are already
healed."

With my guru's words, the excruciating suffering left me. I sat
up feebly. A doctor soon arrived and examined me carefully.

"You appear to have passed through the worst," he said. "I will
take some specimens with me for laboratory tests."

The following morning the physician arrived hurriedly. I was
sitting up, in good spirits.

"Well, well, here you are, smiling and chatting as though you
had had no close call with death." He patted my hand gently. "I
hardly expected to find you alive, after I had discovered from the
specimens that your disease was Asiatic cholera. You are fortunate,
young man, to have a guru with divine healing powers! I am convinced of it!"

I agreed wholeheartedly. As the doctor was preparing to leave,
Rajendra and Auddy appeared at the door. The resentment in their
faces changed into sympathy as they glanced at the physician and
then at my somewhat wan countenance.

"We were angry when you didn't turn up as agreed at the Calcutta train. You have been sick?"

"Yes." I could not help laughing as my friends placed the luggage in the same corner it had occupied yesterday. I paraphrased:

"There was a ship that sailed for Spain; before it arrived, it was
back again!"

Master entered the room. I permitted myself a convalescent's
liberty, and captured his hand lovingly.

"Guruji," I said, "from my twelfth year on, I have made many unsuccessful attempts to reach the Himalayas. I am finally convinced that without your blessings the Goddess Parvati* will not receive me!"

---

* Lit., "of the mountains." Parvati is mythologically represented as the daughter of King Himalaya (lit., "abode of the snows"), whose home is a certain peak on the Tibetan border. Astonished travelers, passing below that inaccessible peak, view afar a vast snow formation resembling a palace, with icy domes and turrets.

Parvati, Kali, Durga, Uma, and other goddesses are aspects of Jaganmatri, "Divine Mother of the World," variously named to signalize particular functions. God or Shiva (see page 258 n.) in His *para* or transcendental aspect is inactive in creation; His *shakti* (energy, activating force) is relegated to His "consorts," the productive "female" powers that make possible the infinite unfoldments in the cosmos.

Mythological tales in the *Puranas* give the Himalayas as the abode of Shiva. The Goddess Ganga came down from the sky to be the presiding deity of the Himalayan-sourced river; the Ganges is therefore poetically said to flow from heaven to earth through the hair of Shiva, "King of Yogis" and the Destroyer-Renovator of the Trinity. Kalidasa, the "Indian Shakespeare," described the Himalayas as "the massed laughter of Shiva." "The reader may manage to imagine that stretch of great white teeth," writes F. W. Thomas in *The Legacy of India* (Oxford), "but the full idea may still escape him, unless he has realized the figure of the grand Ascete, eternally enthroned in the towering mountain world, where the Ganges in her descent from heaven passes through his matted locks, with the moon their crest-jewel." (See picture of Shiva in photo section, p. 10.)

In Hindu art Shiva is often shown wearing an antelope skin of velvet blackness, symbolizing the darkness and mystery of Night—the sole garment of Him who is *digambara*, "sky-clad." Certain Shiva sects wear no clothing in honor of the Lord who owns nothing—and everything.

One of the patron saints of Kashmir, the 14th-century Lalla Yogiswari ("Supreme Mistress of Yoga") was a "sky-clad" Shiva devotee. A scandalized contemporary asked the saint why she observed nudity. "Why not?" Lalla replied tartly. "I see no men about." To Lalla's somewhat drastic way of thinking, he who lacked God-realization did not deserve the name of "man." She practiced a technique, closely allied to *Kriya Yoga*, whose liberating efficacy she celebrated in numerous quatrains. I translate one of them here:

> What acid of sorrow have I not drunk?
> Countless my rounds of birth and death.
>   Lo! naught but nectar in my cup
>   Quaffed by the art of breath.

Undergoing no mortal death, the saint dematerialized herself in fire. Later she appeared before her grieving townspeople, a living form enwrapped in golden robes—fully clad at last!

CHAPTER 21

We Visit Kashmir

"You are strong enough now to travel. I will accompany you to Kashmir," Sri Yukteswar informed me two days after my miraculous recovery from Asiatic cholera.

That evening our party of six entrained for the north. Our first leisurely stop was at Simla, a queenly city resting on the throne of Himalayan hills. We strolled over the steep streets, admiring the magnificent views.

"English strawberries for sale," cried an old woman, squatting in a picturesque open marketplace.

Master was curious about the strange little red fruits. He bought a large basket of them and offered it to Kanai and me, who were nearby. I tasted one berry but spat it hastily on the ground.

"Sir, what a sour fruit! I could never like strawberries!"

My guru laughed. "Oh, you will like them—in America. At a dinner there, your hostess will serve them with sugar and cream. After she has mashed the berries with a fork, you will taste them and say: 'What delicious strawberries!' Then you will remember this day in Simla."

(Sri Yukteswar's forecast vanished from my mind, but reappeared there many years later, shortly after my arrival in America. I was a dinner guest at the home of Mrs. Alice T. Hasey [Sister Yogmata] in West Somerville, Massachusetts. When a dessert of strawberries was put on the table, my hostess picked up a fork and mashed my berries, adding cream and sugar. "The fruit is rather tart; I think you will like it fixed this way," she remarked. I took a mouthful. "What delicious strawberries!" I exclaimed. At once my guru's prediction in Simla emerged from the fathomless cave of memory. I was awestruck to realize that long ago his God-tuned mind had detected the program of karmic events wandering in the ether of futurity.)

Our party soon left Simla and entrained for Rawalpindi. There we hired a large closed-top landau, drawn by two horses, for a seven-day trip to Srinagar, capital of Kashmir. The second day of our northbound journey brought into view the true Himalayan vastness. As the iron wheels of our carriage creaked along the hot, stony roads, we were enraptured with changing vistas of mountainous grandeur.

"Sir," Auddy said to Master, "I am greatly enjoying these glorious scenes in your holy company."

I felt a throb of pleasure at Auddy's appreciation, for I was acting as host on this trip. Sri Yukteswar caught my thought; he turned to me and whispered:

"Don't flatter yourself; Auddy is not nearly as entranced with the scenery as he is with the prospect of leaving us long enough to have a cigarette."*

I was shocked. "Sir," I said in an undertone, "please do not break our harmony by these unpleasant words. I can hardly believe that Auddy is hankering for a smoke." I looked apprehensively at my usually irrepressible guru.

"Very well, I won't say anything to Auddy." Master chuckled. "But you will soon see, when the landau halts, that he is quick to seize his opportunity."

The carriage arrived at a small caravanserai. As our horses were led to be watered, Auddy inquired, "Sir, do you mind if I ride a while with the driver? I would like to get a little outside air."

Sri Yukteswar gave permission, but remarked to me, "He wants fresh smoke and not fresh air."

The landau resumed its noisy progress over the dusty roads. Master's eyes were twinkling; he instructed me: "Crane up your neck through the carriage door and see what Auddy is doing with the air."

I obeyed, and was startled to observe Auddy in the act of exhaling rings of cigarette smoke. My glance toward Sri Yukteswar was apologetic.

"You are right, as always, sir. Auddy is enjoying a puff along with a panorama." I surmised that my friend had received a gift from the cab driver; I knew that Auddy had not carried any cigarettes from Calcutta.

We continued on the labyrinthine way, delighting in views of rivers, valleys, precipitous crags, and multitudinous mountain tiers. Each night we stopped at a rustic inn and cooked our food. Sri Yukteswar took special care of my diet, insisting that I have lime

---

* It is a mark of disrespect, in India, to smoke in the presence of one's elders and superiors.

juice at all meals. I was still weak, but daily improving, though the rattling carriage had been strictly designed for discomfort.

Joyous anticipations filled our hearts as we neared central Kashmir: paradise land of lotus lakes, floating gardens, gaily canopied houseboats, the many-bridged Jhelum River, and flower-strewn pastures, all encircled by the Himalayas.

Our approach to Srinagar was through an avenue of tall, welcoming trees. We engaged rooms at a double-storied inn overlooking the noble hills. No running water was available; we drew our supply from a nearby well. The summer weather was ideal: warm days and slightly cold nights.

We made a pilgrimage to an ancient Srinagar temple dedicated to Swami Shankara. As I gazed upon the mountain-peak hermitage, bold against the sky, I fell into an ecstatic trance. A vision appeared of a hilltop mansion in a distant land; the lofty Shankara temple in Srinagar became transformed into the edifice where, years later, I established Self-Realization Fellowship headquarters in America. (When I first visited Los Angeles, and saw the large building on the crest of Mount Washington, I recognized it at once from my long-past visions in Kashmir and elsewhere.)

A few days in Srinagar; then on to Gulmarg ("mountain paths of flowers"); eighty-five hundred feet high. There I had my first ride on a large horse. Rajendra mounted a small trotter, one whose heart was fired by ambition for speed. We ventured onto the very steep Khilanmarg; the path led through a dense forest, abounding in tree mushrooms, where the mist-shrouded trails were often precarious. But Rajendra's little animal never permitted my oversized steed a moment's rest, even at the most perilous turns. On, on, untiringly came Rajendra's horse, oblivious to all but the joy of competition.

Our strenuous race was rewarded by a breathtaking view. For the first time in this life, I gazed in all directions at sublime snow-capped Himalayas, lying tier upon tier like silhouettes of huge polar bears. My eyes feasted exultingly on endless reaches of icy mountains against sunny blue skies.

I rolled merrily with my young companions, all wearing overcoats, on the sparkling white slopes. On our downward trip we saw afar a vast carpet of yellow flowers, wholly transfiguring the bleak hills.

Our next excursions were to the famous "pleasure gardens" of Emperor Jehangir at Shalimar and Nishat Bagh. The ancient palace at Nishat Bagh is built directly over a natural waterfall.

Rushing down from the mountains, the torrent has been regulated through ingenious contrivances to flow over colorful terraces and to gush into fountains amidst the dazzling flower-beds. The stream also enters several of the palace rooms, ultimately dropping fairy-like into the lake below. The immense gardens are riotous with color — roses, jasmine, lilies, snapdragons, pansies, lavender, poppies. An emerald encirclement is formed by symmetrical rows of *chinars,** cypresses, cherry trees; beyond them tower the white austerities of the Himalayas.

So-called Kashmir grapes are considered a rare delicacy in Calcutta. Rajendra, who had been talking about the grape feast awaiting us in Kashmir, was disappointed to find there no large vineyards. Now and then I chaffed him over his baseless anticipation.

"Oh, I have become so much gorged with grapes I can't walk!" I would say. "The invisible grapes are brewing within me!" Later we heard that sweet grapes grow abundantly in Kabul, west of Kashmir. We consoled ourselves with ice cream made of *rabri* (heavily condensed milk), flavored with whole pistachio nuts.

We took several trips in *shikaras*, small boats shaded by red-embroidered canopies, coursing along the intricate channels of Dal Lake—a network of canals like a watery spider web. Here the numerous floating gardens, crudely improvised with logs and earth, strike one with amazement, so incongruous is the first sight of vegetables and melons growing in the midst of vast waters. Occasionally one sees a peasant, disdaining to be "rooted to the soil," towing his square plot of "land" to a new location in the many-fingered lake.

In this storied vale one finds an epitome of all the earth's beauties. The Lady of Kashmir is mountain-crowned, lake-garlanded, and flower-shod. In later years, after I had toured many countries, I understood why Kashmir is often called the world's most scenic spot. It possesses some of the charms of the Swiss Alps, and of Loch Lomond in Scotland, and of the exquisite English lakes. An American traveler in Kashmir finds much to remind him of the rugged grandeur of Alaska and of Pikes Peak near Denver.

As entries in a scenic beauty contest, I offer for first prize either the gorgeous view of Xochimilco in Mexico, where skies, mountains, and poplars are reflected, amid playful fish, in myriad lanes of water; or the lakes of Kashmir, guarded like beautiful maidens by the stern surveillance of the Himalayas. These two places stand out in my memory as the loveliest spots on earth.

---

* The Oriental plane tree.

Yet I was awed also when I beheld the wonders of Yellowstone National Park, and of the Grand Canyon of the Colorado, and of Alaska. Yellowstone is perhaps the only region on earth where one may see numerous geysers erupting high in the air with almost clocklike regularity. In this volcanic area Nature has left a specimen of an earlier creation: hot sulphurous springs, opal- and sapphire-colored pools, violent geysers, and freely roaming bears, wolves, bison, and other wild creatures. Motoring along the roads of Wyoming to the "Devil's Paint Pot" of bubbling hot mud, observing the gurgling springs, spouting geysers, and vaporous fountains, I was disposed to say that Yellowstone deserves a special prize for uniqueness.

At Yosemite Park in California the ancient majestic sequoias, stretching huge columns far into the sky, are green natural cathedrals designed with skill divine. Though there are wonderful falls in the Orient, none match the torrential beauty of Niagara in New York on the Canadian border. Mammoth Cave in Kentucky and Carlsbad Caverns in New Mexico are strange fairylands. Long stalactites, hanging from cave ceilings and mirrored in underground waters, present a glimpse of other worlds as fancied by man.

In Kashmir a large number of the people, world-famed for their beauty, are as white as Europeans and have similar features and bone structure; many are blue-eyed and blonde-haired. Dressed in Western clothes they look like Americans. The coldness of the Himalayas affords the Kashmiris relief from the sultry sun and preserves their light complexions. As one travels south to the tropical latitudes of India, he finds progressively that the people are darker and darker.

After spending happy weeks in Kashmir, I was forced to make preparations to return to Bengal for the fall term of Serampore College. Sri Yukteswar, Kanai, and Auddy were to remain in Srinagar a while longer. Shortly before I departed, Master hinted that his body would be subject to suffering in Kashmir.

"Sir, you look a picture of health," I protested.

"There is a chance that I may even leave this earth."

"Guruji!" I fell at his feet with an imploring gesture. "Please promise that you won't leave your body now. I am utterly unprepared to carry on without you."

Sri Yukteswar was silent, but smiled at me so compassionately that I felt reassured. Reluctantly I left him.

"Master dangerously ill." This telegram from Auddy reached

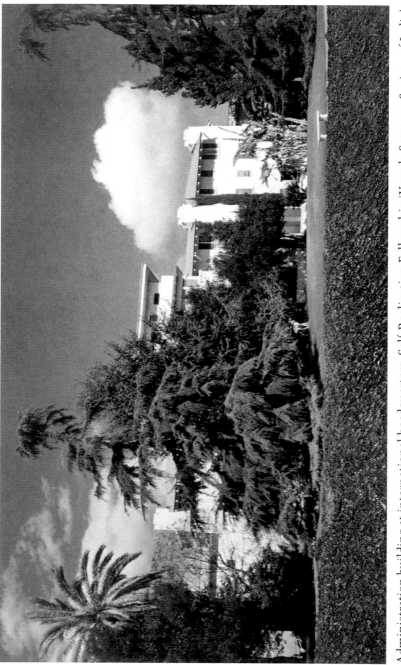

Administration building at international headquarters, Self-Realization Fellowship (Yogoda Satsanga Society of India), established by Sri Yogananda in 1925, atop Mt. Washington in Los Angeles, California

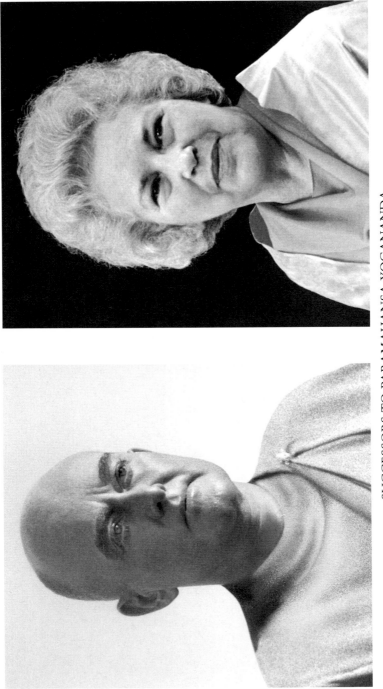

SUCCESSORS TO PARAMAHANSA YOGANANDA

Sri Rajarsi Janakananda, spiritual head and president of Self-Realization Fellowship/Yogoda Satsanga Society of India 1952–1955

Sri Daya Mata, spiritual head and president of the Self-Realization/Yogoda society since the passing of Rajarsi Janakananda in February 1955 me shortly after my return to Serampore.

"Sir," I wired my guru frantically, "I asked for your promise not to leave me. Please keep your body; otherwise, I also shall die."

"Be it as you wish." This was Master's reply from Kashmir.

A letter from Auddy arrived in a few days, informing me that Master had recovered. On his return to Serampore during the next fortnight, I was grieved to find my guru's body reduced to half its usual weight.

Fortunately for his disciples, Sri Yukteswar burned many of their sins in the fire of his severe fever in Kashmir. The metaphysical method of physical transfer of disease is known to highly advanced yogis. A strong man may assist a weak one by helping the latter to carry a heavy load; a spiritual superman is able to minimize the physical and mental troubles of his disciples by assuming a part of their karmic burdens. Just as a rich man relinquishes some money when he pays off a large debt for his prodigal son, who is thus saved from the dire consequences of his folly, so a master willingly sacrifices a portion of his bodily wealth to lighten the misery of disciples. *

By a secret yogic method, the saint unites his mind and astral vehicle with those of a suffering individual; the disease is conveyed, wholly or in part, to the yogi's fleshy form. Having harvested God on the physical field, a master is no longer concerned with his body. Though he may allow it to become diseased in order to relieve other persons, his mind, unpollutable, is not affected. He considers himself fortunate in being able to render such aid. To achieve final salvation in the Lord is indeed to find that the human body has completely fulfilled its purpose; a master then uses it in any way he deems fit.

A guru's work in the world is to alleviate the sorrows of mankind, whether through spiritual means or intellectual counsel or will power or physical transfer of disease. Escaping to the superconsciousness whenever he so desires, a master can become oblivious of physical illness; sometimes, to set an example for disciples, he chooses to bear bodily pain stoically. By putting on the ailments of others, a yogi can satisfy, for them, the karmic law of cause and effect. This law is mechanically or mathematically operative; its workings may be scientifically manipulated by men of divine wisdom.

* Many Christian saints, including Therese Neumann (see page 316), are familiar with the metaphysical transfer of disease.

The spiritual law does not require a master to become ill whenever he heals another person. Healings ordinarily take place through the saint's knowledge of various methods of instantaneous cure in which no hurt to the spiritual healer is involved. On rare occasions, however, a master who wishes to quicken greatly his disciples' evolution may then voluntarily work out on his own body a large measure of their undesirable karma.

Jesus signified himself as a ransom for the sins of many. With his divine powers,* Christ could never have been subjected to death by crucifixion if he had not willingly cooperated with the subtle cosmic law of cause and effect. He thus took on himself the consequences of others' karma, especially that of his disciples. In this manner they were highly purified and made fit to receive the omnipresent consciousness or Holy Ghost that later descended upon them.†

Only a Self-realized master can transfer his life force or convey into his own body the diseases of others. An ordinary man cannot employ this yogic method of cure; nor is it desirable that he should do so, because an unsound physical instrument is a hindrance to deep meditation. The Hindu scriptures teach that an imperative duty of man is to keep his body in good condition; otherwise his mind is unable to remain fixed in devotional concentration.

A very strong mind, however, can transcend all physical difficulties and attain to God-realization. Many saints have ignored illness and succeeded in their divine quest. St. Francis of Assisi, himself severely afflicted with ailments, healed other men, and even raised the dead.

I once knew an Indian saint, half of whose body, in his earlier years, had been covered with sores. His diabetic illness had been so acute that he had found it difficult to sit still at one time for more than fifteen minutes. But his spiritual aspiration had been undeterable. "Lord," he had prayed, "wilt Thou come into my broken temple?" With ceaseless command of will, the saint had gradually become able to sit in the lotus posture daily for eighteen hours, engrossed in the ecstatic trance. "And," he told me, "at the end of three years I found the Infinite Light blazing within me. Rejoicing

* Christ said, just before he was led away to be crucified: "Thinkest thou that I cannot now pray to my Father, and he shall presently give me more than twelve legions of angels? But how then shall the scriptures be fulfilled, that thus it must be?"—Matt. 26:53–54.

† Acts 1:8; 2:1–4.

in Its splendor, I forgot the body. Later I saw that it had become whole through the Divine Mercy."

A historical healing incident concerns King Baber (1483–1530), founder of the Mogul empire in India. His son Humayun* became gravely ill. The father prayed with anguished determination that he receive the malady and that his son be spared. Humayun recovered; Baber immediately fell sick and died of the same disease that had stricken his son.

Many persons believe that a great master should have the health and strength of a Sandow.† The assumption is unfounded. A sickly body does not indicate that a guru is lacking in divine powers, any more than lifelong health necessarily indicates inner illumination. The distinguishing qualifications of a master are not physical but spiritual.

Numerous bewildered seekers in the West erroneously think that an eloquent speaker or writer on metaphysics must be a master. Proof that one is a master, however, is supplied only by the ability to enter at will the breathless state (*sabikalpa samadhi*) and by the attainment of immutable bliss (*nirbikalpa samadhi*).‡ The rishis have pointed out that solely by these achievements may a human being demonstrate that he has mastered *maya*, the dualistic cosmic delusion. He alone may say from the depths of realization: *"Ekam sat"* ("Only One exists").

> "When there is duality because of ignorance, one sees all things as distinct from the Self," Shankara, the great monist has written. "When everything is known as the Self, not even an atom is seen as other than the Self....As soon as knowledge of the Reality has sprung up, there can be no fruits of past actions to be experienced, owing to the unreality of the body, just as there can be no dream after waking."

Only great gurus are able to assume the karma of disciples.

---

* Humayun became the father of Akbar the Great. With Islamic zeal, Akbar at first persecuted the Hindus. "As I grew in knowledge, I was overwhelmed with shame," he said later. "Miracles occur in the temples of every creed." He arranged for a Persian translation of the Bhagavad Gita, and invited to his court several Jesuit Fathers from Rome. Akbar inaccurately but lovingly attributed to Christ the following saying (inscribed on the Victory Arch in Akbar's new city of Fatehpur Sikri): "Jesus, Son of Mary (on whom be peace), said: *The world is a bridge; pass over it, but build no house upon it.*"

† A German athlete (d. 1925), known as "the world's strongest man."

‡ See pp. 210, 353 n.

Sri Yukteswar would not have suffered in Srinagar* unless he had received permission from the Spirit within him to help his disciples in that strange way. Few saints were ever more sensitively equipped with wisdom to carry out divine commands than my God-tuned Master.

When I ventured a few words of sympathy over his emaciated figure, my guru said gaily:

"It has its good points; I am able now to get into some small *ganjis* (undershirts) that I haven't worn for years!"

Listening to Master's jovial laugh, I remembered the words of St. Francis de Sales: "A saint that is sad is a sad saint!

---

* Srinagar, capital city of Kashmir, was founded in the third century B.C. by Emperor Asoka. He built there 500 monasteries, of which 100 were still standing when the Chinese pilgrim Hiuen Tsiang visited Kashmir 1000 years later. Another Chinese writer, Fa-Hsien (fifth century), viewing the ruins of Asoka's vast palace at Pataliputra (modern Patna), tells us the structure was of such incredible beauty in its architecture and decorative sculpture that it "could have been the work of no mortal hands."

CHAPTER 22

The Heart of a Stone Image

"As a loyal Hindu wife, I do not wish to complain of my husband. But I yearn to see him turn from his materialistic views. He delights in ridiculing the pictures of saints in my meditation room. Dear brother, I have deep faith that you can help him. Will you?"

My eldest sister Roma gazed beseechingly at me. I was paying a short visit at her Calcutta home on Girish Vidyaratna Lane. Her plea touched me, for she had exercised a profound spiritual influence over my early life, and had lovingly tried to fill the void left in the family circle by Mother's death.

"Beloved sister, of course I will do anything I can." I smiled, eager to lift the gloom plainly visible on her face, in contrast to her usual calm and cheerful expression.

Roma and I sat a while in silent prayer for guidance. A year earlier, my sister had asked me to initiate her in *Kriya Yoga*, in which she was making notable progress.

An inspiration seized me. "Tomorrow," I said, "I am going to the temple of Kali in Dakshineswar. Please come with me, and persuade your husband to accompany us. I feel that in the vibrations of that holy place, Divine Mother will touch his heart. But don't disclose our object in wanting him to go."

Sister agreed hopefully. Very early the next morning I was pleased to find that Roma and her husband were in readiness for the trip. As our hackney carriage rattled along Upper Circular Road toward Dakshineswar, my brother-in-law, Satish Chandra Bose, amused himself by deriding the worth of gurus. I noticed that Roma was quietly weeping.

"Sister, cheer up!" I whispered. "Don't give your husband the satisfaction of believing that we take his mockery seriously."

"Mukunda, how can you admire worthless humbugs?" Satish was saying. "A sadhu's very appearance is repulsive. He is either as thin as a skeleton, or as unholily fat as an elephant!"

I shook with laughter—a reaction that annoyed Satish. He retired into sullen silence. As our cab entered the temple grounds in

Dakshineswar, he grinned sarcastically.

"This excursion, I suppose, is a scheme to reform me?"

As I turned away without reply, he caught my arm. "Young Mr. Monk," he said, "don't forget to make proper arrangements with the temple authorities to provide for our noon meal." Satish wished to spare himself any conversation with priests.

"I am going to meditate now. Do not worry about your lunch," I replied sharply. "Divine Mother will look after it."

"I don't trust Divine Mother to do a single thing for me. But I do hold you responsible for my food." Satish's tones were threatening.

I proceeded alone to the portico that fronts the large temple of Kali (God in the aspect of Mother Nature). Selecting a shady spot near one of the pillars, I sat down and assumed the lotus posture. Although it was only about seven o'clock, the morning sun would soon be oppressive.

The world receded as I became devotionally entranced. My mind was concentrated on Goddess Kali. Her statue in this very temple in Dakshineswar had been the special object of adoration by the great master, Sri Ramakrishna Paramahansa. In answer to his anguished demands, the stone image had often taken a living form and conversed with him.

"Silent Mother of stone," I prayed, "Thou didst become filled with life at the plea of Thy beloved devotee Ramakrishna; why dost Thou not also heed the wails of this yearning son of Thine?"

My aspiring zeal increased boundlessly, accompanied by a divine peace. Yet, when five hours had passed, and the Goddess whom I was inwardly visualizing had made no response, I felt slightly disheartened. Sometimes it is a test by God to delay the fulfillment of prayers. But He eventually appears to the persistent devotee in whatever form he holds dear. A devout Christian sees Jesus; a Hindu beholds Krishna, or the Goddess Kali, or an expanding Light if his worship takes an impersonal turn.

Reluctantly I opened my eyes, and saw that the temple doors were being locked by a priest, in conformance with a noon-hour custom. I rose from my secluded seat on the portico and stepped into the courtyard. Its stone surface was scorched by the midday sun; my bare feet were painfully burned.

"Divine Mother," I silently remonstrated, "Thou didst not come to me in vision, and now Thou art hidden in the temple behind closed doors. I wanted to offer a special prayer to Thee today on behalf of my brother-in-law."

My inward petition was instantly acknowledged. First, a delightful cold wave descended over my back and under my feet, banishing all discomfort. Then, to my amazement, the temple became greatly magnified. Its large door slowly opened, revealing the stone figure of Goddess Kali. Gradually the statue changed into a living form, smilingly nodding in greeting, thrilling me with joy indescribable. As if by a mystic syringe, the breath was withdrawn from my lungs; my body became very still, though not inert.

An ecstatic enlargement of consciousness followed. I could see clearly for several miles over the Ganges River to my left, and beyond the temple into the entire Dakshineswar precincts. The walls of all buildings glimmered transparently; through them I observed people walking to and fro over distant acres.

Though I was breathless and though my body remained in a strangely quiet state, I was able to move my hands and feet freely. For several minutes I experimented in closing and opening my eyes; in either state I saw distinctly the whole Dakshineswar panorama.

Spiritual sight, X-raylike, penetrates into all matter; the divine eye is center everywhere, circumference nowhere. I realized anew, standing there in the sunny courtyard, that when man ceases to be a prodigal child of God, engrossed in a physical world indeed dream, baseless as a bubble, he reinherits his eternal realms. If escapism be a need of man, cramped in his narrow personality, can any other escape compare with that of omnipresence?

In my sacred experience at Dakshineswar, the only extraordinarily enlarged objects were the temple and the form of the Goddess. Everything else appeared in its normal dimensions, although each was enclosed in a halo of mellow light—white, blue, and pastel rainbow hues. My body seemed to be of ethereal substance, ready to levitate. Fully conscious of my material surroundings, I was looking about me and taking a few steps without disturbing the continuity of the blissful vision.

Behind the temple walls I suddenly glimpsed my brother-in-law as he sat under the thorny branches of a sacred *bel* tree. I could effortlessly discern the course of his thoughts. Somewhat uplifted under the holy influence of Dakshineswar, his mind yet held unkind reflections about me. I turned directly to the gracious form of the Goddess.

"Divine Mother," I prayed, "wilt Thou not spiritually change my sister's husband?"

The beautiful figure, hitherto silent, spoke at last. "Thy wish is granted!"

I looked happily at Satish. As though instinctively aware that some spiritual power was at work, he rose resentfully from his seat on the ground. I saw him running behind the temple; he approached me, shaking his fist.

The all-embracing vision disappeared. No longer could I see the glorious Goddess; the temple lost its transparency and resumed its ordinary dimensions. Again my body sweltered under the fierce rays of the sun. I jumped to the shelter of the portico, to which Satish pursued me angrily. I looked at my watch. It was one o'clock; the divine vision had lasted an hour.

"You little fool," my brother-in-law blurted out, "you have been sitting there cross-legged and cross-eyed for hours. I have gone back and forth watching you. Where is our food? Now the temple is closed; you failed to notify the authorities about us; it is too late to arrange for our lunch!"

The exaltation I had felt in the Goddess's presence lingered with me. I exclaimed, "Divine Mother will feed us!"

"Once and for all," Satish shouted, "I would like to see your Divine Mother giving us food here without prior arrangements!"

His words were hardly uttered when a temple priest crossed the courtyard and joined us.

"Son," he addressed me, "I have been observing your face serenely glowing during hours of meditation. I saw the arrival of your party this morning, and felt a desire to put aside ample food for your lunch. It is against the temple rules to feed those who do not make a request beforehand, but I have made an exception for you."

I thanked him, and gazed straight into Satish's eyes. He flushed with emotion, lowering his gaze in silent repentance. When we were served a lavish meal, including out-of-season mangoes, I noticed that my brother-in-law's appetite was meager. He was bewildered, diving deep into the ocean of thought.

On the return journey to Calcutta, Satish, with softened expression, occasionally glanced at me pleadingly. But he did not speak a single word after the moment the priest, as though in answer to Satish's challenge, had appeared to invite us to lunch.

The following afternoon I visited my sister at her home. She greeted me affectionately.

"Dear brother," she cried, "what a miracle! Last evening my husband wept openly before me.

"'Beloved Devi,'* he said, 'I am happy beyond expression that

---

* Goddess; lit., "shining one"; from Sanskrit verb root *div*, to shine.

this reforming scheme of your brother's has wrought a transformation. I am going to undo every wrong I have done you. From tonight we will use our large bedroom only as a place of worship; your small meditation room shall be changed into our sleeping quarters. I am sincerely sorry that I have ridiculed your brother. For the shameful way I have been acting, I will punish myself by not talking to Mukunda until I have progressed in the spiritual path. Deeply I will seek the Divine Mother from now on; someday I must surely find Her!'"

Years later (in 1936), I visited Satish in Delhi. I was overjoyed to perceive that he had developed highly in Self-realization and had been blessed by a vision of the Divine Mother. During my stay with him I noticed that Satish secretly spent the greater part of each night in deep meditation, though he was suffering from a serious ailment, and was engaged during the day at his office.

The thought came to me that my brother-in-law's life span would not be a long one. Roma must have read my mind.

"Dear brother," she said, "I am well, and my husband is sick. Nevertheless, I want you to know that, as a devoted Hindu wife, I am going to be the first one to die.* It won't be long now before I pass on."

Taken aback at her ominous words, I yet realized their sting of truth. I was in America when my sister died, about eighteen months after her prediction. My youngest brother Bishnu later gave me the details.

"Roma and Satish were in Calcutta at the time of her death," Bishnu told me. "That morning she dressed herself in her bridal finery.

"'Why this special costume?' Satish inquired.

"'This is my last day of service to you on earth,' Roma replied. A short time later she had a heart attack. As her son was rushing out for aid, she said:

"'Son, do not leave me. It is no use; I shall be gone before a doctor could arrive.' Ten minutes later, holding the feet of her husband in reverence, Roma consciously left her body, happily and without suffering.

"Satish became very reclusive after his wife's death," Bishnu continued. "One day he and I were looking at a photograph of a smiling Roma.

* A Hindu wife believes it is a sign of spiritual advancement if she dies before her husband, as proof of her loyal service to him, or "dying in harness."

"'Why do you smile?' Satish suddenly exclaimed, as though his wife were present. 'You think you were clever in arranging to go before me. I shall prove that you cannot long remain away from me; soon I shall join you.'

"Although at this time Satish had fully recovered from his sickness, and was enjoying excellent health, he died without apparent cause shortly after his strange remark before the photograph."

Thus prophetically passed both my beloved sister Roma and her husband Satish—he who had been transformed at Dakshineswar from an ordinary worldly man to a silent saint.

CHAPTER 23

I Receive My University Degree

"You ignore your textbook assignments in philosophy. No doubt you are depending on an unlaborious 'intuition' to get you through the examinations. But unless you apply yourself in a more scholarly manner, I shall see to it that you don't pass this course."

Professor D. C. Ghoshal of Serampore College was addressing me sternly. If I failed to pass his final written classroom test, I would be ineligible to take the conclusive examinations. These are formulated by the faculty of Calcutta University, which numbers Serampore College among its affiliated branches. In Indian universities a student who is unsuccessful in one subject in the A.B. finals must be examined anew in *all* his subjects the following year.

My instructors at Serampore College usually treated me with kindness, not untinged with amusement. "Mukunda is a bit over-drunk with religion." Thus summing me up, they tactfully spared me the embarrassment of trying to answer classroom questions; they trusted the final written tests to eliminate me from the list of A.B. candidates. The judgment passed by my fellow students was expressed in their nickname for me—"Mad Monk."

I took an ingenious step to nullify Professor Ghoshal's threat to me of failure in philosophy. When the results of the final test were about to be publicly announced, I asked a classmate to accompany me to the professor's study.

"Come along, I want a witness," I told my companion. "I shall be very much disappointed if I have not succeeded in outwitting the instructor."

Professor Ghoshal shook his head after I had inquired what rating he had given my paper.

"You are not among those who have passed," he said in triumph. He searched through a large pile of sheets on his desk. "Your paper isn't here at all; you have failed, in any case, through non-appearance at the examination."

I chuckled. "Sir, I was there. May I look through the stack myself?"

The professor, nonplussed, gave his permission; I quickly found my paper, from which I had carefully omitted any identification mark except my roll-call number. Unwarned by the "red flag" of my name, the instructor had given a high rating to my answers even though they were unembellished by textbook quotations.*

Seeing through my trick, he now thundered, "Sheer brazen luck!" He added hopefully, "You are sure to fail in the A.B. finals."

For the tests in my other subjects, I received some coaching, particularly from my dear friend and cousin, Prabhas Chandra Ghosh, son of my Uncle Sarada. I staggered painfully but successfully—with the lowest possible passing marks—through all my final tests.

Now, after four years of college, I was eligible to sit for the A.B. examinations. Nevertheless, I hardly expected to avail myself of the privilege. The Serampore College finals were child's play compared to the stiff ones that would be set by Calcutta University for the A.B degree. My almost daily visits to Sri Yukteswar had left me little time to enter the college halls. There my presence rather than my absence would cause my classmates to exclaim in surprise.

The routine I followed almost every day started with my setting out on a bicycle at nine-thirty in the morning. In one hand I would carry an offering for my guru—a few flowers from the garden of my Panthi boardinghouse. Greeting me affably, Master would invite me to lunch. I invariably accepted with alacrity, glad to banish the thought of college for the day. After hours with Sri Yukteswar, listening to his incomparable flow of wisdom or helping with ashram duties, I would reluctantly depart around midnight for the Panthi. Occasionally I stayed all night with my guru, so happily engrossed in his conversation that I scarcely noticed when darkness changed into dawn.

One night about eleven o'clock, as I was putting on my shoes† in preparation for the ride to the boardinghouse, Master questioned me gravely.

"When do your A.B. examinations start?"

"Five days hence, sir."

"I hope you are in readiness for them."

---

* I must do Professor Ghoshal the justice of admitting that the strained relations between us were not due to any fault of his, but solely to my absences from classes.

Professor Ghoshal is a remarkable orator with vast philosophical knowledge. In later years we came to a cordial understanding.

† A disciple always removes his shoes in an Indian hermitage.

Transfixed with alarm, I held one shoe in the air. "Sir," I protested, "you know that my days have been passed with you rather than with the professors. How can I bring myself to enact a farce by appearing for those difficult finals?"

Sri Yukteswar's eyes were turned piercingly on mine. "You must appear." His tone was coldly peremptory. "We should not give cause for your father and other relatives to criticize your preference for ashram life. Just promise me that you will be present for the examinations; answer them the best way you can."

Uncontrollable tears were coursing down my face. I felt that Master's command was unreasonable and that his interest was, to say the least, belated.

"I will appear if you wish it," I said with a sob. "But no time remains for proper preparation." To myself I muttered, "In answer to the questions, I will fill up the sheets with your teachings!"

When I entered the hermitage the following day at my usual hour, I presented my bouquet mournfully to Sri Yukteswar. He laughed at my woebegone air.

"Mukunda, has the Lord ever failed you, at an examination or elsewhere?"

"No, sir," I responded warmly. Grateful memories came in a revivifying flood.

"Not laziness but burning zeal for God has prevented you from seeking college honors," my guru said kindly. After a silence, he quoted, "'Seek ye first the kingdom of God, and His righteousness; and all these things shall be added unto you.'" *

For the thousandth time, I felt my burdens lifted in Master's presence. When we had finished our early lunch, he suggested that I return to the Panthi.

"Does your friend, Romesh Chandra Dutt, still live in your boardinghouse?"

"Yes, sir."

"Get in touch with him; the Lord will inspire him to help you with the examinations."

"Very well, sir; but Romesh is unusually busy. He is the honor man in our class, and carries a heavier course than the others."

Master waved aside my objections. "Romesh will find time for you. Now go."

I bicycled back to the Panthi. The first person I met in the boardinghouse compound was the scholarly Romesh. As though his

* Matthew 6:33.

days were quite free, he obligingly agreed to my diffident request.

"Of course! I am at your service." He spent many hours of that day and of each of the next few days in coaching me in my various subjects.

"I believe that many questions in the English literature examination will concern the route taken by Childe Harold," he told me. "We must get an atlas at once."

I hastened to the home of Uncle Sarada and borrowed an atlas. Romesh marked the European map at the places visited by Byron's romantic traveler.

A few classmates had gathered around to listen to the tutoring. "Romesh is advising you wrongly," one of them commented to me at the end of a session. "Usually only fifty percent of the questions are about the books; the other half involve the authors' lives."

When I sat for the examination in English literature, my first glance at the questions caused tears of gratitude to pour down my cheeks, wetting my paper. The classroom monitor came to my desk and made a sympathetic inquiry.

"My great guru foretold that Romesh would help me," I explained. "Look, the very questions suggested to me by Romesh are here on the examination sheet!" I added, "Fortunately for me, there are very few questions this year on British authors, whose lives are wrapped in deep mystery so far as I am concerned."

My boardinghouse was in an uproar when I returned. The boys who had been ridiculing me for my faith in Romesh's coaching now almost deafened me with congratulations. During the week of the examinations I continued to spend as much time as possible with Romesh, who formulated questions that he thought were likely to be set by the professors. Day by day, Romesh's questions appeared in almost the same words on the examination sheets.

The news was widely circulated in the college that something resembling a miracle was occurring and that success seemed probable for the absentminded "Mad Monk." I made no attempt to hide the facts of the case. The local professors were powerless to alter the questions, which had been arranged by the faculty of Calcutta University.

Thinking over the examination in English literature, I realized one morning that I had made a serious error. Certain questions had been divided into two parts: A or B, and C or D. Instead of considering one question in each part, I had answered *both* questions in the first section and had carelessly overlooked the second section. The best mark I could possibly score in that paper would be 33—three points less than the passing mark of 36.

I rushed to Master and poured out my troubles.

"Sir, I have made an unpardonable blunder. I don't deserve the divine blessings through Romesh; I am quite unworthy."

"Cheer up, Mukunda." Sri Yukteswar's tones were light and unconcerned. He pointed to the blue vault of the heavens. "It is more likely that the sun and moon will interchange their positions in space than that you will fail to get your degree!"

I left the hermitage in a more tranquil mood, though it seemed mathematically inconceivable that I could pass. I looked once or twice apprehensively into the sky; the Lord of Day appeared to be secure in his customary orbit.

As I reached the Panthi, I overheard a classmate's remark: "I have just learned that this year, for the first time, the required passing mark in English literature has been lowered."

I entered the boy's room with such speed that he looked up in alarm. I questioned him eagerly.

"Long-haired monk," he said laughingly, "why this sudden interest in scholastic matters? Why cry in the eleventh hour? But it is true that the passing mark has just been lowered to 33 points."

A few joyous leaps took me to my own room, where I sank to my knees and praised the mathematical perfections of my Divine Father.

Each day I thrilled with the consciousness of a Spiritual Presence that I clearly felt to be guiding me through Romesh. A significant incident occurred in connection with my examination in the Bengali-language course. One morning Romesh, who had not coached me in that subject, called to me as I was leaving the boardinghouse on my way to the examination hall.

"There is Romesh shouting for you," a classmate said to me impatiently. "Don't return; we shall be late at the hall."

Ignoring the advice, I ran back to the house.

"Usually the Bengali examination is easily passed by our Bengali boys," Romesh said. "But I have just had a hunch that this year the professors have planned to 'massacre' the students by asking questions about the required-reading books." He then outlined two stories from the life of Vidyasagar, a renowned Bengali philanthropist of the nineteenth century.

I thanked Romesh and quickly bicycled to the hall. There I found that the examination sheet in Bengali contained two parts.

The first instruction was: "Give two instances of the charities of Vidyasagar."* As I transferred to the paper the lore that I had so recently acquired, I whispered a few words of thanksgiving that I had heeded Romesh's last-minute summons. Had I been ignorant of Vidyasagar's benefactions (which now included one to me), I could not have passed the Bengali examination.

The second instruction on the sheet read: "Write an essay in Bengali on the life of the man who has most inspired you." Gentle reader, I need not inform you what man I chose for my theme. As I covered page after page with praise of my guru, I smiled to realize that my muttered prediction was coming true: "I will fill up the sheets with your teachings!"

I had not felt inclined to question Romesh about my course in philosophy. Trusting my long training under Sri Yukteswar, I safely disregarded the textbook explanations. The highest mark given to any of my papers was the one in philosophy. My score in all other subjects was just barely within the passing mark.

It is a pleasure to record that my unselfish friend Romesh received his own degree *cum laude.*

Father was wreathed in smiles at my graduation. "I hardly thought you would pass, Mukunda," he confessed. "You spend so much time with your guru." Master had indeed correctly detected the unspoken criticism of my father.

For years I had been uncertain that I would ever see the day when an A.B. could follow my name. I seldom use the title without reflecting that it was a divine gift, conferred on me for reasons somewhat obscure. Occasionally I hear college men remark that very little of their crammed knowledge remained with them after graduation. That admission consoles me a bit for my undoubted academic deficiencies.

On the day in June 1915 that I received my degree from Calcutta University, I knelt at my guru's feet and thanked him for all the blessings flowing from his life† into mine.

---

* I have forgotten the exact wording of the instruction, but I remember that it concerned the stories Romesh had just told me about Vidyasagar.

   Because of his erudition Pundit Ishwar Chandra became widely known in Bengal simply by the title of *Vidyasagar* ("Ocean of Learning").

† The power of influencing others' minds and the course of events is a *vibhuti* (yogic power) mentioned in Patanjali's *Yoga Sutras* III:24, which explains it to be a result of "universal sympathy." [Two scholarly books on the *Sutras* are *Yoga-System of Patanjali* (Vol. 17, Oriental Series, Harvard Univ.) and Dasgupta's *Yoga Philosophy* (Trubner's, London).]

"Get up, Mukunda," he said indulgently. "The Lord simply found it more convenient to make you a graduate than to rearrange the sun and moon!"

All scriptures proclaim that the Lord created man in His omnipotent image. Control over the universe appears to be supernatural, but in truth such power is inherent and natural in everyone who attains "right remembrance" of his divine origin. Men of God-realization like Sri Yukteswar are devoid of the ego-principle (*ahamkara*) and its uprisings of personal desires; the actions of true masters are in effortless conformity with *rita*, natural righteousness. In Emerson's words, all great ones become "not virtuous, but Virtue; then is the end of the creation answered, and God is well pleased."

Any man of divine realization could perform miracles, because, like Christ, he understands the subtle laws of creation; but not all masters choose to exercise phenomenal powers. (See p. 200 n.) Each saint reflects God in his own way; the expression of individuality is basic in a world where not two grains of sand are exactly alike.

Invariable rules may not be formulated about God-illumined saints: some perform miracles, others do not; some are inactive, while others (like King Janaka of ancient India and St. Teresa of Avila) are concerned with large affairs; some teach, travel, and accept disciples, while others pass their lives as silently and unobtrusively as a shadow. No worldly critic can read the secret scroll of karma (past actions) that unrolls for each saint a different script.

CHAPTER 24

I Become a Monk
of the Swami Order

"Master, my father has been anxious for me to accept an executive position with the Bengal-Nagpur Railway. But I have definitely refused it." I added hopefully, "Sir, will you not make me a monk of the Swami Order?" I looked pleadingly at my guru. During preceding years, in order to test the depth of my determination, he had refused this same request. Today, however, he smiled graciously.

"Very well, tomorrow I will initiate you into swamihood." He went on quietly, "I am happy that you have persisted in your desire to be a monk. Lahiri Mahasaya often said: 'If you don't invite God to be your summer Guest, He won't come in the winter of your life.'"

"Dear Master, I could never relinquish my wish to belong to the Swami Order like your revered self." I smiled at him with measureless affection.

"He that is unmarried careth for the things that belong to the Lord, how he may please the Lord: but he that is married careth for the things of the world, how he may please his wife."* I had analyzed the lives of many of my friends who, after undergoing certain spiritual discipline, had then married. Launched on the sea of worldly responsibilities, they had forgotten their resolutions to meditate deeply.

To allot the Lord a secondary place† in life was, to me, inconceivable. He is the sole Owner of the cosmos, silently showering man with gifts from life to life. There is but one gift man may offer in return—his love, which he is empowered to withhold or bestow.

In taking infinite pains to shroud with mystery His presence in the atoms of creation, the Creator could have had but one motive,

* I Corinthians 7:32–33.
† "He who offers God a second place offers Him no place."—*Ruskin.*

one sensitive desire: that man seek Him only through free will. With what velvet glove of every humility has He not covered the iron hand of omnipotence!

The following day was one of the most memorable in my life. It was a sunny Thursday, I remember, in July 1915, a few weeks after my graduation from college. On the inner balcony of his Serampore hermitage, Master dipped a new piece of white silk into a dye of ocher, the traditional color of the Swami Order. After the cloth had dried, my guru draped it around me as a renunciant's robe.

"Someday you will go to the West, where silk is preferred," he said. "As a symbol, I have chosen for you this silk material instead of the customary cotton."

In India, where monks embrace the ideal of poverty, a silk-clad swami is an unusual sight. Many yogis, however, wear garments of silk, which retains certain subtle bodily currents better than cotton.

"I am averse to ceremonies," Sri Yukteswar remarked. "I will make you a swami in the *bidwat* (non-ceremonious) manner."

The *bibidisa* or elaborate initiation into swamihood includes a fire ceremony, during which symbolical funeral rites are performed. The physical body of the disciple is represented as dead, cremated in the flame of wisdom. The newly made swami is then given a chant, such as: "This *atma* is Brahma"* or "Thou art That" or "I am He." Sri Yukteswar, however, with his love of simplicity, dispensed with all formal rites and merely asked me to select a new name.

"I will give you the privilege of choosing it yourself," he said, smiling.

"Yogananda,"† I replied after a moment's thought. The name means "bliss (*ananda*) through divine union (*yoga*)."

"Be it so. Forsaking your family name of Mukunda Lal Ghosh, henceforth you shall be called Yogananda of the Giri branch of the Swami Order."

As I knelt before Sri Yukteswar, and for the first time heard him pronounce my new name, my heart overflowed with gratitude. How lovingly and tirelessly had he labored, that the boy Mukunda be someday transformed into the monk Yogananda! I joyfully sang

---

* Literally, "This soul is Spirit." The Supreme Spirit, the Uncreated, is wholly unconditioned (*neti, neti,* not this, not that) but is often referred to in *Vedanta* as *Sat-Chit-Ananda,* that is, Being-Intelligence-Bliss.

† Yogananda is a fairly common name among swamis.

a few verses from the long Sanskrit chant of Lord Shankara:*

> Mind, nor intellect, nor ego, feeling;
> Sky nor earth nor metals am I.
> I am He, I am He, Blessed Spirit, I am He!
> No birth, no death, no caste have I;
> Father, mother, have I none.
> I am He, I am He, Blessed Spirit, I am He!
> Beyond the flights of fancy, formless am I,
> Permeating the limbs of all life;
> Bondage I do not fear; I am free, ever free,
> I am He, I am He, Blessed Spirit, I am He!

Every swami belongs to the monastic order that has been honored in India from time immemorial. Reorganized in its present form centuries ago by Shankaracharya, it has since been headed by an unbroken line of venerable teachers (each of whom successively bears the title of Jagadguru Sri Shankaracharya). Many monks, perhaps a million, make up the Swami Order; to enter it they fulfill a requirement to receive initiation from men who themselves are swamis. All monks of the Swami Order thus trace their spiritual lineage to a common guru, Adi ("the first") Shankaracharya. They take vows of poverty (nonattachment to possessions), chastity, and obedience to the head or spiritual authority. In many ways the Catholic Christian monastic orders resemble the more ancient Order of Swamis.

To his new name a swami adds a word that indicates his formal connection with one of the ten subdivisions of the Swami Order. These *dasanamis* or ten agnomens include the *Giri* (mountain), to which Swami Sri Yukteswar Giri and hence I myself belong. Among the other branches are *Sagara* (sea), *Bharati* (land), *Puri*

---

* Shankara is often called Shankaracharya; *acharya* means "religious teacher." Shankara's date is a center of the usual scholastic dispute. A few records indicate that the peerless monist lived in the sixth century B.C.; the sage Anandagiri gives the dates of 44–12 B.C.; Western historians assign Shankara to the eighth or early ninth century A.D. An affinity for many ages!

The late Jagadguru Sri Shankaracharya of the ancient Gowardhan Math in Puri, His Holiness Bharati Krishna Tirtha, visited America for three months in 1958. It was the first time any Shankaracharya had traveled to the West. His historic tour was sponsored by Self-Realization Fellowship. The Jagadguru spoke before the leading universities of America and participated in a discussion on world peace with the eminent historian Dr. Arnold Toynbee.

In 1959 Sri Shankaracharya of Puri accepted the invitation of Sri Daya Mata, President, to act as representative of the Gurus of Self-Realization Fellowship/Yogoda Satsanga Society of India in initiating into swamihood two Yogoda Satsanga monks. He performed the ceremony in the Sri Yukteswar temple at Yogoda Satsanga Ashram in Puri. *(Publisher's Note)* (tract), *Saraswati* (wisdom of Nature), *Tirtha* (place of pilgrimage), and *Aranya* (forest).

A swami's monastic name, which usually ends in *ananda* (supreme bliss), signifies his aspiration to attain emancipation through a particular path, state, or divine quality—love, wisdom, discrimination, devotion, service, yoga. His agnomen indicates harmony with Nature.

The ideal of selfless service to all mankind and of renunciation of personal ties and ambitions leads most swamis to engage actively in humanitarian and educational work in India or occasionally in foreign lands. Discarding prejudices of caste, creed, class, color, sex, and race, a swami follows the precepts of human brotherhood. His goal is absolute unity with Spirit. Imbuing his waking and sleeping consciousness with the thought, "I am He," he roams contentedly, in the world but not of it. Thus only may he justify his title of *swami:* one who seeks to achieve union with the *Swa* or Self.

Sri Yukteswar was both a swami and a yogi. A swami, formally a monk by virtue of his connection with the venerable Order, is not always a yogi. Anyone who practices a scientific technique for divine realization is a yogi. He may be either married or unmarried, either a man of worldly responsibilities or one of formal religious ties.

A swami may conceivably follow only the path of dry reasoning, of cold renunciation; but a yogi engages himself in a definite, step-by-step procedure by which the body and mind are disciplined and the soul gradually liberated. Taking nothing for granted on emotional grounds or by faith, a yogi practices a thoroughly tested series of exercises that were first mapped out by the ancient rishis. In every age of India, yoga has produced men who became truly free, true Yogi-Christs.

Like any other science, yoga is applicable by people of every clime and time. The theory advanced by certain ignorant writers that yoga is "dangerous" or "unsuitable" for Westerners is wholly false, and has lamentably deterred many sincere students from seeking its manifold blessings.

Yoga is a method for restraining the natural turbulence of thoughts, which otherwise impartially prevents all men, of all lands, from glimpsing their true nature of Spirit. Like the healing light of the sun, yoga is beneficial equally to men of the East and to men of the West. The thoughts of most persons are restless and capricious; a manifest need exists for yoga: the science of mind control.

The ancient rishi Patanjali* defines yoga as "neutralization of the alternating waves in consciousness."† His short and masterly work, *Yoga Sutras*, forms one of the six systems of Hindu philosophy. In contradistinction to Western philosophies, all six Hindu systems‡ embody not only theoretical teachings but practical ones also. After pursuing every conceivable ontological inquiry, the Hindu systems formulate six definite disciplines aimed at the permanent removal of suffering and the attainment of timeless bliss.

The later *Upanishads* uphold the *Yoga Sutras*, among the six systems, as containing the most efficacious methods for achieving direct perception of truth. Through the practical techniques of yoga, man leaves behind forever the barren realms of speculation and cognizes in experience the veritable Essence.

The *Yoga* system of Patanjali is known as the Eightfold Path.§ The first steps are (1) *yama* (moral conduct), and (2) *niyama* (religious observances). *Yama* is fulfilled by noninjury to others, truthfulness, nonstealing, continence, and noncovetousness. The *niyama* prescripts are purity of body and mind, contentment in all circumstances, self-discipline, self-study (contemplation), and devotion to God and guru.

The next steps are (3) *asana* (right posture); the spinal column must be held straight, and the body firm in a comfortable position for meditation; (4) *pranayama* (control of *prana*, subtle life cur-

---

* Patanjali's date is unknown, though many scholars assign him to the second century B.C. The rishis wrote treatises on a vast number of subjects with such insight that the ages have been powerless to outmode them; yet, to the subsequent consternation of historians, the sages made no effort to attach their own dates and stamp of personality to their literary works. They knew that their brief spans were only temporarily important as flashes of the great infinite Life; and that truth is timeless, impossible to trademark, and no private possession of their own.

† *"Chitta vritti nirodha"* (*Yoga Sutras* I:2), which may also be translated as "cessation of the modifications of the mind-stuff." *Chitta* is a comprehensive term for the thinking principle, which includes the pranic life forces, *manas* (mind or sense consciousness), *ahamkara* (egoity), and *buddhi* (intuitive intelligence). *Vritti* (literally "whirlpool") refers to the waves of thought and emotion that ceaselessly arise and subside in man's consciousness. *Nirodha* means neutralization, cessation, control.

‡ The six orthodox (Vedas-based) systems are *Sankhya, Yoga, Vedanta, Mimamsa, Nyaya,* and *Vaisesika.* Readers of a scholarly bent will delight in the subtleties and broad scope of these ancient formulations as summarized in English in *A History of Indian Philosophy,* Vol. I, by Prof. Surendranath Dasgupta (Cambridge Univ. Press).

§ Not to be confused with the "Noble Eightfold Path" of Buddhism, a guide to man's conduct, as follows: (1) right ideals, (2) right motive, (3) right speech, (4) right action, (5) right means of livelihood, (6) right effort, (7) right remembrance (of the Self), and (8) right realization (*samadhi*).

rents); and (5) *pratyahara* (withdrawal of the senses from external objects).

The last steps are forms of yoga proper: (6) *dharana* (concentration), holding the mind to one thought; (7) *dhyana* (meditation); and (8) *samadhi* (superconscious experience). This Eightfold Path of Yoga leads to the final goal of *Kaivalya* (Absoluteness), in which the yogi realizes the Truth beyond all intellectual apprehension.

"Which is greater," one may ask, "a swami or a yogi?" If and when oneness with God is achieved, the distinctions of the various paths disappear. The Bhagavad Gita, however, has pointed out that the methods of yoga are all-embracing. Its techniques are not meant only for certain types and temperaments, such as those few persons who incline toward the monastic life; yoga requires no formal allegiance. Because the yogic science satisfies a universal need, it has a natural universal appeal.

A true yogi may remain dutifully in the world; there he is like butter on water, and not like the unchurned, easily diluted milk of undisciplined humanity. Fulfilling one's earthly responsibilities need not separate man from God, provided he maintains mental uninvolvement with egotistical desires and plays his part in life as a willing instrument of the Divine.

There are a number of great men, living today in American or European or other non-Hindu bodies, who, though they may never have heard the words *yogi* and *swami*, are yet true exemplars of those terms. Through their disinterested service to mankind, or through their mastery over passions and thoughts, or through their singlehearted love of God, or through their great powers of concentration, they are, in a sense, yogis; they have set themselves the goal of yoga—self-control. These men could rise to even greater heights if they were taught the definite science of yoga, which makes possible a more conscious direction of one's mind and life.

Yoga has been superficially misunderstood by certain Western writers, but its critics have never been its practitioners. Among many thoughtful tributes to yoga may be mentioned one by Dr. C. G. Jung, the famous Swiss psychologist.

"When a religious method recommends itself as 'scientific,' it can be certain of its public in the West. Yoga fulfills this expectation," Dr. Jung writes.* "Quite apart from the charm of the new and the fascination of the half-understood, there is good cause for

---

* Dr. Jung attended the Indian Science Congress in 1937 and received an honorary degree from the University of Calcutta.

Yoga to have many adherents. It offers the possibility of controllable experience and thus satisfies the scientific need for 'facts'; and, besides this, by reason of its breadth and depth, its venerable age, its doctrine and method, which include every phase of life, it promises undreamed-of possibilities.

"Every religious or philosophical practice means a psychological discipline, that is, a method of mental hygiene. The manifold, purely bodily procedures of Yoga* also mean a physiological hygiene which is superior to ordinary gymnastics and breathing exercises, inasmuch as it is not merely mechanistic and scientific, but also philosophical; in its training of the parts of the body, it unites them with the whole of the spirit, as is quite clear, for instance, in the *Pranayama* exercises where *Prana* is both the breath and the universal dynamics of the cosmos....

"Yoga practice...would be ineffectual without the concepts on which Yoga is based. It combines the bodily and the spiritual in an extraordinarily complete way.

"In the East, where these ideas and practices have developed, and where for several thousand years an unbroken tradition has created the necessary spiritual foundations, Yoga is, as I can readily believe, the perfect and appropriate method of fusing body and mind together so that they form a unity which is scarcely to be questioned. This unity creates a psychological disposition which makes possible intuitions that transcend consciousness."

The Western day is nearing when the inner science of self-control will be found as necessary as the outer conquest of Nature. The Atomic Age will see men's minds sobered and broadened by the now scientifically indisputable truth that matter is in reality a concentrate of energy. The human mind can and must liberate within itself energies greater than those within stones and metals, lest the material atomic giant, newly unleashed, turn on the world in mindless destruction. An indirect benefit of mankind's concern over atomic bombs may be an increased practical interest in the science of yoga,† a "bombproof shelter" truly.

---

* Dr. Jung is here referring to *Hatha Yoga*, a specialized branch of bodily postures and techniques for health and longevity. *Hatha* is useful, and produces spectacular physical results, but this branch of yoga is little used by yogis bent on spiritual liberation.

† Many uninformed persons speak of yoga as *Hatha Yoga* or consider yoga to be "magic," dark mysterious rites for attaining spectacular powers. When scholars, however, speak of yoga they mean the system expounded in *Yoga Sutras* (also known as *Patanjali's Aphorisms*): *Raja* ("royal") *Yoga*. The treatise embodies philosophic

concepts of such grandeur as to have inspired commentaries by some of India's greatest thinkers, including the illumined master Sadasivendra (see page 337 n.).

Like the other five orthodox (Vedas-based) philosophical systems, *Yoga Sutras* considers the "magic" of moral purity (the "ten commandments" of *yama* and *niyama*) to be the indispensable preliminary for sound philosophical investigation. This personal demand, not insisted on in the West, has bestowed lasting vitality on the six Indian disciplines. The cosmic order (*rita*) that upholds the universe is not different from the moral order that rules man's destiny. He who is unwilling to observe the universal moral precepts is not seriously determined to pursue truth.

Section III of *Yoga Sutras* mentions various yogic miraculous powers (*vibhutis* and *siddhis*). True knowledge is always power. The path of yoga is divided into four stages, each with its *vibhuti* expression. Achieving a certain power, the yogi knows that he has successfully passed the tests of one of the four stages. Emergence of the characteristic powers is evidence of the scientific structure of the yoga system, wherein delusive imaginations about one's "spiritual progress" are banished; proof is required!

Patanjali warns the devotee that unity with Spirit should be the sole goal, not the possession of *vibhutis*—the merely incidental flowers along the sacred path. May the Eternal Giver be sought, not His phenomenal gifts! God does not reveal Himself to a seeker who is satisfied with any lesser attainment. The striving yogi is therefore careful not to exercise his phenomenal powers, lest they arouse false pride and distract him from entering the ultimate state of *Kaivalya*.

When the yogi has reached his Infinite Goal, he exercises the *vibhutis*, or refrains from exercising them, just as he pleases. All his actions, miraculous or otherwise, are then performed without karmic involvement. The iron filings of karma are attracted only where a magnet of the personal ego still exists.

CHAPTER 25

Brother Ananta and Sister Nalini

"Ananta cannot live; the sands of his karma for this life have run out."

These inexorable words reached my inner consciousness as I sat one morning in deep meditation. Shortly after I had entered the Swami Order, I paid a visit to my birthplace, Gorakhpur, as the guest of my elder brother Ananta. A sudden illness confined him to his bed; I nursed him lovingly.

The solemn inward pronouncement filled me with grief. I felt that I could not bear to remain longer in Gorakhpur, only to see my brother removed before my helpless gaze. Amidst uncomprehending criticism from my relatives, I left India on the first available boat. It cruised along Burma and the China Sea to Japan. I disembarked at Kobe, where I spent only a few days. My heart was too heavy for sight-seeing.

On the return trip to India, the boat touched at Shanghai. There Dr. Misra, the ship's physician, guided me to several curio shops, where I selected various presents for Sri Yukteswar and my family and friends. For Ananta I purchased a large carved bamboo piece. No sooner had the Chinese salesman handed me the bamboo souvenir than I dropped it on the floor, crying out, "I have bought this for my dear dead brother!"

A clear realization had swept over me that his soul was just being freed in the Infinite. The souvenir was sharply and symbolically cracked by its fall; amidst sobs, I wrote on the bamboo surface: "For my beloved Ananta, now gone."

My companion, the doctor, had been observing me with a sardonic smile.

"Save your tears," he remarked. "Why shed them until you are sure he is dead?"

When our boat reached Calcutta, Dr. Misra again accompanied me. My youngest brother Bishnu was waiting to greet me at the dock.

"I know Ananta has departed this life," I said to Bishnu, before he had had time to speak. "Please tell me, and the doctor here, when Ananta died."

Bishnu named the date, which was the very day that I had bought the souvenirs in Shanghai.

"Look here!" Dr. Misra ejaculated. "Don't let any word of this get around! The professors will be adding a year's study of mental telepathy to the medical course, which is already long enough!"

Father embraced me warmly as I entered our home. "You have come," he said tenderly. Two large tears dropped from his eyes. Ordinarily undemonstrative, he had never before shown me these external signs of affection. Outwardly the grave father, inwardly he possessed the melting heart of a mother. In all family affairs he played this dual parental role.

Soon after Ananta's passing, my younger sister Nalini was brought back from death's door by a divine healing. Before relating the story, I will refer to a few phases of our earlier life.

The childhood relationship between Nalini and me had not been of the happiest nature. I was very thin; she was thinner still. Through an unconscious motive that psychologists will have no difficulty in identifying, I would often tease my sister about her appearance. Her retorts would be equally imbued with the callous frankness of extreme youth. Sometimes Mother would intervene, temporarily ending the childish quarrels by a gentle box on my ear (as the elder ear).

After her school years were over Nalini was betrothed to Dr. Panchanon Bose, a likable young physician of Calcutta. Elaborate marriage rites were celebrated in due time. On the wedding night I joined the large, jovial group of relatives in the living room of our Calcutta home. The bridegroom was leaning on an immense gold-brocaded pillow, with Nalini at his side. A gorgeous purple silk *sari** could not, alas, wholly hide her angularity. I sheltered myself behind the pillow of my new brother-in-law and grinned at him in friendly fashion. He had never seen Nalini until the day of the nuptial ceremony, when he finally learned what he was getting in the matrimonial lottery.

Feeling my sympathy, Dr. Bose pointed unobtrusively to Nalini, and whispered in my ear, "Say, what's this?"

"Why, Doctor," I replied, "it is a skeleton for your observation!"

As the years went on, Dr. Bose endeared himself to our family, who called on him whenever illness arose. He and I became fast friends, often joking together, usually with Nalini as our target.

* The gracefully draped dress of Indian women.

"It is a medical curiosity," my brother-in-law remarked to me one day. "I have tried everything on your lean sister—cod-liver oil, butter, malt, honey, fish, meat, eggs, tonics. Still she fails to bulge even one-hundredth of an inch."

A few days later I visited the Bose home. My errand there took only a few minutes; I was leaving, unnoticed, I thought, by Nalini. As I reached the front door, I heard her voice, cordial but commanding.

"Brother, come here. You are not going to give me the slip this time. I want to talk with you."

I mounted the stairs to her room. To my surprise, she was in tears.

"Dear brother," she said, "let us bury the old hatchet. I see that your feet are now firmly set on the spiritual path. I want to become like you in every way." She added hopefully, "You are now robust in appearance; will you help me? My husband does not come near me, and I love him so dearly! But my chief desire is to progress in God-realization, even if I must remain thin* and unattractive."

My heart was deeply touched at her plea. Our new friendship steadily progressed; one day she asked to become my disciple.

"Train me in any way you like. I put my trust in God instead of tonics." She gathered together an armful of medicines and poured them down a drain outside her window.

As a test of her faith, I asked her to omit from her diet all fish, meat, and eggs.

After several months, during which Nalini had strictly followed the various rules I had outlined, and had adhered to her vegetarian diet in spite of numerous difficulties, I paid her a visit.

"Sis, you have been conscientiously observing the spiritual injunctions; your reward is near." I smiled mischievously. "How plump do you want to be? As fat as our aunt who hasn't seen her feet in years?"

"No! But I long to be as stout as you are."

I replied solemnly. "By the grace of God, as I have spoken truth always, I speak truly now.† Through the divine blessings, your body

---

* Because most persons in India are thin, reasonable plumpness is considered desirable.

† The Hindu scriptures declare that those who habitually speak the truth develop the power of materializing their words. What commands they utter from the heart come to pass. (*Yoga Sutras* II:36.)

Because the worlds are built on truth, all scriptures extol it as a virtue by which man may tune his life with the Infinite. Mahatma Gandhi often said: "Truth is God";

shall verily change from today; in one month it shall have the same weight as mine."

These words from my heart found fulfillment. In thirty days, Nalini's weight equaled mine. The new roundness gave her beauty; her husband fell deeply in love. Their marriage, begun so inauspiciously, turned out to be ideally happy.

On my return from Japan, I learned that during my absence Nalini had been stricken with typhoid fever. I rushed to her home, and was aghast to find her extremely emaciated. She was in a coma.

My brother-in-law told me, "Before her mind became confused by illness, she often said: 'If brother Mukunda were here, I would not be faring thus.'" He added tearfully, "The other doctors and I see no ray of hope. After her long bout with typhoid, blood dysentery has now set in."

I tried to move heaven and earth with my prayers. Engaging an Anglo-Indian nurse, who gave me full cooperation, I applied on my sister various yoga methods of healing. The blood dysentery vanished.

But Dr. Bose shook his head mournfully. "She simply has no more blood left to shed."

"She will recover," I replied stoutly. "In seven days her fever will be gone."

A week later I was thrilled to see Nalini open her eyes and gaze at me with loving recognition. From that day her recovery was swift. Although she regained her usual weight, she bore one sad scar of her nearly fatal illness: her legs were paralyzed. Indian and English specialists pronounced her a hopeless cripple.

The incessant war for her life that I had waged by prayer had exhausted me. I went to Serampore to ask Sri Yukteswar's help. His eyes expressed deep sympathy as I told him of Nalini's plight.

"Your sister's legs will be normal at the end of one month." He added, "Let her wear, next to her skin, a band with an unperforated two-carat pearl, held on by a clasp."

I prostrated myself at his feet with joyful relief.

"Sir, you are a master; your word that she will recover is enough. But if you insist I will immediately get her a pearl."

---

his lifelong striving was for perfect truth in thought, speech, and act. Throughout the ages the ideal of *satya* (truth) has permeated Hindu society. Marco Polo tells us that the *Brahmins* "would not utter a lie for anything on earth." An English judge in India, William Sleeman, says in his *Journey Through Oudh in 1849–50:* "I have had before me hundreds of cases in which a man's property, liberty, or life depended on his telling a lie; and he has refused to tell it."

My guru nodded. "Yes, do that." He went on to describe correctly the physical and mental characteristics of Nalini, whom he had never seen.

"Sir," I inquired, "is this an astrological analysis? You do not know her birth day or hour."

Sri Yukteswar smiled. "There is a deeper astrology, not dependent on the testimony of calendars and clocks. Each man is a part of the Creator, or Cosmic Man; he has a heavenly body as well as one of earth. The human eye sees the physical form, but the inner eye penetrates more profoundly, even to the universal pattern of which each man is an integral and individual part."

I returned to Calcutta and purchased a pearl* for Nalini. A month later, her paralyzed legs were completely healed.

Sister asked me to convey her heartfelt gratitude to my guru. He listened to the message in silence. But as I was taking my leave, he made a pregnant comment:

"Your sister has been told by many doctors that she can never bear children. Assure her that within a few years she will give birth to two daughters."

Some years later, to Nalini's joy, she bore a girl; and, in a few more years, another daughter.

---

* Pearls and other jewels as well as metals and plants, applied directly to the human skin, exercise an electromagnetic influence over the physical cells. Man's body contains carbon and various metallic elements that are present also in plants, metals, jewels. The discoveries of the rishis in these fields will doubtless receive confirmation someday from physiologists. Man's sensitive body, with its electrical life currents, is a center of many mysteries as yet unexplored.

Though jewels and metal bangles have remedial values for the body, Sri Yukteswar had another reason for recommending them. Masters never wish to appear as great healers: God alone is the Healer. Saints, therefore, often cloak with various disguises the powers they have humbly received from the Lord. Man usually puts his trust in tangibles; when persons came for healing to my guru, he advised them to wear a bangle or a jewel in order to arouse their faith and also to divert attention from himself. The bangles and jewels possessed, in addition to their intrinsic electromagnetic healing potencies, Master's hidden spiritual blessing.

SRI SHANKARACHARYA AT SRF-YSS HEADQUARTERS

Sri Jagadguru Shankaracharya Bharati Krishna Tirtha of Puri, India, at Self-Realization Fellowship International Headquarters, Los Angeles (founded in 1925 by Paramahansa Yogananda). In 1958, the Jagadguru, senior head of the Swami Order, paid a three-month visit to America, sponsored by Self-Realization Fellowship. It was the first time in the history of the ancient Swami Order that a Shankaracharya had traveled to the West. (See page 196 n.)

A WESTERNER IN SAMADHI
Rajarsi Janakananda (James J. Lynn)

On a private beach at Encinitas, California, in January 1937, after five years of daily practice of *Kriya Yoga*, Mr. Lynn received in *samadhi* (superconsciousness) the Beatific Vision: the Infinite Lord as the Indwelling Glory.

"The balanced life of Mr. Lynn may serve as an inspiration for all men," Yogananda said. Conscientiously discharging the duties of his worldly life, Mr. Lynn yet found time daily for deep meditation on God. The successful businessman became an illumined *Kriya Yogi*. (See pages 313, 404–5.)

Paramahansaji often lovingly referred to him as "Saint Lynn," and in 1951 bestowed on him the monastic name Rajarsi Janakananda (after the spiritually illustrious King Janaka of ancient India). The title *rajarsi*, literally "royal rishi," is derived from *raja* ("king") + *rsi* (or *rishi*, "great saint").

CHAPTER 26

The Science of Kriya Yoga

The science of *Kriya Yoga*, mentioned so often in these pages, became widely known in modern India through the instrumentality of Lahiri Mahasaya, my guru's guru. The Sanskrit root of *kriya* is *kri*, to do, to act and react; the same root is found in the word *karma*, the natural principle of cause and effect. *Kriya Yoga* is thus "union (*yoga*) with the Infinite through a certain action or rite (*kriya*)." A yogi who faithfully practices the technique is gradually freed from karma or the lawful chain of cause-effect equilibriums.

Because of certain ancient yogic injunctions, I may not give a full explanation of *Kriya Yoga* in a book intended for the general public. The actual technique should be learned from an authorized *Kriyaban (Kriya Yogi)* of Self-Realization Fellowship (Yogoda Satsanga Society of India).* Here a broad reference must suffice.

Kriya Yoga is a simple, psychophysiological method by which human blood is decarbonated and recharged with oxygen. The atoms of this extra oxygen are transmuted into life current to rejuvenate the brain and spinal centers. By stopping the accumulation of venous blood, the yogi is able to lessen or prevent the decay of tissues. The advanced yogi transmutes his cells into energy. Elijah, Jesus, Kabir, and other prophets were past masters in the use of *Kriya* or a similar technique, by which they caused their bodies to materialize and dematerialize at will.

Kriya is an ancient science. Lahiri Mahasaya received it from his great guru, Babaji, who rediscovered and clarified the technique after it had been lost in the Dark Ages. Babaji renamed it, simply, *Kriya Yoga.*

---

* Paramahansa Yogananda conferred on those who would succeed him as president and spiritual head of his society (Self-Realization Fellowship/Yogoda Satsanga Society of India) the authority to bestow *Kriya Yoga* instruction and initiation on eligible students, or to appoint an ordained SRF/YSS minister to do so. He also provided for the perpetual dissemination of the *Kriya Yoga* science through his *Self-Realization Fellowship (Yogoda) Lessons*, available from the SRF international headquarters in Los Angeles (see page 425). *(Publisher's Note)*

"The *Kriya Yoga* that I am giving to the world through you in this nineteenth century," Babaji told Lahiri Mahasaya, "is a revival of the same science that Krishna gave millenniums ago to Arjuna; and that was later known to Patanjali and Christ, and to St. John, St. Paul, and other disciples."

Kriya Yoga is twice referred to by Lord Krishna, India's greatest prophet, in the Bhagavad Gita. One stanza reads: "Offering the inhaling breath into the exhaling breath and offering the exhaling breath into the inhaling breath, the yogi neutralizes both breaths; thus he releases *prana* from the heart and brings life force under his control."* The interpretation is: "The yogi arrests decay in the body by securing an additional supply of *prana* (life force) through quieting the action of the lungs and heart; he also arrests mutations of growth in the body by control of *apana* (eliminating current). Thus neutralizing decay and growth, the yogi learns life-force control."

Another Gita stanza states: "That meditation-expert (*muni*) becomes eternally free who, seeking the Supreme Goal, is able to withdraw from external phenomena by fixing his gaze within the mid-spot of the eyebrows and by neutralizing the even currents of *prana* and *apana* [that flow] within the nostrils and lungs; and to control his sensory mind and intellect; and to banish desire, fear, and anger."†

Krishna also relates‡ that it was he, in a former incarnation, who communicated the indestructible yoga to an ancient illuminato, Vivasvat, who gave it to Manu, the great legislator.§ He, in turn, instructed Ikshwaku, founder of India's solar warrior dynasty. Passing thus from one to another, the royal yoga was guarded by the rishis until the coming of the materialistic ages.¶ Then, because of priestly secrecy and man's indifference, the sacred lore gradually became inaccessible.

---

* Bhagavad Gita IV:29.

† *Ibid.* V:27–28. See pp. 537, 539–40 for further explanations about the science of breath.

‡ *Ibid.* IV:1–2.

§ The antehistorical author of *Manava Dharma Shastra* or *Laws of Manu*. These institutes of canonized common law are effective in India to this day.

¶ The start of the materialistic ages, according to Hindu scriptural reckoning, was 3102 B.C. That year was the beginning of the last Descending *Dwapara Yuga* of the Equinoctial Cycle, and also the start of the *Kali Yuga* of the Universal Cycle (see p. 147). Most anthropologists, believing that 10,000 years ago humanity was living in a barbarous Stone Age, summarily dismiss as "myths" the widespread traditions of very ancient civilizations in Lemuria, Atlantis, India, China, Japan, Egypt, Mexico, and many other lands.

Kriya Yoga is mentioned twice by the ancient sage Patanjali, foremost exponent of yoga, who wrote: *"Kriya Yoga* consists of body discipline, mental control, and meditating on *Aum."** Patanjali speaks of God as the actual Cosmic Sound of *Aum* that is heard in meditation.† *Aum* is the Creative Word, the whir of the Vibratory Motor, the witness‡ of Divine Presence. Even the beginner in yoga may soon hear the wondrous sound of *Aum.* Through this blissful spiritual encouragement, he becomes convinced that he is in communion with supernal realms.

Patanjali refers a second time to the *Kriya* technique or life-force control thus: "Liberation can be attained by that *pranayama* which is accomplished by disjoining the course of inspiration and expiration."§

St. Paul knew *Kriya Yoga,* or a similar technique, by which he could switch life currents to and from the senses. He was therefore able to say: "I protest by our rejoicing which I have in Christ, *I die daily."*¶ By a method of centering inwardly all bodily life force (which ordinarily is directed only outwardly, to the sensory world, thus lending it a seeming validity), St. Paul experienced daily a true yoga union with the "rejoicing" (bliss) of the Christ Consciousness. In that felicitous state he was conscious of being "dead" to or freed from sensory delusions, the world of *maya.*

In the initial states of God-communion (*sabikalpa samadhi*) the devotee's consciousness merges in the Cosmic Spirit; his life force is withdrawn from the body, which appears "dead," or motionless and rigid. The yogi is fully aware of his bodily condition of suspended animation. As he progresses to higher spiritual states

---

* *Yoga Sutras* II:1. In using the words *Kriya Yoga,* Patanjali was referring either to the technique later taught by Babaji or to one very similar. That Patanjali was mentioning a definite technique of life-force control is proved by his aphorism in *Yoga Sutras* II:49 (cited on this page).

† *Ibid.* I:27.

‡ "These things saith the Amen, the faithful and true *witness,* the beginning of the creation of God."—Revelation 3:14. "In the beginning was the Word, and the Word was with God, and the Word was God....All things were made by him [the Word or *Aum*]; and without him was not any thing made that was made."—John 1:1–3. *Aum* of the Vedas became the sacred word *Hum* of the Tibetans, *Amin* of the Moslems, and *Amen* of the Egyptians, Greeks, Romans, Jews, and Christians. Its meaning in Hebrew is *sure, faithful.*

§ *Yoga Sutras* II:49.

¶ I Corinthians 15:31. "Our rejoicing" is the correct translation; not, as usually given, "your rejoicing." St. Paul was referring to the *universality* of the Christ Consciousness.

(*nirbikalpa samadhi*), however, he communes with God without bodily fixation; and in his ordinary waking consciousness, even in the midst of exacting worldly duties.*

"*Kriya Yoga* is an instrument through which human evolution can be quickened," Sri Yukteswar explained to his students. "The ancient yogis discovered that the secret of cosmic consciousness is intimately linked with breath mastery. This is India's unique and deathless contribution to the world's treasury of knowledge. The life force, which is ordinarily absorbed in maintaining heart action, must be freed for higher activities by a method of calming and stilling the ceaseless demands of the breath."

The *Kriya Yogi* mentally directs his life energy to revolve, upward and downward, around the six spinal centers (medullary, cervical, dorsal, lumbar, sacral, and coccygeal plexuses), which correspond to the twelve astral signs of the zodiac, the symbolic Cosmic Man. One-half minute of revolution of energy around the sensitive spinal cord of man effects subtle progress in his evolution; that half-minute of *Kriya* equals one year of natural spiritual unfoldment.

The astral system of a human being, with six (twelve by polarity) inner constellations revolving around the sun of the omniscient spiritual eye, is interrelated with the physical sun and the twelve zodiacal signs. All men are thus affected by an inner and an outer universe. The ancient rishis discovered that man's earthly and heavenly environment, in a series of twelve-year cycles, push him forward on his natural path. The scriptures aver that man requires a million years of normal, diseaseless evolution to perfect his human brain and attain cosmic consciousness.

One thousand *Kriyas* practiced in 8½ hours gives the yogi, in one day, the equivalent of one thousand years of natural evolution: 365,000 years of evolution in one year. In three years, a *Kriya Yogi* can thus accomplish by intelligent self-effort the same result that Nature brings to pass in a million years. The *Kriya* shortcut, of course, can be taken only by deeply developed yogis. With the guidance of a guru, such yogis have carefully prepared their body and brain to withstand the power generated by intensive practice.

The *Kriya* beginner employs his yogic technique only four-

---

* The Sanskrit word *bikalpa* means "difference, nonidentity." *Sabikalpa* is the state of *samadhi* "with difference," *nirbikalpa* is the state "without difference." That is, in *sabikalpa samadhi* the devotee still retains a slight feeling of separateness from God; in *nirbikalpa samadhi* he realizes fully his identity as Spirit.

teen to twenty-four times, twice daily. A number of yogis achieve emancipation in six or twelve or twenty-four or forty-eight years. A yogi who dies before achieving full realization carries with him the good karma of his past *Kriya* effort; in his new life he is naturally propelled toward his Infinite Goal.

The body of the average man is like a fifty-watt lamp, which cannot accommodate the billion watts of power roused by an excessive practice of *Kriya*. Through gradual and regular increase of the simple and foolproof methods of *Kriya*, man's body becomes astrally transformed day by day, and is finally fitted to express the infinite potentials of cosmic energy, which constitutes the first materially active expression of Spirit.

Kriya Yoga has nothing in common with the unscientific breathing exercises taught by a number of misguided zealots. Attempts to hold breath forcibly in the lungs are unnatural and decidedly unpleasant. *Kriya* practice, on the other hand, is accompanied from the very beginning by feelings of peace and by soothing sensations of regenerative effect in the spine.

The ancient yogic technique converts the breath into mind-stuff. By spiritual advancement, one is able to cognize the breath as a mental concept, an act of mind: a dream breath.

Many illustrations could be given of the mathematical relationship between man's respiratory rate and the variations in his states of consciousness. A person whose attention is wholly engrossed, as in following some closely knit intellectual argument, or in attempting some delicate or difficult physical feat, automatically breathes very slowly. Fixity of attention depends on slow breathing; quick or uneven breaths are an inevitable accompaniment of harmful emotional states: fear, lust, anger. The restless monkey breathes at the rate of 32 times a minute, in contrast to man's average of 18 times. The elephant, tortoise, snake, and other creatures noted for their longevity have a respiratory rate that is less than man's. The giant tortoise, for instance, which may attain the age of three hundred years, breathes only 4 times a minute.

The rejuvenating effects of sleep are due to man's temporary unawareness of body and breathing. The sleeping man becomes a yogi; each night he unconsciously performs the yogic rite of releasing himself from bodily identification, and of merging the life force with healing currents in the main brain region and in the six subdynamos of his spinal centers. Unknowingly, the sleeper is thus recharged by the cosmic energy that sustains all life.

The voluntary yogi performs a simple, natural process consciously, not unconsciously like the slow-paced sleeper. The *Kriya Yogi* uses his technique to saturate and feed all his physical cells with undecayable light and thus to keep them in a spiritually magnetized condition. He scientifically makes breathing unnecessary, and does not enter (during his hours of practice) the negative states of sleep, unconsciousness, or death.

In men under *maya* or natural law, the flow of life energy is toward the outward world; the currents are wasted and abused in the senses. The practice of *Kriya* reverses the flow; life force is mentally guided to the inner cosmos and becomes reunited with subtle spinal energies. By such reinforcement of life force, the yogi's body and brain cells are renewed by a spiritual elixir.

Through proper food, sunlight, and harmonious thoughts, men who are led only by Nature and her divine plan will achieve Self-realization in a million years. Twelve years of normal healthful living are required to effect even slight refinements in brain structure; a million solar returns are exacted to purify the cerebral tenement sufficiently for manifestation of cosmic consciousness. A *Kriya Yogi*, however, by use of a spiritual science removes himself from the necessity for a long period of careful observance of natural laws.

Untying the cord of breath that binds the soul to the body, *Kriya* serves to prolong life and to enlarge the consciousness to infinity. The yoga technique overcomes the tug-of-war between the mind and the matter-entangled senses, and frees the devotee to reinherit his eternal kingdom. He knows then that his real being is bound neither by physical encasement nor by breath—symbol of mortal man's enslavement to air, to Nature's elemental compulsions.

Master of his body and mind, the *Kriya Yogi* ultimately achieves victory over the "last enemy,"* Death.

> So shalt thou feed on Death, that feeds on men:
> And Death once dead, there's no more dying then.†

---

* "The last enemy that shall be destroyed is death" (I Corinthians 15:26). The incorruptibility of Paramahansa Yogananda's body after death (see page 422) proved him a perfected *Kriya Yogi*. Not all great masters, however, manifest bodily nondecay after death. (See page 268 n.) Such miracles occur, the Hindu scriptures tell us, only for some special purpose. In Paramahansaji's case, the "special purpose" was doubtless to convince the West of the value of yoga. Yoganandaji had been commanded by Babaji and Sri Yukteswarji to serve the West; Paramahansaji fulfilled that trust both in his life and in his death. *(Publisher's Note)*

† Shakespeare: *Sonnet 146.*

Introspection, or "sitting in the silence," is an unscientific way of trying to force apart the mind and senses, tied together by the life force. The contemplative mind, attempting its return to divinity, is constantly dragged back toward the senses by the life currents. *Kriya*, controlling the mind *directly* through the life force, is the easiest, most effective, and most scientific avenue of approach to the Infinite. In contrast to the slow, uncertain "bullock cart" theological path to God, *Kriya Yoga* may justly be called the "airplane" route.

The yogic science is based on an empirical consideration of all forms of concentration and meditation techniques. Yoga enables the devotee to switch off or on, at will, life current to the five sense telephones of sight, sound, smell, taste, and touch. Attaining this power of sense disconnection, the yogi finds it simple to unite his mind at will with divine realms or with the world of matter. No longer is he unwillingly brought back by the life force to the mundane sphere of rowdy sensations and restless thoughts.

The life of an advanced *Kriya Yogi* is influenced, not by effects of past actions, but solely by directions from the soul. The devotee thus avoids the slow, evolutionary monitors of egoistic actions, good and bad, of common life — cumbrous and snail-like to the eagle hearts.

The superior method of soul living frees the yogi; emerging from his ego-prison, he tastes the deep air of omnipresence. The thralldom of natural living is, in contrast, set in a pace humiliating. Conforming his life merely to the evolutionary order, a man can command no concessionary haste from Nature. Though he live without error against the laws that govern his body and mind, he still requires a million years of masquerading incarnations to attain final emancipation.

The telescopic methods of a yogi, disengaging himself from physical and mental identifications in favor of soul individuality, are therefore commended to those who eye with revolt a thousand thousand years. This numerical periphery is enlarged for the ordinary man, who lives in harmony not even with Nature, let alone his soul; pursuing instead unnatural complexities and offending in his thoughts and body the sweet sanities of Nature. For him, two times a million years can scarce suffice for liberation.

Gross man seldom or never realizes that his body is a kingdom, governed by Emperor Soul on the throne of the cranium, with subsidiary regents in the six spinal centers or spheres of consciousness. This theocracy extends over a throng of obedient subjects: twenty-seven thousand billion cells (endowed with sure if seemingly automatic intelligence by which they perform all duties of bodily growths, transformations, and dissolutions) and fifty million substratal thoughts, emotions, and variations of alternating phases in man's consciousness in an average life of sixty years.

Any apparent insurrection in the human body or mind against Emperor Soul, manifesting as disease or irrationality, is due to no disloyalty among the humble subjects, but stems from past or present misuse by man of his individuality or free will—given to him simultaneously with a soul, and revocable never.

Identifying himself with a shallow ego, man takes for granted that it is he who thinks, wills, feels, digests meals, and keeps himself alive, never admitting through reflection (only a little would suffice) that in his ordinary life he is naught but a puppet of past actions (karma) and of Nature or environment. Each man's intellectual reactions, feelings, moods, and habits are merely effects of past causes, whether of this or a prior life. Lofty above such influences, however, is his regal soul. Spurning the transitory truths and freedoms, the *Kriya Yogi* passes beyond all disillusionment into his unfettered Being. The world's scriptures declare man to be not a corruptible body but a living soul; in *Kriya Yoga* he finds a method to prove the scriptural affirmation.

"Outward ritual cannot destroy ignorance, because they are not mutually contradictory," wrote Shankara in his famous *Century of Verses.* "Realized knowledge alone destroys ignorance. . . . Knowledge cannot spring up by any other means than inquiry. 'Who am I? How was this universe born? Who is its maker? What is its material cause?' This is the kind of inquiry referred to." The intellect has no answer for these questions; hence the rishis evolved yoga as the technique of spiritual inquiry.

The true yogi, withholding his thoughts, will, and feelings from false identification with bodily desires, uniting his mind with superconscious forces in the spinal shrines, thus lives in the world as God hath planned; he is impelled neither by impulses from the past nor by fresh motivations of human witlessness. Receiving fulfillment of his Supreme Desire, he is safe in the final haven of inexhaustibly blissful Spirit.

Referring to the sure and methodical efficacy of yoga, Krishna praises the technological yogi in the following words: "The yogi is greater than body-disciplining ascetics, greater even than the followers of the path of wisdom (*Jnana Yoga*), or of the path of action (*Karma Yoga*); be thou, O disciple Arjuna, a yogi!"*

Kriya Yoga is the real "fire rite" oft extolled in the Gita. The yogi casts his human longings into a monotheistic bonfire consecrated to the unparalleled God. This is indeed the true yogic fire ceremony, in which all past and present desires are fuel consumed by love divine. The Ultimate Flame receives the sacrifice of all human madness, and man is pure of dross. His metaphorical bones stripped of all desirous flesh, his karmic skeleton bleached by the antiseptic sun of wisdom, inoffensive before man and Maker, he is clean at last.

---

* Bhagavad Gita VI:46.

Modern science is beginning to discover the truly extraordinary curative and rejuvenating effects, on body and mind, of non-breathing. Dr. Alvan L. Barach of the College of Physicians and Surgeons in New York has originated a local lung-rest therapy that is restoring to health many tuberculosis sufferers. The use of an equalizing pressure chamber enables the patient to stop breathing. *The New York Times* of Feb. 1, 1947, quoted Dr. Barach as follows: "The effect of cessation of breathing on the central nervous system is of considerable interest. The impulse for movement of the voluntary muscles in the extremities is strikingly diminished. The patient may lie in the chamber for hours without moving his hands or changing position. The desire to smoke disappears when voluntary respiration stops, even in patients who have been accustomed to smoke two packages of cigarettes daily. In many instances the relaxation is of such a nature that the patient does not require amusement." In 1951 Dr. Barach publicly confirmed the value of the treatment, which, he said, "not only rests the lungs but also the entire body, and, seemingly, the mind. The heart, for example, has its work decreased by a third. Our subjects stop worrying. None feel bored."

From these facts, one begins to understand how it is possible for yogis to sit motionless for long periods without mental or bodily urge toward restless activity. Only by such quietude may the soul find its way back to God. Though ordinary men must remain in an equalizing pressure chamber to obtain certain benefits of non-breathing, the yogi needs nothing but the *Kriya Yoga* technique to receive rewards in body and mind, and in soul-awareness.

CHAPTER 27

Founding a Yoga School
in Ranchi

"Why are you averse to organizational work?"

Master's question startled me a bit. It is true that my private conviction at the time was that organizations are "hornets' nests."

"It is a thankless task, sir," I answered. "No matter what the leader does, or does not do, he is criticized."

"Do you want the whole divine *channa* (milk curd) for yourself alone?" My guru's retort was accompanied by a stern glance. "Could you or anyone else achieve God-communion through yoga if a line of generous-hearted masters had not been willing to convey their knowledge to others?" He added, "God is the Honey, organizations are the hives; both are necessary. Any *form* is useless, of course, without the spirit, but why should you not start busy hives full of the spiritual nectar?"

His counsel moved me deeply. Although I made no outward reply, an adamant resolution arose in my breast: I would share with my fellows, so far as lay in my power, the unshackling truths I had learned at my guru's feet. "Lord," I prayed, "may Thy love shine forever on the sanctuary of my devotion, and may I be able to awaken Thy love in all hearts."

On a previous occasion, before I had joined the monastic order, Sri Yukteswar had made a most unexpected remark.

"How you will miss the companionship of a wife in your old age!" he had said. "Do you not agree that the family man, engaged in useful work to maintain his wife and children, thus plays a rewarding role in God's eyes?"

"Sir," I had protested in alarm, "you know that my desire in this life is only for the Cosmic Beloved."

Master had laughed so merrily that I understood his words had been uttered merely to test me.

"Remember," he had said slowly, "that he who rejects the usual worldly duties can justify himself only by assuming some kind of responsibility for a much larger family."

The ideal of right education for youth had always been very close to my heart. I saw clearly the arid results of ordinary instruction, aimed at the development of body and intellect only. Moral and spiritual values, without whose appreciation no man can approach happiness, were yet lacking in the formal curriculum. I determined to found a school where young boys could develop to the full stature of manhood. My first step in that direction was made with seven children at Dihika, a small country site in Bengal.

A year later, in 1918, through the generosity of Sir Manindra Chandra Nundy, the Maharaja of Kasimbazar, I was able to transfer my fast-growing group to Ranchi. This town in Bihar, about two hundred miles from Calcutta, is blessed with one of the most healthful climates in India. The Kasimbazar Palace in Ranchi became the main building of the new school, which I called "Yogoda Satsanga Brahmacharya Vidyalaya."*

I organized a program for both grammar- and high-school grades. It includes agricultural, industrial, commercial, and academic subjects. Following the educational ideals of the rishis (whose forest ashrams had been the ancient seats of learning, both secular and divine, for the youth of India), I arranged that most class instruction be given outdoors.

The Ranchi students are taught yoga meditation, and a unique system of health and physical development, *Yogoda,* whose principles I discovered in 1916.

Realizing that man's body is like an electric battery, I reasoned that it could be recharged with energy through the direct agency of the human will. As no action of any kind is possible without *willing,* man may avail himself of the prime mover, will, to renew his strength without burdensome apparatus or mechanical exercises. By the simple Yogoda techniques, one may consciously and instantly recharge his life force (centered in the medulla oblongata) from the unlimited supply of cosmic energy.

The boys at Ranchi responded well to Yogoda training, developing extraordinary ability to shift the life force from one part of the

---

* *Vidyalaya,* school. *Brahmacharya* here refers to one of the four stages in the Vedic plan for man's life, as comprising that of (1) the celibate student (*brahmachari*); (2) the householder with worldly responsibilities (*grihastha*); (3) the hermit (*vanaprastha*); (4) the forest dweller or wanderer, free from all earthly concerns (*sannyasi*). This ideal scheme of life, while not widely observed in modern India, still has many devout followers. The four stages are carried out religiously under the lifelong direction of a guru.

Further information about the Yogoda Satsanga school in Ranchi is given in chapter 40.

body to another part and to sit in perfect poise in difficult *asanas* (postures).* They performed feats of strength and endurance that many powerful adults could not equal.

My youngest brother, Bishnu Charan Ghosh, joined the Ranchi school; later he became a noted physical culturist. He and one of his students traveled in 1938–9 to the West, giving exhibitions of strength and muscular control. Professors at Columbia University in New York and at many other universities in America and Europe were amazed by demonstrations of the power of the mind over the body.†

At the end of the first year in Ranchi, applications for admission had reached two thousand. But the school, which at that time was solely residential, could accommodate only a hundred. Instruction for day students was soon added.

In the Vidyalaya I had to play father-mother to the little children and to cope with many organizational difficulties. I often remembered Christ's words: "There is no man that hath left house, or brethren, or sisters, or father, or mother, or wife, or children, or lands, for my sake, and the gospel's, but he shall receive an hundredfold now in this time, houses, and brethren, and sisters, and mothers, and children, and lands, with persecutions; and in the world to come eternal life."‡

Sri Yukteswar had interpreted these words as follows: "The devotee who forgoes the usual life experiences of marriage and family-rearing in order to assume greater responsibilities—those for society in general ("an hundredfold now in this time, houses, and brethren")—performs a work that is often accompanied by persecution from a misunderstanding world. But such larger identifications help the devotee to overcome selfishness and bring him a divine reward."

One day my father arrived in Ranchi to bestow a paternal blessing, long withheld because I had hurt him by refusing his offer of a position with the Bengal-Nagpur Railway.

"Son," he said, "I am now reconciled to your choice in life. It gives me joy to see you amidst these happy, eager youngsters; you belong here rather than with the lifeless figures of railway timetables." He waved toward a group of a dozen little ones who were tagging at

* Reflecting a growing interest in the West in *asanas* (yoga postures), a number of illustrated books on the subject have appeared.
† Bishnu Charan Ghosh passed away on July 9, 1970, in Calcutta. *(Publisher's Note)*
‡ Mark 10:29–30.

my heels. "I had only eight children," he observed with twinkling eyes, "but I can feel for you!"

With twenty-five fertile acres at our disposal, the students, teachers, and I enjoyed daily periods of gardening and other outdoor work. We had many pets, including a young deer that was fairly idolized by the children. I, too, loved the fawn so much that I allowed it to sleep in my room. At the light of dawn the little creature would toddle over to my bed for a morning caress.

One day, because some business would require my attention in the town of Ranchi, I fed the pet earlier than usual. I told the boys not to feed the fawn until my return. One lad was disobedient and gave it a large quantity of milk. When I came back in the evening, sad news greeted me: "The fawn is nearly dead, through overfeeding."

In tears, I placed the apparently lifeless pet on my lap. I prayed piteously to God to spare its life. Hours later, the small creature opened its eyes, stood up, and walked feebly. The whole school shouted for joy.

But a deep lesson came to me that night, one I can never forget. I stayed up with the fawn until two o'clock, when I fell asleep. The deer appeared in a dream, and spoke to me:

"You are holding me back. Please let me go; let me go!"

"All right," I answered in the dream.

I awoke immediately, and cried out, "Boys, the deer is dying!" The children rushed to my side.

I ran to the corner of the room where I had placed the pet. It made a last effort to rise, stumbled toward me, then dropped at my feet, dead.

According to the mass karma that guides and regulates the destinies of animals, the deer's life was over, and it was ready to progress to a higher form. But by my deep attachment, which I later realized was selfish, and by my fervent prayers, I had been able to hold it in the limitations of the animal form from which the soul was struggling for release. The soul of the deer made its plea in a dream because, without my loving permission, it either would not or could not go. As soon as I agreed, it departed.

All sorrow left me; I realized anew that God wants His children to love everything as a part of Him, and not to feel delusively that death ends all. The ignorant man sees only the unsurmountable wall of death, hiding, seemingly forever, his cherished friends. But the man of unattachment, he who loves others as expressions of the

Lord, understands that at death the dear ones have only returned for a breathing space of joy in Him.

The Ranchi school grew from small and simple beginnings to an institution now well known in Bihar and Bengal. Many departments of the school are supported by voluntary contributions from those who rejoice in perpetuating the educational ideals of the rishis. Flourishing branch schools have been established in Midnapore and Lakhanpur.

The Ranchi headquarters maintains a Medical Department where medicines and the services of doctors are supplied without charge to the poor of the locality. The number treated has averaged more than 18,000 persons a year. The Vidyalaya has made its mark, too, in competitive sports; and in the scholastic field, where many Ranchi graduates have distinguished themselves in later university life.

In the past three decades the Ranchi school has been honored by visits from many eminent men and women of East and West. Swami Pranabananda, the Banaras "saint with two bodies," came to Ranchi for a few days in 1918. As the great master viewed the picturesque classes under the trees, and saw in the evening that young boys were sitting motionless for hours in yoga meditation, he was profoundly moved.

"Joy comes to my heart," he said, "to see that Lahiri Mahasaya's ideals for the proper training of youth are being carried on in this institution. My guru's blessings be on it."

A young lad sitting by my side ventured to ask the great yogi a question.

"Sir," he said, "shall I be a monk? Is my life only for God?"

Though Swami Pranabananda smiled gently, his eyes were piercing the future.

"Child," he replied, "when you grow up, there is a beautiful bride waiting for you." (The boy did eventually marry, after having planned for years to enter the Swami Order.)

Some time after Swami Pranabananda had visited Ranchi, I accompanied my father to the house in Calcutta in which the yogi was temporarily staying. Pranabananda's prediction, made to me so many years before, came rushing to my mind: "I shall see you, with your father, later on."

As Father entered the swami's room, the great yogi rose from his seat and embraced my parent with loving respect.

"Bhagabati," he said, "what are you doing about yourself?

Don't you see your son racing to the Infinite?" I blushed to hear his praise before my father. The swami went on, "You recall how often our blessed guru used to say: *'Banat, banat, ban jai.'** So keep up *Kriya Yoga* ceaselessly, and reach the divine portals quickly."

The body of Pranabananda, which had appeared so well and strong during my amazing first visit to him in Banaras, now showed definite aging, though his posture was still admirably erect.

"Swamiji," I inquired, looking straight into his eyes, "please tell me: Aren't you feeling the advance of age? As the body is weakening, are your perceptions of God suffering any diminution?"

He smiled angelically. "The Beloved is more than ever with me now." His complete conviction overwhelmed my mind and soul. He went on, "I am still enjoying the two pensions—one from Bhagabati here, and one from above." Pointing his finger heavenward, for a short time the saint was transfixed in ecstasy, his face lit with a divine glow. An ample answer to my question!

Noticing that Pranabananda's room contained many plants and packages of seed, I asked their purpose.

"I have left Banaras permanently," he said, "and am now on my way to the Himalayas. There I shall open an ashram for my disciples. These seeds will produce spinach and a few other vegetables. My dear ones will live simply, spending their time in blissful God-union. Nothing else is necessary."

Father asked his brother disciple when he would return to Calcutta.

"Never again," the saint replied. "This year is the one in which Lahiri Mahasaya told me I would leave my beloved Banaras forever and go to the Himalayas, there to throw off my mortal frame."

My eyes filled with tears at his words, but the swami smiled tranquilly. He reminded me of a little heavenly child, sitting securely on the lap of the Divine Mother. The burden of the years has no ill effect on a great yogi's full possession of supreme spiritual powers. He is able to renew his body at will; yet sometimes he does not care to retard the aging process, but allows his karma to expend itself on the physical plane, using his present body as a time-saving device to preclude the necessity of working out remaining fragments of karma in a new incarnation.

---

* One of Lahiri Mahasaya's favorite remarks, with which he would encourage his students to persevere in meditation. It is literally: "Making, making, some day made." One may freely translate the thought as: "Striving, striving, one day behold! the Divine Goal."

Months later I met an old friend, Sanandan, who was one of Pranabananda's close disciples.

"My adorable guru is gone," he told me, amidst sobs. "He established a hermitage near Rishikesh, and gave us loving training. When we were pretty well settled, and making rapid spiritual progress in his company, he proposed one day to feed a huge crowd from Rishikesh. I inquired why he wanted such a large number.

"'This is my last festival ceremony,' he said. I did not understand the full implications of his words.

"Pranabanandaji helped with the cooking of great amounts of food. We fed about 2000 guests. After the feast, he sat on a high platform and gave an inspired sermon on the Infinite. At the end, before the gaze of thousands, he turned to me, as I sat beside him on the dais, and spoke with unusual force.

"'Sanandan, be prepared; I am going to kick the frame.'*

"After a stunned silence, I cried loudly, 'Master, don't do it! Please, please don't do it!' The crowd remained silent, wondering at my words. Pranabanandaji smiled at me, but his eyes were already beholding Eternity.

"'Be not selfish,' he said, 'nor grieve for me. I have been long cheerfully serving you all; now rejoice and wish me Godspeed. I go to meet my Cosmic Beloved.' In a whisper Pranabanandaji added, 'I shall be reborn shortly. After enjoying a brief period of the Infinite Bliss, I shall return to earth and join Babaji.† You shall soon know when and where my soul has been encased in a new body.'

"He cried again, 'Sanandan, here I kick the frame by the second *Kriya Yoga*.'‡

"He looked at the sea of faces before us, and gave a blessing. Directing his gaze inward to the spiritual eye, he became immobile. While the bewildered crowd thought he was meditating in an

---

* That is, give up the body.

† Lahiri Mahasaya's guru, who is still living. (See chapter 33.)

‡ The actual technique used by Pranabananda is known to higher *Kriya Yoga* initiates of the Self-Realization path as the Third *Kriya Yoga* Initiation. When given to Pranabananda by Lahiri Mahasaya, it was the "second" *Kriya* he received from the Yogavatar. This *Kriya* enables the devotee who has mastered it to leave and return to the body consciously at any time. Advanced yogis use this *Kriya* technique during the last exit of death—a moment they invariably know beforehand.

Great yogis go "in and out" of the spiritual eye, the pranic star "door" of salvation. Christ said: "I am the door: by me if any man enter in, he shall be saved, and shall go in and out, and find pasture. The thief [*maya* or delusion] cometh not but for to steal, and to kill, and to destroy: I [the Christ Consciousness] am come that they might have life, and that they might have it more abundantly" (John 10:9–10).

ecstatic state, he had already left the tabernacle of flesh and had plunged his soul into the cosmic vastness. The disciples touched his body, seated in the lotus posture, but it was no longer warm flesh. Only a stiffened frame remained; the tenant had fled to the immortal shore."

As Sanandan finished his recountal, I thought: "The blessed 'saint with two bodies' was dramatic in his death as in his life!"

I inquired where Pranabananda was to be reborn.

"I consider that information a sacred trust," Sanandan replied. "I should not tell it to anyone. Perhaps you may find out some other way."

Years later I discovered from Swami Keshabananda* that Pranabananda, a few years after his birth in a new body, had gone to Badrinarayan in the Himalayas, and there joined the group of saints around the great Babaji.

---

* My meeting with Keshabananda is described on pages 346–48.

CHAPTER 28

Kashi, Reborn and Discovered

"Please do not go into the water. Let us bathe by dipping our buckets."

I was addressing the young Ranchi students who were accompanying me on an eight-mile hike to a neighboring hill. The pond before us seemed inviting, but a distaste for it had arisen in my mind. Most of the boys began to dip their buckets, but a few lads yielded to the temptation of the cool waters. No sooner had they dived than large water snakes wiggled around them. What shrieks and splashes! What comical alacrity in leaving the pond!

We enjoyed a picnic lunch after we had reached our destination. I sat under a tree, surrounded by the boys. Finding me in an inspirational mood, they plied me with questions.

"Please tell me, sir," one youth inquired, "if I shall always stay with you in the path of renunciation."

"Ah, no," I replied, "you will be forcibly taken away to your home, and later you will marry."

Incredulous, he made a vehement protest. "Only if I am dead could I be carried home." (But in a few months his parents arrived to take him away, in spite of his tearful resistance. Some years later, he did marry.)

After answering many questions, I was addressed by a lad named Kashi. He was about twelve years old, a brilliant student, and beloved by all.

"Sir," he said, "what will be my fate?"

"You shall soon be dead." An irresistible power, it seemed, forced the words from my lips.

The disclosure shocked and grieved me as well as everyone else. Silently rebuking myself as an *enfant terrible*, I refused to answer further questions.

On our return to the school, Kashi came to my room.

"If I die, will you find me when I am reborn, and bring me again to the spiritual path?" he asked amid sobs.

I felt constrained to refuse this difficult occult responsibility.

But for weeks afterward, Kashi pressed me doggedly. Seeing him
unnerved to the breaking point, I finally consoled him.

"Yes," I promised. "If the Heavenly Father lends His aid, I will
try to find you."

During the summer vacation, I started on a short trip. Regret-
ting that I could not take Kashi with me, before leaving I called
him to my room and carefully instructed him to remain, against
all persuasion, in the spiritual vibrations of the school. Somehow
I felt that if he did not go home, he might avoid the impending
calamity.

No sooner had I left than Kashi's father arrived in Ranchi. For
fifteen days he tried to break the will of his son, explaining that if
Kashi would go to Calcutta for only four days to see his mother, he
could then return. Kashi persistently refused. The father finally said
he would take the boy away with the help of the police. The threat
disturbed Kashi, who was unwilling to be the cause of any unfavor-
able publicity to the school. He saw no choice but to go.

I returned to Ranchi a few days later. When I heard how Kashi
had been removed, I entrained at once for Calcutta. There I engaged
a horse cab. Surprisingly, as the vehicle passed beyond the Howrah
bridge over the Ganges, the first persons I saw were Kashi's father
and other relatives in mourning clothes. Shouting to my driver to
stop, I jumped from the cab and glared at the unfortunate father.

"Mr. Murderer," I cried somewhat unreasonably, "you have
killed my boy!"

The father had already realized the wrong he had done in forcibly bringing Kashi to Calcutta. During the few days the boy had
been there, he had eaten contaminated food, contracted cholera,
and passed on.

My love for Kashi, and the pledge to find him after death, night
and day haunted me. No matter where I went, his face loomed up
before me. I began a memorable search for him, even as long ago I
had searched for my lost mother.

I felt that inasmuch as God had given me the faculty of reason, I
must utilize it and tax my powers to the utmost in order to discover
the subtle laws by which I could know the boy's astral whereabouts.
He was a soul vibrating with unfulfilled desires, I realized—a mass
of light floating somewhere amidst millions of luminous souls in
the astral regions. How was I to tune in with him, among so many
vibrating lights of other souls?

Using a secret yoga technique, I broadcasted my love to Kashi's soul through the "microphone" of the spiritual eye, the inner point between the eyebrows.* I intuitively felt that Kashi would soon return to the earth, and that if I kept unceasingly broadcasting my call to him, his soul would reply. I knew that the slightest impulse sent to me by Kashi would be felt in the nerves of my fingers, arms, and spine.

Using my upraised hands as antennae, I often turned myself round and round, trying to discover the direction of the place in which, I believed, he had already been reborn as an embryo. I hoped to receive response from him in the concentration-tuned "radio" of my heart.

With undiminishing zeal, I practiced the yoga method steadily for about six months after Kashi's death. Walking with a few friends one morning in the crowded Bowbazar section of Calcutta, I lifted my hands in the usual manner. For the first time, there was response. I thrilled to detect electrical impulses trickling down my fingers and palms. These currents translated themselves into one overpowering thought from a deep recess of my consciousness: "I am Kashi, I am Kashi; come to me!"

The thought became almost audible as I concentrated on my heart radio. In the characteristic, slightly hoarse whisper of Kashi,† I heard his summons again and again. I seized the arm of one of my companions, Prokash Das, and smiled at him joyfully.

"It looks as though I have located Kashi!"

I began to turn round and round, to the undisguised amusement of my friends and the passing throng. The electrical impulses tingled through my fingers only when I faced toward a nearby path, aptly named "Serpentine Lane." The astral currents disappeared when I turned in other directions.

"Ah," I exclaimed, "Kashi's soul must be living in the womb of some mother whose home is in this lane."

My companions and I approached closer to Serpentine Lane; the

---

* The will, projected from the point between the eyebrows, is the *broadcasting* apparatus of thought. Man's feeling or emotional power, calmly concentrated on the heart, enables it to act as a mental radio that *receives* the messages of other persons, far or near. In telepathy the fine vibrations of thoughts in one man's mind are transmitted through the subtle vibrations of astral ether and then through the grosser earthly ether, creating electrical waves that, in turn, transform themselves into thought waves in the mind of the other person.

† Every soul in its pure state is omniscient. Kashi's soul remembered all the characteristics of Kashi, the boy, and therefore mimicked his hoarse voice in order to stir my recognition.

vibrations in my upraised hands grew stronger, more pronounced. As if by a magnet, I was pulled toward the right side of the road. Reaching the entrance of a certain house, I was astounded to find myself transfixed. I knocked at the door in a state of intense excitement, holding my very breath. I felt that my long and unusual quest had come to a successful end.

The door was opened by a servant, who told me her master was at home. He descended the stairway from the second floor and smiled at me inquiringly. I hardly knew how to frame my question, at once pertinent and impertinent.

"Please tell me, sir, if you and your wife have been expecting a child for about six months?"*

"Yes, it is so." Seeing that I was a swami, a renunciant attired in the traditional orange cloth, he added politely, "Pray inform me how you know my affairs."

When he heard about Kashi and the promise I had given, the astonished man believed my story.

"A male child of fair complexion will be born to you," I told him. "He will have a broad face, with a cowlick atop his forehead. His disposition will be notably spiritual." I felt certain that the coming child would bear these resemblances to Kashi.

Later I visited the child, whose parents had given him his old name of Kashi. Even in infancy he was strikingly similar in appearance to my dear Ranchi student. The child showed me an instantaneous affection; the attraction of the past awoke with redoubled intensity.

* Though many men, after physical death, remain in an astral world for 500 or 1000 years, there is no invariable rule about the length of time between incarnations. (See chapter 43.) A man's allotted span in a physical or an astral embodiment is karmically predetermined.

Death, and indeed sleep, "the little death," are a mortal necessity, freeing the unenlightened human being temporarily from sense trammels. As man's essential nature is Spirit, he receives in sleep and in death certain revivifying reminders of his incorporeity.

The equilibrating law of karma, as expounded in the Hindu scriptures, is that of action and reaction, cause and effect, sowing and reaping. In the course of natural righteousness (*rita*), each man, by his thoughts and actions, becomes the molder of his destiny. Whatever universal energies he himself, wisely or unwisely, has set in motion must return to him as their starting point, like a circle inexorably completing itself. "The world looks like a mathematical equation, which, turn it how you will, balances itself. Every secret is told, every crime is punished, every virtue rewarded, every wrong redressed, in silence and certainty."—Emerson, "Compensation." An understanding of karma as the law of justice underlying life's inequalities serves to free the human mind from resentment against God and man. (See p. 151.)

Years later the teenage boy wrote me, during my stay in America. He explained his deep longing to follow the path of a renunciant. I directed him to a Himalayan master, who accepted as a disciple the reborn Kashi.

CHAPTER 29

Rabindranath Tagore and I
Compare Schools

"Rabindranath Tagore taught us to sing, as a natural form of self-expression, as effortlessly as birds."

Bhola Nath, a bright fourteen-year-old lad at my Ranchi school, gave me that explanation after I had complimented him one morning on his melodious outbursts. With or without provocation, the boy poured forth a tuneful stream. He had previously attended the famous Tagore school, Santiniketan (Haven of Peace), in Bolpur.

"The songs of Rabindranath have been on my lips since early youth," I told my companion. "All Bengalis, even the unlettered peasants, delight in his lofty verse."

Bhola and I sang together a few refrains from Tagore, who set to music thousands of Indian poems: some of his own composition and others of ancient origin.

"I met Rabindranath soon after he had received the Nobel Prize for literature," I remarked after our vocalizing. "I was drawn to visit him because I admired his undiplomatic courage in disposing of his literary critics." I chuckled.

Bhola, curious, inquired the story.

"The scholars severely flayed Tagore for introducing a new style into Bengali poetry," I began. "He mixed colloquial and classical expressions, ignoring all the prescribed limitations dear to the pundits' hearts. His songs embody deep philosophic truth in emotionally appealing terms, with little regard for the accepted literary forms.

"An influential critic spitefully referred to Rabindranath as a 'pigeon-poet who sold his cooings in print for a rupee.' But Tagore's revenge was at hand; the whole Western literary world paid homage at his feet soon after he himself had translated into English his *Gitanjali* ("Song Offerings"). A trainload of pundits, including his one-time critics, went to Santiniketan to offer their congratulations.

"Rabindranath received his guests only after an intentionally long delay, and then heard their praise in stoic silence. Finally he turned against them their own habitual weapons of criticism.

"'Gentlemen,' he said, 'the fragrant honors you here bestow are incongruously mingled with the putrid odors of your past contempt. Is there possibly any connection between my award of the Nobel Prize, and your suddenly acute powers of appreciation? I am still the same poet who displeased you when I first offered my humble flowers at the shrine of Bengal.'

"The newspapers published an account of the bold chastisement given by Tagore. I admired the outspoken words of a man unhypnotized by flattery," I went on. "I was introduced to Rabindranath in Calcutta by his secretary, Mr. C. F. Andrews,* who was simply attired in a Bengali *dhoti.* He referred lovingly to Tagore as 'Gurudeva.'

"Rabindranath received me graciously. He emanated an aura of charm, culture, and courtliness. Replying to my question about his literary background, he told me that he had been chiefly influenced by our religious epics and by the works of Vidyapati, a popular fourteenth-century poet."

Inspired by these memories, I began to sing Tagore's version of an old Bengali song, "Light the Lamp of Thy Love." Bhola and I chanted joyously as we strolled over the Vidyalaya grounds.

About two years after founding the Ranchi school, I received an invitation from Rabindranath to visit him at Santiniketan and discuss our educational ideals. I went gladly. The poet was seated in his study when I entered; I thought then, as at our first meeting, that he was as striking a model of superb manhood as any painter could desire. His beautifully chiseled face, nobly patrician, was framed in long hair and flowing beard. Large, melting eyes; an angelic smile; and a voice of flutelike quality that was literally enchanting. Stalwart, tall, and grave, he combined an almost womanly tenderness with the delightful spontaneity of a child. No idealized conception of a poet could find more suitable embodiment than in this gentle singer.

Tagore and I were soon deep in a comparative study of our schools, both founded along unorthodox lines. We discovered many identical features—outdoor instruction, simplicity, ample scope for the child's creative spirit. Rabindranath, however, laid considerable stress on the study of literature and poetry, and on the self-expression through music and song that I had already noted in the case of Bhola. The Santiniketan children observed periods of silence but were given

---

* The English writer and publicist, close friend of Mahatma Gandhi. Mr. Andrews is honored in India for his many services to his adopted land.

no special yoga training.

The poet listened with flattering attention to my description of the energizing Yogoda exercises and of the yoga concentration techniques taught to all students at Ranchi.

Tagore told me of his own early educational struggles. "I fled from school after the fifth grade," he said, laughing. I could readily understand how his innate poetic delicacy would be affronted by the dreary, disciplinary atmosphere of a schoolroom.

"That is why I opened Santiniketan under the shady trees and the glories of the sky." He motioned eloquently to a little group studying in the beautiful garden. "A child is in his natural setting amidst the flowers and the songbirds. There he may more easily express the hidden wealth of his individual endowment. True education is not pumped and crammed in from outward sources, but aids in bringing to the surface the infinite hoard of wisdom within."*

I agreed, and added, "In ordinary schools the idealistic and hero-worshiping instincts of the young are starved on an exclusive diet of statistics and chronological eras."

The poet spoke lovingly of his father, Devendranath, who had inspired the Santiniketan beginnings.

"Father presented me with this fertile land, where he had already built a guest house and temple," Rabindranath told me. "I started my educational experiment here in 1901, with only ten boys. The eight thousand pounds that came with the Nobel Prize all went for the upkeep of the school."

The elder Tagore, Devendranath, known far and wide as "Maharishi" ("great sage"), was a very remarkable man, as one may discover from his *Autobiography*. Two years of his manhood were spent in meditation in the Himalayas. In turn, his father, Dwarkanath Tagore, had been celebrated throughout Bengal for his munificent public benefactions. From this illustrious tree has sprung a family of geniuses. Not Rabindranath alone; all his relatives have distinguished themselves in creative expression. His nephews, Gogonendra and Abanindra, are among the foremost artists† of India. Rabindranath's brother, Dwijendra, was a deep-seeing philosopher, beloved even by birds and woodland creatures.

---

* "The soul having been often born, or, as the Hindus say, 'traveling the path of existence through thousands of births'... there is nothing of which she has not gained the knowledge; no wonder that she is able to recollect...what formerly she knew.... For inquiry and learning is reminiscence all."—*Emerson, "Representative Men."*

† Rabindranath, too, in his sixties engaged in a serious study of painting. His work was exhibited some years ago in European capitals and in New York.

Rabindranath invited me to stay overnight in the guest house. In the evening I was charmed by a tableau of the poet and a group in the patio. Time unfolded backward: the scene before me was like one in an ancient hermitage—the joyous singer encircled by his devotees, all aureoled in divine love. Tagore knitted each tie of friendship with cords of harmony. Never assertive, he drew and captured the heart with an irresistible magnetism. Rare blossom of poesy blooming in the garden of the Lord, attracting others by a natural fragrance!

In his melodious voice, Rabindranath read to us a few of his exquisite poems, newly created. Most of his songs and plays, written for the delectation of his students, have been composed at Santiniketan. The beauty of his lines, to me, lies in his art of referring to God in nearly every stanza, yet seldom mentioning the sacred Name. "Drunk with the bliss of singing," he wrote, "I forget myself and call Thee friend who art my Lord."

The following day, after lunch, I bade the poet a reluctant farewell. I rejoice that his little school has now grown to an international university, Visva-Bharati,* where scholars from many lands find an ideal environment.

"Where the mind is without fear and the head is held high;
Where knowledge is free;
Where the world has not been broken up into fragments by
    narrow domestic walls;
Where words come out from the depth of truth;
Where tireless striving stretches its arms toward perfection;
Where the clear stream of reason has not lost its way into the
    dreary desert sand of dead habit;
Where the mind is led forward by Thee into ever widening
    thought and action;
Into that heaven of freedom, my Father, let my country awake!"†

RABINDRANATH TAGORE

---

* Although the beloved poet died in 1941, his Visva-Bharati institution is still flourishing. In January 1950, sixty-five teachers and students from Santiniketan paid a ten-day visit to the Yogoda Satsanga school in Ranchi. The group was headed by Sri S. N. Ghosal, rector of the school department of Visva-Bharati. The guests gave great pleasure to the Ranchi students by a dramatic performance of Rabindranath's beautiful poem, "Pujarini."

† *Gitanjali* (Macmillan Co.). A thoughtful study of the poet will be found in *The Philosophy of Rabindranath Tagore*, by the celebrated scholar, Sir S. Radhakrishnan (Macmillan, 1918).

CHAPTER 30

The Law of Miracles

The great novelist Leo Tolstoy* wrote a delightful folk tale, *The Three Hermits*. His friend Nicholas Roerich summarized it, as follows:

"On an island there lived three old hermits. They were so simple that the only prayer they used was: 'We are three; Thou art Three—have mercy on us!' Great miracles were manifested during this naive prayer.

"The local bishop† came to hear about the three hermits and their inadmissible prayer, and decided to visit them in order to teach them the canonical invocations. He arrived on the island, told the hermits that their heavenly petition was undignified, and taught them many of the customary prayers. The bishop then left on a boat. He saw, following the ship, a radiant light. As it approached he discerned the three hermits, who were holding hands and running upon the waves in an effort to overtake the vessel.

"'We have forgotten the prayers you taught us,' they cried as they reached the bishop, 'and have hastened to ask you to repeat them.' The awed bishop shook his head.

"'Dear ones,' he replied humbly, 'continue to live with your old prayer!'"

How did the three saints walk on the water?

How did Christ resurrect his crucified body?

How did Lahiri Mahasaya and Sri Yukteswar perform their miracles?

Modern science has, as yet, no answer; though with the advent of the Atomic Age the scope of the world-mind has been abruptly enlarged. The word "impossible" is becoming less prominent in man's vocabulary.

* Tolstoy had many ideals in common with Mahatma Gandhi; the two men corresponded on the subject of nonviolence. Tolstoy considered Christ's central teaching to be "resist not evil (with evil)" (Matthew 5:39); evil should be "resisted" only with its logically effective opposite: good or love.

† The story apparently has a historical basis; an editorial note informs us that the bishop met the three hermits while he was sailing from Archangel to the Slovetsky Monastery, at the mouth of the Dvina River.

The Vedic scriptures declare that the physical world operates under one fundamental law of *maya,* the principle of relativity and duality. God, the Sole Life, is Absolute Unity; to appear as the separate and diverse manifestations of a creation He wears a false or unreal veil. That illusory dualistic veil is *maya.** Many great scientific discoveries of modern times have confirmed this simple pronouncement of the ancient rishis.

Newton's Law of Motion is a law of *maya:* "To every action there is always an equal and contrary reaction; the mutual actions of any two bodies are always equal and oppositely directed." Action and reaction are thus exactly equal. "To have a single force is impossible. There must be, and always is, a pair of forces equal and opposite."

Fundamental natural activities all betray their mayic origin. Electricity, for example, is a phenomenon of repulsion and attraction; its electrons and protons are electrical opposites. Another example: the atom or final particle of matter is, like the earth itself, a magnet with positive and negative poles. The entire phenomenal world is under the inexorable sway of polarity; no law of physics, chemistry, or any other science is ever found free from inherent opposite or contrasted principles.

Physical science, then, cannot formulate laws outside of *maya:* the very fabric and structure of creation. Nature herself is *maya;* natural science must perforce deal with her ineluctable quiddity. In her own domain, she is eternal and inexhaustible; future scientists can do no more than probe one aspect after another of her varied infinitude. Science thus remains in a perpetual flux, unable to reach finality; fit indeed to discover the laws of an already existing and functioning cosmos but powerless to detect the Law Framer and Sole Operator. The majestic manifestations of gravitation and electricity have become known, but what gravitation and electricity are, no mortal knoweth.†

To surmount *maya* was the task assigned to the human race by the millennial prophets. To rise above the duality of creation and perceive the unity of the Creator was conceived of as man's highest goal. Those who cling to the cosmic illusion must accept its

* See pp. 35 n., 37 n.

† Marconi, the great inventor, made the following admission of scientific inadequacy before the finalities: "The inability of science to solve life is absolute. This fact would be truly frightening were it not for faith. The mystery of life is certainly the most persistent problem ever placed before the thought of man."

essential law of polarity: flow and ebb, rise and fall, day and night, pleasure and pain, good and evil, birth and death. This cyclic pattern assumes a certain anguishing monotony after man has gone through a few thousand human births; he begins then to cast a hopeful eye beyond the compulsions of *maya.*

To remove the veil of *maya* is to uncover the secret of creation. He who thus denudes the universe is the only true monotheist. All others are worshiping heathen images. So long as man remains subject to the dualistic illusions of Nature, the Janus-faced *Maya* is his goddess; he cannot know the one true God.

The world illusion, *maya,* manifests in men as *avidya,* literally, "not-knowledge," ignorance, delusion. *Maya* or *avidya* can never be destroyed through intellectual conviction or analysis, but solely through attaining the interior state of *nirbikalpa samadhi.* The Old Testament prophets, and seers of all lands and ages, spoke from that state of consciousness.

Ezekiel said:* "Afterwards he brought me to the gate, even the gate that looketh toward the east: and, behold, the glory of the God of Israel came from the way of the east: and his voice was like a noise of many waters: and the earth shined with his glory." Through the divine eye in the forehead (east), the yogi sails his consciousness into omnipresence, hearing the Word or *Aum,* divine sound of "many waters": the vibrations of light that constitute the sole reality of creation.

Among the trillion mysteries of the cosmos, the most phenomenal is light. Unlike sound waves, whose transmission requires air or other material media, light waves pass freely through the vacuum of interstellar space. Even the hypothetical ether, held as the interplanetary medium of light in the undulatory theory, may be discarded on the Einsteinian grounds that the geometrical properties of space render unnecessary a theory of ether. Under either hypothesis, light remains the most subtle, the freest from material dependence, of any natural manifestation.

In the gigantic conceptions of Einstein, the velocity of light— 186,300 miles per second—dominates the whole Theory of Relativity. He proves mathematically that the velocity of light is, so far as man's finite mind is concerned, the only constant of a universe in flux. On the sole "absolute" of light velocity depend all human standards of time and space. Not abstractly eternal as hitherto considered, time and space are relative and finite factors. They derive

* Ezekiel 43:1–2.

their conditional measurement-validities only in reference to the yardstick of light velocity.

In joining space as a dimensional relativity, time is now stripped to its rightful nature: a simple essence of ambiguity. With a few equational strokes of his pen, Einstein banished from the universe every fixed reality except that of light.

In a later development, his Unified Field Theory, the great physicist sought to embody in one mathematical formula the laws of gravitation and of electromagnetism. Reducing the cosmical structure to variations on a single law, Einstein has reached across the ages to the rishis who proclaimed a sole fabric of creation: a protean *maya.**

On the epochal Theory of Relativity have arisen the mathematical possibilities of exploring the ultimate atom. Great scientists are now boldly asserting not only that the atom is energy rather than matter, but that atomic energy is essentially mind-stuff.

"The frank realization that physical science is concerned with a world of shadows is one of the most significant advances," Sir Arthur Stanley Eddington writes in *The Nature of the Physical World.*† "In the world of physics we watch a shadowgraph performance of the drama of familiar life. The shadow of my elbow rests on the shadow table as the shadow ink flows over the shadow paper. It is all symbolic, and as a symbol the physicist leaves it. Then comes the alchemist Mind who transmutes the symbols....To put the conclusion crudely, the stuff of the world is mind-stuff."

With the recent devising of an electron microscope came definite proof of the light-essence of atoms and of the inescapable duality of nature. *The New York Times* gave the following report of a 1937 demonstration of the electron microscope before a meeting of the American Association for the Advancement of Science:

> The crystalline structure of tungsten, hitherto known only indirectly by means of X rays, stood outlined boldly on a fluorescent screen, showing nine atoms in their correct positions in the space lattice, a cube, with one atom in each corner and one in the center. The atoms in the crystal lattice of the tungsten appeared on the fluorescent screen as points of light, arranged in geometric

---

* Einstein was convinced that the link between the laws of electromagnetism and gravity could be expressed in a mathematical formula (the Unified Field Theory), on which he was working at the time this book was written. Though he did not live to complete his work on it, many physicists today share Einstein's conviction that such a link will be found. *(Publisher's Note)*

† Macmillan Company.

pattern. Against this crystal cube of light the bombarding molecules of air could be observed as dancing points of light, similar to points of sunlight shimmering on moving waters....

The principle of the electron microscope was first discovered in 1927 by Drs. Clinton J. Davisson and Lester H. Germer of the Bell Telephone Laboratories, New York City, who found that the electron has a dual personality, partaking of the characteristics of both a particle and a wave.* The wave quality gave the electron the characteristic of light, and a search was begun to devise means for "focusing" electrons in a manner similar to the focusing of light by means of a lens.

For his discovery of the Jekyll-Hyde quality of the electron, which...showed that the entire realm of physical nature has a dual personality, Dr. Davisson received the Nobel Prize in physics.

"The stream of knowledge," Sir James Jeans writes in *The Mysterious Universe,*† "is heading toward a non-mechanical reality; the universe begins to look more like a great thought than like a great machine."

Twentieth-century science is thus sounding like a page from the hoary Vedas.

From science, then, if it must be so, let man learn the philosophic truth that there is no material universe; its warp and woof is *maya,* illusion. Under analysis all its mirages of reality dissolve. As, one by one, the reassuring props of a physical cosmos crash beneath him, man dimly perceives his idolatrous reliance, his transgression of the Divine Command: "Thou shalt have no other gods before Me."‡

In his famous equation outlining the equivalence of mass and energy, Einstein proved that the energy in any particle of matter is equal to its mass or weight multiplied by the square of the velocity of light. The release of the atomic energies is brought about through annihilation of the material particles. The "death" of matter has given birth to an Atomic Age.

Light velocity is a mathematical standard or constant not because there is an absolute value in 186,300 miles a second, but because no material body, whose mass increases with its velocity, can ever attain the velocity of light. Stated another way: only a material body whose mass is infinite could equal the velocity of light.

This conception brings us to the law of miracles.

Masters who are able to materialize and dematerialize their bodies and other objects, and to move with the velocity of light,

* That is, both matter and energy.
† Cambridge University Press.   ‡ Exodus 20:3.

and to utilize the creative light rays in bringing into instant visibility any physical manifestation, have fulfilled the lawful condition: their mass is infinite.

The consciousness of a perfected yogi is effortlessly identified not with a narrow body but with the universal structure. Gravitation, whether the "force" of Newton or the Einsteinian "manifestation of inertia," is powerless to *compel* a master to exhibit the property of weight: the distinguishing gravitational condition of all material objects. He who knows himself as the omnipresent Spirit is subject no longer to the rigidities of a body in time and space. The imprisoning "rings-pass-not" have yielded to the solvent: *I am He.*

"Let there be light! And there was light."* In the creation of the universe, God's first command brought into being the structural essential: light. On the beams of this immaterial medium occur all divine manifestations. Devotees of every age testify to the appearance of God as flame and light. "His eyes were as a flame of fire," St. John tells us, "....and his countenance was as the sun shineth in his strength."†

A yogi who through perfect meditation has merged his consciousness with the Creator perceives the cosmical essence as light (vibrations of life energy); to him there is no difference between the light rays composing water and the light rays composing land. Free from matter-consciousness, free from the three dimensions of space and the fourth dimension of time, a master transfers his body of light with equal ease over or through the light rays of earth, water, fire, and air.

"If therefore thine eye be single, thy whole body shall be *full of light.*"‡ Long concentration on the liberating spiritual eye has enabled the yogi to destroy all delusions concerning matter and its gravitational weight; he sees the universe as the Lord created it: an essentially undifferentiated mass of light.

"Optical images," Dr. L. T. Troland of Harvard tells us, "are built up on the same principle as the ordinary 'halftone' engravings; that is, they are made up of minute dottings or stipplings far too small to be detected by the eye....The sensitiveness of the retina is so great that a visual sensation can be produced by relatively few quanta of the right kind of light."

The law of miracles is operable by any man who has realized

* Genesis 1:3.
† Revelation 1:14–16.
‡ Matthew 6:22.

that the essence of creation is light. A master is able to employ his divine knowledge of light phenomena to project instantly into perceptible manifestation the ubiquitous light atoms. The actual form of the projection (whatever it be: a tree, a medicine, a human body) is determined by the yogi's wish and by his power of will and of visualization.

At night man enters the state of dream-consciousness and escapes from the false egoistic limitations that daily hem him round. In sleep he has an ever recurrent demonstration of the omnipotence of his mind. Lo! in the dream appear his long-dead friends, the remotest continents, the resurrected scenes of his childhood.

That free and unconditioned consciousness, which all men briefly experience in certain of their dreams, is the permanent state of mind of a God-tuned master. Innocent of all personal motives, and employing the creative will bestowed on him by the Creator, a yogi rearranges the light atoms of the universe to satisfy any sincere prayer of a devotee.

"And God said, Let us make man in our image, after our likeness: and let them have dominion over the fish of the sea, and over the fowl of the air, and over the cattle, and over all the earth, and over every creeping thing that creepeth upon the earth."*

For this purpose were man and creation made: that he should rise up as master of *maya*, knowing his dominion over the cosmos.

In 1915, shortly after I had entered the Swami Order, I witnessed a strange vision. Through it I came to understand the relativity of human consciousness, and clearly perceived the unity of the Eternal Light behind the painful dualities of *maya*. The vision descended on me as I sat one morning in my little attic room in Father's Garpar Road home. For months the First World War had been raging in Europe; I had been reflecting sadly on the vast toll of death.

As I closed my eyes in meditation, my consciousness was suddenly transferred to the body of a captain in command of a battleship. The thunder of guns split the air as shots were exchanged between shore batteries and the ship's cannons. A huge shell hit the powder magazine and tore my ship asunder. I jumped into the water, together with the few sailors who had survived the explosion.

Heart pounding, I reached the shore safely. But alas! a stray bullet ended its swift flight in my chest. I fell groaning to the ground. My whole body was paralyzed, yet I was aware of possessing it as one is conscious of a leg gone to sleep.

* Genesis 1:26.

"At last the mysterious footstep of Death has caught up with me," I thought. With a final sigh, I was about to sink into unconsciousness when lo! I found myself seated in the lotus posture in my Garpar Road room.

Hysterical tears poured forth as I joyfully stroked and pinched my regained possession: a body free from a bullet hole in the breast. I rocked to and fro, inhaling and exhaling to assure myself that I was alive. Amidst these self-gratulations, again I found my consciousness transferred to the captain's dead body by the gory shore. Utter confusion of mind came upon me.

"Lord," I prayed, "am I dead or alive?"

A dazzling play of light filled the whole horizon. A soft rumbling vibration formed itself into words:

"What has life or death to do with light? In the image of My light I have made you. The relativities of life and death belong to the cosmic dream. Behold your dreamless being! Awake, My child, awake!"

As steps in man's awakening, the Lord inspires scientists to discover, at the right time and place, the secrets of His creation. Many modern discoveries help man to apprehend the cosmos as a varied expression of one power—light, guided by divine intelligence. The wonders of the motion picture, of radio, of television, of radar, of the photoelectric cell—the amazing "electric eye," of atomic energies, are all based on the electromagnetic phenomenon of light.

The motion-picture art can portray any miracle. From the impressive visual standpoint, no marvel is barred to trick photography. A man may be seen as a transparent astral body that is rising from his gross physical form, he can walk on the water, resurrect the dead, reverse the natural sequence of developments, and play havoc with time and space. The expert may assemble the photographic images as he pleases, achieving optical wonders similar to those that a true master produces with actual light rays.

Motion pictures, with their lifelike images, illustrate many truths concerning creation. The Cosmic Director has written His own plays and has summoned the tremendous casts for the pageant of the centuries. From the dark booth of eternity He sends His beams of light through the films of successive ages, and pictures are thrown on the backdrop of space.

Just as cinematic images appear to be real but are only combinations of light and shade, so is the universal variety a delusive seeming. The planetary spheres, with their countless forms of life, are naught but figures in a cosmic motion picture. Temporarily true

A *yogini* (woman yogi), Shankari Mai Jiew, only living disciple of Trailanga Swami. She is shown here (with three representatives from the YSS school in Ranchi) at *Kumbha Mela* in Hardwar, 1938; the *yogini* was then 112 years old.

KASHI
Student at Ranchi School

PANCHANON BHATTACHARYA
Disciple of Lahiri Mahasaya

YOGODA MATH, DAKSHINESWAR, INDIA

Yogoda Satsanga Society of India headquarters, on the Ganges River, near Calcutta, founded by Paramahansa Yogananda in 1939

RABINDRANATH TAGORE

Inspired Poet of Bengal, and Nobel laureate in literature

JAGADIS CHANDRA BOSE

India's great physicist, botanist, and inventor of the crescograph to man's five sense perceptions, the transitory scenes are cast on the screen of human consciousness by the infinite creative beam.

A cinema audience may look up and see that all screen images are appearing through the instrumentality of one imageless beam of light. The colorful universal drama is similarly issuing from the single white light of a Cosmic Source. With inconceivable ingenuity God is staging "super-colossal" entertainment for His children, making them actors as well as audience in His planetary theater.

One day I entered a cinema house to view a newsreel of the European battlefields. The First World War was still being waged in the West; the newsreel presented the carnage with such realism that I left the theater with a troubled heart.

"Lord," I prayed, "why dost Thou permit such suffering?"

To my intense surprise, an instant answer came in the form of a vision of the actual European battlefields. The scenes, filled with the dead and dying, far surpassed in ferocity any representation of the newsreel.

"Look intently!" A gentle Voice spoke to my inner consciousness. "You will see that these scenes now being enacted in France are nothing but a play of chiaroscuro. They are the cosmic motion picture, as real and as unreal as the theater newsreel you have just seen—a play within a play."

My heart was still not comforted. The Divine Voice went on: "Creation is light and shadow both, else no picture is possible. The good and evil of *maya* must ever alternate in supremacy. If joy were ceaseless here in this world, would man ever desire another? Without suffering, he scarcely cares to recall that he has forsaken his eternal home. Pain is a prod to remembrance. The way of escape is through wisdom. The tragedy of death is unreal; those who shudder at it are like an ignorant actor who dies of fright on the stage when nothing more has been fired at him than a blank cartridge. My sons are children of light; they will not sleep forever in delusion."

Although I had read scriptural accounts of *maya*, they had not given me the deep insight that came with personal visions and with the accompanying words of consolation. One's values are profoundly changed when he is finally convinced that creation is only a vast motion picture; and that not in it, but beyond it, lies his own reality.

After I had finished writing this chapter, I sat on my bed in the lotus posture. My room* was dimly lit by two shaded lamps. Lifting my gaze, I noticed that the ceiling was dotted with small

---

* In Self-Realization Fellowship hermitage, Encinitas, California. *(Publisher's Note)*

mustard-colored lights, scintillating and quivering with a radium-like luster. Myriads of penciled rays, like sheets of rain, gathered into a transparent shaft and poured silently upon me.

At once my physical body lost its grossness and became metamorphosed into astral texture. I felt a floating sensation as, barely touching the bed, the weightless body shifted slightly and alternately to left and right. I looked around the room; the furniture and walls were as usual, but the little mass of light had so multiplied that the ceiling was invisible. I was wonder-struck.

"This is the cosmic motion-picture mechanism." A Voice spoke as though from within the light. "Shedding its beam on the white screen of your bed sheets, it is producing the picture of your body. Behold, your form is nothing but light!"

I gazed at my arms and moved them back and forth, yet could not feel their weight. Ecstatic joy overwhelmed me. The cosmic stem of light, blossoming as my body, seemed a divine reproduction of the light beams that stream out of the projection booth in a cinema house and make manifest the pictures on the screen.

For a long time I experienced this motion picture of my body in the faintly lit theater of my own bedroom. Though I have had many visions, none was ever more singular. As the illusion of a solid body was completely dissipated, and as my realization deepened that the essence of all objects is light, I looked up to the throbbing stream of lifetrons and spoke entreatingly.

"Divine Light, please withdraw this, my humble bodily picture, into Thyself; even as Elijah was drawn up to heaven in a chariot of flame." *

---

* II Kings 2:11.

A "miracle" is commonly considered to be an effect or event without law, or beyond law. But all events in our precisely adjusted universe are lawfully wrought and lawfully explicable. The so-called miraculous powers of a great master are a natural accompaniment to his exact understanding of subtle laws that operate in the inner cosmos of consciousness.

Nothing may truly be said to be a "miracle" except in the profound sense that everything is a miracle. That each of us is encased in an intricately organized body, and is set upon an earth whirling through space among the stars—is anything more commonplace? or more miraculous?

Great prophets like Christ and Lahiri Mahasaya usually perform many miracles. Such masters have a large and difficult spiritual mission to execute for mankind; miraculously helping those in distress appears to be a part of that mission. (See p. 193 n.) Divine fiats are required against incurable diseases and insoluble human problems. When Christ was asked by the nobleman to heal his dying son at Capernaum, Jesus replied with wry humor: "Except ye see signs and wonders, ye will not believe." But he added: "Go thy way; thy son liveth" (John 4:46–54).

This prayer was evidently startling; the beam disappeared. My body resumed its normal weight and sank on the bed; the swarm of dazzling ceiling lights flickered and vanished. My time to leave this earth had apparently not arrived.

"Besides," I thought philosophically, "Elijah might well be displeased at my presumption!"

In this chapter I have given the Vedic explanation of *maya*, the magical power of illusion that underlies the phenomenal worlds. Western science has already discovered that a "magic" of unreality pervades atomic "matter." However, it is not only Nature, but man also (in his mortal aspect) who is subject to *maya:* the principle of relativity, contrast, duality, inversion, oppositional states.

It should not be imagined that the truth about *maya* was understood only by the rishis. The Old Testament prophets called *maya* by the name of Satan (lit., in Hebrew, "the adversary"). The Greek Testament, as an equivalent for Satan, uses *diabolos* or devil. Satan or *Maya* is the Cosmic Magician who produces multiplicity of forms to hide the One Formless Verity. In God's plan and play (*lila*), the sole function of Satan or *Maya* is to attempt to divert man from Spirit to matter, from Reality to unreality.

Christ describes *maya* picturesquely as a devil, a murderer, and a liar. "The devil...was a murderer from the beginning, and abode not in the truth, because there is no truth in him. When he speaketh a lie, he speaketh of his own: for he is a liar, and the father of it" (John 8:44).

"The devil sinneth from the beginning. For this purpose the Son of God was manifested, that he might destroy the works of the devil" (I John 3:8). That is, the manifestation of Christ Consciousness, within man's own being, effortlessly destroys the illusions or "works of the devil."

Maya is "from the beginning" because of its structural inherence in the phenomenal worlds. These are ever in transitional flux as antithesis to the Divine Immutability.

CHAPTER 31

An Interview With the
Sacred Mother

"Revered Mother, I was baptized in infancy by your prophet-husband. He was the guru of my parents and of my own guru Sri Yukteswarji. Will you therefore give me the privilege of hearing a few incidents in your sacred life?"

I was addressing Srimati Kashi Moni, the life companion of Lahiri Mahasaya. Finding myself in Banaras for a short period, I was fulfilling a long-felt desire to visit the venerable lady.

She received me graciously in the home of the Lahiri family in the Garudeswar Mohulla section of Banaras. Although aged, she was blooming like a lotus, emanating a spiritual fragrance. She was of medium build, with fair skin, a slender neck, and large lustrous eyes.

"Son, you are welcome here. Come upstairs."

Kashi Moni led the way to a very small room where, for a time, she had lived with her husband. I felt honored to witness the shrine in which the peerless master had condescended to play the human drama of matrimony. The gentle lady motioned me to a pillow seat by her side.

"It was years before I came to realize the divine stature of my husband," she began. "One night, in this very room, I had a vivid dream. Glorious angels floated in unimaginable grace above me. So realistic was the sight that I awoke at once; strangely, the room was enveloped in dazzling light.

"My husband, in lotus posture, was levitated in the center of the room, surrounded by angels. In supplicating dignity they were worshiping him with palm-folded hands.

"Astonished beyond measure, I was convinced that I was still dreaming.

"'Woman,' Lahiri Mahasaya said, 'you are not dreaming. Forsake your sleep forever and forever.' As he slowly descended to the floor, I prostrated myself at his feet.

"'Master,' I cried, 'again and again I bow before you! Will you forgive me for having considered you as my husband? I die with shame to realize that I have remained asleep in ignorance by the side of one who is divinely awakened. From this night, you are no longer my husband, but my guru. Will you accept my insignificant self as your disciple?'*

"The master touched me gently. 'Sacred soul, arise. You are accepted.' He motioned toward the angels. 'Please bow in turn to each of these holy saints.'

"After I had finished my humble genuflections, the angelic voices sounded together, like a chorus in an ancient scripture.

"'Consort of the Divine One, thou art blessed. We salute thee.' They bowed at my feet and lo! their refulgent forms vanished. The room darkened.

"My guru asked me to receive initiation into *Kriya Yoga.*

"'Of course,' I replied. 'I am sorry not to have had that blessing earlier in my life.'

"'The time was not ripe.' Lahiri Mahasaya smiled consolingly. 'Much of your karma I have silently helped you to work out. Now you are willing and ready.'

"He touched my forehead. Masses of whirling light appeared; the radiance gradually formed itself into an opal-blue spiritual eye, ringed in gold and centered with a white pentagonal star.

"'Penetrate your consciousness through the star into the kingdom of the Infinite.' My guru's voice had a new note, soft like distant music.

"Vision after vision broke as oceanic surf on the shores of my soul. The panoramic spheres finally melted in a sea of bliss. I lost myself in ever surging blessedness. When I returned hours later to awareness of this world, the master gave me the technique of *Kriya Yoga.*

"From that night on, Lahiri Mahasaya never slept in my room again. Nor, thereafter, did he ever sleep. He remained in the front room downstairs, in the company of his disciples both by day and by night."

The illustrious lady fell into silence. Realizing the uniqueness of her relationship with the sublime yogi, I finally ventured to ask for further reminiscences.

"Son, you are greedy. Nevertheless you shall have one more story." She smiled shyly. "I will confess a sin that I committed against my guru-husband. Some months after my initiation, I began to feel forlorn and neglected. One morning Lahiri Mahasaya entered this little room to fetch an article; I quickly followed him.

---

* "He for God only, she for God in him."—*Milton.*

Overcome by delusion, I addressed him scathingly.

"'You spend all your time with the disciples. What about your responsibilities for your wife and children? I regret that you do not interest yourself in providing more money for the family.'

"The master glanced at me for a moment, then lo! he was gone. Awed and frightened, I heard a voice resounding from every part of the room:

"'It is all nothing, don't you see? How could a nothing like me produce riches for you?'

"'Guruji,' I cried, 'I implore pardon a million times! My sinful eyes can see you no more; please appear in your sacred form.'

"'I am here.' This reply came from above me. I looked up and saw the master materialize in the air, his head touching the ceiling. His eyes were like blinding flames. Beside myself with fear, I lay sobbing at his feet after he had quietly descended to the floor.

"'Woman,' he said, 'seek divine wealth, not the paltry tinsel of earth. After acquiring inward treasure, you will find that outward supply is always forthcoming.' He added, 'One of my spiritual sons will make provision for you.'

"My guru's words naturally came true; a disciple did leave a considerable sum for our family."

I thanked Kashi Moni for sharing with me her wondrous experiences.* On the following day I returned to her home and enjoyed several hours of philosophical discussion with Tincouri and Ducouri Lahiri. These two saintly sons of India's great yogi followed closely in his ideal footsteps. Both men were fair, tall, stalwart, and heavily bearded, with soft voices and an old-fashioned charm of manner.

His wife was not the only woman disciple of Lahiri Mahasaya; there were hundreds of others, including my mother. A woman *chela* once asked the guru for his photograph. He handed her a print, remarking, "If you deem it a protection, then it is so; otherwise it is only a picture."

A few days later this woman and Lahiri Mahasaya's daughter-in-law happened to be studying the Bhagavad Gita at a table behind which hung the guru's photograph. An electrical storm broke out with great fury.

"Lahiri Mahasaya, protect us!" The women bowed before the picture. Lightning struck the book on the table, but the two devotees were unhurt.

* The venerable mother passed on in Banaras on March 25, 1930.

"I felt as though a sheet of ice were placed around me, to ward off the scorching heat," the *chela* related.

Lahiri Mahasaya performed two miracles in connection with a woman disciple, Abhoya. She and her husband, a Calcutta lawyer, started one day for Banaras to visit the guru. Their carriage was delayed by heavy traffic; they reached the Howrah main station in Calcutta only to hear the Banaras train whistling for departure.

Abhoya, near the ticket office, stood quietly.

"Lahiri Mahasaya, I beseech thee to stop the train!" she silently prayed. "I cannot suffer the pangs of delay in waiting another day to see thee."

The wheels of the snorting train continued to move round and round, but there was no onward progress. The engineer and passengers descended to the platform to view the phenomenon. An English railroad guard approached Abhoya and her husband. Contrary to all precedent, the guard volunteered his services. "Babu," he said, "give me the money. I will buy your tickets while you get aboard."

As soon as the couple was seated and had received the tickets, the train slowly moved forward. In panic, the engineer and passengers clambered again to their places, knowing neither how the train started nor why it had stopped in the first place.

Arriving at the home of Lahiri Mahasaya in Banaras, Abhoya silently prostrated herself before the master, and tried to touch his feet.

"Compose yourself, Abhoya," he remarked. "How you love to bother me! As if you could not have come here by the next train!"

Abhoya visited Lahiri Mahasaya on another memorable occasion. This time she wanted his intercession, not with a train, but with the stork.

"I pray you to bless me that my ninth child live," she said. "Eight babies have been born to me; all died soon after birth."

The master smiled sympathetically. "Your coming child will live. Please follow my instructions carefully. The baby, a girl, will be born at night. See that the oil lamp is kept burning until dawn. Do not fall asleep and thus allow the light to become extinguished."

Abhoya's child was a daughter, born at night, exactly as foreseen by the omniscient guru. The mother instructed her nurse to keep the lamp filled with oil. Both women kept the urgent vigil far into the early morning hours, but finally fell asleep. The lamp oil was almost gone; the light flickered feebly. The bedroom door unlatched and flew open with a violent sound. The startled women awoke. Their astonished eyes beheld the form of Lahiri Mahasaya.

"Abhoya, behold, the light is almost gone!" He pointed to the lamp, which the nurse hastened to refill. As soon as it burned again brightly, the master vanished. The door closed; the latch was affixed without visible agency.

Abhoya's ninth child survived; in 1935, when I made inquiry, she was still living.

One of Lahiri Mahasaya's disciples, the venerable Kali Kumar Roy, related to me many fascinating details of his life with the master.

"I was often a guest at his Banaras home for weeks at a time," Roy told me. "I observed that many saintly figures, *dandi* swamis,* arrived in the quiet of night to sit at the guru's feet. Sometimes they would engage in discussion of meditational and philosophical points. At dawn the exalted guests would depart. I found during my visits that Lahiri Mahasaya did not once lie down to sleep.

"During an early period of my association with the master, I had to contend with the opposition of my employer," Roy went on. "He was steeped in materialism.

"'I don't want religious fanatics on my staff,' he would sneer. 'If I ever meet your charlatan guru, I shall give him some words to remember.'

"This threat failed to interrupt my regular program; I spent nearly every evening in my guru's presence. One night my employer followed me and rushed rudely into the parlor. He doubtless intended to utter the remarks he had promised. No sooner had the man seated himself than Lahiri Mahasaya addressed the group of about twelve disciples.

"'Would you all like to see a picture?'

"When we nodded, he asked us to darken the room. 'Sit behind one another in a circle,' he said, 'and place your hands over the eyes of the man in front of you.'

"I was not surprised to observe that my employer also was following, albeit unwillingly, the master's directions. In a few minutes Lahiri Mahasaya asked us what we were seeing.

"'Sir,' I replied, 'a beautiful woman appears. She wears a red-bordered *sari*, and stands near an elephant-ear plant.' All the other disciples gave the same description. The master turned to my employer. 'Do you recognize that woman?'

---

* Members of a certain order of monks who ritually carry a *danda* (bamboo staff) as a symbol of the *Brahma-danda* ("Staff of Brahma"), which, in man, is the spinal column. The awakening of the seven cerebrospinal centers constitutes the true path to the Infinite.

"'Yes.' The man was evidently struggling with emotions new to his nature. 'I have been foolishly spending my money on her, though I have a good wife. I am ashamed of the motives that brought me here. Will you forgive me, and receive me as a disciple?'

"'If you lead a good moral life for six months, I shall accept you.' The master added, 'Otherwise I won't have to initiate you.'

"For three months my employer refrained from temptation; then he resumed his former relationship with the woman. Two months later he died. Thus I came to understand my guru's veiled prophecy about the improbability of the man's initiation."

Lahiri Mahasaya had a famous friend, Trailanga Swami, who was reputed to be over three hundred years old. The two yogis often sat together in meditation. Trailanga's renown is so widespread that few Hindus would deny the possibility of truth in any story of his astounding miracles. If Christ returned to earth and walked the streets of New York, displaying his divine powers, it would cause the same awe among the people that Trailanga created decades ago as he passed through the crowded lanes of Banaras. He was one of the *siddhas* (perfected beings) who have cemented India against the erosions of time.

On many occasions the swami was seen to drink, with no ill effect, the most deadly poisons. Thousands of people, including a few who are still living, have seen Trailanga floating on the Ganges. For days together he would sit on top of the water or remain hidden for very long periods under the waves. A common sight at Manikarnika Ghat was the swami's motionless body on the blistering stone slabs, wholly exposed to the merciless Indian sun.

By these feats Trailanga sought to teach men that human life need not depend on oxygen or on certain conditions and precautions. Whether the great master was above water or under it, and whether or not his body challenged the fierce solar rays, he proved that he lived by divine consciousness: Death could not touch him.

The yogi was great not only spiritually, but physically. His weight exceeded three hundred pounds: a pound for each year of his life! As he ate very seldom, the mystery is increased. A master, however, easily ignores all usual rules of health when he desires to do so for some special reason, often a subtle one known only to himself.

Great saints who have awakened from the cosmic mayic dream and have realized this world as an idea in the Divine Mind, can do as they wish with the body, knowing it to be only a manipulatable form of condensed or frozen energy. Though physical scientists now understand that matter is nothing but congealed energy, illumined masters have passed victoriously from theory to practice in the field of matter control.

Trailanga always remained completely nude. The harassed police of Banaras came to regard him as a baffling problem child. The natural swami, like the early Adam in the Garden of Eden, was unconscious of his nakedness. The police were quite conscious of it, however, and unceremoniously committed him to jail. General embarrassment ensued: the enormous body of Trailanga was soon seen, in its usual entirety, on the prison roof. His cell, still securely locked, offered no clue to his mode of escape.

The discouraged officers of the law once more performed their duty. This time a guard was posted before the swami's cell. Might again retired before Right: the great master was soon observed in his nonchalant stroll over the roof.

The Goddess of Justice wears a blindfold; in the case of Trailanga the outwitted police decided to follow her example.

The great yogi preserved a habitual silence.* In spite of his round face and huge, barrel-like stomach, Trailanga ate only occasionally. After weeks without food, he would break his fast with potfuls of clabbered milk offered to him by devotees. A skeptic once determined to expose Trailanga as a charlatan. A large bucket of calcium-lime mixture, used in whitewashing walls, was placed before the swami.

"Master," the materialist said, in mock reverence, "I have brought you some clabbered milk. Please drink it."

Trailanga unhesitatingly drank, to the last drop, the quarts of burning lime. In a few minutes the evildoer fell to the ground in agony.

"Help, Swami, help!" he cried. "I am on fire! Forgive my wicked test!"

The great yogi broke his habitual silence. "Scoffer," he said, "you did not realize when you offered me poison that my life is one with your own. Except for my knowledge that God is present in my stomach, as in every atom of creation, the lime would have killed me. Now that you know the divine meaning of boomerang, never again play tricks on anyone."

The sinner, healed by Trailanga's words, slunk feebly away.

---

* He was a *muni*, or monk, who observed *mauna*, spiritual silence. Sanskrit *muni* is akin to Greek *monos*, "alone, single," from which are derived English words such as *monk* and *monism*.

The reversal of pain was not a result of the master's will but of the operation of the law of justice* that upholds creation's farthest swinging orb. The functioning of the divine law is instantaneous for men of God-realization like Trailanga; they have banished forever all thwarting crosscurrents of ego.

Faith in the automatic adjustments of righteousness (often paid in an unexpected coin, as in the case of Trailanga and the would-be murderer) assuages our hasty indignance at human injustice. "Vengeance is mine; I will repay, saith the Lord."† What need for man's poor resources? the universe duly conspires for retribution.

Dull minds discredit the possibility of divine justice, love, omniscience, immortality. "Airy scriptural conjectures!" Men with this insensitive viewpoint, aweless before the cosmic spectacle, set into motion in their lives a discordant train of events that ultimately compels them to seek wisdom.

The omnipotence of spiritual law was referred to by Jesus on the occasion of his triumphal entry into Jerusalem. As the disciples and the multitude shouted for joy, and cried, "Peace in heaven, and glory in the highest," certain Pharisees complained of the undignified spectacle. "Master," they protested, "rebuke thy disciples."

But Jesus replied that if his disciples were silenced, "the stones would immediately cry out."‡

In this reprimand to the Pharisees, Christ was pointing out that divine justice is no figurative abstraction, and that a man of peace, though his tongue be torn from its roots, will yet find his speech and his defense in the bedrock of creation, the universal order itself.

"Think you," Jesus was saying, "to silence men of peace? As well may you hope to throttle the voice of God, whose very stones sing His glory and His omnipresence. Will you demand that men not celebrate together in honor of the peace in heaven? Will you counsel them to gather in multitudes and express their oneness only on occasions of war on earth? Then make your preparations, O Pharisees, to overtopple the foundations of the world; for gentle men as well as stones or earth, and water and fire and air shall rise up against you, to bear witness to the divine harmony in creation."

* Cf. II Kings 2:19–24. After Elisha had performed the miracle of "healing the waters" in Jericho, a group of children ridiculed him. "And there came forth two she-bears out of the wood, and tare forty and two children of them."

† Romans 12:19.

‡ Luke 19:37–40.

The grace of the Christlike yogi, Trailanga, was once bestowed on my *sejo mama* (maternal uncle). One morning Uncle saw the master amid a crowd of devotees at a Banaras *ghat*. He managed to edge his way close to Trailanga and humbly to touch the yogi's feet. Uncle was astonished to find himself instantly freed from a painful chronic disease.*

The only known living disciple of the great yogi is a woman, Shankari Mai Jiew.† Daughter of one of Trailanga's disciples, she received the swami's training from her early childhood. She lived for forty years in a series of lonely Himalayan caves near Badrinath, Kedarnath, Amarnath, and Pasupatinath. The *brahmacharini* (woman ascetic), born in 1826, is now well over the century mark. Not aged in appearance, however, she has retained her black hair, sparkling teeth, and amazing energy. She comes out of her seclusion every few years to attend the periodical *melas* or religious fairs.

This woman saint often visited Lahiri Mahasaya. She has related that one day, in the Barrackpore section near Calcutta, while she was sitting by Lahiri Mahasaya's side, his great guru Babaji quietly entered the room and held converse with them both. "The deathless master was wearing a wet cloth," she recalls, "as though he had just come from a dip in the river. He blessed me with some spiritual counsel."

Trailanga, on a certain occasion in Banaras, forsook his usual silence in order to pay public honor to Lahiri Mahasaya. One of Trailanga's disciples objected.

"Sir," he said, "why do you, a swami and a renunciant, show such respect to a householder?"

"My son," Trailanga replied, "Lahiri Mahasaya is like a divine kitten, remaining wherever the Cosmic Mother has placed him. While dutifully playing the part of a worldly man, he has received that perfect Self-realization which I have sought by renouncing everything—even my loincloth!"

---

* The lives of Trailanga and other great masters remind us of Jesus' words: "And these signs shall follow them that believe: In my name [the Christ Consciousness] they shall cast out devils; they shall speak with new tongues; they shall take up serpents; and if they drink any deadly thing, it shall not hurt them; they shall lay hands on the sick, and they shall recover."—Mark 16:17–18.

† Bengali version of suffix *ji*, denoting respect.

CHAPTER 32

Rama Is Raised From the Dead

"'Now a certain man was sick, named Lazarus....When Jesus heard that, he said, This sickness is not unto death, but for the glory of God, that the Son of God might be glorified thereby.'"[*]

Sri Yukteswar was expounding the Christian scriptures one sunny morning on the balcony of his Serampore hermitage. Besides a few of Master's other disciples, I was present with a small group of my Ranchi students.

"In this passage Jesus calls himself the Son of God. Though he was truly united with God, his reference here has a deep impersonal significance," my guru explained. "The Son of God is the Christ or Divine Consciousness in man. No *mortal* can glorify God. The only honor that man can pay his Creator is to seek Him; man cannot glorify an Abstraction that he does not know. The 'glory' or nimbus around the head of the saints is a symbolic witness of their *capacity* to render divine homage."

Sri Yukteswar went on to read the marvelous story of Lazarus' resurrection. At its conclusion Master fell into a long silence, the sacred book open on his knee.

"I too was privileged to behold a similar miracle." My guru finally spoke with solemn unction. "Lahiri Mahasaya resurrected one of my friends from the dead."

The young lads at my side smiled with keen interest. There was enough of the boy in me, too, to enjoy not only the philosophy but, in particular, any story I could get Sri Yukteswar to relate about his wondrous experiences with his guru.

"My friend Rama and I were inseparable," Master began. "Because he was shy and reclusive, he chose to visit our guru Lahiri Mahasaya only during the hours between midnight and dawn, when the crowd of daytime disciples was absent. As I was Rama's closest friend, he confided to me many of his deep spiritual experiences. I found inspiration in his ideal companionship." My guru's face softened with memories.

[*] John 11:1–4.

"Rama was suddenly put to a severe test," Sri Yukteswar continued. "He contracted the disease of Asiatic cholera. As our master never objected to the services of physicians at times of serious illness, two specialists were summoned. Amidst the frantic rush of ministering to the stricken man, I was deeply praying to Lahiri Mahasaya for help. I hurried to his home and sobbed out the story.

"'The doctors are seeing Rama. He will be well.' My guru smiled jovially.

"I returned with a light heart to my friend's bedside, only to find him in a dying state.

"'He cannot last more than one or two hours,' one of the physicians told me with a gesture of despair. Once more I hastened to Lahiri Mahasaya.

"'The doctors are conscientious men. I am sure Rama will be well.' The master dismissed me blithely.

"At Rama's place I found both doctors gone. One had left me a note: 'We have done our best, but his case is hopeless.'

"My friend was indeed the picture of a dying man. I did not understand how Lahiri Mahasaya's words could fail to come true, yet the sight of Rama's rapidly ebbing life kept suggesting to my mind: 'All is over now.' Tossing thus on alternating waves of faith and doubt, I ministered to my friend as best I could. He roused himself to cry out:

"'Yukteswar, run to Master and tell him I am gone. Ask him to bless my body before its last rites.' With these words Rama sighed heavily and gave up the ghost.*

"I wept for an hour by his bedside. Always a lover of quiet, now he had attained the utter stillness of death. Another disciple came in; I asked him to remain in the house until I returned. Half dazed, I trudged back to my guru.

"'How is Rama now?' Lahiri Mahasaya's face was wreathed in smiles.

"'Sir, you will soon see how he is,' I blurted out emotionally. 'In a few hours you will see his body, before it is carried to the crematory grounds.' I broke down and moaned openly.

"'Yukteswar, control yourself. Sit calmly and meditate.' My guru retired into *samadhi*. The afternoon and night passed in unbroken silence; I struggled unsuccessfully to regain an inner composure.

---

* A cholera victim is often rational and fully conscious right up to the moment of death.

"At dawn Lahiri Mahasaya glanced at me consolingly. 'I see you are still disturbed. Why didn't you explain yesterday that you expected me to give Rama tangible aid in the form of some medicine?' The master pointed to a cup-shaped lamp containing crude castor oil. 'Fill a little bottle with oil from the lamp; put seven drops in Rama's mouth.'

"'Sir,' I remonstrated, 'he has been dead since yesterday noon. Of what use is the oil now?'

"'Never mind, just do as I ask.' My guru's cheerful mood was incomprehensible to me; I was still in an unassuaged agony of bereavement. Pouring out a small amount of oil, I departed for Rama's house.

"I found my friend's body rigid in the death-clasp. Paying no attention to his ghastly condition, I opened his lips with my right index finger; and managed, with my left hand and the help of the cork, to put the oil drop by drop over his clenched teeth. As the seventh drop touched his cold lips, Rama shivered violently. His muscles from head to foot vibrated as he sat up wonderingly.

"'I saw Lahiri Mahasaya in a blaze of light!' he cried. 'He shone like the sun. "Arise, forsake your sleep," he commanded me. "Come with Yukteswar to see me."'

"I could scarcely believe my eyes when Rama dressed himself and was strong enough after that fatal sickness to walk to the home of our guru. There he prostrated himself before Lahiri Mahasaya with tears of gratitude.

"The master was beside himself with mirth. His eyes twinkled at me mischievously.

"'Yukteswar,' he said, 'surely henceforth you will not fail to carry with you a bottle of castor oil. Whenever you see a corpse, just administer the oil. Why, seven drops of lamp oil must surely foil the power of Yama!'*

"'Guruji, you are ridiculing me. I don't understand; please point out the nature of my error.'

"'I told you twice that Rama would be well; yet you could not fully believe me,' Lahiri Mahasaya explained. 'I did not mean the doctors would be able to cure him; I remarked only that they were in attendance. I didn't want to interfere with the physicians; they have to live, too.' In a voice resounding with joy, my guru added, 'Always know that the omnipotent Paramatman† can heal anyone, doctor or no doctor.'

* The god of death.
† Literally, "Supreme Soul."

"'I see my mistake,' I acknowledged remorsefully. 'I know now that your simple word is binding on the whole cosmos.'"

As Sri Yukteswar finished the awesome story, one of the Ranchi lads ventured a question that, from a child, was doubly understandable.

"Sir," he said, "why did your guru send castor oil?"

"Child, giving the oil had no special meaning. Because I had expected something material, Lahiri Mahasaya chose the nearby oil as an objective symbol to awaken my greater faith. The master allowed Rama to die, because I had partially doubted. But the divine guru knew that inasmuch as he had said the disciple would be well, the healing must take place, even though he had to cure Rama of death, a disease usually final!"

Sri Yukteswar dismissed the little group, and motioned me to a blanket seat at his feet.

"Yogananda," he said with unusual gravity, "you have been surrounded from birth by direct disciples of Lahiri Mahasaya. The great master lived his sublime life in partial seclusion, and steadfastly refused to permit his followers to build any organization around his teachings. He made, nevertheless, a significant prediction.

"'About fifty years after my passing,' he said, 'an account of my life will be written because of a deep interest in yoga that will arise in the West. The message of yoga will encircle the globe. It will aid in establishing the brotherhood of man: a unity based on humanity's direct perception of the One Father.'

"My son Yogananda," Sri Yukteswar went on, "you must do your part in spreading that message, and in writing that sacred life."

Fifty years after Lahiri Mahasaya's passing in 1895 culminated in 1945, the year of completion of this present book. I cannot but be struck by the coincidence that the year 1945 has also ushered in a new age—the era of revolutionary atomic energies. All thoughtful minds turn as never before to the urgent problems of peace and brotherhood, lest the continued use of physical force banish all men along with the problems.

Though the works of the human race disappear tracelessly by time or bomb, the sun does not falter in its course; the stars keep their invariable vigil. Cosmic law cannot be stayed or changed, and man would do well to put himself in harmony with it. If the cosmos is against might, if the sun wars not in the heavens but retires at dueful time to give the stars their little sway, what avails our mailed fist? Shall any peace come out of it? Not cruelty but goodwill upholds the universal sinews; a humanity at peace will know the endless fruits of victory, sweeter to the taste than any nurtured on the soil of blood.

The effective League of Nations will be a natural, nameless league of human hearts. The broad sympathies and discerning insight needed for the healing of earthly woes cannot flow from a mere intellectual consideration of human diversities, but from knowledge of men's deepest unity—kinship with God. Toward realization of the world's highest ideal—peace through brotherhood—may yoga, the science of personal communion with the Divine, spread in time to all men in all lands.

Though India possesses a civilization more ancient than that of any other country, few historians have noted that her feat of survival is by no means an accident, but a logical incident in the record of devotion to the eternal verities that India has offered through her best men in every generation. By sheer continuity of being, by intransitivity before the ages (can dusty scholars truly tell us how many?), India has given the worthiest answer of any people to the challenge of time.

The Biblical story of Abraham's plea to the Lord* that the city of Sodom be spared if ten righteous men could be found therein, and the Divine Reply: "I will not destroy it for ten's sake," gains new meaning in the light of India's escape from oblivion. Gone are the empires of mighty nations, skilled in the arts of war, that once were India's contemporaries: ancient Egypt, Babylonia, Greece, Rome.

The Lord's answer clearly shows that a land lives, not in its material achievements, but in its masterpieces of man.

Let the divine words be heard again, in this twentieth century, twice dyed in blood ere half over: No nation that can produce ten men who are great in the eyes of the Unbribable Judge shall know extinction.

Heeding such persuasions, India has proved herself not witless against the thousand cunnings of Time. Self-realized masters in every century have hallowed her soil. Modern Christlike sages, like Lahiri Mahasaya and Sri Yukteswar, rise up to proclaim that a knowledge of yoga, the science of God-realization, is vital to man's happiness and to a nation's longevity.

Very scanty information about the life of Lahiri Mahasaya and his universal doctrine has ever appeared in print.† For three decades

---

* Genesis 18:23–32.

† A short biography in Bengali, *Sri Sri Shyama Charan Lahiri Mahasaya*, by Swami

in India, America, and Europe I have found a deep and sincere interest in his message of liberating yoga; a written account of the master's life, even as he foretold, is now needed in the West, where lives of the great modern yogis are little known.

Lahiri Mahasaya was born on September 30, 1828, into a pious *Brahmin* family of ancient lineage. His birthplace was the village of Ghurni in the Nadia district near Krishnanagar, Bengal. He was the only son of Muktakashi, second wife of the esteemed Gaur Mohan Lahiri (whose first wife, after the birth of three sons, had died during a pilgrimage). The boy's mother passed away during his childhood. We have little information about her, except a revealing fact: she was an ardent devotee of Lord Shiva,* scripturally designated as the "King of Yogis."

The boy, whose full name was Shyama Charan Lahiri, spent his early years at the ancestral home in Ghurni. At the age of three or four he was often observed sitting under the sands in a certain yoga posture, his body completely hidden except for the head.

The Lahiri estate was destroyed in the winter of 1833, when the nearby Jalangi River changed its course and disappeared into the depths of the Ganges. One of the Shiva temples founded by the Lahiris went into the river along with the family home. A devotee rescued the stone image of Lord Shiva from the swirling waters and placed it in a new temple, now well known as the Ghurni Shiva Site.

Satyananda, appeared in 1941. From its pages I have translated a few passages for this section on Lahiri Mahasaya.

* One of the trinity of Godhead: Brahma, Vishnu, Shiva, whose universal work is, respectively, that of creation, preservation, and dissolution-restoration. Shiva (sometimes spelled Siva), represented in mythology as the Lord of Renunciants, appears in visions to His devotees under various aspects, such as Mahadeva the matted-haired Ascetic and Nataraja the Cosmic Dancer.

The Lord as Shiva or Destroyer is, to many minds, a difficult conception. In *Mahimnastava*, a hymn by Puspadanta, a Shiva devotee, he plaintively asks: "Why didst Thou create the worlds, only to destroy them?" A stanza of *Mahimnastava* (translated by Arthur Avalon) reads:

"By the stamping of Thy feet the safety of the earth came in sudden peril,
By the movement of Thine arms, strong like iron rods,
The stars in the ether were scattered.
Lashed by Thy loosened hair the heavens were troubled.
Verily Thou didst finely dance!
But to trouble the world in order to save it—
What mystery is this?"
But the ancient poet concludes:
"Great is the difference between my mind—
Capable of but little understanding, and subject to sorrows—
And Thine everlasting glory, surpassing all attributes!"

Gaur Mohan Lahiri and his family left Ghurni and became residents of Banaras, where the father immediately erected a Shiva temple. He conducted his household along the lines of Vedic discipline, with regular observance of ceremonial worship, acts of charity, and scriptural study. Just and open-minded, however, he did not ignore the beneficial current of modern ideas.

The boy Lahiri took lessons in Hindi and Urdu in Banaras study groups. He attended a school conducted by Joy Narayan Ghosal, receiving instruction in Sanskrit, Bengali, French, and English. Applying himself to a close study of the Vedas, the young yogi listened eagerly to scriptural discussions by learned *Brahmins*, including a Mahratta pundit named Nag-Bhatta.

Shyama Charan was a kind, gentle, and courageous youth, beloved by all his companions. With a well-proportioned, healthy, and powerful body, he excelled in swimming and in many feats of manual skill.

In 1846 Shyama Charan Lahiri was married to Srimati Kashi Moni, daughter of Sri Debnarayan Sanyal. A model Indian housewife, Kashi Moni cheerfully performed her home duties and observed the householder's obligation to serve guests and the poor. Two saintly sons, Tincouri and Ducouri, and two daughters blessed the union. At the age of twenty-three, in 1851, Lahiri Mahasaya took the post of accountant in the Military Engineering Department of the British government. He received many promotions during the time of his service. Thus not only was he a master before God's eyes but also a success in the little human drama in which he played a humble role as an office worker in the world.

At various times the Engineering Department transferred Lahiri Mahasaya to its offices in Gazipur, Mirjapur, Naini Tal, Danapur, and Banaras. After the death of his father, the young man assumed responsibility for the members of his entire family. He bought for them a home in the secluded Garudeswar Mohulla neighborhood of Banaras.

It was in his thirty-third year that Lahiri Mahasaya* saw fulfillment of the purpose for which he had reincarnated on earth. He met his great guru, Babaji, near Ranikhet in the Himalayas, and was initiated by him into *Kriya Yoga*.

This auspicious event did not happen to Lahiri Mahasaya alone; it was a fortunate moment for all the human race. The lost, or long-vanished, highest art of yoga was again being brought to light.

* The Sanskrit religious title of *Mahasaya* means "large-minded."

As the Ganges* came from heaven to earth, in the Puranic story, offering a divine draught to the parched devotee Bhagirath, so in 1861 the celestial river of *Kriya Yoga* began to flow from the secret fastnesses of the Himalayas into the dusty haunts of men.

---

* The waters of Mother Ganga, holy river of the Hindus, have their origin in an icy cave of the Himalayas amidst the eternal snows and silences. Down the centuries thousands of saints have delighted in remaining near the Ganges; they have left along its banks an aura of blessing. (See p. 171 n.)

An extraordinary, perhaps unique, feature of the Ganges River is its unpollutability. No bacteria live in its changeless sterility. Millions of Hindus, without harm, use its waters for bathing and drinking. This fact is baffling to modern scientists. One of them, Dr. John Howard Northrop, co-winner of the Nobel Prize for chemistry in 1946, recently said: "We know that the Ganges is highly contaminated. Yet Indians drink out of it, swim in it, and are apparently not affected." He added, hopefully: "Perhaps bacteriophage [the virus that destroys bacteria] renders the river sterile."

The Vedas inculcate reverence for all natural phenomena. The devout Hindu well understands the praise of St. Francis of Assisi: "Blessed be my Lord for our Sister Water, so useful, humble, chaste, and precious."

CHAPTER 33

Babaji, Yogi-Christ of Modern India

The Northern Himalayan crags near Badrinarayan are still blessed by the living presence of Babaji, guru of Lahiri Mahasaya. The secluded master has retained his physical form for centuries, perhaps for millenniums. The deathless Babaji is an *avatara*. This Sanskrit word means "descent"; its roots are *ava*, "down," and *tri*, "to pass." In the Hindu scriptures, *avatara* signifies the descent of Divinity into flesh.

"Babaji's spiritual state is beyond human comprehension," Sri Yukteswar explained to me. "The dwarfed vision of men cannot pierce to his transcendental star. One attempts in vain even to picture the avatar's attainment. It is inconceivable."

The *Upanishads* have minutely classified every stage of spiritual advancement. A *siddha* ("perfected being") has progressed from the state of a *jivanmukta* ("freed while living") to that of a *paramukta* ("supremely free"—full power over death); the latter has completely escaped from the mayic thralldom and its reincarnational round. The *paramukta* therefore seldom returns to a physical body; if he does return, he is an avatar, a divinely appointed medium of supernal blessings on the world. An avatar is unsubject to the universal economy; his pure body, visible as a light image, is free from any debt to Nature.

The casual gaze may see nothing extraordinary in an avatar's form; but, on occasion, it casts no shadow nor makes any footprint on the ground. These are outward symbolic proofs of an inward freedom from darkness and material bondage. Such a God-man alone knows the Truth behind the relativities of life and death. Omar Khayyam, so grossly misunderstood, sang of this liberated man in the immortal scripture, the *Rubaiyat:*

> Ah, Moon of my Delight who know'st no wane,
> The Moon of Heav'n is rising once again;
>   How oft hereafter rising shall she look
> Through this same Garden after me—in vain!

The "Moon of Delight who know'st no wane" is God, eternal Polaris, anachronous never. The "Moon of Heav'n rising once again" is the outward cosmos, fettered to the law of periodic recurrence. Through Self-realization the Persian seer had forever freed himself from compulsory returns to earth: the "garden" of Nature or *Maya*. "How oft hereafter rising shall she look after me—in vain!"* What frustration of search by a wondering universe for an absolute omission!

Christ expressed his freedom in another way: "And a certain scribe came, and said unto him, Master, I will follow thee whithersoever thou goest. And Jesus saith unto him, The foxes have holes, and the birds of the air have nests; but the Son of man hath not where to lay his head."†

Spacious with omnipresence, could Christ indeed be followed except in the overarching Spirit?

Krishna, Rama, Buddha, and Patanjali were among the ancient Indian avatars. A considerable poetic literature in Tamil has grown up around Agastya, a South Indian avatar. He worked many miracles during the centuries preceding and following the Christian era, and is credited with retaining his physical form even to this day.

Babaji's mission in India has been to assist prophets in carrying out their special dispensations. He thus qualifies for the scriptural classification of *Mahavatar* (Great Avatar). He has stated that he gave yoga initiation to Shankara,‡ reorganizer of the Swami Order, and to Kabir, famous medieval master. The chief nineteenth-century disciple was, as we know, Lahiri Mahasaya, revivalist of the lost *Kriya* art.

Babaji is ever in communion with Christ; together they send out vibrations of redemption and have planned the spiritual technique of salvation for this age. The work of these two fully illumined masters—one with a body, and one without a body—is to inspire the nations to forsake wars, race hatreds, religious sectarianism, and the boomerang evils of materialism. Babaji is well aware of the trend of modern times, especially of the influence and complexities of Western civilization, and realizes the necessity of spreading the self-liberations of yoga equally in the West and in the East.

* Edward FitzGerald's translation.

† Matthew 8:19–20.

‡ Shankara, whose historically known guru was Govinda Jati, received initiation into *Kriya Yoga* from Babaji in Banaras. Babaji, in recounting the story to Lahiri Mahasaya and Swami Kebalananda, gave many fascinating details of his meeting with the great monist.

That there is no historical reference to Babaji need not surprise us. The great guru has never openly appeared in any century; the misinterpreting glare of publicity has no place in his millennial plans. Like the Creator, the sole but silent Power, Babaji works in a humble obscurity.

Great prophets like Christ and Krishna come to earth for a specific and spectacular purpose; they depart as soon as it is accomplished. Other avatars, like Babaji, undertake work that is concerned more with the slow evolutionary progress of man during the centuries than with any one outstanding event of history. Such masters always veil themselves from the gross public gaze and have the power to become invisible at will. For these reasons, and because they generally instruct their disciples to maintain silence about them, a number of towering spiritual figures remain world-unknown. I give in these pages on Babaji merely a hint of his life—only a few facts that he deems fitting and helpful to be publicly imparted.

No limiting facts about Babaji's family or birthplace, dear to the annalist's heart, have ever been discovered. His speech is generally in Hindi, but he converses easily in any language. He has adopted the simple name of Babaji (Revered Father); other titles of respect given him by Lahiri Mahasaya's disciples are Mahamuni Babaji Maharaj (Supreme Ecstatic Master), Maha Yogi (the Great Yogi), and Trambak Baba or Shiva Baba (titles of avatars of Shiva). Does it matter that we know not the patronymic of a fully released master?

"Whenever anyone utters with reverence the name of Babaji," Lahiri Mahasaya said, "that devotee attracts an instant spiritual blessing."

The deathless guru bears no mark of age on his body; he appears to be a youth of not more than twenty-five. Fair-skinned, of medium build and height, Babaji's beautiful, strong body radiates a perceptible glow. His eyes are dark, calm, and tender; his long, lustrous hair is copper-colored. Sometimes Babaji's face closely resembles that of Lahiri Mahasaya. On occasion the similarity was so striking that Lahiri Mahasaya, in his later years, might have passed as the father of the youthful-looking Babaji.

Swami Kebalananda, my saintly Sanskrit tutor, spent some time with Babaji* in the Himalayas.

---

* Babaji (revered father) is a common title; many noted teachers in India are addressed as "Babaji." None of them, however, is Babaji the guru of Lahiri Mahasaya. The existence of the Mahavatar was revealed to the public for the first time in 1946, in *Autobiography of a Yogi*.

"The peerless master moves with his group from place to place in the mountains," Kebalananda told me. "His small band contains two highly advanced American disciples. After Babaji has been in one locality for some time, he says: *'Dera danda uthao.'* ('Let us lift our camp and staff.') He carries a *danda* (bamboo staff). His words are the signal for moving with his group instantaneously to another place. He does not always employ this method of astral travel; sometimes he goes on foot from peak to peak.

"Babaji can be seen or recognized by others only when he so desires. He is known to have appeared in many slightly different forms to various devotees—sometimes with beard and moustache and sometimes without them. His undecayable body requires no food; the master, therefore, seldom eats. As a social courtesy to visiting disciples, he occasionally accepts fruits, or rice cooked in milk and clarified butter.

"Two amazing incidents of Babaji's life are known to me," Kebalananda went on. "His disciples were sitting one night around a huge fire that was blazing for a sacred Vedic ceremony. The guru suddenly seized a burning brand and lightly struck the bare shoulder of a *chela* who was close to the fire.

"'Sir, how cruel!' Lahiri Mahasaya, who was present, made this remonstrance.

"'Would you rather have seen him burned to ashes before your eyes, according to the decree of his past karma?'

"With these words Babaji placed his healing hand on the *chela's* disfigured shoulder. 'I have freed you tonight from painful death. The karmic law has been satisfied through your slight suffering by fire.'

"On another occasion Babaji's sacred circle was disturbed by the arrival of a stranger. He had climbed with astonishing skill to the nearly inaccessible ledge near the guru's camp.

"'Sir, you must be the great Babaji.' The man's face was lit with inexpressible reverence. 'For months I have pursued a ceaseless search for you among these forbidding crags. I implore you to accept me as a disciple.'

"When the great guru made no response, the man pointed to the rock-lined chasm below the ledge. 'If you refuse me, I will jump from this mountain. Life has no further value if I cannot win your guidance to the Divine.'

"'Jump then,' Babaji said unemotionally. 'I cannot accept you in your present state of development.'

"The man immediately hurled himself over the cliff. Babaji instructed the shocked disciples to fetch the stranger's body. After they had returned with the mangled form, the master placed his hand on the dead man. Lo! he opened his eyes and prostrated himself humbly before the omnipotent guru.

"'You are now ready for discipleship.' Babaji beamed lovingly on his resurrected *chela.* 'You have courageously passed a difficult test.* Death shall not touch you again; now you are one of our immortal flock.' Then he spoke his usual words of departure, *'Dera danda uthao';* the whole group vanished from the mountain."

An avatar lives in the omnipresent Spirit; for him there is no distance inverse to the square. Only one reason, therefore, motivates Babaji in maintaining his physical form from century to century: the desire to furnish humanity with a concrete example of its own possibilities. Were man never vouchsafed a glimpse of Divinity in the flesh, he would remain oppressed by the heavy mayic delusion that he cannot transcend his mortality.

Jesus knew from the beginning the sequence of his life; he passed through each event not for himself, not from any karmic compulsion, but solely for the upliftment of reflective human beings. The four evangelists—Matthew, Mark, Luke, and John—recorded the ineffable drama for the benefit of later generations.

For Babaji, also, there is no relativity of past, present, future; from the beginning he has known all phases of his life. Accommodating himself to the limited understanding of men, he has played many acts of his divine life in the presence of one or more witnesses. Thus it came about that a disciple of Lahiri Mahasaya was present when Babaji deemed the time to be ripe for him to proclaim the possibility of bodily immortality. He uttered this promise before Ram Gopal Muzumdar, that it might finally become known for the inspiration of other seeking hearts. The great ones speak their words and participate in the seemingly natural course of events, solely for the good of man, even as Christ said: "Father...I knew that thou hearest me always: but *because of the people which stand by I said it,* that they may believe that thou hast sent me."†

During my visit at Ranbajpur with Ram Gopal, "the sleepless

---

* The test concerned obedience. When the illumined master said: "Jump," the man obeyed. Had he hesitated, he would have disproved his assertion that he considered his life worthless without Babaji's guidance. Had he hesitated, he would have revealed that he lacked complete trust in the guru. Therefore, though drastic and unusual, the test was a perfect one in the circumstances.

† John 11:41–42.

saint,"* he related the wondrous story of his first meeting with Babaji.

"I sometimes left my isolated cave to sit at the feet of Lahiri Mahasaya in Banaras," Ram Gopal told me. "One midnight as I was silently meditating in a group of his disciples, the master made a surprising request.

"'Ram Gopal,' he said, 'go at once to the Dasaswamedh bathing *ghat.*'

"I soon reached the secluded spot. The night was bright with moonlight and the glittering stars. After I had sat in patient silence for a while, my attention was drawn to a huge stone slab near my feet. It rose gradually, revealing an underground cave. As the stone became stationary, held up by some unknown means, the draped form of a young and surpassingly lovely woman emerged from the cave and levitated high in the air. Surrounded by a soft halo, she slowly descended in front of me and stood motionless, steeped in ecstasy. She finally stirred, and spoke gently.

"'I am Mataji,† the sister of Babaji. I have asked him and also Lahiri Mahasaya to come to my cave tonight to discuss a matter of great importance.'

"A nebulous light was rapidly floating over the Ganges; the strange luminescence was reflected in the opaque waters. It approached nearer and nearer until, with a blinding flash, it appeared by the side of Mataji and condensed itself instantly into the human form of Lahiri Mahasaya. He bowed humbly at the feet of the woman saint.

"Before I had recovered from my bewilderment, I was further wonder-struck to behold a circling mass of mystical light traveling in the sky. Descending swiftly, the flaming whirlpool neared our group and materialized itself into the body of a beautiful youth. I understood at once that he was Babaji. He looked like Lahiri Mahasaya; though Babaji appeared much younger than his disciple, and had long, bright hair.

"Lahiri Mahasaya, Mataji, and I knelt at the great guru's feet. An ethereal sensation of beatific glory thrilled every fiber of my being as I touched his divine flesh.

---

* The omnipresent yogi who observed that I failed to bow before the Tarakeswar shrine (chapter 13).

† "Holy Mother." Mataji also has lived through the centuries; she is almost as far advanced spiritually as her brother. She remains in ecstasy in a secret underground cave near the Dasaswamedh *ghat.*

"'Blessed sister,' Babaji said, 'I am intending to shed my form and plunge into the Infinite Current.'

"'I have already glimpsed your plan, beloved Master. I wanted to discuss it with you tonight. Why should you leave your body?' The glorious woman looked at him beseechingly.

"'What is the difference if I wear a visible or an invisible wave on the ocean of my Spirit?'

"Mataji replied with a quaint flash of wit. 'Deathless Guru, if it makes no difference, then please do not ever relinquish your form.'*

"'Be it so,' Babaji said solemnly. 'I shall never leave my physical body. It will always remain visible to at least a small number of people on this earth. The Lord has spoken His own wish through your lips.'

"As I listened in awe to the conversation between these exalted beings, the great guru turned to me with a benign gesture.

"'Fear not, Ram Gopal,' he said, 'you are blessed to be a witness at the scene of this immortal promise.'

"As the sweet melody of Babaji's voice faded away, his form and that of Lahiri Mahasaya slowly levitated and moved backward over the Ganges. An aureole of dazzling light surrounded their bodies as they vanished into the night sky. Mataji's form floated to the cave and descended; the stone slab came down and closed over the cave, as if moved by invisible hands.

"Infinitely inspired, I wended my way back to Lahiri Mahasaya's place. As I bowed before him in the early dawn, my guru smiled at me understandingly.

"'I am happy for you, Ram Gopal,' he said. 'Your desire to meet Babaji and Mataji, which you have often expressed to me, has found at last a wondrous fulfillment.'

"My fellow disciples informed me that Lahiri Mahasaya had not moved from his dais since my departure at midnight.

"'He gave a wonderful discourse on immortality after you had left for the Dasaswamedh *ghat*,' one of the *chelas* told me. For the first time I fully realized the truth in the scriptural verses which state that a man of Self-realization can appear at different places in two or more bodies at the same time.

---

* This incident reminds one of Thales. The great Greek philosopher taught that there is no difference between life and death.

"Why, then," inquired a critic, "do you not die?"

"Because," answered Thales, "it makes no difference."

"Lahiri Mahasaya later explained to me many metaphysical points concerning the hidden divine plan for this earth," Ram Gopal concluded. "Babaji has been chosen by God to remain in his body for the duration of this particular world cycle. Ages will come and go—still the deathless master,* beholding the drama of the centuries, shall be present on this stage terrestrial."

---

* "If a man keep my saying (remain unbrokenly in the Christ Consciousness), he shall never see death" (John 8:51).

In these words Jesus was not referring to immortal life in the physical body—a monotonous confinement one would hardly mete out to a sinner, much less a saint! The illumined man of whom Christ spoke is one who has awakened from the deathly trance of ignorance to Eternal Life. (See chapter 43.)

Man's essential nature is formless omnipresent Spirit. Compulsory or karmic embodiment is the result of *avidya*, ignorance. The Hindu scriptures teach that birth and death are manifestations of *maya*, cosmic delusion. Birth and death have meaning only in the world of relativity.

Babaji is not limited to a physical body or to this planet, but, at God's wish, is fulfilling a special mission for the earth.

Great masters like Swami Pranabananda (see p. 223) who come back to earth in new embodiments do so for reasons best known to themselves. Their incarnations on this planet are not subject to the rigid restrictions of karma. Such voluntary returns are called *vyutthana* or reversion to earthly life after *maya* has ceased to blind.

Whatever be the manner of his passing, whether ordinary or phenomenal, a fully God-realized master is able to resurrect his body and to appear in it before the eyes of earth dwellers. Materializing the atoms of a physical body can scarcely strain the powers of one who is united with the Lord—Him whose solar systems defy computation!

"I lay down my life that I might take it again," Christ proclaimed. "No man taketh it from me, but I lay it down of myself. I have power to lay it down, and I have power to take it again" (John 10:17–18).

CHAPTER 34

Materializing a Palace
in the Himalayas

"Babaji's first meeting with Lahiri Mahasaya is an enthralling story, and one of the few that give us a detailed glimpse of the deathless guru."

These words were Swami Kebalananda's preamble to a wondrous tale. The first time he recounted it I was literally spellbound. On many other occasions I coaxed my gentle Sanskrit tutor to repeat the story, which was later told me in substantially the same words by Sri Yukteswar. Both these disciples of Lahiri Mahasaya had heard the awesome tale direct from the lips of their guru.

"My first meeting with Babaji took place in my thirty-third year," Lahiri Mahasaya had said. "In the autumn of 1861 I was stationed in Danapur as an accountant in the Military Engineering Department of the Government. One morning the office manager summoned me.

"'Lahiri,' he said, 'a telegram has just come from our main office. You are to be transferred to Ranikhet, where an army post* is now being established.'

"With one servant, I set out on the 500-mile trip. Traveling by horse and buggy, we arrived in thirty days at the Himalayan site of Ranikhet.†

"My office duties were not onerous; I was able to spend many hours roaming in the magnificent hills. A rumor reached me that great saints blessed the region with their presence; I felt a strong desire to see them. During a ramble one early afternoon, I was astounded to hear a distant voice calling my name. I continued my vigorous upward climb on Drongiri Mountain. A slight uneasiness beset me at the thought that I might not be able to retrace my steps

---

* Later a military sanatorium. By 1861 the British Government had already established in India a telegraphic system.

† Ranikhet, in the Almora district, is situated at the foot of Nanda Devi, one of the highest Himalayan peaks (25,661 feet).

before darkness descended over the jungle.

"I finally reached a small clearing whose sides were dotted with caves. On one of the rocky ledges stood a smiling young man, extending his hand in welcome. I noticed with astonishment that, except for his copper-colored hair, he bore a remarkable resemblance to myself.

"'Lahiri,* you have come!' The saint addressed me affectionately in Hindi. 'Rest here in this cave. It was I who called you.'

"I entered a neat little grotto that contained several woolen blankets and a few *kamandalus* (water pots).

"'Lahiri, do you remember that seat?' The yogi pointed to a folded blanket in one corner.

"'No, sir.' Somewhat dazed at the strangeness of my adventure, I added, 'I must leave now, before nightfall. I have business in the morning at my office.'

"The mysterious saint replied in English, 'The office was brought for you, and not you for the office.'

"I was dumbfounded that this forest ascetic should not only speak English but also paraphrase the words of Christ.†

"'I see my telegram took effect.' The yogi's remark was incomprehensible to me; I asked its meaning.

"'I refer to the telegram that summoned you to these isolated parts. It was I who silently suggested to the mind of your superior officer that you be transferred to Ranikhet. When one feels his unity with mankind, all minds become transmitting stations through which he can work at will.' He added, 'Lahiri, surely this cave seems familiar to you?'

"As I maintained a bewildered silence, the saint approached and struck me gently on the forehead. At his magnetic touch, a wondrous current swept through my brain, releasing the sweet seed-memories of my previous life.

"'I remember!' My voice was half choked with joyous sobs. 'You are my guru Babaji, who has belonged to me always! Scenes of the past arise vividly in my mind; here in this cave I spent many years

---

* Babaji actually said "Gangadhar," the name by which Lahiri Mahasaya had been known in his previous incarnation. Gangadhar (literally, "he who holds Ganga, the river Ganges") is one of the names of Lord Shiva. According to the Puranic legend, the holy river Ganga descended from heaven. Lest earth be unable to endure the force of its powerful descent, Lord Shiva caught Ganga's waters in his matted locks, whence he released them in a benign flow. The metaphysical significance of "Gangadhar" is: "he who has control over the 'river' of life current in the spine."

† "The sabbath was made for man, and not man for the sabbath" (Mark 2:27).

of my last incarnation!' As ineffable recollections overwhelmed me,
I tearfully embraced my master's feet.

"'For more than three decades I have waited for you to return
to me.' Babaji's voice rang with celestial love.

"'You slipped away and disappeared into the tumultuous waves
of the life beyond death. The magic wand of your karma touched
you, and you were gone! Though you lost sight of me, never did
I lose sight of you! I pursued you over the luminescent astral sea
where the glorious angels sail. Through gloom, storm, upheaval,
and light I followed you, like a mother bird guarding her young. As
you lived out your human term of womb life, and emerged a babe,
my eye was ever on you. When you covered your tiny form in the
lotus posture under the Ghurni sands in childhood, I was invisibly present. Patiently, month after month, year after year, I have
watched over you, waiting for this perfect day. Now you are with
me! Here is your cave, loved of yore; I have kept it ever clean and
ready for you. Here is your hallowed *asana*-blanket, where daily
you sat to fill your expanding heart with God. Here is your bowl,
from which you often drank the nectar prepared by me. See how I
have kept the brass cup brightly polished, that someday you might
drink again from it. My own, do you now understand?'

"'My guru, what can I say?' I murmured brokenly. 'Where has
one ever heard of such deathless love?' I gazed long and ecstatically
at my eternal treasure, my guru in life and death.

"'Lahiri, you need purification. Drink the oil in this bowl and
lie down by the river.' Babaji's practical wisdom, I reflected with a
quick, reminiscent smile, was ever to the fore.

"I obeyed his directions. Though the icy Himalayan night was
descending, a warm, comforting radiation began to pulsate within
me. I marveled. Was the unknown oil endued with a cosmical heat?

"Bitter winds whipped around me in the darkness, shrieking
a fierce challenge. The chill wavelets of the Gogash River lapped
now and then over my body, outstretched on the rocky bank. Tigers howled nearby, but my heart was free of fear; the radiant force
newly generated within me conveyed an assurance of unassailable
protection. Several hours passed swiftly; faded memories of another
life wove themselves into the present brilliant pattern of reunion
with my divine guru.

"My solitary musings were interrupted by the sound of approaching footsteps. In the darkness, a man's hand gently helped
me to my feet, and gave me some dry clothing.

"'Come, brother,' my companion said. 'The master awaits you.' He led the way through the forest. As we came to a turn in the path, the somber night was suddenly lit by a steady luminosity in the distance.

"'Can that be the sunrise?' I inquired. 'Surely the whole night has not passed?'

"'The hour is midnight.' My guide laughed softly. 'Yonder light is the glow of a golden palace, materialized here tonight by the peerless Babaji. In the dim past, you once expressed a desire to enjoy the beauties of a palace. Our master is now satisfying your wish, thus freeing you from the last bond of your karma.'* He added, 'The magnificent palace will be the scene of your initiation tonight into *Kriya Yoga*. All your brothers here join in a paean of welcome, rejoicing at the end of your exile. Behold!'

"Before us stood a vast palace of dazzling gold. Ornamented with countless jewels, set amid landscaped gardens, reflected in tranquil pools—a spectacle of unparalleled grandeur! Towering archways were intricately inlaid with great diamonds, sapphires, and emeralds. Men of angelic countenance were stationed by gates redly resplendent with rubies.

"I followed my companion into a spacious reception hall. The odors of incense and roses wafted through the air; dim lamps shed a multicolored glow. Small groups of devotees, some fair, some dark-skinned, chanted softly or sat silently in the meditative posture, immersed in inner peace. A vibrant joy pervaded the atmosphere.

"'Feast your eyes; enjoy the artistic splendors of this palace; for it has been brought into being solely in your honor,' my guide remarked, smiling sympathetically as I exclaimed in wonder.

"'Brother,' I said, 'the beauty of this structure surpasses the bounds of human imagination. Please explain to me the mystery of its origin.'

"'I will gladly enlighten you.' My companion's dark eyes sparkled with wisdom. 'There is nothing inexplicable about this materialization. The whole cosmos is a projected thought of the Creator. The heavy clod of the earth, floating in space, is a dream of God's. He made all things out of His mind, even as man in his dream consciousness reproduces and vivifies a creation with its creatures.

"'The Lord first formed the earth as an idea. He quickened it; atomic energy and then matter came into being. He coordinated

---

* The karmic law requires that every human wish find ultimate fulfillment. Nonspiritual desires are thus the chain that binds man to the reincarnational wheel.

BABAJI
A Mahavatar, "Divine Incarnation"
Guru of Lahiri Mahasaya

Yoganandaji helped an artist to draw this true likeness of the great Yogi-Christ of modern India.

Mahavatar Babaji has refused to reveal to his disciples any limiting facts about his birthplace and birthdate. He has lived for many centuries amid the Himalayan snows.

"Whenever anyone utters with reverence the name of Babaji," Lahiri Mahasaya said, "that devotee attracts an instant spiritual blessing."

LAHIRI MAHASAYA

"I am Spirit. Can your camera reflect the omnipresent Invisible?" After several unsuccessful exposures of film on which no image of Lahiri Mahasaya could be captured, the Yogavatar finally permitted his "bodily temple" to be photographed. "The master never posed for another picture; at least, I have seen none," wrote Paramahansaji. (See page 9.)

BABAJI'S CAVE IN THE HIMALAYAS

A cave near Ranikhet, occasionally occupied by Mahavatar Babaji. A grandson of Lahiri Mahasaya, Ananda Mohan Lahiri (*in white*), and three other devotees are visiting the sacred spot.

earth atoms into a solid sphere. All its molecules are held together by the will of God. When He withdraws His will, all earth atoms will be transformed into energy. Atomic energy will return to its source: consciousness. The earth idea will disappear from objectivity.

"'The substance of a dream is held in materialization by the subconscious thought of the dreamer. When that cohesive thought is withdrawn in wakefulness, the dream and its elements dissolve. A man closes his eyes and erects a dream creation, which, on awakening, he effortlessly dematerializes. He follows the divine archetypal pattern. Similarly, when he awakens in cosmic consciousness, he effortlessly dematerializes the illusion of a cosmic-dream universe.

"'In tune with the infinite all-accomplishing Will, Babaji is able to command the elemental atoms to combine and manifest themselves in any form. This golden palace, instantaneously brought into being, is real—in the same sense that the earth is real. Babaji created this beautiful mansion out of his mind and is holding its atoms together by the power of his will, even as God's thought created the earth and His will maintains it.' He added, 'When this structure has served its purpose, Babaji will dematerialize it.'

"As I remained silent in awe, my guide made a sweeping gesture. 'This shimmering palace, superbly embellished with jewels, has not been built by human effort; its gold and gems were not laboriously mined. It stands solidly, a monumental challenge to man.* Whoever realizes himself as a son of God, even as Babaji has done, can reach any goal by the infinite powers hidden within him. A common stone secretly contains stupendous atomic energies;† even so, the lowliest mortal is a powerhouse of divinity.'

"The sage picked up from a nearby table a graceful vase whose handle was blazing with diamonds. 'Our great guru created this palace by solidifying myriads of free cosmic rays,' he went on. 'Touch this vase and its diamonds; they will pass all the tests of sensory experience.'

"I examined the vase; its jewels were worthy of a king's collection. I passed my hand over the room walls, thick with glistening gold. Deep satisfaction spread over my mind. A desire, hidden in

* "What is a miracle? 'Tis a reproach,/ 'Tis an implicit satire on mankind."—*Edward Young, "Night Thoughts."*

† The theory of the atomic structure of matter is expounded in ancient Indian *Vaisesika* and *Nyaya* treatises. "Vast worlds lie within the hollows of each atom, multifarious as the motes in a sunbeam."—*Yoga Vasishtha.*

my subconsciousness from lives now gone, seemed simultaneously gratified and extinguished.

"My stately companion led me through ornate arches and corridors into a series of chambers richly furnished in the style of an emperor's palace. We entered an immense hall. In the center stood a golden throne, encrusted with jewels that shed a dazzling medley of colors. There, in lotus posture, sat the supreme Babaji. I knelt on the shining floor at his feet.

"'Lahiri, are you still feasting on your dream desires for a golden palace?' My guru's eyes were twinkling like his own sapphires. 'Wake! All your earthly thirsts are about to be quenched forever.' He murmured some mystic words of blessing. 'My son, arise. Receive your initiation into the kingdom of God through *Kriya Yoga.*'

"Babaji stretched out his hand; a *homa* (sacrificial) fire appeared, surrounded by fruits and flowers. I received the liberating yogic technique before this flaming altar.

"The rites were completed in the early dawn. In my ecstatic state I felt no need for sleep. I wandered about the palace rooms, filled with treasures and exquisite objets d'art, and visited the gardens. I noticed, nearby, the caves and barren mountain ledges that I had seen yesterday; but then they had not adjoined a great building and flowered terraces.

"Reentering the palace, fabulously glistening in the cold Himalayan sunlight, I sought the presence of my master. He was still enthroned, surrounded by many quiet disciples.

"'Lahiri, you are hungry.' Babaji added, 'Close your eyes.'

"When I reopened them, the enchanting palace and its gardens had disappeared. My own body and the forms of Babaji and his disciples were all now seated on the bare ground at the exact site of the vanished palace, not far from the sunlit entrances of the rocky grottos. I recalled that my guide had remarked that the palace would be dematerialized, its captive atoms released into the thought essences from which they had sprung. Although stunned, I looked trustingly at my guru. I knew not what to expect next on this day of miracles.

"'The purpose for which the palace was created has now been served,' Babaji explained. He lifted an earthen vessel from the ground. 'Put your hand there and receive whatever food you desire.'

"I touched the broad, empty bowl; hot buttered *luchis*, curry, and sweetmeats appeared. As I ate them I noticed that the bowl remained ever filled. At the end of the meal I looked around for water. My guru pointed to the bowl before me. The food had vanished; in its place was water.

"'Few mortals know that the kingdom of God includes the kingdom of mundane fulfillments,' Babaji observed. 'The divine realm extends to the earthly; but the latter, illusory in nature, does not contain the essence of Reality.'

"'Beloved Guru, last night you demonstrated for me the link of beauty in heaven and earth!' I smiled at memories of the vanished palace; surely no simple yogi had ever received initiation into the august mysteries of Spirit amidst surroundings of more impressive luxury! I gazed tranquilly at the stark contrast of the present scene. The gaunt ground, the skyey roof, the caves offering primitive shelter—all seemed a gracious natural setting for the seraphic saints around me.

"I sat that afternoon on my blanket, hallowed by associations of past-life realizations. My divine guru approached and passed his hand over my head. I entered the *nirbikalpa samadhi* state, remaining unbrokenly in its bliss for seven days. Crossing the successive strata of Self-knowledge, I penetrated the deathless realms of Reality. All delusive limitations dropped away; my soul was fully established on the altar of the Cosmic Spirit.

"On the eighth day I fell at my guru's feet and implored him to keep me always near him in this sacred wilderness.

"'My son,' Babaji said, embracing me, 'your role in this incarnation must be played before the gaze of the multitude. Prenatally blessed by many lives of lonely meditation, you must now mingle in the world of men.

"'A deep purpose underlay the fact that you did not meet me this time until you were already a married man, with modest family and business responsibilities. You must put aside your thoughts of joining our secret band in the Himalayas. Your life lies amid the city crowds, serving as an example of the ideal yogi-householder.

"'The cries of many bewildered worldly men and women have not fallen unheard on the ears of the Great Ones,' he went on. 'You have been chosen to bring spiritual solace through *Kriya Yoga* to numerous earnest seekers. The millions who are encumbered by family ties and heavy worldly duties will take new heart from you, a householder like themselves. You should guide them to understand that the highest yogic attainments are not barred to the family man. Even in the world, the yogi who faithfully discharges his responsibilities, without personal motive or attachment, treads the sure path of enlightenment.

"'No necessity compels you to leave the world, for inwardly you have already sundered its every karmic tie. Not of this world, you must yet be in it. Many years still remain during which you should conscientiously fulfill your family, business, civic, and spiritual duties. A sweet new breath of divine hope will penetrate the arid hearts of worldly men. From your balanced life, they will understand that liberation is dependent on inner, rather than outer, renunciations.'

"How remote seemed my family, the office, the world, as I listened to my guru in the high Himalayan solitudes! Yet adamantine truth rang in his words; I submissively agreed to leave this blessed haven of peace. Babaji instructed me in the ancient rigid rules that govern the transmission of the yogic art from guru to disciple.

"'Bestow the *Kriya* key only on qualified *chelas*,' Babaji said. 'He who vows to sacrifice all in the quest of the Divine is fit to unravel the final mysteries of life through the science of meditation.'

"'Angelic Guru, as you have already favored mankind by resurrecting the lost *Kriya* art, will you not increase that benefit by relaxing the strict requirements for discipleship?' I gazed beseechingly at Babaji. 'I pray that you permit me to communicate *Kriya* to all sincere seekers, even though at first they may not be able to vow themselves to complete inner renunciation. The tortured men and women of the world, pursued by the threefold suffering,* need special encouragement. They may never attempt the road to freedom if *Kriya* initiation be withheld from them.'

"'Be it so. The divine wish has been expressed through you. Give *Kriya* to all who humbly ask you for help,' the merciful guru replied.†

---

* Physical, mental, and spiritual suffering; manifested, respectively, in disease, in psychological inadequacies or "complexes," and in soul ignorance.

† At first Babaji gave permission to Lahiri Mahasaya, only, to teach *Kriya Yoga* to others. The Yogavatar then asked that a few of his disciples also be empowered to teach *Kriya*. Babaji consented, and decreed that the teaching of *Kriya* be restricted, in the future, to those who were advanced on the *Kriya* path and upon whom authority had been conferred by Lahiri Mahasaya or by the channels established by the Yogavatar's authorized disciples. Babaji compassionately promised to assume life-after-life responsibility for the spiritual welfare of all faithful and loyal *Kriya Yogis* who have been initiated by duly authorized *Kriya* teachers.

Self-Realization Fellowship and Yogoda Satsanga Society of India *Kriya Yoga* initiates are strictly required to sign a pledge that they will not reveal the *Kriya* technique to others. In this way the simple but exact *Kriya* technique is protected

"After a silence, Babaji added, 'Repeat to each of your disciples this majestic promise from the Bhagavad Gita:* *Swalpamapyasya dharmasya trayate mahato bhayat.*' ["Even a little practice of this *dharma* (religious rite or righteous action) will save you from great fear (*mahato bhayat*)"—the colossal sufferings inherent in the repeated cycles of birth and death.]

"As I knelt the next morning at my guru's feet for a farewell blessing, he sensed my deep reluctance to leave him.

"'There is no separation for us, my beloved child.' He touched my shoulder affectionately. 'Wherever you are, whenever you call me, I shall be with you instantly.'

"Consoled by his wondrous promise, and rich with the newly found gold of God-wisdom, I wended my way down the mountain. At the office I was welcomed by my fellow employees, who for ten days had thought me lost in the Himalayan jungles. A letter soon arrived from the head office.

"'Lahiri should return to the Danapur office,' it read. 'His transfer to Ranikhet occurred by error. Another man should have been sent to assume the Ranikhet duties.'

"I smiled, reflecting on the hidden crosscurrents in the events that had led me to this farthermost spot of India.

"Before returning to Danapur,† I spent a few days with a Bengali family in Moradabad. A party of six friends gathered to greet me. As I turned the conversation to spiritual subjects, my host observed gloomily:

---

from changes and distortions by unauthorized teachers, and remains in its original, uncorrupted form.

Although the ancient restrictions of asceticism and renunciation were waived by Babaji in order that the masses might benefit from *Kriya Yoga*, he nevertheless required of Lahiri Mahasaya and all descendants of his spiritual line (the SRF-YSS line of Gurus) that they impose on any who sought initiation a period of preliminary spiritual training, by way of preparation for *Kriya Yoga* practice. The practice of a highly advanced technique such as *Kriya* is incompatible with a desultory spiritual life. *Kriya Yoga* is more than a meditation technique; it is also a way of life, and requires acceptance by the initiate of certain spiritual disciplines and injunctions. Self-Realization Fellowship and Yogoda Satsanga Society of India have faithfully carried out these instructions handed down through Babaji, Lahiri Mahasaya, Sri Yukteswar, and Paramahansa Yogananda. The *Hong-Sau* and *Aum* techniques, taught in the *SRF-YSS Lessons* and by authorized SRF-YSS representatives as a preliminary to *Kriya Yoga*, are an integral part of the *Kriya Yoga* path. These techniques are highly effective in raising the consciousness to Self-realization, and in liberating the soul from bondage. *(Publisher's Note)*

* Chapter II:40.

† A town near Banaras.

"'Oh, in these days India is destitute of saints!'

"'Babu,' I protested warmly, 'of course there are still great masters in this land!'

"In a mood of exalted fervor, I felt impelled to relate my miraculous experiences in the Himalayas. The little company was politely incredulous.

"'Lahiri,' one man said soothingly, 'your mind has been under a strain in those rarefied mountain airs. This is some daydream you have recounted.'

"Burning with the enthusiasm of truth, I spoke without due thought. 'If I call him, my guru will appear right in this house.'

"Interest gleamed in every eye; it was no wonder that the group was eager to behold such a phenomenon. Half reluctantly, I asked for a quiet room and two new woolen blankets.

"'The master will materialize from the ether,' I said. 'Remain silently outside the door; I shall soon call you.'

"I sank into the meditative state, humbly summoning my guru. The darkened room became filled with a dim, soothing glow; the luminous figure of Babaji emerged.

"'Lahiri, do you call me for a trifle?' The master's gaze was stern. 'Truth is for earnest seekers, not for those of idle curiosity. It is easy to believe when one sees; no soul searchings are then necessary. Supersensual truth is deservedly discovered by those who overcome their natural materialistic skepticism.' He added gravely, 'Let me go!'

"I fell entreatingly at his feet. 'Holy Guru, I realize my serious error; I humbly ask pardon. It was to create faith in these spiritually blinded minds that I ventured to call you. Because you have graciously appeared at my prayer, please do not depart without bestowing a blessing on my friends. Unbelievers though they be, at least they were willing to investigate the truth of my strange assertions.'

"'Very well, I will stay a while. I do not wish your word discredited before your friends.' Babaji's face had softened, but he added gently, 'Henceforth, my son, I shall come whenever you need me; not always when you call me.'*

"Tense silence reigned in the little group when I opened the

---

* In the path to the Infinite, even illumined masters like Lahiri Mahasaya may suffer from an excess of zeal, and be subject to discipline. In the Bhagavad Gita, we read many passages where the divine guru Krishna gives chastisement to the prince of devotees, Arjuna.

door. As if mistrusting their senses, my friends stared at the lustrous figure on the blanket seat.

"'This is mass hypnotism!' One man laughed blatantly. 'No one could possibly have entered this room without our knowledge!'

"Babaji advanced smilingly and motioned to each one to touch the warm, solid flesh of his body. Doubts dispelled, my friends prostrated themselves on the floor in awed repentance.

"'Let *halua** be prepared.' Babaji made this request, I knew, further to assure the group of his physical reality. While the porridge was boiling, the divine guru chatted affably. Great was the metamorphosis of these doubting Thomases into devout St. Pauls. After we had eaten, Babaji blessed each of us in turn. There was a sudden flash; we witnessed the instantaneous dechemicalization of the electronic elements of Babaji's body into a spreading vaporous light. The God-tuned will power of the master had loosened its grasp of the ether atoms held together as his body; forthwith the trillions of tiny lifetronic sparks faded into the infinite reservoir.

"'With my own eyes I have seen the conqueror of death.' Maitra,† one of the group, spoke reverently. His face was transfigured with the joy of his recent awakening. 'The supreme guru played with time and space, as a child plays with bubbles. I have beheld one with the keys of heaven and earth.'

"I soon returned to Danapur," Lahiri Mahasaya had concluded. "Firmly anchored in the Spirit, again I assumed the manifold family and business obligations of a householder."

Lahiri Mahasaya also related to Swami Kebalananda and Sri Yukteswar the story of another meeting with Babaji. The occasion was one of many on which the supreme guru fulfilled his promise: "I shall come whenever you need me."

"The scene was a *Kumbha Mela* at Allahabad," Lahiri Mahasaya told his disciples. "I had gone there during a short vacation from my office duties. As I wandered amidst the throng of monks and sadhus that had come from great distances to attend the holy festival, I noticed an ash-smeared ascetic who was holding a begging

* A thick pudding made of wheat farina fried in butter and boiled in milk and sugar.

† The man, later known as Maitra Mahasaya, became highly advanced in Self-realization. I met Maitra Mahasaya shortly after my graduation from high school; he visited the *Mahamandal* hermitage in Banaras, while I was a resident there. He told me then of Babaji's materialization before the group in Moradabad. "As a result of the miracle," Maitra Mahasaya explained to me, "I became a lifelong disciple of Lahiri Mahasaya."

bowl. The thought arose in my mind that the man was hypocritical, wearing the outward symbols of renunciation without a corresponding inward grace.

"No sooner had I passed the ascetic than my astounded eye fell on Babaji. He was kneeling in front of a matted-haired anchorite.

"'Guruji!' I hastened to his side. 'Sir, what are you doing here?'

"'I am washing the feet of this renunciant, and then I shall clean his cooking utensils.' Babaji smiled at me like a little child; I knew he was intimating that he wanted me to criticize no one, but to see the Lord as residing equally in all body-temples, whether of superior or inferior men.

"The great guru added, 'By serving wise and ignorant sadhus, I am learning the greatest of virtues, pleasing to God above all others—humility.'"*

---

* "[He] humbleth himself to behold the things that are in heaven and in the earth" (Psalms 113:6). "Whosoever shall exalt himself shall be abased; and he that shall humble himself shall be exalted" (Matt. 23:12).

To humble the ego or false self is to discover one's eternal identity.

CHAPTER 35

The Christlike Life of Lahiri Mahasaya

"Thus it becometh us to fulfil all righteousness."* In these words to John the Baptist, and in asking John to baptize him, Jesus was acknowledging the divine rights of his guru.

From a reverent study of the Bible from an Oriental viewpoint,† and from intuitional perception, I am convinced that John the Baptist was, in past lives, the guru of Christ. Numerous passages in the Bible imply that John and Jesus in their last incarnations were, respectively, Elijah and his disciple Elisha. (These are the spellings in the Old Testament. The Greek translators spelled the names as Elias and Eliseus; they reappear in the New Testament in these changed forms.)

The very end of the Old Testament is a prediction of the reincarnation of Elijah and Elisha: "Behold, I will send you Elijah the prophet before the coming of the great and dreadful day of the Lord."‡ Thus John (Elijah), sent "before the coming...of the Lord," was born slightly earlier to serve as a herald for Christ. An angel appeared to Zacharias the father to testify that his coming son John would be none other than Elijah (Elias).

"But the angel said unto him, Fear not, Zacharias: for thy prayer is heard; and thy wife Elisabeth shall bear thee a son, and thou shalt call his name John....And many of the children of Israel shall he turn to the Lord their God. And he shall go before him§ *in*

---

* Matthew 3:15.

† Many Biblical passages reveal that the law of reincarnation was understood and accepted. Reincarnational cycles are a more reasonable explanation for the different states of evolution in which mankind is found, than is the common Western theory which assumes that something (consciousness of egoity) came out of nothing, existed with varying degrees of lustihood for thirty or ninety years, and then returned to the original void. The inconceivable nature of such a void is a problem to delight the heart of a medieval Schoolman.

‡ Malachi 4:5.

§ "Before him," i.e., "before the Lord."

the spirit and power of Elias, to turn the hearts of the fathers to the children, and the disobedient to the wisdom of the just; to make ready a people prepared for the Lord."*

Jesus twice unequivocally identified Elijah (Elias) as John: "Elias is come already, and they knew him not....Then the disciples understood that he spake unto them of John the Baptist."† Again, Christ says: "For all the prophets and the law prophesied until John. And if ye will receive it, this is Elias, which was for to come."‡

When John denied that he was Elias (Elijah),** he meant that in the humble garb of John he came no longer in the outward elevation of Elijah the great guru. In his former incarnation he had given the "mantle" of his glory and his spiritual wealth to his disciple Elisha. "And Elisha said, I pray thee, let a double portion of thy spirit be upon me. And he said, Thou hast asked a hard thing: nevertheless, if thou see me when I am taken from thee, it shall be so unto thee....And he took the *mantle* of Elijah that fell from him."††

The roles became reversed, because Elijah-John was no longer needed to be the ostensible guru of Elisha-Jesus, now divinely perfected.

When Christ was transfigured on the mountain‡‡ it was his guru Elias, with Moses, that he saw. In his hour of extremity on the Cross, Jesus cried out: *"Eli, Eli, lama sabachthani?* that is to say, My God, my God, why hast thou forsaken me? Some of them that stood there, when they heard that, said, This man calleth for Elias....Let us see whether Elias will come to save him."§§

The timeless bond of guru and disciple that existed between John and Jesus was present also for Babaji and Lahiri Mahasaya. With tender solicitude the deathless guru swam the abysmal waters that swirled between two lives of his *chela,* and guided the successive steps taken by the child and then by the man Lahiri Mahasaya. It was not until the disciple had reached his thirty-third year that Babaji deemed the time ripe for reestablishing openly the never-severed link.

After the brief meeting near Ranikhet, the selfless guru did not keep the beloved disciple by his side but released Lahiri Mahasaya for an outward world mission. "My son, I shall come whenever you need me." What mortal lover can fulfill the infinite implications of such a promise?

* Luke 1:13–17.   ** John 1:21.   §§ Matthew 27:46–49.
† Matthew 17:12–13.   †† II Kings 2:9–14.
‡ Matthew 11:13–14.   ‡‡ Matthew 17:3.

Unknown to society in general, a great spiritual renaissance started in 1861 in a remote corner of Banaras. As the fragrance of flowers cannot be suppressed, so Lahiri Mahasaya, quietly living as an ideal householder, could not hide his innate glory. Devotee-bees from every part of India began to seek the divine nectar of the liberated master.

The English office superintendent was one of the first to notice a strange transcendental change in his employee, whom he affectionately called "Ecstatic Babu."

"Sir, you seem sad. What is the trouble?" Lahiri Mahasaya made this sympathetic inquiry one morning to his employer.

"My wife in England is critically ill. I am torn by anxiety."

"I shall get you some word about her." Lahiri Mahasaya left the room and sat for a short time in a secluded spot. On his return he smiled consolingly.

"Your wife is improving; she is now writing you a letter." The omniscient yogi quoted some parts of the missive.

"Ecstatic Babu, I already know that you are no ordinary man. Yet I am unable to believe that, at will, you can banish time and space!"

The promised letter finally arrived. The astounded superintendent found that it contained not only the good news of his wife's recovery but also the same phrases that, weeks earlier, the great master had uttered.

The wife came to India some months later. Meeting Lahiri Mahasaya, she gazed at him reverently.

"Sir," she said, "it was your form, haloed in glorious light, that I beheld months ago by my sickbed in London. At that moment I was completely healed! Soon after, I was able to undertake the long ocean voyage to India."

Day after day the sublime guru initiated one or two devotees into *Kriya Yoga*. In addition to these spiritual duties and to the responsibilities of his business and family life, the great master took an enthusiastic interest in education. He organized many study groups and played an active part in the growth of a large high school in the Bengalitola section of Banaras. At weekly meetings, which came to be called his "Gita Assembly," the guru expounded the scriptures to many eager truth seekers.

By these manifold activities, Lahiri Mahasaya sought to answer the common challenge: "After performing one's business and social duties, where is the time for devotional meditation?" The harmoniously balanced life of the great householder-guru became the inspiration of thousands of men and women. Earning only a modest salary, thrifty, unostentatious, accessible to all, the master carried on naturally and happily in the path of disciplined worldly life.

Though ensconced in the seat of the Supreme One, Lahiri Mahasaya showed reverence to all men, irrespective of their differing merits. When his devotees saluted him, he bowed in turn to them. With a childlike humility, the master often touched the feet of others, but seldom allowed them to pay him similar honor, even though such obeisance toward the guru is an ancient Oriental custom.

A significant feature of Lahiri Mahasaya's life was his gift of *Kriya* initiation to those of every faith. Not Hindus only, but Moslems and Christians were among his foremost disciples. Monists and dualists, those of various faiths or of no established faith, were impartially received and instructed by the universal guru. One of his highly advanced *chelas* was Abdul Gufoor Khan, a Moslem. Lahiri Mahasaya, belonging himself to the highest or *Brahmin* caste, made courageous efforts to dissolve the rigid caste bigotry of his time. Those from every walk of life found shelter under the master's omnipresent wings. Like all other God-inspired prophets, Lahiri Mahasaya gave new hope to the outcasts and the downtrodden of society.

"Remember that you belong to no one and that no one belongs to you. Reflect that some day you will suddenly have to leave everything in this world—so make the acquaintance of God now," the great guru told his disciples. "Prepare yourself for the coming astral journey of death by riding daily in a balloon of divine perception. Through delusion you are perceiving yourself as a bundle of flesh and bones, which at best is a nest of troubles.* Meditate unceasingly, that you quickly behold yourself as the Infinite Essence, free from every form of misery. Cease being a prisoner of the body; using the secret key of *Kriya,* learn to escape into Spirit."

The master encouraged his various disciples to adhere to the good traditional discipline of their own faiths. Stressing the all-inclusive nature of *Kriya Yoga* as a practical technique of liberation, Lahiri Mahasaya then gave his *chelas* liberty to express their lives in conformance with environment and upbringing.

"A Moslem should perform his *namaj*† worship five times daily," the master pointed out. "Several times daily a Hindu should sit in meditation. A Christian should go down on his knees several

---

* "How many sorts of death are in our bodies! Nothing is therein but death."—*Martin Luther, "Table-Talk."*

† The chief prayer of the Moslems, repeated five times daily.

times daily, praying to God and then reading the Bible."

With wise discernment the guru guided his followers into the paths of *Bhakti* (devotion), *Karma* (action), *Jnana* (wisdom), or *Raja* (royal or complete) *Yoga,* according to each man's natural tendencies. The master, who was slow to give his permission to devotees wishing to enter the formal path of monkhood, always cautioned them first to reflect well on the austerities of the monastic life.

The great guru taught his disciples to avoid theoretical discussion of the scriptures. "He only is wise who devotes himself to realizing, not reading only, the ancient revelations," he said. "Solve all your problems through meditation.* Exchange unprofitable speculations for actual God-communion.

"Clear your mind of dogmatic theological debris; let in the fresh, healing waters of direct perception. Attune yourself to the active inner Guidance; the Divine Voice has the answer to every dilemma of life. Though man's ingenuity for getting himself into trouble appears to be endless, the Infinite Succor is no less resourceful."

The master's omnipresence was demonstrated one day before a group of disciples who were listening to his exposition of the Bhagavad Gita. As he was explaining the meaning of *Kutastha Chaitanya* or the Christ Consciousness in all vibratory creation, Lahiri Mahasaya suddenly gasped and cried out:

"I am drowning in the bodies of many souls off the coast of Japan!"

The next morning the *chelas* read a cabled newspaper account of the deaths of a number of persons whose ship had foundered the preceding day near Japan.

Many distant disciples of Lahiri Mahasaya were aware of his enfolding presence. "I am ever with those who practice *Kriya,*" he would say consolingly to *chelas* who could not remain near him. "I will guide you to the Cosmic Home through your ever enlarging spiritual perceptions."

Sri Bhupendra Nath Sanyal,† an eminent disciple of the great guru, stated that, as a youth in 1892, unable to go to Banaras, he prayed to the master for spiritual instruction. Lahiri Mahasaya appeared before Bhupendra in a dream and gave him *diksha* (initiation). Later the boy went to Banaras and asked the guru for *diksha.* "I have already initiated you, in a dream," Lahiri Mahasaya replied.

---

* "Seek truth in meditation, not in moldy books. Look in the sky to find the moon, not in the pond."—*Persian proverb.*

† Sri Sanyal died in 1962. *(Publisher's Note)*

If a disciple neglected any of his worldly obligations, the master would gently correct and discipline him.

"Lahiri Mahasaya's words were mild and healing, even when he was forced to speak openly of a *chela's* faults," Sri Yukteswar once told me. He added ruefully, "No disciple ever fled from our master's barbs." I could not help laughing, but I truthfully assured my guru that, sharp or not, his every word was music to my ears.

Lahiri Mahasaya carefully graded *Kriya* into four progressive initiations.* He bestowed the three higher techniques only after a devotee had manifested definite spiritual progress. One day a certain *chela*, convinced that his worth was not being duly evaluated, gave voice to his discontent.

"Master," he said, "surely I am ready now for the second initiation." At this moment the door opened to admit a humble disciple, Brinda Bhagat. He was a Banaras postman.

"Brinda, sit by me here." The great guru smiled at him affectionately. "Tell me, are you ready for the second *Kriya*?"

The little postman folded his hands supplicatingly. "Gurudeva," he said in alarm, "no more initiations, please! How can I assimilate any higher teachings? I have come today to ask your blessings, because the first *Kriya* has filled me with such divine intoxication that I cannot deliver the letters!"

"Already Brinda swims in the sea of Spirit." At these words from Lahiri Mahasaya, the other disciple hung his head.

"Master," he said, "I see I have been a poor workman, finding fault with my tools."

The lowly postman, who was uneducated, later developed his insight through *Kriya* to such an extent that scholars occasionally sought his interpretation on involved scriptural points. Innocent alike of sin and syntax, little Brinda won renown in the domain of learned pundits.

Besides the numerous Banaras disciples of Lahiri Mahasaya, hundreds came to him from distant parts of India. He himself traveled to Bengal on several occasions, visiting at the homes of the fathers-in-law of his two sons. Thus blessed by his presence, Bengal became honeycombed with small *Kriya* groups. Particularly in the districts of Krishnanagar and Bishnupur, many silent devotees to this day have kept the invisible current of spiritual meditation flowing.

---

* *Kriya Yoga* has many ramifications; Lahiri Mahasaya discerned the four essential steps—those that possess the highest practical value.

Among many saints who received *Kriya* from Lahiri Mahasaya may be mentioned the illustrious Swami Bhaskarananda Saraswati of Banaras; and the Deoghar ascetic of high stature, Balananda Brahmachari. For a time Lahiri Mahasaya served as private tutor to the son of Maharaja Iswari Narayan Sinha Bahadur of Banaras. Recognizing the master's spiritual attainment, the Maharaja, as well as his son, sought *Kriya* initiation, as did the Maharaja Jotindra Mohan Thakur.

A number of Lahiri Mahasaya's disciples with influential worldly position were desirous of expanding the *Kriya* circle by publicity. The guru refused his permission. One *chela*, the royal physician to the Lord of Banaras, started an organized effort to spread the master's name as "Kashi Baba" (Exalted One of Banaras).* Again the guru forbade it.

"Let the fragrance of the *Kriya* flower be wafted in a natural way," he said. "The seeds of *Kriya* will take sure root in the soil of spiritually fertile hearts."

Although the great master did not adopt the system of preaching through the modern medium of an organization, or through the printing press, he knew that the power of his message would rise like a resistless flood, inundating by its own force the banks of human minds. The changed and purified lives of devotees were the simple guarantees of the deathless vitality of *Kriya*.

In 1886, twenty-five years after his Ranikhet initiation, Lahiri Mahasaya was retired on a pension.† With his availability in the daytime, disciples sought him out in ever increasing numbers. The great guru now sat in silence most of the time, locked in the tranquil lotus posture. He seldom left his little parlor, even for a walk or to visit other parts of the house. A quiet stream of *chelas* arrived, almost ceaselessly, for a *darshan* (holy sight) of the guru.

To the awe of all beholders, Lahiri Mahasaya's habitual physiological state exhibited the superhuman features of breathlessness, sleeplessness, cessation of pulse and heartbeat, calm eyes unblinking for hours, and a profound aura of peace. No visitors departed without upliftment of spirit; all knew they had received the silent blessing of a true man of God.

---

* Other titles bestowed on Lahiri Mahasaya by his disciples were *Yogibar* (greatest of yogis), *Yogiraj* (king of yogis), and *Munibar* (greatest of saints). I have added *Yogavatar* (incarnation of yoga).

† He had given, altogether, thirty-five years of service in one department of the government.

The master now permitted his disciple, Panchanon Bhatta-charya, to open in Calcutta a yoga center, the "Arya Mission In-stitution." The center distributed certain yogic herbal medicines,* and published the first inexpensive editions in Bengal of the Bhaga-vad Gita. The *Arya Mission Gita*, in Hindi and Bengali, found its way into thousands of homes.

In accordance with ancient custom, the master gave to people in general a *neem*† oil for the cure of various diseases. When the guru requested a disciple to distill the oil, he could easily accom-plish the task. If anyone else tried, he would encounter strange difficulties; finding, after putting the oil through the required dis-tilling processes, that the liquid had almost completely evaporated. Evidently the master's blessing was a necessary ingredient.

Lahiri Mahasaya's handwriting and signature, in Bengali script, are shown opposite. The lines occur in a letter to a *chela;* the great master interprets a Sanskrit verse as follows: "He who has attained a state of calmness wherein his eyelids do not blink has achieved *Sambhabi Mudra*."‡

[*signed, lower left*] "Sri Shyama Charan Deva Sharman"

Like many other great prophets, Lahiri Mahasaya himself wrote no books, but instructed various disciples in his interpreta-tions of the scriptures. My dear friend Sri Ananda Mohan Lahiri, a late grandson of the master, wrote the following:

"The Bhagavad Gita and other parts of the *Mahabharata* epic possess several knot-points (*vyas-kutas*). Keep the knot-points un-questioned, and we find only mythical stories of a peculiar and eas-

---

* Hindu medical treatises are called *Ayurveda*. Vedic physicians used delicate surgical instruments, employed plastic surgery, understood how to counteract the effects of poison gas, performed Caesarean sections and brain operations, were skilled in dynamization of drugs. Hippocrates (4th century B.C.) borrowed much of his *materia medica* from Hindu sources.

† East Indian margosa tree. Its medicinal values are now recognized in the West, where the bitter *neem* bark is used as a tonic, and the oil from seeds and fruit is given for leprosy and other diseases.

‡ *Sambhabi Mudra* means fixing the gaze at the spot between the eyebrows. When the yogi has reached a certain stage of mental peace his eyelids do not blink; he is absorbed in the inner world.

A *mudra* ("symbol") usually refers to a ritual gesture of the fingers and hands. Many *mudras* induce calmness by affecting certain nerves. Ancient Hindu treatises minutely classify the *nadis* (72,000 nerve passages in the body) and their relationships with the mind. The *mudras* employed in worship and in yoga thus have a scientific foundation. An elaborate language of *mudras* is also found in the iconography and the ritual dances of India.

ily misunderstood type. Leave the knot-points unexplained, and we lose a science that India has preserved with superhuman patience after a quest of thousands of years of experiment.*

"Lahiri Mahasaya brought to light, clear of allegories, the science of religion that had been cleverly put out of sight in a riddle of scriptural imagery. No longer an unintelligible jugglery of words, the formulas of Vedic worship have been proved by the master to be full of scientific significance.

"We know that man is usually helpless against evil passions; but these are rendered powerless and man finds no motive for indulging in them when there dawns on him a consciousness of superior and lasting bliss through *Kriya Yoga*. Here the give-up, the negation of the lower nature, synchronizes with a take-up, the experience of beatitude. Without such a course, moral maxims that embody mere negatives are useless to us.

"It is the Infinite, the Ocean of Power, that lies behind all phenomenal manifestations. Our eagerness for worldly activity kills in us the sense of spiritual awe. Because modern science tells us how to utilize the powers of Nature, we fail to comprehend the Great Life in back of all names and forms. Familiarity with Nature has bred contempt for her ultimate secrets; our relation with her is one of practical business. We tease her, so to speak, to discover the

---

* "A number of seals recently excavated from archaeological sites of the Indus valley, datable in the third millennium B.C., show figures seated in meditative postures now used in the system of Yoga, and warrant the inference that even at that time some of the rudiments of Yoga were already known. We may not unreasonably draw the conclusion that systematic introspection with the aid of studied methods has been practiced in India for five thousand years."—*Professor W. Norman Brown, in "Bulletin of the American Council of Learned Societies," Washington, D.C.*

The testimony of the Hindu scriptures, however, is that the science of Yoga has been known in India for untold millenniums.

ways in which she may be forced to serve our purposes; we make use of her energies, whose Source yet remains unknown. In science our relation with Nature is like that between an arrogant man and his servant; or, in a philosophical sense, Nature is like a captive in the witness box. We cross-examine her, challenge her, and minutely weigh her evidence in human scales that cannot measure her hidden values.

"On the other hand, when the self is in communion with a higher power, Nature automatically obeys, without stress or strain, the will of man. This effortless command over Nature is called 'miraculous' by the uncomprehending materialist.

"The life of Lahiri Mahasaya set an example which changed the erroneous notion that yoga is a mysterious practice. In spite of the matter-of-factness of physical science, every man may find a way through *Kriya Yoga* to understand his proper relation with Nature and to feel spiritual reverence for all phenomena,* whether mystical or of everyday occurrence. We should bear in mind that many things inexplicable a thousand years ago are no longer so, and matters mysterious now may become lawfully intelligible a few years hence.

"The science of *Kriya Yoga* is eternal. It is true like mathematics; like the simple rules of addition and subtraction, the law of *Kriya* can never be destroyed. Burn to ashes all books on mathematics; the logically minded will always rediscover such truths. Suppress all books on yoga; its fundamentals will be re-revealed whenever there appears a sage with pure devotion and consequently pure knowledge."

Just as Babaji is among the greatest of avatars, a *Mahavatar*, and as Sri Yukteswar may justly be called a *Jnanavatar* or Incarnation of Wisdom, so Lahiri Mahasaya was a *Yogavatar* or Incarnation of Yoga.†

By the standards of both qualitative and quantitative good, the great master elevated the spiritual level of society. In his power to raise his close disciples to Christlike stature and in his wide dissemi-

---

* "The man who cannot wonder, who does not habitually wonder (and worship), were he president of innumerable Royal Societies and carried....the epitome of all laboratories and observatories, with their results, in his single head, is but a pair of spectacles behind which there is no eye."—*Carlyle, "Sartor Resartus."*

† Sri Yukteswar had referred to his *chela* Paramahansa Yogananda as an incarnation of divine love. After Paramahansaji's passing, his chief disciple and spiritual successor Rajarsi Janakananda (James J. Lynn) officially bestowed on him the title of *Premavatar* or Incarnation of Love. *(Publisher's Note)*

nation of truth among the masses, Lahiri Mahasaya ranks among the saviors of mankind.

His uniqueness as a prophet lies in his practical stress on a definite method, *Kriya*, opening for the first time the doors of yoga freedom to all men. Apart from the miracles of his own life, surely the *Yogavatar* reached the zenith of all wonders in reducing the ancient complexities of yoga to an effective simplicity within the ordinary grasp.

In reference to miracles, Lahiri Mahasaya often said, "The operation of subtle laws that are unknown to people in general should not be publicly discussed or published without due discrimination." If in these pages I have appeared to flout his cautionary words, it is because he has given me an inner reassurance. However, in recording the lives of Babaji, Lahiri Mahasaya, and Sri Yukteswar, I have thought it advisable to omit certain miraculous stories. I could hardly have included them without writing, also, an explanatory volume of abstruse philosophy.

As a householder-yogi, Lahiri Mahasaya brought a practical message suited to the needs of today's world. The excellent economic and religious conditions of ancient India no longer obtain. The great master therefore did not encourage the old ideal of a yogi as a wandering ascetic with a begging bowl. He stressed, rather, the advantages to a yogi of earning his own living, of not being dependent on a hard-pressed society for support, and of practicing yoga in the privacy of his home. To this counsel Lahiri Mahasaya added the heartening force of his own example. He was a modern, "streamlined" model of a yogi. His way of life, as planned by Babaji, was intended to be a guide for aspiring yogis in all parts of the world.

New hope for new men! "Divine union," the *Yogavatar* proclaimed, "is possible through self-effort, and is not dependent on theological beliefs or on the arbitrary will of a Cosmic Dictator."

Through use of the *Kriya* key, persons who cannot bring themselves to believe in the divinity of any man will behold at last the full divinity of their own selves.

CHAPTER 36

Babaji's Interest in the West

"Master, did you ever meet Babaji?"

It was a calm summer night in Serampore; the large stars of the tropics gleamed over our heads as I sat by Sri Yukteswar's side on the second-story balcony of the hermitage.

"Yes." Master smiled at my direct question; his eyes lit with reverence. "Three times I have been blessed by the sight of the deathless guru. Our first meeting was in Allahabad at a *Kumbha Mela*."

The religious fairs held in India from time immemorial are known as *Kumbha Melas*; they have kept spiritual goals in constant sight of the multitude. Devout Hindus gather by millions every twelve years to meet thousands of sadhus, yogis, swamis, and ascetics of all kinds. Many are hermits who never leave their secluded haunts except to attend the *melas** and there bestow blessings on worldly men and women.

"I was not a swami at the time I met Babaji," Sri Yukteswar went on. "But I had already received *Kriya* initiation from Lahiri Mahasaya. He encouraged me to attend the *mela* that was convening in January 1894 in Allahabad. It was my first experience of a *kumbha*; I felt slightly dazed by the clamor and surge of the crowd. I gazed around searchingly, but saw no illumined face of a master. Passing a bridge on the bank of the Ganges, I noticed an acquaintance standing nearby, his begging bowl extended.

"'Oh, this fair is nothing but a chaos of noise and beggars,' I thought in disillusionment. 'I wonder if Western scientists, patiently enlarging the realms of knowledge for the practical good of mankind, are not more pleasing to God than these idlers who profess religion but concentrate on alms.'

"My smoldering reflections on social reform were interrupted by the voice of a tall *sannyasi* who halted before me.

"'Sir,' he said, 'a saint is calling you.'

"'Who is he?'

"'Come and see for yourself.'

* See p. 342 n.

"Hesitantly following this laconic advice, I soon found myself near a tree whose branches were sheltering a guru with an attractive group of disciples. The master, a bright unusual figure, with sparkling dark eyes, rose at my approach and embraced me.

"'Welcome, Swamiji,' he said affectionately.

"'Sir,' I replied emphatically, 'I am *not* a swami.'

"'Those on whom I am divinely directed to bestow the title of *swami* never cast it off.' The saint addressed me simply, but deep conviction of truth rang in his words; I was instantly engulfed in a wave of spiritual blessing. Smiling at my sudden elevation into the ancient monastic order,* I bowed at the feet of the obviously great and angelic being in human form who had thus honored me.

"Babaji—for it was indeed he—motioned me to a seat near him under the tree. He was strong and young, and looked like Lahiri Mahasaya; yet the resemblance did not strike me, even though I had often heard of the extraordinary similarities in the appearance of the two masters. Babaji possesses a power by which he can prevent any specific thought from arising in a person's mind. Evidently the great guru wished me to be perfectly natural in his presence, not overawed by knowledge of his identity.

"'What do you think of the *Kumbha Mela*?'

"'I was greatly disappointed, sir,' I said, but added hastily, 'up until the time I met you. Somehow saints and this commotion don't seem to belong together.'

"'Child,' the master said, though apparently I was nearly twice his own age, 'for the faults of the many, judge not the whole. Everything on earth is of mixed character, like a mingling of sand and sugar. Be like the wise ant that seizes only the sugar, and leaves the sand untouched. Though many sadhus here still wander in delusion, yet the *mela* is blessed by a few men of God-realization.'

"In view of my own meeting with this exalted master, I quickly agreed with him.

"'Sir,' I commented, 'I have been thinking of the leading scientific men of the West, greater by far in intelligence than most people congregated here, living in distant Europe and America, professing different creeds, and ignorant of the real values of such *melas* as the present one. They are the men who could benefit greatly by meetings with India's masters. But, although high in intellectual attainments, many Westerners are wedded to rank materialism. Others,

---

* Sri Yukteswar was later formally initiated into the Swami Order by the *Mahant* (monastery head) of Buddh Gaya in Bihar.

famous in science and philosophy, do not recognize the essential unity in religion. Their creeds serve as insurmountable barriers that threaten to separate them from us forever.'

"'I saw that you are interested in the West, as well as in the East.' Babaji's face beamed with approval. 'I felt the pangs of your heart, broad enough for all men. That is why I summoned you here.

"'East and West must establish a golden middle path of activity and spirituality combined,' he continued. 'India has much to learn from the West in material development; in return, India can teach the universal methods by which the West will be able to base its religious beliefs on the unshakable foundations of yogic science.

"'You, Swamiji, have a part to play in the coming harmonious exchange between Orient and Occident. Some years hence I shall send you a disciple whom you can train for yoga dissemination in the West. The vibrations there of many spiritually seeking souls come floodlike to me. I perceive potential saints in America and Europe, waiting to be awakened.'"

At this point in his story, Sri Yukteswar turned his gaze fully on mine.

"My son," he said, smiling in the bright moonlight, "you are the disciple that, years ago, Babaji promised to send me."

I was happy to learn that Babaji had directed my steps to Sri Yukteswar, yet it was hard for me to visualize myself in the remote West, away from my beloved guru and the simple hermitage peace.

"Babaji then spoke of the Bhagavad Gita," Sri Yukteswar went on. "To my astonishment, he indicated by a few words of praise that he knew I had written interpretations of several Gita chapters.

"'At my request, Swamiji, please undertake another task,' the great master said. 'Will you not write a short book on the underlying harmony between Christian and Hindu scriptures? Their basic unity is now obscured by men's sectarian differences. Show by parallel references that the inspired sons of God have spoken the same truths.'

"'Maharaj,'* I answered diffidently, 'what a command! Shall I be able to fulfill it?'

"Babaji laughed softly. 'My son, why do you doubt?' he said reassuringly. 'Indeed, Whose work is all this, and Who is the Doer of all actions? Whatever the Lord has made me say is bound to materialize as truth.'

"I deemed myself empowered by the blessings of the saint, and

* "Great king"—a title of respect.

agreed to write the book. Feeling that the parting hour had arrived, I rose reluctantly from my leafy seat.

"'Do you know Lahiri?' the master inquired. 'He is a great soul, isn't he? Tell him of our meeting.' He then gave me a message for Lahiri Mahasaya.

"After I had bowed humbly in farewell, the saint smiled benignly. 'When your book is finished, I shall pay you a visit,' he promised. 'Good-bye for the present.'

"I left Allahabad the following day and entrained for Banaras. Reaching my guru's home, I poured out the story of the wonderful saint at the *Kumbha Mela.*

"'Oh, didn't you recognize him?' Lahiri Mahasaya's eyes were dancing with laughter. 'I see you couldn't, for he prevented you. He is my incomparable guru, the celestial Babaji!'

"'Babaji!' I repeated, awestruck. 'The Yogi-Christ Babaji! The invisible-visible savior Babaji! Oh, if I could just recall the past and be once more in his presence, to show my devotion at his lotus feet!'

"'Never mind,' Lahiri Mahasaya said consolingly. 'He has promised to see you again.'

"'Gurudeva, the divine master asked me to give you a message. "Tell Lahiri," he said, "that the stored-up power for this life now runs low; it is nearly finished."'

"At my utterance of these enigmatic words, Lahiri Mahasaya's figure trembled as though touched by a lightning current. In an instant everything about him fell silent; his smiling countenance turned incredibly stern. Like a wooden statue, somber and immovable in its seat, his body became colorless. I was alarmed and bewildered. Never in my life had I seen this joyous soul manifest such awful gravity. The other disciples present stared apprehensively.

"Three hours passed in silence. Then Lahiri Mahasaya resumed his natural, cheerful demeanor, and spoke affectionately to each of the *chelas.* Everyone sighed in relief.

"I realized by my master's reaction that Babaji's message had been an unmistakable signal by which Lahiri Mahasaya understood that his body would soon be untenanted. His awesome silence proved that my guru had instantly controlled his being, cut the last cord of attachment to the material world, and fled to his ever living identity in Spirit. Babaji's remark had been his way of saying: 'I shall be ever with you.'

"Though Babaji and Lahiri Mahasaya were omniscient, and had no need of communicating with each other through me or any other intermediary, the great ones often condescend to play a part in the human drama. Occasionally they transmit their prophecies through messengers in an ordinary way, that later the fulfillment of their words infuse greater divine faith in a wide circle of men who learn the story.

"I soon left Banaras, and set to work in Serampore on the scriptural writings requested by Babaji," Sri Yukteswar continued. "No sooner had I begun my task than I was inspired to compose a poem dedicated to the deathless guru. The melodious lines flowed effortlessly from my pen, though never before had I attempted Sanskrit poetry.

"In the quiet of night I busied myself over a comparison of the Bible and the scriptures of *Sanatan Dharma*.* Quoting the words of the blessed Lord Jesus, I showed that his teachings are in essence one with the revelations of the Vedas. Through the grace of my *param-guru*,† my book, *The Holy Science*,‡ was finished in a short time.

"The morning after I had concluded my literary efforts," Master continued, "I went to the Rai Ghat here to bathe in the Ganges. The *ghat* was deserted; I stood still for a while, enjoying the sunny peace. After a dip in the sparkling waters, I started for home. The only sound in the silence was that of my Ganges-drenched cloth, swish-swashing with every step. As I passed beyond the site of the large banyan tree near the riverbank, a strong impulse urged me to look back. There, under the shade of the banyan, and surrounded by a few disciples, sat the great Babaji!

---

* Literally, "eternal religion," the name given to the body of Vedic teachings. *Sanatan Dharma* came to be called *Hinduism* because the Greeks who invaded northwestern India under Alexander the Great designated the people on the banks of the river Indus as *Indoos*, or *Hindus*. The word *Hindus*, properly speaking, refers only to followers of *Sanatan Dharma* or Hinduism. The term *Indians* applies equally to Hindus and Moslems and other *inhabitants* of the soil of India (and also, through the confusing geographical error of Columbus, to the Mongoloid aboriginals in America).

The ancient name for India is *Aryavarta*, literally, "abode of the Aryans." The Sanskrit root of *arya* is "worthy, holy, noble." The later ethnological misuse of *Aryan* to signify not spiritual, but physical, characteristics, led the great Orientalist, Max Müller, to say quaintly: "To me an ethnologist who speaks of an Aryan race, Aryan blood, Aryan eyes and hair, is as great a sinner as a linguist would be if he spoke of a dolichocephalic dictionary or a brachycephalic grammar."

† The word *paramguru* refers to the guru of one's guru. Thus Babaji, the *guru* of Lahiri Mahasaya, is the *paramguru* of Sri Yukteswar.

Mahavatar Babaji is the supreme guru in the Indian line of masters who assume responsibility for the spiritual welfare of all SRF-YSS members who faithfully practice *Kriya Yoga*.

‡ Now published by Self-Realization Fellowship, Los Angeles, California.

"'Greetings, Swamiji!' The beautiful voice of the master rang out to assure me I was not dreaming. 'I see you have successfully completed your book. As I promised, I am here to thank you.'

"With a fast-beating heart, I prostrated myself fully at his feet. 'Paramguruji,' I said imploringly, 'will you and your *chelas* not honor my nearby home with your presence?'

"The supreme guru smilingly declined. 'No, child,' he said, 'we are people who like the shelter of trees; this spot is quite comfortable.'

"'Please tarry a while, Master.' I gazed entreatingly at him. 'I shall be back at once with some special sweetmeats.'*

"When I returned in a few minutes with a dish of delicacies, the lordly banyan no longer sheltered the celestial troupe. I searched all around the *ghat*, but in my heart I knew that the little band had already fled on etheric wings.

"I was deeply hurt. 'Even if we meet again I would not care to talk with Babaji,' I told myself. 'He was unkind to leave me so suddenly.' This was a wrath of love, of course, and nothing more. A few months later I visited Lahiri Mahasaya in Banaras. As I entered his parlor, my guru smiled in greeting.

"'Welcome, Yukteswar,' he said. 'Did you just meet Babaji at the threshold of my room?'

"'Why, no,' I answered in surprise.

"'Come here.' Lahiri Mahasaya touched me gently on the forehead; at once I beheld, near the door, the form of Babaji, blooming like a perfect lotus.

"I remembered my old hurt, and did not bow. Lahiri Mahasaya looked at me in astonishment.

"The divine guru was gazing at me with fathomless eyes. 'You are annoyed with me.'

"'Sir, why shouldn't I be?' I answered. 'Out of the air you came with your magic group, and into the thin air you vanished.'

"'I told you I would see you, but didn't say how long I would remain.' Babaji laughed softly. 'You were full of excitement. I assure you that I was fairly extinguished in the ether by the gust of your restlessness.'

"I was instantly satisfied by this unflattering explanation. I knelt at his feet; the supreme guru patted me kindly on the shoulder.

"'Child, you must meditate more,' he said. 'Your gaze is not yet faultless—you could not see me hiding behind the sunlight.' With these words in a voice like a celestial flute, Babaji disappeared into the hidden radiance.

---

* It is considered disrespectful in India if one does not offer refreshments to the guru.

"That was one of my last visits to Banaras to see my guru," Sri Yukteswar concluded. "Even as Babaji had foretold at the *Kumbha Mela*, the householder incarnation of Lahiri Mahasaya was drawing to a close. During the summer of 1895 his stalwart body developed a small boil on the back. He protested against lancing; he was working out in his own flesh the evil karma of some of his disciples. Finally a few *chelas* became very insistent; the master replied cryptically:

"'The body has to find a cause to go; I will be agreeable to whatever you want to do.'

"A short time later the incomparable guru gave up his body in Banaras. No longer need I seek him out in his little parlor; I find every day of my life blessed by his omnipresent guidance."

Years later, from the lips of Swami Keshabananda,* an advanced disciple, I heard many wonderful details about the passing of Lahiri Mahasaya.

"A few days before my guru relinquished his body," Keshabananda told me, "he materialized himself before me as I sat in my hermitage at Hardwar.

"'Come at once to Banaras.' With these words Lahiri Mahasaya vanished.

"I entrained immediately for Banaras. At my guru's home I found many disciples assembled. For hours that day† the master expounded the Gita; then he addressed us simply.

"'I am going home.'

"Our sobs of anguish broke out like an irresistible torrent.

"'Be comforted; I shall rise again.' After this utterance Lahiri Mahasaya rose from his seat, thrice turned his body around in a circle, assumed the lotus posture while facing the north, and gloriously entered *mahasamadhi*.‡

"Lahiri Mahasaya's beautiful body, so dear to the devotees, was cremated with solemn householder rites at Manikarnika Ghat by the holy Ganges," Keshabananda continued. "The following day, at ten o'clock in the morning, while I was still in Banaras, my room was suffused with a great light. Lo! before me stood the flesh and

---

* My visit to Keshabananda's ashram is described on pages 346–48.

† September 26, 1895, is the date on which Lahiri Mahasaya left his body. In a few more days he would have reached his sixty-seventh birthday.

‡ Thrice revolving the body, then facing the north, are parts of a Vedic rite used by masters who know beforehand when the final hour is about to strike for the physical body. The last meditation, during which the master merges himself in the Cosmic *Aum*, is called the *maha*, or great, *samadhi*.

blood form of Lahiri Mahasaya. It looked exactly like his old body, except that it appeared younger and more radiant. My divine guru spoke to me.

"'Keshabananda,' he said, 'it is I. From the disintegrated atoms of my cremated body, I have resurrected a remodeled form. My householder work in the world is done; but I do not leave the earth entirely. Henceforth I shall spend some time with Babaji in the Himalayas, and with Babaji in the cosmos.'

"With a few words of blessing to me, the transcendent master vanished. Wondrous inspiration filled my heart; I was uplifted in Spirit even as were the disciples of Christ and Kabir* who beheld their living guru after his physical death.

"When I returned to my isolated hermitage in Hardwar," Keshabananda went on, "I carried with me a portion of the sacred ashes of Lahiri Mahasaya. I knew he had escaped the spatiotemporal cage; the bird of omnipresence was freed. Yet it comforted my heart to enshrine his holy ashes."

Another disciple who was blessed by the sight of his resurrected guru was the saintly Panchanon Bhattacharya.† I visited him in his home in Calcutta and listened with delight to the story of his many years with the master. In conclusion, he told me of the most marvelous event in his life.

"Here in Calcutta," Panchanon said, "at ten o'clock of the morning that followed his cremation, Lahiri Mahasaya appeared before me in living glory."

Swami Pranabananda, the "saint with two bodies," also con-

---

* Kabir was a great 16th-century saint whose large following included Hindus and Moslems. At the time of Kabir's death the disciples quarreled over the manner of conducting the funeral ceremonies. The exasperated master rose from his final sleep, and gave his instructions. "Half of my remains should be buried with Moslem rites," he said. "Let the other half be cremated with a Hindu sacrament." He then vanished. When the disciples removed the shroud that had covered his body, nothing was found but a beautiful array of flowers. Half of these were obediently buried, in Maghar, by the Moslems, who revere his shrine to this day. The other half was cremated with Hindu ceremonies in Banaras. A temple, *Kabir Cheura*, was built on the site and attracts immense numbers of pilgrims.

In his youth Kabir was approached by two disciples who wanted minute intellectual guidance along the mystic path. The master responded simply:

> Path presupposes distance;
> If He be near, no path needest thou at all.
> Verily it maketh me smile
> To hear of a fish in water athirst!

† See p. 288. Panchanon erected a Shiva temple in a 17-acre garden in Deoghar, Bihar, in which is enshrined an oil painting of Lahiri Mahasaya. *(Publisher's Note)*

fided to me the details of his own supernal experience. During his visit to my Ranchi school, Pranabananda told me:

"A few days before Lahiri Mahasaya left his body, I received from him a letter that requested me to come at once to Banaras. I was unavoidably delayed, however, and could not leave at once. Just as I was preparing to leave for Banaras, about ten o'clock in the morning, I was suddenly overwhelmed with joy to see in my room the shining figure of my guru.

"'Why hurry to Banaras?' Lahiri Mahasaya said, smiling. 'You shall find me there no longer.'

"As the import of his words dawned on me, I cried out broken-heartedly, believing that I was seeing him only in a vision.

"The master approached me comfortingly. 'Here, touch my flesh,' he said. 'I am living, as always. Do not lament; am I not with you forever?'"

From the lips of these three great disciples, a story of wondrous truth has emerged: At the morning hour of ten, one day after the body of Lahiri Mahasaya had been consigned to the flames, the resurrected master, in a real but transfigured body, appeared before three disciples, each in a different city.

"So when this corruptible shall have put on incorruption, and this mortal shall have put on immortality, then shall be brought to pass the saying that is written, Death is swallowed up in victory. O death, where is thy sting? O grave, where is thy victory?"*

---

* I Corinthians 15:54–55. "Why should it be thought a thing incredible with you, that God should raise the dead?"—Acts 26:8.

CHAPTER 37

I Go to America

"America! Surely these people are Americans!" This was my thought as a panorama of Western faces* passed before my inward view.

Immersed in meditation, I was sitting behind some dusty boxes in the storeroom of the Ranchi school.† A private spot was difficult to find during those busy years with the youngsters!

The vision continued; a vast multitude, gazing at me intently, swept actorlike across the stage of consciousness.

The storeroom door opened; as usual, one of the young lads had discovered my hiding place.

"Come here, Bimal," I cried gaily. "I have news for you: the Lord is calling me to America!"

"To America?" The boy echoed my words in a tone that implied I had said "to the moon."

"Yes! I am going forth to discover America, like Columbus. He thought he had found India; surely there is a karmic link between those two lands!"

Bimal scampered away; soon the whole school was informed by the two-legged newspaper.

I summoned the bewildered faculty and gave the school into its charge.

"I know you will keep Lahiri Mahasaya's yoga ideals of education ever to the fore," I said. "I shall write you frequently; God willing, someday I shall be back."

Tears stood in my eyes as I cast a last look at the little boys and the sunny acres of Ranchi. A definite epoch in my life had now closed, I knew; henceforth I would dwell in far lands. I entrained for Calcutta a few hours after my vision. The following day I received an

---

* Many of those faces I have since seen in the West, and instantly recognized.

† In 1995, marking the seventy-fifth anniversary of Paramahansa Yogananda's coming to America, a beautiful Smriti Mandir (commemorative temple) was dedicated on the site of the former storeroom in Ranchi where Paramahansaji's vision occurred. *(Publisher's Note)*

invitation to serve as the delegate from India to an International Congress of Religious Liberals in America. It was to convene that year in Boston, under the auspices of the American Unitarian Association.

My head in a whirl, I sought out Sri Yukteswar in Serampore.

"Guruji, I have just been invited to address a religious congress in America. Shall I go?"

"All doors are open for you," Master replied simply. "It is now or never."

"But sir," I said in dismay, "what do I know about public speaking? Seldom have I given a lecture, and never in English."

"English or no English, your words on yoga shall be heard in the West."

I laughed. "Well, dear Guruji, I hardly think the Americans will learn Bengali! Please bless me with a push over the hurdles of the English language."*

When I broke the news of my plans to Father, he was utterly taken aback. To him America seemed incredibly remote; he feared he might never see me again.

"How can you go?" he asked sternly. "Who will finance you?" As he had affectionately borne the expenses of my education and whole life, he doubtless hoped that his question would bring my project to an embarrassing halt.

"The Lord will surely finance me." As I made this reply, I thought of the similar one I had given long ago to my brother Ananta in Agra. Without very much guile, I added, "Father, perhaps God will put it into your mind to help me."

"No, never!" He glanced at me piteously.

I was astounded, therefore, when Father handed me, the following day, a check made out for a large amount.

"I give you this money," he said, "not in my role as a father but as a faithful disciple of Lahiri Mahasaya. Go then to that far Western land; spread there the creedless teachings of *Kriya Yoga*."

I was immensely touched at the selfless spirit in which Father had been able quickly to put aside his personal desires. The just realization had come to him during the preceding night that no ordinary desire for foreign travel was motivating my plans.

"Perhaps we shall not meet again in this life." Father, who was sixty-seven at this time, spoke sadly.

An intuitive conviction prompted me to reply, "Surely the Lord will bring us together once more."

---

* Sri Yukteswar and I ordinarily conversed in Bengali.

As I went about my preparations to leave Master and my native land for the unknown shores of America, I experienced not a little trepidation. I had heard many stories about the "materialistic West"—a land very different from India, steeped in the centuried aura of saints.

"To dare the Western airs," I thought, "an Oriental teacher should be hardy beyond the trials of any Himalayan cold!"

One early morning I began to pray, with an adamant determination to continue, even to die praying, until I heard the voice of God. I wanted His blessing and assurance that I would not lose myself in the fogs of modern utilitarianism. My heart was set to go to America, but even more strongly was it resolved to hear the solace of divine permission.

I prayed and prayed, muffling my sobs. No answer came. At noon I reached a zenith; my head was reeling under the pressure of my agonies. I felt that if I cried once more, increasing the depth of my inner passion, my brain would split.

At that moment there came a knock on the door of my Garpar Road home. Answering the summons, I beheld a young man in the scanty garb of a renunciant. He entered the house.

"He must be Babaji!" I thought, dazed, because the man before me had the features of a young Lahiri Mahasaya. He answered my thought. "Yes, I am Babaji." He spoke melodiously in Hindi. "Our Heavenly Father has heard your prayer. He commands me to tell you: Follow the behests of your guru and go to America. Fear not; you shall be protected."

After a vibrant pause, Babaji addressed me again. "You are the one I have chosen to spread the message of *Kriya Yoga* in the West. Long ago I met your guru Yukteswar at a *Kumbha Mela*; I told him then I would send you to him for training."

I was speechless, choked with devotional awe at his presence, and deeply touched to hear from his own lips that he had guided me to Sri Yukteswar. I lay prostrate before the deathless guru. He graciously lifted me up. After telling me many things about my life, he gave me some personal instruction and uttered a few secret prophecies.

"*Kriya Yoga*, the scientific technique of God-realization," he finally said with solemnity, "will ultimately spread in all lands, and aid in harmonizing the nations through man's personal, transcendental perception of the Infinite Father."

With a gaze of majestic power, the master electrified me with a glimpse of his cosmic consciousness.

"If there should rise
Suddenly within the skies
Sunburst of a thousand suns
Flooding earth with beams undeemed-of,
Then might be that Holy One's
Majesty and radiance dreamed of!"*

In a short while Babaji started toward the door, remarking, "Do not try to follow me. You will not be able to do so."

"Please, Babaji, don't go away," I cried repeatedly. "Take me with you!" He replied, "Not now. Some other time."

Overcome by emotion, I disregarded his warning. As I tried to pursue him, I discovered that my feet were firmly rooted to the floor. From the door, Babaji gave me a last affectionate glance. My eyes were fixed on him longingly as he raised his hand by way of benediction and walked away.

After a few minutes my feet were free. I sat down and went into a deep meditation, unceasingly thanking God not only for answering my prayer but for blessing me by a meeting with Babaji. My whole body seemed sanctified through the touch of the ancient, ever-youthful master. Long had it been my burning desire to behold him.

Until now, I have never recounted to anyone this story of my meeting with Babaji. Holding it as the most sacred of my human experiences, I have hidden it in my heart. But the thought occurred to me that readers of this autobiography would be more inclined to believe in the reality of the secluded Babaji with his world interests if I relate that I have seen him with my own eyes. I have helped an artist to draw, for this book, a true picture of the Yogi-Christ of modern India.

The eve of my departure for the United States found me in Sri Yukteswar's holy presence. "Forget you were born among Hindus, and don't adopt all the ways of the Americans. Take the best of both peoples," he said in his calm way of wisdom. "Be your true self, a child of God. Seek and incorporate into your being the best qualities of all your brothers, scattered over the earth in various races."

Then he blessed me: "All those who come to you with faith, seeking God, will be helped. As you look at them, the spiritual current emanating from your eyes will enter their brains and change their material habits, making them more God-conscious." Smilingly, he added, "Your lot to attract sincere souls is very good. Everywhere you go, even in a wilderness, you will find friends."

Both of Sri Yukteswar's blessings have been amply demonstrated.

* Bhagavad Gita XI:12 (Arnold's translation).

LAHIRI MAHASAYA (1828–1895)
A Yogavatar, "Incarnation of Yoga"
Disciple of Babaji; Guru of Sri Yukteswar
Reviver in modern India of the ancient *Kriya Yoga* science

PARAMAHANSA YOGANANDA
Passport picture taken in Calcutta, India, 1920

I came alone to America, in which I had not a single friend; but there I found thousands ready to receive the timeless soul teachings.

I left India in August, 1920, on *The City of Sparta*, the first passenger boat sailing for America after the close of the World War. I had been able to book passage only after the removal, in ways fairly miraculous, of many "red-tape" difficulties concerned with the granting of my passport.

During the two-month voyage a fellow passenger found out that I was the Indian delegate to the Boston congress.

"Swami Yogananda," he said, with the first of many quaint pronunciations by which I was later to hear my name spoken by the Americans, "please favor the passengers with a lecture next Thursday night. I think we would all benefit by a talk on 'The Battle of Life and How to Fight It.'"

Alas! I had to fight the battle of my own life, I discovered on Wednesday. Desperately trying to organize my ideas into a lecture in English, I finally abandoned all preparations; my thoughts, like a wild colt eyeing a saddle, refused any cooperation with the rules of English grammar. Fully trusting in Master's past assurances, however, I appeared before my Thursday audience in the saloon of the steamer. No eloquence rose to my lips; speechlessly I stood before the assemblage. After an endurance contest lasting ten minutes, the audience realized my predicament and began to laugh.

The situation was not funny to me at the moment; indignantly I sent a silent prayer to Master.

"You *can*! Speak!" His voice sounded instantly within my consciousness.

My thoughts fell at once into a friendly relation with the English language. Forty-five minutes later the audience was still attentive. The talk won me a number of invitations to lecture later before various groups in America.

I never could remember, afterward, a word that I had spoken. By discreet inquiry I learned from a number of passengers: "You gave an inspiring lecture in stirring and correct English." At this delightful news I humbly thanked my guru for his timely help, realizing anew that he was ever with me, setting at naught all barriers of time and space.

Once in a while, during the remainder of the ocean trip, I experienced a few apprehensive twinges about the coming English-lecture ordeal at the Boston congress.

"Lord," I prayed deeply, "please let my sole inspiration be Thyself."

The City of Sparta docked near Boston in late September. On October 6, 1920, I addressed the congress with my maiden speech in America. It was well received; I sighed in relief. The magnanimous secretary of the American Unitarian Association wrote the following comment in a published account* of the congress proceedings:

"Swami Yogananda, delegate from the Brahmacharya Ashram of Ranchi, brought the greetings of his Association to the Congress. In fluent English and with a forceful delivery he gave an address of a philosophical character on 'The Science of Religion,' which has been printed in pamphlet form for a wider distribution. Religion, he maintained, is universal and it is one. We cannot possibly universalize particular customs and conventions; but the common element in religion can be universalized, and we may ask all alike to follow and obey it."

Because of Father's generous check, I was able to remain in America after the congress was over. Three happy years were spent in humble circumstances in Boston. I gave public lectures, taught classes, and wrote a book of poems, *Songs of the Soul*, with a preface by Dr. Frederick B. Robinson, president of the College of the City of New York.†

Starting a transcontinental tour in 1924, I spoke before thousands in many of the principal cities. In Seattle I embarked for a vacation in beautiful Alaska.

With the help of largehearted students, by the end of 1925 I had established an American headquarters on Mount Washington Estates in Los Angeles. The building is the one I had seen years before in my vision at Kashmir. I hastened to send Sri Yukteswar pictures of these distant American activities. He replied with a postcard in Bengali, which I here translate:

11th August, 1926

Child of my heart, O Yogananda!

Seeing the photos of your school and students, what joy comes in my life I cannot express in words. I am melting in joy to see your yoga students of different cities.

Hearing about your methods of chant affirmations, healing vibrations, and divine healing prayers, I cannot refrain from thanking you from my heart.

Seeing the gate, the winding hilly way upward, and the

---

* *New Pilgrimages of the Spirit* (Boston: Beacon Press, 1921).

† Published by Self-Realization Fellowship. Dr. and Mrs. Robinson visited India in 1939, and were honored guests at a Yogoda Satsanga meeting.

beautiful scenery spread out beneath Mount Washington Estates,
I yearn to behold it all with my own eyes.

Everything here is going on well. Through the grace of God,
may you ever be in bliss.

SRI YUKTESWAR GIRI

Years sped by. I lectured in every part of my new land, and addressed hundreds of clubs, colleges, churches, and groups of every denomination. During the decade of 1920–1930 my yoga classes were attended by tens of thousands of Americans. To them all I dedicated a new book of prayers and soul thoughts, *Whispers from Eternity,** with a preface by Mme. Amelita Galli-Curci.

Sometimes (usually on the first of the month, when bills rolled in for the upkeep of Mount Washington Center, headquarters of Self-Realization Fellowship) I thought longingly of the simple peace of India. But daily I saw a widening understanding between West and East; my soul rejoiced.

George Washington, the "father of his country," who felt on many occasions that he was being divinely guided, uttered (in his "Farewell Address") the following words of spiritual inspiration for America:

"It will be worthy of a free, an enlightened, and at no distant period a great, nation to give to mankind the magnanimous and too novel example of a people always guided by an exalted justice and benevolence. Who can doubt that, in the course of time and things, the fruits of such a plan would richly repay any temporary advantages which might be lost by a steady adherence to it? Can it be that Providence has not connected the permanent felicity of a nation with its virtue?"

WALT WHITMAN'S "HYMN TO AMERICA"
(From "Thou Mother With Thy Equal Brood")

Thee in thy future,
Thee in thy larger, saner brood of female, male—thee in thy athletes,
    moral, spiritual; South, North, West, East.
Thee in thy moral wealth and civilization (until which thy proudest
    material civilization must remain in vain),
Thee in thy all-supplying, all-enclosing worship—thee in no single bible,
    savior, merely,
Thy saviors countless, latent within thyself, equal to any, divine as any...
These! these in thee (certain to come) today I prophesy.

---

* Published by Self-Realization Fellowship.

CHAPTER 38

Luther Burbank—
A Saint Amid the Roses

"The secret of improved plant breeding, apart from scientific knowledge, is love." Luther Burbank uttered this wisdom as I walked beside him in his garden in Santa Rosa, California. We halted near a bed of edible cacti.

"While I was conducting experiments to make 'spineless' cacti," he continued, "I often talked to the plants to create a vibration of love. 'You have nothing to fear,' I would tell them. 'You don't need your defensive thorns. I will protect you.' Gradually the useful plant of the desert emerged in a thornless variety."

I was charmed at this miracle. "Please, dear Luther, give me a few cactus leaves to plant in my garden at Mount Washington."

A workman standing nearby started to strip off some leaves; Burbank prevented him.

"I myself will pluck them for the swami." He handed me three leaves, which later I planted, rejoicing as they grew to huge estate.

The great horticulturist told me that his first notable triumph was the large potato now known by his name. With the indefatigability of genius, he went on to present the world with hundreds of crossed improvements on nature—his new Burbank varieties of tomato, corn, squash, cherries, plums, nectarines, berries, poppies, lilies, roses.

I focused my camera as Luther led me before the famous walnut tree by which he has proved that natural evolution can be telescopically hastened.

"In only sixteen years," he said, "this walnut tree reached a state of abundant nut production. Unaided Nature would have required twice that time."

Burbank's little adopted daughter came romping with her dog into the garden.

"She is my human plant." Luther waved to her affectionately. "I see humanity now as one vast plant, needing for its highest fulfillments only love, the natural blessings of the great outdoors, and intelligent crossing and selection. In the span of my own lifetime I have observed such wondrous progress in plant evolution that I look forward optimistically to a healthy, happy world as soon as its children are taught the principles of simple and rational living. We must return to nature and nature's God."

"Luther, you would delight in my Ranchi school, with its outdoor classes, and atmosphere of joy and simplicity."

My words touched the chord closest to Burbank's heart—child education. He plied me with questions, interest gleaming from his deep, serene eyes.

"Swamiji," he said finally, "schools like yours are the only hope of a future millennium. I am in revolt against the educational systems of our time, severed from nature and stifling of all individuality. I am with you heart and soul in your practical ideals of education."

As I was taking leave of the gentle sage, he autographed a small volume and presented it to me.*

"Here is my book on *The Training of the Human Plant*,"† he said. "New types of training are needed—fearless experiments. At times the most daring trials have succeeded in bringing out the best in fruits and flowers. Educational innovations for children should likewise become more numerous, more courageous."

I read his little book that night with intense interest. His eye envisioning a glorious future for the race, he wrote: "The most stubborn living thing in this world, the most difficult to swerve, is a plant once fixed in certain habits.... Remember that this plant has preserved its individuality all through the ages; perhaps it is one which can be traced backward through aeons of time in the very rocks themselves, never having varied to any great extent in all these vast periods. Do you suppose, after all these ages of repetition, the plant does not become possessed of a will, if you so choose to call it, of unparalleled tenacity? Indeed, there are plants, like certain of the palms, so persistent that no human power has yet been able to change them. The human will is a weak thing beside the will of a plant. But see how this whole plant's lifelong stubbornness is

---

* Burbank also gave me an autographed picture of himself. I treasure it even as a Hindu merchant once treasured a picture of Lincoln. The Hindu, who was in America during the Civil War years, conceived such an admiration for Lincoln that he was unwilling to return to India until he had obtained a portrait of the Great Emancipator. Planting himself adamantly on Lincoln's doorstep, the merchant refused to leave until the astonished President permitted him to engage the services of Daniel Huntington, the famous New York artist. When the portrait was finished, the Hindu carried it in triumph to Calcutta.

† New York: Century Co., 1922.

LUTHER BURBANK

SANTA ROSA, CALIFORNIA

U. S. A.

December 22, 1924

I have examined the Yogoda system of Swami Yogananda and in my opinion it is ideal for training and harmonizing man's physical, mental, and spiritual natures. Swami's aim is to establish "How-to-Live" schools throughout the world, wherein education will not confine itself to intellectual development alone, but also training of the body, will, and feelings.

Through the Yogoda system of physical, mental, and spiritual unfoldment by simple and scientific methods of concentration and meditation, most of the complex problems of life may be solved, and peace and good-will come upon earth. The Swami's idea of right education is plain commonsense, free from all mysticism and non-practicality; otherwise it would not have my approval.

I am glad to have this opportunity of heartily joining with the Swami in his appeal for international schools on the art of living which, if established, will come as near to bringing the millennium as anything with which I am acquainted.

Luther Burbank

broken simply by blending a new life with it, making, by crossing, a complete and powerful change in its life. Then when the break comes, fix it by these generations of patient supervision and selection, and the new plant sets out upon its new way never again to return to the old, its tenacious will broken and changed at last.

"When it comes to so sensitive and pliable a thing as the nature of a child, the problem becomes vastly easier."

Magnetically drawn to this great American, I visited him again and again. One morning I arrived at the same time as the postman, who deposited in Burbank's study about a thousand letters. Horticulturists wrote him from all parts of the world.

"Swamiji, your presence is just the excuse I need to get out into the garden," Luther said gaily. He opened a large desk drawer containing hundreds of travel folders.

"See," he said, "this is how I do my traveling. Tied down by my plants and correspondence, I satisfy my desire for foreign lands by a glance now and then at these pictures."

My car was standing before his gate; Luther and I drove along the streets of the little town, its gardens bright with his own varieties of Santa Rosa, Peachblow, and Burbank roses.

The great scientist had received *Kriya* initiation during one of my earlier visits. "I practice the technique devoutly, Swamiji," he said. After many thoughtful questions to me about various aspects of yoga, Luther remarked slowly:

"The East indeed possesses immense hoards of knowledge that the West has scarcely begun to explore."*

Intimate communion with Nature, who unlocked to him many of her jealously guarded secrets, had given Burbank a boundless spiritual reverence.

"Sometimes I feel very close to the Infinite Power," he confided shyly. His sensitive, beautifully modeled face lit with his memories. "Then I have been able to heal sick persons around me, as well as many ailing plants."

He told me of his mother, a sincere Christian. "Many times since her death," Luther said, "I have been blessed by her appearance in visions; she has spoken to me."

---

* Dr. Julian Huxley, famous English biologist and director of UNESCO, recently stated that Western scientists should "learn the Oriental techniques" for entering the trance state and for control of breathing. *"What* happens? *How* is it possible?" he said. An *Associated Press* dispatch from London, dated Aug. 21, 1948, reported: "Dr. Huxley told the new World Federation for Mental Health it might well look into the mystic lore of the East. If this lore could be investigated scientifically, he advised mental specialists, 'then I think an immense step forward could be made in your field.'"

We drove back reluctantly toward his home and those waiting thousand letters.

"Luther," I remarked, "next month I am starting a magazine to present the truth-offerings of East and West. Please help me decide on a good name for the journal."

We discussed titles for a while, and finally agreed on *East-West.** After we had re-entered his study, Burbank gave me an article he had written on "Science and Civilization."

"This will go in the first issue of *East-West*," I said gratefully.

As our friendship grew deeper, I called Burbank my "American saint." "Behold a man," I paraphrased, "in whom is no guile."† His heart was fathomlessly deep, long acquainted with humility, patience, sacrifice. His little home amid the roses was austerely simple; he knew the worthlessness of luxury, the joy of few possessions. The modesty with which he wore his scientific fame repeatedly reminded me of the trees that bend low with the burden of ripening fruits; it is the barren tree that lifts its head high in an empty boast.

I was in New York when, in 1926, my dear friend passed away. In tears I thought, "Oh, I would gladly walk all the way from here to Santa Rosa for one more glimpse of him!" Locking myself away from secretaries and visitors, I spent the next twenty-four hours in seclusion.

The following day I conducted a Vedic memorial rite before a large picture of Luther. A group of my American students, garbed in Hindu ceremonial clothes, chanted the ancient hymns as an offering was made of flowers, water, and fire—symbols of the bodily elements and their return to the Infinite Source.

Though the form of Burbank lies in Santa Rosa under a Lebanon cedar that he planted years ago in his garden, his soul is enshrined for me in every wide-eyed flower that blooms by the wayside. Withdrawn for a time into the spacious spirit of nature, is that not Luther whispering in her winds, walking her dawns?

His name has now passed into the heritage of common speech. Listing "burbank" as a transitive verb, Webster's New International Dictionary defines it: "To cross or graft (a plant). Hence, figuratively, to improve (anything, as a process or institution) by selecting good features and rejecting bad, or by adding good features."

"Beloved Burbank," I cried after reading the definition, "your very name is now a synonym for goodness!"

* Renamed *Self-Realization* in 1948.
† John 1:47.

CHAPTER 39

Therese Neumann,
the Catholic Stigmatist

"Return to India. I have waited for you patiently for fifteen years. Soon I shall swim out of the body and on to the Shining Abode. Yogananda, come!"

Sri Yukteswar's voice sounded startlingly in my inner ear as I sat in meditation at my Mt. Washington headquarters. Traversing ten thousand miles in the twinkling of an eye, his message penetrated my being like a flash of lightning.

Fifteen years! Yes, I realized, now it is 1935; I have spent fifteen years in spreading my guru's teachings in America. Now he recalls me.

A short time later I described my experience to a dear friend, Mr. James J. Lynn. His spiritual development by daily practice of *Kriya Yoga* has been so remarkable that I often call him "Saint Lynn." In him and in a number of other Occidentals I happily see a fulfillment of Babaji's prophecy that the West, too, would produce saints of true Self-realization through the ancient yogic path.

Mr. Lynn generously insisted on making a donation for my travels. The financial problem thus solved, I made arrangements to sail, via Europe, for India. In March 1935, I had Self-Realization Fellowship chartered under the laws of the State of California as a nonsectarian nonprofit corporation, designed to exist perpetually. To Self-Realization Fellowship I donated all my possessions, including the rights in all my writings. Like most other religious and educational institutions, Self-Realization Fellowship is supported by endowments and donations from its members and the public.

"I shall be back," I told my students. "Never shall I forget America."

At a farewell banquet given to me in Los Angeles by loving friends, I looked long at their faces and thought gratefully, "Lord, he who remembers Thee as the Sole Giver will never lack the sweetness of friendship among mortals."

I sailed from New York on June 9, 1935, on the *Europa*. Two students accompanied me: my secretary, Mr. C. Richard Wright, and an elderly lady from Cincinnati, Miss Ettie Bletsch. We enjoyed the days of ocean peace, a welcome contrast to the past hurried weeks. Our period of leisure was short-lived; the speed of modern boats has some regrettable features!

Like any other group of inquisitive tourists, we walked about the huge and ancient city of London. On the day following my arrival I was invited to address a large meeting in Caxton Hall, at which I was introduced to the London audience by Sir Francis Younghusband.

Our party spent a pleasant day as guests of Sir Harry Lauder at his estate in Scotland. A few days later our little group crossed the English Channel to the continent, for I wanted to make a pilgrimage to Bavaria. This would be my only chance, I felt, to visit the great Catholic mystic, Therese Neumann of Konnersreuth.

Years earlier I had read an amazing account of Therese. Information given in the article was as follows:

(1) Therese, born on Good Friday in 1898, was injured in an accident at the age of twenty; she became blind and paralyzed.

(2) She miraculously regained her sight in 1923 through prayers to St. Thérèse of Lisieux, "The Little Flower." Later Therese Neumann's limbs were instantaneously healed.

(3) From 1923 onward, Therese has abstained completely from food and drink, except for the daily swallowing of one small consecrated wafer.

(4) The stigmata, sacred wounds of Christ, appeared in 1926 on Therese's head, breast, hands, and feet. Every Friday* she experiences the Passion of Christ, suffering in her own body all his historic agonies.

(5) Knowing ordinarily only the simple German of her village, during her Friday trances Therese utters phrases which scholars have identified as ancient Aramaic. At appropriate times in her vision, she speaks Hebrew or Greek.

(6) By ecclesiastical permission, Therese has several times been under close scientific observation. Dr. Fritz Gerlich, editor of a Protestant German newspaper, went to Konnersreuth to "expose the Catholic fraud," but ended up by reverently writing her biography.

* Since the war years, Therese has not experienced the Passion every Friday but only on certain holy days of the year. Books on her life are *Therese Neumann: A Stigmatist of Our Day,* and *Further Chronicles of Therese Neumann,* both by Friedrich Ritter von Lama; and *The Story of Therese Neumann,* by A. P. Schimberg (1947); all published by Bruce Pub. Co., Milwaukee, Wisconsin; and *Therese Neumann,* by Johannes Steiner, published by Alba House, Staten Island, N.Y.

As always, whether in East or West, I was eager to meet a saint. I rejoiced as our little party entered, on July 16, the quaint village of Konnersreuth. The Bavarian peasants exhibited lively interest in our Ford automobile (brought with us from America) and its assorted group—an American young man, an elderly lady, and an olive-hued Oriental with long hair tucked under his coat collar.

Therese's little cottage, clean and neat, with geraniums blooming by a primitive well, was alas! silently closed. The neighbors, and even the village postman who passed by, could give us no information. Rain began to fall; my companions suggested that we leave.

"No," I said stubbornly, "I will stay here until I find some clue leading to Therese."

Two hours later we were still sitting in our car amidst the dismal rain. "Lord," I sighed complainingly, "why didst Thou lead me here if she has disappeared?"

An English-speaking man halted beside us, politely offering his aid.

"I don't know for certain where Therese is," he said, "but she often visits at the home of Professor Franz Wutz, a teacher of foreign languages at the University of Eichstätt, eighty miles from here."

The following morning our party motored to the quiet town of Eichstätt. Dr. Wutz greeted us cordially at his home; "Yes, Therese is here." He sent her word of the visitors. A messenger soon appeared with her reply:

"Though the bishop has asked me to see no one without his permission, I will receive the man of God from India."

Deeply touched at these words, I followed Dr. Wutz upstairs to the sitting room. Therese entered immediately, radiating an aura of peace and joy. She wore a black gown and spotless white headdress. Although her age was thirty-seven at this time, she seemed much younger; possessing indeed a childlike freshness and charm. Healthy, well-formed, rosy-cheeked, and cheerful, this is the saint who does not eat!

Therese greeted me with a very gentle handshaking. We beamed in silent communion, each knowing the other to be a lover of God.

Dr. Wutz kindly offered to serve as interpreter. As we seated ourselves, I noticed that Therese was glancing at me with naive curiosity; evidently Hindus had been rare in Bavaria.

"Don't you eat anything?" I wanted to hear the answer from her own lips.

"No, except a Host* at six o'clock each morning."

"How large is the Host?"

"It is paper-thin, the size of a small coin." She added, "I take it for sacramental reasons; if it is unconsecrated, I am unable to swallow it."

"Certainly you could not have lived on that, for twelve whole years?"

"I live by God's light."

How simple her reply, how Einsteinian!

"I see you realize that energy flows to your body from the ether, sun, and air."

A swift smile broke over her face. "I am so happy to know you understand how I live."

"Your sacred life is a daily demonstration of the truth uttered by Christ: 'Man shall not live by bread alone, but by every word that proceedeth out of the mouth of God.'"†

Again she showed joy at my explanation. "It is indeed so. One of the reasons I am here on earth today is to prove that man can live by God's invisible light, and not by food only."

"Can you teach others how to live without food?"

She appeared a trifle shocked. "I cannot do that; God does not wish it."

As my gaze fell on her strong, graceful hands, Therese showed me a square, freshly healed wound on the back of each hand. On the palm of each hand, she pointed out a smaller, crescent-shaped wound, freshly healed. Each wound went straight through the hand. The sight brought to me a distinct recollection of the large square iron nails with crescent-tipped ends that are still used in the East but that I do not recall having seen in the West.

---

* A Eucharistic flour-wafer.

† Matthew 4:4. Man's body battery is not sustained by gross food (bread) alone, but by the vibratory cosmic energy (Word, or *Aum*). The invisible power flows into the human body through the gate of the medulla oblongata. This sixth bodily center is located at the back of the neck at the top of the five spinal *chakras* (Sanskrit for "wheels" or centers of radiating life force).

The medulla, the principal entrance for the body's supply of universal life energy (*Aum*), is directly connected by polarity with the Christ Consciousness center (*Kutastha*) in the single eye between the eyebrows: the seat of man's power of will. Cosmic energy is then stored up in the seventh center, in the brain, as a reservoir of infinite potentialities (mentioned in the Vedas as the "thousand-petaled lotus of light"). The Bible refers to *Aum* as the Holy Ghost or invisible life force that divinely upholds all creation. "What? know ye not that your body is the temple of the Holy Ghost which is in you, which ye have of God, and ye are not your own?"—I Corinthians 6:19.

The saint told me something of her weekly trances. "As a helpless onlooker, I observe the whole Passion of Christ." Each week, from Thursday midnight until Friday afternoon at one o'clock, her wounds open and bleed; she loses ten pounds of her ordinary 121-pound weight. Suffering intensely in her sympathetic love, Therese yet looks forward joyously to these weekly visions of her Lord.

I realized at once that her strange life is intended by God to reassure all Christians of the historical authenticity of Jesus' life and crucifixion as recorded in the New Testament, and to display dramatically the ever living bond between the Galilean Master and his devotees.

Professor Wutz related some of his experiences with the saint.

"A group of us, including Therese, often travel for days on sight-seeing trips in Germany," he told me. "It is a striking contrast—Therese eats nothing; the rest of us have three meals a day. She remains as fresh as a rose, untouched by fatigue. Whenever the rest of us get hungry and look for wayside inns, Therese laughs merrily."

The professor added some interesting physiological details: "Because Therese takes no food, her stomach has shrunk. She has no excretions, but her perspiration glands function; her skin is always soft and firm."

At the time of parting, I expressed to Therese my desire to be present at her trance.

"Yes, please come to Konnersreuth next Friday," she said graciously. "The bishop will give you a permit. I am very happy you sought me out in Eichstätt."

Therese shook hands gently, many times, and walked with our party to the gate. Mr. Wright turned on the automobile radio; the saint examined it with little enthusiastic chuckles. Such a large crowd of youngsters gathered that Therese retreated into the house. We saw her at a window, where she peered at us, childlike, waving her hand.

From a conversation the next day with two of Therese's brothers, very kind and amiable, we learned that the saint sleeps only one or two hours at night. In spite of the many wounds in her body, she is active and full of energy. She loves birds, looks after an aquarium of fish, and works often in her garden. Her correspondence is large; Catholic devotees write her for prayers and healing blessings. Many seekers have been cured through her of serious diseases.

Her brother Ferdinand, about twenty-three, explained that

Therese has the power, through prayer, of working out on her own body the ailments of others. The saint's abstinence from food dates from a time when she prayed that the throat disease of a young man of her parish, then preparing to enter holy orders, be transferred to her own throat.

On Thursday afternoon our party drove to the home of the bishop, who looked at my flowing locks with some surprise. He readily wrote out the necessary permit. There was no fee; the rule made by the Church is simply to protect Therese from the onrush of casual tourists, who in previous years had flocked by thousands to Konnersreuth on Fridays.

We arrived in the village on Friday morning about nine-thirty. I noticed that Therese's little cottage possesses a glass-roofed section to afford her plenty of light. We were glad to see the doors no longer closed, but wide open in hospitable cheer. We joined a line of about twenty visitors, each carrying a permit. Many had come from great distances to view the mystic trance.

Therese had passed my first test at the professor's house by her intuitive knowledge that I wanted to see her for spiritual reasons, and not just to satisfy a passing curiosity.

My second test was connected with the fact that, just before I went upstairs to her room, I put myself into a yogic trance state in order to attain telepathic and televisional rapport with her. I entered her chamber, filled with visitors; she was lying in a white robe on the bed. With Mr. Wright close behind me, I halted just inside the threshold, awestruck at a strange and most frightful spectacle.

Blood flowed thinly and continuously in an inch-wide stream from Therese's lower eyelids. Her gaze was focused upward on the spiritual eye within the central forehead. The cloth wrapped around her head was drenched in blood from the stigmata wounds of the Crown of Thorns. The white garment was redly splotched over her heart from the wound in her side at the spot where Christ's body, long ages ago, had suffered the final indignity of the soldier's spear thrust.

Therese's hands were extended in a gesture maternal, pleading; her face wore an expression both tortured and divine. She appeared thinner and was subtly changed in many inner and outer ways. Murmuring words in a foreign tongue, she spoke with slightly quivering lips to persons who were visible to her superconscious sight.

As I was in attunement with her, I began to see the scenes of her vision. She was watching Jesus as he carried the timbers of the

Cross amid the jeering multitude.* Suddenly she lifted her head in consternation: the Lord had fallen under the cruel weight. The vision disappeared. In the exhaustion of fervid pity, Therese sank heavily against her pillow.

At this moment I heard a loud thud behind me. Turning my head for a second, I saw two men carrying out a prostrate body. But because I was coming out of the deep superconscious state, I did not immediately recognize the fallen person. Again I fixed my eyes on Therese's face, deathly pale under the rivulets of blood, but now calm, radiating purity and holiness. I glanced behind me later and saw Mr. Wright standing with his hand against his cheek, from which blood was trickling.

"Dick," I inquired anxiously, "were you the one who fell?"

"Yes, I fainted at the terrifying spectacle."

"Well," I said consolingly, "you are brave to return and look upon the sight again."

Remembering the patiently waiting line of pilgrims, Mr. Wright and I silently bade farewell to Therese and left her sacred presence.†

The following day our little group motored south, thankful that we were not dependent on trains but could stop the Ford wherever we chose throughout the countryside. We enjoyed every minute of a tour through Germany, Holland, France, and the Swiss Alps. In Italy we made a special trip to Assisi to honor the apostle of humility, St. Francis. The European tour ended in Greece, where we viewed the Athenian temples, and saw the prison in which the gentle Socrates‡

---

* During the hours preceding my arrival, Therese had already passed through many visions of the closing days in Christ's life. Her entrancement usually starts with scenes of the events that followed the Last Supper and ends with Jesus' death on the Cross; or, occasionally, with his entombment.

† An INS news dispatch from Germany, dated March 26, 1948, reported: "A German peasant woman lay on her cot this Good Friday; her head, hands, and shoulders blood-marked where Christ's body had bled from the nails of the Cross and the Crown of Thorns. Thousands of awe-filled Germans and Americans filed silently past the cottage bed of Therese Neumann."

The great stigmatist died in Konnersreuth on September 18, 1962. *(Publisher's Note)*

‡ A passage in Eusebius relates an interesting encounter between Socrates and a Hindu sage. The passage runs: "Aristoxenus, the musician, tells the following story about the Indians. One of these men met Socrates at Athens, and asked him what was the scope of his philosophy. 'An inquiry into human phenomena,' replied Socrates. At this the Indian burst out laughing. 'How can a man inquire into human phenomena,' he said, 'when he is ignorant of divine ones?'"

The Greek ideal, echoed in Western philosophies, is: "Man, know thyself." A Hindu would say: "Man, know thy Self." The dictum of Descartes: "I think, therefore I am," is not philosophically valid. The reasoning faculties cannot shed light on man's had drunk his death potion. One is filled with admiration for the artistry with which the ancient Greeks everywhere wrought their very fancies in alabaster.

We took ship over the sunny Mediterranean, disembarking at Palestine. Wandering day after day over the Holy Land, I was more than ever convinced of the value of pilgrimage. To the sensitive heart, the spirit of Christ is all-pervasive in Palestine. I walked reverently by his side at Bethlehem, Gethsemane, Calvary, the holy Mount of Olives, and by the River Jordan and the Sea of Galilee.

Our little party visited the Birth Manger, Joseph's carpenter shop, the tomb of Lazarus, the house of Martha and Mary, the hall of the Last Supper. Antiquity unfolded; scene by scene, I saw the divine drama that Christ once played for the ages.

On to Egypt, with its modern Cairo and ancient pyramids. Then a boat down the long Red Sea, over the vast Arabian Sea; lo, India!

---

ultimate Being. The human mind, like the phenomenal world that it cognizes, is in perpetual flux and can yield no finalities. Intellectual satisfaction is not the highest goal. The seeker of God is the real lover of *vidya*, unchangeable truth; all else is *avidya*, relative knowledge.

CHAPTER 40

I Return to India

Gratefully I was inhaling the blessed air of India. Our boat *Rajputana* docked on August 22, 1935, in the huge harbor of Bombay. Even this, my first day off the ship, was a foretaste of the ceaselessly busy year ahead. Friends had gathered at the dock to welcome us with flower garlands; soon, at our suite in the Taj Mahal Hotel, we received several groups of reporters and photographers.

Bombay was a city new to me; I found it energetically modern, with many innovations from the West. Palms line the spacious boulevards; magnificent state structures vie for interest with ancient temples. Very little time was given to sight-seeing, however; I was impatient, eager to see my beloved guru and other dear ones. Consigning the Ford to a baggage car, our party was soon speeding eastward by train toward Calcutta. *

Our arrival at Howrah Station found such an immense crowd assembled to greet us that for a while we were unable to disembark from the train. The young Maharaja of Kasimbazar and my brother Bishnu headed the reception committee; I was unprepared for the warmth and magnitude of our welcome.

Preceded by a line of automobiles and motorcycles, and amidst the joyous sounds of drums and conchs, Miss Bletsch, Mr. Wright, and I, flower-garlanded from head to foot, drove slowly to my father's home.

My aged parent embraced me as one returning from the dead; long we gazed on each other, speechless with joy. Brothers and sisters, uncles, aunts, and cousins, students and friends of years long past were grouped around me, not a dry eye among us. Passed now into the archives of memory, the scene of loving reunion vividly endures, unforgettable in my heart. As for my meeting with Sri Yukteswar, words fail me; let the following description from my secretary suffice:

---

* We broke our journey in Central Provinces, halfway across the continent, to see Mahatma Gandhi in Wardha. Those days are described in chapter 44.

"Today, filled with the highest anticipations, I drove Yoganandaji from Calcutta to Serampore," Mr. Wright recorded in his travel diary.

"We passed by quaint shops—one of them the favorite eating place of Yoganandaji during his college days—and finally entered a narrow, walled lane. A sudden left turn, and there before us stood the two-story brick ashram of the master, its grilled balcony jutting from the upper floor. The pervasive impression was that of peaceful solitude.

"In grave humility I walked behind Yoganandaji into the courtyard within the hermitage walls. Hearts beating fast, we proceeded up some old cement steps; trod, no doubt, by countless truth seekers. Our tension grew keener and keener as on we strode. Before us, near the head of the stairs, quietly appeared the Great One, Swami Sri Yukteswarji, standing in the noble pose of a sage.

"My heart heaved and swelled at the blessing of being in his sublime presence. Tears blurred my eager sight when Yoganandaji dropped to his knees, and with bowed head offered his soul's gratitude and greeting; touching with his hand the guru's feet, and then, in humble obeisance, his own forehead. He rose then and was embraced on both sides on the bosom by Sri Yukteswarji.

"No words passed in the beginning, but intense feeling was expressed in the mute phrases of the soul. How their eyes sparkled with the warmth of reunion! A tender vibration surged through the quiet patio, and the sun suddenly eluded the clouds to add a blaze of glory.

"On bended knee before the master I gave my own unexpressed love and thanks; touching his feet, calloused by time and service, and receiving his blessing. I stood then and gazed into his beautiful eyes—deep with introspection yet radiant with joy.

"We entered his sitting room, whose whole side opens to the balcony first seen from the street. The master sat on a covered mattress placed on the cement floor, bracing himself against a worn davenport. Yoganandaji and I sat near the guru's feet, with orange-colored pillows to lean against and to ease our positions on the straw mat.

"I tried without much success to understand the gist of the talk in Bengali between the two Swamijis (for they do not use English, I discovered, when they are together; although Swamiji Maharaj, as the great guru is called by others, can and often does speak it). But I easily perceived the saintliness of the Great One through his heart-warming smile and twinkling eyes. Quickly discernible in his merry or serious conversation is a positiveness in statement: the mark of a sage—one who knows he knows, because he knows God. The master's great wisdom, strength of purpose, and determination are apparent in every way.

"He was simply clad; his *dhoti* and shirt, once dyed an ocher color, are now a faded orange. Studying him reverently from time to time, I noted that he is of large, athletic stature; his body hardened by the trials and sacrifices of a renunciant's life. His poise is majestic. He moves with dignified tread and erect posture. A jovial and rollicking laugh comes from the depths of his chest, causing his whole body to shake and quiver.

"His austere face strikingly conveys an impression of divine power. His hair, parted in the middle, is white around the forehead, streaked elsewhere with silvery gold and silvery black, and ends in ringlets at his shoulders. His beard and moustache are scant or thinned out, and seem to enhance his features. His forehead slopes, as though seeking the heavens. His dark eyes are haloed by an ethereal blue ring. He has a rather large and homely nose, with which he amuses himself in idle moments; flipping and wiggling it with his fingers, like a child. In repose his mouth is stern, yet subtly touched with tenderness.

"Glancing here and there, I observed that the somewhat dilapidated room suggests the owner's nonattachment to material comforts. The weather-stained white walls of the long chamber are streaked with fading blue plaster. At one end of the room hangs the unique picture of Lahiri Mahasaya, devotionally adorned with a simple garland. There is also an old photograph showing Yoganandaji at the time of his arrival in Boston, standing with other delegates to the Congress of Religions.

"I noted a quaint concurrence of old and new. A huge cut-glass candlelight chandelier is covered with cobwebs through long disuse; and on the wall hangs a bright up-to-date calendar. The room emanates a fragrance of peace and happiness.

"Beyond the balcony, coconut palms tower over the hermitage as though in silent protection.

"The master needs merely to clap his hands; before finishing, he is attended by some small disciple. One of them, a thin lad named Prafulla,* has long black hair, sparkling black eyes, and a

---

* Prafulla was the lad who was present with Master when a cobra approached (see page 98).

heavenly smile: his eyes twinkle as the corners of his mouth rise, like stars and a crescent moon suddenly appearing at twilight.

"Swami Sri Yukteswarji's joy is obviously intense at the return of his 'product' (and he seems to be somewhat inquisitive about me, the 'product's product'). However, the predominance of wisdom in the Great One's nature hinders his outward expression of feeling.

"Yoganandaji presented him with some gifts, as is the custom when a disciple returns to his guru. We sat down later to a simple but well-cooked meal of vegetables and rice. Sri Yukteswarji was pleased at my observance of a number of Indian customs, 'finger-eating,' for example.

"After several hours of flying Bengali phrases and the exchange of warm smiles and joyful glances, we paid obeisance at his feet, bade adieu with a *pranam*,* and departed for Calcutta with an ever-lasting memory of a sacred meeting. Although I write chiefly of my external impressions of the master, yet I was always conscious of his spiritual glory. I felt his power, and shall ever retain that feeling as my divine blessing."

From America, Europe, and Palestine I had brought many presents for Sri Yukteswar. He received them smilingly, but without remark. For my own use, I had bought in Germany a combination umbrella-cane. In India I decided to give the cane to Master.

"This gift I appreciate indeed!" My guru's eyes were turned on me with affectionate understanding as he made the unwonted comment. From all the presents, it was the cane that he singled out to display to visitors.

"Master, please permit me to get a new carpet for the sitting room." I had noticed that Sri Yukteswar's tiger skin was placed over a torn rug.

"Do so if it pleases you." My guru's voice was not enthusiastic. "Behold, my tiger mat is nice and clean; I am monarch in my own little kingdom. Beyond it is the vast world, interested only in externals."

As he uttered these words I felt the years roll back; once again I am a young disciple, purified daily in fires of chastisement!

As soon as I could tear myself away from Serampore and Calcutta, I set out, with Mr. Wright, for Ranchi. What a welcome there, a touching ovation! Tears stood in my eyes as I embraced the selfless

---

* Lit., "complete salutation," from Sanskrit root *nam*, to salute or bow down; and the prefix *pra*, completely. A *pranam* salutation is made chiefly before monks and other respected persons.

teachers who had kept the banner of the school flying during my fifteen years' absence. The bright faces and happy smiles of the residential and day students were ample testimony to the worth of their careful school and yoga training.

Yet, alas, the Ranchi institution was in dire financial difficulties. Sir Manindra Chandra Nundy, the old Maharaja whose Kasimbazar Palace had been converted into the central school building, and who had made many princely donations, was now dead. Many free, benevolent features of the school were seriously endangered for lack of sufficient public support.

I had not spent years in America without learning some of its practical wisdom, its undaunted spirit before obstacles. For one week I remained in Ranchi, wrestling with critical problems. Then came interviews in Calcutta with prominent leaders and educators, a long talk with the young Maharaja of Kasimbazar, a financial appeal to my father, and lo! the shaky foundations of the Ranchi school began to be righted. Many donations arrived in the nick of time from my American students.

Within a few months after my arrival in India, I had the joy of seeing the Ranchi school legally incorporated. My lifelong dream of a permanently endowed yoga educational center was fulfilled. That aspiration had guided me in the humble beginnings in 1917 with a group of seven boys.

The school, Yogoda Satsanga Brahmacharya Vidyalaya, conducts outdoor classes in grammar- and high-school subjects. The resident students and day scholars also receive vocational training of some kind.

The boys themselves regulate many of their activities through autonomous committees. Very early in my career as an educator I discovered that boys who may impishly delight in outwitting a teacher will cheerfully accept disciplinary rules that are set by their fellow students. Never a model pupil myself, I had a ready sympathy for all boyish pranks and problems.

Sports and games are encouraged; the fields resound with hockey and football* practice. Ranchi students often win the cup at competitive events. The boys are taught the *Yogoda* method of muscle recharging through will power: mental direction of life energy to any part of the body. They also learn *asanas* (postures) and sword and *lathi* (stick) play. Trained in first aid, the Ranchi students have given praiseworthy service to their province in tragic times of flood or

* English-style football is called soccer in America.

famine. The boys work in the garden and grow their own vegetables.

Instruction in Hindi in primary-school subjects is provided for *Kols, Santals,* and *Mundas,* aboriginal tribes of the province. Classes for girls only are conducted in nearby villages.

The unique feature at Ranchi is the initiation into *Kriya Yoga.* The boys daily practice their spiritual exercises, engage in Gita chanting, and are taught by precept and example the virtues of simplicity, self-sacrifice, honor, and truth. Evil is pointed out to them as being that which produces misery; good as those actions which result in true happiness. Evil may be compared to poisoned honey, tempting but laden with death.

Overcoming restlessness of body and mind by concentration techniques has achieved astonishing results: it is no novelty at Ranchi to see an appealing little figure, aged nine or ten years, sitting for an hour or more in unbroken poise, the unwinking gaze directed to the spiritual eye.

In the orchard stands a Shiva temple, with a statue of the blessed master, Lahiri Mahasaya. Daily prayers and scripture classes are held in the garden under the mango bowers.

Yogoda Satsanga Sevashram ("Home of Service") Hospital on the Ranchi estate offers free surgical and medical aid to many thousands of India's poor.

Ranchi lies 2000 feet above sea level; the climate is mild and equable. The twenty-five-acre site, by a large bathing pond, includes one of the finest private orchards in India: five hundred fruit trees—mango, date, guava, litchi, jackfruit.

The Ranchi library contains numerous magazines and a thousand volumes in English and Bengali, donations from the West and the East. There is a collection of the scriptures of the world. A well-classified museum displays precious stones and archaeological, geological, and anthropological exhibits: trophies, to a great extent, of my wanderings over the Lord's varied earth.*

Branch high schools, with the residential and yoga features of Ranchi, have been opened and are now flourishing. These are Yogoda Satsanga Vidyapith (School) for boys at Lakhanpur in West Bengal, and the high school and hermitage at Ejmalichak in Midnapore, Bengal.†

---

* A museum in the West, with similar exhibits collected by Paramahansa Yogananda, is located at Self-Realization Fellowship Lake Shrine in Pacific Palisades, California. *(Publisher's Note)*

† From this original nucleus many YSS educational institutions for both boys and

A stately Yogoda Math (ashram) in Dakshineswar, fronting the Ganges, was dedicated in 1939. Only a few miles north of Calcutta, the hermitage affords a haven of peace for city dwellers.

The Dakshineswar Math is the headquarters in India of Yogoda Satsanga Society and its schools, centers, and hermitages in various parts of India. Yogoda Satsanga Society of India is legally affiliated with the international headquarters: Self-Realization Fellowship in Los Angeles, California, U.S.A. Yogoda Satsanga* activities include publication of the quarterly *Yogoda Magazine* and fortnightly mailings of lessons to students in all parts of India. These lessons give detailed instruction in the Self-Realization Fellowship Energization, Concentration, and Meditation Techniques. Their faithful practice constitutes the essential groundwork for the higher instruction in *Kriya Yoga*, which is given in subsequent lessons to qualified students.

Yogoda educational, religious, and humanitarian activities require the service and devotion of many teachers and workers. I do not list their names here, because they are so numerous; but in my heart each one has a lustrous niche.

Mr. Wright formed many friendships with Ranchi boys; clad in a simple *dhoti*, he lived for a while among them. In Bombay, Ranchi, Calcutta, Serampore, everywhere he went, my secretary, who has a gift of vivid description, would write in a travel diary his adventures. One evening I asked him a question.

"Dick, what is your impression of India?"

"Peace," he said thoughtfully. "The racial aura is peace."

---

girls are now thriving in several locales in India. Their curricula range from primary to college level.

* "Yogoda" is derived from *yoga*, union, harmony, equilibrium; and *da*, that which imparts. "Satsanga" is composed of *sat*, truth, and *sanga*, fellowship.

"Yogoda" is a word coined by Paramahansa Yogananda in 1916, when he discovered the principles of recharging the human body with energy from the cosmic source. (See pp. 217–18.)

Sri Yukteswar called his hermitage organization Satsanga (Fellowship with Truth); his disciple Paramahansaji naturally wished to retain that name.

Yogoda Satsanga Society of India is a nonprofit institution, designed to exist perpetually. Under that name Yoganandaji incorporated his work and foundations in India, which are now being ably administered by a Board of Directors at Yogoda Math in Dakshineswar, W. Bengal. Many YSS meditation centers are now flourishing in various parts of India.

In the West, Yoganandaji rendered the name of his society in English, incorporating his work there as Self-Realization Fellowship. Sri Daya Mata has been the president since 1955 of both Yogoda Satsanga Society of India and Self-Realization Fellowship. *(Publisher's Note)*

CHAPTER 41

An Idyl in South India

"You are the first Westerner, Dick, ever to enter that shrine. Many others have tried in vain."

At my words Mr. Wright looked startled, then pleased. We had just left the beautiful Chamundi Temple in the hills overlooking Mysore in southern India. There we had bowed before the gold and silver altars of the Goddess Chamundi, patron deity of the Mysore ruling family.

"As a souvenir of the unique honor," Mr. Wright said, carefully wrapping a few rose petals, "I will always preserve these petals, blessed by the priest with rose water."

My companion and I* were spending the month of November 1935, as guests of the State of Mysore. The Maharaja's† heir, H.H. the Yuvaraja, Sri Kantheerava Narasimharaja Wadiyar, had invited my secretary and me to visit his enlightened and progressive realm.

During the past fortnight I had addressed thousands of citizens and students in Mysore City at the Town Hall, the Maharaja's College, the University Medical School; and three mass meetings in Bangalore at the National High School, the Intermediate College, and Chetty Town Hall in which three thousand persons had assembled.

Whether the eager listeners had been able to credit the glowing picture I drew of America, I know not; but the applause had always been loudest when I spoke of the mutual benefits to be derived from exchange of the best features of East and West.

Mr. Wright and I were now relaxing in the tropical peace. His travel diary contains the following account of his impressions of Mysore:

"Many rapturous moments have been spent in gazing, almost absentmindedly, at the ever changing canvas of God stretched across the firmament, for His touch alone is able to produce colors that vibrate with the freshness of life. That youth of colors is lost

* Miss Bletsch had remained behind with my relatives in Calcutta.
† Maharaja Sri Krishna Rajendra Wadiyar IV.

when man tries to imitate with mere pigments, for the Lord resorts to a more simple and effective medium—neither oils nor pigments but mere rays of light. He tosses a splash of light here, and it reflects red; He waves the brush again and the color blends gradually into orange and gold; then with a piercing thrust He stabs the clouds with a streak of purple that leaves a ringlet or fringe of red oozing out of the wound; and so, on and on He plays, night and morning alike, ever changing, ever new, ever fresh; no duplicates, no patterns or colors just the same. The beauty of the change in India from day to night, and from night to day, is beyond compare elsewhere; often the sky looks as if God had taken all the colors in His kit and had given them one mighty kaleidoscopic toss into the heavens.

"I must relate the splendor of a twilight visit to the huge Krishnaraja Sagar Dam,* twelve miles outside Mysore City. Yoganandaji and I boarded a small bus, and, with a small boy as official cranker or battery substitute, started off over a smooth dirt road just as the sun was setting, squashing on the horizon like an overripe tomato.

"Our journey led past the ever present square rice fields, through a grove of comforting banyan trees, in between towering coconut palms; nearly everywhere vegetation was as thick as in a jungle. Approaching the crest of a hill, we beheld an immense artificial lake, reflecting the stars and a fringe of palms and other trees, and surrounded by lovely terraced gardens and rows of electric lights.

"Below the brink of the dam we saw a dazzling spectacle: colored beams playing on geyserlike fountains that resembled outpourings of brilliant inks—gorgeous blue, red, green, and yellow waterfalls; and majestic stone elephants spouting water. The dam (whose lighted fountains reminded me of those at the 1933 World's Fair in Chicago) is modernly outstanding in this ancient land of paddy fields and simple people. The Indians have given us such a loving welcome that I fear it will take more than my strength to bring Yoganandaji back to America.

"Another rare privilege—my first elephant ride. Yesterday the Yuvaraja invited us to his summer palace to enjoy a ride on one of his elephants, an enormous beast. I mounted a ladder provided to climb aloft to the *howdah* or saddle, which is silk-cushioned and boxlike; and then for a rolling, tossing, heaving, and swaying down into a gully—too much thrilled to worry or exclaim, but hanging on for dear life!"

* An irrigation dam built in 1930 to serve the area near Mysore City, which is renowned for its silks, soaps, and sandalwood oil.

Southern India, rich with historical and archaeological remains, is a land of definite and yet indefinable charm. To the north of Mysore is Hyderabad, a picturesque plateau cut by the mighty Godavari River. Broad fertile plains, the lovely Nilgiris or "Blue Mountains," other areas with barren hills of limestone or granite. Hyderabad history is a long, colorful story, starting three thousand years ago under the Andhra kings and continuing under Hindu dynasties until A.D. 1294, when the region passed to a line of Moslem rulers.

The most breathtaking display of architecture, sculpture, and painting in all India is found at Hyderabad in the ancient rock-sculptured caves of Ellora and Ajanta. The Kailasa at Ellora, a huge monolithic temple, possesses carved figures of gods, men, and beasts in the stupendous proportions of a Michelangelo. Ajanta is the site of twenty-five monasteries and five cathedrals, all rock excavations supported by tremendous frescoed pillars on which artists and sculptors have immortalized their genius.

Hyderabad City is graced by Osmania University and by the imposing Mecca Masjid Mosque in which ten thousand Moslems assemble for prayer.

Mysore State, three thousand feet above sea level, abounds in dense tropical forests: the home of wild elephants, bison, bears, panthers, and tigers. The two chief cities, Bangalore and Mysore, are clean and attractive, with many beautiful parks and public gardens.

Hindu architecture and sculpture achieved their highest perfection in Mysore under the patronage of Hindu kings from the eleventh to the fifteenth century. The temple at Belur, an eleventh-century masterpiece completed during the reign of King Vishnuvardhana, is unsurpassed in the world for delicacy of detail and exuberant imagery.

The rock edicts found in northern Mysore date from the third century B.C. They illuminate the memory of King Asoka,* whose vast empire included India, Afghanistan, and Baluchistan. Inscribed in various dialects, Asoka's "sermons in stone" bear witness to the widespread literacy of his day. Rock Edict XIII denounces wars: "Consider nothing as true conquest save that of religion." Rock

---

* Emperor Asoka erected 84,000 religious *stupas* (shrines) in various parts of India. Fourteen rock edicts and ten stone pillars survive. Each pillar is a triumph of engineering, architecture, and sculpture. He arranged for the construction of many reservoirs, dams, and irrigation sluices; of highways and tree-shaded roads dotted with rest houses for travelers; of botanical gardens for medicinal purposes; and of hospitals for man and beast.

Edict X declares that a king's true glory depends on the moral progress he aids his people in attaining. Rock Edict XI defines "the true gift" to be, not goods, but Good—the spreading of truth. On Rock Edict VI the beloved emperor invites his subjects to confer with him on public business "at any hour of the day or night," adding that by faithful discharge of his kingly duties he was thus "obtaining his own release from the debt he owed his fellowmen."

Asoka was a grandson of the formidable Chandragupta Maurya, who destroyed the garrisons left in India by Alexander the Great and who in 305 B.C. defeated the invading Macedonian army of Seleucus. Chandragupta then received at his court in Pataliputra* the Greek ambassador Megasthenes, who has left us descriptions of the happy and enterprising India of his day.

In 298 B.C. the victorious Chandragupta handed over the reins of India's government to his son. Traveling to South India, Chandragupta spent the last twelve years of his life as a penniless ascetic, seeking Self-realization in a rocky cave in Sravanabelagola, now a Mysore shrine. The same region boasts the world's largest monolithic statue, carved out of an immense boulder by the Jains in A.D. 983 to honor the sage Gomateswara.

Interesting stories have been minutely recorded by Greek historians and others who accompanied or followed after Alexander in his expedition to India. The narratives of Arrian, Diodoros, Plutarch, and Strabo the geographer have been translated by Dr. J. W. McCrindle† to throw a shaft of light on ancient India. The most admirable feature of Alexander's unsuccessful invasion was the deep interest he displayed in Hindu philosophy and in the yogis and holy men whom he encountered from time to time and whose society he eagerly sought. Shortly after the Western warrior arrived in Taxila in northern India, he sent Onesikritos (a disciple of the Hellenic school of Diogenes) to fetch a great *sannyasi* of Taxila, Dandamis.

"Hail to thee, O teacher of *Brahmins!*" Onesikritos said after seeking out Dandamis in his forest retreat. "The son of the mighty

---

* The city of Pataliputra (modern Patna) has a fascinating history. Lord Buddha visited the site in the sixth century B.C. when it was only an unimportant fort. He made this prophecy: "As far as Aryan people resort, as far as merchants travel, Pataliputra will become for them the chief city, a center for the interchange of all kinds of wares" (*Mahaparinirbana Sutra*). Two centuries later Pataliputra became the capital city of the huge empire of Chandragupta Maurya. His grandson Asoka brought the metropolis to an even greater prosperity and splendor. (See p. xxv.)

† Six volumes on *Ancient India* (Calcutta: Chuckervertty, Chatterjee & Co., 15 College Square; 1879, reissued 1927).

God Zeus, being Alexander who is the Sovereign Lord of all men, asks you to go to him. If you comply, he will reward you with great gifts; if you refuse, he will cut off your head!"

The yogi received calmly this fairly compulsive invitation, and "did not so much as lift up his head from his couch of leaves."

"I also am a son of Zeus, if Alexander be such," he commented. "I want nothing that is Alexander's, for I am content with what I have, while I see that he wanders with his men over sea and land for no advantage, and is never coming to an end of his wanderings.

"Go and tell Alexander that God the Supreme King is never the Author of insolent wrong, but is the Creator of light, of peace, of life, of water, of the body of man and of souls; He receives all men when death sets them free, being then in no way subject to evil disease. He alone is the God of my homage, who abhors slaughter and instigates no wars.

"Alexander is no god, since he must taste of death," continued the sage in quiet scorn. "How can such as he be the world's master, when he has not yet seated himself on a throne of inner universal dominion? Neither as yet has he entered living into Hades, nor does he even know the course of the sun over the vast regions of this earth. Most nations have not so much as heard his name!"

After this chastisement—surely the most caustic ever sent to assault the ears of the "Lord of the World"—the sage added ironically, "If Alexander's present dominions be not capacious enough for his desires, let him cross the Ganges River; there he will find a country able to sustain all his men.*

"The gifts Alexander promises are useless to me," Dandamis went on. "The things I prize and find of real worth are trees, which are my shelter; blooming plants, which provide my daily food; and water, which assuages my thirst. Possessions amassed with anxious thought are wont to prove ruinous to those who gather them, causing only the sorrow and vexation that afflict all unenlightened men.

"As for me, I lie upon forest leaves, and, having nothing to guard, close my eyes in tranquil slumber; whereas, had I anything of worldly value, that burden would banish sleep. The earth supplies me with everything I need, even as a mother provides her child with milk. I go wherever I please, unencumbered by material cares.

---

* Neither Alexander nor any of his generals ever crossed the Ganges. Finding determined resistance in the northwest, the Macedonian army mutinied by refusing to penetrate farther; Alexander was forced to leave India. He sought further conquests in Persia.

"Should Alexander cut off my head, he cannot also destroy my soul. My head, then silent, and my body, like a torn garment, will remain on the earth, from which their elements were taken. I then, becoming Spirit, shall ascend to God. He enclosed us all in flesh and put us on earth to prove whether, when here below, we shall live obedient to His ordinances; and He will require of us, when we depart hence, an account of our lives. He is the Judge of all wrongdoing; the groans of the oppressed ordain the punishment of the oppressor.

"Let Alexander terrify with threats men who wish for wealth and who dread death. Against the *Brahmins* his weapons are powerless; we neither love gold nor fear death. Go then and tell Alexander this: Dandamis has no need of aught that is yours, and therefore will not go to you; and, if you want anything from Dandamis, come you to him."

Onesikritos duly conveyed the message; Alexander listened with close attention, and "felt a stronger desire than ever to see Dandamis; who, though old and naked, was the only antagonist in whom he, the conqueror of many nations, had met more than his match."

Alexander invited to Taxila a number of *Brahmin* ascetics noted for their skill in answering philosophical questions with pithy wisdom. An account of the verbal skirmish is given by Plutarch; Alexander himself framed all the questions.

"Which be the more numerous, the living or the dead?"

"The living, for the dead are not."

"Which breeds the larger animals, the sea or the land?"

"The land, for the sea is only a part of land."

"Which is the cleverest of beasts?"

"That one with which man is not yet acquainted." (Man fears the unknown.)

"Which existed first, the day or the night?"

"The day was first by one day." This reply caused Alexander to betray surprise; the *Brahmin* added: "Impossible questions require impossible answers."

"How best may a man make himself beloved?"

"A man will be beloved if, possessed with great power, he still does not make himself feared."

"How may a man become a god?"*

"By doing that which it is impossible for a man to do."

* From this question we may surmise that the "Son of Zeus" had an occasional doubt that he had already attained perfection.

"Which is stronger, life or death?"

"Life, because it bears so many evils."

Alexander succeeded in taking out of India, as his teacher, a true yogi. This man was Kalyana (Swami Sphines), called "Kalanos" by the Greeks. The sage accompanied Alexander to Persia. On a stated day, at Susa in Persia, Kalanos gave up his aged body by entering a funeral pyre in view of the whole Macedonian army. The historians record the astonishment of the soldiers as they observed that the yogi had no fear of pain or death; he never once moved from his position as he was consumed in the flames. Before leaving for his cremation, Kalanos had embraced many of his close companions but had refrained from bidding farewell to Alexander, to whom the Hindu sage had merely remarked:

"I shall see you later in Babylon."

Alexander left Persia and, a year later, died in Babylon. The prophecy had been the Indian guru's way of saying that he would be present with Alexander in life and death.

The Greek historians have left us many vivid and inspiring pictures of Indian society. Hindu law, Arrian tells us, protects the people and "ordains that no one among them shall, under any circumstances, be a slave; but that, enjoying freedom themselves, they shall respect the equal right to it that all men possess."*

"The Indians," states another text, "neither put out money at usury, nor know how to borrow. It is contrary to established practice for the Indians to do or to suffer a wrong; therefore they neither make contracts nor require securities." Healing, we are told, was by simple and natural means. "Cures are effected rather by regulating diet than by the use of medicines. The remedies most esteemed are ointments and plasters. All others are considered to be in great measure pernicious." Engagement in war was restricted to the *Kshatriyas* or warrior caste. "Nor would an enemy, coming upon a husbandman at work on his land, do him any harm; for men of this class are regarded as public benefactors and are protected from all injury. The land, thus remaining unravaged and producing

---

* All Greek observers comment on the lack of slavery in India, a feature at complete variance with the structure of Hellenic society.

Creative India by Prof. Benoy Kumar Sarkar gives a comprehensive picture of India's ancient and modern achievements and distinctive values in economics, political science, literature, art, and social philosophy. (Lahore: Motilal Banarsi Dass, Publishers, 1937, 714 pp.)

Another recommended volume is *Indian Culture Through the Ages*, by S. V. Venkatesvara (New York: Longmans, Green & Co.).

heavy crops, supplies the inhabitants with the requisites to make life enjoyable."

The ubiquitous religious shrines of Mysore are a constant reminder of the many great saints of South India. One of these masters, Thayumanavar, has left us the following challenging poem:

> You may control a mad elephant;
> You may shut the mouth of the bear and the tiger;
> Ride the lion and play with the cobra;
> By alchemy you may earn your livelihood;
> You may wander through the universe incognito;
> Make vassals of the gods; be ever youthful;
> You may walk on water and live in fire:
> But control of the mind is better and more difficult.

In the beautiful and fertile State of Travancore in the extreme south of India, where traffic is conveyed over rivers and canals, the Maharaja assumes every year a hereditary obligation to expiate the sin incurred by wars and the annexation in the distant past of several petty states to Travancore. For fifty-six days annually the Maharaja visits the temple thrice daily to hear Vedic hymns and recitations; the expiation ceremony ends with the *lakshadipam* or illumination of the temple by a hundred thousand lights.

Madras Presidency on the southeast coast of India contains the flat, spacious, sea-girt city of Madras, and Conjeeveram, the Golden City, capital site of the Pallava Dynasty whose kings ruled during the early centuries of the Christian era. In modern Madras Presidency the nonviolent ideals of Mahatma Gandhi have made great headway; the white distinguishing "Gandhi caps" are seen everywhere. In the south generally the Mahatma has effected many important temple reforms for "untouchables" as well as caste-system reforms.

The origin of the caste system, formulated by the great legislator Manu, was admirable. He saw clearly that men are distinguished by natural evolution into four great classes: those capable of offering service to society through their bodily labor (*Sudras*); those who serve through mentality, skill, agriculture, trade, commerce, business life in general (*Vaisyas*); those whose talents are administrative, executive, and protective—rulers and warriors (*Kshatriyas*); those of contemplative nature, spiritually inspired and inspiring (*Brahmins*). "Neither birth nor sacraments nor study nor ancestry can decide whether a person is twice-born (i.e., a *Brahmin*)," the *Mahabharata* declares, "character and conduct only can decide."*

---

* "Inclusion in one of these four castes originally depended not on a man's birth but

Manu instructed society to show respect to its members insofar as they possessed wisdom, virtue, age, kinship or, lastly, wealth. Riches in Vedic India were always despised if they were hoarded or unavailable for charitable purposes. Ungenerous men of great wealth were assigned a low rank in society.

Serious evils arose when the caste system became hardened through the centuries into a hereditary halter. India, self-governing since 1947, is making slow but sure progress in restoring the ancient values of caste, based solely on natural qualification and not on birth. Every nation on earth has its own distinctive misery-producing karma to deal with and honorably remove. India, with her versatile and invulnerable spirit, is proving herself equal to the task of caste reformation.

So entrancing is southern India that Mr. Wright and I yearned to prolong our idyl. But time, in its immemorial rudeness, dealt us no courteous extensions. I was scheduled soon to address the concluding session of the Indian Philosophical Congress at Calcutta University. At the end of the visit to Mysore, I enjoyed a talk with Sir C. V. Raman, president of the Indian Academy of Sciences. This brilliant

---

on his natural capacities as demonstrated by the goal in life he elected to achieve," writes Tara Mata in *East-West* for January 1935. "This goal could be (1) *kama*, desire, activity of the life of the senses (*Sudra* stage), (2) *artha*, gain, fulfilling but controlling the desires (*Vaisya* stage), (3) *dharma*, self-discipline, the life of responsibility and right action (*Kshatriya* stage), (4) *moksha*, liberation, the life of spirituality and religious teaching (*Brahmin* stage). These four castes render service to humanity by (1) body, (2) mind, (3) will power, (4) Spirit.

"These four stages have their correspondence in the eternal *gunas* or qualities of nature, *tamas, rajas,* and *sattva:* obstruction, activity, and expansion; or, mass, energy, and intelligence. The four natural castes are marked by the gunas as (1) *tamas* (ignorance), (2) *tamas-rajas* (mixture of ignorance and activity), (3) *rajas-sattva* (mixture of right activity and enlightenment), (4) *sattva* (enlightenment). Thus has nature marked every man with his caste, by the predominance in himself of one, or the mixture of two, of the *gunas.* Of course every human being has all three *gunas* in varying proportions. The guru will be able rightly to determine a man's caste or evolutionary status.

"To a certain extent, all races and nations observe in practice, if not in theory, the features of caste. Where there is great license or so-called liberty, particularly in intermarriage between extremes in the natural castes, the race dwindles away and becomes extinct. The *Purana Samhita* compares the offspring of such unions to barren hybrids, like the mule, which is incapable of propagation of its own species. Artificial species are eventually exterminated. History offers abundant proof of numerous great races which no longer have any living representatives. The caste system of India is credited by her most profound thinkers with being the check or preventive against license that has preserved the purity of the race and brought it safely through millenniums of vicissitudes, though many other ancient races have completely vanished."

A few of the delegates to the International Congress of Religious Liberals, October 1920, Boston, Massachusetts, at which Yoganandaji gave his maiden speech in America. (*Left to right*) Rev. T. R. Williams, Prof. S. Ushigasaki, Rev. Jabez T. Sunderland, Sri Yogananda, and Rev. C. W. Wendte.

With the help of large-hearted students, Sri Yogananda purchased Mt. Washington Estates in 1925. Even before the transaction was completed, he held his first meeting, an Easter sunrise service, on the grounds of the soon-to-be world headquarters of his society.

His Excellency Emilio Portes Gil, president of Mexico, was host to Sri Yogananda when he visited Mexico City, 1929.

Paramahansaji meditating in a boat on Lake Xochimilco, Mexico, 1929

DURING HIS 32 YEARS IN THE WEST, THE GREAT GURU INITIATED MORE THAN 100,000 STUDENTS IN YOGA

Yoganandaji on stage, conducting class in Denver, Colorado, 1924. In hundreds of cities he taught the largest yoga classes in the world. Through his books and his lessons for home study, and the establishment of monastic centers for training teachers, Paramahansa Yogananda ensured the continuance of the worldwide mission given to him by Mahavatar Babaji.

PARAMAHANSA YOGANANDA AT THE WHITE HOUSE

Paramahansa Yogananda and Mr. John Balfour leaving the White House after a call on President Calvin Coolidge, who is looking out of the window.

The Washington Herald, January 25, 1927, reported: "Swami Yogananda was...greeted with evident pleasure by Mr. Coolidge, who told him he had been reading a great deal about him. This is the first time in the history of India that a Swami has been received officially by the President."

Paramahansa Yogananda places flowers at George Washington's crypt, Mt. Vernon, Virginia, February 22, 1927

Yoganandaji in his cabin on a steamer en route to Alaska during transcontinental speaking tour, 1924

LUTHER BURBANK AND PARAMAHANSA YOGANANDA
Santa Rosa, California, 1924

PARAMAHANSA YOGANANDA, PHILHARMONIC AUDITORIUM, LOS ANGELES

The *Los Angeles Times*, January 28, 1925, reported: "The Philharmonic Auditorium presents the extraordinary spectacle of thousands being turned away an hour before the advertised opening of a lecture with the 3,000-seat hall filled to its utmost capacity. Swami Yogananda is the attraction. A Hindu invading the United States to bring God in the midst of a Christian community, preaching the essence of Christian doctrine."

Swami Sri Yukteswar and Paramahansa Yogananda in religious procession, Calcutta, 1935. The two Sanskrit verses on the standard read: (*Above*) "Follow the path of the great ones." (*Below, words of Swami Shankara*) "The company of a divine personage, even for a moment, can save and redeem us."

Last Solstice Festival celebrated by Swami Sri Yukteswar, December 1935. The author is seated next to his great guru (*center*) at the table in the courtyard of the ashram in Serampore. In this hermitage Paramahansa Yogananda received much of his ten years' spiritual training under Sri Yukteswarji.

LUNCH AT MAHATMA GANDHI'S ASHRAM IN WARDHA

Yogananda is reading a note that Gandhi (*right*) has just written (it was a Monday, the Mahatma's day for observing silence). On the following day, August 27, 1935, at Gandhiji's request Sri Yogananda initiated him in *Kriya Yoga*.

LORD SHIVA

Embodiment of the spirit of asceticism, Lord Shiva represents the Destroyer-Renovator aspect of the triune nature of God (Creator, Preserver, Destroyer). Symbolic of his transcendent nature, Shiva is depicted in *samadhi* bliss in the Himalayas. His serpent collar (*naga kundala*) and armlets indicate his mastery over delusion and his creative force. The Divine Mother is that aspect of God which is active in creation: the *shakti*, or power, of the transcendent Lord. She is known by many names, according to the qualities She expresses. Here Her upraised hand signifies universal blessing; the others hold, symbolically, prayer beads (devotion), pages of scripture (learning and wisdom), and a jar of holy water (purification).

THE DIVINE MOTHER

PARAMAHANSA YOGANANDA

Photograph taken on December 13, 1935, at Damodar, India, during a
visit to the site of his first school for boys, founded in nearby Dihika
in 1917. He is meditating in the doorway of a crumbling tower that
had once been a favorite nook for seclusion.

YOGODA SATSANGA BRANCH MATH

The Yogoda Satsanga Society of India Branch Math and Ashram, Ranchi,
was founded by Paramahansa Yogananda when he moved his boys'
school to this site in 1918. Today the Branch Math serves YSS members
and distributes Paramahansaji's *Kriya Yoga* teachings throughout India.
In addition to its spiritual activities, this center maintains several
educational institutions and a charitable dispensary.

Sri Yogananda (*center*) and his secretary, C. Richard Wright (*right, seated*), in Ranchi, July 17, 1936. They are surrounded by teachers and students of Sri Yogananda's School for Aborigine Girls.

Sri Yogananda with teachers and students of Yogoda Satsanga Society school for boys, Ranchi, 1936. The school, founded by Yoganandaji, was moved to this site from Dihika, Bengal, in 1918, under the patronage of the Maharaja of Kasimbazar.

Procession of teachers and students of the Ranchi school, March 1938, in annual commemoration of the school's founding

Students of Yogoda Satsanga Society school for boys, Ranchi, 1970. In keeping with Yoganandaji's ideals in founding the school, many classes are held outdoors, and the boys receive yoga training as well as academic and vocational instruction.

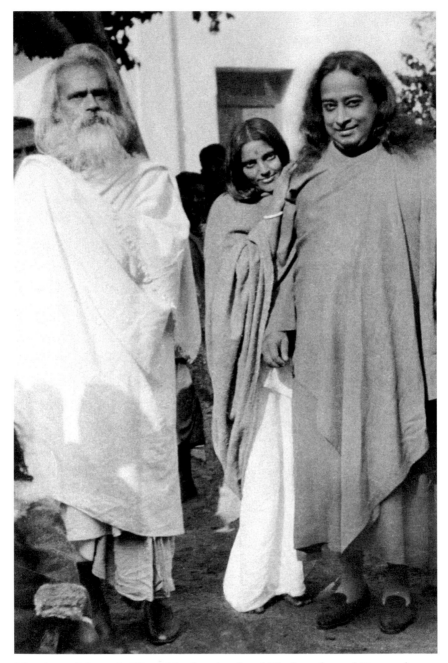

Meeting of Ananda Moyi Ma, her husband Bholanath, and Paramahansa
Yogananda, Calcutta (see page 439)

Ramana Maharshi and Paramahansa Yogananda at Sri Ramana's Arunachala ashram (see page 339)

Sri Yogananda and Swami Dayananda, Mahamandal Hermitage, Banaras, February 7, 1936. In a traditional gesture of respect, Yoganandaji has seated himself at the feet of Dayanandaji, spiritual head of this hermitage. Here, as a boy, Yoganandaji had pursued spiritual discipline before he found his guru, Swami Sri Yukteswar, in 1910.

Swami Keshabananda (*standing, left*), a ninety-year-old disciple of Lahiri Mahasaya; Yoganandaji; and C. Richard Wright, Sri Yoganandaji's secretary, at Keshabananda's ashram, Brindaban, 1936

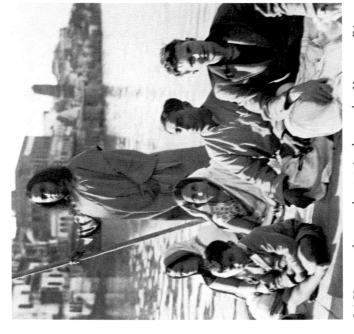

Sri Yogananda on a boat trip down the Yamuna River, 1935, at Mathura, a holy city associated with the birth and childhood of Bhagavan Krishna. (*Seated, center to right*) Daughter of Ananta Lal Ghosh (elder brother of Sri Yogananda); Sananda Lal Ghosh (Yoganandaji's younger brother); and C. Richard Wright.

Sri Yogananda (*center, dark robe*) with some of the *Kriya Yoga* students who attended his class on Yogoda (Self-Realization) teachings at his father's home in Calcutta, 1935. Because of the large attendance, the class met in the adjacent open-air gymnasium of Yoganandaji's younger brother, Bishnu Ghosh, a renowned physical culturist.

18

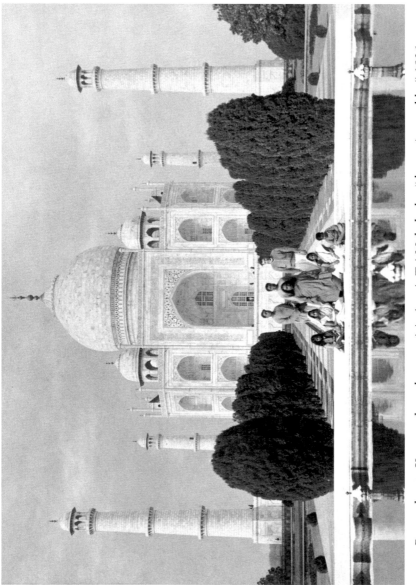

Paramahansa Yogananda and party visit Agra's Taj Mahal, the "dream in marble," 1936

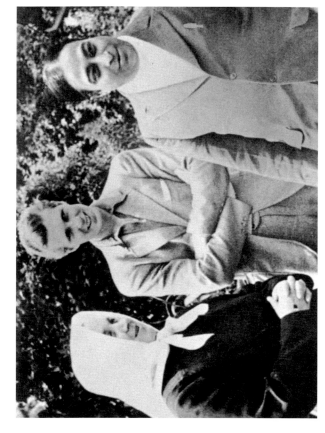

THERESE NEUMANN, C. RICHARD WRIGHT, SRI YOGANANDA
Eichstätt, Bavaria, July 17, 1935

GIRI BALA, NON-EATING SAINT

She employs a certain yogic technique to recharge her body with cosmic energy from the ether, sun, and air. "I have never been sick," the saint said. "I sleep very little, as sleep and waking are the same to me."

Paramahansa Yogananda in the SRF Hermitage, Encinitas, California,
July 1950

Hindu physicist was awarded the Nobel Prize in 1930 for the "Raman Effect," his important discovery in the diffusion of light.

Waving a reluctant farewell to a crowd of Madras students and friends, Mr. Wright and I set out on our travels. On the way we stopped before a little shrine sacred to the memory of Sadasiva Brahman,* in whose eighteenth-century life story miracles cluster thickly. A larger Sadasiva shrine at Nerur, erected by the Raja of Pudukkottai, is a pilgrimage spot that has witnessed many divine healings. The successive rulers of Pudukkottai have treasured as sacred the religious instructions that Sadasiva wrote in 1750 for the guidance of the reigning prince.

Many quaint stories of Sadasiva, a lovable and fully illumined master, are still current among South Indian villagers. Immersed one day in *samadhi* on a bank of the Kaveri River, Sadasiva was seen to be carried away by a sudden flood. Weeks later he was found buried deep beneath a mound of earth near Kodumudi in Coimbatore District. As the villagers' shovels struck his body, the saint rose and walked briskly away.

Sadasiva became a *muni* (nonspeaking saint) after his guru had rebuked him for worsting in dialectical argument an elderly *Vedanta* scholar. "When will you, a youth, learn to hold your tongue?" the guru had remarked.

"With your blessings, even from this moment."

Sadasiva's guru was Swami Sri Paramasivendra Saraswati, author of *Daharavidya Prakasika* and a profound commentary on *Uttara Gita.* Certain worldly men, affronted because the God-intoxicated Sadasiva was often to be seen dancing "without decorum" on the streets, carried their complaints to his learned guru. "Sir," they declared, "Sadasiva is no better than a madman."

But Paramasivendra smiled joyfully. "Oh," he exclaimed, "if only others had such madness!"

Sadasiva's life was marked by many strange and beautiful manifestations of the Intervening Hand. Much seeming injustice there is in this world; but God's devotees can testify to countless instances of His immediate righteousness. One night Sadasiva, in *samadhi,* halted near the granary of a rich householder. Three servants, on the lookout for thieves, raised their sticks to strike the saint. Lo!

---

* His formal title was Swami Sri Sadasivendra Saraswati, under which he wrote his books (commentaries on *Brahma Sutras* and Patanjali's *Yoga Sutras*). He is highly revered by modern-day philosophers of India.

The Shankaracharya of Sringeri Math, His Holiness Sri Sacchidananda Sivabhinava Narasimha Bharati, wrote an inspiring *Ode* to Sadasiva.

their arms were immobilized. Like statues, their arms aloft, the trio stood in unique tableau until the departure of Sadasiva at dawn.

On another occasion the great master was roughly pressed into service by a passing foreman whose laborers were carrying fuel. The silent saint humbly bore his burden to the required destination and there placed his load on top of a huge pile. The whole heap of fuel at once burst into flames.

Sadasiva, like Trailanga Swami, wore no cloth. One morning the nude yogi absentmindedly entered the tent of a Moslem chieftain. Two ladies screamed in alarm; the warrior dealt a savage sword thrust at Sadasiva, whose arm was severed. The master departed unconcernedly. Overcome by awe and remorse, the Moslem picked up the arm from the floor and followed Sadasiva. The yogi quietly inserted his arm into the bleeding stump. When the chieftain humbly asked for some spiritual instruction, Sadasiva wrote with his finger in the sands:

"Do not do what you want, and then you may do what you like."

The Moslem was uplifted to a purified state of mind and understood the paradoxical advice to be a guide to soul freedom through mastery of the ego. So great was the spiritual impact of those few words that the warrior became a worthy disciple; his former haunts knew him no more.

The village children once expressed a desire in Sadasiva's presence to see the Madura religious festival, 150 miles away. The yogi indicated to the little ones that they should touch his body. Lo! instantly the whole group was transported to Madura. The children wandered happily among the thousands of pilgrims. In a few hours the yogi brought his small charges home by his simple mode of transportation. The astonished parents listened to vivid tales about the procession of images in Madura, and noticed that the children were carrying bags of Madura sweets.

An incredulous youth derided the saint and the story. On the occasion of the next religious festival, held in Srirangam, the boy approached Sadasiva.

"Master," he said scornfully, "why don't you take me to the festival in Srirangam, even as you took the other children to Madura?"

Sadasiva complied; the boy immediately found himself among the distant city throng. But alas! where was the saint when the youth wanted to leave? The weary boy reached his home by the prosaic method of foot locomotion.

Before leaving South India, Mr. Wright and I made a pilgrimage to the holy hill of Arunachala near Tiruvannamalai to meet Sri Ramana Maharshi. At his ashram the sage welcomed us affectionately and pointed to a nearby stack of *East-West* magazines. During the hours that we spent with him and his disciples, he was mostly silent, his gentle face radiating divine love and wisdom.

To help suffering humanity regain its forgotten state of Perfection, Sri Ramana teaches that one should constantly ask himself: "Who am I?"—the Great Inquiry indeed. By stern rejection of all other thoughts the devotee soon finds himself going deeper and deeper into the true Self, and the sidetracking bewilderments of other thoughts cease to arise. The illumined rishi of South India has written:

> Dualities and trinities on something do hang,
> Supportless they never appear;
> That support searched for, they loosen and fall.
> There is the Truth. Who sees that never wavers.

CHAPTER 42

Last Days With My Guru

"Guruji, I am glad to find you alone this morning." I had just arrived at the Serampore hermitage, carrying a fragrant burden of fruit and roses. Sri Yukteswar glanced at me meekly.

"What is your question?" Master looked about the room as though seeking escape.

"Guruji, I came to you as a high-school youth; now I am a grown man, even with a gray hair or two. Though you have showered me with silent affection from the first hour to this, do you realize that once only, on the day of meeting, have you ever said, 'I love you'?" I looked at him pleadingly.

Master lowered his gaze. "Yogananda, must I bring out into the cold realms of speech the warm sentiments best guarded by the wordless heart?"

"Guruji, I know you love me, but my mortal ears ache to hear you say so."

"Be it as you wish. During my married life I often yearned for a son, to train in the yogic path. But when you came into my life, I was content; in you I have found my son." Two clear teardrops stood in Sri Yukteswar's eyes. "Yogananda, I love you always."

"Your answer is my passport to heaven." I felt a weight lift from my heart, dissolved forever at his words. I knew he was unemotional and self-contained, yet often I had wondered at his silence. Sometimes I feared I had been unsuccessful in fully satisfying him. His was a strange nature, never utterly to be known; a nature deep and still, unfathomable to the outer world, whose values he had long transcended.

A few days later I spoke before a huge audience at Albert Hall in Calcutta. Sri Yukteswar consented to sit on the platform, with the Maharaja of Santosh and the Mayor of Calcutta. Master made no remark to me, but I glanced at him from time to time during my address and thought he looked pleased.

Then came a talk before the alumni of Serampore College. As I gazed on my old classmates, and as they gazed on their own "Mad

Monk," tears of joy showed unashamedly. My silver-tongued professor of philosophy, Dr. Ghoshal, came forward to greet me, all our past misunderstandings dissolved by the alchemist Time.

A Winter Solstice Festival was celebrated at the end of December in the Serampore hermitage. As always, Sri Yukteswar's disciples gathered from far and near. Devotional *sankirtans,* solos in the nectar-sweet voice of Kristo-da, a feast served by young disciples, Master's profoundly moving discourse under the stars in the thronged courtyard of the ashram—memories, memories! Joyous festivals of years long past! Tonight, however, there was to be a new feature.

"Yogananda, please address the assemblage—in English." Master's eyes were twinkling as he made this doubly unusual request; was he thinking of the shipboard predicament that had preceded my first lecture in English? I told the story to my audience of brother disciples, ending with a fervent tribute to our guru.

"His unfailing guidance was with me not only on the ocean steamer," I concluded, "but daily throughout my fifteen years in the vast and hospitable land of America."

After the guests had departed, Sri Yukteswar called me to the same bedroom where (once only, after a similar festival) I had been permitted to sleep in his bed. Tonight my guru was sitting there quietly, a semicircle of disciples at his feet.

"Yogananda, are you leaving now for Calcutta? Please return here tomorrow. I have certain things to tell you."

The next afternoon, with a few simple words of blessing, Sri Yukteswar bestowed on me the further monastic title of *Paramahansa.**

"It now formally supersedes your former title of *Swami,*" he said as I knelt before him. With a silent chuckle I thought of the struggles to be undergone by my Western students over the pronunciation of *Paramahansaji.*†

"My task on earth is now finished; you must carry on." Master spoke quietly, his eyes calm and gentle. My heart was palpitating in fear.

---

* Lit., *parama,* highest; *hansa,* swan. The white swan is mythologically represented as the vehicle or mount of Brahma the Creator. The sacred *hansa,* said to have the power of extracting only milk from a mixture of milk and water, is thus a symbol of spiritual discrimination.

Ahan-sa or *'han-sa* (pronounced *hong-sau*) is literally "I am He." These potent Sanskrit syllables possess a vibratory connection with the incoming and the outgoing breath. Thus with his every breath man unconsciously asserts the truth of his being: *I am He!*

† They have generally evaded the difficulty by addressing me as *sir.*

"Please send someone to take charge of our ashram in Puri," Sri Yukteswar went on. "I leave everything in your hands. You will be able successfully to sail the boat of your life and that of the organization to the divine shores."

In tears I was embracing his feet; he rose and blessed me lovingly.

The following day I summoned from Ranchi a devotee, Swami Sebananda, and sent him to Puri to assume the hermitage duties. Later my guru discussed with me the legal details of settling his estate; he was anxious to prevent the possibility of litigation by relatives, after his death, for possession of his two hermitages and other properties, which he wished to be deeded over solely for charitable purposes.

"Arrangements were recently made for Master to visit Kidderpore, but he failed to go." Amulaya Babu, a brother disciple, made this remark to me one afternoon; I felt a cold wave of premonition. To my pressing inquiries, Sri Yukteswar only replied, "I shall go to Kidderpore no more." For a moment, Master trembled like a frightened child.

("Attachment to bodily residence, springing up of its own nature,* is present in slight degree even in great saints," Patanjali wrote. In some of my guru's discourses on death, he had been wont to add: "Just as a long-caged bird hesitates to leave its accustomed home when the door is opened.")

"Guruji," I entreated him with a sob, "don't say that! Never utter those words to me!"

Sri Yukteswar's face relaxed in a peaceful smile. Though nearing his eighty-first birthday, he looked well and strong.

Basking day by day in the sunshine of my guru's love, unspoken but keenly felt, I banished from my conscious mind the various hints he had given of his approaching passing.

"Sir, the *Kumbha Mela* is convening this month at Allahabad." I pointed out to Master the *mela* dates in a Bengali almanac.†

---

* That is, springing from immemorial roots, past experiences of death. This passage occurs in Patanjali's *Yoga Sutras* II:9.

† Religious *melas* are mentioned in the ancient *Mahabharata*. The Chinese traveler Hieuen Tsiang has left an account of a vast *Kumbha Mela* held in A.D. 644 at Allahabad. *Kumbha Mela* is held every third year, successively, in Hardwar, Allahabad, Nasik, and Ujjain, returning to Hardwar to complete a twelve-year cycle. Each city holds *Ardha* (half) *Kumbha* in the sixth year after its *Kumbha*; thus *Kumbha* and *Ardha Kumbha* are held, in different cities, every three years.

Hieuen Tsiang tells us that Harsha, king of northern India, distributed to the monks and pilgrims at the *Kumbha Mela* the entire wealth (a five-year accumulation) of the royal treasury. When Hieuen Tsiang departed for China he refused Harsha's parting gifts of jewels and gold; but carried away, as of greater value, 657 religious manuscripts.

"Do you really want to go?"

Not sensing Sri Yukteswar's reluctance to have me leave him, I went on, "Once you beheld the blessed sight of Babaji at an Allahabad *kumbha*. Perhaps this time I shall be fortunate enough to see him."

"I do not think you will meet him there." My guru then fell into silence, not wishing to obstruct my plans.

When I set out for Allahabad the following day with a small group, Master blessed me quietly in his usual manner. Apparently I was remaining oblivious to implications in Sri Yukteswar's attitude because the Lord wished to spare me the experience of being forced, helplessly, to witness my guru's passing. It has always happened in my life that, at the death of those dearly beloved by me, God has compassionately arranged that I be distant from the scene.*

Our party reached the *Kumbha Mela* on January 23, 1936. The surging crowd of nearly two million persons was an impressive sight, even an overwhelming one. The peculiar genius of the Indian people is the reverence innate in even the lowliest peasant for the worth of the Spirit and for the monks and sadhus who have forsaken worldly ties to seek a diviner anchorage. Impostors and hypocrites there are indeed; but India respects all for the sake of the few who illumine the land with supernal blessings. Westerners who were viewing the vast spectacle had a unique opportunity to feel the pulse of the nation, the spiritual ardor to which India owes her quenchless vitality under the blows of time.

The first day was spent by our group in sheer staring. Thousands of pilgrims bathed in the holy Ganges for remission of sins; *Brahmin* priests performed solemn rituals of worship; devotional offerings were strewn at the feet of silent *sannyasis*; lines of elephants, caparisoned horses, and slow-paced Rajputana camels filed by, followed by a quaint religious parade of naked sadhus who waved gold and silver scepters or streamers of silken velvet.

Anchorites wearing only loincloths sat quietly in little groups, their bodies besmeared with ashes, which protect them from heat and cold. The spiritual eye was vividly represented on their foreheads by a single spot of sandalwood paste. Shaven-headed swamis appeared by the thousand, ocher-robed and carrying their bamboo staff and begging bowl. Their faces beamed with the renunciant's peace as they walked about or held philosophical discussions with disciples.

* I was not present at the deaths of my mother, elder brother Ananta, eldest sister Roma, Master, Father, and many other beloved ones. (Father passed on in Calcutta in 1942, aged eighty-nine.)

Here and there under the trees, around huge piles of burning logs, were picturesque sadhus,* their hair braided and massed in coils on top of their heads. Some wore beards several feet in length, curled and tied in a knot. They meditated quietly, or extended their hands in blessing to the passing throng—beggars, maharajas on elephants, women in multicolored *saris,* their bangles and anklets tinkling, *fakirs* with thin arms held grotesquely aloft, *brahmacharis* carrying meditation elbow-props, humble sages whose solemnity hid an inner bliss. High above the din we heard the ceaseless summons of the temple bells.

On our second *mela* day my companions and I entered various ashrams and temporary huts, offering *pranams* to saintly personages. We received the blessing of the leader of the *Giri* branch of the Swami Order—a thin, ascetical monk with eyes of smiling fire. Our party then visited a hermitage whose guru had observed for the past nine years the vows of silence and a strict fruitarian diet. On a dais in the ashram hall sat a blind sadhu, Prajna Chakshu,† profoundly learned in the *shastras* and highly revered by all sects.

After I had given a brief discourse in Hindi on *Vedanta,* our group left the peaceful hermitage to greet a nearby swami, Krishnananda, a handsome monk with rosy cheeks and impressive shoulders. Reclining near him was a tame lioness. Succumbing to the monk's spiritual charm—not, I am sure, to his powerful physique!—the jungle animal refuses all meat in favor of rice and milk. The swami has taught the tawny-haired beast to utter *"Aum"* in a deep, attractive growl—a cat devotee!

Our next encounter, an interview with a learned young sadhu, is well described in Mr. Wright's sparkling travel diary.

"We rode in the Ford across the very low Ganges on a creaking pontoon bridge, crawling snakelike through the crowds and over narrow, twisting lanes, passing the site on the riverbank which Yoganandaji pointed out to me as the meeting place of Babaji and Sri Yukteswarji. Alighting from the car a short time later, we walked some distance through the thickening smoke of the sadhus' fires and over the slippery sands to reach a cluster of tiny, very modest

---

* The hundreds of thousands of Indian sadhus are controlled by an executive committee of seven leaders, representing seven large sections of India. The present *mahamandaleswar* or president is Joyendra Puri. This saintly man is extremely reserved, often confining his speech to three words—Truth, Love, and Work. A sufficient conversation!

† A title whose literal meaning is "one who sees with his intelligence" (not having physical sight).

mud-and-straw huts. We halted in front of one of these insignificant temporary dwellings, with a pygmy doorless entrance, the shelter of Kara Patri, a young wandering sadhu noted for his exceptional intelligence. There he sat, cross-legged on a pile of straw, his only covering—and incidentally his only possession—an ocher cloth draped over his shoulders.

"Truly a divine face smiled at us after we had crawled on all fours into the hut and *pranamed* at the feet of this enlightened soul, while the kerosene lantern at the entrance flickered weird, dancing shadows on the thatched walls. His face, especially his eyes and perfect teeth, beamed and glistened. Although I was puzzled by the Hindi, his expressions were very revealing; he was full of enthusiasm, love, spiritual glory. No one could be mistaken as to his greatness.

"Imagine the happy life of one unattached to the material world; free of the clothing problem; free of food craving, never begging, never touching cooked food except on alternate days, never carrying a begging bowl; free of all money entanglements, never handling money, never storing things away, always trusting in God; free of transportation worries, never riding in vehicles, but always walking on the banks of the sacred rivers; not remaining in one place longer than a week in order to avoid any growth of attachment.

"Such a modest soul! unusually learned in the Vedas, and possessing an M.A. degree and the title of *Shastri* (master of scriptures) from Banaras University. A sublime feeling pervaded me as I sat at his feet; it all seemed to be an answer to my desire to see the real, the ancient India, for he is a true representative of this land of spiritual giants."

I questioned Kara Patri about his wandering life. "Don't you have any extra clothes for winter?"

"No, this is enough."

"Do you carry any books?"

"No, I teach from memory those people who wish to hear me."

"What else do you do?"

"I roam by the Ganges."

At these quiet words, I was overpowered by a yearning for the simplicity of his life. I remembered America, and all the responsibilities that lay on my shoulders.

"No, Yogananda," I thought sadly for a moment, "in this life roaming by the Ganges is not for you."

After the sadhu had told me a few of his spiritual realizations, I shot an abrupt question.

"Are you giving these descriptions from scriptural lore, or from inner experience?"

"Half from book learning," he answered with a straightforward smile, "and half from experience."

We sat happily awhile in meditative silence. After we had left his sacred presence, I said to Mr. Wright, "He is a king sitting on a throne of golden straw."

We had our dinner that night on the *mela* grounds under the stars, eating from leaf plates pinned together with sticks. Dishwashings in India are reduced to a minimum!

Two more days of the fascinating *kumbha;* then northwest along the Yamuna banks to Agra. Once again I gazed on the Taj Mahal; in memory Jitendra stood by my side, awed by the dream in marble. Then on to the Brindaban ashram of Swami Keshabananda.

My object in seeking out Keshabananda was connected with this book. I had never forgotten Sri Yukteswar's request that I write the life of Lahiri Mahasaya. During my stay in India I was taking every opportunity to contact direct disciples and relatives of the Yogavatar. Recording their conversations in voluminous notes, I verified facts and dates, and collected photographs, old letters, and documents. My Lahiri Mahasaya portfolio began to swell; I realized with dismay that ahead of me lay arduous labors in authorship. I prayed that I might be equal to my role as biographer of the colossal guru. Several of his disciples feared that in a written account their master might be belittled or misinterpreted.

"One can hardly do justice in cold words to the life of a divine incarnation," Panchanon Bhattacharya had once remarked to me.

Other close disciples were similarly satisfied to keep the Yogavatar hidden in their hearts as the deathless preceptor. Nevertheless, mindful of Lahiri Mahasaya's prediction about his biography, I spared no effort to secure and substantiate the facts of his outward life.

Swami Keshabananda greeted our party warmly at Brindaban in his Katyayani Peeth Ashram, an imposing brick building with massive black pillars, set in a beautiful garden. He ushered us at once into a sitting room adorned with an enlargement of Lahiri Mahasaya's picture. The swami was approaching the age of ninety, but his muscular body radiated strength and health. With long hair and a snow-white beard, eyes twinkling with joy, he was a veritable patriarchal embodiment. I informed him that I wanted to mention his name in my book on India's masters.

"Please tell me about your earlier life." I smiled entreatingly; great yogis are often uncommunicative.

Keshabananda made a gesture of humility. "There is little of external moment. Practically my whole life has been spent in the Himalayan solitudes, traveling on foot from one quiet cave to another. For a while I maintained a small ashram outside Hardwar, surrounded on all sides by a grove of tall trees. It was a peaceful spot little visited by travelers, owing to the ubiquity of cobras." Keshabananda chuckled. "Later a Ganges flood washed away the hermitage and cobras alike. My disciples then helped me to build this Brindaban ashram."

One of our party asked the swami how he had protected himself against the Himalayan tigers.

Keshabananda shook his head. "In those high spiritual altitudes," he said, "wild beasts seldom molest the yogis. Once in the jungle I encountered a tiger face-to-face. At my sudden ejaculation, the animal was transfixed as though turned to stone." Again the swami chuckled at his memories.*

"Occasionally I left my seclusion to visit my guru in Banaras. He used to joke with me over my ceaseless travels in the Himalayan wilderness.

"'You have the mark of wanderlust on your foot,' he told me once. 'I am glad that the sacred Himalayas are extensive enough to engross you.'

"Many times," Keshabananda went on, "both before and after his passing, Lahiri Mahasaya has appeared bodily before me. For him no Himalayan height is inaccessible!"

Two hours later he led us to a dining patio. I sighed in silent dismay. Another fifteen-course meal! Less than a year of Indian hospitality, and I had gained fifty pounds! Yet it would have been considered the height of rudeness to refuse any of the dishes, carefully prepared for the endless banquets in my honor. In India (nowhere else, alas!) a well-padded swami is considered a delightful sight.

After dinner, Keshabananda led me to a secluded nook.

---

* There are many methods, it appears, for outwitting a tiger. An Australian explorer, Francis Birtles, has recounted that he found the Indian jungles "varied, beautiful, and safe." His safety charm was flypaper. "Every night I spread a quantity of sheets around my camp and was never disturbed," he explained. "The reason is psychological. The tiger is an animal of great conscious dignity. He prowls around and challenges man until he comes to the flypaper; he then slinks away. No dignified tiger would dare face a human being after squatting down upon a sticky flypaper!"

"Your arrival is not unexpected," he said. "I have a message for you."

I was surprised; no one had known of my plan to visit Keshabananda.

"While roaming last year in the northern Himalayas near Badrinarayan," the swami continued, "I lost my way. Shelter appeared in a spacious cave, which was empty, though the embers of a fire glowed in a hole in the rocky floor. Wondering about the occupant of this lonely retreat, I sat near the fire, my gaze fixed on the sunlit entrance to the cave.

"'Keshabananda, I am glad you are here.' These words came from behind me. I turned, startled, and was dazzled to behold Babaji! The great guru had materialized himself in a recess of the cave. Overjoyed to see him again after many years, I prostrated myself at his holy feet.

"'I called you here,' Babaji went on. 'That is why you lost your way and were led to my temporary abode in this cave. It is a long time since our last meeting; I am pleased to greet you once more.'

"The deathless master blessed me with some words of spiritual help, then added: 'I give you a message for Yogananda. He will pay you a visit on his return to India. Many matters connected with his guru and with the surviving disciples of Lahiri will keep Yogananda fully occupied. Tell him, then, that I won't see him this time, as he is eagerly hoping; but I shall see him on some other occasion.'"

I was deeply touched to receive from Keshabananda's lips this consoling promise from Babaji. A certain hurt in my heart vanished; I grieved no longer that, even as Sri Yukteswar had hinted, Babaji did not appear at the *Kumbha Mela.*

Spending one night as guests of the ashram, our party set out the following afternoon for Calcutta. Riding over a bridge of the Yamuna River, we enjoyed a magnificent view of the skyline of Brindaban just as the sun set fire to the sky—a veritable furnace of Vulcan in color, reflected below us in the still waters.

The Yamuna beach is hallowed by memories of the child Sri Krishna. Here he engaged with innocent sweetness in his *lilas* (plays) with the *gopis* (maids), exemplifying the supernal love which ever exists between a divine incarnation and his devotees. The life of Lord Krishna has been misunderstood by many Western commentators. Scriptural allegory is baffling to literal minds. An amusing blunder by a translator will illustrate this point. The story concerns an inspired medieval saint, the cobbler Ravidas, who sang in the simple terms of his own trade of the spiritual glory hidden in all mankind:

> Under the vast vault of blue
> Lives the divinity clothed in hide.

One turns aside to hide a smile on hearing the pedestrian interpretation given to Ravidas's poem by a Western writer:

> He afterwards built a hut, set up in it an idol which he made
> from a hide, and applied himself to its worship.

Ravidas was a brother disciple of the great Kabir. One of Ravidas's exalted *chelas* was the Rani of Chitor. She invited a large number of *Brahmins* to a feast in honor of her teacher, but they refused to eat with a lowly cobbler. As they sat down in dignified aloofness to eat their own uncontaminated meal, lo! each *Brahmin* found at his side the form of Ravidas. This mass vision accomplished a widespread spiritual revival in Chitor.

In a few days our little group reached Calcutta. Eager to see Sri Yukteswar, I was disappointed to hear that he had left Serampore and was now in Puri, about three hundred miles to the south.

"Come to Puri ashram at once." This telegram was sent on March 8 by a brother disciple to Atul Chandra Roy Chowdhry, one of Master's *chelas* in Calcutta. News of the message reached my ears; anguished at its implications, I dropped to my knees and implored God that my guru's life be spared. As I was about to leave Father's home for the train, a divine voice spoke within.

"Do not go to Puri tonight. Thy prayer cannot be granted."

"Lord," I said, grief-stricken, "Thou dost not wish to engage with me in a 'tug-of-war' at Puri, where Thou wilt have to deny my incessant prayers for Master's life. Must he, then, depart for higher duties at Thy behest?"

In obedience to the inner command, I did not leave that night for Puri. The following evening I set out for the train; on the way, at seven o'clock, a black astral cloud suddenly covered the sky.* Later, while the train roared toward Puri, a vision of Sri Yukteswar appeared before me. He was sitting, very grave of countenance, with a light on each side.

"Is it all over?" I lifted my arms beseechingly.

He nodded, then slowly vanished.

As I stood on the Puri train platform the following morning, still hoping against hope, an unknown man approached me.

"Have you heard that your Master is gone?" He left me without

---

* Sri Yukteswar passed at this hour — 7:00 P.M., March 9, 1936.

another word; I never discovered who he was or how he had known where to find me.

Stunned, I swayed against the platform wall, realizing that in diverse ways my guru was trying to convey to me the devastating news. Seething with rebellion, my soul was like a volcano. By the time I reached the Puri hermitage I was nearing collapse. The inner voice was tenderly repeating: "Collect yourself. Be calm."

I entered the ashram room where Master's body, unimaginably lifelike, was sitting in the lotus posture—a picture of health and loveliness. A short time before his passing, my guru had been slightly ill with fever, but before the day of his ascension into the Infinite, his body had become completely well. No matter how often I looked at his dear form I could not realize that its life had departed. His skin was smooth and soft; in his face was a beatific expression of tranquillity. He had consciously relinquished his body at the hour of mystic summoning.

"The Lion of Bengal is gone!" I cried in a daze.

I conducted the solemn rites on March 10. Sri Yukteswar was buried* with the ancient rituals of the swamis in the garden of his Puri ashram. His disciples later arrived from far and near to honor their guru at a vernal equinox memorial service. The *Amrita Bazar Patrika*, leading newspaper of Calcutta, carried his picture and the following report:

> The death *Bhandara* ceremony for Srimat Swami Sri Yukteswar Giri Maharaj, aged 81, took place at Puri on March 21. Many disciples came down to Puri for the rites.
>
> One of the greatest expounders of the Bhagavad Gita, Swami Maharaj was a great disciple of Yogiraj Sri Shyama Charan Lahiri Mahasaya of Banaras. Swami Maharaj was the founder of several Yogoda Satsanga [Self-Realization Fellowship] centers in India, and was the great inspiration behind the yoga movement which was carried to the West by Swami Yogananda, his principal disciple. It was Sri Yukteswarji's prophetic powers and deep realization that inspired Swami Yogananda to cross the oceans and spread in America the message of the masters of India.
>
> His interpretations of the Bhagavad Gita and other scriptures testify to the depth of Sri Yukteswarji's command of the philosophy, both Eastern and Western, and remain as an eye-opener for

---

* Hindu funeral customs require cremation for householders; swamis and monks of other orders are not cremated, but buried. (There are occasional exceptions.) The bodies of monks are symbolically considered to have undergone cremation in the fire of wisdom at the time of taking the monastic vows.

the unity between Orient and Occident. As he believed in the unity of all religious faiths, Sri Yukteswar Maharaj established Sadhu Sabha (Society of Saints) with the cooperation of leaders of various sects and faiths, for the inculcation of a scientific spirit in religion. At the time of his demise he nominated Swami Yogananda his successor as the president of Sadhu Sabha.

India is really poorer today by the passing of such a great man. May all fortunate enough to have come near him inculcate in themselves the true spirit of India's culture and *sadhana* which was personified in him.

I returned to Calcutta. Not trusting myself as yet to go to the Serampore hermitage with its sacred memories, I summoned Prafulla, Sri Yukteswar's little disciple in Serampore, and made arrangements for him to enter the Ranchi school.

"The morning you left for the Allahabad *mela*," Prafulla told me, "Master dropped heavily on the davenport.

"'Yogananda is gone!' he cried. 'Yogananda is gone!' He added cryptically, 'I shall have to tell him some other way.' He sat then for hours in silence."

My days were filled with lectures, classes, interviews, and reunions with old friends. Beneath a hollow smile and a life of ceaseless activity, a stream of black brooding polluted the inner river of bliss which for so many years had meandered under the sands of all my perceptions.

"Where has that divine sage gone?" I cried silently from the depths of a tormented spirit.

No answer came.

"It is best that Master has completed his union with the Cosmic Beloved," my mind assured me. "He is eternally glowing in the dominion of deathlessness."

"Never again may you see him in the old Serampore mansion," my heart lamented. "No longer may you bring your friends to meet him, or proudly say: 'Behold, there sits India's *Jnanavatar!*'"

Mr. Wright made arrangements for our party to sail from Bombay for the West in early June. After a fortnight in May of farewell banquets and speeches in Calcutta, Miss Bletsch, Mr. Wright and I left in the Ford for Bombay. On our arrival, the ship authorities asked us to cancel our passage, as no room could be found for the Ford, which we would need again in Europe.

"Never mind," I said gloomily to Mr. Wright. "I want to return once more to Puri." I silently added, "Let my tears once again water the grave of my guru."

CHAPTER 43

The Resurrection
of Sri Yukteswar

"Lord Krishna!" The glorious form of the avatar appeared in a shimmering blaze as I sat in my room at the Regent Hotel in Bombay. Shining over the roof of a high building across the street, the ineffable vision had suddenly burst on my sight as I gazed out of my tall open third-story window.

The divine figure waved to me, smiling and nodding in greeting. When I could not understand the exact message of Lord Krishna, he departed with a gesture of blessing. Wondrously uplifted, I felt that some spiritual event was presaged.

My Western voyage had, for the time being, been canceled. I was scheduled for several public addresses in Bombay before leaving on a return visit to Bengal.

Sitting on my bed in the Bombay hotel at three o'clock in the afternoon of June 19, 1936—one week after the vision of Krishna—I was roused from my meditation by a beatific light. Before my open and astonished eyes, the whole room was transformed into a strange world, the sunlight transmuted into supernal splendor.

Waves of rapture engulfed me as I beheld the flesh and blood form of Sri Yukteswar!

"My son!" Master spoke tenderly, on his face an angel-bewitching smile.

For the first time in my life I did not kneel at his feet in greeting, but instantly advanced to gather him hungrily in my arms. Moment of moments! The anguish of past months was toll I counted weightless against the torrential bliss now descending.

"Master mine, beloved of my heart, why did you leave me?" I was incoherent in an excess of joy. "Why did you let me go to the *Kumbha Mela*? How bitterly have I blamed myself for leaving you!"

"I did not want to interfere with your happy anticipation of seeing the pilgrimage spot where first I met Babaji. I left you only for a little while; am I not with you again?"

"But is it *you*, Master, the same Lion of God? Are you wearing a body like the one I buried beneath the cruel Puri sands?"

"Yes, my child, I am the same. This is a flesh and blood body. Though I see it as ethereal, to your sight it is physical. From cosmic atoms I created an entirely new body, exactly like that cosmic-dream physical body which you laid beneath the dream-sands at Puri in your dream-world. I am in truth resurrected—not on earth but on an astral planet. Its inhabitants are better able than earthly humanity to meet my lofty standards. There you and your exalted loved ones shall someday come to be with me."

"Deathless guru, tell me more!"

Master gave a quick, mirthful chuckle. "Please, dear one," he said, "won't you relax your hold a little?"

"Only a little!" I had been embracing him with an octopus grip. I could detect the same faint, fragrant, natural odor that had been characteristic of his body before. The thrilling touch of his divine flesh still persists around the inner sides of my arms and in my palms whenever I recall those glorious hours.

"As prophets are sent on earth to help men work out their physical karma, so I have been directed by God to serve on an astral planet as a savior," Sri Yukteswar explained. "It is called Hiranya-loka or 'Illumined Astral Planet.' There I am aiding advanced beings to rid themselves of astral karma and thus attain liberation from astral rebirths. The dwellers on Hiranyaloka are highly developed spiritually; all of them had acquired, in their last earth-incarnation, the meditation-given power of consciously leaving their physical bodies at death. No one can enter Hiranyaloka unless he has passed on earth beyond the state of *sabikalpa samadhi* into the higher state of *nirbikalpa samadhi.**

"Hiranyaloka inhabitants have already passed through the ordinary astral spheres, where nearly all beings from earth must go at death; there they destroyed many seeds of karma connected with their past actions in astral worlds. None but advanced devotees can

---

* See pp. 209–10. In *sabikalpa samadhi* the devotee has attained realization of his oneness with Spirit but cannot maintain his cosmic consciousness except in the immobile trance state. By continuous meditation he reaches the superior state of *nirbikalpa samadhi,* in which he may move freely in the world without any loss of God-perception.

In *nirbikalpa samadhi* the yogi dissolves the last vestiges of his material or earthly karma. Nevertheless, he may still have certain astral and causal karma to work out, and therefore takes astral and then causal reembodiments on high-vibrational spheres.

perform such redemptive work effectively in the astral spheres.*
Then, in order to free their souls fully from all traces of astral
karma, these aspirants were drawn by cosmic law to be reborn in
new astral bodies on Hiranyaloka, the astral sun or heaven, where
I am present to help them. There are also nearly perfect beings on
Hiranyaloka who have come from the superior causal world."

My mind was now in such perfect attunement with my guru's
that he was conveying his word-pictures to me partly by speech
and partly by thought transference. I was thus quickly receiving
his idea-tabloids.

"You have read in the scriptures," Master went on, "that God
encased the human soul successively in three bodies—the idea,
or causal, body; the subtle astral body, seat of man's mental and
emotional natures; and the gross physical body. On earth a man is
equipped with his physical senses. An astral being works with his
consciousness and feelings and a body made of lifetrons.† A causal-
bodied being remains in the blissful realm of ideas. My work is with
those astral beings who are preparing to enter the causal world."

"Adorable Master, please tell me more about the astral cosmos." Though I had slightly relaxed my embrace at Sri Yukteswar's
request, my arms were still around him. Treasure beyond all treasures, my guru who had laughed at death to reach me!

"There are many astral planets, teeming with astral beings,"
Master began. "The inhabitants use astral planes, or masses of light,
to travel from one planet to another, faster than electricity and radio-
active energies.

"The astral universe, made of various subtle vibrations of light
and color, is hundreds of times larger than the material cosmos. The
entire physical creation hangs like a little solid basket under the
huge luminous balloon of the astral sphere. Just as many physical
suns and stars roam in space, so there are also countless astral solar
and stellar systems. Their planets have astral suns and moons, more
beautiful than the physical ones. The astral luminaries resemble
the aurora borealis—the sunny astral aurora being more dazzling

---

* Because most persons, enjoying the beauty of the astral worlds, do not see any
necessity for strenuous spiritual effort.

† Sri Yukteswar used the word *prana*; I have translated it as lifetrons. The Hindu
scriptures refer not only to the *anu*, "atom," and to the *paramanu*, "beyond the
atom," finer electronic energies, but also to *prana*, "creative lifetronic force." Atoms
and electrons are blind forces; *prana* is inherently intelligent. The pranic lifetrons
in the spermatozoa and ova, for instance, guide the development of the embryo
according to a karmic design.

than the mild-rayed moon-aurora. The astral day and night are longer than those of earth.

"The astral world is infinitely beautiful, clean, pure, and orderly. There are no dead planets or barren lands. The terrestrial blemishes—weeds, bacteria, insects, snakes—are absent. Unlike the variable climates and seasons of the earth, the astral planets maintain the even temperature of an eternal spring, with occasional luminous white snow and rain of many-colored lights. Astral planets abound in opal lakes and bright seas and rainbow rivers.

"The ordinary astral universe—not the subtler astral heaven of Hiranyaloka—is peopled with millions of astral beings who have come, more or less recently, from the earth, and also with myriads of fairies, mermaids, fishes, animals, goblins, gnomes, demigods and spirits, all residing on different astral planets in accordance with karmic qualifications. Various spheric mansions or vibratory regions are provided for good and evil spirits. Good ones can travel freely, but the evil spirits are confined to limited zones. In the same way that human beings live on the surface of the earth, worms inside the soil, fish in water, and birds in air, so astral beings of different grades are assigned to suitable vibratory quarters.

"Among the fallen dark angels, expelled from other worlds, friction and war take place with lifetronic bombs or mental mantric* vibratory rays. These beings dwell in the gloom-drenched regions of the lower astral cosmos, working out their evil karma.

"In the vast realms above the dark astral prison, all is shining and beautiful. The astral cosmos is more naturally attuned than the earth to the divine will and plan of perfection. Every astral object is manifested primarily by the will of God, and partially by the will-call of astral beings. They possess the power of modifying or enhancing the grace and form of anything already created by the Lord. He has given His astral children the freedom and privilege of changing or improving at will the astral cosmos. On earth a solid must be transformed into liquid or other form through natural or chemical processes, but astral solids are changed into astral liquids, gases, or energy solely and instantly by the will of the inhabitants.

"The earth is dark with warfare and murder in the sea, land, and air," my guru continued, "but the astral realms know a happy

---

* Adjective of *mantra,* chanted seed-sounds discharged by the mental gun of concentration. The *Puranas* (ancient *shastras* or treatises) describe these mantric wars between *devas* and *asuras* (gods and demons). An *asura* once tried to slay a *deva* with a potent chant. Because of mispronunciation the mental bomb acted as a boomerang and killed the demon.

harmony and equality. Astral beings dematerialize or materialize their forms at will. Flowers or fish or animals can metamorphose themselves, for a time, into astral men. All astral beings are free to assume any form, and can easily commune together. No fixed, definite, natural law hems them round—any astral tree, for example, can be successfully asked to produce an astral mango or other desired fruit, flower, or indeed any other object. Certain karmic restrictions are present, but there are no distinctions in the astral world about desirability of various forms. Everything is vibrant with God's creative light.

"No one is born of woman; offspring are materialized by astral beings through the help of their cosmic will into specially patterned, astrally condensed forms. The recently physically disembodied being arrives in an astral family through invitation, drawn by similar mental and spiritual tendencies.

"The astral body is not subject to cold or heat or other natural conditions. The anatomy includes an astral brain, or the thousand-petaled lotus of light, and six awakened centers in the *sushumna*, or astral cerebrospinal axis. The heart draws cosmic energy as well as light from the astral brain, and pumps it to the astral nerves and body cells, or lifetrons. Astral beings are able to effect changes in their forms by lifetronic force and by holy mantric vibrations.

"In most cases the astral body is an exact counterpart of the last physical form. The face and figure of an astral person resemble those of his youth in his previous earthly sojourn. Occasionally someone, like myself, chooses to retain his old-age appearance." Master, emanating the very essence of youth, chuckled merrily.

"Unlike the spacial, three-dimensional physical world cognized only by the five senses, the astral spheres are visible to the all-inclusive sixth sense—intuition," Sri Yukteswar went on. "By sheer intuitional feeling, all astral beings see, hear, smell, taste, and touch. They possess three eyes, two of which are partly closed. The third and chief astral eye, vertically placed on the forehead, is open. Astral beings have all the outer sensory organs—ears, eyes, nose, tongue, and skin—but they employ the intuitional sense to experience sensations through any part of the body; they can see through the ear, or nose, or skin. They are able to hear through the eyes or tongue, and can taste through the ears or skin, and so forth.*

"Man's physical body is exposed to countless dangers, and is

---

* Examples of such powers are not wanting even on earth, as in the case of Helen Keller and other rare beings.

easily hurt or maimed; the ethereal astral body may occasionally be cut or bruised but is healed at once by mere willing."

"Gurudeva, are all astral persons beautiful?"

"Beauty in the astral world is known to be a spiritual quality, and not an outward conformation," Sri Yukteswar replied. "Astral beings therefore attach little importance to facial features. They have the privilege, however, of costuming themselves at will with new, colorful, astrally materialized bodies. Just as worldly men don new array for gala events, so astral beings find occasions to bedeck themselves in specially designed forms.

"Joyous astral festivities on the higher astral planets like Hiranyaloka take place when a being is liberated from the astral world through spiritual advancement, and is therefore ready to enter the heaven of the causal world. On such occasions the Invisible Heavenly Father, and the saints who are merged in Him, materialize Themselves into bodies of Their own choice and join the astral celebration. In order to please His beloved devotee, the Lord takes any desired form. If the devotee worshiped through devotion, he sees God as the Divine Mother. To Jesus, the Father-aspect of the Infinite One was appealing beyond other conceptions. The individuality with which the Creator has endowed each of His creatures makes every conceivable and inconceivable demand on the Lord's versatility!" My guru and I laughed happily together.

"Friends of other lives easily recognize one another in the astral world," Sri Yukteswar went on in his beautiful, flutelike voice. "Rejoicing at the immortality of friendship, they realize the indestructibility of love, often doubted at the time of the sad, delusive partings of earthly life.

"The intuition of astral beings pierces through the veil and observes human activities on earth, but man cannot view the astral world unless his sixth sense is somewhat developed. Thousands of earth-dwellers have momentarily glimpsed an astral being or an astral world.*

"The advanced beings on Hiranyaloka remain mostly awake in ecstasy during the long astral day and night, helping to work out intricate problems of cosmic government and the redemption of prodigal sons, earthbound souls. When the Hiranyaloka beings sleep,

---

* On earth pure-minded children are sometimes able to see the graceful astral bodies of fairies. Through drugs or intoxicating drink, whose use is forbidden by all scriptures, a man may so derange his consciousness that he perceives the hideous forms in astral hells.

they have occasional dreamlike astral visions. Their minds are usually engrossed in the conscious state of highest *nirbikalpa* bliss.

"Inhabitants in all parts of the astral worlds are still subject to mental agonies. The sensitive minds of the higher beings on planets like Hiranyaloka feel keen pain if any mistake is made in conduct or perception of truth. These advanced beings endeavor to attune their every act and thought with the perfection of spiritual law.

"Communication among the astral inhabitants is held entirely by astral telepathy and television; there is none of the confusion and misunderstanding of the written and spoken word which earth-dwellers must endure. Just as persons on the cinema screen appear to move and act through a series of light pictures, and do not actually breathe, so the astral beings walk and work as intelligently guided and coordinated images of light, without the necessity of drawing power from oxygen. Man depends upon solids, liquids, gases, and energy for sustenance; astral beings sustain themselves principally by cosmic light."

"Master mine, do astral beings eat anything?" I was drinking in his marvelous elucidations with the receptivity of all my faculties—mind, heart, soul. Superconscious perceptions of truth are permanently real and changeless, while fleeting sense experiences and impressions are never more than temporarily or relatively true, and soon lose in memory all their vividness. My guru's words were so penetratingly imprinted on the parchment of my being that at any time, by transferring my mind to the superconscious state, I can clearly relive the divine experience.

"Luminous raylike vegetables abound in the astral soils," he answered. "The astral beings consume vegetables, and drink a nectar flowing from glorious fountains of light and from astral brooks and rivers. Just as invisible images of persons on the earth can be dug out of the ether and made visible by a television apparatus, later being dismissed again into space, so the God-created, unseen astral blueprints of vegetables and plants floating in the ether are precipitated on an astral planet by the will of its inhabitants. In the same way, from the wildest fancy of these beings, whole gardens of fragrant flowers are materialized, returning later to the etheric invisibility. Although dwellers on the heavenly planets like Hiranyaloka are almost freed from any necessity of eating, still higher is the unconditioned existence of almost completely liberated souls in the causal world, who eat nothing save the manna of bliss.

"The earth-liberated astral being meets a multitude of relatives, fathers, mothers, wives, husbands, and friends, acquired during different incarnations on earth,* as they appear from time to time in various parts of the astral realms. He is therefore at a loss to understand whom to love especially; he learns in this way to give a divine and equal love to all, as children and individualized expressions of God. Though the outward appearance of loved ones may have changed, more or less according to the development of new qualities in the latest life of any particular soul, the astral being employs his unerring intuition to recognize all those once dear to him in other planes of existence, and to welcome them to their new astral home. Because every atom in creation is inextinguishably dowered with individuality,† an astral friend will be recognized no matter what costume he may don, even as on earth an actor's identity is discoverable by close observation despite any disguise.

"The span of life in the astral world is much longer than on earth. A normal advanced astral being's average life period is from five hundred to one thousand years, measured in accordance with earthly standards of time. As certain redwood trees outlive most trees by millenniums, or as some yogis live several hundred years though most men die before the age of sixty, so some astral beings live much longer than the usual span of astral existence. Visitors to the astral world dwell there for a longer or shorter period in accordance with the weight of their physical karma, which draws them back to earth within a specified time.

"The astral being does not have to contend painfully with death at the time of shedding his luminous body. Many of these beings nevertheless feel slightly nervous at the thought of dropping their astral form for the subtler causal one. The astral world is free from unwilling death, disease, and old age. These three dreads are the curse of earth, where man has allowed his consciousness to identify itself almost wholly with a frail physical body requiring constant aid from air, food, and sleep in order to exist at all.

"Physical death is attended by the disappearance of breath and the disintegration of fleshly cells. Astral death consists of the dispersement of lifetrons, those manifest units of energy which constitute the life of astral beings. At physical death a being loses

* Lord Buddha was once asked why a man should love all persons equally. "Because," the great teacher replied, "in the very numerous and varied life-spans of each man, every other being has at one time or another been dear to him."

† The eight elemental qualities that enter into all created life, from atom to man, are earth, water, fire, air, ether, sensory mind (*manas*), intelligence (*buddhi*), and individuality or ego (*ahamkara*). (Cf. Bhagavad Gita VII:4.)

his consciousness of flesh and becomes aware of his subtle body in the astral world. Experiencing astral death in due time, a being thus passes from the consciousness of astral birth and death to that of physical birth and death. These recurrent cycles of astral and physical encasement are the ineluctable destiny of all unenlightened beings. Scriptural definitions of heaven and hell sometimes stir man's deeper-than-subconscious memories of his long series of experiences in the blithesome astral and disappointing terrestrial worlds."

"Beloved Master," I asked, "will you please describe more in detail the difference between rebirth on the earth and in the astral and causal spheres?"

"Man as an individualized soul is essentially causal-bodied," my guru explained. "That body is a matrix of the thirty-five *ideas* required by God as the basic or causal thought forces from which He later formed the subtle astral body of nineteen elements and the gross physical body of sixteen elements.

"The nineteen elements of the astral body are mental, emotional, and lifetronic. The nineteen components are intelligence; ego; feeling; mind (sense-consciousness); five instruments of *knowledge,* the subtle counterparts of the senses of sight, hearing, smell, taste, touch; five instruments of *action,* the mental correspondence for the executive abilities to procreate, excrete, talk, walk, and exercise manual skill; and five instruments of *life force,* those empowered to perform the crystallizing, assimilating, eliminating, metabolizing, and circulating functions of the body. This subtle astral encasement of nineteen elements survives the death of the physical body, which is made of sixteen gross chemical elements.

"God thought out different ideas within Himself and projected them into dreams. Lady Cosmic Dream thus sprang out decorated in all her colossal endless ornaments of relativity.

"In thirty-five thought categories of the causal body, God elaborated all the complexities of man's nineteen astral and sixteen physical counterparts. By condensation of vibratory forces, first subtle, then gross, He produced man's astral body and finally his physical form. According to the law of relativity, by which the Prime Simplicity has become the bewildering manifold, the causal cosmos and causal body are different from the astral cosmos and astral body; the physical cosmos and physical body are likewise characteristically at variance with the other forms of creation.

"The fleshly body is made of the fixed, objectified dreams of the

Creator. The dualities are ever present on earth: disease and health, pain and pleasure, loss and gain. Human beings find limitation and resistance in three-dimensional matter. When man's desire to live is severely shaken by disease or other causes, death arrives; the heavy overcoat of the flesh is temporarily shed. The soul, however, remains encased in the astral and causal bodies.* The cohesive force by which all three bodies are held together is desire. The power of unfulfilled desires is the root of all of man's slavery.

"Physical desires are rooted in egotism and sense pleasures. The compulsion or temptation of sensory experience is more powerful than the desire-force connected with astral attachments or causal perceptions.

"Astral desires center around enjoyment in terms of vibration. Astral beings enjoy the ethereal music of the spheres and are entranced by the sight of all creation as exhaustless expressions of changing light. The astral beings also smell, taste, and touch light. Astral desires are thus connected with an astral being's power to precipitate all objects and experiences as forms of light or as condensed thoughts or dreams.

"Causal desires are fulfilled by perception only. The nearly-free beings who are encased only in the causal body see the whole universe as realizations of the dream-ideas of God; they can materialize anything and everything in sheer thought. Causal beings therefore consider the enjoyment of physical sensations or astral delights as gross and suffocating to the soul's fine sensibilities. Causal beings work out their desires by materializing them instantly.† Those who find themselves covered only by the delicate veil of the causal body can bring universes into manifestation even as the Creator. Because all creation is made of the cosmic dream-texture, the soul thinly clothed in the causal has vast realizations of power.

"A soul, being invisible by nature, can be distinguished only by the presence of its body or bodies. The mere presence of a body signifies that its existence is made possible by unfulfilled desires.‡

---

* "Body" signifies any soul encasement, whether gross or subtle. The three bodies are cages for the Bird of Paradise.

† Even as Babaji helped Lahiri Mahasaya to rid himself of a subconscious desire from some past life for a palace, as described in chapter 34.

‡ "And he said unto them, Wheresoever the body is, thither will the eagles be gathered together."—Luke 17:37. Wherever the soul is encased in the physical body or in the astral body or in the causal body, there the eagles of desires—which prey on human sense weaknesses, or on astral and causal attachments—will also gather to keep the soul a prisoner.

"So long as the soul of man is encased in one, two, or three body-containers, sealed tightly with the corks of ignorance and desires, he cannot merge with the sea of Spirit. When the gross physical receptacle is destroyed by the hammer of death, the other two coverings—astral and causal—still remain to prevent the soul from consciously joining the Omnipresent Life. When desirelessness is attained through wisdom, its power disintegrates the two remaining vessels. The tiny human soul emerges, free at last; it is one with the Measureless Amplitude."

I asked my divine guru to shed further light on the high and mysterious causal world.

"The causal world is indescribably subtle," he replied. "In order to understand it, one would have to possess such tremendous powers of concentration that he could close his eyes and visualize the astral cosmos and the physical cosmos in all their vastness—the luminous balloon with the solid basket—as existing in ideas only. If by this superhuman concentration one succeeded in converting or resolving the two cosmoses with all their complexities into sheer ideas, he would then reach the causal world and stand on the borderline of fusion between mind and matter. There one perceives all created things—solids, liquids, gases, electricity, energy, all beings, gods, men, animals, plants, bacteria—as forms of consciousness, just as a man can close his eyes and realize that he exists, even though his body is invisible to his physical eyes and is present only as an idea.

"Whatever a human being can do in fancy, a causal being can do in reality. The most colossal imaginative human intelligence is able, in mind only, to range from one extreme of thought to another, to skip mentally from planet to planet, or tumble endlessly down a pit of eternity, or soar rocketlike into the galaxied canopy, or scintillate like a searchlight over milky ways and the starry spaces. But beings in the causal world have a much greater freedom, and can effortlessly manifest their thoughts into instant objectivity, without any material or astral obstruction or karmic limitation.

"Causal beings realize that the physical cosmos is not primarily constructed of electrons, nor is the astral cosmos basically composed of lifetrons—both in reality are created from the minutest particles of God-thought, chopped and divided by *maya,* the law of relativity that apparently intervenes to separate creation from its Creator.

"Souls in the causal world recognize one another as individualized points of joyous Spirit; their thought-things are the only objects that surround them. Causal beings see the difference between their bodies and thoughts to be merely ideas. As a man, closing his eyes, can visualize a dazzling white light or a faint blue haze, so causal beings by thought alone are able to see, hear, smell, taste, touch; they create anything, or dissolve it, by the power of cosmic mind.

"Both death and rebirth in the causal world are in thought. Causal-bodied beings feast only on the ambrosia of eternally new knowledge. They drink from the springs of peace, roam on the trackless soil of perceptions, swim in the ocean-endlessness of bliss. Lo! see their bright thought-bodies zoom past trillions of Spirit-created planets, fresh bubbles of universes, wisdom-stars, spectral dreams of golden nebulae on the skyey bosom of Infinity!

"Many beings remain for thousands of years in the causal cosmos. By deeper ecstasies the freed soul then withdraws itself from the little causal body and puts on the vastness of the causal cosmos. All the separate eddies of ideas, particularized waves of power, love, will, joy, peace, intuition, calmness, self-control, and concentration melt into the ever-joyous Sea of Bliss. No longer does the soul have to experience its joy as an individualized wave of consciousness, but is merged in the One Cosmic Ocean, with all its waves—eternal laughter, thrills, throbs.

"When a soul is out of the cocoon of the three bodies it escapes forever from the law of relativity and becomes the ineffable Ever-Existent.* Behold the butterfly of Omnipresence, its wings etched with stars and moons and suns! The soul expanded into Spirit remains alone in the region of lightless light, darkless dark, thoughtless thought, intoxicated with its ecstasy of joy in God's dream of cosmic creation."

"A free soul!" I ejaculated in awe.

"When a soul finally gets out of the three jars of bodily delusions," Master continued, "it becomes one with the Infinite without any loss of individuality. Christ had won this final freedom even before he was born as Jesus. In three stages of his past, symbolized in his earth-life as the three days of his experience of death and resurrection, he had attained the power to fully arise in Spirit.

"The undeveloped man must undergo countless earthly and astral and causal incarnations in order to emerge from his three bodies. A master who achieves this final freedom may elect to return

---

* "Him that overcometh will I make a pillar in the temple of my God, and he shall go no more out (i.e., shall reincarnate no more)....To him that overcometh will I grant to sit with me in my throne, even as I also overcame, and am set down with my Father in his throne."—Revelation 3:12, 21.

to earth as a prophet to bring other human beings back to God, or like myself he may choose to reside in the astral cosmos. There a savior assumes some of the burden of the inhabitants' karma* and thus helps them to terminate their cycle of reincarnation in the astral cosmos and go on permanently to the causal spheres. Or a freed soul may enter the causal world to aid its beings to shorten their span in the causal body and thus attain the Absolute Freedom."

"Resurrected One, I want to know more about the karma which forces souls to return to the three worlds." I could listen forever, I thought, to my omniscient Master. Never in his earth-life had I been able at one time to assimilate so much of his wisdom. Now for the first time I was receiving a clear, definite insight into the enigmatic interspaces on the checkerboard of life and death.

"The physical karma or desires of man must be completely worked out before his continued stay in astral worlds becomes possible," my guru elucidated in his thrilling voice. "Two kinds of beings live in the astral spheres. Those who still have earthly karma to dispose of and who must therefore reinhabit a gross physical body in order to pay their karmic debts could be classified, after physical death, as temporary visitors to the astral world rather than as established residents.

"Beings with unredeemed earthly karma are not permitted after astral death to go to the high causal sphere of cosmic ideas, but must shuttle to and fro from the physical and astral worlds only, conscious successively of their physical body of sixteen gross elements, and of their astral body of nineteen subtle elements. After each loss of his physical body, however, an undeveloped being from the earth remains for the most part in the deep stupor of the death-sleep and is hardly conscious of the beautiful astral sphere. After the astral rest, such a man returns to the material plane for further lessons, gradually accustoming himself, through repeated journeys, to the worlds of subtle astral texture.

"Normal or long-established residents of the astral universe, on the other hand, are those who, freed forever from all material longings, need return no more to the gross vibrations of earth. Such beings have only astral and causal karma to work out. At astral death these beings pass to the infinitely finer and more delicate

---

* Sri Yukteswar was signifying that, even as in his earthly incarnation he had occasionally assumed the weight of disease to lighten his disciples' karma, so in the astral world his mission as a savior enabled him to take on certain astral karma of dwellers on Hiranyaloka, and thus hasten their evolution into the higher causal world.

causal world. At the end of a certain span, determined by cosmic law, these advanced beings then return to Hiranyaloka or a similar high astral planet, reborn in a new astral body to work out their unredeemed astral karma.

"My son, you may now comprehend more fully that I am resurrected by divine decree," Sri Yukteswar continued, "as a savior of astrally reincarnating souls coming back from the causal sphere, in particular, rather than of those astral beings who are coming up from the earth. Those from the earth, if they still retain vestiges of material karma, do not rise to the very high astral planets like Hiranyaloka.

"Just as most people on earth have not learned through meditation-acquired vision to appreciate the superior joys and advantages of astral life and thus, after death, desire to return to the limited, imperfect pleasures of earth, so many astral beings, during the normal disintegration of their astral bodies, fail to picture the advanced state of spiritual joy in the causal world and, dwelling on thoughts of the more gross and gaudy astral happiness, yearn to revisit the astral paradise. Heavy astral karma must be redeemed by such beings before they can achieve after astral death an unbroken stay in the causal thought-world, so thinly partitioned from the Creator.

"Only when a being has no further desires for experiences in the pleasing-to-the-eye astral cosmos, and cannot be tempted to go back there, does he remain in the causal world. Completing there the work of redeeming all causal karma or seeds of past desires, the confined soul thrusts out the last of the three corks of ignorance and, emerging from the final jar of the causal body, commingles with the Eternal.

"Now do you understand?" Master smiled so enchantingly!

"Yes, through your grace. I am speechless with joy and gratitude."

Never from song or story had I ever received such inspiring knowledge. Though the Hindu scriptures refer to the causal and astral worlds and to man's three bodies, how remote and meaningless those pages compared with the warm authenticity of my resurrected Master! For him indeed existed not a single "undiscover'd country from whose bourn no traveller returns"!*

"The interpenetration of man's three bodies is expressed in many ways through his threefold nature," my great guru went on. "In the wakeful state on earth a human being is conscious more or less of his three vehicles. When he is sensuously intent on tasting, smelling, touching, listening, or seeing, he is working principally

---

* *Hamlet* (Act III, Scene 1).

through his physical body. Visualizing or willing, he is working mainly through his astral body. His causal being finds expression when man is thinking or diving deep in introspection or meditation; the cosmical thoughts of genius come to the man who habitually contacts his causal body. In this sense an individual may be classified broadly as 'a material man,' 'an energetic man,' or 'an intellectual man.'

"A man identifies himself about sixteen hours daily with his physical vehicle. Then he sleeps; if he dreams, he remains in his astral body, effortlessly creating any object even as do the astral beings. If man's sleep be deep and dreamless, for several hours he is able to transfer his consciousness, or sense of I-ness, to the causal body; such sleep is revivifying. A dreamer is contacting his astral and not his causal body; his sleep is not fully refreshing."

I had been lovingly observing Sri Yukteswar while he gave his wondrous exposition.

"Angelic Guru," I said, "your body looks exactly as it did when last I wept over it in the Puri ashram."

"Oh, yes, my new body is a perfect copy of the old one. I materialize or dematerialize this form any time at will, much more frequently than I did while on earth. By quick dematerialization, I now travel instantly by light express from planet to planet or, indeed, from astral to causal or to physical cosmos." My divine guru smiled. "Though you move about so fast these days, I had no difficulty in finding you at Bombay!"

"O Master, I was grieving so deeply about your death!"

"Ah, wherein did I die? Isn't there some contradiction?" Sri Yukteswar's eyes were twinkling with love and amusement.

"You were only dreaming on earth; on that earth you saw my dream-body," he went on. "Later you buried that dream-image. Now my finer fleshly body—which you behold and are even now embracing rather closely!—is resurrected on another finer dream-planet of God. Someday that finer dream-body and finer dream-planet will pass away; they too are not forever. All dream-bubbles must eventually burst at a final wakeful touch. Differentiate, my son Yogananda, between dreams and Reality!"

This idea of Vedantic* resurrection struck me with wonder. I

---

* Life and death as relativities of thought only. *Vedanta* points out that God is the only Reality; all creation or separate existence is *maya* or illusion. This philosophy of monism received its highest expression in the *Upanishad* commentaries of Shankara.

was ashamed that I had pitied Master when I had seen his lifeless body at Puri. I comprehended at last that my guru had always been fully awake in God, perceiving his own life and passing on earth, and his present resurrection, as nothing more than relativities of divine ideas in the cosmic dream.

"I have now told you, Yogananda, the truths of my life, death, and resurrection. Grieve not for me; rather broadcast everywhere the story of my resurrection from the God-dreamed earth of men to another God-dreamed planet of astrally garbed souls! New hope will be infused into the hearts of misery-mad, death-fearing dreamers of the world."

"Yes, Master!" How willingly would I share with others my joy at his resurrection!

"On earth my standards were uncomfortably high, unsuited to the natures of most men. Often I scolded you more than I should have. You passed my test; your love shone through the clouds of all reprimands." He added tenderly, "I have also come today to tell you: Never again shall I wear the stern gaze of censure. I shall scold you no more."

How much I had missed the chastisements of my great guru! Each one had been a guardian angel of protection.

"Dearest Master! Rebuke me a million times—do scold me now!"

"I shall chide you no more." His divine voice was grave, yet with an undercurrent of laughter. "You and I shall smile together, so long as our two forms appear different in the *maya*-dream of God. Finally we shall merge as one in the Cosmic Beloved; our smiles shall be His smile, our unified song of joy vibrating throughout eternity to be broadcast to God-tuned souls!"

Sri Yukteswar gave me light on certain matters which I cannot reveal here. During the two hours that he spent with me in the Bombay hotel room he answered my every question. A number of world prophecies uttered by him that June day in 1936 have already come to pass.

"I leave you now, beloved one!" At these words I felt Master melting away within my encircling arms.

"My child," his voice rang out, vibrating into my very soul-firmament, "whenever you enter the door of *nirbikalpa samadhi* and call on me, I shall come to you in flesh and blood, even as today."

With this celestial promise Sri Yukteswar vanished from my sight. A cloud-voice repeated in musical thunder: "Tell all! Whosoever knows by *nirbikalpa* realization that your earth is a dream of God can come to the finer dream-created planet of Hiranyaloka, and there find me resurrected in a body exactly like my earthly one. Yogananda, tell all!"

Gone was the sorrow of parting. The pity and grief for his death, long robber of my peace, now fled in stark shame. Bliss poured forth like a fountain through endless, newly opened soul pores. Anciently clogged with disuse, they now widened in purity at the driving flood of ecstasy. My former incarnations appeared before my inward eye in motion-picturelike sequence. Good and bad karma of the past was dissolved in the cosmic light shed around me by Master's divine visit.

In this chapter of my autobiography I have obeyed my guru's behest and spread the glad tidings, though they confound once more an incurious generation. Groveling, man knows well; despair is seldom alien; yet these are perversities, no part of man's true lot. The day he wills, he is set on the path to freedom. Too long has he hearkened to the dank pessimism of his "dust-thou-art" counselors, heedless of the unconquerable soul.

I was not the only one privileged to behold the Resurrected Guru.

One of Sri Yukteswar's *chelas* was an aged woman, affectionately known as *Ma* (Mother), whose home was close to the Puri hermitage. Master had often stopped to chat with her during his morning walk. On the evening of March 16, 1936, Ma arrived at the ashram and asked to see her guru.

"Why, Master died a week ago!" Swami Sebananda, now in charge of the Puri hermitage, looked at her sadly.

"That's impossible!" she protested with a smile.

"No." Sebananda recounted details of the burial. "Come," he said, "I will take you to the front garden to his grave."

Ma shook her head. "There is no grave for him! This morning at ten o'clock he passed in his usual walk before my door! I talked to him for several minutes in the bright outdoors.

"'Come this evening to the ashram,' he said.

"I am here! Blessings pour on this old gray head! The deathless guru wanted me to understand in what transcendent body he visited me this morning!"

The astounded Sebananda knelt before her.

"Ma," he said, "what a weight of grief you lift from my heart! He is risen!"

Paramahansaji and Faye Wright, now Sri Daya Mata (see photo opposite page 205), at SRF Encinitas Hermitage, 1939. Soon after she entered the SRF Ashram in 1931, the Guru told her: "You are my nest egg. When you came, I knew many other true devotees of God would be drawn to this path." He once lovingly remarked, "My Faye, so much good she will do!...I know I can work through her because she is receptive."

Paramahansa Yogananda and James J. Lynn, later Sri Rajarsi Janakananda (see photo opposite page 205). Guru and disciple are meditating at SRF-YSS International Headquarters, Los Angeles, 1933. "Some people say, 'The Western man cannot meditate.' That is not true," Yoganandaji said. "Since Mr. Lynn first received *Kriya Yoga*, I have never seen him when he was not inwardly communing with God."

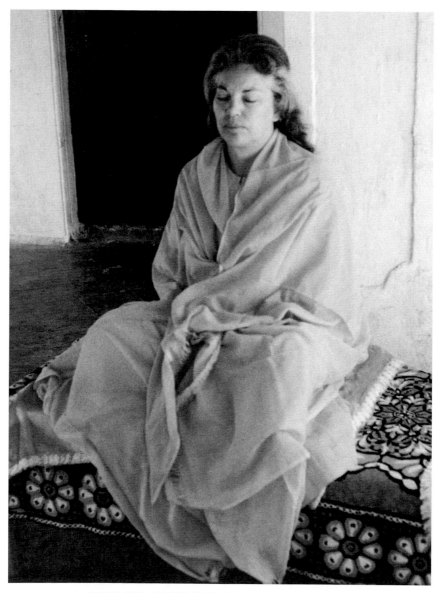

SRI DAYA MATA IN DIVINE COMMUNION

Sri Daya Mata, president of Self-Realization Fellowship/Yogoda Satsanga Society of India, absorbed in meditation, during a visit to India in 1968. "Paramahansa Yogananda taught us the way," she has written, "not only by his words and divine example, but by giving to us the scientific SRF methods of meditation. It is not possible to satisfy the soul's thirst merely by reading about truth. One must drink deep from the Fountain of Truth—God. Self-realization means just that: direct experience of God."

A true "Mother of Compassion," as her name Daya Mata implies, the theme of her life is loving God and sharing His love with all.

Mr. Goodwin J. Knight, Lt. Governor of California (*center*), with Yoganandaji and Mr. A. B. Rose, at dedication of Self-Realization Fellowship India Center, adjacent to the SRF temple shown below, Hollywood, California, April 8, 1951

Self-Realization Temple (Church of All Religions), Hollywood

Paramahansa Yogananda on grounds of SRF Encinitas Hermitage, situated on a bluff overlooking the Pacific Ocean, 1940

The Indian Ambassador to the United States, Mr. Binay Ranjan Sen, with Sri Yogananda at Self-Realization Fellowship International Headquarters, Los Angeles, March 4, 1952—three days before the passing of the great yogi.

In a eulogy at the funeral on March 11, Ambassador Sen said: "If we had a man like Paramahansa Yogananda in the United Nations today, probably the world would be a better place than it is. To my knowledge, no one has worked more, has given more of himself, to bind the peoples of India and America together."

CHAPTER 44

With Mahatma Gandhi
at Wardha

"Welcome to Wardha!" Mahadev Desai, secretary to Mahatma Gandhi, greeted Miss Bletsch, Mr. Wright, and me with these cordial words and the gift of wreaths of *khaddar* (homespun cotton). Our little group had just arrived at the station in Wardha on an early morning in August, glad to leave the dust and heat of the train. Consigning our luggage to a bullock cart, we entered an open motorcar with Mr. Desai and his companions: Babasaheb Deshmukh and Dr. Pingale. A short drive over the muddy country roads brought us to "Maganvadi," the ashram of India's political saint.

Mr. Desai led us at once to the writing room where, cross-legged, sat Mahatma Gandhi. Pen in one hand and a scrap of paper in the other, on his face a vast, winning, warmhearted smile!

"Welcome!" he scribbled in Hindi; it was a Monday, his weekly day of silence.

Though this was our first meeting, we beamed on each other affectionately. In 1925 Mahatma Gandhi had honored the Ranchi school by a visit, and had inscribed in its guest book a gracious tribute.

The tiny 100-pound saint radiated physical, mental, and spiritual health. His soft brown eyes shone with intelligence, sincerity, and discrimination; this statesman has matched wits and emerged the victor in a thousand legal, social, and political battles. No other leader in the world has attained the secure niche in the hearts of his people that Gandhi occupies for India's unlettered millions. Their spontaneous tribute is his famous title—Mahatma, "great soul."[*] For them alone Gandhi confines his attire to the widely cartooned loincloth, symbol of his oneness with the downtrodden masses who can afford no more.

"The ashram residents are wholly at your disposal; please call on them for any service." With characteristic courtesy, the Mahatma handed me this hastily written note as Mr. Desai led our party from the writing room toward the guest house.

---

[*] His family name is Mohandas Karamchand Gandhi. He never refers to himself as "Mahatma."

Our guide led us through orchards and flowering fields to a tile-roofed building with latticed windows. A front-yard well, twenty-five feet across, was used, Mr. Desai said, for watering stock; nearby stood a revolving cement wheel for threshing rice. Each of our small bedrooms proved to contain only the irreducible minimum—a bed, handmade of rope. The whitewashed kitchen boasted a faucet in one corner and a fire pit for cooking in another. Simple Arcadian sounds reached our ears—the cries of crows and sparrows, the lowing of cattle, and the rap of chisels being used to chip stones.

Observing Mr. Wright's travel diary, Mr. Desai opened it and wrote on a page a list of *Satyagraha** vows taken by all of the Mahatma's earnest followers (*satyagrahis*):

> "Nonviolence; Truth; Non-Stealing; Celibacy; Non-Possession; Body Labor; Control of the Palate; Fearlessness; Equal Respect for all Religions; *Swadeshi* (use of home manufactures); Freedom from Untouchability. These eleven should be observed as vows in a spirit of humility."

(Gandhi himself signed this page on the following day, giving the date also—August 27, 1935.)

Two hours after our arrival my companions and I were summoned to lunch. The Mahatma was already seated under the arcade of the ashram porch, across the courtyard from his study. About twenty-five barefooted *satyagrahis* were squatting before brass cups and plates. A community chorus of prayer; then a meal served from large brass pots containing *chapatis* (whole-wheat unleavened bread) sprinkled with *ghee*; *talsari* (boiled and diced vegetables), and a lemon jam.

The Mahatma ate *chapatis*, boiled beets, some raw vegetables, and oranges. On the side of his plate was a large lump of very bitter *neem* leaves, a notable blood cleanser. With a spoon he separated a portion and placed it on my dish. I bolted it down with water, remembering childhood days when Mother had forced me to swallow the unpleasant dose. Gandhi, however, was eating the *neem* paste bit by bit without distaste.

In this trifling incident I noted the Mahatma's ability to detach his mind from the senses at will. I recalled a much-publicized appendectomy performed on him some years ago. Refusing anesthetics, the saint had chatted cheerfully with his devotees throughout the operation, his calm smile revealing his unawareness of pain.

---

* The literal translation from Sanskrit is "holding to truth." *Satyagraha* is the famous nonviolence movement led by Gandhi.

The afternoon brought me an opportunity for a chat with Gandhi's noted disciple, daughter of an English admiral, Miss Madeleine Slade, now called Mira Behn.* Her strong, calm face lit with enthusiasm as she told me, in flawless Hindi, of her daily activities.

"Rural reconstruction work is rewarding! A group of us go every morning at five o'clock to serve the nearby villagers and teach them simple hygiene. We make it a point to clean their latrines and thatched mud huts. The villagers are illiterate; they cannot be educated except by example!" She laughed gaily.

I looked in admiration at this highborn Englishwoman whose true Christian humility enables her to do the scavengering work usually performed only by "untouchables."

"I came to India in 1925," she told me. "In this land I feel that I have 'come back home.' Now I would never be willing to return to my old life and old interests."

We discussed America for a while. "I am always pleased and amazed," she said, "to see the deep interest in spiritual subjects shown by many of the Americans who visit India."†

Mira Behn's hands were soon busy at a *charka* (spinning wheel). Owing to the Mahatma's efforts, *charkas* are now omnipresent in rural India.

Gandhi has sound economic and cultural reasons for encouraging the revival of cottage industries, but he does not counsel a fanatical repudiation of all modern progress. Machinery, trains, automobiles, the telegraph have played important parts in his own colossal life! Fifty years of public service, in prison and out, wrestling daily with practical details and harsh realities in the political world, have only increased his balance, open-mindedness, sanity, and humorous appreciation of the quaint human spectacle.

Our trio enjoyed a six o'clock supper as guests of Babasaheb

---

* She has published a number of letters written by the Mahatma that reveal the self-disciplinary training given her by her guru (*Gandhi's Letters to a Disciple*; Harper & Bros., New York, 1950).

In a later book (*The Spirit's Pilgrimage*; Coward-McCann, N.Y., 1960), Miss Slade mentioned the large number of persons who visited Gandhi in Wardha. She wrote: "At this distance of time I cannot recall many of them, but two remain clearly in my mind: Halide Edib Hanum, the celebrated woman writer of Turkey; and Swami Yogananda, founder of Self-Realization Fellowship of America." *(Publisher's Note)*

† Miss Slade reminded me of another distinguished Western woman, Miss Margaret Woodrow Wilson, eldest daughter of America's great president. I met her in New York; she was intensely interested in India. Later she went to Pondicherry, where she spent the last five years of her life, happily pursuing a path of discipline at the feet of the illumined master, Sri Aurobindo Ghosh.

Deshmukh. The seven p.m. prayer hour found us back at Maganvadi ashram, climbing to the roof where thirty *satyagrahis* were grouped in a semicircle around Gandhi. He was squatting on a straw mat, an ancient pocket watch propped up before him. The fading sun cast a last gleam over the palms and banyans; the hum of night and the crickets had started. The atmosphere was serenity itself; I was enraptured.

A solemn chant led by Mr. Desai, with responses from the group; then a Gita reading. The Mahatma motioned to me to give the concluding prayer. Such divine unison of thought and aspiration! A memory forever: the Wardha rooftop meditation under the early stars.

Punctually at eight o'clock Gandhi ended his silence. The herculean labors of his life require him to apportion his time minutely.

"Welcome, Swamiji!" The Mahatma's greeting this time was not via paper. We had just descended from the roof to his writing room, simply furnished with square mats (no chairs), a low desk with books, papers, and a few ordinary pens (not fountain pens); a nondescript clock ticked in a corner. An all-pervasive aura of peace and devotion. Gandhi was bestowing one of his captivating, cavernous, almost toothless smiles.

"Years ago," he explained, "I started my weekly observance of a day of silence as a means for gaining time to look after my correspondence. But now those twenty-four hours have become a vital spiritual need. A periodical decree of silence is not a torture but a blessing."

I agreed wholeheartedly.* The Mahatma questioned me about America and Europe; we discussed India and world conditions.

"Mahadev," Gandhi said as Mr. Desai entered the room, "please make arrangements at Town Hall for Swamiji to speak there on yoga tomorrow night."

As I was bidding the Mahatma good night, he considerately handed me a bottle of citronella oil.

"The Wardha mosquitoes don't know a thing about *ahimsa,*† Swamiji!" he said, laughing.

The following morning our little group breakfasted early on whole-wheat porridge with molasses and milk. At ten-thirty we were called to the ashram porch for lunch with Gandhi and the *satyagrahis*. Today the menu included brown rice, a new selection of vegetables, and cardamom seeds.

---

* For years in America I had been observing periods of silence, to the consternation of callers and secretaries.

† Harmlessness; nonviolence; the foundation rock of Gandhi's creed. He was deeply influenced by the Jains, who revere *ahimsa* as the root virtue. Jainism, a sect of Hinduism, was widely spread in the sixth century B.C. by Mahavira, a contemporary of Buddha. May Mahavira ("great hero") look down the ages on his heroic son Gandhi!

Noon found me strolling about the ashram grounds, on to the grazing land of a few imperturbable cows. The protection of cows is a passion with Gandhi.

"The cow to me means the entire sub-human world, extending man's sympathies beyond his own species," the Mahatma has explained. "Man through the cow is enjoined to realize his identity with all that lives. Why the ancient rishis selected the cow for apotheosis is obvious to me. The cow in India was the best comparison; she was the giver of plenty. Not only did she give milk, but she also made agriculture possible. The cow is a poem of pity; one reads pity in the gentle animal. She is the second mother to millions of mankind. Protection of the cow means protection of the whole dumb creation of God. The appeal of the lower order of creation is all the more forceful because it is speechless."*

Certain daily rituals are enjoined on the orthodox Hindu. One is *Bhuta Yajna,* an offering of food to the animal kingdom. This ceremony symbolizes man's realization of his obligations to less evolved forms of creation—instinctively tied to body identification (a delusion that afflicts man also) but lacking the liberating quality of reason peculiar to humanity.

Bhuta Yajna thus reinforces man's readiness to succor the weak, as man in turn is comforted by countless solicitudes of higher unseen beings. Humanity is also under bond for rejuvenating gifts of Nature—prodigal in earth, sea, and sky. The evolutionary barrier of incommunicability among Nature, animals, man, and astral angels is surmounted by daily *yajnas* (rituals) of silent love.

Two other daily *yajnas* are *Pitri* and *Nri. Pitri Yajna* is an offering of oblations to ancestors: a symbol of man's acknowledgment of his debt to past generations, whose store of wisdom illumines humanity today. *Nri Yajna* is an offering of food to strangers or the poor: a symbol of the present responsibilities of man, his duties to contemporaries.

In the early afternoon I fulfilled a neighborly *Nri Yajna* by a visit to Gandhi's ashram for little girls. Mr. Wright accompanied me on the ten-minute drive. Tiny young flowerlike faces atop long-stemmed colorful *saris!* At the end of a brief talk in Hindi†

---

* Gandhi wrote beautifully on thousands of subjects. Of prayer he said: "It is a reminder to ourselves that we are helpless without God's support. No effort is complete without prayer, without a definite recognition that the best human endeavor is of no effect if it has not God's blessing behind it. Prayer is a call to humility. It is a call to self-purification, to inward search."

† Hindi is an Indo-Aryan language based largely on Sanskrit roots; it is the chief vernacular of northern India.

that I was giving outdoors, the skies unloosed a sudden downpour. Laughing, Mr. Wright and I climbed aboard the car and sped back to Maganvadi amidst sheets of driving silver. Such tropical intensity and splash!

Reentering the guest house I was struck anew by the stark simplicity and evidences of self-sacrifice which are everywhere present. The Gandhi vow of non-possession came early in his married life. Renouncing an extensive legal practice which had been yielding him an annual income of more than $20,000, the Mahatma dispersed all his wealth to the poor.

Sri Yukteswar used to poke gentle fun at the commonly inadequate conceptions of renunciation.

"A beggar cannot renounce wealth," Master would say. "If a man laments: 'My business has failed; my wife has left me; I will renounce all and enter a monastery,' to what worldly sacrifice is he referring? He did not renounce wealth and love; they renounced him!"

Saints like Gandhi, on the other hand, have made not only tangible material sacrifices, but also the more difficult renunciation of selfish motive and private goal, merging their inmost being in the stream of humanity as a whole.

The Mahatma's remarkable wife, Kasturbai, did not object when he failed to set aside any part of his wealth for the use of her and their children. Married in early youth, Gandhi and his wife took a vow of celibacy after the birth of four sons.* A tranquil heroine in the intense drama that has been their life together, Kasturbai has followed her husband to prison, shared his three-week fasts, and fully borne her share of his endless responsibilities. She has paid Gandhi the following tribute:

> I thank you for having had the privilege of being your life-long companion and helpmate. I thank you for the most perfect marriage in the world, based on *brahmacharya* (self-control) and

---

The main dialect of Western Hindi is Hindustani, written both in the *Devanagari* (Sanskrit) characters and in Arabic characters. Its subdialect, Urdu, is spoken by Moslems; and by Hindus in North India.

* Gandhi has described his life with devastating candor in *The Story of My Experiments with Truth* (Ahmedabad: Navajivan Press, 1927–28, in 2 vols.). This autobiography has been summarized in *Mahatma Gandhi, His Own Story*, edited by C. F. Andrews, with an introduction by John Haynes Holmes (New York: Macmillan Co., 1930).

Many autobiographies replete with famous names and colorful events are almost completely silent on any phase of inner analysis or development. One lays down each of these books with a certain dissatisfaction, as though saying: "Here is a man who knew many notable persons, but who never knew himself." This reaction is impossible with Gandhi's autobiography; he exposes his faults and subterfuges with an impersonal devotion to truth rare in annals of any age.

not on sex. I thank you for having considered me your equal in your life work for India. I thank you for not being one of those husbands who spend their time in gambling, racing, women, wine, and song, tiring of their wives and children as the little boy quickly tires of his childhood toys. How thankful I am that you were not one of those husbands who devote their time to growing rich on the exploitation of the labor of others.

How thankful I am that you put God and country before bribes, that you had the courage of your convictions and a complete and implicit faith in God. How thankful I am for a husband who put God and his country before me. I am grateful to you for your tolerance of me and my shortcomings of youth, when I grumbled and rebelled against the change you made in our mode of living, from so much to so little.

As a young child, I lived in your parents' home; your mother was a great and good woman; she trained me, taught me how to be a brave, courageous wife and how to keep the love and respect of her son, my future husband. As the years passed and you became India's most beloved leader, I had none of the fears that beset the wife who may be cast aside when her husband has climbed the ladder of success, as so often happens in other countries. I knew that death would still find us husband and wife.

For years Kasturbai performed the duties of treasurer of the public funds which the idolized Mahatma is able to raise by millions. Many humorous stories are told in Indian homes to the effect that husbands are nervous about their wives' wearing any jewelry to a Gandhi meeting; the Mahatma's magical tongue, pleading for the downtrodden, charms the gold bracelets and diamond necklaces right off the arms and necks of the wealthy into the collection basket!

One day the public treasurer, Kasturbai, could not account for a disbursement of four rupees. Gandhi duly published an auditing in which he inexorably pointed out his wife's four-rupee discrepancy.

I had often told this story before classes of my American students. One evening a woman in the hall had given an outraged gasp.

"Mahatma or no Mahatma," she had cried, "if he were my husband I would have given him a black eye for such an unnecessary public insult!"

After some good-humored banter had passed between us on the subject of American wives and Hindu wives, I had gone on to a fuller explanation.

"Mrs. Gandhi considers the Mahatma not as her husband but as her guru, one who has the right to discipline her for even insignificant errors," I had pointed out. "Some time after Kasturbai had been publicly rebuked, Gandhi was sentenced to prison on a political charge. As he was calmly bidding farewell to his wife, she fell at his feet. 'Master,' she said humbly, 'if I have ever offended you, please forgive me.'"

At three o'clock that afternoon in Wardha, I betook myself, by previous appointment, to the writing room of the saint who had been able to make an unflinching disciple out of his own wife—rare miracle! Gandhi looked up with his unforgettable smile.

"Mahatmaji," I said as I squatted beside him on the uncushioned mat, "please tell me your definition of *ahimsa.*"

"The avoidance of harm to any living creature in thought or deed."

"Beautiful ideal! But the world will always ask: May one not kill a cobra to protect a child, or one's self?"

"I could not kill a cobra without violating two of my vows—fearlessness, and non-killing. I would rather try inwardly to calm the snake by vibrations of love. I cannot possibly lower my standards to suit my circumstances." With his charming candor, he added, "I must confess that I could not serenely carry on this conversation were I faced by a cobra!"

I remarked on several very recent Western books on diet which lay on his desk.

"Yes, diet is important in the *Satyagraha* movement—as everywhere else," he said with a chuckle. "Because I advocate complete continence for *satyagrahis,* I am always trying to find out the best diet for the celibate. One must conquer the palate before he can control the procreative instinct. Semi-starvation or unbalanced diets are not the answer. After overcoming the inward *greed* for food, a *satyagrahi* must continue to follow a rational vegetarian diet with all necessary vitamins, minerals, calories, and so forth. By inward and outward wisdom in regard to eating, the *satyagrahi's* sexual fluid is easily turned into vital energy for the whole body."

The Mahatma and I compared our knowledge of good meat substitutes. "The avocado is excellent," I said. "There are numerous avocado groves near my center in California."

Gandhi's face lit with interest. "I wonder if they would grow in Wardha? The *satyagrahis* would appreciate a new food."

"I will be sure to send some avocado plants from Los Angeles to Wardha." I added, "Eggs are a high-protein food; are they forbidden to *satyagrahis?*"

"Not unfertilized eggs." The Mahatma laughed reminiscently. "For years I would not countenance their use; even now I personally do not eat them. One of my daughters-in-law was once dying of malnutrition; her doctor insisted on eggs. I would not agree, and advised him to give her some egg substitute.

"'Gandhiji,' the doctor said, 'unfertilized eggs contain no life sperm; no killing is involved.'

"I then gladly gave permission for my daughter-in-law to eat eggs; she was soon restored to health."

On the previous night Gandhi had expressed a wish to receive the *Kriya Yoga* of Lahiri Mahasaya. I was touched by the Mahatma's open-mindedness and spirit of inquiry. He is childlike in his divine quest, revealing that pure receptivity which Jesus praised in children, "...of such is the kingdom of heaven."

The hour for my promised instruction had arrived; several *satyagrahis* now entered the room — Mr. Desai, Dr. Pingale, and a few others who desired the *Kriya* technique.

I first taught the little class the physical Yogoda exercises. The body is visualized as divided into twenty parts; the will directs energy in turn to each section. Soon everyone was vibrating before me like a human motor. It was easy to observe the rippling effect on Gandhi's twenty body parts, at nearly all times completely exposed to view! Though very thin, he is not unpleasingly so; the skin of his body is smooth and unwrinkled.*

Later I initiated the group into the liberating technique of *Kriya Yoga.*

The Mahatma has reverently studied all world religions. The Jain scriptures, the Biblical New Testament, and the sociological writings of Tolstoy† are the three main sources of Gandhi's nonviolence convictions. He has stated his credo thus:

> I believe the Bible, the Koran, and the Zend-Avesta‡ to be as divinely inspired as the Vedas. I believe in the institution of Gurus, but in this age millions must go without a Guru, because it is a rare thing to find a combination of perfect purity and perfect learning. But one need not despair of ever knowing the truth of one's religion, because the fundamentals of Hinduism as of every great religion are unchangeable, and easily understood.
>
> I believe like every Hindu in God and His oneness, in rebirth and salvation....I can no more describe my feeling for Hinduism than for my own wife. She moves me as no other woman in the

---

* Gandhi has undergone many short and long fasts. He enjoys exceptionally good health. His books, *Diet and Diet Reform; Nature Cure;* and *Key to Health* are available from Navajivan Publishing House, Ahmedabad, India.

† Thoreau, Ruskin, and Mazzini are three other Western writers whose sociological views Gandhi has studied carefully.

‡ The sacred scripture given to Persia about 1000 B.C. by Zoroaster.

world can. Not that she has no faults; I daresay she has many more than I see myself. But the feeling of an indissoluble bond is there. Even so I feel for and about Hinduism with all its faults and limitations. Nothing delights me so much as the music of the Gita, or the *Ramayana* by Tulsidas. When I fancied I was taking my last breath, the Gita was my solace.

Hinduism is not an exclusive religion. In it there is room for the worship of all the prophets of the world.* It is not a missionary religion in the ordinary sense of the term. It has no doubt absorbed many tribes in its fold, but this absorption has been of an evolutionary, imperceptible character. Hinduism tells each man to worship God according to his own faith or *dharma*,† and so lives at peace with all religions.

Of Christ, Gandhi has written: "I am sure that if He were living here now among men, He would bless the lives of many who perhaps have never even heard His name...just as it is written: 'Not every one that saith unto me, Lord, Lord...but he that doeth the will of my Father.'‡ In the lesson of His own life, Jesus gave humanity the magnificent purpose and the single objective toward which we all ought to aspire. I believe that He belongs not solely to Christianity, but to the entire world, to all lands and races."

On my last evening in Wardha I addressed the meeting which had been called by Mr. Desai in Town Hall. The room was thronged to the windowsills with about 400 persons assembled to hear the talk on yoga. I spoke first in Hindi, then in English. Our little group returned to the ashram in time for a good-night glimpse of the Mahatma — deep in peace and correspondence.

Night was still lingering when I rose at five a.m. Village life was already stirring; first a bullock cart by the ashram gates, then a peasant with his huge burden balanced precariously on his head. After breakfast our trio sought out Gandhi for farewell *pranams*. The saint rises at four o'clock for his morning prayer.

"Mahatmaji, good-bye!" I knelt to touch his feet. "India is safe in your keeping."

* The unique feature of Hinduism among the world religions is that it derives not from a single great founder but from the impersonal Vedic scriptures. Hinduism thus gives scope for worshipful incorporation into its fold of prophets of all ages and all lands. The Vedic scriptures regulate not only devotional practices but all important social customs, in an effort to bring man's every action into harmony with divine law.

† A comprehensive Sanskrit word for law; conformity to law or natural righteousness; duty as inherent in the circumstances in which a man finds himself at any given time. The scriptures define *dharma* as "the natural universal laws whose observance enables man to save himself from degradation and suffering."

‡ Matthew 7:21.

Years have rolled by since the Wardha idyl; the earth, oceans, and skies have darkened with a world at war. Alone among great leaders, Gandhi has offered a practical nonviolent alternative to armed might. To redress grievances and remove injustices, the Mahatma has employed nonviolent means which again and again have proved their effectiveness. He states his doctrine in these words:

I have found that life persists in the midst of destruction. Therefore there must be a higher law than that of destruction. Only under that law would well-ordered society be intelligible and life worth living.

If that is the law of life we must work it out in daily existence. Wherever there are wars, wherever we are confronted with an opponent, conquer by love. I have found that the certain law of love has answered in my own life as the law of destruction has never done.

In India we have had an ocular demonstration of the operation of this law on the widest scale possible. I don't claim that nonviolence has penetrated the 360,000,000 people in India, but I do claim it has penetrated deeper than any other doctrine in an incredibly short time.

It takes a fairly strenuous course of training to attain a mental state of nonviolence. It is a disciplined life, like the life of a soldier. The perfect state is reached only when the mind, body, and speech are in proper coordination. Every problem would lend itself to solution if we determined to make the law of truth and nonviolence the law of life.

The grim march of world political events points inexorably to the truth that without spiritual vision, the people perish. Science, if not religion, has awakened in humanity a dim sense of the insecurity and even insubstantiality of all material things. Where indeed may man go now, if not to his Source and Origin, the Spirit within him?

Consulting history, one may reasonably state that man's problems have not been solved by the use of brute force. World War I produced an earth-chilling snowball of dread karma that swelled into World War II. Only the warmth of brotherhood can melt the present colossal snowball of sanguinary karma that may otherwise grow into World War III. Unholy twentieth-century trinity! Use of jungle logic instead of human reason in settling disputes will restore the earth to a jungle. If not brothers in life, then brothers in violent death. It was not for such ignominy that God lovingly permitted man to discover the release of atomic energies!

War and crime never pay. The billions of dollars that went up in the smoke of explosive nothingness would have been sufficient to have made a new world, one almost free from disease and completely free from poverty. Not an earth of fear, chaos, famine, pestilence, the *danse macabre*, but one broad land of peace, prosperity, and widening knowledge.

The nonviolent voice of Gandhi appeals to man's highest conscience. Let nations ally themselves no longer with death, but with life; not with destruction, but with construction; not with hate, but with the creative miracles of love.

"One should forgive, under any injury," says the *Mahabharata*. "It hath been said that the continuation of the species is due to man's being forgiving. Forgiveness is holiness; by forgiveness the universe is held together. Forgiveness is the might of the mighty; forgiveness is sacrifice; forgiveness is quiet of mind. Forgiveness and gentleness are the qualities of the Self-possessed. They represent eternal virtue."

Nonviolence is the natural outgrowth of the law of forgiveness and love. "If loss of life becomes necessary in a righteous battle," Gandhi proclaims, "one should be prepared, like Jesus, to shed his own, not others', blood. Eventually there will be less blood spilt in the world."

Epics shall someday be written on the Indian *satyagrahis* who withstood hate with love, violence with nonviolence, who allowed themselves to be mercilessly slaughtered rather than bear arms. The result on certain historic occasions was that opponents threw down their guns and fled—shamed, shaken to their depths by the sight of men who valued the lives of others above their own.

"I would wait, if need be for ages," Gandhi says, "rather than seek the freedom of my country through bloody means." The Bible warns us: "All they that take the sword shall perish with the sword."* The Mahatma has written:

> I call myself a nationalist, but my nationalism is as broad as the universe. It includes in its sweep all the nations of the earth.† My nationalism includes the well-being of the whole world. I do not want my India to rise on the ashes of other nations. I do not want India to exploit a single human being. I want India to be strong in order that she can infect the other nations also with her strength. Not so with a single nation in Europe today; they do not give strength to the others.

* Matthew 26:52. This is one of numerous passages in the Bible that necessarily imply the reincarnation of man. (See p. 151 n.) Many of life's complexities are explicable only through an understanding of the karmic law of justice.

† "Let not a man glory in this, that he love his country;
  Let him rather glory in this, that he love his kind."
                                                    —*Persian proverb*

MAHATMA GANDHI'S HANDWRITING, IN HINDI

[handwritten Hindi/Devanagari lines]

[signature in Devanagari]

Mahatma Gandhi visited Yogoda Satsanga Brahmacharya Vidyalaya, high school with yoga training in Ranchi, India. He graciously wrote the foregoing lines in the guest book. He said:

"This institution has deeply impressed my mind. I cherish high hopes that this school will further encourage the use of the spinning wheel."

September 17, 1925   [signed] Mohandas Gandhi

President Wilson mentioned his beautiful fourteen points, but said: "After all, if this endeavor of ours to arrive at peace fails, we have our armaments to fall back upon." I want to reverse that position, and I say: "Our armaments have failed already. Let us now be in search of something new; let us try the force of love and God which is truth." When we have got that, we shall want nothing else.

By the Mahatma's training of thousands of true *satyagrahis* (those who have taken the eleven rigorous vows mentioned in the first part of this chapter), who in turn spread the message; by patiently educating the Indian masses to understand the spiritual and eventually material benefits of nonviolence; by arming his people with nonviolent weapons—noncooperation with injustice, the willingness to endure indignities, prison, death itself rather than resort to arms; by enlisting world sympathy through countless examples of heroic martyrdom among *satyagrahis*, Gandhi has dramatically portrayed the practical nature of nonviolence, its solemn power to settle disputes without war.

Gandhi has already won through nonviolent means a greater number of political concessions for his land than any other leader of a country has ever won except through bullets. Nonviolent methods for eradication of all wrongs and evils have been strikingly applied not only in the political arena but in the delicate and complicated field of Indian social reform. Gandhi and his followers have removed many long-standing feuds between Hindus and Moham-medans; hundreds of thousands of Moslems look to the Mahatma as their leader. The untouchables have found in him their fearless and triumphant champion. "If there be a rebirth in store for me," Gandhi wrote, "I wish to be born a pariah in the midst of pariahs, because thereby I would be able to render them more effective service."

The Mahatma is indeed a "great soul," but it was illiterate millions who had the discernment to bestow the title. This gentle prophet is honored in his own land. The lowly peasant has been able to rise to Gandhi's high challenge. The Mahatma wholeheart-edly believes in the inherent nobility of man. The inevitable fail-ures have never disillusioned him. "Even if the opponent plays him false twenty times," he writes, "the *satyagrahi* is ready to trust him the twenty-first time, for an implicit trust in human nature is the very essence of the creed."*

"Mahatmaji, you are an exceptional man. You must not expect the world to act as you do." A critic once made this observation.

"It is curious how we delude ourselves, fancying that the body can be improved, but that it is impossible to evoke the hidden pow-ers of the soul," Gandhi replied. "I am engaged in trying to show that if I have any of those powers, I am as frail a mortal as any of us and that I never had anything extraordinary about me nor have I now. I am a simple individual liable to err like any other fellow mortal. I own, however, that I have enough humility to confess my errors and to retrace my steps. I own that I have an immov-able faith in God and His goodness, and an unconsumable passion for truth and love. But is that not what every person has latent in him?" He added: "If we may make new discoveries and inventions in the phenomenal world, must we declare our bankruptcy in the spiritual domain? Is it impossible to multiply the exceptions so as to make them the rule? Must man always be brute first and man after, if at all?"†

---

* "Then came Peter to him and said, Lord, how oft shall my brother sin against me, and I forgive him? till seven times? Jesus saith unto him, I say not unto thee, Until seven times: but, Until seventy times seven." —Matthew 18:21–22. I prayed deeply to understand this uncompromising counsel. "Lord," I protested, "is it possible?" When the Divine Voice finally responded, It brought a humbling flood of light:

"How many times, O Man, do I forgive each of you daily?"

† Charles P. Steinmetz, the great electrical engineer, was once asked by Mr. Roger W. Babson: "What line of research will see the greatest development during the next fifty years?" "I think the greatest discovery will be made along spiritual lines," Steinmetz replied. "Here is a force which history clearly teaches has been the greatest power in the development of men. Yet we have merely been playing with it and have never

Americans may well remember with pride the successful nonviolence experiment of William Penn, in founding his 17th-century colony in Pennsylvania. There were "no forts, no soldiers, no militia, even no arms." Amidst the savage frontier wars and the butcheries that went on between the new settlers and the Red Indians, the Quakers of Pennsylvania alone remained unmolested. "Others were slain; others were massacred; but they were safe. Not a Quaker woman suffered assault; not a Quaker child was slain, not a Quaker man was tortured." When the Quakers were finally forced to give up the government of the state, "war broke out, and some Pennsylvanians were killed. But only three Quakers were killed, three who had so far fallen from their faith as to carry weapons of defence."

"Resort to force in the Great War (I) failed to bring tranquillity," Franklin D. Roosevelt pointed out. "Victory and defeat were alike sterile. That lesson the world should have learned."

"The more weapons of violence, the more misery to mankind," Lao-tzu taught. "The triumph of violence ends in a festival of mourning."

"I am fighting for nothing less than world peace," Gandhi has declared. "If the Indian movement is carried to success on a nonviolent *Satyagraha* basis, it will give a new meaning to patriotism and, if I may say so in all humility, to life itself."

Before the West dismisses Gandhi's program as one of an impractical dreamer, let it first reflect on a definition of *Satyagraha* by the Master of Galilee:

"Ye have heard that it hath been said, An eye for an eye, and a tooth for a tooth: but I say unto you, That ye resist not evil [with evil]: but whosoever shall smite thee on thy right cheek, turn to him the other also."*

Gandhi's epoch has extended, with the beautiful precision of cosmic timing, into a century already desolated and devastated by two World Wars. A divine handwriting appears on the granite wall of his life: a warning against the further shedding of blood among brothers.

---

seriously studied it as we have the physical forces. Someday people will learn that material things do not bring happiness and are of little use in making men and women creative and powerful. Then the scientists of the world will turn their laboratories over to the study of God and prayer and the spiritual forces which as yet have hardly been scratched. When this day comes, the world will see more advancement in one generation than it has seen in the past four."

* Matthew 5:38–39.

Mahatma Gandhi
In Memoriam

"He was in the true sense the father of the nation, and a madman has slain him. Millions and millions are mourning because the light has gone out....The light that shone in this land was no ordinary light. For a thousand years that light will be seen in this country, and the world will see it." So spoke Prime Minister of India Jawaharlal Nehru shortly after Mahatma Gandhi had been assassinated in New Delhi on January 30, 1948.

Five months earlier, India had peacefully achieved her national independence. The work of the 78-year-old Gandhi was done; he realized that his hour was nigh. "Abha, bring me all the important papers," he said to his grandniece on the morning of the tragedy. "I must reply today. Tomorrow may never be." In numerous passages of his writings, also, Gandhi gave intimations of his final destiny.

As the dying Mahatma sank slowly to the ground, three bullets in his frail and fast-worn body, he lifted his hands in the traditional Hindu gesture of greeting, silently bestowing his forgiveness. Innocent artist as he was in all the ways of his life, Gandhi became a supreme artist at the moment of his death. All the sacrifices of his selfless life had made possible that final loving gesture.

"Generations to come, it may be," Albert Einstein wrote in a tribute to the Mahatma, "will scarce believe that such a one as this ever in flesh and blood walked upon the earth." A dispatch from the Vatican in Rome said: "The assassination caused great sorrow here. Gandhi is mourned as an apostle of Christian virtues."

Fraught with symbolic meaning are the lives of all great ones who come to earth for the accomplishment of a specific righteousness. Gandhi's dramatic death in the cause of Indian unity has highlighted his message to a world torn in every continent with disunity. That message he has stated in prophetic words:

"Nonviolence has come among men and it will live. It is the harbinger of the peace of the world."

CHAPTER 45

The Bengali
"Joy-Permeated Mother"

"Sir, please do not leave India without a glimpse of Nirmala Devi. Her sanctity is intense; she is known far and wide as Ananda Moyi Ma (Joy-Permeated Mother)." My niece, Amiyo Bose, gazed at me earnestly.

"Of course! I want very much to see the woman saint." I added, "I have read of her advanced state of God-realization. A little article about her appeared years ago in *East-West.*"

"I have met her," Amiyo went on. "She recently visited my own small town of Jamshedpur. At the entreaty of a disciple, Ananda Moyi Ma went to the home of a dying man. She stood by his bedside; as her hand touched his forehead, his death-rattle ceased. The disease vanished at once; to the man's glad astonishment, he was well."

A few days later I heard that the Blissful Mother was staying at the home of a disciple in the Bhowanipur section of Calcutta. Mr. Wright and I set out immediately from my father's Calcutta home. As the Ford neared the Bhowanipur house, my companion and I observed an unusual street scene.

Ananda Moyi Ma was standing in an open-topped automobile, blessing a throng of about one hundred disciples. She was evidently on the point of departure. Mr. Wright parked the Ford some distance away, and accompanied me on foot toward the quiet assemblage. The woman saint glanced in our direction; she alit from her car and walked toward us.

"Father, you have come!" With these fervent words (in Bengali) she put her arm around my neck and her head on my shoulder. Mr. Wright, to whom I had just remarked that I did not know the saint, was hugely enjoying this extraordinary demonstration of welcome. The eyes of the hundred *chelas* were also fixed with some surprise on the affectionate tableau.

I had instantly seen that the saint was in a high state of *samadhi.* Oblivious to her outward garb as a woman, she knew herself as the changeless soul; from that plane she was joyously greeting another devotee of God. She led me by the hand into her automobile.

"Ananda Moyi Ma, I am delaying your journey!" I protested.

"Father, I am meeting you for the first time in this life,* after ages!" she said. "Please do not leave yet."

We sat together in the rear seats of the car. The Blissful Mother soon entered the immobile ecstatic state. Her beautiful eyes glanced heavenward and, half-opened, became stilled, gazing into the near-far inner Elysium. The disciples chanted gently: "Victory to Mother Divine!"

I had found many men of God-realization in India, but never before had I met such an exalted woman saint. Her gentle face was burnished with the ineffable joy that had given her the name of Blissful Mother. Long black tresses lay loosely behind her unveiled head. A red dot of sandalwood paste on her forehead symbolized the spiritual eye, ever open within her. Tiny face, tiny hands, tiny feet—a contrast to her spiritual magnitude!

I put some questions to a nearby woman *chela* while Ananda Moyi Ma remained entranced.

"The Blissful Mother travels widely in India; in many parts she has hundreds of disciples," the *chela* told me. "Her courageous efforts have brought about many desirable social reforms. Although a *Brahmin*, the saint recognizes no caste distinctions. A group of us always travels with her, looking after her comforts. We have to mother her; she takes no notice of her body. If no one gave her food, she would not eat or make any inquiries. Even when meals are placed before her, she does not touch them. To prevent her disappearance from this world, we disciples feed her with our own hands. For days together she often stays in the divine trance, scarcely breathing, her eyes unwinking. One of her chief disciples is her husband, Bholanath. Many years ago, soon after their marriage, he took the vow of silence."

The *chela* pointed to a broad-shouldered, fine-featured man with long hair and hoary beard. He was standing quietly in the midst of the gathering, his hands folded in a disciple's reverential attitude.

Refreshed by her dip in the Infinite, Ananda Moyi Ma was now focusing her consciousness on the material world.

"Father, please tell me where you stay." Her voice was clear and melodious.

* Ananda Moyi Ma was born in 1896 in the village of Kheora in the Tripura District of east Bengal.

"At present, in Calcutta or Ranchi; but soon I shall be returning to America."

"America?"

"Yes. An Indian woman saint would be sincerely appreciated there by spiritual seekers. Would you like to go?"

"If Father can take me, I will go."

This reply caused her nearby disciples to start in alarm.

"Twenty or more of us always travel with the Blissful Mother," one of them told me firmly. "We could not live without her. Wherever she goes, we must go."

Reluctantly I abandoned the plan, as possessing an impractical feature of spontaneous enlargement!

"Please come at least to Ranchi, with your devotees," I said on taking leave of the saint. "As a divine child yourself, you will enjoy the little ones in my school."

"Whenever Father takes me, I will gladly go."

A short time later the Ranchi Vidyalaya was in gala array for the saint's promised visit. The youngsters looked forward to any day of festivity—no lessons, hours of music, and a feast for the climax!

"Victory! Ananda Moyi Ma, ki jai!" This reiterated chant from scores of enthusiastic little throats greeted the saint's party as it entered the school gates. Showers of marigolds, tinkle of cymbals, lusty blowing of conch shells and beat of the *mridanga* drum! The Blissful Mother wandered smilingly over the sunny Vidyalaya grounds, ever carrying within her heart the portable paradise.

"It is beautiful here," Ananda Moyi Ma said graciously as I led her into the main building. She seated herself with a childlike smile by my side. The closest of dear friends, she made one feel, yet an aura of remoteness was ever around her—the paradoxical isolation of Omnipresence.

"Please tell me something of your life."

"Father knows all about it; why repeat it?" She evidently felt that the factual history of one short incarnation was beneath notice.

I laughed, gently repeating my request.

"Father, there is little to tell." She spread her graceful hands in a deprecatory gesture. "My consciousness has never associated itself with this temporary body. Before I* came on this earth, Father, 'I was

---

* Ananda Moyi Ma does not refer to herself as "I"; she uses humble circumlocutions like "this body" or "this little girl" or "your daughter." Nor does she refer to anyone as her "disciple." With impersonal wisdom she bestows equally on all human beings the divine love of the Universal Mother.

the same.' As a little girl, 'I was the same.' I grew into womanhood;
still 'I was the same.' When the family in which I had been born
made arrangements to have this body married, 'I was the same.' And,
Father, in front of you now, 'I am the same.' Ever afterward, though
the dance of creation change around me in the hall of eternity, 'I shall
be the same.'"

Ananda Moyi Ma sank into a deep meditative state. Her form
was statue-still; she had fled to her ever calling kingdom. The dark
pools of her eyes appeared lifeless and glassy. This expression is
often present when saints remove their consciousness from the
physical body, which is then hardly more than a piece of soulless
clay. We sat together for an hour in the ecstatic trance. She returned
to this world with a gay little laugh.

"Please, Ananda Moyi Ma," I said, "come with me to the garden. Mr. Wright will take some pictures."

"Of course, Father. Your will is my will." Her glorious eyes
retained an unchanging divine luster as she posed for many photographs.

Time for the feast! Ananda Moyi Ma squatted on her blanket-
seat, a disciple at her elbow to feed her. Like an infant, the saint
obediently swallowed the food after the *chela* had brought it to her
lips. It was plain that the Blissful Mother did not recognize any difference between curries and sweetmeats!

As dusk approached, the saint left with her party amidst a
shower of rose petals, her hands raised in blessing on the little lads.
Their faces shone with the affection she had effortlessly awakened.

"Thou shalt love the Lord thy God with all thy heart, and with
all thy soul, and with all thy mind, and with all thy strength,"
Christ has proclaimed; "this is the first commandment."*

Casting aside every inferior attachment, Ananda Moyi Ma offers
her sole allegiance to the Lord. Not by the hair-splitting distinctions of scholars but by the sure logic of faith, the childlike saint
has solved the only problem in human life—establishment of unity
with God.

Man has forgotten this stark simplicity, now befogged by a million issues. Refusing a monotheistic love to the Creator, nations try
to disguise their infidelity by punctilious respect before the outward
shrines of charity. These humanitarian gestures are virtuous, because for a moment they divert man's attention from himself; but
they do not free him from his prime responsibility in life, referred

---

* Mark 12:30.

to by Jesus as the "first commandment." The uplifting obligation to love God is assumed with man's earliest breath of an air freely bestowed by his only Benefactor.*

On one other occasion after her visit to the Ranchi school I had opportunity to see Ananda Moyi Ma. She stood with a group some months later on the Serampore station platform, waiting for the train.

"Father, I am going to the Himalayas," she told me. "Some kind persons have built for us a hermitage in Dehra Dun."

As she boarded the train, I marveled to see that whether amidst a crowd, on a train, feasting, or sitting in silence, her eyes never looked away from God.

Within me I still hear her voice, an echo of measureless sweetness:

"Behold, now and always one with the Eternal, 'I am ever the same.'"

---

* "Many feel the urge to create a new and better world. Rather than let your thoughts dwell on such matters, you should concentrate on That by the contemplation of which there is hope of perfect peace. It is man's duty to become a seeker after God or Truth."—*Ananda Moyi Ma.*

CHAPTER 46

The Woman Yogi Who Never Eats

"Sir, whither are we bound this morning?" Mr. Wright was driving the Ford; he took his eyes off the road long enough to gaze at me with a questioning twinkle. From day to day he seldom knew what part of Bengal he would be discovering next.

"God willing," I replied devoutly, "we are on our way to see an eighth wonder of the world—a woman saint whose diet is thin air!"

"Repetition of wonders—after Therese Neumann." But Mr. Wright laughed eagerly just the same; he even accelerated the speed of the car. More extraordinary grist for his travel diary! Not one of an average tourist, that!

The Ranchi school had just been left behind us; we had risen before the sun. Besides my secretary and me, three Bengali friends were in the party. We drank in the exhilarating air, the natural wine of the morning. Our driver guided the car warily among the early peasants and the two-wheeled carts, slowly drawn by yoked, hump-shouldered bullocks, inclined to dispute the road with a honking interloper.

"Sir, we would like to know more of the fasting saint."

"Her name is Giri Bala," I informed my companions. "I first heard about her years ago from a scholarly gentleman, Sthiti Lal Nundy. He often came to the Garpar Road home to tutor my brother Bishnu.

"'I know Giri Bala well,' Sthiti Babu told me. 'She employs a certain yoga technique that enables her to live without eating. I was her close neighbor in Nawabganj near Ichapur.* I made it a point to watch her closely; never did I find evidence that she was taking either food or drink. My interest finally mounted so high that I approached the Maharaja of Burdwan† and asked him to conduct an investigation. Astounded at the story, he invited her to his palace. She agreed to a test and lived for two months locked up in a small

---

* In northern Bengal.

† H.H. Sir Bijay Chand Mahtab, now dead. His family doubtless possesses some record of the Maharaja's three investigations of Giri Bala.

section of his home. Later she returned for a palace visit of twenty days; and then for a third test of fifteen days. The Maharaja himself told me that these three rigorous scrutinies had convinced him beyond doubt of her non-eating state.'

"This story of Sthiti Babu's has remained in my mind for over twenty-five years," I concluded. "Sometimes in America I wondered if the river of time would not swallow the yogini* before I could meet her. She must be quite aged now. I do not even know where, or if, she lives. But in a few hours we shall reach Purulia; her brother has a home there."

By ten-thirty our little group was conversing with the brother, Lambodar Dey, a lawyer of Purulia.

"Yes, my sister is living. She sometimes stays with me here, but at present she is at our family home in Biur." Lambodar Babu glanced doubtfully at the Ford. "I hardly think, Swamiji, that any automobile has ever penetrated into the interior as far as Biur. It might be best if you all resign yourselves to the jolts of a bullock cart."

As one voice our party pledged loyalty to the Pride of Detroit.

"The Ford comes from America," I told the lawyer. "It would be a shame to deprive it of an opportunity to get acquainted with the heart of Bengal!"

"May Ganesh† go with you!" Lambodar Babu said, laughing. He added courteously, "If you ever get there, I am sure Giri Bala will be glad to see you. She is approaching her seventies, but continues in excellent health."

"Please, tell me, sir, if it is absolutely true that she eats nothing?" I looked directly into his eyes, those telltale windows of the mind.

"It is true." His gaze was open and honorable. "In more than five decades I have never seen her eat a morsel. If the world suddenly came to an end, I could not be more astonished than by the sight of my sister's taking food!"

We chuckled together over the improbability of these two cosmic events.

"Giri Bala has never sought an inaccessible solitude for her yoga practices," Lambodar Babu went on. "She has lived her entire life surrounded by her family and friends. They are all well accustomed now to her strange state—not one of them who would not be stupefied if Giri Bala suddenly decided to eat anything! Sister is naturally retiring, as befits a Hindu widow, but our little circle in Purulia and

* Woman yogi.
† "Remover of Obstacles," the god of good fortune.

in Biur all know that she is literally an 'exceptional' woman."

The brother's sincerity was manifest. Our little party thanked him warmly and set out toward Biur. We stopped at a street shop for curry and *luchis*, attracting a swarm of urchins who gathered round to watch Mr. Wright eating with his fingers in the simple Hindu manner.* Hearty appetites caused us to fortify ourselves against an afternoon which, unknown to us at the moment, was to prove fairly laborious.

Our way now led east through sun-baked rice fields into the Burdwan section of Bengal. On through roads lined with dense vegetation; the songs of the mynas and the stripe-throated bulbuls streamed out from trees with huge, umbrellalike branches. A bullock cart now and then, the *rini, rini, manju, manju* squeak of its axle and iron-shod wooden wheels contrasting sharply in mind with the *swish, swish* of auto tires over the aristocratic asphalt of the cities.

"Dick, halt!" My sudden request brought a jolting protest from the Ford. "That overburdened mango tree is fairly shouting an invitation!"

The five of us dashed like children to the mango-strewn earth; the tree had benevolently shed its fruits as they had ripened.

"Full many a mango is born to lie unseen," I paraphrased, "and waste its sweetness on the stony ground."

"Nothing like this in America, Swamiji, eh?" laughed Sailesh Mazumdar, one of my Bengali students.

"No," I admitted, filled with mangoes and contentment. "How I have missed this fruit in the West! A Hindu's heaven without mangoes is inconceivable!"

I hurled a rock and downed a proud beauty from the highest limb.

"Dick," I asked between bites of ambrosia, warm with the tropical sun, "are all the cameras in the car?"

"Yes, sir, in the baggage compartment."

"If Giri Bala proves to be a true saint, I want to write about her in the West. A Hindu yogini with such inspiring powers should not live and die unknown—like most of these mangoes."

Half an hour later I was still strolling in the sylvan peace.

"Sir," Mr. Wright remarked, "we should reach Giri Bala before the sun sets, to have enough light for photographs." He added with

---

* Sri Yukteswar used to say: "The Lord has given us the fruits of the good earth. We like to see our food, to smell it, to taste it—the Hindu likes also to touch it!" One does not mind *hearing* it, either, if no one else is present at the meal!

a grin, "Westerners are a skeptical lot; we can't expect them to believe in the lady without any pictures!"

This bit of wisdom was indisputable; I turned my back on temptation and reentered the car.

"You are right, Dick," I sighed as we sped along. "I sacrifice the mango paradise on the altar of Western realism. Photographs we must have!"

The road became more and more sickly: wrinkles of ruts, boils of hardened clay—the sad infirmities of old age. Our group dismounted occasionally to allow Mr. Wright more easily to maneuver the Ford, which the rest of us pushed from behind.

"Lambodar Babu spoke truly," Sailesh acknowledged. "The car is not carrying us; we are carrying the car!"

Our climb-in, climb-out auto tedium was beguiled ever and anon by the appearance of a village, each one a scene of quaint simplicity.

"Our way twisted and turned through groves of palms among ancient, unspoiled villages nestling in the forest shade," Mr. Wright recorded in his travel diary, under date of May 5, 1936. "Very fascinating are these clusters of thatched mud huts, decorated with one of the names of God on the door; many small, naked children innocently playing about, pausing to stare or run wildly from this big, black, bullockless carriage tearing madly through their village. The women merely peep from the shadows, while the men lazily loll beneath the trees along the roadside, curious beneath their nonchalance. In one place, all the villagers were gaily bathing in the large tank (in their garments, changing by draping dry cloths around their bodies, dropping the wet ones). Women bearing water to their homes, in huge brass jars.

"The road led us a merry chase over mount and ridge; we bounced and tossed, dipped into small streams, detoured around an unfinished causeway, slithered across dry, sandy riverbeds; and finally, at about five p.m., we were close to our destination, Biur. This small village in the interior of Bankura District, hidden in the protection of dense foliage, is unapproachable by travelers in the rainy season, we were told; then the streams are raging torrents and the roads serpentlike spit mud venom.

"Asking for a guide among a group of worshipers on their way home from a temple prayer (out in the lonely field), we were besieged by a dozen scantily clad lads who clambered on the sides of the car, eager to conduct us to Giri Bala.

"The road led toward a grove of date palms sheltering a group of mud huts, but before we had reached it, the Ford was momentarily tipped at a dangerous angle, tossed up and dropped down. The narrow trail led around trees and tanks, over ridges, into holes and deep ruts. The car became anchored on a clump of bushes, then grounded on a hillock, requiring a lift of earth clods; on we proceeded, slowly and carefully; suddenly the way was stopped by a mass of brush in the middle of the cart track, necessitating a detour down a precipitous ledge into a dry tank, rescue from which demanded some scraping, adzing, and shoveling. Again and again the road seemed impassable, but the pilgrimage must go on; obliging lads fetched spades and demolished the obstacles (blessings of Ganesh!) while hundreds of children and parents stared.

"Soon we were threading our way along the two ruts of antiquity, women gazing wide-eyed from their hut doors, men trailing alongside and behind us, children scampering to swell the procession. Ours was perhaps the first auto to traverse these roads; the 'bullock cart union' must be omnipotent here! What a sensation we created—a group piloted by an American and pioneering in a snorting car right into their hamlet fastness, invading the ancient privacy and sanctity!

"Halting by a narrow lane we found ourselves within a hundred feet of Giri Bala's ancestral home. We felt the thrill of fulfillment after the long road struggle crowned by a rough finish. We approached a large, two-storied building of brick and plaster, dominating the surrounding adobe huts; the house was under the process of repair, for around it was the characteristically tropical framework of bamboo.

"With feverish anticipation and suppressed rejoicing we stood before the open doors of the one blessed by the Lord's 'hungerless' touch. Constantly agape were the villagers, young and old, bare and dressed, women aloof somewhat but inquisitive too, men and boys unabashedly at our heels as they gazed on this unprecedented spectacle.

"Soon a short figure came into view in the doorway—Giri Bala! She was swathed in a cloth of dull, goldish silk; in typically Indian fashion, she drew forward modestly and hesitatingly, peering at us from beneath the upper fold of her *swadeshi* cloth. Her eyes glistened like smoldering embers from the shadows of her headpiece; we were enamored by a face of benevolence and Self-realization, free from the taint of earthly attachment.

"Meekly she approached and silently assented to our snapping a number of pictures with our 'still' and 'movie' cameras.* Patiently and shyly she endured our photo techniques of posture adjustment and light arrangement. Finally we had recorded for posterity many photographs of the only woman in the world who is known to have lived without food or drink for over fifty years. (Therese Neumann, of course, has fasted since 1923.) Most motherly was Giri Bala's expression as she stood before us, completely covered in the loose-flowing cloth, nothing of her body visible but her face with its downcast eyes, her hands, and her tiny feet. A face of rare peace and innocent poise—a wide, childlike, quivering lip, a feminine nose, narrow, sparkling eyes, and a wistful smile."

Mr. Wright's impression of Giri Bala was shared by me; spirituality enfolded her like her gently shining veil. She *pranamed* before me in the customary gesture of greeting from a householder to a monk. Her simple charm and quiet smile gave us a welcome beyond that of honeyed oratory; forgotten was our difficult, dusty trip.

The little saint seated herself cross-legged on the verandah. Though bearing the scars of age, she was not emaciated; her olive-colored skin had remained clear and healthy in tone.

"Mother," I said in Bengali, "for over twenty-five years I have thought eagerly of this very pilgrimage! I heard about your sacred life from Sthiti Lal Nundy Babu."

She nodded in acknowledgment. "Yes, my good neighbor in Nawabganj."

"During those years I have crossed the oceans, but never forgot my plan someday to see you. The sublime drama that you are here playing so inconspicuously should be blazoned before a world that has long forgotten the inner food divine."

The saint lifted her eyes for a minute, smiling with serene interest.

"Baba (honored father) knows best," she answered meekly.

I was happy that she had taken no offense; one never knows how yogis and yoginis will react to the thought of publicity. They shun it, as a rule, wishing to pursue in silence the profound soul research. An inner sanction comes to them when the proper time arrives to display their lives openly for the benefit of seeking minds.

"Mother," I went on, "forgive me, then, for burdening you with many questions. Kindly answer only those that please you; I shall

---

* Mr. Wright also took moving pictures of Sri Yukteswar during his last Winter Solstice Festival in Serampore.

understand your silence, also."

She spread her hands in a gracious gesture. "I am glad to reply, insofar as an insignificant person like myself can give satisfactory answers."

"Oh, no, not insignificant!" I protested sincerely. "You are a great soul."

"I am the humble servant of all." She added quaintly, "I love to cook, and to feed people."

A strange pastime, I thought, for a non-eating saint!

"Tell me, Mother, from your own lips—do you live without food?"

"That is true." She was silent for a few moments; her next remark showed that she had been struggling with mental arithmetic. "From the age of twelve years four months down to my present age of sixty-eight—a period of over fifty-six years—I have not eaten food or taken liquids."

"Are you never tempted to eat?"

"If I felt a craving for food, I would have to eat." Simply yet regally she stated this axiomatic truth, one known too well by a world revolving around three meals a day!

"But you do eat something!" My tone held a note of remonstrance.

"Of course!" She smiled in swift understanding.

"Your nourishment is derived from the finer energies of the air and sunlight,* and from the cosmic power that recharges your body through the medulla oblongata."

---

* "What we eat is radiation; our food is so much quanta of energy," Dr. Geo. W. Crile of Cleveland told a gathering of medical men on May 17, 1933, in Memphis. Parts of his speech were reported as follows:

"This all-important radiation, which releases electrical currents for the body's electrical circuit, the nervous system, is given to food by the sun's rays. Atoms, Dr. Crile says, are solar systems. Atoms are the vehicles that are filled with solar radiance as so many coiled springs. These countless atomfuls of energy are taken in as food. Once in the human body, these tense vehicles, the atoms, are discharged in the body's protoplasm, the radiance furnishing new chemical energy, new electrical currents. 'Your body is made up of such atoms,' Dr. Crile said. 'They are your muscles, brains, and sensory organs, such as the eyes and ears.'"

Someday scientists will discover how man can live directly on solar energy. "Chlorophyll is the only substance known in nature that somehow possesses the power to act as a 'sunlight trap,'" William L. Laurence writes in *The New York Times*. "It 'catches' the energy of sunlight and stores it in the plant. Without this no life could exist. We obtain the energy we need for living from the solar energy stored in the plant-food we eat or in the flesh of the animals that eat the plants. The energy we obtain from coal or oil is solar energy trapped by the chlorophyll in plant life millions of years ago. We live by the sun through the agency of chlorophyll."

"Baba knows." Again she acquiesced, her manner soothing and unemphatic.

"Mother, please tell me about your early life. It holds a deep interest for all of India, and even for our brothers and sisters beyond the seas."

Giri Bala put aside her habitual reserve, relaxing into a conversational mood.

"So be it." Her voice was low and firm. "I was born in these forest regions. My childhood was unremarkable save that I was possessed by an insatiable appetite.

"I had been betrothed when I was about nine years old.

"'Child,' my mother often warned me, 'try to control your greed. When the time comes for you to live among strangers in your husband's family, what will they think of you if your days are spent in nothing but eating?'

"The calamity she had foreseen came to pass. I was only twelve when I joined my husband's people in Nawabganj. My mother-in-law shamed me morning, noon, and night about my gluttonous habits. Her scoldings were a blessing in disguise, however; they roused my dormant spiritual tendencies. One morning her ridicule was merciless.

"'I shall soon prove to you,' I said, stung to the quick, 'that I shall never touch food again as long as I live.'

"My mother-in-law laughed in derision. 'So!' she said, 'how can you live without eating, when you cannot live without overeating?'

"This remark was unanswerable. Yet an iron resolution had entered my heart. In a secluded spot I sought my Heavenly Father.

"'Lord,' I prayed incessantly, 'please send me a guru, one who can teach me to live by Thy light and not by food.'

"An ecstasy fell over me. In a beatific spell I set out for the Nawabganj *ghat* on the Ganges. On the way I encountered the priest of my husband's family.

"'Venerable sir,' I said trustingly, 'kindly tell me how to live without eating.'

"He stared at me without reply. Finally he spoke in a consoling manner. 'Child,' he said, 'come to the temple this evening; I will conduct a special Vedic ceremony for you.'

"This vague answer was not the one I was seeking; I continued toward the *ghat*. The morning sun pierced the waters; I purified myself in the Ganges, as though for a sacred initiation. As I left the riverbank, my wet cloth around me, in the broad glare of day my master materialized himself before me!

"'Dear little one,' he said in a voice of loving compassion, 'I am the guru sent here by God to fulfill your urgent prayer. He was deeply touched by its very unusual nature! From today you shall live by the astral light; your bodily atoms shall be recharged by the infinite current.'"

Giri Bala fell into silence. I took Mr. Wright's pencil and pad and translated into English a few items for his information.

The saint resumed the tale, her gentle voice barely audible. "The *ghat* was deserted, but my guru cast round us an aura of guarding light, that no stray bathers later disturb us. He initiated me into a *kria* technique that frees the body from dependence on the gross food of mortals. The technique includes the use of a certain *mantra** and a breathing exercise more difficult than the average person could perform. No medicine or magic is involved; nothing beyond the *kria*."

In the manner of the American newspaper reporter, who had unknowingly taught me his procedure, I questioned Giri Bala on many matters that I thought would be of interest to the world. She gave me, bit by bit, the following information:

"I have never had any children; many years ago I became a widow. I sleep very little, as sleep and waking are the same to me. I meditate at night, attending to my domestic duties in the daytime. I slightly feel the change in climate from season to season. I have never been sick or experienced any disease. I feel only slight pain when accidentally injured. I have no bodily excretions. I can control my heartbeat and breathing. In visions I often see my guru and other great souls."

"Mother," I asked, "why don't you teach others the method of living without food?"

My ambitious hopes for the world's starving millions were quickly shattered.

"No." She shook her head. "I was strictly commanded by my guru not to divulge the secret. It is not his wish to tamper with God's drama of creation. The farmers would not thank me if I taught many people to live without eating! The luscious fruits would lie

---

* Potent vibratory chant. The literal translation of Sanskrit *mantra* is "instrument of thought." It signifies "the ideal, inaudible sounds which represent one aspect of creation; when vocalized as syllables, a *mantra* constitutes a universal terminology" (Webster's New International Dictionary, 2nd ed.). The infinite powers of sound are derived from *Aum*, the "Word" or creative hum of the Cosmic Motor.

uselessly on the ground. It appears that misery, starvation, and disease are whips of our karma that ultimately drive us to seek the true meaning of life."

"Mother," I said slowly, "what is the use of your having been singled out to live without eating?"

"To prove that man is Spirit." Her face lit with wisdom. "To demonstrate that by divine advancement he can gradually learn to live by the Eternal Light and not by food."*

The saint sank into a deep meditative state. Her gaze was directed inward; the gentle depths of her eyes became expressionless. She gave a certain sigh, the prelude to the ecstatic breathless trance. For a time she had fled to the questionless realm, the heaven of inner joy.

The tropical darkness had fallen. The light of a small kerosene lamp flickered fitfully over the heads of many villagers squatting silently in the shadows. The darting glowworms and distant oil lanterns of the huts wove bright eerie patterns into the velvet night. It was the painful hour of parting; a slow, tedious journey lay before our little party.

"Giri Bala," I said as the saint opened her eyes, "please give me a keepsake—a strip from one of your *saris*."

She soon returned with a piece of Banaras silk, extending it in her hand as she suddenly prostrated herself on the ground.

"Mother," I said reverently, "rather let me touch your own blessed feet!"

---

* The non-eating state attained by Giri Bala is a yogic power mentioned in Patanjali's *Yoga Sutras* III:31. She employs a certain breathing exercise that affects the *vishuddha chakra*, the fifth center of subtle energies located in the spine. The *vishuddha chakra*, opposite the throat, controls the fifth element, *akash* or ether, pervasive in the intra-atomic spaces of the physical cells. Concentration on this *chakra* ("wheel") enables the devotee to live by etheric energy.

Therese Neumann neither lives by gross food nor practices a scientific yogic technique for non-eating. The explanation is hidden in the complexities of personal karma. Many lives of dedication to God lie behind a Therese Neumann and a Giri Bala, but their channels for outward expression have been different. Among Christian saints who lived without eating (they were also stigmatists) may be mentioned St. Lidwina of Schiedam, Blessed Elizabeth of Rent, St. Catherine of Siena, Dominica Lazarri, Blessed Angela of Foligno, and the 19th-century Louise Lateau. St. Nicholas of Flüe (Bruder Klaus, the 15th-century hermit whose impassioned plea for union saved the Swiss Confederation) was an abstainer from food for twenty years.

CHAPTER 47

I Return to the West

"I have given many yoga lessons in India and America; but I must confess that, as a Hindu, I am unusually happy to be conducting a class for English students."

My London class members laughed appreciatively; no political turmoils ever disturbed our yoga peace.

India was now a hallowed memory. It is September 1936; I am in England to fulfill a promise, given sixteen months earlier, to lecture again in London.

England, too, is receptive to the timeless yoga message. Reporters and newsreel cameramen swarmed over my quarters at Grosvenor House. The British National Council of the World Fellowship of Faiths organized a meeting on September 29 at Whitefield Congregational Church, where I addressed the audience on the weighty subject of "How Faith in Fellowship May Save Civilization." The eight o'clock lectures at Caxton Hall attracted such crowds that on two nights the overflow waited in Windsor House auditorium for my second talk at nine-thirty. Yoga classes during the following weeks grew so large that Mr. Wright was obliged to arrange a transfer to another hall.

English tenacity has an admirable expression in a spiritual relationship. The London yoga students loyally organized themselves, after my departure, into a Self-Realization Fellowship center, holding their meditation meetings weekly throughout the bitter war years.

Unforgettable weeks in England; days of sight-seeing in London, then over the beautiful countryside. Mr. Wright and I used the trusty Ford to visit the birthplaces and tombs of the great poets and heroes of British history.

Our little party sailed from Southampton for America in late October on the *Bremen*. The sight of the majestic Statue of Liberty in New York harbor brought to our throats joyous emotional gulps.

The Ford, a bit battered from struggles over ancient soils, was still puissant; it now took in its stride the transcontinental trip to California. In late 1936, lo! Mount Washington Center.

The year-end holidays are celebrated annually at the Los An-

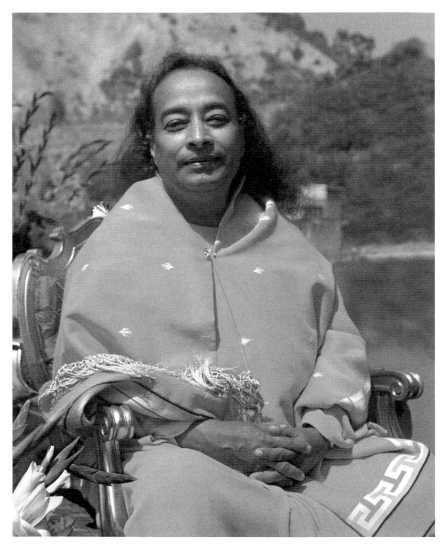

PARAMAHANSA YOGANANDA
Photographed on August 20, 1950, at dedication of Self-Realization
Fellowship Lake Shrine, Pacific Palisades, California

SELF-REALIZATION FELLOWSHIP LAKE SHRINE AND GANDHI WORLD PEACE MEMORIAL

Located in Pacific Palisades, Los Angeles, California, the ten-acre Lake Shrine was dedicated on August 20, 1950, by Paramahansa Yogananda. While supervising the planting and construction work in 1949, Paramahansaji stayed at times in the houseboat shown in photo at left. Visible between the center pillars in other photo is the carved sarcophagus that enshrines a portion of Mahatma Gandhi's ashes. Across the lake is the Windmill Chapel, seen in left photo. Self-Realization Fellowship services, meditations, and classes are held weekly at the Lake Shrine, which is open to the public.

geles center with an eight-hour group meditation on December 24 (Spiritual Christmas),* followed the next day by a banquet (Social Christmas). The festivities this year were augmented by the presence of dear friends and students from distant cities who had arrived to welcome home the three world travelers.

The Christmas Day feast included delicacies brought fifteen thousand miles for this glad occasion: *gucchi* mushrooms from Kashmir, canned *rasagulla* and mango pulp, *papar* biscuits, and an oil of the Indian *keora* flower for flavoring ice cream. The evening found us grouped around a huge sparkling Christmas tree, the nearby fireplace crackling with logs of aromatic cypress.

Gift-time! Presents from the earth's far corners—Palestine, Egypt, India, England, France, Italy. How laboriously had Mr. Wright counted the trunks at each foreign junction, that no pilfering hand receive the treasures intended for loved ones in America! Plaques of the sacred olive tree from the Holy Land, delicate laces and embroideries from Belgium and Holland, Persian carpets, finely woven Kashmir shawls, everlastingly fragrant sandalwood trays from Mysore, Shiva "bull's eye" stones from Central Provinces, Indian coins of dynasties long fled, bejeweled vases and cups, miniatures, tapestries, temple incense and perfumes, *swadeshi* cotton prints, lacquer work, Mysore ivory carvings, Persian slippers with their inquisitive long toe, quaint old illuminated manuscripts, velvets, brocades, Gandhi caps, potteries, tiles, brasswork, prayer rugs—booty of three continents!

One by one I distributed the gaily wrapped packages from the immense pile under the tree.

"Sister Gyanamata!" I handed a long box to the saintly American lady of sweet visage and deep realization who, during my absence, had been in charge at the Mt. Washington Center. From the paper tissues she lifted a *sari* of golden Banaras silk.

"Thank you, sir; it brings before my eyes the pageant of India."

"Mr. Dickinson!" The next parcel contained a gift that I had

---

* Since 1950 this all-day meditation has been held on December 23. Self-Realization Fellowship members around the world also keep Christmas thus, in their homes and in SRF temples and centers, setting aside one day during the Christmas season for deep meditation and prayer. Many have testified to the great spiritual help and blessing they have gained through this annual observance begun by Paramahansa Yogananda.

Paramahansaji also established a Prayer Council at the Mt. Washington Center (the nucleus of Self-Realization Fellowship's Worldwide Prayer Circle), which offers prayers daily for all who request help in solving or dissolving their particular problem. (*Publisher's Note*) bought in a Calcutta bazaar. "Mr. Dickinson will like this," I had thought at the time. A beloved disciple, Mr. E. E. Dickinson had been present at every Christmas festivity since the 1925 founding of the Mt. Washington Center.

At this eleventh annual celebration, he stood before me, untying the ribbons of an oblong package.

"The silver cup!" Struggling with emotion, he stared at the present, a tall drinking cup. He seated himself some distance away, apparently in a daze. I smiled at him affectionately before resuming my role as Santa Claus.

The ejaculatory evening closed with a prayer to the Giver of all gifts; then a group singing of Christmas carols.

Mr. Dickinson and I were chatting together some time later.

"Sir," he said, "please let me thank you now for the silver cup. I could not find any words on Christmas night."

"I brought the gift especially for you."

"For forty-three years I have been waiting for that silver cup! It is a long story, one I have kept hidden within me." Mr. Dickinson looked at me shyly. "The beginning was dramatic: I was drowning. My older brother had playfully pushed me into a fifteen foot pool in a small town in Nebraska. I was only five years old then. As I was about to sink for the second time under the water, a dazzling multicolored light appeared, filling all space. In the midst was the figure of a man with tranquil eyes and a reassuring smile. My body was sinking for the third time when one of my brother's companions bent a tall slender willow tree in such a low dip that I could grasp it with my desperate fingers. The boys lifted me to the bank and successfully gave me first-aid treatment.

"Twelve years later, a youth of seventeen, I visited Chicago with my mother. It was September 1893; the great World Parliament of Religions was in session. Mother and I were walking down a main street, when again I saw the mighty flash of light. A few paces away, strolling leisurely along, was the same man I had seen years before in vision. He approached a large auditorium and vanished within the door.

"'Mother,' I cried, 'that was the man who appeared at the time I was drowning!'

"She and I hastened into the building; the man was seated on a lecture platform. We soon learned that he was Swami Vivekananda of India.* After he had given a soul-stirring talk, I went forward

* Chief disciple of the Christlike master Ramakrishna Paramahansa.

to meet him. He smiled on me graciously, as though we were old friends. I was so young that I did not know how to give expression to my feelings, but in my heart I was hoping that he would offer to be my teacher. He read my thought.

"'No, my son, I am not your guru.' Vivekananda gazed with his beautiful, piercing eyes deep into my own. 'Your teacher will come later. He will give you a silver cup.' After a little pause, he added, smiling, 'He will pour out to you more blessings than you are now able to hold.'

"I left Chicago in a few days," Mr. Dickinson went on, "and never saw the great Vivekananda again. But every word he had uttered was indelibly written on my inmost consciousness. Years passed; no teacher appeared. One night in 1925 I prayed deeply that the Lord would send me my guru. A few hours later, I was awakened from sleep by soft strains of melody. A band of celestial beings, carrying flutes and other instruments, came before my view. After filling the air with glorious music, the angels slowly vanished.

"The next evening I attended, for the first time, one of your lectures here in Los Angeles, and knew then that my prayer had been granted."

We smiled at each other in silence.

"For eleven years now I have been your *Kriya Yoga* disciple," Mr. Dickinson continued. "Sometimes I wondered about the silver cup; I had almost persuaded myself that the words of Vivekananda were only metaphorical.

"But on Christmas night, as you handed me the little box by the tree, I saw, for the third time in my life, the same dazzling flash of light. In another minute I was gazing on my guru's gift that Vivekananda had foreseen for me forty-three years earlier[*]—a silver cup!"

---

[*] Mr. Dickinson met Swami Vivekananda in September of 1893—the year in which Paramahansa Yogananda was born (January 5). Vivekananda was apparently aware that Yogananda was again in incarnation, and that he would go to America to teach the philosophy of India.

In 1965 Mr. Dickinson, still well and active at 89, received the title of Yogacharya (teacher of yoga) in a ceremony at Self-Realization Fellowship headquarters in Los Angeles.

He often meditated for long periods with Paramahansaji, and never missed *Kriya Yoga* practice, three times daily.

Two years before his passing on June 30, 1967, Yogacharya Dickinson gave a talk to the SRF monks. He told them an interesting detail he had forgotten to mention to Paramahansaji. Yogacharya Dickinson said: "When I went up to the lecture platform in Chicago to speak to Swami Vivekananda, before I could greet him he said:

"'Young man, I want you to stay out of the water!'" *(Publisher's Note)*

CHAPTER 48

At Encinitas in California

"A surprise, sir! During your absence abroad we have had this Encinitas hermitage built; it is a 'welcome-home' gift!" Mr. Lynn, Sister Gyanamata, Durga Ma, and a few other devotees smilingly led me through a gate and up a tree-shaded walk.

I saw a building jutting out like a great white ocean liner toward the blue brine. First speechlessly, then with "Oh's!" and "Ah's!", finally with man's insufficient vocabulary of joy and gratitude, I examined the ashram: sixteen unusually large rooms, each one charmingly appointed.

The stately central hall, with immense ceiling-high windows, looks out on an altar of grass, ocean, and sky: a symphony in emerald, opal, and sapphire. A mantel over the huge fireplace of the hall holds pictures of Christ, Babaji, Lahiri Mahasaya, and Sri Yukteswar; bestowing, I feel, their blessings on this tranquil Western ashram.

Directly below the hall, built into the very bluff, two meditation caves confront the infinities of sky and sea. On the grounds are sunbathing nooks, flagstone paths leading to quiet arbors, rose gardens, a eucalyptus grove, and a fruit orchard.

"May the good and heroic souls of the saints come here (so reads 'A Prayer for a Dwelling,' from the Zend-Avesta, that hangs on one of the hermitage doors) and may they go hand in hand with us, giving the healing virtues of their blessed gifts that are as ample as the earth, as high-reaching as the heavens!"

The large estate in Encinitas, California, is a gift to Self-Realization Fellowship from Mr. James J. Lynn, a faithful *Kriya Yogi* since his initiation in January 1932. An American businessman of endless responsibilities (as head of vast oil interests and as president of the world's largest reciprocal fire-insurance exchange), Mr. Lynn nevertheless finds time daily for long and deep *Kriya Yoga* meditation. Leading thus a balanced life, he has attained in *samadhi* the grace of unshakable peace.

During my stay in India and Europe (June 1935 to October 1936), Mr. Lynn* had lovingly plotted with my correspondents in California to prevent any word from reaching me about the construction of the ashram in Encinitas. Astonishment, delight!

During my earlier years in America I had combed the coast of California in quest of a small site for a seaside ashram. Whenever I had found a suitable location some obstacle had invariably arisen to thwart me. Gazing now over the sunny acres in Encinitas, humbly I saw the fulfillment of Sri Yukteswar's long-ago prophecy: "a retreat by the ocean."†

A few months later, Easter of 1937, I conducted on the lawn of the new ashram the first of many Easter sunrise services. Like the Magi of old, several hundred students gazed in devotional awe at the daily miracle: the awakening solar rite in the eastern sky. To the west lay the Pacific Ocean, booming its solemn praise; in the distance a tiny white sailing boat and the lonely flight of a seagull. "Christ, thou art risen!" Not with the vernal sun alone, but in Spirit's eternal dawn.

Many happy months went by. In the Encinitas setting of perfect beauty, I completed a long-projected work, *Cosmic Chants*.‡ I gave English words and Western musical notation to many Indian songs. Included were Shankara's chant, "No Birth, No Death"; the Sanskrit "Hymn to Brahma"; Tagore's "Who Is in My Temple?"; and a number of my compositions: "I Will Be Thine Always," "In the Land Beyond My Dreams," "I Give You My Soul Call," "Come, Listen to My Soul Song," and "In the Temple of Silence."

In the preface to the songbook I recounted my first outstanding experience with Western reaction to Eastern chants. The occasion had been a public lecture; the time, April 18, 1926; the place, Carnegie Hall in New York.

On April 17 I had confided to an American student, Mr. Alvin

---

* After Paramahansaji's passing, Mr. Lynn (Rajarsi Janakananda) served as president of Self-Realization Fellowship and Yogoda Satsanga Society of India. Of his guru Mr. Lynn said: "How heavenly is the company of a saint! Of all the things that have come to me in life, I treasure most the blessings that Paramahansaji has bestowed on me."

Mr. Lynn entered *mahasamadhi* in 1955. *(Publisher's Note)*

† See pages 101–2.

‡ Published by Self-Realization Fellowship. Recordings were made of Paramahansa Yogananda chanting a number of the songs in *Cosmic Chants*. These are also available from Self-Realization Fellowship. *(Publisher's Note)*

Hunsicker, "I am planning to ask the audience to sing an old Hindu chant, 'O God Beautiful.'"*

Mr. Hunsicker had protested that Oriental songs are not easily understood by Americans.

"Music is a universal language," I had replied. "Americans will not fail to feel the soul aspiration in this lofty chant."

The following night the devotional strains of "O God Beautiful" had come for over an hour from three thousand throats. Blasé no longer, dear New Yorkers! your hearts had soared out in a simple paean of rejoicing. Divine healings had taken place that evening among the devotees chanting with love the Lord's blessed name.

In 1941 I paid a visit to the Self-Realization Fellowship Center in Boston. The Boston center leader, Dr. M. W. Lewis, lodged me in an artistically decorated suite. "Sir," Dr. Lewis said, smiling, "during your early years in America you stayed in this city in a single room, without bath. I wanted you to know that Boston boasts some luxurious apartments!"

Happy years in California sped by, filled with activity. A Self-Realization Fellowship Colony† in Encinitas was established in 1937. The numerous activities at the Colony give many-sided training to disciples in accordance with Self-Realization Fellowship ideals. Fruits and vegetables are grown for the use of residents of the Encinitas and Los Angeles centers.

"He hath made of one blood all nations of men."‡ "World brotherhood" is a large term, but man must enlarge his sympathies, consid-

---

* The words of Guru Nanak's song are as follows:
  O God beautiful, O God beautiful!
  In the forest Thou art green,
  In the mountain Thou art high,
  In the river Thou art restless,
  In the ocean Thou art grave.
  To the serviceful Thou art service,
  To the lover Thou art love,
  To the sorrowful Thou art sympathy,
  To the yogi Thou art bliss.
  O God beautiful, O God beautiful,
  At Thy feet, O I do bow!

† Now a flourishing ashram center, whose buildings include the original main hermitage, ashrams for monks and nuns, dining facilities, and an attractive retreat for members and friends. A series of white pillars facing the highway side of the spacious grounds are crowned with lotuses of gold-leafed metal. In Indian art the lotus is a symbol of the Cosmic Consciousness center (*sahasrara*) in the brain, the "thousand-petaled lotus of light."

‡ Acts 17:26.

ering himself in the light of a world citizen. He who truly understands that "it is my America, my India, my Philippines, my Europe, my Africa" and so on, will never lack scope for a useful and happy life.

Though the body of Sri Yukteswar never dwelt on any soil except India's, he knew this brotherly truth:

"The world is my homeland."

CHAPTER 49

The Years 1940–1951

"We have indeed learned the value of meditation, and know that nothing can disturb our inner peace. In the last few weeks during the meetings we have heard air-raid warnings and listened to the explosion of delayed-action bombs, but our students still gather and thoroughly enjoy our beautiful service."

This brave message, written by the leader of the London Self-Realization Fellowship Center, was one of many letters sent to me from war-ravaged England and Europe during the years that preceded America's entry into World War II.

Dr. L. Cranmer-Byng of London, noted editor of *The Wisdom of the East Series*, wrote me in 1942 as follows:

"When I read *East-West** I realized how far apart we seemed to be, apparently living in two different worlds. Beauty, order, calm, and peace come to me from Los Angeles, sailing into port as a vessel laden with the blessings and comfort of the Holy Grail to a beleaguered city.

"I see as in a dream your palm-tree grove, and the temple in Encinitas with its ocean stretches and mountain views; and above all its fellowship of spiritually minded men and women—a community comprehended in unity, absorbed in creative work, and replenished in contemplation.... Greetings to all the Fellowship from a common soldier, written on the watchtower waiting for the dawn."

A Church of All Religions in Hollywood, California, was built by Self-Realization Fellowship workers and dedicated in 1942. A year later another temple was founded in San Diego, California; and, in 1947, one in Long Beach, California.†

One of the most beautiful estates in the world, a floral wonderland in the Pacific Palisades section of Los Angeles, was donated in 1949 to Self-Realization Fellowship. The ten-acre site is a natural

---

* The magazine is now called *Self-Realization*.

† The Long Beach Chapel was outgrown by 1967, in which year the congregation moved to a spacious Self-Realization Fellowship Temple in Fullerton, California. *(Publisher's Note)*

amphitheater, surrounded by verdant hills. A large natural lake, a blue jewel in a mountain diadem, has given the estate its name of Lake Shrine. A quaint Dutch-windmill house on the grounds contains a peaceful chapel. Near a sunken garden a large waterwheel splashes a leisurely music. Two marble statues from China adorn the site—a statue of Lord Buddha and one of Kwan Yin (the Chinese personification of the Divine Mother). A life-size statue of Christ, its serene face and flowing robes strikingly illuminated at night, stands on a hill above a waterfall.

A Mahatma Gandhi World Peace Memorial at the Lake Shrine was dedicated in 1950, the year that marked the thirtieth anniversary* of Self-Realization Fellowship in America. A portion of the Mahatma's ashes, sent from India, was enshrined in a thousand-year-old stone sarcophagus.

A Self-Realization Fellowship "India Center"† in Hollywood was founded in 1951. Mr. Goodwin J. Knight, Lieutenant Governor of California, and Mr. M. R. Ahuja, Consul General of India, joined me in the dedicatory services. On the site is India Hall, an auditorium seating 250 persons.

Newcomers to the various centers often want further light on yoga. A question I sometimes hear is this: "Is it true, as certain organizations state, that yoga may not be successfully studied in printed form but should be pursued only with the guidance of a nearby teacher?"

In the Atomic Age, yoga should be taught by a method of instruction such as the *Self-Realization Fellowship Lessons*,‡ or the liberating science will again be restricted to a chosen few. It would indeed be a priceless boon if each student could keep by his side a guru perfected in divine wisdom; but the world is composed of many "sinners" and few saints. How then may the multitudes be helped by yoga, if not through study in their homes of instructions written by true yogis?

The only alternative is that the "average man" be ignored and

---

* In celebrating this anniversary, I conducted a sacred ceremony in Los Angeles on August 27, 1950, at which I gave *Kriya Yoga* initiation to 500 students.

† Nucleus, with the adjacent temple, of a large ashram center managed by devotees who have dedicated themselves to the service of humanity and to realization in their own lives of Paramahansa Yogananda's ideals. *(Publisher's Note)*

‡ This comprehensive home-study series is available through the international headquarters of Self-Realization Fellowship, the society established by Paramahansa Yogananda for the dissemination of the *Kriya Yoga* science of meditation and spiritual living. (See page 425.) *(Publisher's Note)*

left without yoga knowledge. Such is not God's plan for the new age. Babaji has promised to guard and guide all sincere *Kriya Yogis* in their path toward the Goal.* Hundreds of thousands, not dozens merely, of *Kriya Yogis* are needed to bring into manifestation the world of peace and plenty that awaits men when they have made the proper effort to reestablish their status as sons of the Divine Father.

The founding in the West of a Self-Realization Fellowship organization, a "hive for the spiritual honey," was a duty enjoined on me by Sri Yukteswar and Mahavatar Babaji. The fulfillment of the sacred trust has not been devoid of difficulties.

"Tell me truly, Paramahansaji, has it been worth it?" This laconic question was put to me one evening by Dr. Lloyd Kennell, a leader of the temple in San Diego. I understood him to mean: "Have you been happy in America? What about the falsehoods circulated by misguided people who are anxious to prevent the spread of yoga? What about the disillusionments, the heartaches, the center leaders who could not lead, the students who could not be taught?"

"Blessed is the man whom the Lord doth test!" I answered. "He has remembered, now and then, to put a burden on me." I thought, then, of all the faithful ones, of the love and devotion and understanding that illumines the heart of America. With slow emphasis I went on: "But my answer is yes, a thousand times yes! It *has* been worthwhile, more than ever I dreamed, to see East and West brought closer in the only lasting bond, the spiritual."

The great masters of India who have shown keen interest in the West have well understood modern conditions. They know that, until there is better assimilation in all nations of the distinctive Eastern and Western virtues, world affairs cannot improve. Each hemisphere needs the best offerings of the other.

In the course of world travel I have sadly observed much suffering:† in the Orient, suffering chiefly on the material plane; in

---

* Paramahansa Yogananda, also, told his students of East and West that, after this life, he would continue to watch over the spiritual progress of all *Kriyabans* (students of the *Self-Realization Fellowship Lessons* who have received *Kriya* initiation; see page 276 n.). The truth of his beautiful promise has been proved, since his *mahasamadhi*, by letters from many *Kriya Yogis* who have become aware of his omnipresent guidance. *(Publisher's Note)*

† "That voice is round me like a bursting sea:
    'And is thy earth so marred,
    Shattered in shard on shard?
  Lo, all things fly thee, for thou fliest Me!...
  All which I took from thee I did but take,
    Not for thy harms,

the Occident, misery chiefly on the mental or the spiritual plane. All nations feel the painful effects of unbalanced civilizations. India and many other Eastern lands can greatly benefit from emulation of the practical grasp of affairs, the material efficiency, of Western nations like America. The Occidental peoples, on the other hand, require a deeper understanding of the spiritual basis of life, and particularly of scientific techniques that India anciently developed for man's conscious communion with God.

The ideal of a well-rounded civilization is not a chimerical one. For millenniums India was a land of both spiritual light and widespread material prosperity. The poverty of the last 200 years is, in India's long history, only a passing karmic phase. A byword in the world, century after century, was "the riches of the Indies."*

But just that thou might'st seek it in My arms.
   All which thy child's mistake
Fancied as lost, I have stored for thee at home.
   Rise, clasp My hand, and come!'"

—*Francis Thompson, "The Hound of Heaven"*

* The records of history present India, up until the 18th century, as the world's wealthiest nation. Incidentally, nothing in Hindu literature or tradition tends to substantiate the current Western historical theory that the early Aryans "invaded" India from some other part of Asia or from Europe. The scholars are understandably unable to fix the starting point of this imaginary journey. The internal evidence in the Vedas, pointing to India as the immemorial home of the Hindus, has been presented in an unusual and very readable volume, *Rig-Vedic India*, by Abinas Chandra Das, published in 1921 by Calcutta University. Professor Das claims that emigrants from India settled in various parts of Europe and Asia, spreading the Aryan speech and folklore. The Lithuanian tongue, for example, is in many ways strikingly similar to Sanskrit. The philosopher Kant, who knew nothing of Sanskrit, was amazed at the scientific structure of the Lithuanian language. "It possesses," he said, "the key that will open all the enigmas, not only of philology but also of history."

The Bible refers to the riches of India, telling us (II Chron. 9:21,10) that the "ships of Tarshish" brought to King Solomon "gold and silver, ivory, apes, and peacocks" and "algum [sandalwood] trees and precious stones" from Ophir (Sopara on the Bombay coast). Megasthenes, the Greek ambassador (4th century B.C.), has left us a detailed picture of India's prosperity. Pliny (1st century A.D.) tells us the Romans annually spent fifty million sesterces ($5,000,000) on imports from India, which was then a vast marine power.

Chinese travelers wrote vividly of the opulent Indian civilization, its widespread education and excellent government. The Chinese priest Fa-Hsien (5th century) tells us the Indian people were happy, honest, and prosperous. See Samuel Beal's *Buddhist Records of the Western World* (India was the "Western world" to the Chinese!), Trubner, London; and Thomas Watters' *On Yuan Chwang's Travels in India, A.D. 629–45*, Royal Asiatic Society.

Columbus, discovering the New World in the 15th century, was in reality seeking a shorter trade route to India. For centuries Europe was eager to possess the Indian exports—silks, fine cloths (of such sheerness as to deserve their descriptions:

Abundance, material as well as spiritual, is a structural expression of *rita*, cosmic law or natural righteousness. There is no parsimony in the Divine, nor in Its goddess of phenomena, exuberant Nature.

The Hindu scriptures teach that man is attracted to this particular earth to learn, more completely in each successive life, the infinite ways in which the Spirit may be expressed through, and dominant over, material conditions. East and West are learning this great truth in different ways, and should gladly share with each other their discoveries. Beyond all doubt it is pleasing to the Lord when His earth-children struggle to attain a world civilization free

---

"woven air" and "invisible mist"), cotton prints, brocades, embroideries, rugs, cutlery, armor, ivory and ivory work, perfumes, incense, sandalwood, potteries, medicinal drugs and unguents, indigo, rice, spices, coral, gold, silver, pearls, rubies, emeralds, and diamonds.

Portuguese and Italian merchants have recorded their awe at the fabulous magnificence throughout the empire of Vijayanagar (1336–1565). The glory of its capital was described by the Arabian ambassador Razzak as "such that eye has not seen, nor has ear heard of, any place to equal it on earth."

In the 16th century, for the first time in her long history, India as a whole fell under non-Hindu rule. The Turkish Baber invaded the country in 1524 and founded a dynasty of Moslem kings. By settling in the ancient land, the new monarchs did not drain it of its riches. Weakened, however, by internal dissensions, wealthy India became the prey in the 17th century of several European nations; England finally emerged as the ruling power. India peacefully attained her independence on August 15, 1947.

Like so many Indians, I have a now-it-can-be-told story. A group of young men, whom I had known in college, approached me during World War I and urged me to lead a revolutionary movement. I declined with these words: "Killing our English brothers cannot accomplish any good for India. Her freedom will not come through bullets, but through spiritual force." I then warned my friends that the arms-laden German ships, on which they were depending, would be intercepted by the British at Diamond Harbour, Bengal. The young men, however, went ahead with their plans, which proceeded to go awry in the manner I had foreseen. My friends were released from prison after a few years. Abandoning their belief in violence, several of them joined Gandhi's ideal political movement. In the end they saw India's victory in a "war" won by peaceful means.

The sad division of the land into India and Pakistan, and the short but bloody interlude that ensued in a few parts of the country, were caused by economic factors, and not essentially by religious fanaticism (a minor reason often erroneously presented as a major one). Countless Hindus and Moslems, now as in the past, have lived side by side in amity. Men of both faiths, in immense numbers, became disciples of the "creedless" master Kabir (1450–1518); and to this day he has millions of followers (*Kabir-panthis*). Under the Moslem rule of Akbar the Great, the widest possible freedom of belief prevailed throughout India. Nor is there today any serious religious disharmony amongst 95% of the simple people. The real India, the India that could understand and follow a Mahatma Gandhi, is found not in the large restless cities but in the peaceful 700,000 villages, where simple and just forms of self-government by *panchayats* (local councils) have been a feature from time immemorial. The problems that beset a newly freed India today will surely be solved in time by those great men whom India has never failed to produce.

from poverty, disease, and soul ignorance. Man's forgetfulness of his divine resources (the result of his misuse of free will*) is the root cause of all other forms of suffering.

The ills attributed to an anthropomorphic abstraction called "society" may be laid more realistically at the door of Everyman.† Utopia must spring in the private bosom before it can flower in civic virtue, inner reforms leading naturally to outer ones. A man who has reformed himself will reform thousands.

The time-tested scriptures of the world are one in essence, inspiring man on his upward journey. One of the happiest periods of my life was spent in dictating, for *Self-Realization Magazine,* my interpretation of part of the New Testament.‡ Fervently I implored Christ to guide me in divining the true meaning of his words, many of which have been grievously misunderstood for twenty centuries.

One night while I was engaged in silent prayer, my sitting room in the Encinitas hermitage became filled with an opal-blue light. I beheld the radiant form of the blessed Lord Jesus. A young man, he seemed, of about twenty-five, with a sparse beard and moustache; his long black hair, parted in the middle, was haloed by a shimmering gold.

His eyes were eternally wondrous; as I gazed, they were infinitely changing. With each divine transition in their expression, I intuitively understood the wisdom conveyed. In his glorious gaze I felt the power that upholds the myriad worlds. A Holy Grail appeared at his mouth; it came down to my lips and then returned to Jesus. After a few moments he uttered beautiful words, so personal in their nature that I keep them in my heart.

---

* "Freely we serve,
Because we freely love, as in our will
To love or not; in this we stand or fall.
And some are fallen, to disobedience fallen,
And so from heaven to deepest hell. O fall
From what high state of bliss into what woe!"
        —*Milton, "Paradise Lost"*

† The plan of the divine *lila* or "sportive play" by which the phenomenal worlds have come into existence is one of *reciprocity* between creature and Creator. The sole gift that man can offer to God is love; it suffices to call forth His overwhelming generosity. "Ye have robbed me, even this whole nation. Bring ye all the tithes into the storehouse, that there may be meat in mine house, and prove me now herewith, saith the Lord of hosts, if I will not open you the windows of heaven, and pour you out a blessing, that there shall not be room enough to receive it."—Malachi 3:9–10.

‡ Paramahansa Yogananda's comprehensive interpretation of the four Gospels is published in book form by Self-Realization Fellowship, entitled *The Second Coming of Christ: The Resurrection of the Christ Within You. (Publisher's Note)*

I spent much time in 1950 and 1951 at a tranquil retreat near the Mojave Desert in California. There I translated the Bhagavad Gita and wrote a detailed commentary* that presents the various paths of yoga.

Twice† referring explicitly to a yogic technique (the only one mentioned in the Bhagavad Gita and the same one that Babaji named, simply, *Kriya Yoga*), India's greatest scripture has thus offered practical as well as moral teaching. In the ocean of our dreamworld, the breath is the specific storm of delusion that produces the consciousness of individual waves—the forms of men and of all other material objects. Knowing that mere philosophical and ethical knowledge is insufficient to rouse man from his painful dream of separate existence, Lord Krishna pointed out the holy science by which the yogi may master his body and convert it, at will, into pure energy. The possibility of this yogic feat is not beyond the theoretical comprehension of modern scientists, pioneers in an Atomic Age. All matter has been proved to be reducible to energy.

The Hindu scriptures extol the yogic science because it is employable by mankind in general. The mystery of breath, it is true, has occasionally been solved without the use of formal yoga techniques, as in the cases of non-Hindu mystics who possessed transcendent powers of devotion to the Lord. Such Christian, Moslem, and other saints have indeed been observed in the breathless and motionless trance (*sabikalpa samadhi‡*), without which no man has entered the first stages of God-perception. (After a saint has reached *nirbikalpa* or the highest *samadhi*, however, he is irrevocably established in the Lord—whether he be breathless or breathing, motionless or active.)

Brother Lawrence, the 17th-century Christian mystic, tells us his first glimpse of God-realization came about by viewing a tree. Nearly all human beings have seen a tree; few, alas, have thereby seen the tree's Creator. Most men are utterly incapable of sum-

---

* *God Talks With Arjuna: The Bhagavad Gita—Royal Science of God-Realization,* published by Self-Realization Fellowship. The Bhagavad Gita is India's most beloved scripture. It consists of a dialogue between Lord Krishna (symbolizing Spirit) and his disciple Arjuna (symbolizing the soul of the ideal devotee): words of spiritual guidance that are timeless in their applicability by all truth-seekers. The central message of the Gita is that man may win emancipation through love for God, wisdom, and performance of right actions in a spirit of nonattachment.

† Bhagavad Gita IV:29 and V:27–28.

‡ See chapter 26. Among Christian mystics who have been observed in *sabikalpa samadhi* may be mentioned St. Teresa of Avila, whose body would become so immovably fixed that the astonished nuns in the convent were unable to alter her position or to rouse her to outward consciousness.

moning those irresistible powers of devotion that are effortlessly possessed only by a few *ekantins,* "singlehearted" saints found in all religious paths, whether of East or West. Yet the ordinary man* is not therefore shut out from the possibility of divine communion. He needs, for soul recollection, no more than the *Kriya Yoga* technique, a daily observance of the moral precepts, and an ability to cry sincerely: "Lord, I yearn to know Thee!"

The universal appeal of yoga is thus its approach to God through a daily usable scientific method, rather than through a devotional fervor that, for the average man, is beyond his emotional scope.

Various great Jain teachers of India have been called *tirthakaras,* "ford-makers," because they reveal the passage by which bewildered humanity may cross over and beyond the stormy seas of *samsara* (the karmic wheel, the recurrence of lives and deaths). *Samsara* (literally, "a flowing with" the phenomenal flux) induces man to take the line of least resistance. "Whosoever therefore will be a friend of the world is the enemy of God."† To become the friend of God, man must overcome the devils or evils of his own karma or actions that ever urge him to spineless acquiescence in the mayic delusions of the world. A knowledge of the iron law of karma encourages the earnest seeker to find the way of final escape from its bonds. Because the karmic slavery of human beings is rooted in the desires of *maya*-darkened minds, it is with mind-control‡ that

---

* The "ordinary man" must make a spiritual start somewhere, sometime. "The journey of a thousand miles begins with one step," Lao-tzu observed. Cf. Lord Buddha: "Let no man think lightly of good, saying in his heart, 'It will not come nigh me.' By the falling of waterdrops a pot is filled; the wise man becomes full of good, even if he gather it little by little."

† James 4:4.

‡ "Steadfast a lamp burns sheltered from the wind;
  Such is the likeness of the Yogi's mind
  Shut from sense-storms and burning bright to Heaven.
  When mind broods placid, soothed with holy wont;
  When Self contemplates self, and in itself
  Hath comfort; when it knows the nameless joy
  Beyond all scope of sense, revealed to soul —
  Only to soul! and, knowing, wavers not,
  True to the farther Truth; when, holding this,
  It deems no other treasure comparable,
  But, harbored there, cannot be stirred or shook
  By any gravest grief, call that state 'peace,'
  That happy severance Yoga; call that man
  The perfect Yogin!"
  —Bhagavad Gita VI:19–23 *(Arnold's translation)*

the yogi concerns himself. The various cloaks of karmic ignorance are laid away, and man views himself in his native essence.

The mystery of life and death, whose solution is the only purpose of man's sojourn on earth, is intimately interwoven with breath. Breathlessness is deathlessness. Realizing this truth, the ancient rishis of India seized on the sole clue of the breath and developed a precise and rational science of breathlessness.

Had India no other gift for the world, *Kriya Yoga* alone would suffice as a kingly offering.

The Bible contains passages which reveal that the Hebrew prophets were well aware that God has made the breath to serve as the subtle link between body and soul. Genesis states: "The Lord God formed man of the dust of the ground, and breathed into his nostrils the breath of life; and man became a living soul."* The human body is composed of chemical and metallic substances that are also found in the "dust of the ground." The flesh of man could never carry on activity nor manifest energy and motion were it not for the life currents transmitted by soul to body through the instrumentality, in unenlightened men, of the breath (gaseous energy). The life currents, operating in the human body as the fivefold *prana* or subtle life energies, are an expression of the *Aum* vibration of the omnipresent soul.

The reflection, the verisimilitude, of life that shines in the fleshly cells from the soul source is the only cause of man's attachment to his body; obviously he would not pay solicitous homage to a clod of clay. A human being falsely identifies himself with his physical form because the life currents from the soul are breath-conveyed into the flesh with such intense power that man mistakes the effect for a cause, and idolatrously imagines the body to have life of its own.

Man's conscious state is an awareness of body and breath. His subconscious state, active in sleep, is associated with his mental, and temporary, separation from body and breath. His superconscious state is a freedom from the delusion that "existence" depends on body and breath.† God lives without breath; the soul made in His

---

* Genesis 2:7.

† "You never will enjoy the world aright till the sea itself floweth in your veins, till you are clothed with the heavens, and crowned with the stars, and perceive yourself to be the sole heir of the whole world, and more than so, because men are in it who are every one sole heirs as well as you; till you can sing and delight and rejoice in God, as misers do in gold, and kings in scepters...till you are as familiar with the ways of God in all ages as with your walk and table; till you are intimately acquainted with that shady nothing out of which the world was made." —*Thomas Traherne, "Centuries of Meditations."*

PARAMAHANSA YOGANANDA—"THE LAST SMILE"

A photograph taken an hour before his *mahasamadhi* (a yogi's final conscious exit from the body) at a banquet held in honor of Ambassador Binay R. Sen of India, March 7, 1952, in Los Angeles, California.

The photographer has here caught a loving smile that appears to be a farewell benediction for each one of the master's millions of friends, students, and disciples. The eyes that already were gazing into Eternity are yet full of human warmth and understanding.

Death had no power of disintegration over this incomparable devotee of God; his body manifested a phenomenal state of immutability. (See page 422.)

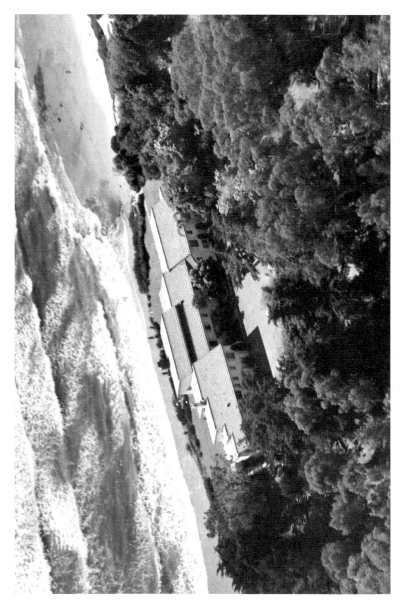

Aerial view of Self-Realization Fellowship Hermitage, overlooking the Pacific Ocean, Encinitas, California. Elsewhere on the spacious grounds are ashram residences and a Self-Realization Retreat; an SRF Temple is nearby.

image becomes conscious of itself, for the first time, only during the breathless state.

When the breath-link between soul and body is severed by evolutionary karma, the abrupt transition called "death" ensues; the physical cells revert to their natural powerlessness. For the *Kriya Yogi,* however, the breath-link is severed at will by scientific wisdom, not by the rude intrusion of karmic necessity. Through actual experience, the yogi is already aware of his essential incorporeity, and does not require the somewhat pointed hint given by Death that man is badly advised to place his reliance on a physical body.

Life by life, each man progresses (at his own pace, be it ever so erratic) toward the goal of his own apotheosis. Death, no interruption in this onward sweep, simply offers man the more congenial environment of an astral world in which to purify his dross. "Let not your heart be troubled....In my Father's house are many mansions."* It is indeed unlikely that God has exhausted His ingenuity in organizing this world, or that, in the next world, He will offer nothing more challenging to our interest than the strumming of harps.

Death is not a blotting-out of existence, a final escape from life; nor is death the door to immortality. He who has fled his Self in earthly joys will not recapture It amidst the gossamer charms of an astral world. There he merely accumulates finer perceptions and more sensitive responses to the beautiful and the good, which are one. It is on the anvil of this gross earth that struggling man must hammer out the imperishable gold of spiritual identity. Bearing in his hand the hard-won golden treasure, as the sole acceptable gift to greedy Death, a human being wins final freedom from the rounds of physical reincarnation.

For several years I conducted classes in Encinitas and Los Angeles on the *Yoga Sutras* of Patanjali and other profound works of Hindu philosophy.

"Why did God ever join soul and body?" a class student asked one evening. "What was His purpose in setting into initial motion this evolutionary drama of creation?" Countless other men have posed such questions; philosophers have sought, in vain, fully to answer them.

"Leave a few mysteries to explore in Eternity," Sri Yukteswar used to say with a smile. "How could man's limited reasoning powers comprehend the inconceivable motives of the Uncreated

---

* John 14:1–2.

Absolute?* The rational faculty in man, tethered by the cause-effect principle of the phenomenal world, is baffled before the enigma of God, the Beginningless, the Uncaused. Nevertheless, though man's reason cannot fathom the riddles of creation, every mystery will ultimately be solved for the devotee by God Himself."

He who sincerely yearns for wisdom is content to start his search by humbly mastering a few simple ABC's of the divine schema, not demanding prematurely a precise mathematical graph of life's "Einstein Theory."

"No man hath seen God at any time (no mortal under 'time,' the relatives of *maya,†* can realize the Infinite); *the only begotten Son, which is in the bosom of the Father* (the reflected Christ Consciousness or outwardly projected Perfect Intelligence that, guiding all structural phenomena through *Aum* vibration, has issued forth from the 'bosom' or deeps of the Uncreated Divine in order to express the variety of Unity), *he hath declared* (subjected to form, or manifested) *him.*"‡

"Verily, verily, I say unto you," Jesus explained, "the Son can do nothing of himself, but what he seeth the Father do: for what things soever he doeth, these also doeth the Son likewise."§

The threefold nature of God as He demonstrates Himself in the phenomenal worlds is symbolized in Hindu scriptures as Brahma the Creator, Vishnu the Preserver, and Shiva the Destroyer-Renovator. Their triune activities are ceaselessly displayed throughout vibratory creation. As the Absolute is beyond the conceptual powers of man, the

---

* "For my thoughts are not your thoughts, neither are your ways my ways, saith the Lord. For as the heavens are higher than the earth, so are my ways higher than your ways, and my thoughts than your thoughts."—Isaiah 55:8–9. Dante testified in *The Divine Comedy:*

> I have been in that heaven the most illumined
> By light from Him, and seen things which to utter
> He who returns hath neither skill nor knowledge;
> For as it nears the object of its yearning
> Our intellect is overwhelmed so deeply
> It never can retrace the path it followed.
> But whatsoever of the holy kingdom
> Was in the power of memory to treasure
> Will be my theme until the song is ended.

† The earth's diurnal cycle, from light to darkness and vice versa, is a constant reminder to man of creation's involvement in *maya* or oppositional states. (The transitional or equilibrated periods of the day, dawn and dusk, are therefore considered auspicious for meditation.) Rending the dual-textured veil of *maya,* the yogi perceives the transcendent Unity.

‡ John 1:18.   § John 5:19.

devout Hindu worships It in the august embodiments of the Trinity.*

The universal creative-preservative-destructive aspect of God, however, is not His ultimate or even His essential nature (for cosmic creation is only His *lila,* creative sport).† His intrinsicality cannot be grasped even by grasping all the mysteries of the Trinity, because His outer nature, as manifested in the lawful atomic flux, merely expresses Him without revealing Him. The final nature of the Lord is known only when "the Son ascends to the Father."‡ The liberated man overpasses the vibratory realms and enters the Vibrationless Original.

All great prophets have remained silent when requested to unveil the ultimate secrets. When Pilate asked: "What is truth?"§ Christ made no reply. The large ostentatious questions of intellectualists like Pilate seldom proceed from a burning spirit of inquiry. Such men speak rather with the empty arrogance that considers a lack of conviction about spiritual values** to be a sign of "open-mindedness."

"To this end was I born, and for this cause came I into the world, that I should bear witness unto the truth. Everyone that is of the truth heareth my voice."†† In these few words Christ spoke volumes. A child of God "bears witness" *by his life.* He embodies truth; if he expound it also, that is generous redundancy.

Truth is no theory, no speculative system of philosophy, no intellectual insight. Truth is exact correspondence with reality. For man, truth is unshakable knowledge of his real nature, his Self as soul. Jesus, by every act and word of his life, proved that he knew *the truth* of his being—his source in God. Wholly identified with

---

* A different conception from that of the trinitarian Reality: *Sat, Tat, Aum;* or Father, Son, Holy Ghost. Brahma-Vishnu-Shiva represents the triune expression of God in the aspect of *Tat* or Son, the Christ Consciousness immanent in vibratory creation. The *shaktis,* energies or "consorts" of the Trinity, are symbols of *Aum* or the Holy Ghost, the sole causative force that upholds the cosmos through vibration. (See pp. 128 n., 171 n.)

† "O Lord...thou hast created all things, and for thy pleasure they are and were created."—Revelation 4:11.

‡ John 14:12.   § John 18:38.

** "Love Virtue; she alone is free;
   She can teach ye how to climb
   Higher than the sphery chime;
   Or, if Virtue feeble were,
   Heaven itself would stoop to her."
         —*Milton, "Comus"*

†† John 18:37.

the omnipresent Christ Consciousness, he could say with simple finality: "Everyone that is of the truth heareth my voice."

Buddha, too, refused to shed light on the metaphysical ultimates, dryly pointing out that man's few moments on earth are best employed in perfecting the moral nature. The Chinese mystic Lao-tzu rightly taught: "He who knows, tells it not; he who tells, knows it not." The final mysteries of God are not "open to discussion." The decipherment of His secret code is an art that man cannot communicate to man; here the Lord alone is the Teacher.

"Be still, and know that I am God."* Never flaunting His omnipresence, the Lord is heard only in the immaculate silences. Reverberating throughout the universe as the creative *Aum* vibration, the Primal Sound instantly translates Itself into intelligible words for the devotee in attunement.

The divine purpose of creation, so far as man's reason can grasp it, is expounded in the Vedas. The rishis taught that each human being has been created by God as a soul that will uniquely manifest some special attribute of the Infinite before resuming its Absolute Identity. All men, endowed thus with a facet of Divine Individuality, are equally dear to God.

The wisdom garnered by India, the eldest brother among the nations, is a heritage of all mankind. Vedic truth, as all truth, belongs to the Lord and not to India. The rishis, whose minds were pure receptacles to receive the divine profundities of the Vedas, were members of the human race, born on this earth, rather than on some other, to serve humanity as a whole. Distinctions by race or nation are meaningless in the realm of truth, where the only qualification is spiritual fitness to receive.

God is Love; His plan for creation can be rooted only in love. Does not that simple thought, rather than erudite reasonings, offer solace to the human heart? Every saint who has penetrated to the core of Reality has testified that a divine universal plan exists and that it is beautiful and full of joy.

To the prophet Isaiah, God revealed His intentions in these words:

> So shall my word [creative *Aum*] be that goeth forth out of my mouth: it shall not return unto me void, but it shall accomplish that which I please, and it shall prosper in the thing whereto I sent it. For ye shall go out with joy, and be led forth with peace: the mountains and the hills shall break forth before

---

* Psalms 46:10. The goal of the science of yoga is to obtain that necessary inner stillness by which one may truly "know God."

you into singing, and all the trees of the field shall clap their hands (Isaiah 55:11–12).

"Ye shall go out with joy, and be led forth with peace." The men of a hard-pressed twentieth century hear longingly that wondrous promise. The full truth within it is realizable by every devotee of God who strives manfully to repossess his divine heritage.

The blessed role of *Kriya Yoga* in East and West has hardly more than just begun. May all men come to know that there exists a definite, scientific technique of Self-realization for the overcoming of all human misery!

In sending loving thought vibrations to the thousands of *Kriya Yogis* scattered like shining jewels over the earth, I often think gratefully:

"Lord, Thou hast given this monk a large family!"

PARAMAHANSA YOGANANDA:
A YOGI IN LIFE AND DEATH

Paramahansa Yogananda entered *mahasamadhi* (a yogi's final conscious exit from the body) in Los Angeles, California, on March 7, 1952, after concluding his speech at a banquet held in honor of H.E. Binay R. Sen, Ambassador of India.

The great world teacher demonstrated the value of yoga (scientific techniques for God-realization) not only in life but in death. Weeks after his departure his unchanged face shone with the divine luster of incorruptibility.

Mr. Harry T. Rowe, Los Angeles Mortuary Director, Forest Lawn Memorial-Park (in which the body of the great master is temporarily placed), sent Self-Realization Fellowship a notarized letter from which the following extracts are taken:

"The absence of any visual signs of decay in the dead body of Paramahansa Yogananda offers the most extraordinary case in our experience....No physical disintegration was visible in his body even twenty days after death....No indication of mold was visible on his skin, and no visible desiccation (drying up) took place in the bodily tissues. This state of perfect preservation of a body is, so far as we know from mortuary annals, an unparalleled one....At the time of receiving Yogananda's body, the Mortuary personnel expected to observe, through the glass lid of the casket, the usual progressive signs of bodily decay. Our astonishment increased as day followed day without bringing any visible change in the body under observation. Yogananda's body was apparently in a phenomenal state of immutability....

"No odor of decay emanated from his body at any time.... The physical appearance of Yogananda on March 27th, just before the bronze cover of the casket was put into position, was the same as it had been on March 7th. He looked on March 27th as fresh and as unravaged by decay as he had looked on the night of his death. On March 27th there was no reason to say that his body had suffered any visible physical disintegration at all. For these reasons we state again that the case of Paramahansa Yogananda is unique in our experience."

In 1977, on the twenty-fifth anniversary of the *mahasamadhi* of Paramahansa Yogananda, the Government of India issued this commemorative stamp in his honor. With the stamp, the government published a descriptive leaflet, which read, in part:

> The ideal of love for God and service to humanity found full expression in the life of Paramahansa Yogananda....Though the major part of his life was spent outside of India, still he takes his place among our great saints. His work continues to grow and shine ever more brightly, drawing people everywhere on the path of the pilgrimage of the Spirit.

ADDITIONAL RESOURCES ON
THE KRIYA YOGA TEACHINGS OF
PARAMAHANSA YOGANANDA

Self-Realization Fellowship is dedicated to freely assisting seekers worldwide. For information regarding our annual series of public lectures and classes, meditation and inspirational services at our temples and centers around the world, a schedule of retreats, and other activities, we invite you to visit our website or our International Headquarters:

www.yogananda-srf.org

Self-Realization Fellowship
3880 San Rafael Avenue
Los Angeles, CA 90065
(323) 225-2471

SELF-REALIZATION FELLOWSHIP LESSONS

*Personal guidance and instruction from Paramahansa
Yogananda on the techniques of yoga meditation
and principles of spiritual living*

If you feel drawn to the spiritual truths described in *Autobiography of a Yogi*, we invite you to enroll in the *Self-Realization Fellowship Lessons*.

Paramahansa Yogananda originated this home-study series to provide sincere seekers the opportunity to learn and practice the ancient yoga meditation techniques introduced in this book — including the science of *Kriya Yoga*. The *Lessons* also present his practical guidance for attaining balanced physical, mental, and spiritual well-being.

The *Self-Realization Fellowship Lessons* are available at a nominal fee (to cover printing and postage costs). All students are freely given personal guidance in their practice by Self-Realization Fellowship monks and nuns.

For more information...

Complete details about the *Self-Realization Fellowship Lessons* are included in the free booklet *Undreamed-of Possibilities*. To receive a copy of this booklet and an application form, please visit our website or contact our International Headquarters.

OTHER BOOKS BY PARAMAHANSA YOGANANDA

Available at bookstores or directly from the publisher:
Self-Realization Fellowship
3880 San Rafael Avenue • Los Angeles, California 90065
Tel (323) 225-2471 • Fax (323) 225-5088
www.yogananda-srf.org

God Talks With Arjuna: *The Bhagavad Gita—A New Translation and Commentary*

In this monumental two-volume work, Paramahansa Yogananda reveals the innermost essence of India's most renowned scripture. Exploring its psychological, spiritual, and metaphysical depths, he presents a sweeping chronicle of the soul's journey to enlightenment through the royal science of God-realization.

The Second Coming of Christ: *The Resurrection of the Christ Within You—A revelatory commentary on the original teachings of Jesus*

In this unprecedented masterwork of inspiration, almost 1700 pages in length, Paramahansa Yogananda takes the reader on a profoundly enriching journey through the four Gospels. Verse by verse, he illumines the universal path to oneness with God taught by Jesus to his immediate disciples but obscured through centuries of misinterpretation: "how to become like Christ, how to resurrect the Eternal Christ within one's self."

The Yoga of the Bhagavad Gita: *An Introduction to India's Universal Science of God-Realization*

A compilation of selections from Paramahansa Yogananda's in-depth, critically acclaimed translation of and commentary on the Bhagavad Gita, *God Talks With Arjuna,* this book presents truth-seekers with an ideal introduction to the Gita's timeless and universal teachings. Contains Yogananda's complete translation of the Bhagavad Gita, presented for the first time in uninterrupted sequential form.

The Yoga of Jesus: *Understanding the Hidden Teachings of the Gospels*

A selection of material from Paramahansa Yogananda's highly praised two-volume work, *The Second Coming of Christ,* this concise book confirms that Jesus, like the ancient sages and masters of the East, not only knew the principles of yoga but taught this universal science of God-realization to his disciples. Sri Yogananda shows that Jesus' message is not about sectarian divisiveness, but a unifying path by which seekers of all faith traditions can enter the kingdom of God.

Man's Eternal Quest

Paramahansa Yogananda's *Collected Talks and Essays* present in-depth discussions of the vast range of inspiring and universal truths that have captivated millions in his *Autobiography of a Yogi*. Volume I explores little-known and seldom-understood aspects of meditation, life after death, the nature of creation, health and healing, the unlimited powers of the mind, and the eternal quest that finds fulfillment only in God.

The Divine Romance

Volume II of Paramahansa Yogananda's collected talks and essays. Among the wide-ranging selections: *How to Cultivate Divine Love; Harmonizing Physical, Mental, and Spiritual Methods of Healing; A World Without Boundaries; Controlling Your Destiny; The Yoga Art of Overcoming Mortal Consciousness and Death; The Cosmic Lover; Finding the Joy in Life.*

Journey to Self-realization

Volume III of the collected talks and essays presents Sri Yogananda's unique combination of wisdom, compassion, down-to-earth guidance, and encouragement on dozens of fascinating subjects, including: *Quickening Human Evolution, How to Express Everlasting Youthfulness,* and *Realizing God in Your Daily Life.*

Wine of the Mystic: *The Rubaiyat of Omar Khayyam — A Spiritual Interpretation*

An inspired commentary that brings to light the mystical science of God-communion hidden behind the *Rubaiyat's* enigmatic imagery. Includes 50 original color illustrations. Winner of the 1995 Benjamin Franklin Award for best book in the field of religion.

Where There Is Light: *Insight and Inspiration for Meeting Life's Challenges*

Gems of thought arranged by subject; a unique handbook to which readers can quickly turn for a reassuring sense of direction in times of uncertainty or crisis, or for a renewed awareness of the ever present power of God one can draw upon in daily life.

Whispers from Eternity

A collection of Paramahansa Yogananda's prayers and divine experiences in the elevated states of meditation. Expressed in a majestic rhythm and poetic beauty, his words reveal the inexhaustible variety of God's nature, and the infinite sweetness with which He responds to those who seek Him.

The Science of Religion

Within every human being, Paramahansa Yogananda writes, there is one inescapable desire: to overcome suffering and attain a happiness that does not end. Explaining how it is possible to fulfill these longings, he examines the relative effectiveness of the different approaches to this goal.

In the Sanctuary of the Soul: *A Guide to Effective Prayer*

Compiled from the works of Paramahansa Yogananda, this inspiring devotional companion reveals ways of making prayer a daily source of love, strength, and guidance.

Inner Peace: *How to Be Calmly Active and Actively Calm*

A practical and inspiring guide, compiled from the talks and writings of Paramahansa Yogananda, that demonstrates how we can be "actively calm" by creating peace through meditation, and "calmly active"—centered in the stillness and joy of our own essential nature while living a dynamic, fulfilling, and balanced life. Winner of the 2000 Benjamin Franklin Award—best book in the field of Metaphysics/Spirituality.

How You Can Talk With God

Defining God as both the transcendent, universal Spirit and the intimately personal Father, Mother, Friend, and Lover of all, Paramahansa Yogananda shows how close the Lord is to each one of us, and how He can be persuaded to "break His silence" and respond in a tangible way.

Metaphysical Meditations

More than 300 spiritually uplifting meditations, prayers, and affirmations that can be used to develop greater health and vitality, creativity, self-confidence, and calmness; and to live more fully in a conscious awareness of the blissful presence of God.

Scientific Healing Affirmations

Paramahansa Yogananda presents here a profound explanation of the science of affirmation. He makes clear why affirmations work, and how to use the power of word and thought not only to bring about healing but to effect desired change in every area of life. Includes a wide variety of affirmations.

Sayings of Paramahansa Yogananda

A collection of sayings and wise counsel that conveys Paramahansa Yogananda's candid and loving responses to those who came to him for guidance. Recorded by a number of his close disciples, the anecdotes in this book give the reader an opportunity to share in their personal encounters with the Master.

Songs of the Soul
Mystical poetry by Paramahansa Yogananda—an outpouring of his direct perceptions of God in the beauties of nature, in man, in everyday experiences, and in the spiritually awakened state of *samadhi* meditation.

The Law of Success
Explains dynamic principles for achieving one's goals in life, and outlines the universal laws that bring success and fulfillment— personal, professional, and spiritual.

Cosmic Chants: *Spiritualized Songs for Divine Communion*
Words and music to 60 songs of devotion, with an introduction explaining how spiritual chanting can lead to God-communion.

AUDIO RECORDINGS OF PARAMAHANSA YOGANANDA

- *Beholding the One in All*
- *Awake in the Cosmic Dream*
- *Songs of My Heart*
- *Be a Smile Millionaire*
- *The Great Light of God*
- *To Make Heaven on Earth*
- *One Life Versus Reincarnation*
- *Removing All Sorrow and Suffering*
- *In the Glory of the Spirit*
- *Follow the Path of Christ, Krishna, and the Masters*
- *Self-Realization: The Inner and the Outer Path*

OTHER PUBLICATIONS FROM SELF-REALIZATION FELLOWSHIP

The Holy Science by Swami Sri Yukteswar

Only Love: Living the Spiritual Life in a Changing World by Sri Daya Mata

Finding the Joy Within You: Personal Counsel for God-Centered Living by Sri Daya Mata

Enter the Quiet Heart: Creating a Loving Relationship With God by Sri Daya Mata

God Alone: The Life and Letters of a Saint by Sri Gyanamata

"Mejda": The Family and the Early Life of Paramahansa Yogananda by Sananda Lal Ghosh

Self-Realization (a quarterly magazine founded by Paramahansa Yogananda in 1925)

FREE INTRODUCTORY BOOKLET:
Undreamed-of Possibilities

The scientific techniques of meditation taught by Paramahansa Yogananda, including *Kriya Yoga*—as well as his guidance on all aspects of balanced spiritual living—are taught in the *Self-Realization Fellowship Lessons.* For further information, please write for the free introductory booklet, *Undreamed-of Possibilities.*

A complete catalog describing all of the Self-Realization Fellowship publications and audio/video recordings is available on request.

THE LINE OF GURUS

Mahavatar Babaji is the Supreme Guru in the Indian line of masters who assume responsibility for the spiritual welfare of all members of Self-Realization Fellowship and Yogoda Satsanga Society of India who faithfully practice *Kriya Yoga.* "I shall remain incarnate on the earth," he has promised, "until this particular world cycle is ended." (See chapters 33 and 37.)

In 1920 Mahavatar Babaji told Paramahansa Yogananda: "You are the one I have chosen to spread the message of *Kriya Yoga* in the West.... The scientific technique of God-realization will ultimately spread in all lands, and aid in harmonizing the nations through man's personal, transcendental perception of the Infinite Father."

Mahavatar means "Great Incarnation" or "Divine Incarnation"; *Yogavatar* means "Incarnation of Yoga"; *Jnanavatar* means "Incarnation of Wisdom."

Premavatar means "Incarnation of Love"—a title bestowed in 1953 on Paramahansa Yogananda by his great disciple, Rajarsi Janakananda (James J. Lynn). (See p. 290 n.)

PHONETIC KEY TO PRONUNCIATION OF SANSKRIT NAMES

In the phonetic examples below, which approximate the Sanskrit, the *uh* indicates an *a* pronounced as in sofa; the *ah* indicates an *a* as in father. Letters enclosed in parentheses (uh) (i) are only partially sounded.

BHAGAVAN KRISHNA
Sounds like: Bhuh-guh-vahn Kr(i)sh-nuh
The *v* sound is between a *v* and a *w*.

MAHAVATAR BABAJI
Sounds like: Muh-hah-vuh-tahr Bah-bah-jee

YOGAVATAR LAHIRI MAHASAYA
Sounds like: Yog-ah-vuh-tahr Lah-hi(as in *his*)-ree
Muh-hah-shy(uh)

JNANAVATAR SWAMI SRI YUKTESWAR
Sounds like: Gyahn-ah-vuh-tahr Swah-mee Shree
Yook-taysh-wuhr

PREMAVATAR PARAMAHANSA YOGANANDA
Sounds like: Praym-ah-vuh-tahr Puh-ruh-m(uh)-hung-s(uh)
Yog-ah-nun-d(uh)
The *han* in Parama*han*sa is a nasalized sound, approximated by the English word *hung,* with a softly nasalized *n* and silent *g.*

AIMS AND IDEALS
OF
SELF-REALIZATION FELLOWSHIP

As set forth by Paramahansa Yogananda, Founder
Sri Daya Mata, President

To disseminate among the nations a knowledge of definite scientific techniques for attaining direct personal experience of God.

To teach that the purpose of life is the evolution, through self-effort, of man's limited mortal consciousness into God Consciousness; and to this end to establish Self-Realization Fellowship temples for God-communion throughout the world, and to encourage the establishment of individual temples of God in the homes and in the hearts of men.

To reveal the complete harmony and basic oneness of original Christianity as taught by Jesus Christ and original Yoga as taught by Bhagavan Krishna; and to show that these principles of truth are the common scientific foundation of all true religions.

To point out the one divine highway to which all paths of true religious beliefs eventually lead: the highway of daily, scientific, devotional meditation on God.

To liberate man from his threefold suffering: physical disease, mental inharmonies, and spiritual ignorance.

To encourage "plain living and high thinking"; and to spread a spirit of brotherhood among all peoples by teaching the eternal basis of their unity: kinship with God.

To demonstrate the superiority of mind over body, of soul over mind.

To overcome evil by good, sorrow by joy, cruelty by kindness, ignorance by wisdom.

To unite science and religion through realization of the unity of their underlying principles.

To advocate cultural and spiritual understanding between East and West, and the exchange of their finest distinctive features.

To serve mankind as one's larger Self.

INDEX

Oriental names of persons, in most cases, are alphabetically listed under the first name, as given in the text of the book; for example, Bhagabati Charan Ghosh is listed under "B." Occidental names, however, are listed under the last name.

Abanindra, nephew of Tagore, 231
Abdul Gufoor Khan, Moslem disciple
  of Lahiri Mahasaya, 284
Abhoya, prayer of, that Lahiri
  Mahasaya stop the train, 247; that
  her ninth child live, 247
Abinas Chandra Das, Prof., 411 n.
Abinash, 6; vision of, of Lahiri Mahasaya in a country field, 7
Abu Said, Persian mystic, quoted, 43–44
action, necessity for, 43 n., 105, 216
Adam and Eve allegory, 149 ff.
After-death states, 225, 227 n., 353 ff.,
  417
Afzal Khan, Moslem wonder-worker,
  158 ff.
Agastya, South Indian avatar, 262
ages (cycles) of the world, 147, 208 n.
ahamkara, ego-principle, 35 n., 42 n.,
  193 n. *See also* Ego.
ahimsa, nonviolence, 43 n., 97, 372, 376
Ahuja, M. R., Consul General of India,
  409
aims and ideals, SRF, 432
Akbar the Great, 138, 179 n., 412 n.
Alakananda, 42
Alexander the Great, 107, 296 n., 331 ff.;
  chastisement of, by Dandamis, 332–
  33; questions of, to *Brahmins,* 333–34;
  prophecy about death of, 334
Amar Mitter, my high school friend,
  flight of, toward Himalayas, 25 ff., 37
Ambassador of India B.R.Sen, xv, 422
American Unitarian Association, 302, 306
Amiyo Bose, my niece, 385
Amulaya, disciple of Sri Yukteswar, 342

amulet, 17 ff., 25, 80; appearance of,
  17; disappearance of, 78, 161 n.
Ananda Mohan Lahiri, quoted, 288 ff.
Ananda Moyi Ma, "Joy Permeated
  Mother," 385 ff.; visit of, to Ranchi
  school, 387 ff.
Ananta Lal Ghosh, my elder brother,
  13, 15 ff., 25, 27, 30 ff., 80, 83 ff.,
  87, 88–89, 105, 146, 302, 343 n.;
  betrothal of, 13; captures me on my
  way to Himalayas, 15; delivers
  Mother's death-bed message, 15–16;
  thwarts my second flight toward
  Himalayas, 27; takes me to a
  Banaras pundit and his son, 30–31;
  greets me in Agra, 83; death of, 83,
  202–203; proposes a "penniless" test
  in Brindaban, 84 ff.; requests *Kriya
  Yoga* initiation, 89
Ancient India, 331 n.
Andrews, C. F., 230 n., 374 n.
Angela, Blessed, of Foligno, absti-
  nence of, from food, 399 n.
angels, incident of, surrounding Lahiri
  Mahasaya, 244–45
Aquinas, St. Thomas, quoted, 166 n.
Arjuna, disciple of Sri Krishna, 44 n.,
  208, 215, 278 n., 414 n.
Arnold, Sir Edwin, translator of
  Bhagavad Gita, quoted, 36 n., 44 n.,
  304 n., 415 n.
Arrian, Greek historian, 331, 334
Arya Mission Institution, 288
Aryan, 331 n., 411 n.; ancient meaning
  of, 296 n.
Aryavarta, ancient name of India, 296 n.

asana, yoga posture, 140 n., 198, 218, 325
ashram, hermitage, 57 n.
Asoka, Emperor, ideal king, xxiii; inscriptions of, 330
Associated Press, report on radio rays, 134 n.; quotes Dr. Huxley, 311 n.
astral body, 210, 227 n., 354, 356 ff., 359 ff., 364 ff.
astral worlds, 161, 227 n., 353 ff., 417
astrology, 142 ff., 210; Sri Yukteswar's views on, 142 ff., 206
astronomy, ancient treatises on, 142 n.
atheism, 157 n.; *Sankhya* philosophy misconstrued as, 148
Atlantic Monthly, 23 n., 72 n.
Atlantis, 208 n.
atma. See Soul.
atom, *"anu,"* and atomic theory, 61 n., 72, 200, 236–37, 239, 272–73, 354 n., 396 n.
Atomic Age, 200, 233, 237, 409, 414
Auddy, J., companion on Kashmir trip, 167, 170, 173, 176–77
Aulukya, (Kanada, "Atom-Eater"), 61 n.
Aum (Om), cosmic creative vibration, 11 n., 17 n., 127, 128 n., 130 n., 138, 209, 235, 298 n., 316 n., 398 n., 416, 418, 419 n., 420
Aurobindo Ghosh, Sri, 371 n.
avatar, 58 n., 261 ff.
avidya, ignorance, 157 n., 235
Ayurveda, 288 n.

Babaji, guru of Lahiri Mahasaya, 123, 207–208, 209 n., 212 n., 223, 252, 259, 261 ff., 263 n., 282, 290 ff., 313, 343, 344, 352, 361 n., 414; an avatar, 261 ff.; silent influence of, 263; appearance of, 263; frees a disciple from death by fire, 264; resurrects a dead devotee, 265; promises always to retain his physical body, 267; first meeting with Lahiri Mahasaya, 269 ff.; arranges Lahiri Mahasaya's transfer to Ranikhet, 270; materializes a palace in the Himalayas, 272 ff.; initiates Lahiri Mahasaya in *Kriya Yoga,* 274; relaxes ancient rules regarding *Kriya,* 276;

quotes Gita on efficacy of *Kriya,* 277; appears before a group in Moradabad, 278–79; washes sadhu's feet at a *Kumbha Mela,* 280; meets Sri Yukteswar in Allahabad, 292 ff., in Serampore, 297, in Banaras, 297; expresses deep interest in the West, 294; promises to send Sri Yukteswar a disciple for training, 294, 303; predicts that Lahiri Mahasaya's life span is nearly ended, 295; is the supreme guru of all Self-Realization Fellowship members, 296 n.; appears before me as I prepare to leave for America, 303–304; sends me a message through Keshabananda, 348; guidance by, of all sincere *Kriya Yogis,* 410
Baber, King, 412 n.; historial healing incident concerning, 179
Babu, "Mister," 6 n., 160 n.
Balananda Brahmachari, received *Kriya Yoga* initiation, 287
Banaras hermitage, 75 ff., 80, 82, 279 n.; my early training in, 75 ff.
bangle, astrological, 142, 143 ff., 152, 153, 154, 206 n.
Barach, Dr. Alvan L., experiments of, in curative effect of breathlessness, 215 n.
Behari, servant in Serampore, 168
Behari Pundit, my professor at Scottish Church College, 118, 120
Bengal-Nagpur Railway Company, 4, 6, 159 n., 194, 218; my father's position in, 4, 19
Bengali, 104, 191–92, 288
Bhaduri Mahasaya, venerable "Levitating Saint," 53 ff.
Bhagabati Charan Ghosh, my father, 4 ff., 13 ff., 19, 21, 24, 32, 73, 74, 75, 83, 84, 93, 105, 107, 159 n., 167, 189, 192, 302; Spartan habits of, 5–6; vision of, of Lahiri Mahasaya in a country field, 7; initiation of, in *Kriya Yoga,* 8; lifelong devotion of, to my mother, 15; visit of, to my Ranchi school, 218; finances my visit to America, 302, 306; welcomes me on my return to India, 321; helps Ranchi school, 325; death of, 343 n.

Bhagavad Gita, "Song of the Lord," 5, 24 n., 25, 26, 30, 36 n., 43 n., 71, 114, 148, 179 n., 199, 208, 215, 278 n., 285, 288, 294, 304, 350, 359 n., 378, 414, 415 n.; quoted by Babaji, 277; my translation of, 414

bhakti, devotion, 71, 108, 128, 285

Bharata, founder of Hindu music, 139

Bhaskarananda Saraswati, Swami, 287

Bhola Nath, singing student at Ranchi, 229, 230

Bhupendra Nath Sanyal, 285

Bible, quoted, 17 n., 75 n., 100 n., 101 n., 102 n.,112, 113, 117, 127 n., 128 n., 136 n., 137 n., 140 n., 148, 149, 150 n., 157 n., 178 n., 189, 194, 218, 222 n., 233 n., 235, 237, 238, 239, 242 n., 251, 252 n., 253, 257, 262, 265, 268 n., 270 n., 280 n., 281 ff., 300, 316, 361 n., 363 n., 377, 378, 380, 382 n., 383, 388, 406, 411 n., 413 n., 415, 416, 417, 418, 420, 421

Bimal, Ranchi student, 301

"bioscope" experience in cosmic consciousness, 70–71

Birtles, Francis, experience of, with tigers, 347 n.

Bishnu Charan Ghosh, my youngest brother, 6, 75, 185, 202, 218, 321, 390

Bletsch, Ettie, 314, 321, 328 n., 351, 369

body. *See* Physical body, Astral body, *and* Causal body.

boils incident, concerning my sister Uma, 11

Bose. *See* Jagadis Chandra.

Bose, Dr. P., husband of my sister Nalini, 203, 205

Brahma, an aspect of Godhead, 23, 58 n., 65 n., 128 n., 137, 140 n., 195, 258 n., 418

brahmachari, celibate student, 217 n., 344

brahmacharini, woman ascetic, 252

Brahmin, "knower of God," one of the four castes, 34 n., 284, 333, 335, 386

breath, 341 n.; mastery of, 53, 96, 105, 126, 128, 179, 208 ff., 414 ff.

breath rate, relation of, to longevity, 211

breathlessness, 179, 416; physical and mental healing effects of, 215 n.

Brinda Bhagat, Banaras postman, 286

brotherhood, 256, 379, 406, 420, 432

Brown, Prof. W. Norman, quoted on India, 60 n., 289 n.

Browning, Robert, quoted, 117

Buddha, 81, 262, 331 n., 359 n., 372 n., 409, 415 n., 420

Bulletin of the American Council of Learned Societies, 60 n., 289 n.

Burbank, Luther, v, 308 ff.

Calcutta University, 70, 156, 187–88, 190, 336; I receive my A.B. degree from, 192

Calligaris, Prof. Giuseppe, 22 n.

Carlyle, quoted, 290 n.

Carnegie Hall, audience of, chants an ancient Hindu song, 405

caste system of India, 4, 284, 335

Catherine, St., of Siena, abstinence of, from food, 399 n.

causal body, 354, 360 ff., 365

causal world, 354, 357, 360, 362 ff.

celibacy, 194, 374, 376

Centuries of Meditations, quoted, 416 n.

Century of Verses, quoted, 81 n., 214

Chakras. See Spinal centers.

Chandragupta, Emperor, contemporary of Alexander the Great, 331

chela, disciple, 103

Childe Harold, examination incident connected with, 190

Chinese records, on India, 342 n., 411 n.

Christ Consciousness, 128 n., 149 n., 151 n., 209, 243 n., 253, 268 n., 285, 316 n., 418, 419 n., 420

Christ, Jesus the, 75 n., 101, 112, 140 n., 148–49, 151 n., 165, 178, 182, 207–08, 209, 233, 249, 251, 253, 262, 265, 268 n., 270, 296, 299, 314, 316 ff., 318, 320, 357, 363, 377, 378, 380, 383, 388, 409, 418, 419; relationship of, with John the Baptist, 281–82; my vision of, in Encinitas, 413

Christian church, early, taught reincarnation, 151 n.

cobra(s), 347, 376; incident of, near Puri hermitage, 98

Colony, SRF, in Encinitas, 406

Columbus, 55, 296 n., 301, 411 n.
commentaries, scriptural, of Pranabananda, 23 n.; of Lahiri Mahasaya, 34,
289; of Sanandana, disciple of Shankara, 81 n.; of Shankara, 81 n.,
110 n.; of Sri Yukteswar, 148 ff.; of
Sadasivendra, 201 n., 337 n.; my, on
the New Testament, 413; my, on
Bhagavad Gita, 414
Compensation, quoted, 43 n., 227 n.
Comus, quoted, 419 n.
concentration techniques, at Ranchi
school, 326
Congress of Religions, in Boston, 302,
305, 323
consciousness, 108 n.; studies in states
of, 42 n.
Cooch Behar, Prince of, challenge of,
to "Tiger Swami," 49
Cosmic Chants, 405
cosmic consciousness, 8 n., 26, 210,
212, 406 n.; early experiences in, 70–
71, 126 ff., 183 ff.; poem on, 129
cosmic motion picture, 240 ff.
Couéism, 11 n., 53 n.
Cousin, Victor, quoted on Oriental philosophy, 65 n.
Cranmer-Byng, Dr. L., letter from England of, 408
creation, universal, evolves out of Brahma,
65 n.; produced by *Aum,* 128 n., 130 n.,
209 n.; cycles of, 147 n.; relegated to
God's "consorts," 171 n.; polarity of,
234, 235; true nature of, 234 ff., 249,
273 ff., 361 ff., 366
Crile, Dr. Geo. W., quoted, 396 n.
customs of India, worship, 8; kite matches,
12; marriage, 13, 15 n., 25, 203; alms-
giving, 17, 373; respect for elder
brother, 32 n., 85; gifts to the guru, 56,
324; touching feet of one's guru, 103,
284; funeral, 112, 299 n., 350 n.; "the
guest is God," 122; refraining from
smoking in the presence of one's elders,
173 n.; removing shoes when entering
hermitage, 188 n.; receiving initiation
into Swami Order, 195–96; eating with
fingers, 324, 392; daily *yajnas,* obligatory offerings, 373

Dabru Ballav, teacher of Gita, 114
Dakshineswar, temple of Kali in, 68,
181 ff.; Yogoda Math in, 327
danda, bamboo staff, 248 n., 264
Dandamis, Hindu sage, rebuke of, to
Alexander the Great, 331 ff.
Dante, poem of, quoted, 418 n.
darshan (holy sight), 145, 287
Dasgupta, Prof. S., 192 n., 198 n.
Daya Mata, president SRF-YSS, 196 n.,
327 n.
Dayananda, Swami, leader at Banaras
hermitage, 75 ff., 82
death, 3, 219, 227 n., 240, 267 n., 268 n.,
284, 300, 342, 359–60, 362, 364 ff.,
366 ff., 416–17
deer, death of, in Ranchi, 219
Desai, M., secretary to Gandhi, 369,
370, 372, 377, 378
Descartes, quoted, 319 n.
desire, fetter of man, 111, 131, 214,
272 n., 361, 364–65, 415
Devendranath Tagore, father of Rabindranath, 231
devil, the, 243 n. *See also Maya.*
dharma, righteousness, duty, xxiii,
43 n., 336 n., 378 n., 379
dhoti, garment of Indian men, 85 n.,
230, 323, 327
diabetes, 152 ff.; saint healed of, by
God, 178
Dickinson, E. E., "Silver cup" incident,
402 ff.
Diet and Diet Reform, 377 n.
Dijen, my college roommate at boardinghouse, 163 ff.
diksha, spiritual initiation, 89, 285
discipline, of my father, 5; of Dayananda, 76 ff.; of Sri Yukteswar, 81,
103, 105 ff.; received even by illumined masters, 278 n.
disease, 99 ff.; metaphysical transfer of,
177 ff., 298, 318, 364 n.
Divine Comedy, The, quoted, 418 n.
Divine Mother, an aspect of God, 11–12,
66 ff., 71, 92 n., 171 n., 357
Dostoyevsky, quoted, 120 n.
dreams, phenomena of, 239, 272
drugs and intoxicants harmful, 357 n.

Ducouri Lahiri, son of Lahiri Maha-saya, 246, 259
Durga, aspect of God as Divine Mother, 92 n., 171 n.
Durga Ma, 404
Dwapara Yuga, present equinoctial Age of the World, 147, 208 n.
Dwarka Prasad, my childhood friend in Bareilly, 14, 28, 31
Dwarkanath Tagore, grandfather of Rabindranath, 231
Dwijendra Tagore, brother of Rabindra-nath, 231

East-West magazine. See Self-Realiza-tion magazine.
Eddington, Sir Arthur S., quoted on the world as "mind-stuff," 236
education, necessity for right, 157 n., 217; views of Tagore on, 231 ff.; views of Luther Burbank on, 309 ff.
ego, 35, 38, 39, 42 n., 88, 106 ff., 135, 162, 193 n., 201 n., 213 ff., 251, 281 n., 338, 360
Egypt, my visit to, 320
"Eightfold Path of Yoga," outlined by Patanjali, 198–99
Einstein, theory of relativity of, 235 ff.; tribute of, to Gandhi, 384
electron microscope, 236
Elijah (Elias), 207, 242–43, 281 ff.
Elisha (Eliseus), 251 n., 281 ff.
Elizabeth, Blessed, of Rent, abstinence of, from food, 399 n.
Emerson, quoted, 23 n., 34 n., 43 n., 53 n., 58 n., 157 n., 193 n., 227 n., 231 n.; poem of, on *Maya,* 38 n.
Encinitas, hermitage and colony in, 404 ff., 408
Encyclopedia Americana, 18 n.
Europe, my tour in, in England and Scotland, 314; in Germany, Holland, France, Switzerland, Italy, and Greece, 319
Evans-Wentz, Dr. W.Y., vi, xiii–xiv

Fa-Hsien, 5th-century Chinese priest in India, 411 n.
fakir, Moslem ascetic, 43, 158, 344

father, my. *See* Bhagabati; of Sri Yuktes-war, 92; of Lahiri Mahasaya, 258, 259
festivals of India, 92 n., 132 n.; *See Kumbha Mela;* celebrations of, by Sri Yukteswar, 92, 136 ff., 341
Forest Lawn Memorial-Park, testimony of mortician of, 422
forgiveness, 380, 382
Francis, St., of Assisi, 178, 260 n.; my pilgrimage to shrine of, 319
Francis de Sales, St., quoted, 180
Freud, 53 n.

Galli-Curci, Amelita, 307
Gandha Baba, "Perfume Saint," wonder-workings of, 40 ff.
Gandhi, M. K. ("Mahatma"), 5 n., 204 n., 233 n., 321 n., 335, 369 ff.; views of, on religion, 205 n., 377 ff., on non-violence, 370, 376 ff., 383, 409, on silence, 372, on cow protection, 373, on celibacy, 374, 376, on diet, 376–77; visit of, to YSS school in Ranchi, 369; eleven vows of, 370; *Kriya Yoga* ini-tiation of, 377; *In Memoriam,* 384
Gandhi's Letters to a Disciple, 371 n.
Gandhi World Peace Memorial, at SRF Lake Shrine, 409
Ganga Dhar, photographer of Lahiri Mahasaya, 9
Ganges River, legend of, 171 n.; purity of, 260 n.
Gaudapada, *paramguru* of *Adi* ("the first") Shankaracharya, 81 n.
Gauri Ma, hermitage hostess in Brinda-ban, 86
Genesis, interpretation of, 149 ff.
Gerlich, Dr. Fritz, 314
ghat, bathing place, 21, 73, 249, 266, 296
Ghosh, my family name, 4
Ghoshal, D. C., my professor at Seram-pore College, 187–88, 341
Ghoshal, S. N., rector at Tagore's uni-versity, Visva-Bharati, 232 n.
Giri ("mountain"), designation of one of the ten branches of the Swami Order, 93, 195–96, 344

Giri Bala, non-eating saint, 390 ff.; uses a yogic technique, 390, 398–99
Gita ("song"). *See* Bhagavad Gita.
Gitanjali, 229; poem in, 232
God, names and manifestations of, 10 n., 11 n., 23 n., 37 n., 65 n., 69, 71, 88 n., 92 n., 126, 128 n., 130–31, 140 n., 171 n., 182, 209, 238, 255, 258 n., 357, 418; omnipresence of, 43 n., 120; the true sustainer of man, 57, 77, 84; source of bounty on my "penniless test," 83ff.; answers prayer, 31, 88, 137, 183, 241; is knowable, 148; at Dakshineswar temple, 183–84
Gogonendra, nephew of Tagore, 231
Govinda Jati, guru of Shankara, 81 n.
Greek historians, on India, 331 ff.
gunas, qualities of Nature, 17 n., 336 n.
guru (*gurudeva*), spiritual teacher, 3 n., 22, 33, 70 n., 79, 91–92, 122, 179, 207, 217 n., 296 n., 377; tribute to, by Shankara, 81 n.
Gyanamata, Sister, 401, 404

Habu, priest at Banaras hermitage, 78
Hanum, Halide Edib, 371 n.
Harsha, King, 342 n.
Hatha Yoga, science of body control, 140 n., 200 n.
Hazrat, astral entity under control of Afzal Khan, 159 ff.
healing, of sadhu, 29; views of Sri Yukteswar on, 99, 104, 170; through use of bangles and jewels, 144, 206 n.; by a master taking others' karma, 177 ff.; views of Lahiri Mahasaya on, 99 ff., 255, 288; in ancient India, 334
hermitage, in Puri, seaside retreat of Sri Yukteswar, xiii, 132, 349, 368; description of, in Banaras, scene of my early training, 75; in Serampore, ashram of Sri Yukteswar, 80, 92, 322, 323; in Brindaban, scene of hospitality on my "penniless test," 86; near Rishikesh, scene of Pranabananda's earth exit, 222 ff.; in Dakshineswar, Yogoda Math, 327; in Brindaban,

built by Keshabananda, 346; in Encinitas, Self-Realization Fellowship, 404–405, 406 n.
Hieuen Tsiang. *See* Yuan Chwang.
Himalaya Mountains, 121, 172 ff., 175, 260 n.; my birthplace near, 4; my flight toward, first, 15, second, 25 ff., 37, third, 118 ff., 124
Hindi, Indian language, 288, 373 n.
Hindu High School, in Calcutta, 73; my graduation from, 74
Hindu scriptures, 75 n., 77 n., 204 n., 212 n., 268 n., 294, 412, 414
Hinduism, 296 n., 377; daily rituals of, 373
Hippocrates, 288 n.
Hiranyaloka, astral planet, 353–54, 357 ff., 364 n., 365, 368
History of Indian Philosophy, 198 n.
Holy Ghost, 128 n., 316 n., 419 n. *See also Aum.*
Holy Grail, my vision of, 413
Holy Land (Palestine), my visit to, 320
Holy Science, The, 147 n., 296
Hound of Heaven, The, quoted, 411 n.
Howells, Prof. George, president of Serampore College, 156
Humayun, Prince, 179 n.; historical healing incident concerning, 179
humility, 38, 68, 72, 120 n., 280
Hunsicker, Alvin, 406
Huxley, Dr. Julian, quoted on Oriental techniques, 311 n.
"Hymn to America," 307
hypnotism, 279; harmful effects of, 42

Ikshwaku, father of India's solar warrior dynasty, 208
immaculate creation, 149
incorruptibility of body, 212 n., 422; of St. Teresa of Avila, 57 n.; of St. John of the Cross, 72 n.
India, ancient and modern civilizations of, xxiii, 18 n., 257, 330 ff., 334 ff., 342 n., 411 ff., 420; contributions of, to civilization, 58, 60 ff., 142 n., 257, 288 n.; independence of, 412 n.; flag, xxiii
India Center, SRF, in Hollywood, 409

International Congress of Religious Liberals, Boston, my first lecture in America at, 302, 306
introspection, 38, 59, 213, 366
intuition, 134, 136 n., 200, 356, 357
Ishwara, God as Ruler of Universe, 10 n.

Jagadguru Sri Shankaracharya, religious title, 196
Jagadis Chandra Bose, famous botanist, 58 ff., 88
Jainism, a sect of Hinduism, 372 n., 377
Janaka, King, 193 n.
Japan, my visit to, 202; vision of coast of, by Lahiri Mahasaya, 285
Jatinda (Jotin Ghosh), flight of, toward Himalayas, 25, 31–32
Jeans, Sir James, quoted on the universe as thought, 237
Jehangir, Emperor, Kashmir gardens of, 174
Jerome, St., taught reincarnation, 151 n.
jewels, remedial influences of, 144, 154, 205–206; materialization of, 272 ff.
ji, suffix denoting respect, 76 n.
Jitendra Mazumdar, my companion, at Banaras hermitage, 75, 76, 82; in Agra, 83, 84, 85, 89, 346; in Brindaban, 86 ff.
jnana, wisdom, 71, 108, 215, 285
Jnanavatar, "Incarnation of Wisdom," a title of Sri Yukteswar, 90, 290, 351
John the Baptist, relationship of, with Jesus, 281 ff.
John, St., of the Cross, 72 n.
Jones, Sir William, tribute of, to Sanskrit, 18 n.
Joseph, St., of Cupertino, levitating state of, 57 n.
Journal of Emerson, 34 n.
Joyendra Puri, president of Indian sadhus, 344 n.
Jules-Bois, M., of the Sorbonne, quoted on superconscious mind, 53 n.
Jung, Dr. C. G., tribute of, to yoga, 199–200

Kabir, great medieval master, 207, 262, 349, 412 n.; resurrection of, 299 n.

Kalanos, Hindu teacher of Alexander the Great, 334
Kali Kumar Roy, disciple of Lahiri Mahasaya, 9, 248–49
Kali Yuga, Iron Age, 147, 147 n., 208 n.
Kali, aspect of God as Mother Nature, 11, 37, 68, 171 n., 181 ff.
Kalidasa, the "Indian Shakespeare," quoted, 171 n.
Kanai, young disciple of Sri Yukteswar, 116, 163, 167, 168, 169, 170, 172, 176
Kant, quoted, 411 n.
Kara Patri, sadhu at *Kumbha Mela,* 345–46
karma, universal law of cause and effect, 30, 143–44, 146, 151 n., 158, 178, 179, 193 n., 201 n., 207, 211, 214, 221, 227 n., 264, 268 n., 271, 272, 298, 353, 355, 359, 364 ff., 380 n., 399 n., 415, 417
Karma Yoga, path to God through works or activity, 215, 285
Kashi, student at Ranchi school, reborn and discovered, 224 ff.
Kashi Moni, wife of Lahiri Mahasaya, 244 ff., 259; beholds angels surrounding her husband, 244–45; witnesses his miraculous disappearance, 246
Kasturbai, wife of Gandhi, 374 ff.
Kebalananda, Swami, my Sanskrit tutor, 32 ff., 93, 269, 279; association of, with Babaji in the Himalayas, 263 ff.
Kedar Nath, 19 ff., 24; beholds Pranabananda's "second body" at a Banaras *ghat,* 21
Keller, Helen, 356 n.
Kellogg, Charles, experiments of, with tonal vibrations, 138 n.
Kennell, Dr. Lloyd, 410
Keshabananda, Swami, 223; sees Lahiri Mahasaya's resurrected body, 298 ff.; receives me at Brindaban hermitage, 346 ff.; gives me message from Babaji, 348
Key to Health, 377 n.
kite incident, with my sister Uma, 12
Knight, Goodwin J., Lt. Governor of California, 409

knowledge, intellectual, compared with
  realization, 34 ff., 114–15, 166, 214,
  285, 320 n.
Krishna, divine avatar, 85, 86, 87, 88,
  132 n., 138, 182, 208, 214, 262, 263,
  278 n., 414; early life of, in Brindaban, 348; my vision of, 352
Krishnananda, Swami, tamer of lioness,
  at *Kumbha Mela,* 344
Kriya Yoga, technique for God-realization, 8, 15, 33, 34, 88–89, 93, 103,
  116, 119, 131, 140, 163, 171 n., 181,
  207 ff., 221, 259–60, 275, 276, 283–
  84, 286 ff., 289 ff., 302, 311, 313,
  326, 377, 409 n., 414–15, 416, 421;
  initiation in, of my parents, 8, of
  Pratap Chatterji, 88, of Ananta, 89,
  of myself, 93, of Kashi Moni, 245,
  of Lahiri Mahasaya, 274; definition
  of, 207; antiquity of, 207; second
  technique of, 222; ancient rules of,
  relaxed by Babaji, 276; four steps of,
  286; eternal basis of, 290; Babaji's
  prophecy about, 303
Kriya Yogi (Kriyaban), practitioner of
  the ancient yogic technique given by
  Babaji to Lahiri Mahasaya, 207,
  210 ff., 410, 417, 421
Kumar, resident at Serampore hermitage, 109 ff.
Kumbha Mela, religious fair, 252, 279,
  292; scene of first meeting of Babaji
  and Sri Yukteswar, 292 ff.; Chinese
  record of, 342 n.; my visit to, 343 ff.
kutastha chaitanya, 8, 128 n., 285, 316 n.
  See also Christ Consciousness.
Kwan Yin, Chinese personification of
  the Divine Mother, 409

Lahiri Mahasaya, disciple of Babaji and
  guru of Sri Yukteswar, 6 ff., 22, 24,
  25, 32 ff., 35, 81, 94, 103, 105, 115,
  118, 121, 123, 194, 207, 221, 233,
  242 n., 244 ff., 257, 261, 262, 263,
  265, 278 n., 282 ff., 292, 295, 297 ff.,
  301, 302, 323, 346, 347, 350, 361 n.,
  404; materialization of, in a country
  field, 7; initiation by, of my parents,
  in *Kriya Yoga,* 8; heals me of Asiatic

cholera, 9; miraculous origin of photograph of, 9; appearance of, 10; bap-
  tizes me, 16; intercedes with Brahma
  for Pranabananda, 23 ff.; guru of Kebalananda, 32 ff.; scriptural commentaries of, 34, 288 ff.; heals blindness
  of Ramu, 35; guru of Sri Yukteswar,
  92, 93; heals Sri Yukteswar of thinness, 99–100; is surrounded by angels, 244–45; initiates his wife in
  Kriya, 245; disappears from her
  sight, 246; protects devotees from
  lightning, 247; delays train at disciple's prayer, 247; saves life of Abhoya's child, 247–48; shows a "picture scene" from the life of the
  employer of Kali Kumar Roy, 248; is
  given tribute by Trailanga Swami,
  252; resurrects Rama from the dead,
  253 ff.; prophesies that his biography
  will be written for the West, 256; refuses publicity, 256, 287; early life
  of, 258 ff.; government employment
  of, 259, 269, 287 n.; simultaneous
  appearance of, at his Banaras home
  and at Dasaswamedh *ghat,* 266 ff.; is
  transferred to Ranikhet, 269; meets
  Babaji, 270 ff.; receives *Kriya* initiation in a palace in Himalayas, 274 ff.;
  life mission of, to portray ideal
  householder yogi, 275–76, 291; asks
  Babaji to relax *Kriya* restrictions,
  276; summons Babaji before Moradabad friends, 278–79; sees Babaji
  washing sadhu's feet, 280; heals his
  employer's wife in London, 283;
  gives *Kriya* initiation to those of
  every faith, 284, 285; has vision of
  shipwreck near Japan, 285; title of
  Yogavatar, 287 n., 290; the handwriting of, 288; earth exit of, 298 ff.; appearance of, in resurrected body, before three disciples, 299 ff.
Lake Shrine, SRF, Los Angeles, 409
Lal Dhari, servant, 168–69
Lalla Yogiswari, "sky clad" Shiva devotee, 171 n.
Lama, F. R. von, 314 n.

Lambodar Dey, brother of Giri Bala, 391–92, 393

lamp, missing, incident of, at Puri hermitage, 136

Lao-tzu, quoted, 383, 415 n., 420

Lateau, Louise, abstinence of, from food, 399 n.

Lauder, Sir Harry, 314

Laurence, William L., quoted on solar energy, 396 n.

law, universe governed by, 100, 110, 143 ff., 242 n., 251, 256, 378 n.

Lawrence, Brother, Christian mystic, 414

Lazarri, Dominica, abstinence of, from food, 399 n.

Legacy of India, The, quoted, 171 n.

Lessons, SRF, for members, 207 n., 409, 410 n., 425

Levinthal, Rabbi I. H., quoted on superconscious mind, 108 n.

Lewis, Dr. M. W., 406

Lidwina, St., of Schiedam, abstinence of, from food, 399 n.

life force, 42, 53 n., 99, 208, 209, 211–12, 217, 316 n., 360, 416

"lifetrons" (*prana*), finer-than-atomic energies, 42, 242, 354, 356, 359, 362

light, phenomenon of, 235 ff.

Lincoln, Abraham, picture of, in Calcutta, 309 n.

Lithuanian language, 411 n.

London, lectures, 314, 400; yoga class in, 400; SRF Center in, 400; letter from, during the war, 408

lotus(es), symbolic meaning of, 59 n., 406 n.; materialization of, by Shankara, to convey disciple across river, 81 n.; of cerebrospinal centers, 140 n.

lotus posture (*padmasana*), 140 n., 287

Lourdes, shrine in, 119

love, 125, 194, 215, 357, 380, 388, 413 n., 420; Sri Yukteswar verbally expresses, for me, 79–80, 340; effect of, on plants, 308

Luther, Martin, quoted, 284 n.

Lynn, James J. (Rajarsi Janakananda), 290 n., 313, 404

Ma, Puri disciple, beholds the resurrected body of Sri Yukteswar, 368

Mahabharata, ancient epic, 4, 5 n., 43 n., 77 n., 288, 335, 380

Mahamandal, hermitage in Banaras, 75, 279 n.

Maharaj, "great king," title of respect, 294, 322, 350

Maharaja, of Kasimbazar, Sir Manindra Chandra Nundy, first patron of Ranchi school, 217, 325; his son, Sir Srish Chandra Nundy, 321, 325; of Banaras, 287; his son, 287; Jotindra Mohan Thakur, 287; of Mysore, 328; his son, my host, 328; of Travancore, 335; of Burdwan, investigation by, of Giri Bala's non-eating state, 390

mahasamadhi, final earth exit of a great yogi, 298, 410 n.

Mahasaya, religious title, 20 n., 68, 259 n.

Mahatma, "great soul." *See* Gandhi

Mahavatar, "Divine Incarnation," a title of Babaji, 262, 290

Mahavira, Jain prophet, 372 n.

Mahendra Nath Gupta ("M"). *See* Master Mahasaya

Maitra Mahasaya, beholds materialization of Babaji's body in Moradabad, 279

man, evolution of, 88, 150, 210, 211 ff., 417; creation of (Genesis concept), 149 ff., 416, (Hindu concept), 151 n.; made in God's image, 149 n., 157 n., 193 n., 239; nature of, 157 n., 365

mantra, potent chant, 17 n., 138, 355 n., 398

Manu, great ancient legislator, 208, 335–36

Marconi, 58; quoted, 234 n.

Marshall, Sir John, quoted, 18 n.

Masson-Oursel, P., quoted on King Asoka, xxiii

master, 70 n., 95, 112, 177 ff., 193 n., 206 n., 250, 268 n.; test of a, 179. *See also* Guru *and* Yogi.

Master Mahasaya (Mahendra Nath Gupta), saint of humility, 66 ff.; "bioscope" experience bestowed on me by, 71

Mataji, sister of Babaji, 266–67

math, monastery, 57 n., 81 n., 196 n., 327
mauna, spiritual silence, 250 n.
maya, cosmic delusion, 35 n., 38, 82, 88, 95, 103, 111, 138, 147, 150, 179, 209, 234 ff., 268 n., 362, 366 n., 418; Emerson's poem on, 38 n.
McCrindle, Dr. J. W., translator of Greek texts on India, 331
Megasthenes, quoted on prosperity of ancient India, 411 n.
metaphysics, 58, 104 n., 179
Milton, quoted, 245 n., 413 n., 419 n.
mind, 42 n., 46, 100, 104, 108 n., 110, 130, 134, 178, 212–13, 215 n., 226 n., 358; poem on control of, 335, 415 n.
Mirabai, medieval mystic, 56; poem by, 56
Mira Behn, disciple of Gandhi, 371
miracles, law of, 42 ff., 101, 193 n., 233 ff., 273 n., 290, 291
Misra, Dr., ship's physician, 202; disbelief of, at Shanghai, 203
Mohenjo-Daro and the Indus Civilization, 18 n.
moral commandments, 415; observance of, necessary for success in yoga, 198
Moslems (Mohammedans), 158, 209 n., 296 n., 382, 412 n.; *namaj* worship of, 284; Mecca Masjid Mosque of, in Hyderabad, 330
mosquito incidents, at Serampore hermitage, 96 ff.
mother, my, 4–6, 8, 11, 13, 14, 15, 16, 66, 67, 78, 203, 343 n., 370; my vision of, in Bareilly, 13; death of, 14; message and amulet from, 16; of Sri Yukteswar, 80, 93, 100, 112; of Lahiri Mahasaya, 258
Mount Washington Estates, 174, 306, 307, 400–401, *See also* Self-Realization Fellowship.
mudra, ritual gesture, 288 n.
Mukunda Lal Ghosh, my name at birth, 4; changed to Yogananda on my entrance into Swami Order, 195
Müller, Max, quoted on misuse of *Aryan,* 296 n.
Museum, YSS, 326; SRF, 326 n.
music, Indian, 137 ff., 405–406
Myers, F. W. H., quoted, 108 n.

Mysore, invitation to visit, 328; my travels in, 328 ff.
Mysterious Universe, The, quoted, 237

nadis, nerve passages, 288 n.
Nalanda University, ancient, 61
Nalini, my younger sister, childhood experiences of, 203; marriage of, 203; healing of, of thinness, 204–205, of typhoid fever, 205, of paralyzed legs, 205; daughters of, 206
Nanak, Guru, chant of, sung in Carnegie Hall, 406
Nantu, help of, in passing my high school examinations, 73–74
Naren, disciple of Sri Yukteswar, 154
Nature, world of relativity. *See* Durga, Kali, *and Maya.*
Nature Cure, 377 n.
Nature of the Physical World, 236
neem, margosa tree, 11, 288, 370
Nehru, Jawaharlal, quoted, 384
Neumann, Therese, of Konnersreuth, 24 n., 177 n., 390, 395, 399 n.; my pilgrimage to meet, 314 ff.
Newton, law of motion of, 234
New York Times, The, quoted, 64, 215 n., 236, 396 n.
Nicholas, St., of Flüe, abstinence of, from food, 399 n.
Night Thoughts, 273 n.
nirbikalpa samadhi, state of changeless God-consciousness, 23 n., 179, 210, 235, 275, 353, 367, 414. *See also Samadhi.*
niyama, religious observances, 198
"Noble Eightfold Path" of Buddhism, 198 n.
nonviolence, 97 ff., 233 n., 370, 372 n.; Gandhi's views on, 376 ff., 379 ff.; experiment in, of William Penn, 383
Northrop, Dr. John Howard, quoted on purity of Ganges water, 260 n.

Om. See Aum.
Omar Khayyam, Persian mystic, 261–62
Onesikritos, messenger of Alexander, visit of, to a Hindu sage, 331 ff.
Origen, taught reincarnation, 151 n.
Over-Soul, 53 n.

padmasana, lotus posture, 140 n.

Pakistan, 412 n.

Panchanon Bhattacharya, 288, 299, 346; beholds Lahiri Mahasaya's resurrected body, 299

Panini, ancient grammarian, tribute of, to Sanskrit, 74 n.

Panthi, my boardinghouse in Serampore, 158, 163, 188, 189, 191; scene of Afzal Khan's four wonder-workings, 159 ff.; scene of Sri Yukteswar's miraculous appearance, 164

Paradise Lost, quoted, 413 n.

paramahansa(ji), religious title, 4 n., 68, 341

paramguru, the guru of one's guru, 296 n.

Parvati, Goddess, 171

Patanjali, ancient exponent of yoga, 53, 97, 198, 200 n., 208, 209, 262, 342, 417; "Eightfold Path of Yoga," outlined by, 198–99

Paul, St., quoted, 208

Penn, William, experiment of, in nonviolence, 383

"penniless test" in Brindaban, 84 ff.

"Perfume Saint" (Gandha Baba), 40 ff.

Persian proverb, 285 n., 380 n.

Phaedrus, quoted, 166 n.

physical body, 98, 104, 122, 149, 150, 206 n., 209 ff., 213–14, 215 n., 217, 316 n., 359 ff., 416, 417

Pilate, Pontius, quoted, 419

pilgrimage, my, to Therese Neumann in Bavaria, 314 ff.; to shrine of St. Francis in Assisi, 319; to Palestine, 320; to Giri Bala in Bengal, 390 ff.

Pingale, Dr., disciple of Gandhi, 369, 377

Plato, 166 n.

Pliny, quoted on prosperity of ancient India, 411 n.

Plutarch, 331, 333

poem(s), by Emerson, 38 n.; by Mirabai, 56; by Tagore, on J. C. Bose, 64, in *Gitanjali,* 232; by Shankara, 81 n., 196; my, "Samadhi," 129–30; by Lalla Yogiswari, 171 n.; by Shakespeare, 212; to Shiva, 258 n.; by Omar Khayyam, 261; by Kabir,

299 n.; by Walt Whitman, 307; by Thayumanavar, 335; by Ravidas, 349; by Nanak, 406 n.; by Francis Thompson, 411 n.; by Milton, 413 n., 419 n.; by Dante, 418 n.

Polo, Marco, quoted, 205 n.

Positive Sciences of the Ancient Hindus, 142 n.

powers, miraculous, 24 n., 130, 192 n., 200 n., 206 n., 242 n., 273; misuse of, 43, 102, 161–62

Prabhas Chandra Ghosh, vice-president, YSS, 146 n., 188

Prafulla, experience of, with cobra, 98; disciple of Sri Yukteswar, 323, 351

Prajna Chakshu, blind sadhu, 344

prana, life energy, 42, 53 n., 140 n., 198, 200, 208, 354 n., 416

Pranabananda, Swami, "the saint with two bodies," 19 ff., 73, 220 ff., 268 n.; *Pranab Gita* by, 23 n.; visit of, to Ranchi school, 220; visit to, by my father and me, 220–21; dramatic earth-exit of, 222 ff.; experience of, in beholding Lahiri Mahasaya's resurrected body, 300

pranam, 324, 378, 395

pranayama, technique for control of life force, 53, 198, 200, 209

Pratap Chatterji, help of, to two penniless boys in Brindaban, 88

prayer, answered, 12, 30, 87, 137, 182–83, 240–41, 303, 305

Prayer Council, 401 n.

"Prayer for a Dwelling," 404

Prayer to the Divine Mother for Forgiveness of Sins, 81 n.

Premavatar, "Incarnation of Love," 290 n.

Prokash Das, 226

psychoanalysis, 42 n.

pundit, scholar, at Banaras, 30–31, 83; at Serampore hermitage, 113

Quakers, Pennsylvania, experiment of, in nonviolence, 383

Rabindranath Tagore, 229 ff., 405; poem by, on J. C. Bose, 64, in *Gitanjali,*

232; my first meeting with, 229–30; invitation of, to visit his Santiniketan school, 230; family of, 231

Radhakrishnan, Sir S., 232 n.

radio, analogy of, in understanding "cauliflower comedy," 133 ff.; microscope, 134 n.; mind-, 134, 226 n.

raga, melodic scale, 138–39

"Raja Begum," tiger in Cooch Behar, 49 ff.

Raja Yoga, "royal" or complete yogic science, 285

Rajarsi Janakananda. *See* Lynn, J.J.

Rajendra Nath Mitra, companion on Kashmir trip, 167 ff., 174, 175

Ram Gopal Muzumdar, "the sleepless saint," 118, 120 ff.; rebuke of, that I failed to bow before Tarakeswar shrine, 120; healing by, of my back, 123; first meeting of, with Babaji and Mataji, 266

Rama, ancient avatar, 35, 262

Rama, disciple of Lahiri Mahasaya, raised from the dead, 253 ff.

Ramakrishna Paramahansa, 68, 182, 402 n.

Raman, Sir C. V., 336

Ramana Maharshi, 339

Ramayana, ancient epic, 4, 35 n., 77 n., 378

Ramu, disciple of Lahiri Mahasaya, healing of, of blindness, 35

Ranchi school (Yogoda Satsanga Brahmacharya Vidyalaya), founded, 217 ff.; branches of, 220, 326; educational, medical, philanthropic activities of, 220, 325 ff.; visit to, by Pranabananda, 220, by Mahatma Gandhi, 369, by Ananda Moyi Ma, 387 ff.; discussion of, with Rabindranath Tagore, 230; visit to, by members of Tagore's Santiniketan school, 232 n.; my vision of America in storeroom of, 301; Luther Burbank's interest in, 309; financial difficulties of, 325; permanent organization of, 325; *Kriya Yoga* initiation to boys at, 326

Ravidas, medieval saint, miracle of, at Chitor, 349; poem by, 349

Rawlinson, H. G., quoted, xxiii

Razzak, quoted on wealth of ancient India, 412 n.

reincarnation, 151 n., 227 n., 272 n., 281 n., 359, 363, 380 n., 417

renunciation, 30 n., 56, 216, 218, 276, 374

resurrection from death, 268 n.; of Rama, 255; of man who jumped from Himalayan cliff, 265; of Lahiri Mahasaya, 299 ff.; of Kabir, 299; of Sri Yukteswar, 352 ff.; of Christ, 363

Revelation, quoted, 140 n., 157 n., 209 n., 419 n.

Richet, Charles Robert, famous physiologist, quoted, on metaphysics, 104 n.; on future discoveries, 135

Rig-Vedic India, 411 n.

rishi, illumined sage, 33, 39, 55, 65 n.

rita, universal law, 193 n., 201 n., 412

rituals, daily, of orthodox Hindus, 373

Robinson, Dr. Frederick B., 306

Roerich, Prof. Nicholas, 233

Roma, my eldest sister, 6, 13, 16, 181, 184, 343 n.; death of, 185

Romesh Chandra Dutt, help of, in my A. B. examinations, 189 ff.

Roosevelt, Franklin D., quoted, 383

Rowe, Harry T., Forest Lawn Mortuary Director, quoted, 422

Roy, Dr. N. C., veterinary surgeon, 152 ff.; healing of diabetes of, by Sri Yukteswar, 152

Rubaiyat, verse of, interpreted, 261

Ruskin, quoted, 194 n.

Sadasiva Brahman, 201 n.; miracles of, 337 ff.

sadhana, path of spiritual discipline, 75, 94, 351

sadhu, ascetic, 16, 344; in Lahore, gives amulet to my mother, 17; in Hardwar, heals own arm, severed by policeman, 29; in Banaras, overhears conversation between pundit's son and me, 31; at Kalighat Temple, 37 ff., 44

Sailesh Mazumdar, companion on trip to Giri Bala, 392

samadhi, state of God-union, 23 n., 94, 105 n., 122, 140 n., 179, 199, 209, 235, 275, 298, 353, 367, 385, 404, 414; poem on, 129–30

Sambhabi Mudra, 288 n.

Sananda Lal Ghosh, my younger brother, 75

Sanandan, disciple of Pranabananda, 222 ff.

Sanandana, disciple of Shankara, 81 n.

Sanatan Dharma (Hinduism), 296 n.

Sankhya Aphorisms, 42 n., 148

sankirtan, group chanting, 137, 139, 140

sannyasi, renunciant, 30, 217 n.

Sanskrit, 18 n., 374 n., 411 n.; tribute to, by Sir William Jones, 18 n., by Panini, 74 n.

Santosh Roy, 152 ff.

Sanyal Mahasaya. *See* Bhupendra

Sarada Ghosh, my uncle, 168, 188, 190; healing of, through herb materialized at Tarakeswar shrine, 119

sari, dress of Indian women, 203, 373, 399

Sartor Resartus, quoted, 290 n.

Sasi, healing of tuberculosis, by Sri Yukteswar, 153 ff.

Sat, Tat, Aum (Father, Son, Holy Ghost), 128 n., 419 n.

Satan ("the adversary"), 243 n. *See also Maya.*

Satish Chandra Bose, husband of my sister Roma, 181 ff.; death of, 186

Satsanga, "fellowship with truth," 136, 327 n. *See* Yogoda Satsanga.

Satyagraha, nonviolence movement founded by Gandhi, 370, 383; eleven vows of, 370

satyagrahi, "one vowed to truth," 370, 376, 380, 381, 382

Schimberg, A. P., 24 n., 314 n.

Schlegel, Friedrich von, quoted, 65 n.

Schopenhauer, tribute of, to *Upanishads,* 113 n.

Scottish Church College, in Calcutta, 94, 155; I receive my Intermediate Arts diploma from, 156

Seal, Dr. B. N., 142 n.

Sebananda, Swami, 342, 368

Self-Realization Church of All Religions, in Hollywood, 408; in San Diego, 408; in Pacific Palisades, 408

Self-Realization Fellowship International Headquarters, Los Angeles, California, 174, 306–307, 327, 400; sponsors visit to America of Shankaracharya, 196 n.; *Lessons* of, 207 n., 409, 425; incorporation of, 313; called Yogoda Satsanga Society (YSS) in India, 327, 350; center of, in London, 400, 408; annual Christmas celebrations of, 400; Colony of, in Encinitas, 406

Self-Realization magazine (formerly *East-West*), 339, 385, 408, 413; founded in 1925, 312; quoted, 61 n., 142 n., 336 n.

Sen, B. R., Ambassador of India, xv, 422

senses, five, of man, 42, 97, 110, 111, 149, 150, 198 n.

Serampore College, 156, 158, 163, 165, 187, 188; an affiliate of Calcutta University, 156; my final examinations at, 187 ff.; my talk before alumni of, 340

sex, 110–11, 149; Gandhi's views on diet and, 376

Shakespeare, poem of, on overcoming death, 212

shakti, "consort" or divine activating quality, 171 n., 419 n.

Shankaracharya (Shankara), Adi, reorganizer of Swami Order, 81 n., 110 n., 112, 113, 174, 179, 196, 214, 262, 366 n.; *maths* founded by, 81 n.; my vision before Srinagar temple of, 174; poem of, 196; date of, 196 n.

Shankaracharya of Mysore, 337 n.

Shankaracharya of Puri, visits America, 196 n.

Shankari Mai Jiew, disciple of Trailanga Swami, conversation of, with Babaji, 252

shastras, sacred books, 33, 77 n.

Shaw, George Bernard, quoted, 18 n.

Shiva, an aspect of Godhead, 37 n., 68, 136 n., 137, 171 n., 258 n., 263, 326,

418; "sky clad" sect of, 171 n.; poem
about, 258 n.
shrine, healing, in Spain, 57 n.; in
Tarakeswar, 119; in Nerur, 337
silver cup, prophecy of, by Swami Vivekananda, 402 ff.
single, or spiritual, eye, 35 n., 136 n., 148,
150 n., 183, 210, 222, 226, 235, 238,
245, 316 n., 318, 326, 343, 356, 386
Slade, Madeleine, *Satyagraha* disciple
of Gandhi, 371
Socrates, 319; quoted, 166 n.; encounter of, with Hindu sage, 319 n.
solar energy, 396 n.
Solomon, 37, 411 n.
Songs of the Soul, 306
soul (Self), individualized Spirit, 65 n.,
111, 134, 143, 146, 148 n., 149, 163,
179, 195 n., 212 ff., 225–26, 231 n.,
360 ff., 415 n., 416–17, 420
spinal centers, 23 n., 98, 140, 150, 207,
210, 211, 213, 248 n., 316 n., 356,
399 n.
Spirit, 195 n., 284, 362–63
spiritual eye. *See* Single eye.
Spirit's Pilgrimage, The, 371 n.
SRF. *See* Self-Realization Fellowship
Sri, "holy," title of respect, 93 n.
Srimad Bhagavata, 151 n.
Sri Yukteswar, my guru, a disciple of
Lahiri Mahasaya, 22, 37, 68, 78 ff.,
83, 84, 90, 121, 122, 124, 125 ff.,
140 ff., 163 ff., 188 ff., 205–206, 210,
216, 218, 233, 244, 253 ff., 261, 269,
279, 286, 290, 303, 307, 340 ff., 344,
348, 349 ff., 374, 392 n., 395 n., 407,
410, 417; visit to, by Dr. W. Y. Evans-
Wentz, xiii–xiv; appearance of, xiv,
78, 79, 323; my first meeting with,
78 ff.; promise by, of unconditional
love, 79, 340; request of, that I enter
college, 91; birth and early life of, 92;
name of, 93; my initiation by, in *Kriya
Yoga* science, 93; vegetarian diet of,
95; healing by, of my thinness, 99;
healing of, by Lahiri Mahasaya, of
thinness, 99–100; strict discipline of,
105 ff.; hermitage experiences of,
with Kumar, 109 ff.; property of, 116,

342; bestows experience of cosmic
consciousness, 126 ff.; directs peasant
to get cauliflower, 133 ff.; refuses to
find missing lamp, 136; provides an
"umbrella" of clouds, 136; expounds
true meaning of astrology, 142 ff., of
scriptural verses, 148 ff.; heals me of
a liver disorder, 145; heals Dr. Roy of
diabetes, 152 ff.; heals Sasi of tuberculosis, 153 ff.; arranges that I pursue
my A.B. studies in Serampore, 156;
relates miracles of Afzal Khan, 158 ff.;
appears simultaneously in Calcutta
and Serampore, 164; heals me of
cholera, 170; strawberry prophecy,
172; undergoes metaphysical illness
in Kashmir, 177 ff.; directs me to Romesh for help in passing A.B. examinations, 189 ff.; initiates me into
Swami Order as Yogananda, 195;
heals Nalini of paralyzed legs, 205–
206; witnesses the resurrection from
death of his brother disciple, Rama,
253 ff.; requests me to write life of
Lahiri Mahasaya, 256, 346; title of
Jnanavatar, 290, 351; beholds Babaji
on three occasions, 292 ff.; writes
book at Babaji's request, 295 ff.; bestows blessings as I leave for America,
304; answers my prayer on shipboard,
305; recalls me to India, 313; predicts
his passing, 313, 341; welcomes me
and Mr. Wright in Serampore, 322;
bestows on me title of *Paramahansa,*
341; earth-exit of, 349–50; burial of,
350; resurrection of, 352 ff.; description by, of astral universe, 354 ff.
Statue of Liberty, 400
Steinmetz, Charles P., quoted on need
for spiritual research, 382 n.
Sthiti Lal Nundy, neighbor of Giri Bala,
390–91, 395
*Story of My Experiments with Truth,
The,* 374 n.
Story of Therese Neumann, The, 24 n.,
314 n.
strawberry incident in Kashmir, 172
subconscious mind, 42 n., 108 n., 123,
416

suffering, purpose of, 39, 241, 399
superconscious mind, 53 n., 97, 108 n., 123, 177, 358, 416
swadeshi, use of home manufactures, 370, 394
swami, member of ancient order of monks, 14 n.,112, 115, 194 ff.; order, reorganized by Shankara, 81 n.; my initiation as a, 195–96; ceremony by Shankaracharya of Puri for two YSS monks, 196 n.; difference between, and yogi, 197 ff.; Sri Yukteswar's initiation as a, 293

Tagore. *See* Rabindranath.
Taj Mahal, famous mausoleum, 83, 85, 89, 346
Tan Sen, musical powers of, 138–39
Tarakeswar shrine, 118 ff.; my first visit to, 119; second visit to, 124; miracle at, of materialization of herb that healed Uncle Sarada, 119
Taxila, ancient university in, 61; visit to, by Alexander the Great, 331, 333
telepathy, 134, 163, 202–203, 226 n., 358
Teresa, St., of Avila, 193 n., 414 n.; levitating state of, 57 n.
Thales, quoted on life-death, 267 n.
Thamu, my youngest sister, 75
Thayumanavar, poem by, on mind control, 335
theism, 71
Thérèse, St., "Little Flower," 314
Thomas, F. W., quoted, 171 n.
Thompson, Francis, quoted, 411 n.
"thousand-petaled lotus," 140 n., 356, 406 n.
three bodies of man, 354, 360 ff., 365–66
Three Hermits, The, 233
Tibet, 41, 121
Tibetan Yoga and Secret Doctrines, xiii; Sri Yukteswar's picture in, xiii
tiger(s), 26, 30, 32, 45 ff., 347; "Raja Begum," in Cooch Behar, 49 ff.
"Tiger Swami" (Swami Sohong), 45 ff.
time and space, relativity of, 235, 238
Tincouri Lahiri, son of Lahiri Mahasaya, 246, 259

Tolstoy, 233, 377
Toynbee, Arnold J., 196 n.
Traherne, Thomas, quoted, 416 n.
Trailanga Swami, miracles of, 249 ff.; healing by, of my uncle, 252; tribute by, to Lahiri Mahasaya, 252
Training of the Human Plant, The, 309
travel diary, of C. Richard Wright, extracts from, on his first visit to Sri Yukteswar in Serampore, 322 ff.; on Mysore travels, 328–29; on Kara Patri at *Kumbha Mela,* 345; on Giri Bala, 393 ff.
Troland, Dr. L. T., quoted on light, 238
truth, 18 n., 135, 198, 204 n., 278, 370, 374 n., 382, 419 ff.

Uma, my elder sister, 13, 41; boil incident, 11; kite incident, 12; goddess, 171 n.
Upanishads, summaries of Vedic thought, 130, 198, 261, 366 n.; tribute to, by Schopenhauer, 113 n. *See also Vedanta.*
Upendra Mohun Chowdhury, observes levitation of Bhaduri Mahasaya, 53–54

Vatican, comment from, on death of Gandhi, 384
Vedanta, "end of the Vedas," 65 n., 81 n., 113 n., 195 n., 344, 366 n.
Vedas, scriptures of India, 34 n., 39 n., 65 n., 71, 77 n., 113 n., 115, 198 n., 237, 260 n., 296, 298 n., 316 n., 411 n., 420; tribute to, by Emerson, 34 n.; fourfold plan of, for man's life, 43 n., 217 n.
Vidyalaya. See Ranchi School.
Vidyasagar, philanthropist, 191
Vishnu, an aspect of Godhead, 137, 258 n., 418
Vishuddhananda, Swami ("Gandha Baba"), 41
visions, my, of a previous incarnation, 3; of Lahiri Mahasaya's living form in his picture, 8; of Himalayan yogis and a Great Light, 10; in Bareilly, of my mother, 13; of my guru's face, 25, 79;

of the Divine Mother, 67; of the world as a soundless motion picture, 70–71; of lightning, 123; at Tarakeswar shrine, of the cosmical spheres, 124; of cosmic consciousness, 126–27; in Kashmir, of a California building, 174; in Dakshineswar, of the living goddess in a stone image, 183–84; in a dream, of pet deer, 219; of a captain in command of a battleship, 239–40; of the European battlefields, 241; of the body as light, 242–43; of American faces, 301; of my guru's passing, 349; of Lord Krishna, 352; in Bombay, of a strange world, 352; of my past incarnations, 368; in Encinitas, of Christ and the Holy Grail, 413

Visva-Bharati, university founded by Tagore, 232; *Quarterly,* 65 n.

Vivasvat, ancient illuminato, 208

Vivekananda, Swami, 402, 403

Washington, George, quoted, 307

water, meditation on, 70; legend about, of Ganges, 171 n.; tribute to, by St. Francis, 260 n.

Whispers from Eternity, 307

Whitman, Walt, poem by, quoted, 307

will power, 116, 134–35, 217, 226 n., 316 n., 325, 377

Wilson, Margaret Woodrow, disciple-ship in India of, 371 n.

Wilson, Woodrow, 371 n.; quoted, 381

words, power of, 11, 17 n., 204 n.

world, cycles of, 147, 208 n.

Wright, C. Richard, my secretary, 313, 317, 318, 319, 321, 324, 327–28, 336, 338, 344, 351, 369, 370, 373, 385, 388, 390, 392, 395, 400–401, *See also* Travel diary.

Wutz, Prof. Franz, in Eichstätt, 315, 317

yajnas, obligatory offerings, 373

yama, moral conduct, 198, 201 n.

Yama, the god of death, 255

yoga, "union," science of uniting the in-dividual soul with the Cosmic Spirit, 42 n., 55, 121, 135, 195, 197 ff., 207 ff., 257, 289 n., 290, 291, 409,

414 ff., 415 n.; universal applicability of, 197, 199, 414–15; ignorant criti-cisms of, 197, 199, 200 n.; definition of, by Patanjali, 198; tribute to, by Jung, 199–200; four stages of, 201 n.

Yoga Sutras (Patanjali's *Aphorisms*), 24 n., 97 n., 112 n., 192 n., 198–99, 200 n., 204 n., 209 n., 399 n., 417

Yogavatar, "Incarnation of Yoga," a title of Lahiri Mahasaya, 287 n., 290, 291

yogi, practitioner of yoga, 3 n., 97, 212 ff., 221, 222 n., 238 ff., 415 n., 417; difference between, and swami, 197 ff. *See also* Yoga.

yogini, woman yogi, 252, 391

Yogmata, Sister, fulfills strawberry prophecy, 172

Yogoda, SRF energizing exercises, 217–18, 231, 325, 327 n., 377

Yogoda Math, YSS hermitage in Dak-shineswar, 327

Yogoda Satsanga Society (YSS), schools and activities of, in India, 196 n., 325 ff., 350

Young, Edward, quoted on miracles, 273 n.

Younghusband, Sir Francis, 314; quoted on cosmic joy, 72 n.

YSS. *See* Yogoda Satsanga Society.

Yuan Chwang (Hieuen Tsiang), 342 n., 411 n.

yugas, world cycles, 147, 208 n.

Zend-Avesta, 377; quoted, 404